North Carolina Manual
1927

Editor

A. R. Newsome

Alpha Editions

This edition published in 2020

ISBN : 9789354047909

Design and Setting By
Alpha Editions
www.alphaedis.com
email - alphaedis@gmail.com

As per information held with us this book is in Public Domain.
This book is a reproduction of an important historical work. Alpha Editions uses the best technology to reproduce historical work in the same manner it was first published to preserve its original nature. Any marks or number seen are left intentionally to preserve its true form.

PUBLICATIONS OF THE
NORTH CAROLINA HISTORICAL COMMISSION

NORTH CAROLINA MANUAL
1927

COMPILED AND EDITED
BY
A. R. NEWSOME
SECRETARY OF THE NORTH CAROLINA
HISTORICAL COMMISSION

RALEIGH
EDWARDS & BROUGHTON COMPANY
STATE PRINTERS
1927

1927

JANUARY	APR	JULY	OCTOBER
S M T W T F S	S M T W T F S	S M T W T F S	S M T W T F S
1 2 3 4 5 6 7 8 9 10 11 12 13 14 15 16 17 18 19 20 21 22 23 24 25 26 27 28 29 30 31	1 2 3 4 5 6 7 8 9 10 11 12 13 14 15 16 17 18 19 20 21 22 23 24 25 26 27 28 29 30	1 2 3 4 5 6 7 8 9 10 11 12 13 14 15 16 17 18 19 20 21 22 23 24 25 26 27 28 29 30 31	2 3 4 5 6 7 8 9 10 11 12 13 14 15 16 17 18 19 20 21 22 23 24 25 26 27 28 29 30 31

FEBRUARY	MAY	AUGUST	NOVEMBER
S M T W T F S	S M T W T F S	S M T W T F S	S M T W T F S
1 2 3 4 5 6 7 8 9 10 11 12 13 14 15 16 17 18 19 20 21 22 23 24 25 26 27 28	1 2 3 4 5 6 7 8 9 10 11 12 13 14 15 16 17 18 19 20 21 22 23 24 25 26 27 28 29 30 31	1 2 3 4 5 6 7 8 9 10 11 12 13 14 15 16 17 18 19 20 21 22 23 24 25 26 27 28 29 30 31	1 2 3 4 5 6 7 8 9 10 11 12 13 14 15 16 17 18 19 20 21 22 23 24 25 26 27 28 29 30

MARCH	JUNE	SEPTEMBER	DECEMBER
S M T W T F S	S M T W T F S	S M T W T F S	S M T W T F S
1 2 3 4 5 6 7 8 9 10 11 12 13 14 15 16 17 18 19 20 21 22 23 24 25 26 27 28 29 30 31	1 2 3 4 5 6 7 8 9 10 11 12 13 14 15 16 17 18 19 20 21 22 23 24 25 26 27 28 29 30	1 2 3 4 5 6 7 8 9 10 11 12 13 14 15 16 17 18 19 20 21 22 23 24 25 26 27 28 29 30	1 2 3 4 5 6 7 8 9 10 11 12 13 14 15 16 17 18 19 20 21 22 23 24 25 26 27 28 29 30 31

1928

JANUARY	APRIL	JULY	OCTOBER
S M T W T F S	S M T W T F S	S M T W T F S	S M T W T F S
1 2 3 4 5 6 7 8 9 10 11 12 13 14 15 16 17 18 19 20 21 22 23 24 25 26 27 28 29 30 31	1 2 3 4 5 6 7 8 9 10 11 12 13 14 15 16 17 18 19 20 21 22 23 24 25 26 27 28 29 30	1 2 3 4 5 6 7 8 9 10 11 12 13 14 15 16 17 18 19 20 21 22 23 24 25 26 27 28 29 30 31	1 2 3 4 5 6 7 8 9 10 11 12 13 14 15 16 17 18 19 20 21 22 23 24 25 26 27 28 29 30 31

FEBRUARY	MAY	AUGUST	NOVEMBER
S M T W T F	S M T W T F S	S M T W T F S	S M T W T F S
1 2 3 4 5 6 7 8 9 10 11 12 13 14 15 16 17 18 19 20 21 22 23 24 25 26 27 28 29	1 2 3 4 5 6 7 8 9 10 11 12 13 14 15 16 17 18 19 20 21 22 23 24 25 26 27 28 29 30 31	1 2 3 4 5 6 7 8 9 10 11 12 13 14 15 16 17 18 19 20 21 22 23 24 25 26 27 28 29 30 31	1 2 3 4 5 6 7 8 9 10 11 12 13 14 15 16 17 18 19 20 21 22 23 24 25 26 27 28 29 30

MARCH	JUNE	SEPTEMBER	DECEMBER
S M T W T F S	S M T W T F S	S M T W T F S	S M T W T F S
1 2 3 4 5 6 7 8 9 10 11 12 13 14 15 16 17 18 19 20 21 22 23 24 25 26 27 28 29 30 31	1 2 3 4 5 6 7 8 9 10 11 12 13 14 15 16 17 18 19 20 21 22 23 24 25 26 27 28 29 30	1 2 3 4 5 6 7 8 9 10 11 12 13 14 15 16 17 18 19 20 21 22 23 24 25 26 27 28 29 30	1 2 3 4 5 6 7 8 9 10 11 12 13 14 15 16 17 18 19 20 21 22 23 24 25 26 27 28 29 30 31

PREFACE

This volume is issued by the North Carolina Historical Commission in order to furnish in succinct form information about the State, its government and institutions, which otherwise would require much investigation in many different sources. Unless otherwise stated, the data in each case is the latest available.

Similar manuals were issued by the Secretary of State in 1903, 1905, and 1907, and by the North Carolina Historical Commission in 1909, 1911, 1913, 1915, 1917, 1919, 1921, 1923, and 1925. The demand for these volumes has been so great that all editions except that of 1925 have been exhausted.

NORTH CAROLINA HISTORICAL COMMISSION

THOMAS M. PITTMAN, *Chairman*, HENDERSON
M. C. S. NOBLE..Chapel Hill
HERIOT CLARKSON..Raleigh
W. N. EVERETT...Raleigh
BEN DIXON MACNEILL..Raleigh
A. R. NEWSOME, *Secretary*, RALEIGH.

CONTENTS

	PAGE
Official Register for 1927-1928	9

THE LEGISLATIVE DEPARTMENT:

Officers and Members of the Senate	15
Senatorial Districts	18
Rules of the Senate	19
Standing Committees of the Senate	30
Officers and Members of the House of Representatives	35
Rules of the House of Representatives	41
Standing Committees of the House of Representatives	58

EXECUTIVE DEPARTMENTS:

The Governor	63
The Secretary of State	70
The Auditor	72
The Treasurer	75
Superintendent of Public Instruction	78
The Attorney-General	83
Council of State	85

JUDICIAL DEPARTMENT:

Court of Impeachment	91
The Supreme Court	92
Superior Courts	93
Other Courts	93
North Carolina Corporation Commission	94

STATE DEPARTMENTS, BOARDS, AND COMMISSIONS:

The Adjutant-General's Department	104
Department of Agriculture	105
Board of Agriculture	113
Joint Committee for Agricultural Work	114
Department of Labor and Printing	115
Department of Insurance	120
State Department of Revenue	126
State Board of Assessment	128
State Highway Commission	131
State Board of Health	137
Department of Conservation and Development	140

Contents

	PAGE
State Board of Charities and Public Welfare	147
Child Welfare Commission	155
The Budget Bureau	163
North Carolina Historical Commission	165
Library Commission of North Carolina	172
State Library	176
Law Library	179
Audubon Society of North Carolina	180
North Carolina Fisheries Commission Board	185
Printing Commission	188
Salary and Wage Commission	189
Judicial Conference	189
State Prison	190
State Bureau of Identification	192
Commissioner of Pardons	193
Educational Commission	194
The Equalizing Fund Commission	195
State Board of Vocational Education	195
College Commission	196
State Committee on High School Text-books	197
Text-book Commission	198
Transportation Advisory Commission	199
State Sinking Fund Commission	200
State Board of Elections	202
State Board of Canvassers	203
State Board of Pensions	204
Commissioner of the Veterans Loan Fund	205
Board of Public Buildings and Grounds	206
Municipal Board of Control	207
State Standard Keeper	208
Board of Commissioners of Navigation and Pilotage	209
Crop Pest Commission	210
National Park Commission for North Carolina	210
Commission on the Reproduction of the Canova Statue of Washington	211
Bennett Place Memorial Commission	212
Board of Medical Examiners	213
Board of Chiropody Examiners	214
The Board of Nurse Examiners of North Carolina	215
Board of Pharmacy	216
North Carolina Board of Veterinary Medical Examiners	217
North Carolina State Board of Dental Examiners	218
State Board of Accountancy	219
State Board of Architectural Examination and Registration	220
State Board of Chiropractic Examiners	220
State Board of Embalmers	221
State Board of Examiners in Optometry	222

Contents

	Page
State Board of Osteopathic Examination and Registration	223
State Board of Registration for Engineers and Land Surveyors	224
State Licensing Board for Contractors	225

STATE EDUCATIONAL INSTITUTIONS:

University of North Carolina	229
North Carolina State College of Agriculture and Engineering	234
North Carolina College for Women	240
Cullowhee State Normal School	245
Appalachian State Normal School	247
East Carolina Teachers College	248
North Carolina School for the White Blind and for the Colored Blind and Deaf	250
North Carolina School for the Deaf	252
Stonewall Jackson Manual Training and Industrial School	253
North Carolina Normal Schools and Colleges for the Colored Race and for the Cherokee Indians of Robeson County	255
Fayetteville Colored Normal School	257
Elizabeth City Colored Normal School	259
Winston-Salem Teachers College at Winston Salem	260
North Carolina College for Negroes	261
Cherokee Indian Normal School of Robeson County	262
Negro Agricultural and Technical College of North Carolina	264
Caswell Training School	265
East Carolina Industrial Training School for Boys	266
State Training School for Negro Boys	267
State Home and Industrial School for Girls and Women	268

STATE CHARITABLE INSTITUTIONS:

State Hospital at Raleigh	273
State Hospital at Morganton	273
State Hospital at Goldsboro	275
North Carolina Sanatorium for the Treatment of Tuberculosis	276
North Carolina Orthopaedic Hospital	278
Oxford Orphanage	279
North Carolina Orphanage for the Colored Race	281
Soldiers' Home	282
Confederate Women's Home	283

MISCELLANEOUS:

The North Carolina Railroad Company	284
The Atlantic and North Carolina Railroad Company	285
The Appalachian and Western North Carolina Railroad Company	285
The North Carolina Agricultural Society	286
The North Carolina State Capitol	287
State Administration Building	

Contents

	PAGE
North Carolina Day	304
Legal Holidays in North Carolina	306
The State Flag	308
The Great Seal	310
State Motto and Its Origin	315
The Confederate Museum at Richmond	317

PLATFORMS OF POLITICAL PARTIES, 1926:

State Democratic Platform	321
State Republican Platform	329

ELECTION RETURNS:

Vote for President by States, 1912-1924	339
Vote for President by Counties, 1916-1924	342
Vote by Counties for Governor in Democratic Primaries, 1920-1924	344
Vote for State Officers in Democratic Primaries, 1924	346
Democratic Primary Vote, June 5, 1926, for United States Senator	347
Vote for Governor by Counties, 1920-1924	348
Vote for United States Senator, 1920-1926	350
Vote for Members of Congress, 1922-1926	352
Vote on Constitutional Amendment and Referendum by Counties, 1926	357
Vote for Solicitors, 1926	361

THE HALIFAX RESOLUTION 369

THE DECLARATION OF INDEPENDENCE 370

CONSTITUTIONS:

Constitution of the United States of America	377
Constitution of the State of North Carolina	394
Index to the Constitution of North Carolina	448

CENSUS:

Population and Area of the Several States and Territories, 1910-1920	459
Population (estimated) of North Carolina, 1675-1786	461
Census of North Carolina, 1790-1840	462
Census of North Carolina, 1850-1920	463
Population of North Carolina Cities and Towns, 1900-1920	466
North Carolina Counties and County Seats	474
Economic Development of North Carolina	477

BIOGRAPHICAL SKETCHES:

Executive Officials	481
Justices of the Supreme Court	487
Members of Congress	491
Members of the General Assembly	499

OFFICIAL REGISTER FOR 1927-1928

LEGISLATIVE DEPARTMENT

J. Elmer Long	President of the Senate	Durham
Richard T. Fountain	Speaker of the House of Representatives	Edgecombe

EXECUTIVE DEPARTMENT

A. W. McLean	Governor	Robeson
J. Elmer Long	Lieutenant-Governor	Durham
W. N. Everett	Secretary of State	Richmond
Baxter Durham	Auditor	Wake
B. R. Lacy	Treasurer	Wake
A. T. Allen	Superintendent of Public Instruction	Alexander
Dennis G. Brummitt	Attorney-General	Granville

JUDICIAL DEPARTMENT

SUPREME COURT JUSTICES

Walter P. Stacy	Chief Justice	New Hanover
W. J. Adams	Associate Justice	Moore
Heriot Clarkson	Associate Justice	Mecklenburg
George W. Connor	Associate Justice	Wilson
W. J. Brogden	Associate Justice	Durham

SUPERIOR COURT JUDGES

W. M. Bond	First District	Chowan—Edenton
M. V. Barnhill	Second District	Nash—Rocky Mount
Garland E. Midyette	Third District	Northampton—Jackson
Frank A. Daniels	Fourth District	Wayne—Goldsboro
R. A. Nunn	Fifth District	Craven—New Bern
H. A. Grady	Sixth District	Sampson—Clinton
W. C. Harris	Seventh District	Wake—Raleigh
E. H. Cranmer	Eighth District	Brunswick—Southport
N. A. Sinclair	Ninth District	Cumberland—Fayetteville
William A. Devin	Tenth District	Granville—Oxford
Raymond G. Parker	Eleventh District	Forsyth—Winston-Salem
Thomas J. Shaw	Twelfth District	Guilford—Greensboro
A. M. Stack	Thirteenth District	Union—Monroe
W. F. Harding	Fourteenth District	Mecklenburg—Charlotte
J. M. Oglesby	Fifteenth District	Cabarrus—Concord
J. L. Webb	Sixteenth District	Cleveland—Shelby
T. B. Finley	Seventeenth District	Wilkes—Wilkesboro
Michael Schenck	Eighteenth District	Henderson—Hendersonville
P. A. McElroy	Nineteenth District	Madison—Marshall
Walter E. Moore	Twentieth District	Jackson—Sylva

SOLICITORS

W. L. Small	First District	Pasquotank—Elizabeth City
Donnell Gilliam	Second District	Edgecombe—Tarboro
R. Hunt Parker	Third District	Vance—Henderson
C. L. Williams	Fourth District	Lee—Sanford
D. M. Clark	Fifth District	Pitt—Greenville
J. A. Powers	Sixth District	Lenoir—Kinston
L. S. Brassfield	Seventh District	Wake—Raleigh
Woodus Kellum	Eighth District	New Hanover—Wilmington
T. A. McNeill	Ninth District	Robeson—Lumberton
W. B. Umstead	Tenth District	Durham—Durham

S. PORTER GRAVES	Eleventh District	Surry—Mount Airy.
J. F. SPRUILL	Twelfth District	Davidson—Lexington.
F. D. PHILLIPS	Thirteenth District	Richmond-Rockingham.
J. G. CARPENTER	Fourteenth District	Gaston—Gastonia.
Z. V. LONG	Fifteenth District	Iredell—Statesville
L. S. SPURLING	Sixteenth District	Caldwell—Lenoir.
JOHN R. JONES	Seventeenth District	Wilkes—North Wilkesboro.
J. W. PLESS, JR.	Eighteenth District	McDowell—Marion.
R. M. WELLS	Nineteenth District	Buncombe—Asheville.
G. C. DAVIS	Twentieth District	Haywood—Waynesville.

CORPORATION COMMISSION

W. T. LEE	Chairman	Haywood.
GEORGE P. PELL	Commissioner	Forsyth.
A. J. MAXWELL	Commissioner	Craven.
R. OTIS SELF	Chief Clerk	Jackson.

ADMINISTRATIVE DEPARTMENTS, BOARDS, AND COMMISSIONS

ADJUTANT GENERAL'S DEPARTMENT
J. VAN B. METTS .... The Adjutant General .... New Hanover.

DEPARTMENT OF AGRICULTURE
W. A. GRAHAM .... Commissioner .... Lincoln.

DEPARTMENT OF LABOR AND PRINTING
F. D. GRIST .... Commissioner .... Caldwell.

DEPARTMENT OF INSURANCE
STACEY W. WADE .... Commissioner .... Carteret.

DEPARTMENT OF REVENUE
R. A. DOUGHTON .... Commissioner .... Alleghany.

STATE HIGHWAY COMMISSION
FRANK PAGE .... Commissioner .... Moore.

STATE BOARD OF HEALTH
C. O'H. LAUGHINGHOUSE .... Secretary .... Pitt.

DEPARTMENT OF CONSERVATION AND DEVELOPMENT
WADE H. PHILLIPS .... Director .... Davidson.

STATE BOARD OF CHARITIES AND PUBLIC WELFARE
MRS. KATE BURR JOHNSON .... Commissioner .... Wake.

CHILD WELFARE COMMISSION
E. F. CARTER .... Executive Secretary .... Wake.

NORTH CAROLINA HISTORICAL COMMISSION
A. R. NEWSOME .... Secretary .... Union.

LIBRARY COMMISSION
MRS. LILLIAN B. GRIGGS .... Secretary .... Durham.

STATE LIBRARY
MISS CARRIE L. BROUGHTON .... Librarian .... Wake.

LAW LIBRARY
MARSHALL DEL. HAYWOOD .... Librarian .... Wake.

OFFICIAL REGISTER

AUDUBON SOCIETY
Miss Placide H. Underwood....Secretary................. Wa[...]

FISHERIES COMMISSION BOARD
J. A. Nelson................Commissioner................ Carteret

SALARY AND WAGE COMMISSION
H. Hoyle Sink..............Executive Secretary......... Davidson

STATE PRISON
George Ross Pou............Superintendent.............. Johnston

SUPERIOR COURT CALENDAR, 1927-1928

District	Spring, 1927	Fall, 1927	Spring, 1928	Fall, 1928
1	Judge Daniels	Judge Midyette	Judge Barnhill	Judge Bond
2	Judge Nunn	Judge Daniels	Judge Midyette	Judge Barnhill
3	Judge Grady	Judge Nunn	Judge Daniels	Judge Midyette
4	Judge Harris	Judge Grady	Judge Nunn	Judge Daniels
5	Judge Cranmer	Judge Harris	Judge Grady	Judge Nunn
6	Judge Sinclair	Judge Cranmer	Judge Harris	Judge Grady
7	Judge Devin	Judge Sinclair	Judge Cranmer	Judge Harris
8	Judge Bond	Judge Devin	Judge Sinclair	Judge Cranmer
9	Judge Barnhill	Judge Bond	Judge Devin	Judge Sinclair
10	Judge Midyette	Judge Barnhill	Judge Bond	Judge Devin
11	Judge Harding	Judge Stack	Judge Shaw	Judge Parker
12	Judge Oglesby	Judge Harding	Judge Stack	Judge Shaw
13	Judge Webb	Judge Oglesby	Judge Harding	Judge Stack
14	Judge Finley	Judge Webb	Judge Oglesby	Judge Harding
15	Judge Schenck	Judge Finley	Judge Webb	Judge Oglesby
16	Judge McElroy	Judge Schenck	Judge Finley	Judge Webb
17	Judge Moore	Judge McElroy	Judge Schenck	Judge Finley
18	Judge Parker	Judge Moore	Judge McElroy	Judge Schenck
19	Judge Shaw	Judge Parker	Judge Moore	Judge McElroy
20	Judge Stack	Judge Shaw	Judge Parker	Judge Moore

PART I

THE LEGISLATIVE DEPARTMENT

1. OFFICERS OF THE SENATE.
2. MEMBERS OF THE SENATE (Arranged Alphabetically).
3. MEMBERS OF THE SENATE (Arranged by Districts).
4. SENATORIAL DISTRICTS.
5. RULES OF THE SENATE.
6. STANDING COMMITTEES OF THE SENATE.
7. OFFICERS OF THE HOUSE OF REPRESENTATIVES.
8. MEMBERS OF THE HOUSE OF REPRESENTATIVES (Arranged Alphabetically).
9. MEMBERS OF THE HOUSE OF REPRESENTATIVES (Arranged by Counties).
10. RULES OF THE HOUSE OF REPRESENTATIVES.
11. STANDING COMMITTEES OF THE HOUSE OF REPRESENTATIVES.

OFFICERS AND MEMBERS OF THE SENATE

OFFICERS

J. Elmer Long	President	Durham
W. L. Long	President, pro tem	Halifax
Leroy B. Martin	Principal Clerk	Yadkin
O. P. Shell	Sergeant-at-Arms	Harnett
B. Fritz Smith	Reading Clerk	Wake
Rev. A. Corey	Engrossing Clerk	Martin

SENATORS
(Alphabetically Arranged)

Name	District	Party	Postoffice
Askew, E. S.	Third	Democrat	Merry Hill, N. C.
Bailey, John L.	Sixth	Democrat	Elm City, N. C.
Blount, M. K.	Fifth	Democrat	Greenville, N. C.
Broughton, J. M.	Thirteenth	Democrat	Raleigh, N. C.
Call, Clarence	Twenty-fourth	Republican	North Wilkesboro, N. C.
Canaday, C. C.	Eighth	Democrat	Benson, N. C.
Childs, W. H.	Twenty-fifth	Democrat	Lincolnton, N. C.
Clark, W. G.	Fourth	Democrat	Tarboro, N. C.
Currie, Claude	Eighteenth	Democrat	Troy, N. C.
Dunlap, Frank L.	Nineteenth	Democrat	Wadesboro, N. C.
Ebbs, Plato	Thirty-first	Democrat	Asheville, N. C.
Fulton, H. T.	Twenty-seventh	Democrat	Kings Mountain, N. C.
Grant, L. Clayton	Ninth	Democrat	Wilmington, N. C.
Grier, Frank L.	Twenty-fifth	Democrat	Statesville, N. C.
Hancock, F. W., Jr.	Fifteenth	Democrat	Oxford, N. C.
Hargett, J. S.	Seventh	Democrat	Trenton, N. C.
Harris, C. P.	Sixth	Democrat	Mapleville, N. C.
Haywood, Fab J.	Twentieth	Democrat	Concord, N. C.
Hines, Chas. A.	Seventeenth	Democrat	Greensboro, N. C.
Horton, W. B.	Sixteenth	Democrat	Yanceyville, N. C.
Horton, W. P.	Thirteenth	Democrat	Pittsboro, N. C.
Hyatt, J. L.	Thirtieth	Republican	Burnsville, N. C.
Johnson, R. D.	Ninth	Democrat	Warsaw, N. C.
Lawrence, Lloyd, J.	First	Democrat	Murfreesboro, N. C.
Long, W. L.	Fourth	Democrat	Roanoke Rapids, N. C.
McDonald, D. A.	Twelfth	Democrat	Carthage, N. C.
McRackan, Donald	Tenth	Democrat	Whiteville, N. C.
McLeod, George B.	Eleventh	Democrat	Lumberton, N. C.
McNeill, P. T.	Twenty-ninth	Democrat	West Jefferson, N. C.
Maguire, S. O.	Twenty-third	Republican	Elkin, N. C.
Moore, Clayton	Second	Democrat	Williamston, N. C.

SENATORS—Continued.

Name	District	Party	Postoffice
Ray, J. Clyde	Sixteenth	Democrat	Hillsboro, N. C.
Roane, R. J.	Thirty-third	Democrat	Whittier, N. C.
Royall, Kenneth C.	Eighth	Democrat	Goldsboro, N. C.
Ruark, J. W.	Tenth	Democrat	Southport, N. C.
Salmon, N. McK.	Twelfth	Democrat	Lillington, N. C.
Sedberry, J. C.	Eighteenth	Democrat	Rockingham, N. C.
Sharp, J. M.	Seventeenth	Democrat	Reidsville, N. C.
Smith, D. B.	Twentieth	Democrat	Charlotte, N. C.
Smith, W. Erskine	Nineteenth	Democrat	Albemarle, N. C.
Spainhour, J. F.	Twenty-eighth	Democrat	Morganton, N. C.
Spencer, C. B.	Second	Democrat	Swan Quarter, N. C.
Stringfield, Thos.	Thirty-second	Democrat	Waynesville, N. C.
Tapp, L. P.	Seventh	Democrat	Kinston, N. C.
Whitmire, R. L.	Twenty-seventh	Democrat	Hendersonville, N. C.
Williams, B. B.	Fourteenth	Democrat	Warrenton, N. C.
Williams, P. H.	First	Democrat	Elizabeth City, N. C.
Woltz, A. E.	Twenty-sixth	Democrat	Gastonia, N. C.
Womble, B. S.	Twenty-second	Democrat	Winston-Salem, N. C.
Woodson, Walter H.	Twenty-first	Democrat	Salisbury, N. C.

SENATORS

(Arranged by Districts)

First District—Lloyd J. Lawrence, Murfreesboro (D); P. H. Williams, Elizabeth City (D).

Second District—Clayton Moore, Williamston (D); C. B. Spencer, Swan Quarter (D).

Third District—E. S. Askew, Merry Hill (D).

Fourth District—W. G. Clark, Tarboro (D); W. L. Long, Roanoke Rapids (D).

Fifth District—M. K. Blount, Greenville (D).

Sixth District—C. P. Harris, Mapleville (D); John L. Bailey, Elm City (D).

Seventh District—L. P. Tapp, Kinston (D); J. S. Hargett, Trenton (D).

Eighth District—Kenneth C. Royal, Goldsboro (D); C. C. Canaday, Benson (D).

Ninth District—L. Clayton Grant, Wilmington (D); R. D. Johnson, Warsaw (D).

Tenth District—Donald McRackan, Whiteville (D); J. W. Ruark, Southport (D).

Eleventh District—George B. McLeod, Lumberton (D).

Twelfth District—N. McK. Salmon, Lillington (D); D. A. McDonald, Carthage (D).

Thirteenth District—J. M. Broughton, Raleigh (D); W. P. Horton, Pittsboro (D).

Fourteenth District—B. B. Williams, Warrenton (D).

Fifteenth District—F. W. Hancock, Jr., Oxford (D).

Sixteenth District—J. Clyde Ray, Hillsboro (D); W. B. Horton, Yanceyville (D).

Seventeenth District—Chas. A. Hines, Greensboro (D); J. M. Sharp, Reidsville (D).

Eighteenth District—Claude Currie, Troy (D); J. C. Sedberry, Rockingham (D).

Nineteenth District—Frank L. Dunlap, Wadesboro (D); W. Erskine Smith, Albemarle (D).

Twentieth District—D. B. Smith, Charlotte (D); Fab J. Haywood, Concord (D).

Twenty-first District—Walter H. Woodson, Salisbury (D).

Twenty-second District—B. S. Womble, Winston-Salem (D).

Twenty-third District—S. O. Maguire, Elkin (R).

Twenty-fourth District—Clarence Call, North Wilkesboro (R).

Twenty-fifth District—W. H. Childs, Lincolnton (D); Frank L. Grier, Statesville (D).

Twenty-sixth District—A. E. Woltz, Gastonia (D).

Twenty-seventh District—H. T. Fulton, Kings Mountain (D); R. L. Whitmire, Hendersonville (D).

Twenty-eighth District—J. F. Spainhour, Morganton (D).

Twenty-ninth District—P. T. McNeill, West Jefferson (D).

Thirtieth District—J. L. Hyatt, Burnsville (R).

Thirty-first District—Plato Ebbs, Asheville (D).

Thirty-second District—Thomas Stringfield, Waynesville (D).

Thirty-third District—R. J. Roane, Whittier (D).

SENATORIAL DISTRICTS
Ch. 161, P. L. 1921.

First District—Camden, Chowan, Currituck, Gates, Hertford, Pasquotank and Perquimans counties shall elect two senators.

Second District—Beaufort, Dare, Hyde, Martin, Pamlico, Tyrrell, and Washington shall elect two senators.

Third District—Bertie and Northampton shall elect one senator.

Fourth District—Edgecombe and Halifax shall elect two senators.

Fifth District—Pitt shall elect one senator.

Sixth District—Franklin, Nash and Wilson shall elect two senators.

Seventh District—Carteret, Craven, Greene, Jones, Lenoir, and Onslow shall elect two senators.

Eighth District—Johnston and Wayne shall elect two senators.

Ninth District—Duplin, New Hanover, Pender, and Sampson shall elect two senators.

Tenth District—Bladen, Brunswick, Columbus, and Cumberland shall elect two senators.

Eleventh District—Robeson shall elect one senator.

Twelfth District—Harnett, Hoke, Moore, and Randolph shall elect two senators.

Thirteenth District—Chatham, Lee, and Wake shall elect two senators.

Fourteenth District—Vance and Warren shall elect one senator.

Fifteenth District—Granville and Person shall elect one senator.

Sixteenth District—Alamance, Caswell, Durham, and Orange shall elect two senators.

Seventeenth District—Guilford and Rockingham shall elect two senators.

Eighteenth District—Davidson, Montgomery, Richmond, and Scotland shall elect two senators.

Nineteenth District—Anson, Stanly, and Union shall elect two senators.

Twentieth District—Cabarrus and Mecklenburg shall elect two senators.

Twenty-first District—Rowan shall elect one senator.

Twenty-second District—Forsyth shall elect one senator.

Twenty-third District—Stokes and Surry shall elect one senator.

Twenty-fourth District—Davie, Wilkes, and Yadkin shall elect one senator.

Twenty-fifth District—Catawba, Iredell, and Lincoln shall elect two senators.

Twenty-sixth District—Gaston shall elect one senator.

Twenty-seventh District—Cleveland, Henderson, McDowell, Polk, and Rutherford shall elect two senators.

Twenty-eighth District—Alexander, Burke and Caldwell shall elect one senator.

Twenty-ninth District—Alleghany, Ashe, and Watauga shall elect one senator.

Thirtieth District—Avery, Madison, Mitchell, and Yancey shall elect one senator.

Thirty-first District—Buncombe shall elect one senator.

Thirty-second District—Haywood, Jackson, and Transylvania shall elect one senator.

Thirty-third District—Cherokee, Clay, Graham, Macon, and Swain shall elect one senator.

RULES OF THE SENATE

Order of Business

1. The President having taken the chair at the hour to which the Senate shall have adjourned, and a quorum being present, the Journal of the preceding day shall be read, unless otherwise ordered by the Senate, to the end that any mistake may be corrected.

2. After reading and approval of the Journal, the order of business shall be as follows:

(1) Reports of standing committees.
(2) Reports of select committees.
(3) Announcement of petitions, bills and resolutions.
(4) Unfinished business of preceding day.
(5) Special orders.

(6) General orders. First, bills and resolutions on third reading; second, bills and resolutions on second reading. But messages from the Governor and House of Representatives and communications and reports from State officers and reports from the Committees on Engrossed Bills and Enrolled Bills may be received and acted on under any order of business.

POWERS AND DUTIES OF THE PRESIDENT

3. He shall take the chair promptly at the appointed time and proceed with the business of the Senate according to the rules adopted. At any time during the absence of the President, the President *pro tempore*, who shall be elected, shall preside, and he is hereby vested, during such time, with all powers of the President except that of giving a casting vote in case of a tie when he shall have voted as a Senator.

4. He shall assign to doorkeepers their respective duties, and shall appoint such pages and laborers as may be necessary, each of whom shall receive the same compensation as is now provided by law.

OF THE CLERK

5. The President and Clerk of the Senate shall see that all bills shall be acted upon by the Senate in the order in which they stand upon the Calendar, unless otherwise ordered as hereinafter provided. The Calendar shall include the numbers and titles of bills and joint resolutions which have passed the House of Representatives and have been received by the Senate for concurrence.

6. The Clerk shall certify the passage of bills by the Senate, with the date thereof, together with the fact whether passed by a vote of three-fifths or two-thirds of the Senate, whenever such vote may be required by the Constitution and laws of the State.

ON THE RIGHTS AND DUTIES OF SENATORS

7. Every Senator presenting a paper shall endorse the same; if a petition, memorial, or report to the General Assembly, with a brief statement of its subject or contents, adding his name; if a resolution, with his name; if a report of a committee, a statement

of such report, with the name of the committee and member making the same; if a bill, a statement of its title, which shall contain a brief statement of the subject or contents of the bill, with his name; and all bills, resolutions, petitions, and memorials shall be delivered to the Clerk and by him handed to the President to be by him referred, and he shall announce the titles and references of the same, which shall be entered on the Journal.

8. All motions shall be reduced to writing, if desired by the President or any Senator, delivered at the table, and read by the President or Clerk before the same shall be debated; but any such motion may be withdrawn by the introducer at any time before decision or amendment.

9. If any question contains several distinct propositions it shall be divided by the President, at the request of any Senator, provided each subdivision, if left to itself, shall form a substantive proposition.

10. When the President is putting a question, or a division by counting shall be had, no Senator shall walk out of or across the chamber, nor when a Senator is speaking pass between him and the President.

11. Every Senator wishing to speak or debate, or to present a petition or other paper, or to make a motion or to report, shall rise from his seat and address the President, and shall not proceed further until recognized by him. No senator shall speak or debate more than twice nor longer than thirty minutes on the same day on the same subject without leave of the Senate, and when two or more Senators rise at once the President shall name the Senator who is first to speak.

12. Every Senator who shall be within the bar of the Senate when the question is stated by the chair shall vote thereon, unless he shall be excused by the Senate or unless he be directly interested in the question; and the bar of the Senate shall include the entire Senate Chamber.

13. When a motion to adjourn or for recess shall be affirmatively determined, no member or officer shall leave his place until adjournment or recess shall be declared by the President.

STANDING COMMITTEES

14. The following committees shall be named by the Lieutenant-Governor:

- On Agriculture.
- On Appropriations.
- On Banks and Currency.
- On Claims.
- On Commerce.
- On Congressional Districts.
- On Constitutional Amendments.
- On Corporation Commission.
- On Corporations.
- On Counties, Cities, and Towns
- On Distribution of Governor's Message.
- On Education.
- On Election Law.
- On Engrossed Bills.
- On Federal Relations.
- On Finance.
- On Fish, Fisheries, and Shell-fish.
- On Caswell Training School.
- On Game Law.
- On Immigration.
- On Insane Asylums.
- On Institutions for the Blind.
- On Institutions for the Deaf.
- On Insurance.
- On Internal Improvements.
- On Journal.
- On Judicial Districts.
- On Judiciary, No. 1.
- On Judiciary, No. 2.
- On Manufacturing.
- On Military Affairs.
- On Mining.
- On Penal Institutions.
- On Pensions and Soldiers' Home.
- On Propositions and Grievances.

On Public Health.
On Public Roads.
On Railroads.
On Rules.
On Salaries and Fees.
On Senate Expenditures.
On Senatorial Districts.

15. JOINT COMMITTEES
On Library.
On Printing.
On Trustees of the University.
On Consolidated Statutes.
On Water Commerce.
On Trustees State College.

16. The Committee on Engrossed Bills shall examine all bills, amendments, and resolutions before they go out of the possession of the Senate, and make a report when they find them correctly engrossed: *Provided*, that when a bill is typewritten and has no interlineations therein, and has passed the Senate without amendment, it shall be sent to the House without engrossment, unless otherwise ordered.

17. The Committee on Appropriations shall carefully examine all bills and resolutions appropriating or paying any moneys out of the State Treasury, except bills creating or increasing salaries, which shall be referred to the proper committee; *Provided*, said committee shall report to the Appropriations Committee the amount allowed, and keep an accurate record of the same and report to the Senate from time to time.

18. Every report of the committee upon a bill or resolution which shall not be considered at the time of making the same, or laid on the table by a vote of the Senate, shall stand upon the general orders with the bill or resolution; and the report of the committee shall show that a majority of the committee were present and voted.

19. That no committee shall be composed of more than nine members unless the Lieutenant-Governor shall, without objection from the Senate, appoint a greater number on any committee.

On General Orders and Special Orders

20. Any bill or other matter may be made a special order for a particular day or hour by a vote of the majority of the Senators voting, and if it shall not be completed on that day it shall be returned to its place on the Calendar, unless it shall be made a special order for another day; and when a special order is under consideration it shall take precedence of any special order or subsequent order for the day, but such subsequent order may be taken up immediately after the previous special order has been disposed of.

21. Every bill shall receive three readings previous to its being passed, and the President shall give notice at each whether it be the first, second, or third. After the first reading, unless a motion shall be made by some Senator, it shall be the duty of the President to refer the subject-matter to an appropriate committee. No bill shall be amended until it shall have been twice read.

Proceedings When There Is Not a Quorum Voting

22. If, on taking the question on a bill, it shall appear that a constitutional quorum is not present, or if the bill require a vote of a certain proportion of all the Senators to pass it, and it appears that such number is not present, the bill shall be again read and the question taken thereon; if the bill fail a second time for the want of the necessary number being present and voting, the bill shall not be finally lost, but shall be returned to the Calendar in its proper order.

Precedence of Motions

23. When a question is before the Senate no motion shall be received except those herein specified, which motions shall have precedence as follows, viz:

(1) For an adjournment.
(2) To lay on the table.
(3) For the previous question.
(4) To postpone indefinitely.
(5) To postpone to a certain day.
(6) To commit to a standing committee.

(7) To commit to a select committee.
(8) To amend.
(9) To substitute.

24. The previous question shall be as follows: "Shall the main question be now put?" and until it is decided shall preclude all amendments and debate. If this question shall be decided in the affirmative, the "main question" shall be on the passage of the bill, resolution, or other matter under consideration; but when amendments are pending the question shall be taken up on such amendments, in their order, without further debate or amendment. However, any Senator may move the previous question and may restrict the same to an amendment or other matter then under discussion. If such question be decided in the negative, the main question shall be considered as remaining under debate.

25. When a motion for the previous question is made and is pending, debate shall cease, and only a motion to adjourn or lay on the table shall be in order, which motion shall be put as follows: adjourn, previous question, lay on the table. After a motion for the previous question is made, pending a second thereto, any member may give notice that he desires to offer an amendment to the bill or other matter under consideration; and after the previous question is seconded such member shall be entitled to offer his amendment in pursuance of such notice.

Other Questions to be Taken Without Debate.

26. The motions to adjourn and lay on the table shall be decided without debate, and the motion to adjourn shall always be in order when made by a Senator entitled to the floor.

27. The respective motions to postpone to a certain day, or to commit, shall preclude debate on the main question.

28. All questions relating to priority of business shall be decided without debate.

29. When the reading of a paper is called for, except petitions, and the same is objected to by any Senator, it shall be determined by the Senate without debate.

30. Any Senator requesting to be excused from voting may make, either immediately before or after the vote shall have been

called and before the result shall have been announced, a brief statement of the reasons for making such request, and the question shall then be taken without debate. Any Senator may explain his vote on any bill pending by obtaining permission of the President before the vote is put: *Provided*, that not more than three minutes shall be consumed in such explanation.

QUESTIONS THAT REQUIRE A TWO-THIRDS VOTE

31. No bill or resolution on its third reading shall be acted on out of the regular order in which it stands on the Calendar, and no bill or resolution shall be acted upon on its third reading the same day on which it passed its second reading unless so ordered by two-thirds of the Senators present.

32. No bill or resolution shall be sent from the Senate on the day of its passage except on the last day of the session, unless otherwise ordered by a vote of two-thirds of the Senators present.

33. No bill or resolution, after being laid upon the table upon motion, shall be taken therefrom except by a vote of two-thirds of the Senators present.

DECORUM IN DEBATE

34. No remark reflecting personally upon the action of any Senator shall be in order in debate unless preceded by a motion or resolution of censure.

35. When a Senator shall be called to order he shall take his seat until the President shall have determined whether he was in order or not; if decided to be out of order, he shall not proceed without the permission of the Senate; and every question of order shall be decided by the President, subject to an appeal to the Senate by any Senator; and if a Senator is called to order for words spoken, the words excepted to shall be immediately taken down in writing, that the President or Senate may be better able to judge of the matter.

MISCELLANEOUS RULES

36. When a blank is to be filled, and different sums or times shall be proposed, the question shall be first taken on the highest sum or the longest time.

37. When a question has been once put and decided, it shall be in order for any Senator who shall have voted in the majority to move a reconsideration thereof; but no motion for the reconsideration of any vote shall be in order after the bill, resolution, message, report, amendment, or motion upon which the vote was taken shall have gone out of the possession of the Senate; nor shall any motion for reconsideration be in order unless made on the same day or the next following legislative day on which the vote proposed to be reconsidered shall have taken place, unless the same shall be made by the Committee on Enrolled Bills for verbal or grammatical errors in the bills, when the same may be made at any time. Nor shall any question be reconsidered more than once.

38. All bills and resolutions shall take their place upon the Calendar according to their number, and shall be taken up in regular order, unless otherwise ordered.

39. No smoking shall be allowed on the floor of the Senate Chamber during the sessions.

40. Senators and visitors shall uncover their heads upon entering the Senate Chamber while the Senate is in session, and shall continue uncovered during their continuance in the Chamber.

41. No Senator or officer of the Senate shall depart the service of the Senate without leave, or receive pay as a Senator or officer for the time he is absent without leave.

42. No person other than the executive and judicial officers of the State, members and officers of the Senate and House of Representatives, and ex-members shall be permitted within the Senate Chamber.

43. No rule of the Senate shall be altered, suspended, or rescinded except on a two-thirds vote of the Senators present: *Provided*, that this shall not apply to Rule 55.

44. In case a less number than a quorum of the Senate shall convene, they are authorized to send the doorkeeper, or any other person, for any or all absent Senators, as a majority of the Senators present shall determine.

45. The ayes and noes may be called for on any question before the vote is taken, and if seconded by one-fifth of the Senators present, the question shall be decided by the ayes and noes, and the same shall be entered upon the Journal.

46. The President of the Senate, whenever it shall appear to him to be necessary in order to expedite the public business, shall appoint clerks to such Senate committees as may be in need of same.

47. Every bill introduced into the Senate shall be printed or typewritten. Amendments need not be typewritten.

48. The Clerk of the Senate shall provide a box of sufficient size, with an opening through the top, for the reception of bills; such box shall be kept under lock and key and shall be stationed on the Clerk's desk. The President of the Senate shall have in his charge and keeping the key to such box. All bills which are to be introduced into the Senate shall be deposited in such box before the session begins. At the proper time the President shall open the box and take therefrom the bills. Such bills shall be read by their titles, which reading shall constitute the first reading of the bill, and unless otherwise disposed of shall be referred to the proper committee. A bill may be introduced by unanimous consent at any time during the session.

49. The Chief Engrossing Clerk of the Senate shall appoint, with the approval of the President of the Senate, as his assistants not more than four competent stenographers and typewriters. Should the public business require more than this number the presiding officer may appoint such additional ones as may be necessary. Such stenographers and typewriters shall work under the direction and supervision of the Engrossing Clerk. They shall also make for the members who introduce a bill, without extra cost, one original and two carbon copies of all bills.

50. The Journal of the Senate shall be typewritten in duplicate, original and carbon, the original to be deposited in the office of the Secretary of State as the record, and the other (carbon) copy to be delivered to the State Printer.

51. All bills and resolutions reported unfavorably by the committee to which they were referred, and having no minority report, shall lie upon the table, but may be taken from the table and placed upon the Calendar at the request of any Senator.

52. That in case of adjournment without any hour being named, the Senate shall reconvene the next legislative day at 11 o'clock a.m.

53. When a bill is materially modified or the scope of its application extended or decreased, or if the county or counties to

which it applies be changed, the title of the bill shall be changed by the Senator introducing the bill or by the committee having it in charge, or by the Engrossing Clerk, so as to indicate the full purport of the bill as amended and the county or counties to which it applies.

54. It shall be the duty of the Principal Clerk to furnish to the presiding officer and the members of the Senate all necessary stationery, which shall be provided for out of the funds set apart for the expenses of the General Assembly.

55. After a bill has been tabled or has failed to pass on any of its readings, the contents of such bill or the principal provisions of its subject-matter shall not be embodied in any other measure. Upon the point of order being raised and sustained by the Chair, such measure shall be laid upon the table, and shall not be taken therefrom except by a vote of two-thirds of the elected membership of the Senate; *Provided*, no local bill shall be held by the Chair as embodying the provisions, or being identical with any State-wide measure which has been laid upon the table or failed to pass any of its readings.

56. That in the event of the absence of the President of the Senate and the President *pro tempore*, at any time fixed for the reconvening of the Senate, the Principal Clerk of the Senate, or, in his absence also, some member of the Senate Committee on Rules shall call the Senate to order and designate some member to act as President.

57. Whenever a public bill is introduced, a carbon copy thereof shall accompany the bill. On the same day that such public bill is introduced the Chief Clerk shall deliver the carbon copy to the Public Printer and cause four hundred (400) copies thereof to be printed. On the morning following the delivery of the printed copies the Chief Clerk shall cause the Chief Page to have a copy thereof put upon the desk of each member and then return the other printed copies in his office. A sufficient number for the use of the committee to whom the bill is referred shall be by the Chief Clerk delivered to the chairman or clerk of the committee. If the bill is passed, the remaining copies shall be by the Chief Clerk delivered to the Chief Clerk of the House of Representatives, for the use of the House of Representatives. No committee shall

consider or report any public bill until after the same shall have been printed as herein provided for. In the event the member introducing the bill and the Chief Clerk shall differ as to whether it is a public bill, the question shall be left to the decision of the President of the Senate whose decision shall be final. The cost of printing as herein provided for shall be paid from the contingent fund of the Senate.

STANDING COMMITTEES OF THE SENATE

Agriculture. Senators Bailey, chairman; Clark, Dunlap, Hargett, Hancock, Askew, McRackan, Currie, Roane, McLeod, Harris, McDonald, Horton of Caswell, Maguire, Call.

Appropriations. Senators Williams of Pasquotank, chairman; Long, Woodson, Hargett, Ray, Woltz, Ebbs, Grant, Spencer, Horton of Chatham, McDonald, Tapp, Hancock, Smith of Mecklenburg, Royall, Haywood, Salmon, Williams of Warren, Currie, Grier, Sedberry, Whitmire, Blount.

Banks and Currency. Senators Royall, chairman; Williams of Pasquotank, Woodson, Woltz, Tapp, Womble, Bailey, Broughton, Hines, Blount, Stringfield, Lawrence, Dunlap, Clark, Williams of Warren, Haywood, Horton of Caswell, Childs, Harris, Askew, Currie, Call.

Caswell Training School. Senators Sedberry, chairman; Hargett, Moore, Askew, Clark, Harris, Ebbs, Haywood, Williams of Warren, Roane, Stringfield, Call.

Claims. Senators Tapp, chairman; Dunlap, Lawrence, Bailey, Johnson, Ruark, McLeod, Horton of Chatham, Hines, Sedberry, Haywood, Childs.

Commerce. Senators Askew, chairman; Long, Williams of Pasquotank, Tapp, Grant, Salmon, Grier, Fulton, Maguire.

Congressional Districts. Senators Williams of Warren, chairman; Moore, Lawrence, Long, Hargett, Johnson, Salmon, Ray, Womble, Grier, Stringfield, Canady.

Consolidated Statutes. Senators Grant, chairman; Spencer, Blount, Royall, Horton of Chatham, Williams of Warren, Sharp, Smith of Mecklenburg, Whitmire.

Standing Committees of the Senate

Constitutional Amendment. Senators McRackan, chairman; Dunlap, Moore, Grant, Woodson, Woltz, Spainhour, Lawrence, Royall, Ruark, Hines.

Corporations. Senators Broughton, chairman; Long, Williams of Pasquotank; Dunlap, Moore, Clark, McRackan, Ruark, Williams of Warren, Hancock, Currie, Smith of Stanly, Haywood, Childs, Whitmire, Stringfield, Canady.

Corporation Commission. Senators Childs, chairman; Williams of Pasquotank, Hargett, McLeod, Salmon, Horton of Caswell, Sedberry, Haywood, Call.

Counties, Cities and Towns. Senators Ebbs, chairman; Clark, McDonald, Sharp, Dunlap, Ray, Tapp, Horton of Chatham, Spencer, Womble, Spainhour, Royall, Broughton, McRackan, Horton of Caswell, Hines, Smith of Mecklenburg, Childs, Whitmire, Roane, Maguire.

Distribution of Governor's Message. Senators Roane, chairman; Bailey, Tapp, McLeod, McDonald, Smith of Mecklenburg, Fulton, McNeill, Hyatt.

Education. Senators Woltz, chairman; Sharpe, Johnson, Ray, Grant, Spainhour, Ebbs, Horton of Chatham, Tapp, Spencer, Smith of Mecklenburg, Blount, Royall, Salmon, Broughton, Hancock, Sedberry, Whitmire, Hyatt, Stringfield, Canady, McNeill, Horton of Caswell, Lawrence, Call, Maguire.

Election Law. Senators Horton of Chatham, chairman; Hargett, Long, Dunlap, Woodson, Williams of Pasquotank, Ebbs, Grant, Spainhour, Blount, Broughton, Hancock, Horton of Caswell, Smith of Mecklenburg, Smith of Stanly, Grier, Whitmire, Canady, McNeill, Ruark, Askew.

Engrossed Bills. Senators Canady, chairman; Askew, Bailey, McRackan, McLeod, McDonald, Ray, Grier, Call.

Enrolled Bills. Senators Whitmire, chairman; Spencer, Clark, Tapp, Ruark, Broughton, Sharpe, Sedberry, Maguire.

Federal Relations. Senators Canady, chairman; Moore, Blount, Harris, Johnson, Call, Fulton, Hyatt.

Finance. Senators Woodson, chairman; Womble, Williams of Pasquotank, Clark, Long, Dunlap, Johnson, Woltz, Ray, Moore, Sharp, McRackan, Hines, Ruark, Broughton, McLeod, Horton of Caswell, Smith of Stanly, Haywood, Hyatt, Stringfield, Childs, Canady, Call.

Fish and Fisheries. Senators Ruark, chairman; Spencer, Hargett, Lawrence, McLeod, Askew, Hancock, Smith of Mecklenburg, Stringfield, McNeill, Currie, Maguire.

Game Law. Senators McLeod, chairman; Dunlap, Tapp, McDonald, Spencer, Williams of Pasquotank, Horton of Chatham, Grant, Ray, Bailey, Sharp, Lawrence, Clark, Harris, Haywood, Grier, Fulton, Roane, Call.

Immigration. Senators Harris, chairman, Lawrence, Askew, Tapp, Ruark, Salmon, Horton of Caswell.

Insane Asylum. Senators Clark, chairman; Woltz, Bailey, Tapp, Womble, Grier, Ray, Ruark, Royall, Salmon, Sedberry, Smith of Stanly, Maguire.

Institutions for the Blind. Senators Spainhour, chairman; Broughton, Royall, Lawrence, Bailey, Hargett, Salmon, Sharp, Currie, Haywood, Childs, Whitmire, Stringfield, Roane.

Institutions for the Deaf. Senators Grier, chairman; Williams of Pasquotank, Ebbs, Askew, Blount, Harris, McDonald, Broughton, Horton of Chatham, Ray, Fulton, McNeill, Hyatt.

Insurance. Senators Hines, chairman; Dunlap, Woodson, Williams of Warren, Clark, Moore, Woltz, Hancock, Ray, McDonald, Grant, Ruark, Williams of Pasquotank, Sedberry, Smith of Stanly, Childs, Fulton, McNeill, Canady, Maguire.

Internal Improvements. Senators Lawrence, chairman; Moore, Long, Harris, Grant, Horton of Chatham, Williams of Warren, Hancock, Hines, Womble, Maguire.

Journal. Senators Stringfield, chairman; Sharp, Spencer, Ray, Currie, Dunlap, Smith of Mecklenburg, Grier, Fulton.

Courts and Judicial Districts. Senators Smith of Mecklenburg, chairman; Johnson, Woltz, Sharpe, Dunlap, Womble, Ray, Moore, Grant, Horton of Chatham, Williams of Warren, Hancock, Hines, Currie, Childs, Lawrence, Whitmire, Canady, Smith of Stanly.

Judiciary, No. 1. Senators Moore, chairman; Long, Sharp, Dunlap, Woltz, Womble, Woodson, Spainhour, Horton of Chatham, Ray, Lawrence, Blount, Salmon, Hancock, Hines, Smith of Stanly, Grier, Ruark.

Judiciary, No. 2. Senators Johnson, chairman; Broughton, Grant, Spencer, Royall, McRakan, Horton of Caswell, Williams of Warren, Currie, Sedberry, Smith of Mecklenburg, Childs, Whitmire, Canady.

Library. Senators Fulton, chairman; Ebbs, Canady, Lawrence, Clark, McLeod, Spainhour, Horton of Caswell.

Manufacture. Senators Haywood, chairman; Long, Hargett, Dunlap, Williams of Pasquotank, Woltz, Woodson, Fulton, Womble, Ray, Hines, Royall, Grant, Smith of Stanly, Smith of Mecklenburg, Stringfield, Call.

Military Affairs. Senators Smith of Stanly, chairman; Dunlap, Horton of Caswell, Royall, Broughton, Salmon, Hancock, Hines, Currie, Sedberry, Grier, Canady.

Mining. Senators Roane, chairman; Askew, McDonald, McLeod, Horton of Chatham, Haywood, Childs, Stringfield, Call.

Penal Institutions. Senators Hancock, chairman; Moore, Spencer, Dunlap, Tapp, Hargett, Canady, Clark, Johnson, McLeod, Salmon, Horton of Chatham, Charp, Currie, Woltz, Ebbs, Stringfield, Sedberry, Maguire.

Printing. Senators McNeill, chairman; Askew, Bailey, Tapp, Johnson, McRackan, McDonald, Williams of Warren, Ray, Sharp.

Pensions and Soldiers' Home. Senators Horton of Caswell, chairman; Dunlap, Woodson, Currie, Horton of Chatham, Woltz, Hines, Smith of Mecklenburg, Smith of Stanly, Whitmire, Fulton, McNeill, Roane, Ruark and Maguire.

Propositions and Grievances. Senators Spencer, chairman; Hargett, Johnson, Bailey, Harris, Tapp, McLeod, McDonald, Broughton, Williams of Warren, Hancock, Haywood, Grier, Whitmire, Fulton, McNeill, Hyatt, Roane.

Public Health. Senators McDonald, chairman; Spencer, Harris, Hargett, Grant, Womble, Ebbs, Hancock, Salmon, Haywood, Grier, Fulton, Roane, Canady, Call, Hyatt.

Roads. Senators Hargett, chairman; Ray, Moore, Spencer, Long, Woodson, Dunlap, Woltz, Johnson, Grant, McRackan, Horton of Chatham, McLeod, Spainhour, Broughton, Ebbs, Blount, Royall, Womble, Hancock, Horton of Caswell, Currie, Grier, McNeill, Roane, Canady, Stringfield, Clark, Hyatt, Maguire, Askew, Salmon.

Railroads. Senators Ray, chairman; Tapp, Williams of Warren, Ruark, Woodson, McDonald, Hines, Spainhour, Sharp, Womble, Dunlap, Smith of Stanly, Haywood, Childs, Fulton, Maguire.

Rules. Senators Long, chairman; Woodson, Williams of Pasquotank, Moore, Johnson, Womble, Ray, Hargett, Woltz, Hines.

Salaries and Fees. Senators Dunlap, chairman; Woltz, Hargett, Williams of Pasquotank, Woodson, Spencer, Tapp, Dunlap, Hines, Clark, Salmon, McNeill, Spencer.

Senate Expenditures. Senators Salmon, chairman; Lawrence, Askew, Clark, Bailey, Tapp, McRackan, Sedberry, Haywood, Childs, Roane.

Senatorial Apportionment. Senators Blount, chairman; Ruark, Moore, Long, Harris, Hargett, Spainhour, Horton of Caswell, McDonald, Smith of Stanly, Fulton, McNeill, Canady, Roane.

Trustees of University. Senators Currie, chairman; Long, Woltz, Moore, Spencer, Johnson, Blount, Ray, Dunlap, Smith of Mecklenburg, Grier, Clark, Blount, Harris, Royall, Williams of Warren.

Water Commerce. Senators Sharp, chairman; McDonald, Woltz, Womble, Woodson, Smith of Mecklenburg, Dunlap, Ray, McLeod, Hancock, Horton of Chatham, Grant, Hargett, Blount, Clark, Williams of Pasquotank, Lawrence, Hyatt.

Welfare. Senators Womble, chairman; Long, Spainhour, Bailey, Tapp, Williams of Pasquotank, Grant, Womble, Hines, Horton of Chatham, Broughton, Hancock, Haywood, Smith of Mecklenburg, Currie, Clark, Blount, Williams of Warren, Salmon, Whitmire, Stringfield, Royall.

Committee on Trustees of State College. Senators Dunlap, chairman; Moore, Ruark, McDonald, Broughton, Hines, Haywood, Womble, Woltz, Ebbs, Call.

OFFICERS AND MEMBERS OF THE HOUSE OF REPRESENTATIVES

OFFICERS

RICHARD T. FOUNTAIN	Speaker	Edgecombe
ALEX LASSITER	Principal Clerk	Bertie
D. P. DELLINGER	Reading Clerk	Gaston
JOHN A. LISK	Sergeant-at-Arms	Montgomery
MISS ROSA B. MUND	Engrossing Clerk	Cabarrus

REPRESENTATIVES
(Alphabetically Arranged)

Name	County	Party	Postoffice
Austin, W. B.	Ashe	Democrat	Jefferson, N. C.
Banks, Veston C.	Pamlico	Democrat	Grantsboro, N. C.
Bell, D. L.	Chatham	Democrat	Pittsboro, N. C.
Bell, W. H.	Carteret	Democrat	Newport, N. C.
Black, Sam	Cabarrus	Democrat	Harrisburg, R. 2, N. C.
Bolich, W. Bryan	Forsyth	Democrat	Winston-Salem, N. C.
Bost, Luther H.	Stanly	Democrat	Albemarle, N. C.
Boyd, Jas. R.	Haywood	Democrat	Waynesville, N. C.
Boyles, C. O.	Stokes	Republican	King, N. C.
Brawley, S. C.	Durham	Democrat	Durham, N. C.
Brewer, J. M.	Wake	Democrat	Wake Forest, N. C.
Brewer, Stacy	Moore	Democrat	Vass, N. C.
Bridger, J. A.	Bladen	Democrat	Bladenboro, N. C.
Brown, P. E.	Wilkes	Republican	Wilkesboro, N. C.
Bullard, V. C.	Cumberland	Democrat	Fayetteville, N. C.
Butler, John S.	Robeson	Democrat	St. Pauls, N. C.
Byrd, A. W.	Wayne	Democrat	Mt. Olive, N. C.
Campbell, Wm. B.	New Hanover	Democrat	Wilmington, N. C.
Coffey, Thos. H.	Watauga	Democrat	Blowing Rock, N. C.
Connor, H. G.	Wilson	Democrat	Wilson, N. C.
Cox, Dr. B. T.	Pitt	Democrat	Winterville, N. C.
Cox, R. M.	Forsyth	Democrat	Winston-Salem, N. C.
Cox, W. E.	Alleghany	Democrat	Stratford, N. C.
Creekmore, T. L.	Wake	Democrat	Raleigh, N. C.
Dunn, Wm., Jr.	Craven	Democrat	New Bern, N. C.
Eddleman, Dr. H. M.	Gaston	Democrat	Gastonia, N. C.
Eure, T. A.	Gates	Democrat	Eure, N. C.
Everett, J. A.	Martin	Democrat	Palmyra, N. C.
Everett, R. O.	Durham	Democrat	Durham, N. C.
Falls, B. T.	Cleveland	Democrat	Shelby, N. C.
Flanagan, E. G.	Pitt	Democrat	Greenville, N. C.
Folger, John H.	Surry	Democrat	Mt. Airy, N. C.
Fountain, R. T.	Edgecombe	Democrat	Rocky Mount, N. C.
Gibbs, Closs	Hyde	Democrat	Engelhard, N. C.
Giles, J. Hamp.	Burke	Democrat	Glen Alpine, N. C.

REPRESENTATIVES—Continued

Name	County	Party	Postoffice
Gold, T. J.	Guilford	Democrat	High Point, N. C.
Graham, A. H.	Orange	Democrat	Hillsboro, N. C.
Graham, A. McL.	Sampson	Democrat	Clinton, N. C.
Grant, A. T., Jr.	Davie	Republican	Mocksville, N. C.
Gwaltney, John L.	Alexander	Democrat	Taylorsville, N. C.
Hargett, Fred W., Jr.	Onslow	Democrat	Jacksonville, N. C.
Harris, R. L.	Person	Democrat	Roxboro, N. C.
Hart, Dr. J. E.	Anson	Democrat	Wadesboro, N. C.
Hayman, M. D.	Dare	Democrat	Wanchese, N. C.
Haywood, Oscar	Montgomery	Democrat	Mt. Gilead, N. C.
Helms, T. L. A.	Union	Democrat	Monroe, N. C.
Hill, John Bright	New Hanover	Democrat	Wilmington, N. C.
Jenkins, T. M.	Graham	Republican	Robbinsville, N. C.
Johnson, E. R.	Currituck	Democrat	Currituck, N. C.
Jones, H. R.	Johnston	Democrat	McCullers, R.F.D., N. C.
Jonas, Chas. A.	Lincoln	Republican	Lincolnton, N. C.
Kerr, A. Yancey	Caswell	Democrat	Yanceyville, N. C.
Klutz, L. P.	Catawba	Republican	Newton, N. C.
Lee, Chas. G., Jr.	Buncombe	Democrat	Asheville, N. C.
Leggett, L. W.	Halifax	Democrat	Hobgood, N. C.
Little, W. F.	Polk	Democrat	Tryon, N. C.
Loven, Ed. S.	Avery	Democrat	Linville, N. C.
McBryde, Dr. M. H.	Rockingham	Democrat	Reidsville, N. C.
McDevitt, N. B.	Madison	Democrat	Marshall, N. C.
MacLean, Angus D.	Beaufort	Democrat	Washington, N. C.
McLean, Miss Carrie L.	Mecklenburg	Democrat	Charlotte, N. C.
Macon, W. H.	Franklin	Democrat	Louisburg, N. C.
Makepeace, O. P.	Lee	Democrat	Sanford, N. C.
Marshall, J. A.	Forsyth	Democrat	Walnut Cove, N. C.
Martin, L. A.	Davidson	Democrat	Lexington, N. C.
Martin, Van B.	Washington	Democrat	Plymouth, N. C.
Mason, O. F., Jr.	Gaston	Democrat	Gastonia, N. C.
Matthews, Johnson	Scotland	Democrat	Wagram, N. C.
Morgan, W. F.	Perquimans	Democrat	Winfall, N. C.
Moser, J. C.	Randolph	Democrat	Asheboro, N. C.
Moss, O. B.	Nash	Democrat	Spring Hope, N. C.
Moss, T. J.	Rutherford	Democrat	Forest City, N. C.
Murphy, Walter	Rowan	Democrat	Salisbury, N. C.
Nash, M. W.	Richmond	Democrat	Hamlet, N. C.
Nettles, Harry	Buncombe	Democrat	Biltmore, N. C.
Nicholson, Cyrus	Jackson	Republican	Sylva, N. C.
Norwood, W. J.	Halifax	Democrat	Rosemary, N. C.
Odom, W. P.	Cherokee	Republican	Murphy, N. C.
Oliver, W. M.	Robeson	Democrat	Marietta, N. C.
Parker, Dr. Carl P.	Northampton	Democrat	Seaboard, N. C.
Parnell, Wm. I.	Yancey	Republican	Burnsville, N. C.
Penland, Witt	Clay	Republican	Hayesville, N. C.
Pool, C. M.	McDowell	Republican	Marion, N. C.
Poole, D. S.	Hoke	Democrat	Raeford, N. C.
Price, W. E.	Mecklenburg	Democrat	Charlotte, N. C.
Privott, H. C.	Chowan	Democrat	Edenton, N. C.

MEMBERS OF HOUSE OF REPRESENTATIVES

REPRESENTATIVES (Continued)

Name	County	Party	P.O.
Rhodes, H. J.	Alamance	Democrat	Burlington, N. C.
Rideoutte, J. W.	Rowan	Democrat	Salisbury, N. C.
Rogers, W. W.	Hertford	Democrat	Ahoskie, N. C.
Rouse, R. C.	Greene	Democrat	Snow Hill, N. C.
Satterwhite, S. J.	Warren	Democrat	Manson, N. C.
Shipman, J. M.	Columbus	Democrat	Whiteville, N. C.
Smith, T. L.	Rockingham	Democrat	Leaksville, N. C.
Smith, Willis	Wake	Democrat	Raleigh, N. C.
Solesbee, Rev. A. S.	Macon	Republican	Franklin, N. C.
Squires, Mark	Caldwell	Democrat	Lenoir, N. C.
Stancill, J. Clyde	Mecklenburg	Democrat	Charlotte, N. C.
Sutton, Fred J.	Lenoir	Democrat	Kinston, N. C.
Tarkington, C. L.	Camden	Democrat	Camden, N. C.
Tatem, C. W.	Tyrrell	Democrat	Columbia, N. C.
Tipton, John H.	Mitchell	Republican	Relief, N. C.
Townsend, N. A.	Harnett	Democrat	Dunn, N. C.
Turlington, Z. V.	Iredell	Democrat	Mooresville, N. C.
Ward, Geo. R.	Duplin	Democrat	Wallace, N. C.
Watkins, John S.	Granville	Democrat	Virgilina, Va. R. F. D.
Watkins, M. B.	Brunswick	Democrat	Town Creek, N. C.
Wells, J. T.	Pender	Democrat	Atkinson, N. C.
Wetmur, F. S.	Henderson	Republican	Hendersonville, N. C.
Whitaker, T. C.	Jones	Democrat	Trenton, N. C.
White, G. T.	Yadkin	Republican	Hamptonville, N. C.
Williams, O. P.	Swain	Republican	Bryson City, N. C.
Wilson, J. K.	Pasquotank	Democrat	Elizabeth City, N. C.
Wilson, T. J.	Transylvania	Democrat	Pisgah Forest, N. C.
Winston, Francis D.	Bertie	Democrat	Windsor, N. C.
Wood, J. W.	Johnston	Democrat	Benson, N. C.
Woodard, W. C.	Nash	Democrat	Rocky Mount, N. C.
Wright, C. G.	Guilford	Democrat	Greensboro, N. C.
Yelverton, Harrison	Wayne	Democrat	Goldsboro, N. C.
Younce, Geo. A.	Guilford	Democrat	Greensboro, N. C.
Young, J. J.	Vance	Democrat	Henderson, N. C.

REPRESENTATIVES
(Arranged by Counties)

Alamance—H. J. Rhodes, Burlington (D).

Alexander—John L. Gwaltney, Taylorsville (D).

Alleghany—W. E. Cox, Stratford (D).

Anson—Dr. J. E. Hart, Wadesboro (D).

Ashe—W. B. Austin, Jefferson (D).

Avery—Ed. S. Loven, Linville (D).

Beaufort—Angus D. MacLean, Washington (D).

Bertie—Francis D. Winston, Windsor (D).

Bladen—J. A. Bridger, Bladenboro (D).
Brunswick—M. B. Watkins, Town Creek (D).
Buncombe—Harry L. Nettles, Biltmore (D); Charles G. Lee, Jr., Asheville (D).
Burke—J. Hamp Giles, Glen Alpine (D).
Cabarrus—Sam Black, Harrisburg, R. F. D. 2 (D).
Caldwell—Mark Squires, Lenoir (D).
Camden—C. L. Tarkington, Camden (D).
Carteret—W. H. Bell, Newport (D).
Caswell—A. Yancey Kerr, Yanceyville (D).
Catawba—L. F. Klutz, Newton (R).
Chatham—D. L. Bell, Pittsboro (D).
Cherokee—W. P. Odom, Murphy (R).
Chowan—H. C. Privott, Edenton (D).
Clay—Witt Penland, Hayesville (R).
Cleveland—B. T. Falls, Shelby (D).
Columbus—J. M. Shipman, Whiteville (D).
Craven—William Dunn, Jr., New Bern (D).
Cumberland—V. C. Bullard, Fayetteville (D).
Currituck—E. R. Johnson, Currituck (D).
Dare—M. D. Hayman, Wanchese (D).
Davidson—L. A. Martin, Lexington (D).
Davie—A. T. Grant, Jr., Mocksville (R).
Duplin—George R. Ward, Wallace (D).
Durham—S. C. Brawley, Durham (D); R. O. Everett, Durham (D).
Edgecombe—R. T. Fountain, Rocky Mount (D).
Forsyth—R. M. Cox, Winston-Salem (D); W. Bryan Bolich, Winston-Salem (D); J. A. Marshall, Walnut Cove (D).
Franklin—W. H. Macon, Louisburg (D).
Gaston—Dr. H. M. Eddleman, Gastonia (D); O. F. Mason, Jr., Gastonia (D).
Gates—T. A. Eure, Eure (D).

Graham—T. M. Jenkins, Robbinsville (R).
Granville—John S. Watkins, Virgilina, Va., R. F. D. (D).
Greene—R. C. Rouse, Snow Hill (D).
Guilford—C. G. Wright, Greensboro (D); T. J. Gold, High Point (D); Geo. A. Younce, Greensboro (D).
Halifax—L. W. Leggett, Hobgood (D); W. J. Norwood, Rosemary (D).
Harnett—N. A. Townsend, Dunn (D).
Haywood—James R. Boyd, Waynesville (D).
Henderson—F. S. Wetmur, Hendersonville (R).
Hertford—W. W. Rogers, Ahoskie (D).
Hoke—D. S. Poole, Raeford (D).
Hyde—Closs Gibbs, Engelhard (D).
Iredell—Z. V. Turlington, Mooresville (D).
Jackson—Cyrus H. Nicholson, Sylva (R).
Johnston—J. W. Wood, Benson (D); Hubert R. Jones, McCullers, R. F. D. (D).
Jones—T. C. Whitaker, Trenton (D).
Lee—O. P. Makepeace, Sanford (D).
Lenoir—Fred I. Sutton, Kinston (D).
Lincoln—C. A. Jonas, Lincolnton (R).
Macon—Rev. A. S. Solesbee, Franklin, R. F. D. 4 (R).
Madison—N. B. McDevitt, Marshall (D).
Martin—J. A. Everett, Palmyra (D).
McDowell—C. M. Pool, Marion (R).
Mecklenburg—J. Clyde Stancill, Charlotte (D); Miss Carrie L. McLean, Charlotte (D); W. E. Price, Charlotte (D).
Mitchell—John H. Tipton, Relief (R).
Montgomery—Oscar Haywood, Mt. Gilead (D).
Moore—Stacy Brewer, Vass (D).
Nash—O. B. Moss, Spring Hope (D); W. C. Woodard, Rocky Mount (D).
New Hanover—William B. Campbell, Wilmington (D); John B. Hill, Wilmington (D).

Northampton—Dr. Carl P. Parker, Seaboard (D).
Onslow—Fred W. Hargett, Jr., Jacksonville (D).
Orange—A. H. Graham, Hillsboro (D).
Pamlico—Veston C. Banks, Grantsboro (D).
Pasquotank—J. K. Wilson, Elizabeth City (D).
Pender—J. T. Wells, Atkinson (D).
Perquimans—W. F. Morgan, Winfall (D).
Person—R. L. Harris, Roxboro (D).
Pitt—Dr. B. T. Cox, Winterville (D); E. G. Flanagan, Greenville (D).
Polk—W. F. Little, Tryon (D).
Randolph—I. C. Moser, Asheboro (D).
Richmond—M. W. Nash, Hamlet (D).
Robeson—John S. Butler, St. Pauls (D); W. M. Oliver, Marietta (D).
Rockingham—Dr. M. H. McBryde, Reidsville (D); T. L. Smith, Leaksville (D).
Rowan—Walter Murphy, Salisbury (D); J. W. Rideoutte, Salisbury (D).
Rutherford—T. J. Moss, Forest City (D).
Sampson—A. McL. Graham, Clinton (D).
Scotland—Walter Johnson Matthews, Wagram (D).
Stanly—Luther H. Bost, Albemarle (D).
Stokes—C. O. Boyles, King (R).
Surry—John H. Folger, Mt. Airy (D).
Swain—O. P. Williams, Bryson City (R).
Transylvania—T. J. Wilson, Pisgah Forest (D).
Tyrrell—C. W. Tatem, Columbia (D).
Union—T. L. A. Helms, Monroe (D).
Vance—I. J. Young, Henderson (D).
Wake—J. M. Brewer, Wake Forest (D); Thomas L. Creekmore, Raleigh (D); Willis Smith, Raleigh (D).
Warren—S. J. Satterwhite, Manson (D).

Washington—Van B. Martin, Plymouth (D).

Watauga—Thomas H. Coffey, Blowing Rock (D).

Wayne—Harrison Yelverton, Goldsboro (D); A. W. Byrd, Mt. Olive (D).

Wilkes—P. E. Brown, Wilkesboro (R).

Wilson—H. G. Connor, Wilson (D).

Yadkin—G. T. White, Hamptonville (R).

Yancey—W. I. Parnell, Burnsville (R).

RULES OF THE HOUSE OF REPRESENTATIVES

Touching the Duties of Speaker

1. It shall be the duty of the Speaker to have the sessions of the House opened with prayer.

2. He shall take the chair every day at the hour fixed by the House on the preceding legislative day, shall immediately call the members to order, and, on appearance of a quorum, cause the Journal of the preceding day to be approved.

3. He shall preserve order and decorum, may speak to points of order in preference to other members, rising from his seat for that purpose, and shall decide questions of order, subject to an appeal to the House by any member, on which appeal no member shall speak more than once, unless by leave of the House. A two-thirds vote of the members present shall be necessary to sustain any appeal from the ruling of the Chair.

4. He shall rise to put a question, but may state it sitting.

5. Questions shall be put in this form, namely, "Those in favor (as the question may be) will say, 'Aye,'" and after the affirmative voice has been expressed, "Those opposed will say, 'No.'" Upon a call for a division, the Speaker shall count, if required, he shall appoint tellers.

6. The Speaker shall have a general direction of the hall. He shall have a right to name any member to perform the duties of the Chair, but substitution shall not extend beyond one day, except in case of sickness or by leave of the House.

7. All committees shall be appointed by the Speaker, unless otherwise specially ordered by the House.

8. In all elections the Speaker may vote. In all other cases he may exercise his right to vote, or he may reserve this right until there is a tie; but in no case shall he be allowed to vote twice on the same question.

9. All acts, addreses and resolutions, and all warrants and subpœnas issued by order of the House shall be signed by the Speaker.

10. In case of any disturbance or disorderly conduct in the galleries or lobby, the Speaker or other presiding officer shall have power to order the same to be cleared.

11. No persons except members of the Senate, officers and clerks of the General Assembly, Judges of the Supreme and Superior Courts, State officers, former members of the General Assembly, and persons particularly invited by the Speaker shall be admitted within the hall of the House: *Provided*, that no person except members of the Senate and officers of the General Assembly shall be allowed on the floor of the House or in the lobby in the rear of the Speaker's desk, unless permitted by the Speaker of the House.

12. Reporters wishing to take down debates may be admitted by the Speaker, who shall assign such places to them on the floor or elsewhere, to effect this object, as shall not interfere with the convenience of the House.

13. Smoking shall not be allowed in the hall, the lobbies, or the galleries while the House is in session: *Provided*, that smoking may be permitted in the lobby in the rear of the Speaker's desk.

Order of Business of the Day

14. After the approval of the Journal of the preceding day, which shall stand approved without objection, the House shall proceed to business in the following order, viz.:

(1) The receiving of petitions, memorials, and papers addressed to the General Assembly or to the House.

(2) Reports of standing committees.

(3) Reports of select committees.

(4) Resolutions.
(5) Bills.
(6) The unfinished business of the preceding day.
(7) Bills, resolutions, petitions, memorials, messages, and other papers on the Calendar, in their exact numerical order, unless displaced by the orders of the day; but messages and motions to elect officers shall always be in order.

No member shall rise from his seat to introduce any petition, resolution or bill out of order unless he is permitted so to do by a suspension of the rules.

On Decorum in Debate

15. When any member is about to speak in debate or deliver any matter to the House, he shall rise from his seat and respectfully address the Speaker.

16. When the Speaker shall call a member to order, the member shall sit down, as also he shall when called to order by another member, unless the Speaker decides the point of order in his favor. By leave of the House a member called to order may clear a matter of fact, or explain, but shall not proceed in debate so long as the decision stands, but by permission of the House. Any member may appeal from the decision of the Chair, and if, upon appeal, the decision be in favor of the member called to order, he may proceed; if otherwise, he shall not, except by leave of the House; and if the case, in the judgment of the House, require it, he shall be liable to its censure.

17. No member shall speak until recognized by the Chair, and when two or more members rise at the same time, the Speaker shall name the member to speak.

18. No member shall speak more than twice on the main question, nor longer than thirty minutes for the first speech and fifteen minutes for the second speech, unless allowed to do so by the affirmative vote of a majority of the members present; nor shall he speak more than once upon an amendment or motion to commit or postpone, and then not longer than ten minutes. But the House may, by consent of a majority, suspend the operation of this rule during any debate on any particular question before the

House, or the Committee on Rules may bring in a special rule that shall be applicable to the debate on any bill.

19. While the Speaker is putting any question, or addressing the House, no person shall speak, stand up, walk out of or across the House, nor when a member is speaking entertain private discourse, stand up, or pass between him and the Chair.

20. No member shall vote on any question when he was not present when the question was put by the Speaker, except by the consent of the House. Upon a division and count of the House on any question, no member without the bar shall be counted.

21. Every member who shall be in the hall of the House for the above purpose when the question is put shall give his vote upon a call of the ayes and noes, unless the House for special reasons shall excuse him, and no application to be excused from voting or to explain a vote shall be entertained unless made before the call of the roll. The hall of the House shall include the lobbies and offices connected with the hall.

22. When a motion is made, it shall be stated by the Speaker, or, if written, it shall be handed to the Chair and read aloud by the Speaker or Clerk before debate.

23. Every motion shall be reduced to writing, if the Speaker or any two members request it.

24. After a motion is stated by the Speaker or read by the Clerk, it shall be deemed to be in possession of the House, but may be withdrawn before a decision or amendment, except in case of a motion to reconsider, which motion, when made by a member, shall be deemed and taken to be in possession of the House, and shall not be withdrawn without leave of the House.

25. When a question is under debate no motion shall be received but to adjourn, to lay on the table, to postpone indefinitely, to postpone to a day certain, to commit or amend, which several motions shall have precedence in the order in which they stand arranged; and no motion to lay on the table, to postpone indefinitely, to postpone to a day certain, to commit or amend, being decided, shall be again allowed at the same stage of the bill or proposition.

26. A motion to adjourn or lay on the table shall be decided without debate, and a motion to adjourn shall always be in order.

except when the House is voting or some member is speaking; but a motion to adjourn shall not follow a motion to adjourn until debate or some other business of the House has intervened.

27. When a question has been postponed indefinitely, the same shall not be acted on again during the session, except upon a two-thirds vote.

28. Any member may call for a division of the question, when the same shall admit of it, which shall be determined by the Speaker.

29. When a motion has been once made and carried in the affirmative or negative, it shall be in order for any member of the majority to move for the reconsideration thereof, on the same or succeeding day, unless it may have subsequently passed the Senate, and no motion to reconsider shall be taken from the table except by a two-thirds vote. But unless such vote has been taken by a call of the yeas and nays, any member may move to reconsider.

30. When the reading of a paper is called for, which has been read in the House, and the same is objected to by any member, it shall be determined by a vote of the House.

31. Petitions, memorials, and other papers addressed to the House shall be presented by the Speaker; a brief statement of the contents thereof may be verbally made by the introducer before reference to a committee, but shall not be debated or decided on the day of their first being read, unless the House shall direct otherwise.

32. When the ayes and noes are called for on any question, it shall be on motion before the question is put; and if seconded by one-fifth of the members present, the question shall be decided by the ayes and noes; and in taking the ayes and noes, or on a call of the House, the names of the members will be taken alphabetically.

33. Decency of speech shall be observed and personal reflection carefully avoided.

34. Any member may arise at any time to speak to a question of personal privilege, and upon objection to him proceeding, the Speaker shall determine if the question is one of privilege.

35. Fifteen members, including the Speaker, shall be authorized to compel the attendance of absent members.

36. No member or officer of the House shall absent himself from the service of the House without leave, unless from sickness or inability.

37. Any member may excuse himself from serving on any committee if he is a member of two standing committees.

38. If any member shall be necessarily absent on temporary business of the House when a vote is taken upon any question, upon entering the House he shall be permitted, on request, to vote, provided that the result shall not be thereby affected.

39. No standing rule or order shall be rescinded or altered without one day's notice given on the motion thereof, and to sustain such motion two-thirds of the House shall be required.

40. The members of the House shall uncover their heads upon entering the House while it is in session, and shall continue so uncovered during their continuance in the hall, except Quakers.

41. A motion to reconsider shall be determined by a majority vote, except a motion to reconsider an indefinite postponement, or a motion to reconsider a motion tabling a motion to reconsider, which shall require a two-thirds vote.

42. After a bill has been tabled or has failed to pass on any of its readings, the contents of such bill or the principal provisions or its subject-matter shall not be embodied in any other measure. Upon the point of order being raised and sustained by the Chair, such measures shall be laid upon the table, and shall not be taken therefrom except by a vote of two-thirds of the elected membership of the House: *Provided*, no local bill shall be held by the Chair as embodying the provisions or being identical with any State-wide measure which has been laid upon the table, or failed to pass any of its readings.

STANDING COMMITTEES

43. At the commencement of the session a standing committee shall be appointed by the Speaker on each of the following subjects, namely:

On Agriculture.
On Appropriations.
On Banks and Banking.
On Claims.

On Commerce.
On Congressional Districts.
On Constitutional Amendments.
On Corporation Commission.
On Corporations.
On Counties, Cities, and Towns.
On Courts and Judicial Districts.
On Education.
On Election Laws.
On Engrossed Bills.
On Expenditures of the House.
On Federal Relations.
On Finance.
On Fish and Fisheries.
On Game.
On Health.
On Immigration.
On Insane Asylums.
On Institutions for the Blind.
On Institutions for the Deaf and Dumb.
On Insurance.
On Internal Improvements.
On the Journal.
On Judiciary, No. 1.
On Judiciary, No. 2.
On Manufactures and Labor.
On Military Affairs.
On Mines and Mining.
On Oyster Industry.
On Penal Institutions.
On Pensions.
On Private and Public-Local Laws.
On Privileges and Elections.
On Propositions and Grievances.
On Public Roads.
On Public Welfare.
On Regulation of Public-Service Corporations
On Rules.

On Salaries and Fees.
On Senatorial Districts.

JOINT COMMITTEES

On Enrolled Bills.
On Justices of the Peace.
On Library.
On Printing.
On Public Buildings and Grounds.
On Trustees of University.
On Revision of the Laws.

The first member announced on each committee shall be chairman.

44. In forming a Committee of the Whole House, the Speaker shall leave the Chair, and a Chairman to preside in committee shall be appointed by the Speaker.

45. Upon bills submitted to a Committee of the Whole House, the bill shall be first read throughout by the Clerk, and then again read and debated by sections, leaving the preamble to be last considered. The body of the bill shall not be defaced or interlined, but all amendments, noting the page and line, shall be duly entered by the Clerk on a separate paper as the same shall be agreed to by the committee, and so reported to the House. After report, the bill shall again be subject to be debated and amended by sections before a question on its passage be taken.

46. The rules of procedure in the House shall be observed in a Committee of the Whole House, so far as they may be applicable, except the rule limiting the time of speaking and the previous question.

47. In a Committee of the Whole House a motion that the committee rise shall always be in order, except when a member is speaking, and shall be decided without debate.

48. Every bill shall be introduced by motion for suspension of the rules, or by order of the House, or on the report of a committee, unless introduced in regular order during the morning hour.

49. All bills and resolutions shall be reported from the committee to which referred, with such recommendation as the committee may desire to make.

50. Every bill shall receive three several readings in the House previous to its passage, and the Speaker shall give notice at each whether it be its first, second or third reading.

51. Any member introducing a bill or resolution shall briefly endorse thereon the substance of the same.

52. All bills and resolutions shall upon their introduction be referred by the Speaker, without suggestion from the introducer, to the appropriate committee. No bills shall be withdrawn from the committee to which referred except upon motion duly made and carried by a majority vote.

53. The Clerk of the House shall keep a separate calendar of the public, local, and private bills, and shall number them in the order in which they are introduced, and all bills shall be disposed of in the order they stand upon the Calendar; but the Committee on Rules may at any time arrange the order of precedence in which bills may be considered. No bill shall be twice read on the same day without the concurrence of two-thirds of the members.

54. All resolutions which may grant money out of the Treasury, or such as shall be of a public nature, shall be treated in all respects in a similar manner with public bills.

55. The Clerk of the House shall be deemed to continue in office until another is appointed.

56. On the point of no quorum being raised, the doors shall be closed and there shall be a call of the House, and upon a call of the House the names of the members shall be called over by the Clerk and the absentees noted, after which the names of the absentees shall again be called over. Those for whom no excuse or sufficient excuses are made may, by order of those present, if fifteen in number, be taken into custody as they appear, or may be sent for and taken into custody wherever to be found by special messenger appointed for that purpose.

Previous Question

57. The previous question shall be as follows: "Shall the main question be now put?" and, until it is decided, shall preclude all amendments and debate. If this question shall be decided in the

affirmative, the "main question" shall be on the passage of the bill, resolution or other matter under consideration; but when amendments are pending, the question shall be taken upon such amendments, in their order, without further debate or amendment. If such question be decided in the negative, the main question shall be considered as remaining under debate: *Provided*, that no one shall move the previous question except the member submitting the report on the bill or other matter under consideration, and the member introducing the bill or other matter under consideration, or the member in charge of the measure, who shall be designated by the chairman of the committee reporting the same to the House at the time the bill or other matter under consideration is reported to the House or taken up for consideration.

When a motion for the previous question is made, and pending the second thereto by a majority, debate shall cease; but if any member obtains the floor, he may move to lay the matter under consideration on the table, or move an adjournment, and when both or either of these motions are pending the question shall stand:

(1) Previous question.
(2) To adjourn.
(3) To lay on the table.

And then upon the main question, or amendments, or the motion to postpone indefinitely, postpone to a day certain, to commit, or amend, in the order of their precedence, until the main question is reached or disposed of; but after the previous question has been called by a majority, no motion, or amendment, or debate shall be in order.

All motions below the motions to lay on the table must be made prior to a motion for the previous question; but, pending and not after the second therefor, by the majority of the House, a motion to adjourn or lay on the table, or both, are in order. This constitutes the precedence of the motions to adjourn and lay on the table over other motions, in Rule 25.

Motions stand as follows in order of precedence in Rule 26:

Previous question.
Adjourn.
Lay on the table.

Postpone definitely.
To commit or amend.

When the previous question is called, all motions below it fall, unless made prior to the call, and all motions above it fall after its second by a majority required. Pending the second, the motions to adjourn and lay on the table are in order, but not after a second. When in order and every motion is before the House, the question stands as follows:

Previous question.
Adjourn.
Lay on the table.
Postpone indefinitely.
Postpone definitely.
To commit.
Amendment to amendment.
Amendment.
Substitute.
Bill.

The previous question covers all other motions when seconded by a majority of the House, and proceeds by regular graduation to the main question, without debate, amendment, or motion, until such question is reached or disposed of.

58. All committees, other than the Committee on Appropriations, when favorably reporting any bill which carries an appropriation from the State, shall indicate same in the report, and said bill shall be re-referred to the Committee on Appropriations for a further report before being acted upon by the House.

59. The Principal Clerk, the Engrossing Clerk, and the Sergeant-at-Arms shall appoint, with the approval of the Speaker, such assistants as may be necessary to the efficient discharge of the duties of their various offices.

60. The Speaker shall appoint a Clerk to the Speaker, and he shall also appoint twelve pages to wait upon the sessions of the House, and when the pressure of business may require, he may appoint six additional pages.

61. The chairman of each of the committees—Agriculture, Appropriations, Banks and Banking, Counties, Cities and Towns,

Courts and Judicial Districts, Education, Fish and Fisheries, Finance, Judiciary, No. 1, Judiciary, No. 2, Propositions and Grievances, Public Roads, Salaries and Fees, Commerce, Public Welfare, and Penal Institutions—may appoint a clerk to his respective committee with the approval of the Speaker.

62. The chairman and five other members of any committee shall constitute a quorum of said committee for the transaction of business.

63. The Committee on the Journal shall examine daily the Journal of the House before the hour of convening, and report after the opening of the House whether or not the proceedings of the previous day have been correctly recorded.

64. When a bill shall be reported by a committee with a recommendation that it be not passed, but accompanied by a minority report, the question before the House shall be "The adoption of the Minority Report," and it failing to be adopted by a majority vote, the bill shall be placed upon the unfavorable calendar. Such minority report shall be signed by at least three members of the committee who were present when the bill was considered in committee. In the event there is an unfavorable report with no minority report accompanying it, the bill shall be placed upon the unfavorable calendar. To take a bill from the unfavorable calendar, a two-thirds vote shall be necessary.

65. Whenever a public bill is introduced, a carbon copy thereof shall accompany the bill. On the same day that such public bill is introduced the Chief Clerk shall deliver the carbon copy to the Public Printer and cause four hundred (400) copies thereof to be printed. On the morning following the delivery of the printed copies, the Chief Clerk shall cause the Chief Page to have a copy thereof put upon the desk of each member and then retain the other printed copies in his office. A sufficient number for the use of the committee to whom the bill is referred shall be by the Chief Clerk delivered to the chairman or clerk of the committee. If the bill is passed, the remaining copies shall be by the Chief Clerk delivered to the Chief Clerk of the Senate, for the use of the Senate. No committee shall consider or report any public bill until after the same shall have been printed as herein provided for. In the event

STANDING COMMITTEES OF HOUSE OF REPRESENTATIVES

the member introducing the bill and the Chief Clerk shall doubt as to whether it is a public bill, the question shall be left to the decision of the Speaker of the House of Representatives, whose decision shall be final. The cost of printing as herein provided for shall be paid from the contingent fund of the House of Representatives.

66. Whenever any resolution or bill is introduced a carbon copy thereof shall be attached thereto, and the Principal Clerk shall cause said carbon copy to be numbered as the original resolution or bill is numbered, and shall cause the same to be available at all times to the member introducing the same. In case the resolution or bill is a public resolution or bill, an additional carbon copy shall also be attached thereto for the use of the Public Printer, under the provisions of Rule 65.

STANDING COMMITTEES OF THE HOUSE OF REPRESENTATIVES

Committee on Agriculture. Representatives Watkins of Granville, chairman; Whitaker, Boyd, Bost, Cox of Forsyth, Cox of Alleghany, Jones, Ward, Oliver, Helms, Satterwhite, Younce, Harris, Eure, Pool of McDowell, Gibbs, Rouse, Everett of Martin, Butler, Tatem, Black, Cox of Pitt, Wells, Norwood, Wilson of Pasquotank, Hargett, Hayman, Johnson, Loven, Little, Marshall, Nettles, Parker, Privott, Shipman, Tarkington, Watkins of Brunswick, Wilson of Transylvania, White, Poole of Hoke, Tipton, Ward, Morgan, Matthews.

Committee on Appropriations. Representatives Tarkington, chairman; Graham of Orange, Connor, Townsend, Nash, Byrd, Brewer of Wake, Price, Giles, MacLean of Beaufort, Dunn, Butler, Wood, Brawley, Smith of Rockingham, Gold, Rogers, Fodges, Younce, Rhodes, Ward, Sutton, Mason, Makepeace, Morgan, Flanagan, Tatem, Butler, Wilson of Pasquotank, Kerr, Woodard, Moore of Rutherford, Everett of Durham, Creekmore, Marshall, Brown.

Committee on Banks and Banking. Representative W. W. Rogers, chairman; Boyd, Woodard, Macon, Flanagan, Harris, Price, Wilson of Nash, Dunn, Sutton, Privott, Townsend, Little, Wilson of T...

sylvania, Young, Smith of Wake, Johnson, Everett of Martin, Gold, MacLean of Beaufort, McDevitt, Hargett, Hill, Gibbs, Williams, Wetmur, Parnell.

Committee on Claims. Representatives Leggett, chairman; Banks, Bell of Carteret, Brewer of Moore, Bridger, Cox of Alleghany. Eddleman, Eure, Hayman, Helms, Loven, Macon, Matthews, Satterwhite, Rideoutte, Shipman, Smith of Rockingham, Young, Bullard, Moser, Boyles, Odom.

Committee on Commerce. Representatives Creekmore, chairman; Gold, Graham of Sampson, Martin of Washington, Dunn, Hill, Nettles, MacLean of Beaufort, Brawley, Bullard, Bolich, Wright, Stancill, Gibbs, Banks, Wilson of Pasquotank, Wells, Bridger, Boyd, Haywood, Cox of Pitt, Bell of Chatham, Jonas, Williams, Ward, Campbell.

Committee on Congressional Districts. Representatives Murphy, chairman; Everett, Sutton, Moss of Nash, Graham of Orange, Moser, Martin of Washington, Miss McLean of Mecklenburg, Nettles, Turlington, Townsend, Coffey, McDevitt, Martin of Davidson, Leggett, Mason, Younce, Whitaker.

Committee on Constitutional Amendments. Representatives Wilson of Pasquotank, chairman; Winston, Murphy, McLean of Beaufort, Miss McLean of Mecklenburg, Hill, Folger, Everett of Durham, Moss of Nash Rideoutte, Martin of Washington, Townsend, Yelverton, Smith of Wake, Leggett, McDevitt, Grant, Solesbee, Penland.

Committee on Corporation Commission. Representatives Rhodes, chairman; Gwaltney, Woodard, Brawley, Bost, Brewer of Wake, Butler, Byrd, Creekmore, Falls, Turlington, Martin of Washington, Moss of Rutherford, Bolich, Leggett, Miss McLean of Mecklenburg, Hargett, Winston, Squires, Folger, Tatem, Everett of Martin, Nicholson, Parnell.

Committee on Corporations. Representatives Boyd, chairman; Murphy, Harris, Norwood, Flanagan, Woodard, Wright, Price, Dunn, Smith of Wake, Hargett, Winston, Moser, Nettles, Parker, Stancill, Sutton, Tarkington, Smith of Rockingham, Privott, Tatem, Squires, Williams, White.

Committee on Counties, Cities and Towns. Representatives Young, chairman; Moser, Coffey, Makepeace, McDevitt, Privott, Nash, Rhodes, Creekmore, Kerr, Campbell, Bolich, McBryde, Bell of

Carteret, Hargett, Woodard, Hart, Falls, Poole of Hoke, Macon, Boyd, Nettles, Helms, MacLean of Beaufort, Giles, Younce, Miss McLean of Mecklenburg, Mason, Byrd, Brewer of Moore, Wilson of Pasquotank, Bullard, Oliver, Eddleman, Solesbee, Brown, Pyrland, Brewer of Wake.

Committee on Courts and Judicial Districts. Representatives Smith of Wake, chairman; Dunn, Bolich, Folger, Connor, Moser, Moss of Nash, Stancill, Miss McLean of Mecklenburg, Bell of Chatham, Rhodes, Campbell, Wright, Winston, Lee, Everett of Durham, Austin, Townsend, Wilson of Pasquotank, McDevitt, Harris, Satterwhite, Hart, Ward, Poole of Hoke, Turlington, Wood, Rogers, Martin of Davidson, Jones, Solesbee, White, Boyd, MacLean of Beaufort.

Committee on Drainage. Representatives Bost, chairman; Dunn, Tatem, Gibbs, Hargett, Watkins of Brunswick, Privott, Hayman, Johnson, Winston, Everett of Martin, Bridger, Matthews, Graham of Orange.

Committee on Education. Representatives Connor, chairman; Moss of Nash, Ward, Cox of Alleghany, MacLean of Beaufort, Geld, Parker, Folger, Poole of Hoke, Black, Austin, Nash, Falls, Winston, Jones, Privott, Graham of Sampson, Giles, Eure, McDevitt, Helms, Bost, Kerr, McBryde, Whitaker, Leggett, Watkins of Brunswick, Makepeace, Satterwhite, Smith of Wake, Rouse, Townsend, Price, Rideoutte, Gwaltney, Miss McLean, Wetmur, Parnell, Harris, Watkins of Granville.

Committee on Election Laws. Representatives E. T. Falls, chairman; Turlington, Graham of Sampson, Miss McLean, Price, Moss of Nash, Moser, Martin of Davidson, Murphy, Bost, Graham of Orange, Sutton, Dunn, Johnson, Creekmore, Jones of Johnston, Brawley, Connor, Martin of Washington, Eure, Brown, Parnell.

Committee on Engrossed Bills. Representatives Mason, chairman; Graham of Orange, Nettles, Sutton, Everett of Martin, Banks, Bell of Carteret, Bost, Bridger, Byrd, Falls, Jones, Lee, Macon, Moss of Rutherford, Rouse, Tipton, Nicholson, Odom.

Committee on Enrolled Bills. Representatives Bell of Chatham, chairman; Black, Bolich, Brawley, Brewer of Moore, Campbell, Creekmore, Eure, Flanagan, Hargett, Hayman, Loven, Marshall, Matthews, Nash, Norwood, Tarkington, Tatem, Watkins of Brunswick, Wells, Yelverton, Williams, Klutz, Brown.

Committee on Expenditures of the House. Representatives Rideoutte, chairman; Mason, Macon, Marshall, Martin of Davidson, Townsend, Martin of Washington, Sutton, Tarkington, Gwaltney,

Moser, Younce, Whitaker, Turlington, Price, Moss of Rutherford, White, Parnell.

Committee on Federal Relations. Representatives Winston, chairman; Dunn, Hill, Wilson of Pasquotank, Haywood, Ward, Everett of Durham, Younce, Bolich, Brawley, MacLean of Beaufort, Graham of Sampson, Sutton, Morgan, Wells, Martin of Washington, Grant, Jonas, Nicholson.

Committee on Finance. Representatives Graham of Orange, chairman; Townsend, Bridger, Murphy, Martin of Davidson, Connor, Winston, Hargett, Squires, Stancill, Cox of Forsyth, Gibbs, Hart, Macon, Wright, McDevitt, Boyd, Coffey, Graham of Sampson, Turlington, Parker, Gold, Makepeace, Austin, Harris, Oliver, Matthews, Moss of Nash, Ward, Moser, Everett of Martin, MacLean of Beaufort, Smith of Wake, Norwood, Jenkins, Byrd.

Committee on Fish and Fisheries. Representatives Whitaker, chairman; W. H. Bell of Carteret, Privott, Gibbs, Austin, Bridger, Pullard, Boyd, Stancill, Johnson, Moss of Nash, Hargett, Coffey, Campbell, Eddleman, Cox of Alleghany, Gold, Pool of McDowell, Dunn, Parnell, Hyman, Younce.

Committee on Game. Representatives Johnson, chairman; Harris, Price, Wilson of Pasquotank, Hayman, Poole of Hoke, Leggett, Brawley, Bell of Chatham, Cox of Forsyth, Gibbs, McBryde, Woodard, Oliver, Sutton, Lee, Marshall, Rogers, Hargett, Brown, Tipton, White.

Committee on Health. Representatives McBryde, chairman; Eddleman, Hart, Parker, Nettles, Cox of Forsyth, Yelverton, Austin, Leggett, Wright, Smith of Wake, Miss McLean of Mecklenburg, Moss of Rutherford, Little, Jones, Klutz, Younce, Grant, Tipton, Murphy, Winston, Cox of Pitt.

Committee on Immigration. Representatives Black, chairman; Wells, Banks, Coffey, Cox of Forsyth, Everett of Martin, Cox of Pitt, Graham of Sampson, Johnson, Kerr, Loven, Matthews, Watkins of Brunswick, Yelverton, Young, Whitaker, Price, Nettles, Oliver, Odom, Solesbee.

Committee on Insane Asylum. Representatives Cox of Pitt, chairman; Hart, Yelverton, Parker, Macon, Giles, Boyd, Bost, Eddleman, Smith of Wake, Wright, Shipman, Moss of Rutherford, Haywood, Loven, McBryde, Klutz, Williams, Byrd.

STANDING COMMITTEES OF HOUSE OF REPRESENTATIVES.

Committee on the Institutions for the Blind. Representative Smith of Rockingham, chairman; Hart, Jones, Watkins of Granville, Young, Marshall, Everett of Durham, Whitaker, Tatem, Prevott, Martin of Washington, Norwood, Satterwhite, Parker.

Committee on the Institutions for the Deaf and Dumb. Representatives Moss of Rutherford, chairman; Bridger, Wells, Younce, Parker, Cox of Pitt, Falls, Austin, Black, Brewer of Wake, Yelverton, Rideoutte, Rouse, Bullard, Gibbs, Watkins of Brunswick, Watkins of Granville, Rogers, Morgan, Leggett, Bell of Carteret.

Committee on Insurance. Representatives Younce, chairman; Woodard, Morgan, Price, Smith of Rockingham, Wilson of Transylvania, Moss of Rutherford, Coffey, Lee, Young, Dunn, Wright, Norwood, Gibbs, Wilson of Pasquotank, Connor, Brewer of Wake, Little, Boyd, Butler, Parker, Flanagan, Haywood, Banks, Graham of Sampson, Squires, Klutz, Jonas, Williams.

Committee on Internal Improvements. Representatives Morgan, chairman; Brewer of Wake, Wood, Rogers, Hill, Wells, Dunn, McDevitt, Boyd, Watkins of Brunswick, Watkins of Granville, Moss of Nash, Kerr, Smith of Rockingham, Makepeace, Parker, Satterwhite, Graham, Bost, Bullard.

Committee on the Journal. Representatives Nettles, chairman; Banks, Leggett, Yelverton, Rhodes, Kerr, Younce, Rideoutte, Nash, Oliver, Loven, Lee, Matthews, Price, Moss of Rutherford, Cox of Alleghany, Boyles, Williams, Odom.

Committee on Judiciary, No. 1. Representatives Moss of Nash, chairman; Ward, Dunn, Gold, Moser, Turlington, Falls, Nash, Bullard, Everett of Durham, Martin of Washington, Byrd, Smith of Wake, Moss of Rutherford, Bolich, Hill, Butler, Wright, Leggett, Rhodes, Lee, Grant, Jenkins, Nicholson, Harris, MacLean of Beaufort.

Committee on Judiciary, No. 2. Representatives Sutton, chairman; Graham of Orange, Wilson of Pasquotank, Miss McLean of Mecklenburg, Connor, Townsend, Winston, Squires, Bell of Chatham, Graham of Sampson, Murphy, Crockmore, Stancill, Gwaltney, Younce, Rogers, Folger, Campbell, Mason, Brawley, Austin, Moss of Davidson, Jonas, Klutz, Woodard.

Committee on Library. Representatives Wright, chairman; Haywood, Brewer of Moore, Eddleman, Connor, Yelverton, Makepeace, Winston, Everett of Durham, Little, Rhodes, Rideoutte, Lee, Johnson, Watkins of Granville, Whitaker, Hart, Soles, Wells.

Committee on Manufacture and Labor. Representatives Cox of Forsyth, chairman; Rideoutte, R. L. Harris, Mason, Norwood, Smith of Rockingham, Stancill, Turlington, Wright, Black, Helms, Wood, Bost, Eure, Falls, Flanagan, Gwaltney, Watkins of Granville, Whitaker, Tipton, Pool of McDowell.

Committee on Military Affairs. Representatives Wells, chairman; Norwood, Byrd, Bolich, Younce, Mason, Moss of Rutherford, Bridger, McBryde, Hill, Satterwhite, Sutton, Young, Wright, Jones, Poole of Hoke, Rhodes, Graham of Orange, Bell of Chatham.

Committee on Mines and Mining. Representatives McDevitt, chairman; Wilson of Transylvania, Nettles, Makepeace, Boyd, Brewer of Moore, Bell of Chatham, Bost, Little, Loven, Satterwhite, Tatem, Cox of Pitt, Moss of Rutherford, Boyles, Brown.

Committee on Oyster Industry. Representatives Bell of Carteret, chairman; Morgan, Johnson, Watkins of Brunswick, Gibbs, Tatem, Dunn, Hayman, Banks, Martin, Wells, Moss of Nash, Eure, Macon, Martin of Washington, Leggett, Murphy, Privott, Wetmur, Parnell.

Committee on Penal Institutions. Representatives Brewer of Wake, chairman; Giles, Hart, Bell of Chatham, Dunn, Brawley, Makepeace, Sutton, Moss of Nash, Hill, Creekmore, Moser, Moss of Rutherford, Folger, Byrd, Bridger, Nettles, Wood, Brewer of Moore, White, Pool of McDowell.

Committee on Pensions. Representatives Poole of Hoke, chairman; Coffey, Gwaltney, Kerr, Falls, Bullard, Macon, Wood, Marshall, Eddleman, Rouse, Boyd, Whitaker, D. McDevitt, Morgan, Little, Helms, Bost, Brawley, Haywood, Shipman, Wetmur, White, Solesbee, Watkins of Granville.

Committee on Printing. Representatives Kerr, chairman; Brewer of Moore, Brewer of Wake, Poole of Hoke, Everett of Durham, Winston, Graham of Orange, Makepeace, Macon, Norwood, Turlington, Bridger, Haywood, Helms, Hill, Jones, Leggett, Squires, Little, Privott, Tatem, Boyles, Grant.

Committee on Private and Public Local Laws. Representatives Brawley, chairman; Stancill, Winston, Oliver, Butler, Nash, Hill, Byrd, Rogers, Rhodes, Rouse, Folger, Lee, Austin, Wright, Miss McLean, Klutz.

Committee on Privileges and Elections. Representatives Miss McLean of Mecklenburg, chairman; Wright, Cox of Forsyth, Fol-

STANDING COMMITTEES OF HOUSE OF REPRESENTATIVES 59

ger, Boyd, Byrd, Nash, Coffey, Everett of Martin, Eddleman, Dunn, Hargett, Hill, Johnson, Tatem, Young, Wood, Townsend, Wilson of Pasquotank, Grant, Odom.

Committee on Propositions and Grievances. Representatives Martin of Washington, chairman; Younce, Oliver, Byrd, Creekmore, Matthews, Murphy, Smith of Rockingham, Nash, Morgan, Campbell, Brewer of Moore, Haywood, Wells, Wilson of Transylvania, Stancill, Everett of Martin, Coffey, Falls, Moser, Woodard, Gibbs, Rogers, Nettles, Graham of Sampson, Mason, Moss of Nash, Solesbee, Jonas, Grant.

Committee on Public Roads. Representatives Woodard, chairman; Connor, Ward, Sutton, Townsend, Turlington, Cox of Forsyth, Bost, Price, Rhodes, Mason, Martin of Davidson, Makepeace, Gold, Boyd, Graham of Orange, Graham of Sampson, Johnson, Tatem, Giles, Wells, Creekmore, Bell of Chatham, Black, Watkins of Granville, Brawley, Hargett, Brewer of Moore, Flanagan, Moser, Boyles, Nicholson.

Committee on Public Welfare. Representatives Gold, chairman; Turlington, Townsend, Falls, Young, Moser, Miss McLean of Mecklenburg, Smith of Wake, Giles, Boyd, Graham of Orange, Yelverton, Norwood, Poole of Hoke, Gibbs, Wood, Harris, Tarkington, Wright, Martin of Davidson, Jenkins.

Committee on Regulation of Public Service Corporations. Representatives Ward, chairman; Boyd, Woodard, Falls, Connor, Creekmore, Bolich, Turlington, Mason, Privott, Bullard, Folger, Giles, Kerr, Lee, Jonas, Klutz.

Committee on Revision of Laws. Representatives Stancill of Mecklenburg, chairman; Murphy, Creekmore, Martin of Washington, Bolich, Connor, Moser, Banks, Campbell, Bridger, Brewer of Moore, Ward, Wilson of Pasquotank, Wilson of Transylvania, Brown, Grant.

Committee on Rules. Representatives Moser, chairman; Winton, Connor, Falls, Graham of Orange, Martin of Washington, Makepeace, Moss of Nash, Townsend, Turlington, Younce, Brown.

Committee on Salaries and Fees. Representatives Martin of Davidson, chairman; Ward, Brawley, Eddleman, Austin, Boyd, Bell of Carteret, Everett of Martin, Johnson, Marshall, Rogers, Squires, Bolich, Makepeace, Stancill, Hargett, Little, Morgan, Brewer

Moore, Campbell, Woodard, Townsend, Cox of Pitt, Sutton, Jenkins, Penland.

Committee on Senatorial Districts. Representatives Everett of Durham, chairman; Creekmore, Murphy, Turlington, Graham of Orange, Woodard, Bell of Chatham, Jones, Smith of Rockingham, Yelverton, Ward, Winston, Bullard, Cox of Alleghany, Eddleman, Gwaltney, Boyd, Norwood, Brown, Jenkins.

Committee on Trustees of State College. Representatives Squires, chairman; Johnson, Brewer of Wake, Tatem, Parker, Nettles, Mason, Bost, Rhodes, Kerr, Makepeace, Moss of Nash, Cox of Alleghany, Cox of Forsyth, McBryde, Eure, Privott, Hart, Solesbee, Jenkins, Whitaker, Jones.

Committee on Trustees of University. Representatives Townsend, chairman; Graham of Orange, Murphy, Younce, Sutton, Wilson of Pasquotank, Bell of Chatham, Macon, Parker, Moss of Nash, Mason, Jonas.

Committee of Justices of Peace. Representatives Watkins of Brunswick, chairman; Whitaker, Wilson, Tarkington, Marshall, Morgan, Everett of Martin, Cox of Pitt, Brewer of Moore, Little, Butler, Smith of Rockingham, Lee, Bridger, Loven, Earle, Gibbs, Byrd, Shipman, Rogers, Penland, Odom, Tipton.

Committee of Caswell Training School. Representatives Jones, chairman; Whitaker, Cox, Poole of Hoke, Sutton, Privott, Eddleman, Morgan, Norwood, Butler, Hayman, Loven, Rouse, Marshall, Witmur, Williams.

Committee on Public Buildings and Grounds. Representatives Makepeace, chairman; Byrd, Eure, Wood, Satterwhite, Hayman, Flanagan, Rouse, Gwaltney, Leggett, Bullard, Little, Creekmore, Wetmur, Jenkins.

PART II

EXECUTIVE DEPARTMENTS

1. Governor.
2. Secretary of State.
3. Auditor.
4. Treasurer.
5. Superintendent of Public Instruction.
6. Attorney-General.
7. Council of State.

THE GOVERNOR

Angus Wilton McLean, *Governor*, Raleigh

The Governor is the chief executive officer of the State. He is elected by the people for a term of four years. He receives a salary of $6,500 a year, and in addition is allowed annually $600 for traveling expenses, and a residence with domestic servants.

Article III, Section 2, of the Constitution of North Carolina, prescribes the following qualifications for the Governor:

1. He must have attained the age of thirty years.

2. He must have been a citizen of the United States for five years, and a resident of North Carolina for two years next before the election.

3. No person shall be eligible for the office of Governor for more than four years in any term of eight years, unless he becomes Governor by having been Lieutenant-Governor or President of the Senate.

The same qualifications apply to the office of Lieutenant-Governor.

The Constitution prescribes the powers and duties of the Governor as follows:

1. To take the oath of office prescribed for the Governor.

2. To reside at the seat of government; to keep the General Assembly informed respecting the affairs of the State; and to recommend to the General Assembly such measures as he deems expedient.

3. To grant reprieves, commutations and pardons (except in cases of impeachment), and to report each case of reprieve, commutation, or pardon to the General Assembly.

4. To receive reports from all officials of the Executive Departments and of public institutions and to transmit the same to the General Assembly.

5. He is commander-in-chief of the militia of the State, except when they are called into the service of the United States.

6. To call extra sessions of the General Assembly when he thinks necessary, by and with the advice of the Council of State.

7. To appoint, by and with the advice and consent of the Senate, all officers whose offices are established by the Constitution and whose appointments are not otherwise provided for.

8. To keep "The Great Seal of the State of North Carolina" and use the same as occasions shall require.

He has no veto power, being the only Governor in the United States without such power.

In addition to these duties the following are prescribed by statute:

1. To supervise the official conduct of all executive and administrative officers, and to visit all State institutions whenever he deems such visitation necessary to inquire into their management and needs.

2. To see that all public offices are filled and their duties performed.

3. To make appointments and supply vacancies not otherwise provided for in all departments.

4. To be the sole official organ of communication between the government of this State and other States or the government of the United States.

5. To use the civil and military power of the State to prevent the violation of the statute against prize-fighting in North Carolina.

6. To convene the Council of State for consultation whenever he deems it necessary.

7. To appoint a Private Secretary, who shall keep a record of all public letters written by or to the Governor, in books provided for that purpose.

8. To cause to be kept the following records: a register of all applications for pardon or the commutation of any sentence; an account of his official expenses, and the rewards offered by him for the apprehension of criminals, which shall be paid upon the warrant of the Auditor.

9. Under certain conditions to employ counsel for the State.

10. To appoint by proclamation one day in each year as a day of solemn and public thanksgiving to Almighty God for past blessings and of supplication for His continued kindness and care over us as a State and a Nation.

The Governor

11. To procure a seal for each department of the State government to be used in such manner as may be established by law.

The Governor is, *ex officio*, president of the State Board of Education; chairman Budget Commission; member of the State Board of Canvassers; member State Board of Public Buildings and Grounds; member Pension Board; member State Library Board; chairman State Geological Board; member State Printing Commission; chairman Board of Internal Improvements; Commander-in-Chief State Militia; chairman Memorial Building Commission; president Board of Trustees University of North Carolina; chairman Board of Trustees Orthopedic Hospital; president Board of Trustees State A. and E. College.

Historical Note

The office of governor was provided for in the first charters and plans for colonizing English-speaking America. Sir Walter Raleigh, the founder of English-speaking America, and the supreme authority over it under the crown, instituted the office in his scheme of government for the *first* "Lost Colony" by appointing Ralph Lane the first governor of "Virginia" in 1585. The office was continued in Raleigh's subsequent colonies, likewise in the founding of Virginia at Jamestown. The beginning of North Carolina government was the organization of a government for Albemarle, under the Lords Proprietors. William Drummond was the first governor. Though there were modifications of the office by the Lords Proprietors under their varying plans of government, there was no break in the succession of governors of North Carolina proper during the whole period in which North Carolina was a proprietary government, 1663-1728. The governor was appointed at pleasure by the Proprietors, and his chief duty was to represent them and not the people. He was limited in his executive authority by a council of from six to twelve men; but since the council was created practically always from men recommended by the governor, this limitation was largely illusory. He was supreme in the colony, and limited only by the instructions of the Proprietors themselves. From 1728 to 1776 North Carolina was a Crown Colony. The status of the governor remained the same except that the Crown took the place of the Proprietors. The independent state government was organized under the constitution of 1776. This constitution continued the office of governor but strictly defined his eligibility, powers, and duties, as follows:

1. He was to be elected jointly by the two houses of the General Assembly for a term of one year, and was not to be eligible for more than three terms in any six successive years.

2. He was to be not less than thirty years of age; he must have been a resident of North Carolina for five years; he must be possessed of a freehold to the value of one thousand pounds.

3. He was to be advised in office by a council of state elected by the General Assembly.

4. His powers and duties were strictly defined by the Constitution, by the General Assembly under the Constitution.

5. He was subject to impeachment.

Such was the status of the governor until the Constitution of 1835. This Constitution made the office elective by the people for a term of two years, limited eligibility to four years in any six successive years, and omitted the property qualification.

The Constitution of 1868 increased the term of office to four years and limited it to four years in any successive eight except in the case of succession from Lieutenant-Governor or President of the Senate. This Constitution created the office of Lieutenant-Governor and established all constitutional elective officers, except the Attorney-General, as the Council of State. Since 1868 the constitutional status of the governor has remained the same.

Chief Executives of North Carolina

GOVERNORS OF "VIRGINIA"

April	1585—	June	1586	Ralph Lane [1]
April	1587—	August	1587	John White [1]

CHIEF EXECUTIVES UNDER THE PROPRIETORS

October	1665—	October	1667	William Drummond [2]
October	1667—	December	1669	Samuel Stephens [2, 4]
October	1670—	May	1673	Peter Carteret [3]
May	1673—	November	1676	John Jenkins [5]
November	1676—		1678	Thomas Eastchurch [2, 6]
	1677			Thomas Miller [7]

THE GOVERNOR

....	1677	1678	John Culpepper
....	1678—	....	Seth Sothel
February	1679—August	1679	John Harvey
November	1679—	1681	John Jenkins
....	1682—	1689	Seth Sothel
December	1689—	1691	Philip Ludwell
November 2	1691—	1694	Philip Ludwell
....	1691—	1694	Thomas Jarvis
August 31	1694—	1696	John Archdale
....	1694—	1699	John Harvey
....	1699—	1703	Henderson Walker
....	1703—	1705	Robert Daniel
....	1705—	1706	Thomas Cary
....	1706—	1708	William Glover
....	1708—January	1711	Thomas Cary
....	1710—May 9	1712	Edward Hyde
May 9	1712—September 8	1712	Edward Hyde
September 12	1712—May 28	1714	Thomas Pollock
May 28	1714—March 26	1722	Charles Eden
March 30	1722—August 30	1722	Thomas Pollock
August 30	1722—January 15	1724	William Reed
January 15	1724—July 17	1725	George Burrington
July 17	1725—May	1728	Richard Everard

GOVERNORS UNDER THE CROWN

May	1728—February 25	1731	Richard Everard
February 25	1731—April 15	1734	George Burrington
April 15	1734—October 27	1734	Nathaniel Rice
October 27	1734—July 17	1752	Gabriel Johnston
July 17	1752—January 29	1753	Nathaniel Rice
January 29	1753—November 2	1754	Matthew Rowan
November 2	1754—March 28	1765	Arthur Dobbs
March 28	1765—December 20	1765	William Tryon
December 20	1765—July 1	1771	William Tryon
July 1	1771—August 12	1771	James Hasell
August 12	1771—May	1775	Josiah Martin

PRESIDENTS ON THE PROVINCIAL COUNCIL

October 18	1775—March 5	1776	Cornelius Harnett	New Bern
June 3	1776—August 21	1776	Cornelius Harnett	New Hanover
August 21	1776—September 27	1776	Samuel Ashe	New Hanover
September 27	1776—October 25	1776	Willie Jones	Halifax

GOVERNORS OF NORTH CAROLINA SINCE INDEPENDENCE
(Elected by the Legislature)

December 19	1776—April 18	1777	Richard Caswell	Dobbs
April 18	1777—April 18	1778	Richard Caswell	Dobbs
April 18	1778—May 4	1779	Richard Caswell	Dobbs
May 4	1779—April	1780	Richard Caswell	Dobbs
April	1780—June 26	1781	Abner Nash	Craven
June 26	1781—April 26	1782	Thomas Burke	Orange
April 26	1782—April 30	1783	Alexander Martin	Guilford
April 30	1783—January 1	1785	Alexander Martin	Guilford
January 1	1785—December 12	1785	Richard Caswell	Dobbs
December 12	1785—December 23	1786	Richard Caswell	Dobbs
December 23	1786—December 20	1787	Richard Caswell	Dobbs
December 20	1787—November 18	1788	Samuel Johnston	Chowan
November 18	1788—November 16	1789	Samuel Johnston	Chowan
November 16	1789—December 17	1789	Samuel Johnston	Chowan
December 17	1789—December 9	1790	Alexander Martin	Guilford
December 9	1790—January 2	1792	Alexander Martin	Guilford
January 2	1792—December 14	1792	Alexander Martin	Guilford
December 14	1792—December 26	1793	R. D. Spaight	Craven
December 26	1793—January 6	1795	R. D. Spaight	Craven
January 6	1795—November 19	1796	R. D. Spaight	Craven

November 19	1795	December 19	1796	Samuel Ashe	New Hanover
December 19	1796	December 5	1797	Samuel Ashe	New Hanover
December 5	1797	December 7	1798	Samuel Ashe	New Hanover
December 7	1798	November 23	1799	W. R. Davie	Halifax
November 23	1799	November 29	1800	Benjamin Williams	Moore
November 29	1800	November 28	1801	Benjamin Williams	Moore
November 28	1801	December 6	1802	Benjamin Williams	Moore
December 6	1802	December 1	1803	James Turner[22]	Warren
December 1	1803	November 29	1804	James Turner	Warren
November 29	1804	December 10	1805	James Turner	Warren
December 10	1805	December 1	1806	Nathaniel Alexander	Mecklenburg
December 1	1806	December 1	1807	Nathaniel Alexander	Mecklenburg
December 1	1807	December 12	1808	Benjamin Williams	Moore
December 12	1808	December 13	1809	David Stone	Bertie
December 13	1809	December 5	1910	David Stone	Bertie
December 5	1810	December 9	1811	Benjamin Smith	Brunswick
December 9	1811	November 25	1812	William Hawkins	Warren
November 25	1812	November 20	1813	William Hawkins	Warren
November 20	1813	November 29	1814	William Hawkins	Warren
November 29	1814	December 7	1815	William Miller	Warren
December 7	1815	December 7	1816	William Miller	Warren
December 7	1816	December 3	1817	William Miller	Warren
December 3	1817	November 24	1818	John Branch	Halifax
November 24	1818	November 25	1819	John Branch	Halifax
November 25	1819	December 7	1820	John Branch	Halifax
December 7	1820	December 7	1821	Jesse Franklin	Surry
December 7	1821	December 7	1822	Gabriel Holmes	Sampson
December 7	1822	December 6	1823	Gabriel Holmes	Sampson
December 6	1823	December 7	1824	Gabriel Holmes	Sampson
December 7	1824	December 6	1825	H. G. Burton	Halifax
December 6	1825	December 29	1826	H. G. Burton	Halifax
December 29	1826	December 8	1827	H. G. Burton	Halifax
December 8	1827	December 12	1828	James Iredell	Chowan
December 12	1828	December 10	1829	John Owen	Bladen
December 10	1829	December 18	1830	John Owen	Bladen
December 18	1830	December 13	1831	Montford Stokes	Wilkes
December 13	1831	December 6	1832	Montford Stokes	Wilkes
December 6	1832	December 9	1833	D. L. Swain	Buncombe
December 9	1833	December 10	1834	D. L. Swain	Buncombe
December 10	1834	December 10	1835	D. L. Swain	Buncombe
December 10	1835	December 31	1836	R. D. Spaight, Jr.	Craven

GOVERNORS ELECTED BY THE PEOPLE[23]

December 31	1836	December 29	1838	E. B. Dudley	New Hanover
December 29	1838	January 1	1841	E. B. Dudley	New Hanover
January 1	1841	December 31	1842	J. M. Morehead	Guilford
December 31	1842	January 1	1845	J. M. Morehead	Guilford
January 1	1845	January 1	1847	W. A. Graham	Orange
January 1	1847	January 1	1849	W. A. Graham	Orange
January 1	1849	January 1	1851	Charles Manly	Wake
January 1	1851	December 22	1852	D. S. Reid	Rockingham
December 22	1852	December 6	1854	D. S. Reid[24]	Rockingham
December 6	1854	January 1	1855	Warren Winslow[25]	Cumberland
January 1	1855	January 1	1857	Thomas Bragg	Northampton
January 1	1857	January 1	1859	Thomas Bragg	Northampton
January 1	1859	January 1	1861	John W. Ellis	Rowan
January 1	1861	July 7	1861	John W. Ellis[26]	Rowan
July 7	1861	September 8	1862	Henry T. Clark[27]	Edgecombe
September 8	1862	December 22	1864	Z. B. Vance	Buncombe
December 22	1864	May 29	1865	Z. B. Vance[27]	Buncombe
May 29	1865	December 15	1865	W. W. Holden[25]	Wake
December 15	1865	December 22	1866	Jonathan Worth	Randolph
December 22	1866	July 1	1868	Jonathan Worth[28]	Randolph
July 1	1868	December 15	1870	W. W. Holden[29]	Wake
December 15	1870	January 1	1873	T. R. Caldwell[30]	Burke
January 1	1873	July 11	1874	T. R. Caldwell	Burke

THE GOVERNOR

July 11	1874—January 1	1877	C. H. Brogden	W...
January 1	1877—February 5	1879	Z. B. Vance	M...
February 5	1879—January 18	1881	T. J. Jarvis	Pitt
January 18	1881—January 21	1885	T. J. Jarvis	Pitt
January 21	1885—January 17	1889	A. M. Scales	Rockingham
January 17	1889—April 8	1891	D. G. Fowle	Wake
April 8	1891—January 18	1893	Thomas M. Holt	Alamance
January 18	1893—January 12	1897	Elias Carr	Edgecombe
January 12	1897—January 15	1901	D. L. Russell	Brunswick
January 15	1901—January 11	1905	C. B. Aycock	Wayne
January 11	1905—January 12	1909	R. B. Glenn	Forsyth
January 1	1909—January 15	1913	W. W. Kitchin	Person
January 15	1913—January 11	1917	Locke Craig	Buncombe
January 11	1917—January 12	1921	Thomas W. Bickett	Franklin
January 12	1921—January 12	1925	Cameron Morrison	Mecklenburg
January 12	1925—		Angus Wilton McLean	Robeson

NOTES

[1] Appointed by Sir Walter Raleigh.
[2] Appointed by Sir William Berkeley at the request of the other Lords Proprietors.
[3] Appointed by the Lords Proprietors.
[4] Died in office.
[5] Acting-Governor by virtue of his office as President of the Council.
[6] Died before qualifying.
[7] Deputy of Governor Eastchurch. Deposed by the rebels under John Culpepper.
[8] Elected by the rebels.
[9] On his way to Carolina he was captured by pirates and detained until 1683.
[10] Governor of all Carolina with headquarters at Charleston. Governed North Carolina through a deputy. This plan was followed until 1712.
[11] Deputy Governor.
[12] The first governor of North Carolina as a separate and distinct province. Appointed by the Lords Proprietors.
[13] Continued in office during the transfer of the province from the Lords Proprietors to the Crown.
[14] Appointed by the Crown.
[15] Lieutenant-Governor.
[16] The Provincial Congress (after April, 1776, called the Council of Safety) was the chief executive authority of the revolutionary government during the interval from the overthrow of the royal government in 1775 until the inauguration of the independent State government January 1, 1777.
[17] Resigned.
[18] "That the Senate and House of Commons, jointly at their first meeting after each election, shall by ballot elect a Governor for one year, who shall not be eligible to that office longer than three years in each six successive years." Art. XV, Constitution of 1776.
[19] Chosen by the Convention of December, 1776, to fill interval until the Legislature could meet.
[20] Abolished in 1794.
[21] Elected by Convention of 1789 to United States Senate. Did not qualify for third term as Governor.
[22] John Baptista Ashe, of Halifax, was first chosen, but died before he could qualify. Turner was then elected.
[23] The Convention of 1835 amended the Constitution to provide for the election of a governor by a popular vote, increased his term of office to two years and made six years ineligible for more than two terms successively.
[24] Elected to the United States Senate.
[25] Ex officio as President of the Senate.
[26] Died in office.
[27] Turned out by Provisional government.
[28] Provisional governor appointed by the President of the United States.
[29] Turned out by reconstruction government.
[30] Impeached and removed from office.
[31] Ex officio as lieutenant-governor. Elected governor by the people at the next election.
[32] Ex officio as lieutenant-governor.
[33] Elected to the United States Senate.
[34] Ex officio as lieutenant-governor. Elected governor by the people in 1880.
[35] Died in office.

THE SECRETARY OF STATE

Sec. 1, Art. III, Constitution; Art. 1, Ch. 22, C. S.; Ch. 97, C. S.; Art. 4, Ch. 129, C. S.; Ch. 97, P. L. 1921—Extra Session

W. N. EVERETT, *Secretary of State*, Raleigh

Title—Secretary of State.

Appointment—Elected by the people.

Term—Four years.

Salary—$4,500.

Ex officio Member—Council of State; State Board of Education; Board of Public Buildings, Municipal Board of Control, Trustee State Library, Chairman Board of Advisors of World War Veterans Loan Fund.

Function

To have custody of all statutes and resolutions, rolls of registered voters and other State and official records; to supervise publication and distribution of the laws; to examine and certify articles or certificates of incorporation; to register trademarks, brands and marks.

The Secretary of State countersigns all commissions issued by the Governor, and is charged with the custody of all statutes and joint resolutions of the Legislature, all documents which pass under the Great Seal, and of all books, records, deeds, parchments, maps and papers now deposited in his office or which may hereafter be there deposited pursuant to law.

Through the Secretary of State all corporations for business or charitable purposes under the general laws of the State are chartered. These include mercantile, manufacturing, banking, insurance, railroad, street car, electric, steamboat, and other companies. The certificates of incorporation are there filed and recorded.

There have been 2,880 certificates for domestic corporations filed in the office of Secretary of State for the two-year period ending June 30, 1926.

There have been 391 certificates of dissolutions filed with the Secretary of State during the last two years, and 314 foreign corporations have filed domestication papers. There have been registered 36 trade-marks within the last two years.

SECRETARY OF STATE

Payments to the Treasurer by the Secretary of State for the fiscal years July 1, 1924 to June 30, 1926 were as follows:

	July 1, 1924 to June 30, 1925	July 1, 1925 to June 30, 1926
Great Seals	$ 101.00	$ 77.50
Grants	876.77	1,785.41
Fees	3,284.60	1,078.55
Seals	971.00	326.00
Corporation tax	75,963.80	226,673.22
Corporation Fees	5,598.30	7,695.10
Corporation Seals	1,889.00	2,407.00
Foreign Corporations	9,521.18	25,117.20
Foreign Corporation Penalty		1,595.00
Supreme Court Reports	10,977.07	7,780.78
Code, Laws, Journals	9,157.87	6,404.23
Trade-marks	68.30	52.70
Petty differences	.87	.91
Miscellaneous	44.81	77.95
Land Grant Seals	48.75	82.50
Land Grant Fees and Postage	31.20	55.05
Refunds	790.83	1,244.06
Total	$119,325.38	$282,452.26

Foreign corporations, before being permitted to do business in North Carolina are required to file copies of their charters in the office of the Secretary of State.

All bills passed by the General Assembly are enrolled for ratification under the supervision and direction of the Secretary of State, and shall be typewritten or written with pen and ink, in the discretion of the Secretary of State. All bills are now typewritten. A carbon copy is sent to the State Printer, from which copy are published the laws, resolutions, etc. An assistant to the Secretary of State prepares these laws for publication, determines which are "Public," "Public-Local," and which are "Private"; side notes them and prepares the captions and indexes the laws of the session.

The Secretary of State is charged with the work of distributing the Supreme Court Reports, the Consolidated Statutes, Session Laws, Journals, etc.

All vacant and unappropriated land in North Carolina is subject to entry by residents or citizens of the State. Almost all the vacant land in the State has been granted to individuals or is the property of the State Board of Education, but small tracts are frequently discovered and entries for same made. The warrants, plats, and surveys and a record of grants for all lands originally granted by the Lord Proprietors, by the Crown of Great Britain, or by the State of North Carolina, are preserved in the office of the Secretary of State.

Historical Note

The office of Secretary of State developed from that of Secretary of the Province, which began in 1675 with the appointment of Robert Holden, and continued by the Constitution of 1776. The Secretary of the Province was appointed by the Crown at pleasure, and received his patent from the Governor's Council. He was a Justice of the Peace, Clerk of Pleas of the Crown, and issued land grants. The Constitution of 1776 made the term three years and the method of appointment election by the General Assembly. The Constitution of 1835 reduced the term to two years. The Constitution of 1868 increased the term to four years, and made the office elective by the people.

Secretaries of the Colony

ALBEMARLE

1675-1677	Robert Holden
1677-1679	Thomas Miller
1679-1684	Robert Holden
1681-1685	Francis Hartley
1685	————Woodrowe

NORTH CAROLINA

1694-1702	Daniel Akehurst
1702-1712	Samuel Swann
1712-1722	Tobias Knight
1722-1730	John Lovick
1730-1753	Nathaniel Rice
1753-1754	James Murray
1754-1755	Henry McCulloch
1755-1762	Richard Spaight
1762-1770	Benjamin Heron
1770-1770	John London
1770-1772	Robert Palmer
1772-1775	Samuel Strudwick [1]

[1] Thomas Falkner was appointed in 1761, but never qualified. He farmed out the office to Strudwick.

THE AUDITOR

Secretaries of State

1777-1798	James Glasgow	
1798-1810	William White	Len...
1811-1859	William Hill	Rock...
1859-1862	Rufus H. Page	Wa...
1862-1864	John P. H. Russ	W...
1864-1865	Charles R. Thomas	C...r
1866-1867	Robert W. Best	Gr...
1868-1871	Henry J. Menninger	W...
1872-1875	William H. Howerton	Rowan
1876-1879	Joseph A. Englehard	New H...
1879-1891	William L. Saunders	Wake
1891-1895	Octavius Coke	Wake
1895-1896	Charles M. Cooke	Franklin
1897-1900	Cyrus Thompson	Onslow
1901-1923	J. Bryan Grimes	Pitt
1923	W. N. Everett	Richmond

THE AUDITOR

Art. III, Sec. 1, Constitution; Art. 5, Ch. 129...

BAXTER DURHAM, *State Auditor*, Raleigh

Title—State Auditor.

Appointment—Elected by the people.

Term—Four Years.

Salary—$4,500.

Ex Officio Member—Council of State, State Board of Education, State Board Pensions, Printing Commission.

Function

To superintend the fiscal affairs of the State, to keep and state all accounts in which the State is interested; to draw warrants on the State Treasurer on approved vouchers; to suggest and effect plans for the improvement and management of the public revenue, to handle the pension system; to cause to be audited the accounts of each State department and institution.

Ch. 163, P. L. 1921. To cause to be examined, audited and adjusted the various accounts, systems of accounts and accounting of the several State departments, and institutions; to devise systems for control and disbursements of the funds of the State, its departments and institutions; to require all officers of the State, its departments and institutions to install such systems of accounting procedures and control of disbursement of funds as he shall...

have departments and institutions examined and audited from time to time; to employ experts and accountants to examine, analyze and report on such departments and institutions.

Ch. 100, P. L. 1925. To require all counties, townships, school districts or other municipal corporations to report to the State Auditor on or before June 1, 1925, all bonds or notes having a fixed maturity of one year or more from date thereof, and also to make report to State Auditor within thirty days after the issuance of any bond or note having a fixed maturity of at least one year from date. The State Auditor is directed to furnish the necessary forms and keep on file statements as required in the foregoing.

REPORTS. To report annually to the Governor and biennially to the General Assembly a complete statement of receipts and expenditures of the State during preceding fiscal year and as far as possible of the current year, together with detailed estimate of proposed expenditures for ensuing fiscal year, specifying therein each object of expenditure and distinguishing between such as are provided for by permanent or temporary appropriations, and such as must be provided for by a new statute, and to suggest the means from which such expenditures are to be defrayed.

Comptrollers[1]

1782-1784	Richard Caswell	Dobbs
1784-1808	John Craven	Halifax
1808-1821	Samuel Goodwin	Cumberland
1821-1827	Joseph Hawkins	Warren
1827	John L. Henderson	Rowan
1827-1834	James Grant	Halifax
1834-1836	Nathan Stedman	Chatham
1836-1851	William F. Collins	Nash
1851-1855	William J. Clarke	Wake
1855-1857	George W. Brooks	Pasquotank
1857-1867	Curtis H. Brogden	Wayne
1867-1868	S. W. Burgin	

Auditors of Public Accounts[2]

1862-1864	Samuel F. Phillips	Orange
1864-1865	Richard H. Battle	Wake

State Auditors

1868-1873	Henderson Adams	
1873-1875	John Reilley	Cumberland

[1] The office of State Auditor was created by the Constitution in 1868. Prior to 1868 there was a Comptroller appointed by the General Assembly.
[2] This office was created by the Laws of 1862, and abolished a few years later.

1875-1879	Samuel L. Love	Haywood
1880-1889	William P. Roberts	Gates
1890-1893	George W. Sanderlin	Lenoir
1893-1897	Robert M. Furman	Buncombe
1898-1900	Hal W. Ayer	Wake
1901-1910	Benjamin F. Dixon	Cleveland
1910	Benjamin F. Dixon, Jr.	Wake
1911-1921	William P. Wood	Randolph
1921	Baxter Durham	Wake

THE TREASURER

Sec. 1, Art. IV, Constitution; Art. 6, Cha. 129, C. S.

B. R. LACY, *State Treasurer*, Raleigh

Title—State Treasurer.

Appointment—Elected by the people.

Term—Four years.

Salary—$4,500.

Ex Officio Member—Council of State; State Board of Education (Treasurer), Board of Public Buildings and Grounds.

Ex Officio Treasurer—Hospitals for Insane (3), A. and E. College, State Deaf and Dumb School (Morganton), Deaf, Dumb and Blind School (Raleigh), State Prison, Soldiers' Home, Caswell Training School, State Hospital for Dangerous Insane, Confederate Women's Home, Department of Agriculture, State Board of Education, State Board for Vocational Education.

The duties of the State Treasurer as prescribed by law are as follows:

1. To keep his office in the city of Raleigh and attend there between the hours of 10 o'clock a.m. and 3 o'clock p.m., except Sundays and legal holidays.

2. To receive all moneys that may be paid into the Treasury of the State; to pay interest on State bonds and all warrants legally drawn on the Treasurer by the Auditor, and to report to the Governor and the General Assembly the financial condition of the State, including a summary of the receipts and disbursements for each fiscal year.

3. To make complete revenue bill to cover estimated expenses and recommend the tax rate.

4. To construe revenue when license is paid direct to State Treasurer.

Historical Note

The office of Treasurer originated in 1715 with the appointment of Edward Moseley. From 1740 to 1779 there were two districts, Northern and Southern, with a Treasurer for each. From 1779 to 1782 there were six districts, each with a Treasurer, as follows: Edenton, Salisbury, Hillsboro, Halifax, New Bern, Wilmington. In 1782 a seventh district—Morgan—was created. In 1784 the district system was abandoned, and a treasurer for the State was elected. The colonial treasurers were appointed, and their duties defined by the General Assembly at pleasure. The Constitution of 1776 made the term one year; that of 1835 made it two years. The Constitution of 1868 made the office elective by the people and the term four years.

CONSOLIDATED STATEMENT STATE TREASURY FOR FISCAL YEAR ENDING JUNE 30, 1926

RECEIPTS

Balance July 1, 1925			$ 4,103,639.23
GENERAL FUND:			
Revenue (taxes)	$ 11,813,051.46		
Non revenue	1,320,491.46		
		$ 13,133,542.92	
INSTITUTIONAL FUNDS:			
Colleges and institutions		3,212,364.14	
			16,345,907.06
SPECIAL FUNDS:			
Automobile and other sources	$ 23,340,381.24		
Bond sales	20,125,000.00		
Note sales and renewals	69,388,531.61		
Federal Funds	218,773.48		
Board of Education	258,532.03		
			113,331,218.36
			$ 133,780,764.65

DISBURSEMENTS

General Funds	$ 13,974,003.65		
Special Funds	39,795,391.92		
Federal Funds	219,927.93		
Board of Education	272,496.26		
Notes paid and renewals	61,650,000.00		
		$ 115,911,819.76	
Balance June 30, 1926		17,868,944.89	
			$ 133,780,764.65

THE TREASURER

TREASURY DEPARTMENT STATE DEBT CLOSE OF F. Y.

BONDED DEBT:
Interest and sinking fund provided from
  General Fund:
    4% Funding .... $ 3,980,000.00
    4% Improvement 3,324,000.00
                                                              $ 7,304,000.00
    4¼% General Fund 9,438,000.00
    4½% Improvement 11,517,000.00
    4¾% Improvement 7,660,000.00
    5% Funding 1,500,000.00
    5% Improvement 3,372,000.00
                                                              $ 33,487,000.00

PUBLIC SCHOOLS BUILDING:
Interest and sinking fund provided from
  Special Funds:
    4½% Public Schools Building ....

HIGHWAY BONDS:
Interest and sinking fund provided from
  Special Funds:
    4½% Construction .... $ 54,697,000.00
    4¾% Construction 3,750,000.00
    5% Construction 1,552,000.00
                                                              $ 59,999,000.00

  Total Bonds .... $ 125,557,000.00

NOTES, ANTICIPATING BOND SALES:
Interest paid from Special funds:
    4¼% Highway .... $ 10,000,000.00
    4¼% Chowan river bridge 300,000.00
    3¾% Highway 5,000,000.00
                                                              $ 15,300,000.00
    3¾% Public School Building 5,000,000.00
                                                                          $ 20,300,000.00

                                                                          $ 144,887,000.00

BONDS DUE, NOT PRESENTED FOR PAYMENT:
    4% Consolidated debt, due 1910 .... $ 100.00
    6% Construction due 1879 .... 18,000.00
    4% Improvement due 1924 .... 1,000.00
    4% Improvement due 1925 .... 7,000.00
                                                              $ 26,100.00

  Total State debt .... $ 144,883,100.00

Colonial Treasurers

1715-1740	Province-at-large	Edward M.......
1740-1749	Southern District	Edward M.......
1740-1748	Northern District	John H.......
1749-1750	Southern District	Eleazer All....
1748-1752	Northern District	Thomas B.......
1750-1756	Southern District	John Sta.....
1752-1754	Northern District	John H.......
1766-1773	Southern District	John Ashe
1773-1776	Southern District	Richard C.....
1754-1766	Northern District	Joseph M.......

District Treasurers

1777-1779	Southern District	John Ashe, New H......
1777	Northern District	Samuel Johnston, Chowan
1777-1779	Northern District	William Skinner
1779-1784	Edenton District	William Skinner

1 Declined to serve

1779-1782	Salisbury District	William Cathey
1782-1784	Salsbury District	Robert Lanier
1779	Hillsboro District	William Johnston[1]
1779	Hillsboro District	Nathaniel Rochester[2]
1779-1782	Hillsboro District	Matthew Jones
1782-1784	Hillsboro District	Memucan Hunt, Granville
1779-1784	Halifax District	Green Hill
1779-1782	New Bern District	Richard Cogdell, Craven
1782-1784	New Bern District	Benjamin Exum
1779-1782	Wilmington District	John Ashe, New Hanover
1782-1784	Wilmington District	Timothy Bloodworth, New Hanover
1782-1784	Morgan District	John Brown

State Treasurers

1784-1787	Memucan Hunt	Granville
1787-1827	John Haywood	Edgecombe
1827-1827	John S. Haywood	Wake
1827-1830	William Robards	Granville
1830	Robert H. Burton[1]	Lincoln
1830-1835	William S. Mhoon	Bertie
1835-1837	Samuel F. Patterson	Wilkes
1837-1839	Daniel W. Courts	Surry
1839-1843	Charles L. Hinton	Wake
1843-1845	John H. Wheeler	Lincoln
1845-1852	Charles L. Hinton	Wake
1852-1862	Daniel W. Courts	Surry
1862-1865	Jonathan Worth	Randolph
1865-1865	William Sloan	Anson
1865-1868	Kemp P. Battle	Wake
1869-1876	David A. Jenkins	Gaston
1876-1885	John M. Worth	Randolph
1886-1892	Donald W. Bain	Wake
1893-1895	Samuel McD. Tate	Burke
1895-1901	William H. Worth	Guilford
1901	Benjamin R. Lacy	Wake

SUPERINTENDENT OF PUBLIC INSTRUCTION

Sec. 3, Art. I, Constitution; Ch. 95, C. S.; Ch. 61, P. L. 1921; Ch. 145, P. L. 1921

A. T. ALLEN, *Superintendent of Public Instruction*, Raleigh

Title—Superintendent of Public Instruction.

Appointment—Elected.

Term—Four years.

Salary—$5,000.

Ex Officio Member—Board of Trustees University of North Carolina, President Board of Trustees North Carolina College for Women, President Board of Trustees East Carolina Teachers' College, Secretary State Board of Education, Board of Trustees State

---
[1] Declined to serve.
[2] Election declared illegal because he was a member of the General Assembly.

Library, Executive Officer State Board for Vocational Education, Child Welfare Commission, College Commission, Library Commission.

Function

To direct the operation of the public schools within the State of North Carolina, and to enforce the laws and regulations in relation thereto; to appoint jointly with the Governor the Elementary Text Book Commission and to receive their report; to appoint jointly with the Governor a Committee on High School Text Books and to receive their report and transmit it to the State Board of Education.

To prepare or have prepared and cause to be printed and distributed Course of Study for the Elementary Schools, High School Course of Study, Course of Study in Physical Education, and Course of Study in Americanism; to supervise work of rural libraries; to provide educational films for schools; to provide for the celebration of certain special days and to print programs therefor; to arbitrate disputes between counties over the support of joint school districts; to hear evidence relative to the inefficiency of county superintendents, and to perform such other duties as may be imposed by law or by the rules and regulations of the State Board of Education.

REPORTS. To report biennially to the Governor at least five days prior to regular session of General Assembly, giving information and statistics of the public schools with recommendations as to changes in the law.

Section XLI of the Constitution of North Carolina of 1776 is as follows: "That a school or schools be established by the Legislature for the convenient instruction of youth, with such salaries to the masters, paid by the public, as may enable them to instruct at low prices; and all useful learning shall be duly encouraged and promoted in one or more universities."

Except for the establishment of the University of North Carolina, no attempt was made by the Legislature to carry out this injunction of the Constitution until nearly three-quarters of a century had elapsed. The first efforts were a failure and nothing definite was accomplished until the creation of a Department of Education by the election in 1851 of Calvin H. Wiley, Superintendent of Common Schools. He entered upon the duties of his office in January, 1853.

and was continued in office until October 19, 1865. The following figures tell the story of his work: Number of teachers in 1852, 800; in 1855, 2,064; in 1860, 2,286. Enrollment in the schools in 1853, 83,-373; in 1855, 115,856; in 1860, 116,567. Number of schools taught in 1855, 1,905; 1860, 2,854. School fund in 1853, $192,250; in 1860, $408,566. Expenditures in 1853, $139,865; in 1860, $255,641. The schools were kept open throughout the war, and in 1863 enrolled more than 50,000 pupils. In 1865, as one of the results of the war, the office of Superintendent of Common Schools was abolished.

By the Constitution of 1868 the office of Superintendent of Public Instruction was created, and defined practically as it exists today.

Education in Our Present Constitution

Article IX of the Constitution of North Carolina relates to education. It reads as follows:

SECTION 1. Religion, morality, and knowledge being necessary to good government and the happiness of mankind, schools and the means of education shall forever be encouraged.

SEC. 2. The General Assembly, at its first session under this Constitution, shall provide by taxation and otherwise for a general and uniform system of public schools, wherein tuition shall be free of charge to all the children of the State between the ages of six and twenty-one years. And the children of the white race and the children of the colored race shall be taught in separate public schools; but there shall be no discrimination in favor of or to the prejudice of either race.

SEC. 3. Each county of the State shall be divided into a convenient number of districts in which one or more public schools shall be maintained at least six months in every year; and if the commissioners of any county shall fail to comply with the aforesaid requirements of this section they shall be liable to indictment.

SEC. 4. The proceeds of all lands that have been or hereafter may be granted by the United States to this State and not otherwise appropriated by this State or the United States, also all moneys, stocks, bonds and other property now belonging to any State fund for purposes of education, also the net proceeds of all sales of the swamp lands belonging to the State, and all other grants, gifts or devises that have been or hereafter may be made to the State and

SUPERINTENDENT OF PUBLIC INSTRUCTION

not otherwise appropriated by the State or by the terms of the grant, gift or devise, shall be paid into the State Treasury, and, together with so much of the ordinary revenue of the State as may be by law set apart for that purpose, shall be faithfully appropriated for establishing and maintaining in this State a system of free public schools, and for no other uses or purposes whatsoever.

SEC. 5. All moneys, stocks, bonds, and other property belonging to a county school fund, also the net proceeds from the sale of estrays, also the clear proceeds of all penalties and forfeitures and of all fines collected in the several counties for any breach of the penal or military laws of the State, and all moneys which shall be paid by persons as an equivalent for exemption from military duty shall belong to and remain in the several counties and shall be faithfully appropriated for establishing and maintaining free public schools in the several counties in this State: *Provided*, that the amount collected in each county shall be annually reported to the Superintendent of Public Instruction.

SEC. 6. The General Assembly shall have power to provide for the election of trustees of the University of North Carolina, in whom, when chosen, shall be vested all the privileges, rights, franchises and endowments thereof in any wise granted to or conferred upon the trustees of said University; and the General Assembly may make such provisions, laws and regulations from time to time as may be necessary and expedient for the maintenance and management of said University.

SEC. 7. The General Assembly shall provide that the benefits of the University as far as practicable, be extended to the youth of the State free of expense for tuition; also that all the property which has heretofore accrued to the State or shall hereafter accrue from escheats, unclaimed dividends or distributive shares of the estate of deceased persons shall be appropriated to the use of the University.

SEC. 8. The Governor, Lieutenant-Governor, Secretary of State, Treasurer, Auditor, Superintendent of Public Instruction, and Attorney-General shall constitute a State Board of Education.

SEC. 9. The Governor shall be president and the Superintendent of Public Instruction shall be secretary of the Board of Education.

SEC. 10. The Board of Education shall succeed to all the power and trusts of the president and directors of the literary fund of

North Carolina, and shall have full power to legislate and make all needful rules and regulations in relation to free public schools and the educational fund of the State; but all acts, rules and regulations of said board may be altered, amended, or repealed by the General Assembly, and when so altered, amended or repealed they shall not be reënacted by the board.

SEC. 11. The first session of the Board of Education shall be held at the capital of the State within fifteen days after the organization of the State Government under this Constitution; the time of future meetings may be determined by the board.

SEC. 12. A majority of the board shall contitute a quorum for the transaction of business.

SEC. 13. The contingent expenses of the board shall be provided by the General Assembly.

SEC. 14. As soon as practicable after the adoption of this Constitution the General Assembly shall establish and maintain in connection with the University a department of agriculture, of mechanics, of mining and of normal instruction.

SEC. 15. The General Assembly is hereby empowered to enact that every child of sufficient mental and physical ability shall attend the public schools during the period between the ages of six and eighteen years for a term of not less than sixteen months, unless educated by other means.

SEC. 27. The people have the right to the privilege of education, and it is the duty of the State to guard and maintain that right.—*Bill of Rights, North Carolina Constitution.*

Article II, section 29:

The General Assembly shall not pass any local, private, or special act or resolution: "Erecting new townships, or changing township lines, or establishing or changing the lines of school districts."

EDUCATIONAL QUALIFICATIONS FOR SUFFRAGE

Article VI, section 4, of the Constitution of North Carolina, contains the following:

Every person presenting himself for registration shall be able to read and write any section of the Constitution in the English language; and before he shall be entitled to vote he shall have paid, on or before the first day of May of the year in which he proposes to vote, his poll tax for the previous year, as prescribed by Article V, section 1, of the Constitution. But no male person who was, on January 1, 1867, or at any time prior thereto, entitled to vote under the laws of any State in the United States wherein he then resided, and no lineal descendant of any such person, shall be denied the right to register and vote at any election in this State by reason of his failure to possess the educational qualification herein prescribed: *Provided*, he shall have registered in accordance with the terms of this section prior to December 1, 1908.

Superintendent of Common Schools[1]

1852-1865	Calvin H. Wiley	Guilford

Superintendents of Public Instruction

1868-1872	S. S. Ashley	New Hanover
1872-1874	Alexander McIver	Guilford
1874-1876	Stephen D. Pool	Craven
1876	John Pool	Pasquotank
1877-1884	John C. Scarborough	Johnston
1885-1892	Sidney M. Finger	Catawba
1893-1896	John C. Scarborough	Hertford
1897-1900	Charles H. Mebane	Catawba
1901-1902	Thomas F. Toon	Robeson
1902-1918	James Y. Joyner	Guilford
1919-1923	E. C. Brooks	Durham
1923	A. T. Allen	Alexander

THE ATTORNEY-GENERAL

DENNIS G. BRUMMITT, *Attorney-General*, Raleigh

The Attorney-General is a member of the Executive Department of the State Government. He is elected by the people for a term of four years. His term begins the first of January next after his election and continues until his successor is elected and qualified. He receives a salary of $4,000 per annum.

It is the duty of the Attorney-General:

1. To defend all actions in the Supreme Court in which the State shall be interested or is a party; and, also, when requested by the Governor or either branch of the General Assembly, to appear for the State in any other court or tribunal in any cause or matter, civil or criminal, in which the State may be a party or interested.

---
[1] Office abolished in 1865.

2. At the request of the Governor, Secretary of State, Treasurer, Auditor, Corporation Commissioners, Insurance Commissioner, or Superintendent of Public Instruction, he shall prosecute and defend all suits relating to matters connected with their departments.

3. To represent all State institutions, including the State Prison, whenever requested so to do by the official head of any such institution.

4. To consult with and advise the solicitors, when requested by them, in all matters pertaining to the duties of their office.

5. To give, when required, his opinion upon all questions of law submitted to him by the General Assembly, or either branch thereof, or by any official of the State.

6. To pay all moneys received for debts due or penalties to the State immediately after the receipt thereof, into the Treasury.

The Attorney-General is a member of the State Board of Education, of the State Board of Public Buildings and Grounds, of the State Board of Pensions, of the State Textbook Commission, and of the Printing Commission, and is the legal adviser of the Council of State; chairman of the Municipal Board of Control; member of the State Board of Assessment.

Historical Note

In the colony the Attorney-General was appointed at pleasure by the Crown. In addition to his other duties he was a justice of the Peace. George Durant, the first Attorney-General, was appointed in 1677, and the office has continued since that time. The Constitution of 1776 made the office appointive by the General Assembly to continue during good behavior. The Constitution of 1835 limited the term to four years with the provision that it might be increased. The Constitution of 1868 defined the office as it is today. The Attorney-General, by an act of the General Assembly of 1925 (Chapter 207), was allowed three assistants, to be appointed by him and severally to be assigned to the State Highway Commission, the State Department of Revenue and the Attorney General.

Attorneys-General

1677-1679	George Durant	1716-1724	William Little
1694	John Porter	1724-1725	Thomas Boyd
1703	Richard Plater	1725-1731	William Little
1705	Thomas Snowden	1731-1731	John Conner
1712-1713	Edward Bonwicke	1731-1734	John Montgomery

COUNCIL OF STATE

1734-1734	John Hodgson	1756-1756	
1734-1741	John Montgomery	1756-1756	Robert J...
1741-1747	Joseph Anderson	1756-1766	Thos... C...
1747-1755	Thomas Child	1766-1767	Mar...
1755-1756	George Nicholas	1767	Tho... Mc...
1777-1779	Waightstill Avery		B...
1779-1782	James Iredell		Chowan
1782-1791	Alfred Moore		Brunswick
1791-1794	John Haywood		Halifax
1795-1802	Blake Baker		Edgecombe
1803-1808	Henry Seawell		Wake
1808-1810	Oliver Fitts		Warren
1810	William Miller		Warren
1810-1816	Hutchins G. Burton		Halifax
1816-1825	William Drew		Halifax
1825-1828	James F. Taylor		Wake
1828	Robert H. Jones		Warren
1828-1835	Romulus M. Saunders		Caswell
1835-1840	John R. J. Daniel		Halifax
1840-1842	Hugh McQueen		Chatham
1842-1846	Spier Whitaker		Halifax
1846-1848	Edward Stanly		Beaufort
1848-1851	Bartholomew F. Moore		Halifax
1851-1852	William Eaton, Jr.		Warren
1852-1855	Matt W. Ransom		Northampton
1855-1856	Joseph B. Batchelor		Warren
1856-1860	William H. Bailey		Mecklenburg
1860-1863	William A. Jenkins		Granville
1863-1868	Sion H. Rogers		Wake
1868-1869	William M. Coleman		
1870-1871	Lewis P. Olds		Wake
1871-1873	William M. Shipp		Lincoln
1873-1876	Tazewell L. Hargrove		Granville
1876-1885	Thomas S. Kenan		Wilson
1885-1893	Theodore F. Davidson		Buncombe
1893-1897	Frank I. Osborne		Mecklenburg
1897-1900	Zeb. V. Walser		Davidson
1900-1901	Robert D. Douglas		Guilford
1901-1909	Robert D. Gilmer		Haywood
1909-1917	Thomas W. Bickett		Franklin
1917-1925	James S. Manning		Wake
1925	Dennis G. Brummitt		Granville

COUNCIL OF STATE

Sec. 9, Art. III, Constitution; Sec. 14, Art. III, Constitution; Sec. ...; ... 107, C. S.; Sec. 6937, Art. 2, Ch. 113, C. S.; Sec. 7637, Art. 3, Ch. 1...; ... C. S.; Ch. 50, P. L. 1921, Extra Session; Chs. ...

Composition (4)—Secretary of State, Auditor, Treasurer, Superintendent Public Instruction, *ex officio* members. Attorney General, legal adviser to Executive Department.

Term—Four years.

Function

To advise the Governor in the execution of his office, any three constituting a quorum; to keep a signed record of their advice and

---

[1] Jones and Child held commissions at the same time, but C... ... part of his term.

proceedings in this capacity, from any part of which any member may enter his dissent; to furnish such records to the General Assembly as are required; to convene at call of the Governor; to advise with the Governor in regard to convening General Assembly for extra session. To approve or reject, in conjunction with the Governor, any proposed encumbrance on the franchise or property of any corporation in which the State is a stockholder or otherwise has an interest. State bonds and certificates may be signed in lieu of the Treasurer, in case of his absence or inability to sign, by any member of the Council of State designated by it. The Governor and Council of State shall have charge of all the State's interest in all railroads, canals, and other works of internal improvement and shall report biennially to the General Assembly on their condition, suggesting at the same time such improvements as they deem proper.

Historical Note

The Proprietary Governor was assisted in the administration by a Council. The organization of the Council, and the method of selecting its members, varied with the varying moods of the Lords Proprietors. In 1663 they directed Governor Berkeley to select a Council of six. Two years later they fixed its membership at an even number from six to twelve, inclusive, to be determined by the Governor. In 1670, probably with the idea of making the Council more representative of the varied colonial interests, they changed the number to ten, five of whom were to be their own deputies selected by themselves and five to be selected by the General Assembly. This plan was continued till 1691 when, the Council having become an upper house of the General Assembly, the Lords Proprietors instructed the Governor to consider the deputies alone as members. At the same time, it was determined that each of the Lords Proprietors should be represented in the province by a deputy. Finally, in 1724, the deputies were abolished and the Council was organized with twelve members selected by the Lords Proprietors. The functions of the Council were two-fold, executive and legislative. Together with the Governor, it composed the executive branch of the government, and was charged with many important duties; independently of the Governor its executive functions were inconsiderable. Upon the death or absence of the Governor, the

Council chose a president who administered the government until the vacancy was filled.

The Council formed a part of the legislative branch of the government. Prior to 1691, the legislature, usually called the General Assembly, but sometimes referred to as the Grand Assembly, was composed of the Governor, the Councilors, and the Delegates of the people sitting together as one body. After that date the Council became an upper house, and the delegates a lower house called the House of Commons. This development was the result not of design but of custom, and came about in a thoroughly characteristic English way. As acts of the Assembly were not valid until signed by the Governor and three deputies, it became the custom of the Governor and deputies to meet independently of the Assembly to consider such measures as the Assembly presented for their signatures. Thus the deputies, probably feeling that it was unnecessary for them to pass twice on the same matters, gradually dropped out of the larger body and after a while came to be thought of as a separate and distinct legislative chamber. The Lords Proprietors formally recognized them as such in 1691. At the same time the five councilors elected by the Assembly were dropped from the Council leaving that body composed of the deputies only.

The functions of the Council remained the same under the Crown as under the Proprietors. They were provided for in the instructions from the Crown to the Governor, which also named the first councilors. Vacancies were filled by the King with the board of trade. The Council with the Governor represented the Crown in the province. The Governor could not act without the consent of at least three councilors, but the Governor could suspend his councilors for misconduct, and in the case of vacancy could recommend a successor. The authority, usually advisory, of the Council extended over actions of the Governor and other officers, quit rents, land grants, claims, and warrants, the court of exchequer, patents, commissions, administrators, Indians, reprieves and pardons, and cases of equity, legislative acts.

The Constitution of 1776 continued the Council, but made the office elective by the General Assembly, for the term of one year and the number of councilors seven. The Constitution of 1868 defined the Council of State as it is today.

PART III

JUDICIAL DEPARTMENT

1. COURT OF IMPEACHMENT.
2. SUPREME COURT.
3. SUPERIOR COURTS.
4. OTHER INFERIOR COURTS.
5. CORPORATION COMMISSION.

JUDICIAL DEPARTMENT

The judicial power of the State is vested in:
1. A Court for the Trial of Impeachments.
2. A Supreme Court.
3. The Superior Courts.
4. Courts of Justices of the Peace.
5. Such other inferior courts as may be established by the General Assembly.

COURT OF IMPEACHMENT

Article IV, section 3, of the Constitution of North Carolina provides that the court for the trial of impeachment shall be the Senate. A majority of the members are necessary to a quorum, and the judgment shall not extend beyond removal from and disqualification to hold office in North Carolina; but the party shall be liable to indictment and punishment according to law. The House of Representatives solely has the power of impeaching. No person shall be convicted without the concurrence of two-thirds of the Senators present. When the Governor is impeached, the Chief Justice presides. The following causes, or charges, are sufficient, when proved, to warrant conviction: (1) corruption in office; (2) habitual drunkenness; (3) intoxication while in the exercise of office (4) drunkenness in any public place; (5) mental or physical incompetence to discharge the duties of office; (6) any criminal matter the conviction whereof would tend to bring the office into public contempt.

Only once in the history of the State has the High Court of Impeachment been organized for the purpose of impeaching the Governor. This was in 1870, when the House of Representatives impeached Governor W. W. Holden before the Senate, for "high crimes and misdemeanors." The trial was conducted on both sides by the most eminent lawyers of the State, and resulted in the conviction of the Governor and his removal from office. In 1911 similar charges of impeachment were preferred against Chief Justice David M. Furches and Associate Justice Robert M. Douglas, but both were acquitted.

THE SUPREME COURT

The Supreme Court consists of a Chief Justice and four Associate Justices elected by the qualified voters of the State for a term of eight years.

The Constitution of 1776 required the General Assembly to "appoint Judges of the Supreme Courts of Law and Equity, Judges of Admiralty, and Attorney-General," who were commissioned by the Governor and held office during good behavior. Acting under this authority, the General Assembly in 1776 divided the State into six judicial districts. In 1782 a seventh district and in 1787 an eighth district were added. Under the act of 1777 three judges, Samuel Ashe, Samuel Spencer, and James Iredell, were chosen. The judges rode the circuits separately, but sat together as an appellate court. In 1790 the eight judicial districts were divided into an eastern and a western riding, and a fourth judge was added, two being assigned to each riding. In each riding the two judges sat together as an appellate court. In 1797 the General Assembly created an extraordinary court for the purpose of trying the Secretary of State and other officials who had been discovered confederating with others in an elaborate scheme for defrauding the State by issuing fraudulent land warrants. For trial of these criminals the General Assembly deemed it expedient to create a new court to sit at Raleigh twice a year, not exceeding ten days at each term. The court was authorized to hear appeals of causes which had accumulated in the district courts. The existence of this court under the act was to expire at the close of the session of the General Assembly next after June 10, 1802; but before the expiration of this time the General Assembly continued the court for three years longer, for the purpose of hearing appeals from the district courts, and gave it the name of "Court of Conference." By an act of 1804 the court was made a permanent Court of Record. The judges were ordered to reduce their opinions to writing and to deliver the same *viva voce* in open court. The next year (1805) the name of the court was changed to the Supreme Court. In 1810 the judges were authorized to elect one of their members a Chief Justice, John Louis Taylor being chosen to that office. The Supreme Court now consisted of six judges, but two continued to be a quorum, and all the judges still rode the circuits.

In 1818 an act was passed establishing the present Supreme Court and requiring it to sit in Raleigh for the hearing of appeals. The act provided for three judges to be elected by the General Assembly. John Louis Taylor, Leonard Henderson, and John Hall composed the first court, which began its session January 1, 1819. The judges elected their own Chief Justice, Taylor being continued in that office. The number of judges continued to be three until 1868, when the Constitution adopted by the convention of that year increased the number to a Chief and four Associate Justices. The convention of 1875 reduced it again to three, but by an amendment adopted in 1888 the number was raised to a Chief Justice and four Associate Justices, where it has continued until the present time. The Supreme Court holds annually two sessions of sixteen weeks, one beginning the first Monday in September, the other the first Monday in February.

The court is authorized to choose its own clerk, marshal, reporter, and other officers.

SUPERIOR COURTS

There are twenty Superior Court judges, one for each of the twenty circuits, or judicial districts, who are elected by the people and hold their offices for a term of eight years. The Superior Court has appellate jurisdiction of all issues of law or of fact determined by a clerk of the Superior Court or justice of the peace, and of all appeals from inferior courts for error assigned in matters of law as provided by law. In the matter of original jurisdiction the law is:

"The Superior Court shall have original jurisdiction of the civil actions whereof exclusive original jurisdiction is not given to some other court, and of all criminal actions in which the punishment may exceed a fine of fifty dollars or imprisonment for thirty days; and of all such affrays as shall be committed within one mile of the place where and during the time such court is being held."

OTHER COURTS

The Constitution gives to the General Assembly power to establish other courts inferior to the Supreme and Superior Courts, and to allot and distribute to them such powers and jurisdiction, within constitutional limits, as it sees fit. From the decision of these in ferior courts the Legislature has power to provide a proper system of appeals.

The Constitution also requires the General Assembly to provide for the establishment of special courts for the trial of misdemeanors in cities and towns where the same may be necessary.

Such courts are the mayors of cities and incorporated towns. Their election or appointment is usually provided for in the charters of incorporation, the acts of the General Assembly prescribing how particular towns and cities shall be governed.

The jurisdiction of such special courts—also called in the law, inferior courts—is usually set forth in the charters.

The general law also provides that "the mayor of every city and incorporated town . . . within the corporate limits of his city or town, shall have the jurisdiction of a justice of the peace in all criminal matters arising under the laws of the State or under the ordinances of such city or town."

Justices of the peace, in their respective counties, try (1) that class of civil actions which involve demands for small debts and property of little value and (2) that class of criminal actions, called petty misdemeanors, which involve only slight punishment.

They try all cases of contract or promise to pay money where the sum demanded does not exceed two hundred dollars.

They may try certain other civil actions where the value of the property in controversy or the amount claimed for damages does not exceed fifty dollars.

They try criminal cases arising within their counties, the punishment of which fixed by law cannot exceed a fine of fifty dollars or imprisonment for thirty days.

NORTH CAROLINA CORPORATION COMMISSION
R. O. SELF, *Clerk*, Raleigh

The North Carolina Corporation Commission was established by an act of the General Assembly of 1899, superseding the Railroad Commission, established in 1891. The offices of the Commission occupy the first floor of the State Departments Building. The Commissioners are elected, one every two years, for a period of six years. The present commission is composed of W. T. Lee, Chairman, of Haywood County, George P. Pell, Commissioner, of Forsyth County, and A. J. Maxwell, Commissioner, of Wake County.

The Commission has general supervision over railroad, telegraph, telephone, street railway, steamboat, canal, waterworks, and all other companies exercising the right of eminent domain, and also under the act of 1913, of electric light, power, water, and gas companies. Under the act of 1923, it is given power to require train schedules, and adequate warehousing facilities to promote the more expeditious handling of less carload freight. By the act of 1921, it is given the general supervision of state banks; and by act of 1925, the supervision of motor vehicles used for the transportation of persons or property for compensation, and of capital issues, known as the Blue Sky Law.

Details in regard to the several public utilities are too voluminous to attempt in this manual, but are briefly enumerated as follows:

ELECTRIC POWER

This is truly the "electric age." This business with its great organizations has grown out of the isolated electric plant serving an individual community. The past few years have witnessed a most remarkable degree of concentration in the electric utility business. Goldsboro and Henderson have been on inter-connecting transmission lines with Sheffield, Ala., and Nashville, Tenn. Without this connection west of the Savannah River we have within our jurisdiction, or adjacent for available transmission, hydro-electric power, with steam auxiliaries, producing 760,000 horsepower. This makes possible the operation of more than 6,000 manufacturing plants.

At the close of the year 1923, the seventy-eight privately-owned and operated electric utilities had an invested capital of $45,335,173.

GAS UTILITIES

The ten gas companies operating seventeen plants in the State have an invested capital of approximately $6,000,000.

STREET RAILWAYS

There are twelve street railway systems in the State with approximately $10,000,000 invested capital, and 155 miles of road.

TELEPHONE UTILITIES

The extent of the industry in North Carolina can be more readily comprehended when we realize that 120 companies are operating 295 exchanges, with 150,000 telephones, with 26,000 miles of wire. The companies report investments of approximately $10,000,000.

EXPRESS COMPANIES

The American Railway Express Company and the Southeastern Express Company operate in North Carolina, the American over the Seaboard Air Line, the Atlantic Coast Line, Norfolk Southern and associated lines, and the Southeastern over the Southern and associated lines.

TELEGRAPH COMPANIES

The Western Union Telegraph Company and the Postal Telegraph Company operate in North Carolina over 3,968 miles of pole and cable line. Just what investment these companies have is difficult to ascertain, as many of their lines are leased or operated jointly with telephone companies and railroads.

RAILROAD STATISTICS

There are fifty-seven railroad companies in North Carolina, operating 4,941 miles of road. These companies report a total capital stock of $111,327,000 with funded debt of $145,000,000.

BANKING DEPARTMENT

In 1899 the Commission was given supervision of all State banks. At that time there were fifty-two State banks, twenty-one private banks, and eight savings banks operating under the State system, making a total of eighty-one banking institutions. On December 31, 1925, this number had increased to 501 banks, including 67 branches. The total resources of these banks amounted to $306,986,915.

MOTOR VEHICLE DEPARTMENT

This department has charge of the enforcement and supervision of what is known as the Bus Act, Chapter 50, Public Laws of 1925. On August 14, 1926, ninety-seven passenger bus line certificates were outstanding and under these certificates a total of 456 motor passenger buses were being operated on approximately 4,500 miles of road. The annual bus mileage operation for the year ended June 20,

1926, was approximately 11,350,040. Seventeen express or freight certificates were outstanding, and under these there were being operated eighty-three trucks on 1,756 miles of road. Union bus stations have been established at practically all termini and have done more to improve the service to the traveling public than any other one thing that has been done in connection with the supervision of such service. Consolidation of operation has reduced competition to a point where the operators can give more attention to service.

CAPITAL ISSUES DEPARTMENT

The Capital Issues Department of the Corporation Commission was established by Chapter 190, Public Laws of 1925. It is organized by the appointment of one member of the Corporation Commission as the Commissioner in charge, and the appointment of an Assistant Commissioner, who is in direct charge of the work of the department. The department is charged with the supervision of sales of securities within the State, and under the law registers for sale such securities as may meet the requirements of the law and are neither exempted by the law nor sold in an exempted transaction. All who deal in securities are required to obtain license for such business before engaging in it.

PART IV

STATE DEPARTMENTS, BOARDS, AND COMMISSIONS

1. The Adjutant-General's Department.
2. Department of Agriculture.
3. Board of Agriculture.
4. Joint Committee for Agricultural Work.
5. Department of Labor and Printing.
6. Department of Insurance.
7. State Department of Revenue.
8. State Board of Assessment.
9. State Highway Commission.
10. State Board of Health.
11. Department of Conservation and Development.
12. State Board of Charities and Public Welfare.
13. Child Welfare Commission.
14. The Budget Bureau.
15. North Carolina Historical Commission.
16. Library Commission of North Carolina.
17. State Library.
18. Law Library.
19. Audubon Society of North Carolina.
20. North Carolina Fisheries Commission Board.
21. Printing Commission.
22. Salary and Wage Commission.
23. Judicial Conference.
24. State Prison.
25. State Bureau of Identification.
26. Commissioner of Pardons.
27. Educational Commission.
28. The Equalizing Fund Commission.

29. STATE BOARD OF VOCATIONAL EDUCATION.
30. COLLEGE COMMISSION.
31. STATE COMMITTEE ON HIGH SCHOOL TEXT-BOOKS.
32. TEXT-BOOK COMMISSION.
33. TRANSPORTATION ADVISORY COMMISSION.
34. STATE SINKING FUND COMMISSION.
35. STATE BOARD OF ELECTIONS.
36. STATE BOARD OF CANVASSERS.
37. STATE BOARD OF PENSIONS.
38. COMMISSIONER OF THE VETERAN'S LOAN FUND.
39. BOARD OF PUBLIC BUILDINGS AND GROUNDS.
40. MUNICIPAL BOARD OF CONTROL.
41. STATE STANDARD KEEPER.
42. BOARD OF COMMISSIONERS OF NAVIGATION AND PILOTAGE.
43. CROP PEST COMMISSION.
44. NATIONAL PARK COMMISSION FOR NORTH CAROLINA.
45. COMMISSION ON THE REPRODUCTION OF THE CANOVA STATUE OF WASHINGTON.
46. BENNETT PLACE MEMORIAL COMMISSION.
47. BOARD OF MEDICAL EXAMINERS.
48. BOARD OF CHIROPODY EXAMINERS.
49. THE BOARD OF NURSE EXAMINERS OF NORTH CAROLINA.
50. BOARD OF PHARMACY.
51. NORTH CAROLINA BOARD OF VETERINARY MEDICAL EXAMINERS.
52. NORTH CAROLINA STATE BOARD OF DENTAL EXAMINERS.
53. STATE BOARD OF ACCOUNTANCY.
54. STATE BOARD OF ARCHITECTURAL EXAMINATION AND REGISTRATION.
55. STATE BOARD OF CHIROPRATIC EXAMINERS.
56. STATE BOARD OF EMBALMERS.
57. STATE BOARD OF EXAMINERS IN OPTOMETRY.
58. STATE BOARD OF OSTEOPATHIC EXAMINATION AND REGISTRATION.
59. STATE BOARD OF REGISTRATION FOR ENGINEERS AND LAND SURVEYORS.
60. STATE LICENSING BOARD FOR CONTRACTORS.

THE ADJUTANT GENERAL'S DEPARTMENT

Art. III, Sec. 8, Constitution; Ch. 11, C. S.; Ch. 53, P. L. 1921
Ch. 54, P. L. 1925.

J. VAN B. METTS, *The Adjutant General*, Raleigh

Title—The Adjutant General.

Appointment—By Governor.

Term—Four Years.

Qualification—Five years commissioned service in National Guard, Naval Militia, Regular Army, U. S. Navy, or Marine Corps.

Salary—$4,500.

Function

To organize, direct and control the militia of this State; to preserve the peace and to protect life and property in emergency through the use of the National Guard, Naval Militia and unorganized militia; and otherwise execute the military laws and regulations of the United States, State of North Carolina and the Commander-in-Chief.

To make returns and reports to the Secretaries of War and Navy as required; to keep records of officers and enlisted men; to have prepared and properly distributed military laws, etc., and to perform such other duties as required by military law and regulations of the Governor.

ART. III, CH. 2, C. S. The Governor is Commander-in-Chief of the State Militia which is divided into (1) National Guard, (2) Naval Militia, and (3) Unorganized Militia. The Governor is empowered to call out the militia to execute the laws, suppress riots or insurrections and to repel invasions; to prescribe such regulations relating to the organization of the National Guard and Naval Militia as conform to the requirements of the Federal statutes.

The military staff is divided into (1) the personal staff of the Governor consisting of 10 National Guard officers and 2 Naval Militia officers as aides-de-camp; and (2) the administrative staff as prescribed by the Secretary of War and the Secretary of Navy.

102 STATE DEPARTMENTS, BOARDS, AND COMMISSIONS

The Governor is directed by law to appoint a Property and Disbursing officer for North Carolina, who shall receipt and account for all funds and property belonging to the State for military purposes. His principal duties are the disbursement of all funds appropriated by the State for military purposes including the issuance of thousands of checks quarterly and semi-annually in payment of vouchers and pay rolls for Armory drills.

The Governor shall also, according to law, appoint, subject to the approval of the Secretary of War, a Property and Disbursing officer for the United States. This officer disburses annually about $200,000 in government funds and is accountable for and keeps a record of about two and a half million dollars worth of Federal property in the hands of the National guard.

The Adjutant General, as head of the Department, is subordinate only to the Governor in matters pertaining thereto.

REPORTS. To make an annual report to the Governor including a detailed statement of all expenditures made for military purposes during the year.

To report biennially to the General Assembly.

Historical Note

The office and department of the Adjutant General was created by Chapter 18, of the laws of 1806, and has been in continuous existence ever since, though until 1860 the salary was nominal and the duties of the department slight.

The militia of the State has been in existence since 1679, when the Lords Proprietors instructed Governor John Harvey to organize the able-bodied citizens and to appoint officers. Under the colonial government all officers were appointed by the Governor. Three provisions relating to militia have been brought forward from old charters and constitutions:

1. The Governor is Commander-in-Chief.
2. The people have a right to bear arms.
3. All able-bodied male citizens are subject to military duty at the call of the Governor, subject to regulation of the General Assembly.

The age limit was originally 16-50. This has been changed to 18-45. Citizens were originally required to furnish their own arms; since 1836 the National Government has assumed this obligation. Originally all men subject to military duty were required by law to organize, muster, and drill. The requirement was never universally effective. The law allowed volunteer companies full privilege of organization, drill, and exemption from the regular scheme of organization; and the military activity of the State was usually confined to these volunteer companies of which there were many with long and honorable records. Since 1873 the militia has been in two classes—organized and unorganized. The organized militia consists of volunteers entirely. The State Guard was reorganized in 1877. Up to 1836 all general and field officers were elected by the General Assembly. All company officers were elected by the enlisted men of the several companies. The law was then changed—company officers were still elected by the companies, but general and field officers were elected by the officers of the units concerned. Since 1873 all officers have been appointed by the Governor.

Prior to 1873 each county was required to organize at least one regiment, and the State to maintain at least six brigades. There were in 1854 ten divisions of militia consisting of 105 regiments totaling 1,050 companies of 45 men each—about 1,000 officers and 47,250 enlisted men. In order to conform to the Federal laws, an act of the Legislature of 1903 changed the designation "North Carolina State Guard" to "North Carolina National Guard." These militia organizations formed the main home defense in the war of the Revolution. They formed the basis of the system which enrolled an estimate of 125,000 North Carolinians in the Confederate armies.

The North Carolina State Guard was among the first to respond to the call of the President in 1898 for service in the Spanish-American War. Two regiments of infantry were furnished; and, in addition, North Carolina furnished a regiment of colored troops.

The Federal law having been changed so that the President would have authority to draft or call the National Guard into service of the United States in a National emergency, on June 19th, 1916, the North Carolina National Guard was mobilized at Camp Glenn, North Carolina, for service on the Mexican border, on account of the existing relations with Mexico and sent to Camp Stewart, near El Paso, Texas, for Federal Service.

These National Guard units were:

First, second, third, regiments, Infantry; Troops A and B Cavalry; Companies A and B Engineers; Ambulance Co. No. 1; and Hospital Co. No. 1.

With the exception of the second regiment, Infantry, and Companies A and B Engineers, which were not mustered out of Federal service until following the World War, all these troops were returned to their home stations and mustered out; but soon they were mustered back into Federal service for the World War. National Guard troops served in the Thirtieth and Forty-second Divisions in France and Belgium.

Pursuant to the Proclamation of the President, July 3, 1917, the following organizations, units and detachments of the National Guard of North Carolina were drafted into the Federal service on August 5, 1917:

First Brigade	First Squadron Cavalry
First Infantry	First Machine Gun Troop
Second Infantry	First Battalion Engineers
Third Infantry	First Engineer Train
Field Hospital No. 1	First Motor Truck Company
Ambulance Company No. 1	Field and Staff
Veterinary Corps	Sanitary Detachment and Six
Radio Company Signal Corps	Companies Coast Artillery
First Regiment Field Artillery	Quartermasters Corps

making a total of 277 officers, and 7,454 enlisted men—a grand total of 7,731. Of the Naval Militia 18 officers and 187 men (total 215) were called into Federal service April 6, 1917, as National Naval Volunteers. The record these troops made in the World War is a source of pride to all North Carolinians.

At the close of the World War the entire National Guard was discharged from the service, and the past seven years have been devoted to a reorganization of the State's military forces. The present strength totals approximately 3,800 officers and men, and units are located in about 40 counties. These units are fully equipped at the expense of the Federal authorities, are paid for armory drills during the year from the same source, and are given fifteen days training each summer under the supervision of professional instructors. The State provides armories, maintains the camp site at Camp Glenn, makes allowances to officers and men, takes care of courtsmartial and carrying bond expenses, inspections, etc. The North Carolina National Guard is in a high state of efficiency, comparing favorably in this respect and in numbers with the Guard of the other States. It is interesting to note that at the close of the war there was no National Guard in the United States, but at the present time its strength exceeds 190,000 officers and men organized and equipped similarly to units of the Regular Army.

For further information concerning the strength and location of various units of North Carolina National Guard see "Roster North Carolina National Guard, Revised to December 31, 1925," published by the Adjutant General of North Carolina.

DEPARTMENT OF AGRICULTURE

Sec. 17, Art. III, Constitution; Ch. 84, C. S.; Ch. 25, P. L., 1921; Ch. 174, P. L. 1925.

W. A. GRAHAM, *Commissioner*, Raleigh

Title—Commissioner.

Appointment—Elected by people.

Term—Four years.

Qualification—Practical farmer.

Salary—$4,500.

Ex Officio member—Chairman Board of Agriculture, Joint Committee for Agricultural Work.

The Constitution of the State (1868) provides for a Department of Agriculture, Immigration and Statistics. Under this fundamental law the General Assembly established the Department of Agriculture in 1877. (Chapter 274). Since that time it has been greatly enlarged by the General Assembly, and its field expanded by the ever increasing demands made upon it by a rapidly growing agriculture.

At present the Board consists of ten members, one member from each Congressional District, appointed by the Governor and confirmed by the Senate, for terms of six years; and of the Commissioner of Agriculture, who is a member of and ex officio chairman of the Board.

The Commissioner of Agriculture, who is chief executive officer of the Department, was formerly elected by the Legislature but in order to bring the Department in closer touch with the people, especially the farmers of the State, the law was so changed as to make the office of Commissioner elective.

The Department is charged with the following:

1. Investigations relating to the improvement of agriculture, the beneficial use of commercial fertilizers and composts, and to induce capital and labor to enter the State.

2. Investigations for the improvement of milk and beef cattle, especially with investigations relating to the diseases of cattle and other domestic animals—having power to quarantine infected animals and to regulate the transportation of stock within the State.

3. Investigations of the ravages of insects injuriously affecting market gardens, fruits, etc. and with dissemination of information essential for their abatement.

4. Investigations directed to the introduction and fostering of new agricultural industries adapted to the various soils and climates of the State.

5. Investigations relative to the subject of drainage, and irrigation, and mineral and domestic sources of fertilizers, including composting, etc.

6. The enforcement of the laws enacted for the sale of commercial fertilizers, seed, food products, and with authority to make regulations concerning the same.

7. The dissemination of information relative to the advantages of soil and climate and to the natural resources and industrial opportunities offered in the State.

To these have been added: The issuing of bulletins; the Museum; Farmers' Institutes; enforcement by regulations of the Pure Food Law, concentrated commercial feeding-stuff law, cottonseed meal law, the law regulating the statistics of leaf tobacco, forestry work, the law regulating the standard-weight packages of meal and flour, registration and sale of condimental, patented, proprietary or trademark stock or poultry tonics, regulators or conditioners, the inspection of illuminating and power oils, fluids and gasoline, the law to prevent and punish the sale of adulterated, impure, or misbranded agricultural and vegetable seed and those lacking viability; the manufacture and sale of anti-hog cholera serum; also of inoculating germs for leguminous crops.

The Department is, to a considerable extent, a sub-legislature. The Legislature, in committing to its execution specified laws, confers upon the Board power to make regulations for this purpose, which are given the authority of law, and violation of them is made a misdemeanor, cognizable by the courts. The power to confer this authority has been tested in the courts and approved by decision of the Supreme Court.

Things That Have Been Done by the Agricultural Department

1. The source of the ingredients in fertilizers is made known.

2. The feed inspection law has been amended to include all feeds and the value of feeds much improved.

3. *Condimental Feed Law.* Analyses are made of each brand and published. The people need not pay high prices for many of the ingredients, such as charcoal, copperas, saltpetre, salt, salts, etc., which can be bought for a few cents a pound of grocers. Drugs for either stock or men must have a value corresponding with that printed on the container or they may be excluded from sale.

4. Great advance has been made along all lines of animal feeding and feeds for animals, including poultry. All cases of diseases of animals appearing in the State have been suppressed. We have had no epidemic which could not be eliminated.

5. Eradication of the Cattle Tick is now complete.

Tuberculosis. All herds which pass two successive tests without reactors are placed in the Accredited Herd list. The State appropriates annually $10,000.00 for indemnity for paying for animals slaughtered on account of glanders. When a cow or other animal is affected with tuberculosis or glanders, the animal is reported to the authorities and killed and paid for, thereby preventing spreading of the diseases.

6. A pure seed law by which the farmers may be protected from purchase of inferior seed either in purity or germination.

7. Preparation of legume culture which is sold at fifty cents an acre bottle. This pays the cost of production.

8. Great advance in the work in Entomology, especially in spraying. Many pests have been destroyed and others much curtailed in their injurious operations.

9. Also in Horticulture, all regulatory work is done by the Department.

10. *The Pure Food Law.* The weight or quantity of contents to be marked on all containers, with which numbers the contents must comply. Adulteration is seldom found in the foods sold in the State.

11. Inspection of illuminating oils and gasoline, by which the quality and safety of the oils have been improved without cost to the consumer.

12. Inspection of flour to detect that which is bleached and prevent the sale of it as unbleached.

13. A marketing system is being evolved whereby the farmer can dispose of his products advantageously.

14. *Cottonseed Meal.* No goods are permitted to be branded as "meal" unless they contain $6\frac{1}{2}$ per cent ammonia, but must be branded "cottonseed feed."

15. *The Bulletin* ranks with the highest of its class, and many letters of commendation are received from persons within and without the State. Requests are frequently received for these bulletins in other states; and, also, from the agricultural press. It has a circulation of more than 35,000 each month. Copies have been requested for use as testbooks in the public schools of other states and the University of Wisconsin.

16. The Museum continues to be the most valuable south of Philadelphia, except that at the National Capital. It is the State's great object lesson. Additions to the different departments are made each year. A representative agricultural exhibit is now being collected.

STATISTICS

The following statistics will show some of the results of the work of the Department:

North Carolina produced in

	1860	1910	1915	1918	1923	1924
Corn (bushels)	30,000,000	34,063,531	64,050,000	63,000,000	58,568,000	44,512,000
Wheat (bushels)	4,743,706	7,433,000	10,355,000	13,167,000	6,048,100	5,541,000
Cotton (bales)	145,514	665,132	732,000	732,000	1,020,000	1,001,000

DRAINAGE

The Department has arranged with the National Department for an expert in this work, who gives information to the farmers concerning the drainage of creeks, cutting ditches, and laying tiles.

VETERINARY DIVISION

The Veterinary Division is devoted to giving information as to the treatment of animal diseases.

Serum for vaccination of hogs to prevent the spread of cholera is furnished by this Division.

Ninety-five per cent of the hogs vaccinated escape cholera. The Department is now prepared to supply all requests for serum, and the scourge of cholera has been much abated.

CHEMISTRY

The Division of Chemistry makes analyses of fertilizer, cottonseed meal, feed and foodstuffs, soils, minerals and marls, waters, etc.

TEST FARMS

Test Farms have been established in Edgecombe County, at Willard Station in Pender County, Statesville, near Swannanoa in Buncombe County, and in the old tobacco belt at Oxford, in the newly-drained black lands of Eastern North Carolina, and in Beaufort County. The effort is to conduct these farms for the benefit of the crops grown in each section, first on small plats and then on a large scale, showing results of different kinds and amounts of home-made and commercial fertilizers, preparation of land, cultivation and rotation of crops and demonstration work. These farms are conducted jointly by the State Department and the State College.

COOPERATIVE ASSOCIATIONS AND CREDIT UNIONS

To organize and conduct a bureau of information in regard to coöperative associations and rural credits; to promote the establishing of such agencies through educational campaigns and personal advice and assistance; to examine at least once a year organizations so formed.

PURE FOOD DIVISION

The pure food law passed by the General Assembly of 1899, amended in 1905 and redrafted and passed as a new act in 1907, forbids the manufacture or sale of adulterated or misbranded food or beverages and charges the Department of Agriculture with its enforcement.

Inspections are made throughout the State and samples collected for analyses. The samples are examined for adulteration and the results published, showing the brand name of the article and the name and address of the manufacturer. The first report was published as the Department Bulletin for December, 1909. Since that time similar reports have been published annually.

There are two classes of adulterants found in food:

1. Substances which are deleterious to health, and
2. Substances which merely render the food less valuable.

The use of the first is prohibited; the second can be used provided their presence is made known to the purchaser.

Much of the food and beverages sold in the State is in the hands of unintelligent men, who can be imposed upon by shrewd and unscrupulous manufacturers. Owing to various complications the enforcement of the Food Law is far more difficult than one not familiar with the situation would think.

The National Government has enacted a food law which requires weight of contents to be stamped on all packages or other containers of goods. The Legislature has enacted this law for this State.

FEED INSPECTIONS

The Legislature of 1903 passed a law which requires the Commissioner of Agriculture to employ Feed inspectors, whose duty it is to visit the different towns in the State, see that the law is complied with as to the branding of bags, weight of bags, and to take samples of all feeds. These samples are examined microscopically and if found adulterated are immediately withdrawn from sale.

All samples collected are analyzed by the Feed Chemist and the results, along with such additional information as circumstances may advise, are published in the bulletins of the Department of Agriculture.

In enforcing the law there are four main objects in view:

1. To stop the sale of adulterated feeds in North Carolina.

2. To educate the consumers to buy feed according to the analyses on the bags, just as he buys his fertilizer by an analysis.

3. To teach the dairymen and farmers the best way to combine their home-grown feeds with those they are compelled to buy to get the greatest benefit from the amount consumed.

4. To stimulate a desire on the part of the consumers for better feeds.

ENTOMOLOGY

The work of this division includes the inspection of fruit trees, which are not allowed to be sold in this State unless declared free from disease. Experts are sent to examine all nurseries for insect pests, and many commercial orchards are inspected. Directions are furnished for preparation of material for spraying, and for its application. The San Jose scale is being controlled in many places and further damage prevented by directions sent from this office. Other insect pests and diseases have been prevented or cured, and much valuable information given the people of the State on matters pertaining to insects of all kinds.

MARKET DIVISION

This division coöperates with the farmers in finding the best markets for their surplus products.

BOTANY DIVISION

is charged with the

1. Examination and testing of field, garden, flower and herb seeds.
2. Manufacture and distribution of pure cultures for legume crops.

3. The placing of Federal grades on grain.
4. Identification of plants and the control of weeds.

DEMONSTRATION AND INSPECTION OF POWER AND ILLUMINATING OILS AND GASOLINE

The Pure Food Chemist is also Oil Chemist. The quality of the oil has been kept at a good standard.

DIVISION OF PUBLICATIONS

In addition to editing the *Bulletin* this division issues the *Agricultural Review*, a monthly publication covering the various activities of the Department.

THE MUSEUM

The State Geologist has, since the establishment of his department in 1856, collected specimens of different kinds, principally of minerals, representing the natural resources of the State. In 1879 the care of the Museum and expense of maintenance were transferred to the Department of Agriculture. A building has been erected for its occupancy, and its contents greatly increased. It is now by far the most extensive in its contents of anything of its nature south of Philadelphia, save the National Museum at Washington, D. C. To it, more than any other source, is attributable the fine display the State has made at international, national, and State expositions. It is the state's object lesson, representing its resources in agriculture, timber, mineral, fishes, birds, game, animals and flora and fauna in general.

As articles affected by time become undesirable they are replaced. The idea is to keep the Museum constantly growing, with no chance for stagnation.

IMMIGRATION

The Legislature in 1909 repealed the act of 1907 concerning immigration. There are now no agents of the State employed in foreign countries; a few young men come from Scotland each year, and land and immigration companies bring some people to the State each year, but no report is made to the Department; however, it coöperates with them as far as practicable.

The Department has no lands of the State for sale, and can make no contracts, warrant titles or do any work of like nature. It can only put parties desiring to purchase property in the State in communication with citizens who have property to sell, and leave them to perfect sales, if it is found desirable.

Many letters are received from persons from the states of the Middle West requesting information as to the resources of the State and several hundred have each year purchased homes. The Department had arranged to place exhibits at the fairs in these States, but this was abandoned when the law was repealed.

SALES OF LEAF TOBACCO

Chapter 97, Laws 1907, requires the Department to preserve a record of the leaf tobacco sold on the floors of the warehouses of the State, and publish it monthly. Each warehouse is required to furnish an account of its sales, and is guilty of a misdemeanor for failure.

BOARD OF AGRICULTURE

Sec. 17, Art. III, Constitution; Ch. 84, C. S.; Ch. 137, P. L. 1921; Ch. 28 P. L. 1921 Extra Session; Ch. 174, P. L. 1925.

Composition (11). Ten members. Commissioner of Agriculture, Chairman.

Appointment—Ten by Governor with consent of Senate; one elected.

Term—Six years; Chairman four years.

Qualification—Practical farmers.

Compensation—$5 per diem and mileage.

MEMBERS OF BOARD OF AGRICULTURE

First District—F. P. LATHAM, Belhaven.
Second District—J. J. HARRIS, Macon.
Third District—W. A. BROWN, Rocky Point.
Fourth District—CLARENCE POE, Raleigh.
Fifth District—R. W. SCOTT, Haw River.
Sixth District—J. VANCE McGOUGAN, Fayetteville.
Seventh District—T. J. FINCH, Thomasville.

Eighth District—W. B. McLelland, Stony Point.
Ninth District—O. Max Gardner, Shelby.
Tenth District—E. G. Roberson, Leicester.

Function

The functions of the Board of Agriculture are now strictly legislative and advisory, while all executive power in the Department is vested in the office of Commissioner of Agriculture (Chapter 174, Laws 1925.)

STATE WAREHOUSE SYSTEM. To maintain a cotton warehouse system, administered through a State warehouse superintendent to stabilize and encourage cotton industry; to make suitable rules and regulations to enforce law; to fix charges for storing cotton in local warehouses; to impose a tax of 25 cents on each bale of cotton ginned up to June 30, 1922, to be collected by Commissioner of Revenue, and 90 per cent of the total receipts from this source to be invested in first mortgages to aid and encourage the establishment of warehouses operating under this system.

STATE WAREHOUSE SUPERINTENDENT. To have power to lease property for warehousing of cotton and encourage erection of warehouses in the various cotton-growing counties under terms of this act; to provide an adequate system of inspection, rules, forms and reports to insure security; to supervise local warehouses in general and to issue receipts for cotton classified and stored, through local warehouse managers.

REPORTS. To make an annual report to Governor of its work and all receipts and expenditures and objects for which expended.

JOINT COMMITTEE FOR AGRICULTURAL WORK

Part 3, Art. 1, Ch. 84, C. S.; Art 7, Ch. 93, C. S.; Ch. 142, P. L. 1925

Composition (11)—Governor, Chairman; Commissioner of Agriculture, President State A. and E. College, *ex officio* members; four members Board of Agriculture designated by Board; four members Board of Trustees of A. and E. College designated by Board.

Personnel—Appointed by Board of Trustees of the College: Robert N. Page, Southern Pines; W. D. Laroque, Kinston; J. F. Diggs,

Rockingham; Charles W. Gold, Greensboro. Appointed by State Board of Agriculture: Clarence Poe, Raleigh; O. Max Gardner, Shelby; Dr. J. Vance McGougan, Fayetteville; R. W. Scott, Haw River.

Term—During terms as members of the Board.

Function

It shall be the purpose of the Joint Committee for Agricultural Work to prevent duplication and to maintain greater coöperation on the part of the North Carolina State College of Agriculture and Engineering and the State Department of Agriculture, Immigration and Statistics; and the Joint Committee shall have authority to settle any and all questions relative to jurisdiction or duplication of work that may be referred to it either by the President of the College or the Commissioner of Agriculture, and the decision of the Joint Committee not inconsistent with law shall be binding on both institutions. The Joint Committee shall meet at least once each year at the call of the chairman to receive reports from the President of the College and the Commissioner of Agriculture on the relation of the two institutions, with special reference to the research or any other work in which the two institutions are interested, and to make recommendations to the governing bodies of each that may tend to increase their coöperation in promoting agricultural improvements in the State.

DEPARTMENT OF LABOR AND PRINTING

Arts. 1, 2, Ch. 120, C. S.; Art. 2, Ch. 112, C. S.; Chs. 25, 131, P. L. 1921; Ch. 127, P. L. 1925

F. D. GRIST, *Commissioner*, Raleigh

Title—Commissioner.
Appointment—Elected.
Term—Four years.
Salary—$4,500.
Ex officio Member—Printing Commission.

Function

To collect and collate information and statistics concerning:

1. Labor and its relation to capital, hours of labor, earnings of laborers, and their educational, moral and financial condition, and means of promoting their welfare.

2. Various mining, milling and manufacturing industries of State, location, capacity and output, raw materials and capital invested.

3. Location, estimated and actual horse-power and condition of valuable water powers, developed and undeveloped in this State.

4. Farm lands and farming, kinds, character and quantity of annual farm products in this State.

5. Truck gardening and dairying.

6. Timber lands and timber.

7. Other information affecting agricultural and industrial welfare of the State.

To perform the duties of mine inspector for the State; to act as State Director for U. S. Employment Service; to supervise, in conjunction with printing commission, all State printing; to appoint an assistant commissioner who is a practical printer, to take charge of State printing under his direction.

PUBLIC EMPLOYMENT SERVICE. To maintain a public employment bureau in the Department, to establish and conduct public employment offices in the State; to extend vocational guidance to minors seeking employment; to coöperate with Federal, municipal and other agencies in employment, rehabilitation and Americanization problems.

STATE PRINTING. To carefully examine all printing and binding done for the State or any Department thereof, by the public printers, and to certify that same meets required standards and that the accounts rendered by the public printer are accurate and just. Such accounts shall not be approved by the Commissioner nor audited by the State oftener than forty-eight times a year; to purchase for use of the State, the paper and stationery used for public printing.

COÖPERATIVE PURCHASE OF SUPPLIES. At the beginning of the present biennium and at the request of the Director of the Budget, this Department undertook to centralize the purchase of office equipment and supplies and has been able to reduce the cost on a great many of these items by from 20 to 50 per cent. The total savings to the departments during the fiscal year ending June 30, 1926, amounted to slightly over $4,000. During the year ending June 30, 1927, these savings will approximate $25,000, due to the broadening of the scope of the activity to cover office furniture and equipment, upon which items contracts have been and are being made which enable the State to buy upon the same price basis as dealers.

MINE INSPECTION. To examine all the mines in the State as often as possible, to see that the provisions of law are strictly observed and carried out; to employ counsel and to prosecute violations; to examine particularly the works and machinery belonging to any mine; to examine condition of mines as to ventilation, drainage, and general security, to investigate deaths by accidents; to keep a record of all examinations and all data affecting mining industry in this State.

REPORTS. To publish and distribute biennially a statistical report covering the Department's activities and research, also an annual report to the Governor on mines and mining industry.

The Department of Labor and Printing, created by the Legislature of 1887, is one of the oldest State departments outside of those established by constitutional mandate. The duties of the Department are comprehended under the four general heads:

1. Collection, collation, and publication of industrial statistics.
2. Supervision of the State's printing.
3. Mine inspection.
4. Free employment service.

INDUSTRIAL STATISTICS

The Commissioner, aided by the Assistant Commissioner, collects, collates, and publishes information and statistics concerning labor and its relation to capital, the hours of labor, the earnings of laborers and their educational, moral, and financial condition, and the best means of promoting their mental, moral, and material welfare; also statistics concerning the various mining, milling, and manufacturing industries in this State, their location, capacity, and actual output of manufactured products, the kind and quantity of raw material annually used by them and the capital invested therein; the location, estimated and actual horsepower and condition of valuable waterpowers, developed and undeveloped, in the State; farm lands and farming, the kinds, character, and quantity of the annual farm products; timber lands and timbers, truck gardening, dairying, and such other information and statistics concerning the agricultural and industrial welfare of the citizens of the State as may be deemed of interest and benefit to the public.

A high standard was set for this work and it has ever since been the policy of the office to improve upon its own work from year to year. The biennial report is now recognized as one of the most succinct examples of statistical work issued in the United States. The matter has been boiled down, so to speak, and one chief aim has been to present the greatest possible information in the least possible space, accomplishing thereby two very desirable ends, i.e., ease and convenience of reference, and minimum expense.

Men who are causing the wheels of industry to turn all over the country pronounce the biennial report of the Department one of the most comprehensive and valuable publications, on the subjects treated, issued by any state in the Union. It is the only official publication which shows the industrial status of North Carolina and the great variety of her manufactured products. It reaches every state in the Union and many foreign countries. It is the chief medium through which the State's growth and development are advertised to the world.

THE STATE'S PRINTING

When the public printing had become of such importance that the old practice of assuming that it would take care of itself was proved inadequate and unsatisfactory, the duty of systematizing and superintending this work was added to the duties of the office (Chapter 373, Public Laws of 1899). Since that time the growth of the State has been great. Keeping pace with its progress, the Department of Labor and Printing shows a record of quality and economy in performance not equaled by any other Commonwealth, and approached by but few.

The handling of the public printing has been brought down to the point where figures as to specifications and cost may be given before or after performance, which information serves well where economy enters as largely into any proposition as it does into the public printing. Changes in practice are made as often as it is found that improvement can be made and the policy of the office at the present time makes impossible any of the abuses obtained under the arrangement in force prior to the placing of the public printing under the Department's charge.

Before a single item of printing expense is paid for by the State the account of the printer is examined, accompanied by an inspection of the work itself, by a man who knows the printing business. Every pound of paper purchased is bought by the State to fit the particular need, and is subject to the decision of the expert of the Department—himself, according to the provisions of the act, a "practical printer." The record of purchases of paper shows a great saving along this line, also.

All printing, engraving, die-stamping, and binding done for the State is let to contract for two-year periods under competitive bidding, and the work is carefully supervised in process by the Commissioner of Labor and Printing, aided by the Assistant Commissioner (required by law to be a practical printer). All requisitions for State printing are made upon the Department of Labor and Printing; the Department places orders for same with contracting printers, issuing requisite quantity of paper stock for each order; supervises the work in process, examines the finished work, audits and approves bills for same.

The cost of the State's printing, including the paper stock used, approximates $250,000 annually. The Department purchases all paper for State printing, maintaining a large paper storage warehouse in Raleigh.

MINE INSPECTION

North Carolina has a comprehensive mining law, and by this statute the Commissioner of Labor and Printing is constituted mine inspector with large powers.

PUBLIC EMPLOYMENT SERVICE

Since October 1, 1919, the United States Employment Service, operating in North Carolina, has been conducted under the direction and supervision of the Commissioner of Labor and Printing, who provided office quarters in his department and is serving as Federal Director of the State without additional compensation. Funds for clerical assistance are provided by the Federal and State Governments. During the fiscal year ending June 30, 1926, 33,417 applicants for work were placed in situations satisfactory to them.

Realizing the urgent necessity for a well-organized system of employment for North Carolina, under State and Federal supervision, the Department of Labor and Printing brought the matter to the attention of the General Assembly of 1924 and succeeded in securing an appropriation adequate for the development of such an agency by the Department. The machinery provided in the statute creating the free employment bureaus enables the Department to assist in bringing the jobless man and the manless job together in a systematic way, a service which reaches all classes of employers and all classes of employees. Local employment offices were established in our large industrial centers and much assistance rendered in relieving acute unemployment conditions all too prevalent since the conclusion of the World War. During the first year the employment service was in operation under State and Federal cooperation, more than 15,000 men and women found positions through the public employment bureau of the State Department of Labor and Printing.

DEPARTMENT OF INSURANCE

Ch. 99, C. S.; Ch. 106, C. S.; Ch. 25, P. L. 1921; Ch. 119, P. L. 1924, extra session; Ch. 101, P. L. 1925

STACEY W. WADE, *Commissioner*, Raleigh

Title—Commissioner

Appointment—Elected.

Term—Four Years.

Salary—$4,500.

Function

To direct the administration and enforcement of the insurance laws of this State; to supervise the admission and regulation of all insurance companies, associations and orders doing or proposing to do business in this State (600 life, health, account, casualty, fire, marine, credit, burglary, plate glass, liability, steam boiler, automobile, etc.); to investigate complaints and prosecute violations; to supervise building and loan associations (246), lightning-rod companies, Morris Plan companies, rate-making bureaus and associations and jewelry auctioneers; to enforce the State Building Code and Inspection laws; to act as fire marshal *ex officio* and to investigate fires, etc; to administer premium collections (50 cents on $100) for Firemen's Relief Fund; to receive and file fire insurance rates and pass on complaints of discrimination.

To collect taxes from all classes of insurance companies, whether foreign or local, doing business in this State on the basis of 2 1-2 per cent upon the amount of their gross premium receipts in this State, provided that should one-fourth of the entire assets of the Company be invested and maintained in bonds of this State, or of any county, city or town of this State, or of any property situated in this State or taxable therein, or loans to North Carolina policyholders against the reserve on their policies, then the tax shall be two and one-fourth per centum upon the gross premium receipts aforesaid, and if the amount so invested shall be three-fourths of its total assets, the tax shall be two per centum of its gross premium receipts; provided, that if such company is chartered in this State, maintains its main office herein and if the amount so invested shall be equal to its total reserve on business derived from this state then, as to those companies usually known as life insurance companies, health and accident insurance companies, title insurance companies, and fraternal orders or associations, the tax shall be three-fourths of one per centum upon the gross premium receipts in this State, and as to all other companies one and one-half per centum upon their gross premiums in this State. Companies other than North Carolina companies paying the tax levied in this section shall not be liable for franchise tax on their capital stock and no county, city or town shall be allowed to impose any additional tax, license, or fee, other than ad valorem taxes, upon any insurance company, association, or order paying the tax levied in this section.

To collect fees for licenses issued to all classes of insurance companies and annual fees for licenses issued to each general agent, agent and broker in accordance with the schedule fixed by law.

To collect other fees pertaining to insurance companies as prescribed by law.

Sec. 6079, Ch. 99, C. S. The Insurance Commissioner "shall, in his annual report, make a statement of the fires investigated, the value of property destroyed, the amount of insurance, if any, the origin of the fire, when ascertained, and the location of the property damaged or destroyed, whether in town, city, or country. He shall also file annually an itemized statement, under oath, of all money received by him and disbursed under this chapter."

REPORTS. To submit annually to the Governor, and biennially to the General Assembly, through the Governor, a report of his official acts, the condition of all insurance and other companies or associations under his jurisdiction, with a condensed statement of their reports to him; together with a statement of the licenses, taxes and fees received by him and paid by him to the Treasurer.

To report to the General Assembly at each Session, suggested changes in the laws.

Historical Note

Created by act of General Assembly in 1899.

FIREMEN'S RELIEF FUND

The State of North Carolina pays $2,500 a year to the North Carolina State Volunteer Firemen's Association and to the North Carolina State Firemen's Association, which fund is known as the Firemen's Relief Fund.

The purpose of the fund is for the relief of firemen, members of such associations who may be injured or made sick by disease contracted in the actual discharge of duty as firemen, and for the relief of widows, children or dependent mothers of such firemen who may be killed or die from disease contracted in the discharge of their duty. Such duty must be performed in the service of the fire department from the time of the fire alarm until the members are dismissed by the company officers at roll call, or in service connected with the fire department which is directed to be performed by the officers in charge.

Any fireman of good, moral character in North Carolina, and belonging to an organized fire company, who will comply with the requirements of the constitution and by-laws of the North Carolina State Firemen's Association may become a member of this Association, and be eligible to relief from the fund. This fund was established by Act of the General Assembly in 1891.

GENERAL PROGRESS

During the last four years the insurance companies and building and loan associations operating in North Carolina under the supervision of the Insurance Commissioner have enjoyed a greater growth than ever before in a similar period. There has been a corresponding increase of activity in the other phases of departmental work, which include, lightning rod sales and installation, auctioneers, and the erection and inspection of buildings. Coincident with the growth and increased activity in these different divisions there has been a similar increase in the revenues to the State paid by the Insurance Department, while the work of supervision has also been greatly complicated. From the organization of the department in 1899 to April 1, 1926, there has been paid into the Treasury $11,737,416.55 of which $6,085,472.25 was paid in during the six year period ending April 1, 1926.

BUILDING AND LOAN ASSOCIATIONS

Probably the most outstanding growth has occurred among the building and loan associations of the State. When the building and loan associations were turned over to the Insurance Department in 1904 they had only $80,000 in assets. In December, 1920, 165 associations reported assets totaling $29,000,000. At the close of 1925, 246 associations reported assets of $81,188,000, their receipts increasing during the same period from $16,000,000 to $59,000,000 a year. The force of these institutions in the upbuilding of our cities, both in taxable property and citizenship, cannot be estimated. Their supervision calls for trained experts, and while no fund has ever been appropriated for that purpose by the State, they have been supervised without expense to the State and with little loss to their members. It is gratifying to know that we are in advance of any other State in the provisions for safeguarding our people in this direction as well as in the help rendered the associations in their organization and conduct.

INSURANCE SUPERVISION

This department was created originally for the enforcement of the insurance laws. It is probable that this is still the most important phase of its work; for while insurance was looked upon only a few years ago by many as a gamble, and regarded by the general public with suspicion, today it exceeds every other financial institution of the country in importance. So great is its effect upon commerce and industry that our entire credit system would collapse over night if the protection of insurance were instantly removed.

Since the formation of the department in 1899 it has been the duty of the commissioner to investigate the financial responsibility of each company seeking admission to the State, of which there are now more than six hundred; to scrutinize each of the many thousand forms of contracts issued by them to see that the value of protection was not weakened or destroyed by some qualifying clause; to see that the contracts are given a reasonable interpretation in the settlement of claims and not misrepresented to the public; to watch the progress of companies and see that sufficient reserves are carried to guarantee the protection promised; to protect the public and companies themselves against the impractical and unsafe policies of promoters operating under the guise of insurance who continually seek his approval or attempt to operate in open defiance of the Law.

North Carolina has reaped a great benefit in the growth of its insurance business, particularly in the organization and growth of its domestic companies, for while in 1899 there were only seven North Carolina companies having assets aggregating $746,791, there are today 80 such companies with home offices in this State and assets of more than $58,938,588, furnishing employment to thousands of our citizens and filling a real need in the social and economic life of the State.

FIRE MARSHAL LAW

One of the most far-reaching statutes we are called upon to enforce is the State Building Code, which is accepted as a model by practically every other State and upon which often depend the lives of thousands of our citizens and our children at school. No school building may be erected in the State the plans of which have not been submitted to the Department, examined and approved by an expert in fire protection. The result of this is that we have in North Carolina more modern fire-proof school buildings than any other State in the union, while the pupils are taught fire prevention from textbooks especially prepared for this purpose by the department.

Fire departments throughout the State have been given special attention, organized and drilled by experts, with the result that North Carolina has more motor-driven fire-fighting equipment than any other State of like size, and full paid firemen replace the loyal but inadequate volunteers with their hand reels and horse-drawn vehicles.

A systematic inspection of all cities and towns in the State as to defects in buildings and electrical equipment is carried out through experts in buildings and electrical construction under the direction of the Commissioner. Every fire reported to be of incendiary origin is thoroughly investigated by experienced detectives, and prosecutions conducted where the evidence warrants. This has led to the conviction and imprisonment of hundreds of arson criminals during the history of the department, notwithstanding arson is of all crimes probably the hardest to prove.

A campaign of education in the prevention of fires and accidents is carried on continually throughout the State by competent instructors provided by the department and paid from the taxes collected from insurance companies, which also contribute over $35,000 annually toward the maintenance of our various fire departments.

A business little understood and discredited by many, the sale and erection of lightning rods, has grown to be a considerable industry in the rural sections of the State, and since, as in most lines, there are imposters and inferior products, a special law provides that each brand sold shall be submitted to and approved by the department before being offered for sale, and that each erector shall secure a license from the department upon showing his fitness.

INSURANCE RATES

North Carolina occupies an enviable position compared with adjoining states with reference to fire insurance rates, which distinction has been earned by the campaign on fire prevention carried on by the State Insurance Department, and while the department possesses no power to make fire insurance rates every company operating in the State is required to file a copy of the rates charged by it on all property, and where such rates appear discriminatory they are investigated and equalized with the rates charged on other property of the same class. It is to the credit of the companies to say that this has called for very few adjustments, and that because of the work which we have done along the line of fire prevention North Carolina enjoys lower fire insurance rates than any other Southern State.

There are employed by the department at present twenty-five persons, six of whom are traveling practically all of the time. The time of the others is well taken up in performing the multiple duties imposed by law, and it must be apparent that the efficient performance of their work requires constant study and advancement in order to keep abreast of the corporations whose progressiveness and desire for business demand constant scrutiny and supervision.

STATE DEPARTMENT OF REVENUE
Chs. 34, 38, 40, P. L. 1921; Chs. 101, 158, 182, 258, P. L. 1925
R. A. DOUGHTON, *Commissioner*, Raleigh

Title—Commissioner of Revenue.
Appointment—Elected by the people.
Term—Four years.
Salary—$5,500 and traveling expenses.
Chairman—State Board of Assessment.

Function

To administer and enforce the taxes imposed by the Revenue Act, being given the power to divide the State into districts, to examine any records or persons bearing upon matters required to be included in the return, and to appoint and remove necessary deputies and clerks; to prepare and publish annually statistics with respect to the operation of the revenue act; to keep such records of collection of taxes as may be prescribed by the State Auditor; to make monthly reports to the State Treasurer or State Auditor, or both, of all collections of taxes; and to construe all sections of the revenue act, such decisions being prima facie correct.

Collections Fiscal Year Ending June 30, 1926

	Income Tax	Inheritance Tax	Schedule "B" Tax	Schedule "C" Taxes			Bus Tax	Insurance Tax	Totals
				R. R. Ex. Telephones	Franchise	Marriage License			
July	$ 39,883.69	$258,684.56	$ 205,214.77	$ 9,861.95	$ 579.40	$ 1,314.00	$ 15,689.21	$ 196,645.21	$ 727,875.79
Aug	32,859.06	35,849.73	183,608.55	31,896.82	401.00		14,881.00	355,970.74	655,466.91
Sept	159,617.31	37,314.06	76,134.22	20,911.55	98,218.28	88.00	5,542.61	10,673.92	457,899.95
Oct	80,985.71	78,213.94	96,396.05	320,495.76	389,039.35	166.00	17,527.78	4,682.15	1,047,506.77
Nov	55,462.65	32,160.31	39,215.83	32,745.95	371,267.84		15,220.63	3,951.90	549,034.13
Dec	108,916.26	61,799.77	39,225.15	15,106.34	34,764.49	27,301.00	10,006.11	2,005.17	315,126.29
Jan	33,800.93	29,658.92	54,977.28	6,116.71	12,353.13	4,498.00	17,376.91	61,289.29	219,481.20
Feb	77,734.65	26,059.59	39,797.47	33,074.19	6,780.96	966.00	13,759.30	461,718.96	662,830.52
Mar	4,858,318.55	71,416.57	22,341.76	174.11	6,952.98	565.00	6,640.96	139,903.09	5,106,612.82
April	301,135.79	43,412.06	31,812.76	7,911.06	6,627.33	282.00	14,215.53	32,374.14	440,830.67
May	285,546.88	18,291.45	23,263.45	32,423.30	3,150.65		11,670.00	5,250.65	391,596.28
June	61,316.55	118,457.89	389,756.76	11,367.78	3,436.78	26,367.00	4,597.05	4,278.39	622,518.04
Total	$6,085,577.00	$840,787.85	$1,217,684.05	$522,417.47	$943,572.19	$61,490.00	$147,127.12	$1,280,153.61	$11,199,809.37

To license motor vehicles and to appoint inspectors to enforce automobile license law; to collect automobile license tax and gasoline road tax. To collect all fees, taxes, licenses, etc., required of bus lines and jitneys. To collect all taxes, licenses and fees from all classes of insurance companies.

The taxes collected by the Department of Revenue for the fiscal year ending June 30, 1926, as shown on the preceding page.

STATE BOARD OF ASSESSMENT
Ch. 102, P. L. 1925

Composition (3)—Commissioner of Revenue, Chairman; Chairman of Corporation Commission, Attorney General, members *ex officio*.

This Board is constituted by law of three officers, viz., the Commissioner of Revenue, Attorney General and the Chairman of the Corporation Commission. The Commissioner of Revenue is Chairman of the Board and is empowered to exercise the functions of the Board when the same is not in session. This Board has general supervision of the taxing system of the State and is the final authority, where those who claim injustice has been done, to remedy such injustice in the way of valuations and otherwise. It has among other powers and duties the following:

1. To advise all assessing officers and institute proceedings to enforce penalties against officers, corporations, etc., for failing to discharge their duty.

2. To prepare a pamphlet of instructions to tax assessors and to advise them as to the law and their duties in respect to assessing property.

3. To investigate the taxing system in the various counties, and if it finds the same grossly irregular, unlawfully or unequally assessed, to correct such irregularity and to equalize the valuation of the property in any county either upon the complaint of the taxpayer or upon its own initiation.

4. To require Registers of Deeds, Auditors, Clerks, Mayors, etc., to make such annual reports as will enable the State Board to ascertain the assessed valuations of all property listed for taxation

STATE OF NORTH CAROLINA
State Board of Assessment, Raleigh

Tax Rates of Counties and Schools, and Valuations of Property in North Carolina, as Reported by the Auditors and Register of Deeds of the Several Counties to the State Board of Assessment. These Figures are Approximately Correct, and Cover the Year of 1925.

Name of County	County Tax Rate	School Tax Rate	Total County Rate	Value Real Property	Aggregate Value Real And Personal Property
Alamance	$ .75	$ .60	$ 1.35	$ 23,552,815	$ 34,389,251
Alexander	.56	.74	1.30	5,750,171	8,110,131
Alleghany	.55	.45	1.60	3,583,133	4,572,177
Anson	.55	.68	1.23	11,590,548	22,807,019
Ashe	1.14	.54	1.68	8,522,312	12,031,208
Avery	.79	.91	2.00	4,309,123	5,516,609
Beaufort	.90	.70	1.60	22,187,195	28,397,315
Bertie	.72	.73	1.45	10,998,769	15,995,755
Bladen	.55	.92	1.47	10,910,030	13,160,865
Brunswick	.57	.40	.97	6,713,787	8,816,463
Buncombe	.45	.35	.80	97,567,193	127,194,535
Burke	.28	.54	.82	20,055,307	26,307,535
Cabarrus	.55	.55	1.10	26,918,719	38,828,070
Caldwell	.48	.70	1.18	16,020,833	20,058,876
Camden	.59	1.10	1.69	2,794,417	4,330,254
Carteret	.85	.70	1.55	10,146,274	12,628,821
Caswell	.90	.83	1.73	6,441,900	8,814,679
Catawba	.53	.52	1.05	28,459,670	40,310,805
Chatham	.72	.50	1.22	9,306,095	18,973,281
Cherokee	1.10	.60	1.70	4,450,569	8,584,000
Chowan	.79	.53	1.32	7,048,445	10,325,387
Clay	1.85	1.06	2.91	2,092,508	2,442,032
Cleveland	.26	.54	.80	25,743,925	5,127,068
Columbus	.80	.84	1.64	13,123,587	24,816,581
Craven	.90	.60	1.50	21,957,137	29,062,131
Cumberland	.83	.73	1.56	24,542,705	54,129,215
Currituck	.48	1.16	1.64	4,099,473	5,259,278
Dare	.53	.82	1.35	1,777,554	2,416,266
Davidson	.72	.67	1.45	21,509,725	34,114,040
Davie	.65	.75	1.40	8,806,767	12,770,184
Duplin	.56	.75	1.31	19,247,523	21,908,134
Durham	.49½	.60½	1.10	16,784,786	53,265,589
Edgecombe	.22	.58½	.80½	21,295,076	31,151,425
Forsyth	.26	.29	.55	87,612,962	178,403,829
Franklin	.31	.80	1.15	10,148,044	14,110,941
Gaston	.45	.55	1.00	61,607,376	78,403,829
Gates	.43	1.05	1.78	4,881,352	7,189,068
Graham	.50	.90	1.40	3,995,935	4,251,459
Granville	.65	.93	1.58	14,609,050	21,108,909
Greene	1.08	.55	1.64	14,454,940	14,873,685
Guilford	.46	.39	.85	115,350,400	163,633,800
Halifax	.90	.65	1.55	24,169,858	36,728,300
Harnett	.42	.75	1.17	17,558,487	31,584,541
Haywood	.65	.70	1.35	17,599,534	20,327,342
Henderson	.70	.65	1.35	14,142,294	18,571,978
Hertford	.86	.84	1.70	7,503,048	11,157,408
Hoke	.49	.53	1.02	8,409,348	10,548,502
Hyde	.54	1.00	1.54	4,651,764	4,888,761
Iredell	.60	.60	1.20	28,308,500	41,685,408
Jackson	.75	.73	1.48	6,725,060	11,064,503
Johnston	.64	.65	1.29	28,622,296	43,956,941

130   STATE DEPARTMENTS, BOARDS, AND COMMISSIONS

Name of County	County Tax Rate	School Tax Rate	Total County Rate	Value Real Property	Aggregate Value Real And Personal Property
Jones	$ .40	$ .75	$ 1.15	$ 5,440,901	$ 7,436,535
Lee	.60	.55	1.15	8,617,078	13,194,226
Lenoir	.99	.61	1.60	23,400,570	28,739,480
Lincoln	.80	.70	1.50	10,704,455	15,439,800
Macon	.84	.64	1.48	4,933,674	6,420,178
Madison	1.03	.72	1.75	5,258,935	10,491,526
Martin	.55	.95	1.50	10,573,308	16,434,716
McDowell	.68	.60	1.28	9,749,681	20,796,076
Mecklenburg	.56	.40	.96	109,796,785	160,709,186
Mitchell	.65	.70	1.35	4,060,234	9,549,733
Montgomery	.98	.50	1.48	7,446,884	15,134,605
Moore	.55	.63	1.18	17,577,487	24,904,718
Nash	.55	.80	1.35	23,241,885	32,965,962
New Hanover	.54½	.75½	1.30	42,729,134	57,892,766
Northampton	.71+	.85	1.56+	8,611,025	14,922,932
Onslow	.70	.78	1.48	7,439,525	11,177,396
Orange	.56	.78	1.34	11,277,662	17,895,812
Pamlico	1.11	1.21	2.32	4,438,793	5,660,891
Pasquotank	.59	.55	1.14	13,008,174	18,619,720
Pender	.65	.75	1.40	6,403,326	10,759,401
Perquimans	1.12½	.57½	1.70	5,788,482	7,991,307
Person	.65	.60	1.25	10,571,511	15,191,322
Pitt	.58	.42	1.00	38,494,601	50,222,430
Polk	.66	.90	1.56	5,077,727	6,958,065
Randolph	.55	.45	1.00	13,298,433	20,819,541
Richmond	.82	.53	1.35	21,662,442	32,026,577
Robeson					41,690,315
Rockingham	.84+	.74+	1.59	27,503,974	42,895,754
Rowan	.47	.60	1.07	39,421,238	56,184,746
Rutherford	.49	.60	1.09	21,708,487	32,868,021
Sampson	.62	.70	1.32	16,339,759	22,763,701
Scotland	.84½	.56½	1.41	10,863,825	16,937,215
Stanly	.66	.54	1.20	20,590,855	30,342,631
Stokes	.86	.81	1.67	8,832,522	12,739,723
Surry	.54	.53	1.07	17,779,050	28,407,519
Swain	.44	.55	.99	6,749,239	12,191,696
Transylvania	.78	.62	1.40	5,144,273	7,811,277
Tyrrell	.72	.70	1.42	3,482,280	3,942,472
Union	.90	.85	1.75	17,783,147	25,291,199
Vance	.43	1.02	1.45	12,892,786	21,386,272
Wake	.33	.50	.83	64,215,955	92,595,934
Warren	.25	.60	.85	9,569,043	14,247,497
Washington	.76	.70	1.43	5,870,391	8,712,063
Watauga	.98	.82	1.80	6,724,168	8,396,928
Wayne	.43	.60	1.03	35,733,033	48,158,959
Wilkes	.94	.66	1.60	9,823,402	15,382,600
Wilson	.57	.93	1.50	32,106,007	46,056,195
Yadkin	.67	.63	1.30	7,070,652	9,483,389
Yancey	.88	.55	1.43	5,861,662	7,995,727
Total				$ 1,822,315,959	$ 2,750,980,067

throughout the State to the end that it may have complete statistical information as to the practical operation of the taxing laws.

5. To make investigation of the revenue laws and systems of other states and to report to the Legislature at each regular session thereof the whole amount of taxes collected in the State for all State and county purposes, being classified.

6. To prepare for legislative committees prior to the meeting of each General Assembly such revision of the Revenue and Machinery Acts of the State as experience and investigation indicate should be enacted into law.

7. To value the capital stock of all corporations under the rules and regulations mentioned in the Machinery Act of the State and make a report to the Governor. In fact, the State Board of Assessment is head of the taxing system of the State and is the court of last resort in case of complaints and appeals. Its duties are very extensive and its work from a practical standpoint continues almost throughout the year. The officers who constitute this Board receive no salary as members of such Board.

STATE HIGHWAY COMMISSION

Ch. 2, P. L. 1923; Chs. 277 and 312, P. L. 1925

FRANK PAGE, *State Highway Commissioner*, Raleigh

Composition (10)—Chairman, State Highway Commissioner; nine commissioners.

Appointment—By Governor, with consent of Senate.

Term—Chairman, six years; other members, six years, overlapping.

Qualification—Chairman, practical business man from State at large; members, one from each highway district, three of minority party.

Compensation—Chairman, $15,000 and expenses; other members $10 per diem and expenses.

Function

To supervise and control the location, construction and maintenance of the State Highway system; to meet the requirements of

Federal aid acts; and to administer and enforce other provisions of the State Highway Act.

To keep records of proceedings and adopt rules governing transactions and enforcement of law; to appoint a State highway engineer (4 year term) and other employees, fix their salaries and prescribe their duties; to meet quarterly, or oftener on call of Commissioner or of five members, the Highway Commissioner to devote entire time to the work of the Commission and to be vested with power of Commission when same is not in session.

To designate and map the roads comprising the State Highway System not to exceed 6,500 miles and to publish same; to alter or relocate same subsequent to public hearing or on its own volition; to let all contracts for construction.

To take over and control existing county or township roads constituting part of system; to provide for necessary road materials; to enforce by mandamus its legal rights.

To regulate use of State highways and to police traffic thereon, to establish a traffic census to secure information concerning use, cost, value, importance and necessity of roads forming a part of the State Highway System as a basis for construction of same.

To assume full and exclusive responsibility for the maintenance of all roads other than streets in towns and cites forming part of system, except roads maintained by counties under contract with Commission.

To exercise full power to comply with Federal aid acts relating to construction, maintenance and improvement of rural post roads.

To regulate street openings and excavations on State-owned roads; to condemn land for rights of way and for purposes of obtaining road materials, such as lime, sand, gravel, timber, etc., and to employ counsel for advice and legal action; to select and provide road materials; to adopt standard design and uniformly mark all roads comprised in the system.

To keep full account of each road project showing expenditures and liabilities and records of contracts and force account work.

To apportion construction and maintenance funds obtained from receipts of bond issues ($85,000,000), automobile license tax, gasoline, road tax and other sources, to each district as prescribed by law.

REPORTS. To make full detailed report to each General Assembly, showing construction and maintenance work and cost of same, receipts of license fees and disbursements.

NOTE. Specific duties of State Highway Commissioner and State Highway Engineer as such are not set forth in the law. Reference is invariably to the Highway Commission.

ORGANIZATION

FRANK PAGE, *Chairman*	Raleigh
F. C. KUGLER, *First District*	Washington
C. R. WHEATLY, *Second District*	Beaufort
W. A. McGIRT, *Third District*	Wilmington
JOHN SPRUNT HILL, *Fourth District*	Durham
J. ELWOOD COX, *Fifth District*	High Point
W. C. WILKINSON, *Sixth District*	Charlotte
ALEX S. HANES, *Seventh District*	Winston-Salem
A. M. KISTLER, *Eighth District*	Morganton
J. G. STIKELEATHER, *Ninth District*	Asheville
L. R. AMES, *Acting State-Highway Engineer*	Raleigh

ADMINISTRATIVE

The State Highway Commission, as provided in the Highway Act of 1921 and amendments of 1923 and 1925 is composed of the Chairman, Hon. Frank Page, who is a full-time official, and the nine District Commissioners from the construction districts throughout the State. As set forth in the Highway Law, the Commission has control of the expenditure of the $85,000,000 bond issue, Federal Aid funds, and revenue from the gasoline tax and auto license fees. It is responsible for the construction and maintenance of the 6,500 miles of roads making up the State Highway System and connecting the county-seats and principal towns.

Assistant to Chairman

H. K. Witherspoon, Assistant to Chairman, handles correspondence and detailed work of the Chairman which does not require his personal attention.

Legal Department

Charles Ross, of Lillington, is Attorney for the Highway Commission, which office is provided for in Section 21 of the State Highway Act. The Attorney handles all matters of a legal nature.

Purchasing Department

W. Z. Betts is in charge of the purchasing department and handles the purchasing of all equipment and supplies for the Commission. The majority of the purchasing is done on a competitive basis, thus effecting the saving of a large sum annually. This department also handles the cement purchases of the Commission.

Accounting Department

Homer Peele, an experienced auditor, is in charge of this department and handles all receipts and disbursements of funds coming under the supervision of the Highway Commission.

Equipment Department

C. D. Farmer, Superintendent of Motor Equipment, is in charge of the equipment department, which takes care of the upkeep of the automotive equipment required in the work of the Commission.

The depot, which covers approximately twelve acres, is located about four miles west of Raleigh.

Claim Department

C. H. Rogers, Claim Engineer, has charge of the investigation and adjustment of all claims for damage to property filed with the Commission.

ENGINEERING

State Highway Engineer

L. R. Ames, Acting State Highway Engineer, has direct charge of all engineering work of the Commission, and has under his supervision the departments outlined below.

Road Department

George F. Syme, Senior Highway Engineer, has charge of the drafting and preparation of plans and estimates for all road work carried on by the Commission. This department handles the preparation of proposals, contracts, and checks up final estimates before final payment is made. All blueprint work of the Commission is taken care of in this department.

Bridge Department

W. L. Craven, Senior Bridge Engineer, has charge of the work of designing and preparing plans for all bridges and culverts in the State Highway System. Several large structures have been designed during the past two years.

Locating Department

R. G. Browning, Principal Locating Engineer, has charge of all location surveys on the State Highway System. Thousands of dollars have been saved the State by careful study and revision of proposed locations.

Construction Department

W. E. Hawkins, State Construction Engineer, has under his direction the progress and final inspections of construction work and testing of materials.

Maintenance Department

A. P. Eskridge, State Maintenance Engineer, has charge of one of the most important branches of the Commission. Maintenance of over 6,000 miles of highways is carried on under the direction of this department by a well-organized force throughout the State.

District Engineers

The State is divided into nine construction districts, each in charge of a District Engineer. Each district is in effect a separate unit, but is at the same time under the direction of the State Highway Engineer.

Historical Note

The State Highway Commission of North Carolina was first appointed by Governor Locke Craig in accordance with the provisions of Chapter 113 of the Public Laws of 1915, in anticipation of the passage of the Federal Road Act in 1916; but since the appropriation provided was only $10,000 with which to carry out the provisions of the Act, the Commission could only act in an advisory capacity to the various county and township boards throughout the State. The General Assembly of 1917 made no change either in the Commission or in the law creating it except to set aside the funds collected from automobile license fees, as provided in Chapter 107 of the Public Laws of 1913, as a maintenance fund to provide for the upkeep of the State System of roads.

At this time little could be done towards building new roads, but a great deal was accomplished by educating the people of the State to the need for good roads and the many benefits to be derived therefrom.

Real highway construction may be said to have begun with the passage of the 1919 Highway Law (Chapter 189, Public Laws, 1919) in which fees for automobile licenses were increased sufficiently to provide funds to meet more adequately Federal aid funds allotted by the Government.

By the terms of this law one-fourth of the cost of constructing a road on the State System was furnished by the county in which the road was located, one-fourth from the State Highway Fund, and one-half from Federal aid funds. A new Commission was appointed, consisting of Frank Page of Aberdeen, Chairman; and W. S. Fallis, State Highway Engineer under the former commission, remained in this capacity. During the two years that this Commission functioned under the law of 1919 approximately 200 miles of improved highways were completed at a cost of $2,464,000; and 650 miles, estimated to cost $9,730,000, were placed under construction. Except for paying a portion of the cost of the work and supervising it nothing was done by the Commission in the way of maintenance, as this phase of the work was left in the hands of county officials.

Realizing the need for a more extensive road-building program and seeing the necessity for a more adequate system of maintenance, certain foresighted citizens of the State began a campaign in 1920, which resulted in the passage by the General Assembly of 1921 of the Doughton-Connor-Bowie Act. The purposes of the law are well expressed in section 2, which reads as follows: "The general purposes of this act are for the State to lay out, take over, established and construct and assume control of approximately 5,500 miles of hardsurfaced and other dependable highways running to all county seats, and to all principal towns, State parks and principal State institutions, and linking up with State highways of adjoining States and with national highways into national forest reserves by the most practicable routes, with special view to development of agriculture, commercial and natural resources of the State, and for the further purpose of permitting the State to assume control of the State highways, repair, construct and reconstruct and maintain said highways at the expense of the entire State, and to relieve the counties and cities and towns of the State of this burden." Briefly, the act provides for a State Highway Commission consisting of a chairman from the State at large, and for one commissioner from each of the nine construction districts into which the State is divided; all engineering work is in charge of a State Highway engineer chosen by the Commission; funds are provided by the issuance of serial bonds aggregating $85,000,000; from automobile license fees, and from a tax of four cents per gallon on motor vehicle fuel.

For maps and other information apply to H. K. Witherspoon, assistant to chairman, State Highway Commission, Raleigh.

STATE BOARD OF HEALTH

CHARLES O'H. LAUGHINGHOUSE, *Secretary and State Health Officer*, Raleigh

Composition—Nine members.

Personnel—J. Howell Way, M.D., F.A.C.P., *President*, Waynesville; Thomas E. Anderson, M.D., Statesville; Cyrus Thompson, M.D., Jacksonville; E. J. Tucker, D.D.S., Roxboro; A. J. Crowell, M.D., F.A.C.S., Charlotte; D. A. Stanton, M.D., F.A.C.S., High Point; James P. Stowe, Ph.G., Charlotte; W. S. Rankin, M.D., Sc.D., Charlotte; John B. Wright, M.D., F.A.C.S., Raleigh.

Appointment—Five appointed by Governor; four elected by Medical Society of the State of North Carolina.

Term—Six years.

Compensation—Members of Board, $4 per diem and expenses; Secretary, $5,000 annually.

Function

To enforce the public health laws of the State; to formulate policies and secure remedial or necessary legislation; to educate the public in matters of health.

To take cognizance of the health interests of the people; to make sanitary investigations; to investigate causes of diseases dangerous to the public health, especially epidemics; also the sources of mortality, and the effect of location, employment, and environment upon the public health; to gather and distribute such information; to act as the medical advisers of the State and advise the government in regard to the location, sanitary construction, and management of all State Institutions and to inspect same not less than once a year; to maintain a State Laboratory of Hygiene; to make examinations for the presence and diagnosis of communicable diseases; to prepare and distribute antitoxins, vaccines, and sera; to make monthly examinations of potable waters; to investigate watersheds, systems of water supply, sewerage, and to approve all plans for same; to supervise registration of births and deaths, the Secretary being State Registrar; to control privy construction and maintenance; to conduct prenatal work and child hygiene; to publish bulletins, rules, regulations.

To elect a President from its membership and an executive committee consisting of the President and two other members; to meet annually, and to hold a conjoint meeting with the Medical Society of the State of North Carolina; to hold special sessions and meetings of the executive committee upon call of the President through the Secretary.

The Board elects from the registered physicians of the State a Secretary-Treasurer for a term of six years. He is the executive officer of the Board, and is designated by law as State Health Officer.

Bureaus for the discharge of special duties are maintained as follows: Executive, Vital Statistics and Epidemiology, State Laboratory of Hygiene, Sanitary Engineering and Inspection, Maternity and Infancy, County Health Work.

Historical Note

The North Carolina State Board of Health is the twelfth oldest institution of its kind in the United States. It was created in 1877 by an Act of the General Assembly constituting the entire Medical Society of the State as a board of health. Practically every General Assembly since that time has increased in some vital particular the work and support of the Board. Credit for initiating the work goes by universal assent to Dr. Thomas Fanning Wood of Wilmington, who became the first secretary in 1879 when the General Assembly reconstituted the Board as partially appointed by the Governor, partially elected by the Medical Society. Though the work of the Board has been expanded and modified, no radical changes have since been made in its status.

The first State appropriation in 1877 was $100 annually. The State appropriation for the past fiscal year was $100,000, and to this the Board was able to add by interesting other agencies about $650,000. North Carolina now ranks sixth among the States in the amount of money expended in the protection and promotion of the health of its people. This State has the enviable distinction of having established the first county health department in the United States for service to its rural population, and now has 37 such departments with efficient personnel and adequate budgets for real service. It stands second in the number of such agencies, Ohio having the honor of first place.

The Board at present is composed of seven physicians, one dentist, one pharmacist. The various functions of the Board are administered under the direction and supervision of the State Health Officer by trained men at the heads of the several divisions of specialized work.

DEPARTMENT OF CONSERVATION AND DEVELOPMENT
Ch. 85, C. S.; Ch. 101, C.S.; ch. 122, P. L. 1925
WADE H. PHILLIPS, *Director*, Raleigh.

Composition—Board of Conservation and Development (7 members); Director.

Personnel—Board: Governor A. W. McLean, *chairman;* Dr. H. B. Shaw, State College; Dr. D. D. Carroll, University of North Carolina; H. L. McClaren, Charlotte; Jas. G. K. McClure, Asheville; John H. Small, Washington, D. C.; S. Wade Marr, Raleigh.

Division Chiefs: J. S. Holmes, *State Forester*, Raleigh; Thorndike Saville, *Hydraulic Engineer*, Chapel Hill; H. J. Bryson, *State Geologist*, Raleigh.

Appointment—By Governor with consent of Senate; Director appointed by Governor to serve at his pleasure.

Term—Four years overlapping.

Qualification—Citizens of the State, one from the staff of the University and one from the staff of State College.

Compensation—Four dollars per diem not exceeding eight days annually and necessary traveling expenses; salary of Director fixed by the Governor not to exceed salary heretofore paid State Geologist.

Objects of the Department

1. To take over the powers and duties exercised by the State Geological and Economic Survey, the State Geological Board and the State Geologist, as provided for in chapter one hundred and one of the Consolidated Statutes of one thousand nine hundred and nineteen and other statutes relating thereto.

2. By investigation, recommendation and publication, to aid

   (a) In the promotion of the conservation and development of the natural resources of the State;
   (b) In promoting a more profitable use of lands, forests and waters;
   (c) In promoting the development of commerce and industry;
   (d) In coördinating existing scientific investigations and other related agencies in formulating and promoting sound policies of conservation and development; and

DEPARTMENT OF CONSERVATION AND DEVELOPMENT   111

(e) To collect and classify the facts derived from such investigations and from other agencies of the State as a source of information easily accessible to the citizens of the State and to the public generally, setting forth the natural, economic, industrial and commercial advantages of the State.

The board shall have control of the work of the department and may make such rules and regulations as it may deem advisable to govern the work of the department and the duties of its employees.

It shall make investigations of the natural, industrial and commercial resources of the State, and take such measures as it may deem best suited to promote the conservation and development of such resources.

It shall make investigations of the existing conditions of trade, commerce and industry in the State, with the causes which may hinder or encourage their growth and may devise and recommend such plans as may be considered best suited to promote the development of these interests.

The board may take such other measures as it may deem advisable to obtain and make public a more complete knowledge of the State and its resources and it is authorized to coöperate with other departments and agencies of the State in obtaining and making public such information.

It shall be the duty of the board to arrange and classify the facts derived from the investigations made, so as to provide a general source of information in regard to the State, its advantages and resources.

The board may also cause to be prepared for publication, from time to time, reports and statements, with illustrations, maps and other descriptions, which may adequately set forth the natural and material resources of the State and its industrial and commercial developments, with a view to furnishing information to educate the people with reference to the material advantages of the State, to encourage and foster existing industries, and to present inducements for investment in new enterprises. Such reports and information shall be published and distributed as the board may direct, at the expense of the State as other public documents.

DIRECTOR. With approval of the board, to make or cause to be made examinations and surveys of the economic and natural resources of the State and investigations of its industrial and commercial enterprizes and advantages and to perform such other duties as may be required to carry out the objects of the Department. He shall appoint with approval of the board necessary experts and assistants including State Geologist and State Forester, and shall assign to each appropriate duties.

COOPERATION WITH STATE DEPARTMENTS, COUNTIES AND TOWNS AND WITH FEDERAL GOVERNMENT. The Board is authorized to coöperate with the North Carolina Corporation Commission in investigating the water-powers in the State and to furnish the Corporation Commission such information as is possible regarding the location of the water-power sites, developed water-powers, and such other information as may be desired in regard to water-power in the State; the board shall also coöperate as far as possible with the Department of Labor and Printing, the State Department of Agriculture, the Fisheries Commission Board and other departments and institutions of the State in collecting information in regard to the resources of the State and in preparing the same for publication in such a manner as may best advance the welfare and improvement of the State.

The board is authorized to coöperate with the counties of the State in any surveys to ascertain the natural resources of the county; and with the governing bodies of cities and towns, with boards of trade and other like civic organizations, in examining and locating water supplies and in advising and recommending plans for other municipal improvements and enterprises. Such coöperation is to be conducted upon such terms as the board may direct.

The board is authorized to arrange for and accept such aid and coöperation from the several United States Government bureaus and other sources as may assist in completing topographic surveys and in carrying out the other objects of the department, and to continue any arrangement which may have been heretofore made with such Federal agencies by the Geological and Economic Survey and by the Geological Board.

The board is further authorized and directed to coöperate with the Federal power commission in carrying out the rules and regulations promulgated by that commission; and to act in behalf of the State in carrying out any regulations that may be passed relating to water-powers in this State other than those related to making and regulating rates.

CONTROL OF MOUNT MITCHELL PARK AND OTHER STATE PARKS. The board shall have the control and management of Mount Mitchell Park and any other parks which have been or may be acquired by the State as State parks.

FORESTRY DIVISION. The natural resources of North Carolina are so widespread and important that every possible effort must be made to conserve them, namely to have them used wisely so that they will benefit equally the present and future generations.

The forests of the State besides providing timber and other products for domestic and industrial use, protect and regulate our streams, help prevent the erosion of our soils, furnish feeding and breeding places for our game and other wild life and beautify the great out-of-doors for the recreation and inspiration of our people.

Of the State's total area of 31,000,000 acres, two-thirds or about 21,000,000 acres are in timber of some kind or are best adapted to the growth of timber. From the North Carolina forests there is created by industries dependent upon them an estimated annual wealth of $168,000,000. On the 21,000,000 acres it is estimated that there is now a stand of 29 billion board feet, as against a stand of 40 billion board feet according to an estimate made sixteen years ago. In 1915, North Carolina was the fourth State in the production of lumber, while in 1923 it was the eleventh. It is still first in the number of sawmills which are cutting its timber twice as fast as it is being produced.

The Forestry Division, popularly known as the State Forest Services, is now organized to carry on four principal lines of effort, (1) forest protection, (2) forest planting, (3) State parks and forests, and (4) forestry information.

The forest protective organization covers some thirty counties which coöperate by paying one-half the local costs up to an agreed upon maximum aggregating some $11,600. The State apportionment for this work is $16,990, and private contributions $2,410. This is met by the Federal Government with funds contributed under the Clarke-McNary law on a percentage basis which all counted makes a total available for this work of $68,000.

There are in addition to the administrative force some 2,500 district and deputy forest wardens throughout the coöperating counties selected for their knowledge, ability and good standing, and paid only on part time. This force fought some 1,062 forest fires during 1925 and kept the average burned area down to 171 acres per fire. Although a large damage was reported from these counties for that year the counties were saved a loss of many thousands of dollars through the efforts of these men. However, to protect the 21,000,000 acres of forest land in the State from the annual fire damage of $1,227,500, which is the average reported damage for the past ten year period, the State Forest Service will need much stronger financial support.

A small forest nursery is now established at Raleigh and seedlings of several species of pine are being distributed at cost to farmers throughout the State.

The protection and administration of Mount Mitchell State Park containing 1,224 acres and Fort Macon State Park of 400 acres as well as the developments of a management policy for the State Lakes and other recreational forest and water areas is placed in the State Forest Service.

Economic studies relating to the forest resources of the State are carried on and information distributed to inquirers both within and outside of North Carolina.

WATER RESOURCES DIVISION. Created in 1921, its function has been to promote the conservation and more profitable use of the State's water resources; first, by obtaining basic data through research, directed surveys, and stream gaging, to which is added the collection of such data from all available sources; and second, by presenting this data in a form easily used by engineers and the general public.

Acting in its capacity as an investigator and a seeker for basic information necessary for orderly and economical development of our resources, it has vigorously sought to obtain stream flow records for the use of municipalities in investigating water supplies, and power companies, their developments; has aided in the collection of rainfall records for the same purpose; and it has, through cooperative work with counties, caused surveys to be made of rivers to determine their power possibilities and the most feasible methods for their development. Also, it has caused the chemical analysis of waters from many streams in order to supply such information to industrial concerns seeking locations for manufacturing plants. Miscellaneous investigations, many of them, have been made on the request of the Governor in some instances; of State departments and institutions in others.

While being concerned primarily with the State's Water Resources as such, it is also concerned with those resources during their development and afterwards. Hence it has been authorized and directed to coöperate with the Federal Power Commission and to act in behalf of the State in carrying out any regulations that may be passed relating to water-powers in the State other than those relating to making and regulating rates. In this connection, a very close watch is kept on power developments; contact is maintained with the Federal Power Commission and the interests of the State are looked after.

In order to keep the State fully informed concerning the status of its power developments and of their output, an annual circular is published, called the "Power Situation in North Carolina." In keeping this Circular accurate and up-to-date, considerable statistical work is necessary. For that and other purposes an attempt is made to collect complete statistical data regarding power developments and production; a service which is regarded as worthy and valuable in that, among many other purposes, such figures serve as an industrial barometer.

To meet the future hydro-electric needs of our people there is indicated a State agency for supplying accurate and comprehensive facts upon which State authority may proceed impartially to supervise and regulate future developments, not only in the fixing of rates, but to the end of assuring that water-powers generally shall secure such a uniform treatment as will make the most out of every stream, considered in its character of a public asset to be utilized and managed in the common benefit; that developments are not made in a manner so incomplete as to fail in proper realization of their possibilities, and that they are not unduly delayed by private owners of stream rights. Unless the State takes steps to conserve and properly regulate its powers for itself, the time will come when the authority it neglects to exercise will be assumed by the Federal Government.

The Division's funds have in the past, for the most part, been devoted to stream gaging work in coöperation with the U. S. Geological Survey. Today, stream gaging has been fairly well established; its only need being more adequate funds to allow for sufficient operation and expansion. Other problems of major importance have now presented themselves. A comprehensive investigation of our coastal section with its many sounds, inlets and beaches is needed. The Water Works Association has called for an investigation of the ground-water supplies of the coastal plain section, with particular reference to deep wells. Some of the miscellaneous problems of importance to the State which the Division would be well justified in investigating are: silting in large reservoirs resulting in loss of capacity; evaporation therefrom resulting in loss of power; drainage of waste lands and functioning of drainage districts; inland waterways; rate of recovery of streams from pollution by domestic and industrial sewage; determination of hydrogen-ion concentration of ground and surface waters of the State; and most important of all, sources of water supply available for municipal use with regard to availability, adequacy of yield, and proper method of developing.

The service rendered by the Water Resources Division to the State has far more than justified its existence. Economical development of gigantic hydro-electric power systems has been made possible through the use of stream flow records. The manner in which the industrial development has followed hydro-electric development needs no telling here. Municipalities have been enabled to develop streams for water supplies with assurance of their adequacy. State institutions have been aided in solving their water supply problems. Requests for information concerning water resources of the State have been received and answered in great numbers. Often, however, requests for information have not been satisfied because of limited facilities and insufficient data. Having a great field of usefulness and service to the State, the Division functions, filling that field as best it can with its limited facilities, while waiting for a greater opportunity.

GEOLOGICAL DIVISION. The Department from time to time during its history has undertaken investigations of the geological formations of the State, occurrence of various minerals, their commercial value and methods of mining, and published a number of bulletins and economic papers concerning them, many of these in coöperation with Federal agencies. From an economic as well as scientific point of view there is a great amount of study still needed to be done, and which would, in all probability, yield good returns on the investment.

In 1920, the value of mineral products was the greatest up to that time in the history of the State and amounted to $8,150,753. In 1923, a new high record for mineral production value amounting to $11,042,517 was set. The 1924 mineral production had a value of $10,163,435. The slight decrease in the value of the 1924 mineral production as compared with that of 1923 was due to a falling off in the amount of crushed stone and gravel used for road work and also to a decrease in the price of kaolin and mica.

The marked increases in recent years have come largely from a greater utilization of stone and clay products including kaolins and shale. Possibilities in the commercial uses of clays and shale for fire proofing face brick and various types and qualities of tiles are highly attractive. The Department is constantly investigating and reporting upon mineral resources with the view of providing data for industrial development.

STATE BOARD OF CHARITIES AND PUBLIC WELFARE

Art. XI, Sec. 7, Constitution; Ch. 88, C. S.; Arts. 1, 2, 5, Ch. 103, C. S.; Ch. 128, P. L. 1921; Ch. 90, P. L. 1925

MRS. KATE BURR JOHNSON, *Commissioner of Public Welfare*, Raleigh

Composition—Seven members Elected by General Assembly on recommendation of Governor.

Term—Six years overlapping.

Qualification—One to be a woman.

Compensation—Expenses only

Function

To investigate and supervise the whole system of charitable and penal institutions of the State, and to recommend such changes and additional provisions as it may deem needful for their economical and efficient administration.

To study problems of non-employment, poverty, vagrancy, housing conditions, crime, public amusement, care and treatment of prisoners, divorce and wife desertion, the social evil and kindred subjects and their causes, treatment and prevention; to issue, publish and distribute bulletins on social conditions and proper treatment and remedies for social evils.

To study and promote the welfare of the dependent and delinquent child and to provide either directly or through a bureau of the Board for the placing and supervision of dependent, delinquent and defective children.

To inspect and report on private orphanages, institutions, maternity homes and persons or organizations receiving and placing children and to require such institutions to submit reports, and information as directed; to issue and revoke for cause, licenses to persons or agencies carrying on such work. (According to Ch. 90, P. L. 1925, the Board is not required to license child-caring institutions owned by a religious denomination or a fraternal order and having a plant valued at not less than $60,000.)

To inspect county jails, prisons, county homes and other institutions of a penal or charitable nature, and to require reports from sheriffs and other officers; to approve plans and specifications of new jails and almshouses.

To approve by certificate the election of County Superintendent of Public Welfare elected for two years by County Board of Education and Board of County Commissioners in joint session.

To appoint county boards of charities and public welfare.

To approve applications for establishment of private, town and county hospitals for the insane, feeble-minded, and inebriate and to issue licenses for same which shall at all times be subject to visitation.

To recommend to the Legislature social legislation and the creation of necessary institutions.

Historical Note

In 1917 the General Assembly repealed the law providing for the Board of Public Charities, made mandatory by the State Constitution of 1868, and created the State Board of Charities and Public Welfare with enlarged duties and powers. This session of the Legislature also provided for county superintendents and boards of public welfare, leaving such organization optional with the counties. The General Assembly of 1919 improved the county plan of organization, making the employment of a superintendent of public welfare mandatory in counties having a population of more than 32,000; and also created the State system of juvenile courts.

THE WORK OF THE BOARD

The work of the State Board of Charities and Public Welfare has to do with the unfortunate elements of the State's population—the insane, the feeble-minded, the poor, the crippled, the orphan, the criminal, the neglected, the dependent, and the delinquent. Its object is to secure for these handicapped people the protection and care that are their due in a Christian democracy; to seek out the causes of social maladjustments; and to plan as wisely as may be for their prevention.

This work is organized under six bureaus: the bureau of county organization, the children's bureau, the bureau of institutions, the bureau of mental health and hygiene, the bureau of education and publicity, and the bureau of work among the Negroes.

COUNTY ORGANIZATION

The duties of the bureau of county organization include: (1) coöperation with county boards of commissioners and education and public welfare; (2) promotion of appointment of efficient superintendents of public welfare; (3) appointment of county boards of public welfare; (4) standardization of county public welfare work, including juvenile court and probation work; (5) partial supervision of the enforcement of the compulsory school attendance law.

The county is the basis of the North Carolina plan of public welfare which heads up in the State Board. Fifty-nine counties in North Carolina are now (September, 1926) organized for this work

In only 29 of these is the employment of a superintendent of public welfare required by law. Of these fifty-nine counties, fifty-one have full-time officers and eight, part-time officers.

The County Superintendent of Public Welfare is the agent of the State Board in his county, and is chief school attendance officer, and chief probation officer. With the county juvenile court, he has oversight of all dependent, neglected and delinquent children under 16 years of age in the county. He enforces the child labor laws and supervises, under the county commissioners, the care of the poor and the administration of the poor funds. In addition, he has oversight of persons discharged from hospitals for the insane and from other State institutions and of all persons on probations or parole. He is expected to promote wholesome recreation in the county and to enforce such laws as regulate commercial amusement; to assist the State Board in finding employment for the unemployed; and to investigate the causes of distress.

Election of County Superintendents of Public Welfare must be approved by the State Board, which wishes to approve only persons qualified by training or experience or having personal aptitude for the work. In conjunction with the School of Public Welfare at the University of North Carolina, the Board conducts institutes of public welfare at Chapel Hill each summer, at which county superintendents may study subjects related to their work and discuss their problems.

MOTHERS' AID AND CASE WORK

The children's Bureau has two main divisions of work: Mothers' Aid and Case Work. The Mothers' Aid work is financed by a fund of $30,000 a year given by the General Assembly, to be matched dollar for dollar by the counties taking advantage of it, to help worthy mothers deprived of their husbands' support to rear their children in their own homes. Now (September, 1926) about 1,100 children are being benefited in this way. Since the beginning of the fund in 1923, over four hundred mothers have been helped. Seventy-four counties participate in the fund.

The large majority of the women receiving this help are widows, a few are deserted, a few have husbands in prison or in hospitals for the insane; the husbands of a few are physically incapacitated. These women are encouraged to secure work in their homes to augment their incomes so that their names may eventually be removed from the Mothers' Aid list and the money given to more needy cases. They are encouraged to send their children to school, to have them examined by the health authorities, and in every way to rear them as respectable and useful citizens. These women are not considered as objects of charity, but as employees of the State whose job is to rear good citizens.

In the division of case work, 1,215 cases of unfortunate people have been handled during the last two years by the State Board of Charities and Public Welfare. These cases included mental problems, delinquent women and girls, transients and imposters, investigations for other states, epileptic and insane cases, children needing temporary or permanent care, cripples, and miscellaneous cases.

CLINICS FOR CRIPPLED CHILDREN

A census of crippled children to determine the number in the State was made in 1922, under the direction of the State Board of Charities and Public Welfare, working in connection with the Rehabilitation Department of the State Department of Education.

Since that time regional clinics have been held by the State Orthopedic Hospital and the Children's Bureau, in order to examine any crippled children to see if they could be helped by hospital treatment. At 22 clinics, 1,149 children have been examined, and many of them have been treated at the hospital.

INSTITUTIONAL SUPERVISION

The State Board of Charities and Public Welfare is required by law to supervise all charitable and penal institutions. This includes State and county penal institutions, county homes, institutions for defectives, orphanages, reformatories, maternity homes, and institutions for the delinquent.

Through a special arrangement between the State Board of Charities and Public Welfare and the State Board of Health, a special inspector has spent all of his time since July 1, 1925, in inspecting penal institutions.

Monthly reports are asked by the Bureau from county jails and county prison camps in order to collect statistics on crime. Plans for new jails and county homes are approved by the bureau.

A report of every inmate of child-caring institutions in the State has been filed in the office of this bureau. In this work, the Board's object has been to try to secure for the child committed to an institution the best possible care. A few child-caring institutions have been discontinued because of their failure to meet essential requirements.

MENTAL HYGIENE

The professor of abnormal psychology at the University of North Carolina, who is a part-time member of the staff of the State Board of Charities and Public Welfare, is available for mental examinations of problem cases that come to the attention of the Board. Studies are made by the Bureau of Mental Health and Hygiene of the relation of mental deficiency or aberration to crime, dependency and immorality.

Inspection of all State and private institutions for the insane, the defective or the mentally sick is made by this bureau.

Clinics for the purpose of examining sub-normal school children have been held in several towns, and in some cases, special classes for mentally retarded children have been begun.

Similar clinics have also been held from time to time at State and private institutions.

As far as possible, information on mental diseases and mental defects is given out in order to bring the attention of the public to the necessity of coping with the problems of insanity and feeble-mindedness, both by remedial and preventive methods.

EDUCATION AND PUBLICITY

Through the Bureau of Education and Publicity an effort is made to acquaint the people of North Carolina with what the State Board of Charities and Public Welfare is doing and what it hopes to do. *Public Welfare Progress*, a four-page monthly sheet, is issued to a mailing list of 6,000; special bulletins are printed from time to time; news and feature stories are sent to the State press; special articles are supplied for periodicals; and all requests for material and information on the work of the State Board of Charities and Public Welfare are filled.

In order to promote supplementary training for social workers, Institutes of Public Welfare have been held each summer since 1921 at Chapel Hill in conjunction with the School of Public Welfare of the University of North Carolina. At the Institute in 1926, the registration was 116.

Addresses by members of the Board, by the Commissioner of Public Welfare, and her staff, complete the plan by which the State learns of the work of the Board.

SPELMAN-ROCKEFELLER GRANT

In July, 1924, the State Board received a grant of $30,000 from the Laura Spelman-Rockefeller Memorial Fund, to be used in demonstration work for a period of three years. The School of Public Welfare of the University of North Carolina was given a similar grant to enable the two agencies to show the results that may be obtained in a county, when the superintendent of welfare is trained and fitted for his job and has well-equipped offices and a sufficient number of assistants to do the work.

In four counties—Wake, Orange, Chatham, and Cherokee—the work has been carried on with interesting results. The project has afforded field work under supervision for students at the School of Public Welfare.

NEGRO WORK

Part of the grant has been used to institute the Bureau of Work among Negroes, headed by a trained Negro social worker. The two objectives of the bureau are the intelligent study of Negro life, with its social problems, and the development of programs in the communities through the stimulating of organized coöperative effort on the part of the Negroes. Since the founding of the Bureau in January, 1925, eighteen Negro social workers have been placed in county and city departments of public welfare, and sixty-two Negro communities have been organized.

The plan used by the head of the bureau has attracted favorable notice throughout the country. It has been presented before several national conferences.

Through the Bureau, over $20,000 has been raised in the various counties to carry on welfare work among the Negroes. At the request of the Commissioner, Mr. B. N. Duke, of New York gave $15,000 to the State Orthopedic Hospital at Gastonia, which was for the purpose of erecting a Negro ward for treating Negro crippled children. This has been completed and is doing effective work.

INSTITUTIONS UNDER BOARD

The State institutions that come under the supervision of the State Board of Charities and Public Welfare are:

Hospital for the Insane at Raleigh.

State Prison at Raleigh.

Hospital for the Insane at Morganton.

Hospital for the Negro Insane at Goldsboro.

Stonewall Jackson Training School for Delinquent White Boys at Concord.

North Carolina Orthopedic Hospital for Crippled Children at Gastonia.

Caswell Training School for Mental Defectives at Kinston.

Samarcand Manor for Delinquent White Girls at Samarcand. (Moore County.)

Morrison Industrial School for Delinquent Negro Boys in Richmond County.

Eastern Carolina Industrial Training School for Delinquent White Boys at Rocky Mount.

The State of North Carolina also contributes to the support of the Masonic Orphanage and the Orphanage for Colored Children, both at Oxford. These institutions are also under the supervision of the State Board of Charities and Public Welfare.

This list does not include the county institutions and the private institutions that the State Board supervises.

MEMBERS OF THE BOARD

W. A. BLAIR, *Chairman* .... Winston-Salem
A. W. McALISTER, *Vice Chairman* .... Greensboro
REV. W. L. HUTCHINS .... Thomasville
MRS. WALTER F. WOODARD .... Wilson

Dr. C. H. Durham	Lumberton
Mrs. Joseph A. Brown	Chadbourn
Mrs. Herbert F. Seawell	Carthage

EXECUTIVE STAFF

Mrs. Kate Burr Johnson	Commissioner
Roy Eugene Brown	Institutional Supervision
Emeth Tuttle	Mothers' Aid and Case Work
Mary Frances Camp	County Organization
Harry W. Crane	Mental Health and Hygiene
Lucy F. Lay	Education and Publicity
Lieutenant Lawrence A. Oxley	Negro Work
Lily E. Mitchell	Case Work Supervisor
L. G. Whitley	Inspector of Penal Institutions

CHILD WELFARE COMMISSION*

Art. 1, Ch. 90, C. S. 1919

E. F. Carter, *Executive Secretary*, Raleigh

Members ex officio—Superintendent of Public Instruction, Secretary State Board of Health, and Commissioner of Public Welfare.

Duties of the Commission

To administer the laws relating to child labor, seats for women employees, and separate toilets for sexes and colors. Authorized to make and formulate such rules and regulations for the enforcement and carrying out of the provisions of these laws as in its judgment it shall deem necessary. Empowered to make exceptions and prescribe regulations governing the employment of children under fourteen years of age in the terms enumerated but not prohibited in this act; to make exceptions and prescribe regulations for children under sixteen years of age when (1) such child has symptoms of disease contributory to retardation or disability, or (2) when determined by physical examination that employment of such child

---

* Reprinted from the *North Carolina Manual*, 1925. The editor regrets that he has not been able to secure from the Commission the data necessary to bring the article up to date.

is injurious to its health, or (3) employed when surrounding conditions are injurious to its morals, or (4) employed when dangerous employment hazards are present. Authorized to prescribe legal forms for the employment of all children under sixteen years of age. To appoint, employ and specially designate agents to enforce the laws, to make inspections, issue certificates and carry out the provisions of the laws and rules of the Commission. It is unlawful to prevent any person authorized by the Commission from entering any of the places enumerated in this act for the purpose of making inspections.

ADMINISTRATIVE FUNCTIONS

The executive officer is in charge of the administrative and regulatory work of the Commission and is also secretary. He is appointed by the Commission to serve at its pleasure and receives a salary of $3,000. In addition to the primary object of enforcing the laws, it is his duty to inform the Commission of the conditions existing in the State by means of inspections, study, research and surveys, to initiate a program and recommend policies for the approval of the Commission in governing the administration of these acts and the inauguration of plans for the solution of problems that may arise in their enforcement, to select and organize the personnel of the department, to publish reports and bulletins, showing the Commission's activities, and to prepare the budget.

The organization is formed to accomplish the specific ends designed by the laws in providing a statistical bureau for the accumulation of facts relating to objects of work and the disseminating of same. There is a department of engineering for the study and solution of problems arising from the enforcement of the provisions of the toilet law for sexes and color and the act requiring suitable seats and resting places for female employees. The chief inspector is charged with inspectional work and follow up of violations, certificating agents to supervise and assist in the certification of children and to follow up physical defective cases.

Historical Sketch

The Child Welfare Commission was created by an act of the General Assembly of 1919, and became effective July 1 of the same year. The beginning of the administration found the Commission facing the necessity of formulating rules and policies for the legal prosecution of the work. The funds provided were totally inadequate to meet the responsibilities imposed by the act. A period of five years has demonstrated that the unique and original ideas embodied in this act for the supervision and control of children employed in the State are correct in theory, sound in principle and effective in methods and results. The Commission has passed the experimental stage and is now efficiently handling its own child labor problems with satisfaction and promptness.

RESULTS OF INSPECTIONAL AND CERTIFICATION WORK

Total inspections and special visits to plants in the State now number 14,850 of which 5,356 were accomplished during this period, by field agents. An average of approximately 88 per cent of the official reports received in the office have been accomplished by field agents or through their assistance.

A total of 22,500 school records have been secured since the Commission was authorized to take over the administration of child employment in North Carolina. This has given the Commission a basis upon which to formulate plans for vocational guidance and adjustment, in connection with the educational agencies of our State, for this group of children.

Approximately 22,500 medical examinations have been made of children entering employment during the same period. A volume of corrective health work has been accomplished for the child in employment.

The first eight months of the biennial period of 1923 were devoted to a careful inspection of all cotton, hosiery, furniture, and tobacco plants in the State. Also many department stores and miscellaneous manufacturing plants were visited and inspected.

The total number of children found working in this State in the 2,089 plants visited was 4,691. This includes 387 cotton mills, 170 hosiery mills, 125 furniture plants and 1,269 miscellaneous plants.

There is a total of 3,160 children between fourteen and sixteen years of age in cotton mills. Five hundred ninety-eight children between fourteen and sixteen in the hosiery mills, 116 children in the miscellaneous plants and 360 children in the tobacco plants in the State.

The last few months of the year 1923-24 were devoted to following up cases in child labor, sanitation and the fatigue law of the State. Of the 667 children fourteen and fifteen years old working without certificates, 350 children were certificated for employment, 272 were removed from work, and 45 were found to have been over sixteen years of age.

The requirement of this certificate was optional before the amendment to the child labor law by the special session of the Legislature, August, 1924.

There were 10,425 certificates issued from June 30, 1922, to June 30, 1923, and 7,739 certificates were issued from July 1, 1923, to June 30, 1924, a reduction of 15 per cent.

A survey was made of the twelve and thirteen-year-old boys who work during vacation and after school. Of 880 children under fourteen, the following were found to be actually working: 89 in cotton mills, 41 in hosiery mills, 27 in furniture plants, 1 in tobacco plant, 6 in workshops, 43 in other manufacturing establishments, 113 in mercantile, 46 in delivery service, 2 in amusement, 46 in miscellaneous, making a total of 404 actually working and 476 not working at the time of the survey. This survey shows that only about half of the children certified are working at one time. The same result was shown in the eight months survey in which a total of 4,691 children were found actually working with a total of 7,739 certificates issued in 1923-24, or a reduction of 33 per cent in the number actually employed.

Immediately after the amendment was passed by the special session, another survey was made of the boys twelve and thirteen years of age who are now prohibited in mills, canneries, workshops, factories and manufacturing establishments. It was shown conclusively that the manufacturing interests are keeping faith with our State child labor law and that every child had been removed from employment in these places.

The toilet law was found violated in some of its points in 335 cases. Approximately 50 per cent of these violations were due to not having the toilets lettered or marked for sex and color. The other 50 per cent were more directly related to conditions in construction, equipment, ventilation and cleanliness, which require sanitary engineering services. The coöperation received in this particular phase of our work is most gratifying. Some of the expenditures amount to as much as $10,000 or $12,000. Even more has been involved where sewerage lines have been extended, plant disposals installed and other sanitary provisions made.

SANITARY AND FATIGUE PROBLEMS

The law providing seats or resting places for female employees was found violated in 78 cases. This is one-third of the number discovered in our first biennial period which shows a marked gain in taking care of the fatigue problem in our State.

Seats for female employees or resting places have been one of the most interesting features of our work. A variety of seats have been investigated and studies made of the efficiency of their types and the relation to vocations. Most hearty coöperation has been received as a whole in the carrying out of the constructive work involved in these acts.

The three surveys made of children employed in North Carolina during the last year have informed the Commission of the volume of work, and have determined beyond any doubt that the many stories circulated of the children of ten to fourteen years of age employed in mills and manufacturing places in North Carolina are unfounded.

A study was made by the Commission of the needs of vocational education in the State. The result of this study and the necessity for such training was illustrated very forcibly at the Industrial Conference at Blue Ridge. There was emphasized the necessity of giving children who enter the industrial life of the State, at fourteen or fifteen years of age, with an average grade of five or six years, some incentive and some chance of bettering their education and uplifting them with vocational training and guidance. Also it was pointed out that the children of North Carolina are developed in height and weight as well as those of Northern and Eastern States, Canada and England.

Along with the follow-up survey several special studies have been made. A thorough investigation of the fishing and canning industries of the State was made in regard to child labor.

The fruit industry such as the canning, packing and shipping of strawberries, cantaloupes and peaches has been studied also in reference to child labor.

The Commission has administered the child labor laws and other laws which come under its administrative power with the view of taking care of the children of North Carolina through the mediums of education, health and welfare. The Commission's efforts were forwarded by the hearty coöperation of the manufacturers and public in general. The county superintendents of welfare and of schools and the county health officers have coöperated in every instance in forwarding the program of the Commission.

Requirements of Child Labor Law

PROHIBITIVE EMPLOYMENTS OF CHILDREN UNDER FOURTEEN

No child under the age of fourteen years shall be employed or permitted to work, in or about or in connection with any mill, factory, cannery, workshop, or manufacturing establishment.

EMPLOYMENT OF CHILDREN UNDER FOURTEEN REGULATED

No child under the age of fourteen years shall be employed, or permitted to work, in or about or in connection with any laundry, bakery, mercantile establishment, office, hotel, restaurant, barber shop, bootblack stand, public stable, garage, place of amusement, brick yard, lumber yard, or any messenger or delivery service, public works, or any form of street trades, except in cases and under regulations prescribed by the Commission.

Exceptions. This section shall not be construed to include bona fide boys' and girls' canning clubs recognized by the Agricultural Department of this State, or vocational training classes authorized by the State Board of Education, and such canning clubs and vocational classes are hereby expressly exempted from the provisions of this article.

CHILD WELFARE COMMISSION

PROHIBITED EMPLOYMENTS OF CHILDREN UNDER SIXTEEN

No person under sixteen years of age shall be employed, or permitted to work, at night in any of the places or occupations referred to in the first preceding section, between the hours of nine p.m. and six a.m., and no person under sixteen years of age shall be employed or permitted to work in or about or in connection with any quarry or mine, nor shall any child under the age of sixteen years be employed, except in cases and under regulations prescribed by the Commission herein created, when (1) such child has symptoms of disease contributory to retardation or disability; or (2) when determined by physical examination that employment of such child is injurious to its health; or (3) employed when surrounding conditions are injurious to its morals; or (4) employed when dangerous employment hazards are present.

The Commission has passed 14 rules and made legal interpretations of the 21 vocations enumerated in the law.

THE MANDATORY REQUIREMENTS OF THE LAW AND RULES OF THE COMMISSION FOR AGES, HOURS AND CONDITIONS OF EMPLOYMENT

1. No child under fourteen years of age shall be employed in a mill, factory, cannery, workshop, or manufacturing establishment.

2. No child under fourteen years of age shall be engaged in any of the occupations enumerated in the law, during school hours except in connection with continuation schools, vocational classes and bona fide canning clubs.

3. No child under sixteen years of age shall be employed before 6 a.m. or after 9 p.m.

4. No minor shall be worked in a factory or manufacturing establishment for a longer period than sixty hours in one week.

5. No boy under fourteen years of age shall be employed more than eight hours per day.

6. No girl under sixteen years of age shall be employed in any form of street trades.

7. No girl under fourteen years of age shall be employed in any of the places enumerated in the law.

8. Girls and boys between fourteen and sixteen years of age are required to secure an age certificate for legal employment in the places enumerated in the law.

9. Boys between twelve and fourteen years of age are required to secure an employment certificate to be employed in the enumerated occupations not prohibited, during the hours the public school is not in session and on Saturdays.

10. A temporary certificate waiving physical examination and school record is required of children under sixteen years of age to secure temporary employment not to exceed thirty days.

11. A badge is required for children under sixteen years of age to engage in any form of street trades.

12. The employer is required to make out an application for the employment of a child stating the kind of business and nature of work.

13. The parents must sign their approval of the employment in making a statement of the age and birthdate of the child.

14. A bona fide contemporary record of age is required of all children entering employment under sixteen years of age.

15. A physical examination is required of all children entering employment under sixteen years of age.

16. A school record is required showing the grade completed, vocational training, and teacher's observation of the mental, physical and moral condition of all children entering employment.

17. A personal knowledge is required of the physical condition of each place employing children under sixteen years of age.

18. Reasonable physical standards have been prepared for determining the entry of children into employment.

19. The prohibition of children from entering places, where dangerous machinery hazards are present, has resulted in the preparation of a tentative draft of safety standards.

20. Investigation is required of the moral surroundings that may effect children in employment.

THE BUDGET BUREAU
Ch. 89, P. L. 1925

Composition—Governor, Director of the Budget ex officio; Advisory Budget Commission composed of the chairman of the Appropriation and Finance committees of the House and the Senate and two other persons appointed by the Governor.

Personnel—Appointed members: R. S. McCoin, Henderson; A. M. Dixon, Gastonia.

Term—Not specified.

Compensation—$10 per diem and expenses.

Function

The purpose of Chapter 89 in creating the Budget Bureau, was to vest in the Governor of the State a more direct and effective supervision over all agencies and institutions, and for the efficient and economical administration of all such agencies and institutions, and for the initiation and preparation for each session of the General Assembly, of a balanced budget of the State's revenues and expenditures. To this end, the Governor is ex officio Director of the Budget, and is the head of the Budget Bureau, which is created and established in connection with his office.

The Director of the Budget has power to have examined the books and accounts of any of the departments and institutions, and to compel the production of all books, papers or other documents; to supervise generally the accounting and auditing systems now in force, and to inaugurate such changes as may be necessary to exhibit correct information; to examine any State institution or agency, to inspect its property and to inquire into its methods of operation and management.

He is also empowered to make such surveys, studies and examinations of departments, institutions and agencies of the State, as well as its problems, so as to determine whether there may be any overlapping in the performance of the duties of the several departments, institutions and agencies.

He is authorized to secure such help, expert accountants, draftsmen, and clerical help, as may be necessary to carry out the duties under the act. Under this authority the Budget Bureau is organized into a Staff Control to supervise and direct the various activities of the State Government and the expenditures made out of the appropriations.

He is charged with the duty of examining or causing to be examined, annually at the close of the fiscal year, the accounts of the State Treasurer and of the State Auditor.

He is charged with the duty of recommending to the General Assembly at each biennial session, such changes in the organization, management and general conduct of the various departments, institutions and other agencies of the State as in his judgment will promote the more efficient and economical operation and management thereof.

The Advisory Budget Commission, created by the same act, is made up of the Chairmen of the Appropriation and Finance Committees of the Senate and of the House, and two other persons to be appointed by the Governor. It meets in January and July of each year and at such other times as the public interest may require, at the call of the Director.

The enactments establishing the Executive Budget System and creating the Budget Bureau, provide that no money shall be appropriated except in the manner as set forth, and that no money shall be disbursed from the State Treasury except as therein provided, the general purpose of the enactments being to systematize and to pursue in an orderly manner the fiscal operations of the State; to present a comprehensive program of the resources and proposed expenditures to the General Assembly, as a basis for the appropriations to be made; to enforce thereafter the legislative will in carrying out the program so adopted; and finally, to account to the General Assembly for the performance under the authorizations made.

Forty-seven states of the Union have adopted some form of a budget. Thirty-one have adopted the Executive Budget, with or without staff control—four of the thirty-one under constitutional amendment, the others under statutory enactment. Ten states have an Administrative Board Budget, two of which are under constitutional amendment, and eight under statutory enactment; five states have an Administrative Legislative Board Budget, all of which are under statutory enactment; and one state has a Legislative Budget under statutory enactment. The North Carolina Budget is on the Executive Budget plan, and is the most complete and comprehensive of any so far adopted by any of the states; its provisions and methods of carrying into execution have been sought as patterns for legislation and proposed legislation by many other states of the Union.

NORTH CAROLINA HISTORICAL COMMISSION
Ch. 102, C. S.
A. R. NEWSOME, *Secretary*, Raleigh

The North Carolina Historical Commission was created by an act of the Legislature of 1903. It consists of five members appointed by the Governor for terms of six years. They receive no salary or per diem, but are allowed their actual expenses when attending to their official duties.

The offices of the Commission are in the State Administration Building, a fireproof structure erected under an act of the General Assembly in 1911.

The duties of the Commission are as follows:

1. To have collected historical data pertaining to the history of North Carolina and the territory included therein from the earliest times.

2. To have such material properly edited, published by the State Printer as other State printing, and distributed under the direction of the Commission.

3. To care for the proper marking and preservation of battlefields, houses, and other places celebrated in the history of the State.

4. To diffuse knowledge in reference to the history and resources of North Carolina.

5. To encourage the study of the history of North Carolina in the schools of the State, and to stimulate and encourage historical investigation and research among the people of the State.

6. To make a biennial report of its receipts and disbursements, its work and needs, to the Governor, to be by him transmitted to the General Assembly.

The powers of the Commission are as follows:

1. To adopt a seal for use in official business.

2. To adopt rules for its own government not inconsistent with the provisions of the law.

3. To fix a reasonable price for its publications and to devote the revenue arising from such sales to extending the work of the Commission.

4. To employ a secretary.

5. To control the expenditures of such funds as may be appropriated for its maintenance.

General Summary

Following is a general summary of the work of the Historical Commission:

1. The Commission has saved from destruction, classified and filed many thousands of letters and other documents of the Executive and Legislative Departments from colonial times to the present.

2. It has collected from the counties of the State and preserved from destruction 1,318 volumes and cases of valuable records and arranged them for use.

3. It has made an extensive collection, numbering more than 100,000 pieces of material bearing on North Carolina's part in the World War.

4. It has secured for the State the following collections:

Ashe, Samuel A'Court.
Badger, George Edmund, statesman, 1822-1858.
Bennehan, Richard, merchant, 1771-1790.
Bolles, Charles P., engineer, 1846-1855.
Bond, Tillie. MSS., 1690-1828.
Bragg, Braxton, 1864-1870.
Branch, John, statesman, 1819-1833.
Branch, L. O'B., soldier, 1861-1862.
Brevard family, 1757-1869.

Brooks, A. L., 1750-1875.
Bryan, John H., statesman, 1773-1906.
Burgwyn, W. H. S., soldier, banker, 1861-1912.
Burton, Robert, attorney, 1772-1785.
Cantwell, John L., soldier, 1855-1896.
Caswell, Richard, soldier, statesman, 1777-1789.
Caswell, William, soldier, 1781-1784.
Clark plantation, 1825-1861.
Clark, David, soldier, 1861-1863.
Clark, Walter, 1783-1913.
Cogdell, Richard, soldier, 1761-1784.
Collier, George W., soldier, 1861-1865.
Convention, 1788; 1789.
Council journals, 1745-1775.
County records dating from 1724.
Dartmouth papers, 1720-1783.
Davie, William R., soldier, statesman, 1778-1817.
Dickson papers, 1784-1790.
Dobbin, James C., statesman, 1816-1857.
Duffy, William, attorney, 1785-1809.
English Records—American Loyalists.
Fanning-McCulloh papers, 1762-1806.
Gaston, William, statesman, 1803-1842.
Gilmer, John A., statesman, 1860-1861.
Governor's papers, 1735-1925.
Grimes, Bryan, soldier, planter, 1844-1912.
Hale, E. J., editor, 1850-1867.
Hamlin, Wood John, 1762-1835.
Hawks, F. L., historian, 1850.
Henderson, Thomas, statesman, 1810-1811.
Hogg, Thomas D., papers.
Howe, Robert, soldier, 1777-1780.
Iredell, James, judge, 1770-1790.
Johnston, Samuel, statesman, 1763-1802.
King, R. H., minister, 1767-1825.
Lacy, Drury, letters.
Legislative papers, 1729-1900.
Lombardy Grove accounts, 1806.

McDowell, Charles, soldier, 1782.
Maclaine, Archibald, statesman, 1783-1790.
Macon, Nathaniel, statesman, 1804-1837.
Merrimon, A. S., judge, 1853-1854.
Miller, R. J., minister, 1799-1831.
Miscellaneous, 4 vols., 1755-1912.
Murphey, Archibald DeBow, statesman, 1797-1830.
Muster rolls, 1861-1865.
Nash, Frederic, judge, 1764-1863.
Oath books of governors, commons, conventions, 1816-1875.
Olds, Fred A.
Pettigrew papers. Plantation records, 1772-1900.
Pollock, Thomas, statesman, 1708-1761.
Reid, D. S., statesman, 1803-1880.
Revolutionary Army accounts, 1776-1777.
Revolutionary committees of safety, 1774-1776.
Saunders, W. L., statesman, historian, 1866-1888.
Shaw papers, economic, 1735-1883.
Shipping records, 1725-1751.
Spanish Records, 1566— .
Spencer, Cornelia Phillips, author, 1859-1903.
Spottswood, Alexander, colonial governor, 1710-1712.
Steele, John, statesman, 1777-1831.
Sumner, Jethro, soldier, 1760-1783.
Swepson, Geo. W., papers, 1866-1870.
Vance, Zebulon B., governor and U. S. Senator, 1827-1895.
Waddell family papers, 1771-1886.
Wiley, Calvin H., educator, 1835-1902.
Williams, John, statesman, 1772-1784.
Williamson, Hugh, historian, 1780-1790.
Winslow family papers.
Newspapers, North Carolina, 1751-1800.
Stevens facsimiles. MSS. in European archives. 1773-1783.

5. It has issued the following publications: *Public Education in North Carolina, 1790-1840: A Documentary History*, 2 vols.; *North Carolina Schools and Academies, 1790-1840: A Documentary History; The Correspondence of Jonathan Worth*, 2 vols.; *The Papers of Archibald D. Murphey*, 2 vols.; *The Papers of Thomas Ruffin*, Vols.

I, II, III and IV; *Literary and Historical Activities in North Carolina, 1900-1905; Von Graffenreid's Account of the Founding of New Bern; Records of the Moravians in North Carolina,* Vols. I and II; *The Papers of John Steele,* 2 vols.; *Calendars of Manuscript Collections,* Vol. I; *North Carolina Manual for* 1909, 1911, 1913, 1915, 1917, 1919, 1921, 1923, and 1925; and thirty-two bulletins.

6. It recovered for the State, through the gift of the Italian Government, Canova's famous statue of Washington.

7. It has erected in the rotunda of the Capitol a marble bust of William A. Graham; and obtained, without cost to the State, similar busts of Matt W. Ransom, Samuel Johnston, John M. Morehead, Calvin H. Wiley, and W. S. Ashe.

8. The Commission maintains in its Hall of History one of the most extensive historical museums in America. It contains about 15,000 objects, illustrative of every period of the history of North Carolina from the earliest colonial times to the present.

9. It has assisted a large number of students in their investigations of North Carolina history, given information about the history of the State whenever it was possible, and has encouraged in many ways the study of our history in the schools of the State.

THE LEGISLATIVE REFERENCE LIBRARY

In addition to its other duties the Historical Commission maintains the Legislative Reference Library. The Legislative Reference Library is not a new institution. For 25 years such departments in other states have been rendering valuable service. They have been provided for in thirty states, and in more than fifty cities of the United States. Recently there has been established a Legislative Reference Bureau in the Congressional Library which is rendering similar aid to the National Government.

For ten years progressive citizens urged the establishment of such a department in North Carolina. In response to that demand the Legislature of 1915, by a unanimous vote in the Senate and House of Representatives, passed a bill entitled "An act to establish a Legislative Reference Library," under the supervision of the North Carolina Historical Commission.

Among the duties of the Librarian set forth in this act are the following: "To collect, tabulate, annotate and digest information for the use of the members and committees of the General Assembly, and the officials of the State, and of the various counties and cities included therein, upon all questions of State, county, and municipal legislation."

As indicated by the caption as well as the subject-matter of the act, this Department is created primarily for the benefit of the members and committees of the General Assembly.

These representatives of the people serve practically without compensation and in most cases make considerable personal sacrifice in order to be of service to the State. During the short sessions of the General Assembly they do not have time to study and thus secure for themselves information about the hundreds of measures they are called upon to consider. Heretofore there has been no agency to collect and classify the sort of information needed by the busy legislator.

To fill this want is the particular field of service of the Legislative Reference Library. For that purpose more than ten thousand books, laws, pamphlets, and clippings have been gathered and classified so that they are instantly available for use by interested persons. Additional material is received daily, and an attempt is made to procure as full information as is obtainable about all legislation in other states and counties.

Information relating to the following subjects, which are taken from a list of more than fifteen hundred headings, will serve to illustrate the scope of service which is rendered: Agriculture, Appropriations, Automobiles, Banks, Bill Drafting, Budgets, Campaign Expenses, Capital Punishment, Charities, Child Labor, Civil Service, Constitutions, Contracts, Convicts, Coöperative Buying and Marketing, Corporations, Courts, Credit, Crime and Criminals, Democratic Party, Drainage, Education, Elections, Employment, Factories, Farm Problems, Finance, Fires, Fish and Game, Food, Forests, Freight Rates, Health, Immigration, Initiative and Referendum, Insane, Insurance, Judges, Juries, Labor, Lawyers, Liens, Legislation, Loans, Manufacturers, Marriage and Divorce, Medicine, Militia, Municipalities, Negroes, Newspapers, Pardons, Parole, Passenger

Rates, Pensions, Pharmacy, Platforms, Primaries, Prisons, Procedure, Prohibition, Public-Service Corporations, Railroads, Republican Party, Roads, Rural Credits, Schools, State Government, Statutes, Strikes, Taxation, Trusts, Universities and Colleges, Vital Statistics, Vocational Education, Wages, Woman Suffrage, Women, Workmen's Compensation.

The province of the Legislative Reference Library is not to promote legislation, but to furnish data and information so that the best and most widely approved laws may be enacted.

With the coöperation and assistance of the persons for whose benefit the Legislative Reference Library was created, it hopes to achieve the same measure of success that similar agencies have had in other states.

The first Legislative Reference Librarian was W. S. Wilson, 1915-1918. Henry M. London has held this position since 1919.

MEMBERS OF THE HISTORICAL COMMISSION

W. J. Peele	1903-1919
J. D. Huffman	1903-1905
F. A. Sondley	1903-1905
Richard Dillard	1903-1905
R. D. W. Connor	1903-1907
Charles L. Raper	1905-1907
Thomas W. Blount	1905-1911
J. Bryan Grimes	1905-1923
M. C. S. Noble	1907-
D. H. Hill	1907-1922
Thomas M. Pittman	1911-
Frank Wood	1919-1926
Heriot Clarkson	1922-
W. N. Everett	1923
Ben Dixon MacNeill	1926-

SECRETARIES

R. D. W. Connor	1903-1921
D. H. Hill	1921-1924
R. B. House	1924-1926
A. R. Newsome	1926-

LIBRARY COMMISSION OF NORTH CAROLINA
Art. 4, Ch. 109, C. S.
Mrs. Lillian B. Griggs, *Secretary and Director*, Raleigh

Composition (5)—Superintendent of Public Instruction *ex officio*; State Librarian *ex officio*; two members appointed by North Carolina Library Association; one member by Governor.

Personnel—Mrs. Nancy P. Leak, Chairman, Rockingham; Carrie L. Broughton, Vice Chairman, Raleigh; A. T. Allen, Raleigh; Alfred M. Scales, Greensboro; Joseph P. Breedlove, Durham.

Term—Three years, overlapping terms.

Compensation—Traveling expenses only.

Function

To give advice and assistance to all libraries of the State and to all communities proposing to establish libraries, as to the best means of establishing and administering such libraries in the selection of books, cataloging, maintenance, etc.; to aid in organizing new libraries; to establish and maintain traveling libraries as may be practicable; to receive reports annually from every public library in the State in such form as may be prescribed by the commission; to employ a secretary trained in library methods, and fix compensation.

Reports. To report biennially to Governor.

Important Activities:

1. Establishment of Public Libraries. Organizer visits communities and directs work of classifying, etc.

2. Reorganization of old libraries. Organizer visits and advises.

3. Compilation of library statistics, based on annual reports received.

4. Publication of bulletin (20-page quarterly magazine).

5. Maintenance of system of traveling libraries of 35-40 vol.: 15 Fiction; 15 Juvenile; 10 Biography, travel, etc. Also traveling library for schools consisting of juvenile.

6. Package libraries: (1) Debate; (2) Farmers; (3) Study Club.

7. General Loan Collection—Miscellaneous, all subjects to individuals.

The Library Commission of North Carolina was created by the General Assembly of 1909, and active work was begun September 15th of the same year. The Commission consists of five members, two of whom are appointed by the North Carolina Library Association and one by the Governor; the State Librarian and the Superintendent of Public Instruction complete the membership.

The purpose of the Commission, as expressed in the law, is to "give assistance, advice, and counsel to all libraries in the State, to all communities which may propose to establish libraries, and to all persons interested, as to the best means of establishing and administering such libraries, as to the selection of books, cataloging, maintenance and other details of library management as may be practicable."

The following are the important lines of activity.

1. *Establishment of Public Libraries.* The Commission endeavors to secure the establishment of public libraries in localities able to support them, and gives advice and assistance in arousing public interest. After preliminary correspondence, communities proposing to establish libraries are visited by the Secretary or organizer, and the practical details of organization explained. In many instances she classifies the books, starts the accession record and shelf-list, installs a proper charging system, and teaches the librarian how to keep the necessary records. The service is rendered without cost to the library.

County Libraries—The Commission sponsors the County Library idea—the idea of extending the privileges of the library to the rural residents of the county. One good library in each county, preferably at the county seat, serving equally the urban and rural residents is a goal particularly desired for the library service of the State. The following twelve counties have provided to some extent library privileges for their rural residents:

Burke	New Hanover
Chowan	Rowan
Durham	Stanly
Forsyth	Vance
Guilford	Wake
Mecklenburg	Warren

2. *Reorganization of Old Libraries.* The Secretary visits libraries already established to confer with the Librarian and Library Board regarding methods of work and plans for further development. While much information and advice may be given by letters and circulars, personal visits are much more effective, as they invariably give new impulse to the local work and enable the Secretary to become familiar with library conditions in all parts of the State.

3. *Library Statistics.* Every public library in the State, including free public libraries, subscription libraries, school, college and university libraries, Young Men's Christian Association, legal association, medical association, Supreme Court and State libraries, is required by law to make an annual report to the Commission. From the data thus secured the Commission compiles an annual report of library conditions in North Carolina.

Library Statistics—There are 292,861 volumes in the public libraries of the State and $123,753 is appropriated for their maintenance. With the population of the State at two and one-half million and the recognized standard at one dollar per capita for library service, it will readily be seen that the State is not in the front rank of those having adequate library facilities.

4. *The North Carolina Library Bulletin.* This is a magazine of 20 pages, published quarterly. It is sent free to every library in the State, and, upon application, to library trustees and to others interested in library extension. The first issue appeared in December, 1909. Each number contains important library articles, book lists, editorial notes, and general library news. It is intended to serve as a means of communication with each and every library, to bring the libraries into closer relation with one another, and,

in general, to increase the interest in libraries throughout the State, and to improve the quality of their service to the public.

5. *Traveling Libraries.* For the benefit of communities without library facilities the Library Commission maintains a system of free traveling libraries. A library contains from thirty-five to forty volumes. The rules governing the loan of libraries are as few and simple as possible. Borrowers agree to pay the freight both from and to Raleigh, to take good care of the books and to return them promptly, to make good any loss or damage beyond reasonable wear and tear, and to lend the books without charge to all responsible persons in the community.

Traveling libraries containing only children's books have been prepared especially for the use of schools.

Special collections are loaned to teachers of agriculture and home economics for the school year.

The Commission loaned 411,989 volumes, 1924-26.

6. *Package Libraries.* Package libraries are of two kinds: The Debate libraries, and the Study Club libraries. The Debate libraries are carefully prepared collections on the political, social, and economic questions which are being debated by schools and societies throughout the State. They are not lent to individuals, but to schools and debating societies, and on condition that all taking part in the debate have the use of the material. Study club libraries are prepared for clubs pursuing a definite course of study.

7. *The General Loan Collection.* This is a miscellaneous collection of books and pamphlets on all subjects and it enables the commission to send books to individuals and to supplement the various fixed collections so that they will meet the needs of the borrower. The books from this section are lent for three weeks, and the borrower pays the postage both from and to Raleigh.

8. *Distribution of Library Literature.* In addition to the *North Carolina Library Bulletin*, the following publications have been issued and distributed by the Commission:

Free Traveling Libraries.
Clubwomen and Libraries.
Agriculture and Country Life.
North Carolina Package Libraries: Material for debate.
Select Bibliography of North Carolina, by Stephen B. Weeks.

How to Start a Public Library.
Material for Study Clubs.
Free Debate Libraries.
Graded List of Children's Books.
Book for Mothers and Homemakers.

Other library literature, including tracts of the American Library Association, book lists, building plans, etc., is sent out as required.

9. *School Libraries.* The development of school libraries is a special feature of the work. A close connection has been established with the schools by giving advice on the care and use of school libraries, assistance in starting the necessary records, and help in the selection and purchase of books.

STATE LIBRARY
Art. 1, Ch. 109, C. S.; Ch. 202, P. L. 1921

CARRIE L. BROUGHTON, *State Librarian,* Raleigh

Trustees—Governor, *ex officio;* Superintendent of Public Instruction, *ex officio;* Secretary of State, *ex officio.*

Function

To maintain the State and document libraries; to make rules and regulations by which the librarian shall be governed for the protection and preservation of the books and library; to make suitable distribution of State-owned books, reports and publications; to procure, publish and sell historical documents and books, the Governor to designate documents to be preserved; to appoint a committee consisting of State Librarian, Superintendent of Public Instruction and three other persons to purchase books; to appoint a Librarian to serve four years, and the latter is authorized to employ an assistant.

To maintain a document library during the sessions of the General Assembly; to keep two copies each of the laws and journals of the General Assembly.

REPORTS. To report biennially to the General Assembly.

Historical Note

The North Carolina State Library, like practically all State Libraries, had its beginning in the miscellaneous collection of books which had accumulated in the various offices of the State officials. These books were purchased and donated to meet the various needs of the members of the General Assembly and the State Officers.

When the capitol was burned in 1831, the library which was located in that building, was also consumed. The fire that destroyed the old building originated on the roof; and owing to an unnecessary panic caused by the announcement that the dome was falling, the people fled from the building and left the library to its fate.

In 1837, the General Assembly passed an act requiring the Secretary of State to collect books for the State Library and discharge the duty of Librarian. It was further enacted by the General Assembly that he be allowed fifty dollars per annum for his services as State Librarian during his term of office. No appropriation was made for several years, and on the completion of the present capitol in 1840, the few books saved from the fire were removed to the Capitol building.

Code 2, Vol. 2, Section 3608, says "The sum of $500 is annually appropriated for the increase of the Public Library."

In March, 1888, the State Library was moved from the Capitol building to the new Supreme Court Library Building located on the northeast corner of Salibury and Edenton streets, where it remained until January, 1913, when it was moved to its present location.

As stated above, in 1840 the Legislature appropriated $500 for the purchase of books. This appropriation stood for eighty years, from 1840 to 1921, when the General Assembly increased it to $3,000. In 1923 the appropriation was increased to $5,000, and in 1925 to $12,500. This includes not only book fund but also expense of administration.

The increased interest in the State Library is concrete evidence that the educational movement started with Aycock is bearing abundant fruit. The library is becoming an agency through which the State can see itself from year to year as it progresses from one period of development to another. Its people are learning to resurrect the past and to see therein the mistakes, the lessons and the good they teach. This in itself is real and genuine progress. The growth of the State Library is a visible evidence of that important fact.

Coöperation between the library and the schools has been marked during the past few years. Some days the teachers, both white and black, bring a whole class to spend an hour searching through some valuable book of reference. There has been a marked increase in this use of the library among the negro students in our colleges and public schools. They have a separate reading room with full access to the entire library.

The reference service continues to be stressed and also the work among club women. Quick service by telephone is more and more appreciated. Requests for information or reference which come by mail both from the city and from widely scattered parts of the country increase every year. A valuable reference aid is given from the Periodical division. Recently there have been indexed all articles appearing in the magazines about North Carolinians or North Carolina. All books written about North Carolinians or about North Carolina are preserved. Thousands of volumes give emphasis to the fact that here in North Carolina we are not as ignorant as we sometimes are pictured, for many North Carolinians have written books. We now have in printed form a complete bibliography of North Carolina to be found in the State Library.

Nearly five thousand State papers have been classified according to towns, dates, and missing numbers. Besides this, many articles of historical value have been indexed. This is one of the most useful features of the library. There is also a printed bibliography of all newspapers in the Library.

Special emphasis has been laid upon books relating to the war between the States. The collection is large and has been selected with much care. It is especially strong on regimental histories, newspaper files, magazines, maps, and photographic scenes.

The genealogical department is becoming more and more popular. Many valuable books and periodicals have been selected for this department, with special emphasis on North Carolina, Virginia, Georgia, South Carolina and Pennsylvania. Almost every day visitors from different sections of our own State and from other states search through these records to connect their family history.

Law Library

The State Library is the chief repository for data about the State and State affairs. To the legislator and man of public affairs the library is a place where he can at his own convenience and in his own way study intelligently and freely all questions of legislation that will affect his people and his State.

Number of volumes in general Library	40,716
Number of volumes in government documents	7,521
Number of volumes in bound newspapers	4,968
Number of volumes in bound magazines	4,880
Total	58,085

LAW LIBRARY
Art. 2, Ch. 109, C. S.
MARSHALL DeLANCEY HAYWOOD, *Librarian*

Trustees—Justices of the Supreme Court, *ex officio*.

Function

To maintain the Law Library and prescribe rules for its government. All moneys appropriated for its increase are paid out under their direction and supervision. May appoint a librarian who shall perform his duties under rules and regulations of trustees.

The Clerk of the Supreme Court, under direction of the trustees, is directed to spend annually the amounts paid in by applicants for license to practice law, examined by the Court, in the purchase of such books as may be necessary to keep the library well appointed and no other appropriation for that purpose is allowed. He is also allowed $200 annually for binding old books and for other contingent purposes.

Historical Note

Created by act of the General Assembly of 1883.

AUDUBON SOCIETY OF NORTH CAROLINA
Part 2, Art. 1, Ch. 38, C. S.
Miss Placide H. Underwood, *Secretary*, Raleigh

Function

To secure the enactment and enforcement of laws for the preservation of birds and game of the State; to designate for appointment by the Governor, county bird and game wardens for such counties as come under its jurisdiction, and to prescribe their duties and fix compensation; to receive fees for all non-resident hunters' licenses through the State Treasurer issued by clerk of Superior Court in specified counties, and to revoke such licenses for cause; to issue certificates to suitable persons to collect bird nests and eggs for scientific purposes; to promote the study of birds; to stimulate instruction of children by parents and teachers; to arouse public sentiment against destruction of wild birds and their eggs; to prepare and distribute literature upon such subjects; to raise funds necessary to carry out purposes of Society and to defray expenses.

Report. To make an annual report to the Governor of the receipts and expenditures of the Society for the year.

Note. The Audubon Society of North Carolina was created a body politic and corporate in 1903, with eight directors or trustees, officers consisting of a president, vice president, secretary, and treasurer. The treasurer is designated by Society and commissioned by Governor.

At the present time nineteen counties are under the jurisdiction of the Society; a bill for the enactment of a State-wide game commission to take over the enforcement work of the Society was introduced in 1917, by Senator Kelly, Chairman of Senate Committee on game. So many amendments were offered particularly aimed at exemption of certain counties from its provisions, that it was finally tabled after much debate. The Society made the same effort to have a bill passed creating a State-wide Game Commission at the sessions of the General Assembly of 1919 and 1921, without result.

in counties not under Society's jurisdiction, game laws are enforced by the county commissioners who constitute county game protection commissions. They appoint local game wardens.

Historical Note

The Audubon Society of North Carolina was incorporated in 1903 with J. Y. Joyner, T. Gilbert Pearson, R. H. Lewis, A. H. Boyden, H. H. Brimley, P. D. Gold, Jr., J. F. Jordan, and R. N. Wilson as incorporators. (Rev. 1905, Sec. 1863.)

The officers of The Audubon Society of North Carolina are a president, vice president, secretary and treasurer, and such other officers as may be fixed by the by-laws. (Rev. 1905, Sec. 1863.)

The objects for which the corporation is formed are to promote among the citizens of North Carolina a better appreciation of the value of the song and insectivorous birds to man and the State; to encourage parents and teachers to give instruction to children on the subject; to stimulate public sentiment against the destruction of wild birds and their eggs; to secure the enactment and the enforcement of proper and necessary laws for the protection and preservation of the birds and game of North Carolina. Its further office is through the appointment of game wardens, to rigidly enforce the laws for game and bird protection.

The funds received by the Treasurer of the State from the license tax on non-resident hunters constitutes a fund known as the Bird and Game Fund. This fund is paid out by the Treasurer of the State on the order of the Treasurer of The Audubon Society of North Carolina, who makes an annual report to the Governor of the receipts and expenditures of the society for each year.

The Governor, upon the recommendation of The Audubon Society, appoints bird and game wardens and the Treasurer of the Society, whose terms of office, unless otherwise provided for, are during good behavior, or until their successors are appointed. The Governor issues to the Treasurer of The Audubon Society and to each person appointed as warden, a commission. These commissions are transmitted to the clerk's office of the Superior Court for the county from which the prospective treasurer or bird and game warden is appointed.

Every person appointed as game warden, before entering upon the duties of the office, is required to take oath before the clerk of the Superior Court of the county in which he resides that he will faithfully perform the duties of said office, and execute a bond in the sum of one hundred dollars for the faithful discharge of his duties. The compensation of wardens is fixed and paid by the society.

There are only nineteen counties of the State under the jurisdiction of The Audubon Society, and there are Game Wardens in the various counties, each county having one or more wardens.

Any non-resident of the State who desires to hunt in any of the counties under the jurisdiction of The Audubon Society is required to make application to the clerk of the Superior Court of any of the counties under Audubon control, and the clerk of the court issues such license upon the payment of a fee of ten dollars and clerk's fee. A non-resident hunting license issued by the clerk of the Superior Court of any one of the counties under the jurisdiction of The Audubon Society is valid in all the Audubon counties, while a non-resident hunting license issued in a county not under the jurisdiction of The Audubon Society can be used only in the county in which it is issued.

In 1909 the General Assembly of North Carolina passed an act withdrawing certain counties from Audubon protection. Subsequent to 1909 other counties have been withdrawn so that at the present time there are only nineteen counties under the jurisdiction of The Audubon Society of North Carolina. The following counties are under the jurisdiction of The Audubon Society:

Alamance	Durham	Northampton
Alleghany	Greene	Rockingham
Ashe	Iredell	Rowan
Brunswick	Lenoir	Rutherford
Buncombe	McDowell	Watauga
Columbus	Mecklenburg	Wake
	New Hanover	

In its efforts toward education, The Audubon Society has expended part of its funds towards the publication of a book on North Carolina birds. The Society has had prepared and paid for the plates presenting pictures of bird life in North Carolina. During the year 1919 The Book on North Carolina Birds, by T. Gilbert Pearson, C. S. Brimley, and H. H. Brimley, was published after a period of several years, the material for this book having been destroyed by fire when the establishment of E. M. Uzzell & Co. was burned in November, 1915. This is a joint publication of the North Carolina Geological and Economic Survey, the State Audubon Society and the State Museum. Copies of this publication can be secured either from the office of the Secretary of The Audubon Society, Raleigh, or from the North Carolina Geological and Economic Survey, Chapel Hill, upon the payment of $2.75 for cloth bound copies and $2.00 paper bound.

The Audubon Society owns two small islands in Pamlico Sound which are patrolled by a game warden during the nesting season. These islands are Leggett Lump and Royal Shoal.

In an attempt to increase a State-wide interest in bird and game conservation, the secretaries of the Society have given illustrated bird lectures and talked on bird study to Teachers' Institutes, Community Clubs, Women's Clubs and to many of the schools in the State, and a great many Junior Audubon Societies have been organized and several schools and clubs have held "Bird Days" as a result of this work.

A bill providing for the enactment of a State-wide game commission to take over the work of The Audubon Society was introduced into the Senate by Senator Kelly, Chairman of the Senate Committee on Game, at the session of the General Assembly of 1917. This bill, amended several times so as to exempt certain counties from its provisions, passed its first reading. On its second reading, there were so many amendments offered that the bill was transferred to the committee. The committee stripped the bill of all amendments and reported it back to the Senate with a substitute amendment. When the bill came up for passage, however, there were several more amendments offered and a parliamentary wrangle followed, during which the bill was tabled. It was then so near the end of the session of the General Assembly that there was not sufficient time to take the matter up in the House, and the matter was dropped. The Society made an effort to have a like bill passed at the sessions of the General Assembly of 1919 and 1921 without result.

Having failed in its efforts to have a bill passed creating a Statewide Game Commission at the session of the Legislature of 1921, the officers and directors of The Audubon Society decided that it would be best for said Society not to undertake to have such a bill passed at any future session of the General Assembly, but it would heartily endorse any bill providing for better game legislation and conservation of wild life in the State of North Carolina.

When The Audubon Society was organized the office of the Secretary was at Greensboro, N. C., Mr. T. Gilbert Pearson, now President of The National Association of Audubon Societies, being Secretary. In 1913, upon the election of Mr. James W. Cheshire, Secretary, the office was moved to Raleigh, and since that time the work of the Society has been carried on by the various secretaries in Raleigh.

Having been confined to his home for several months on account of ill health, Dr. Richard H. Lewis resigned as President of The Audubon Society in December, 1925, and requested that his resignation be accepted as he would be unable to give his attention to the affairs of the Audubon Society. The resignation of Dr. Lewis was accepted with profound regret. Pursuant to the resignation of Dr. Lewis as President of the Audubon Society, the Secretary called a meeting of both the officers and directors of the Society for the purpose of considering the election of a new President and discussing other matters of interest to said Society. A quorum could not be secured of said officers and directors, and under the advice of the Attorney General, the Vice President and Secretary have been carring on the work of the Society.

It is with deep regret that the Secretary reports the death of Dr. Richard H. Lewis on August 6, 1926. The Audubon Society will always feel the great loss occasioned by the death of Dr. Lewis, as his interest and advice were most valuable in the administration of the affairs of the said Society.

Officers of The Audubon Society of North Carolina:

NORTH CAROLINA FISHERIES COMMISSION BOARD

OFFICERS

H. H. BRIMLEY, *Vice-President*	Raleigh
P. H. UNDERWOOD, *Secretary*	Raleigh
R. A. BROWN, *Treasurer*	Raleigh

BOARD OF DIRECTORS

REV. MELTON W. CLARK	Greensboro
BROOK G. EMPIE	Wilmington
B. F. SHELTON	Speed
W. H. SWIFT	Greensboro
FRANKLIN SHERMAN, JR.	Raleigh

SECRETARIES

T. GILBERT PEARSON	1903-1911
P. D. GOLD, JR.	Nov. 22, 1912-June 1, 1915
J. W. CHESHIRE	June 1, 1913-March 20, 1915
R. E. PARKER	June 1, 1915-June 1, 1917
G. A. MARTIN	June 1, 1917-Oct. 10, 1917
MISS PLACIDE H. UNDERWOOD	October 10, 1917 (—)

NORTH CAROLINA FISHERIES COMMISSION BOARD

Ch. 37, Consolidated Statutes, as amended by the General Assembly of 1923

PERSONNEL

J. K. DIXON, *Chairman*	Trenton
ROBERT LASSITER	Charlotte
SANTFORD MARTIN	Winston-Salem
FRANK H. STEDMAN	Fayetteville
H. C. WALL	Rockingham
J. Q. GILKEY	Marion
GEORGE L. HAMPTON	Canton
F. S. WORTHY	Washington
H. V. GRANT	Snead's Ferry
E. S. ASKEW	Windsor
R. BRUCE ETHERIDGE	Manteo

EXECUTIVE BRANCH

J. A. NELSON, *Fisheries Commissioner* ....Morehead City

ASSISTANT COMMISSIONERS

J. H. STONE ....Wilmington
E. O. SPENCER ....Swan Quarter
L. A. QUIDLEY ....Manteo

N. R. WEBB, *Secretary and Chief Clerk* ....Morehead City
MISS CARITA WADE, *Stenographer* ....Morehead City
FRANK J. RIEGER, *Superintendent of Hatcheries* ....Waynesville

Creation and Organization of the Board

The General Assembly of 1923 reorganized the Fisheries Commission Board as follows:

It created the Fisheries Commission, consisting of eleven members to be appointed by the Governor and confirmed by the Senate. At least six of these members shall have a practical knowledge of the fishing industry and shall be denominated the Fisheries Commission Board. Four of the members appointed in 1923 were to hold office for a term of two years; four for a term of four years, and three for a term of six years. After the expiration of these special terms of office, the general term of a member of the Board is to be six years. The compensation of the members is $4 a day and traveling expenses while attending the meeting of the Board, provided, the per diem and expenses shall not exceed $250 each per year. The chairman of the Board is elected by the Board and may receive such compensation as the Board sees fit to allow.

The Fisheries Commission is empowered to appoint a Fisheries Commissioner for a term of four years, and the Fisheries Commissioner may appoint two assistants, subject to the approval of the Board, to hold office at the pleasure of the Fisheries Commissioner, and he may appoint such other fish inspectors as may be necessary. It is the purpose of the law creating the Fisheries Commission Board to make this organization self-sustaining, but until it becomes so certain appropriations are allowed it for maintenance. The powers of the Board in general are to make such regulations as may be necessary concerning fish and fisheries, to regulate the shipment of fish products, to make surveys of fish resources of the State, and to report on them to the Legislature. The duties of the Fisheries Commissioner are as follows:

To enforce all acts relating to the fish and fisheries of North Carolina. By and with the advice and consent of the Fisheries Commission Board, to make such regulations as shall maintain open for the passage of fishes all inlets and not less than one-third of the width of all sounds and streams, or such greater proportions of their width as may be necessary. To collect and compile statistics showing the annual product of the fisheries of the State, the capital invested, and the apparatus employed, and any fisherman refusing to give these statistics shall be refused a license for the next year. To prepare and have on file in his office maps based on the charts of the United States Coast and Geodetic Survey, of the largest scale published, showing as closely as may be the location of all fixed apparatus employed during each fishing season. To have surveyed and marked in a prominent manner those areas of waters of the State in which the use of any or all fishing appliances are prohibited by law or regulation and those areas of water in the State in which oyster tonging or dredging is prohibited by law. To prosecute all violation of the fish laws, and wherever necessary he may employ counsel for this purpose. To remove, pending trial, nets or other appliances he finds being fished or used in violation of the fisheries laws of the State. To carry on investigations relating to the migrations and habits of the fish in the waters of the State, also investigations relating to the cultivation of the oyster, clam and other mollusca, and of the terrapin and crab, and for this purpose he may employ such scientific assistance as may be authorized by the Fisheries Commission Board. The commissioner shall be responsible for the collection of all license taxes, fees, rentals, or other imports on the fisheries, and shall pay same into the State Treasury to the credit of the Fisheries Commission fund. He shall on or before the twenty-fifth day of each month mail to the Treasurer of the State a consolidated statement showing the amount of taxes and license fees collected during the preceding month, and by and from whom collected. He shall, in an official capacity, have power to administer oaths and to send for and examine persons and papers.

If any fisherman fail or refuse to give statistics as required in this section, the Board may extend the time of his operations, and the Fisheries Commission Board is empowered to make such rules and regulations as they think proper to procure statistics as to the annual products of the fisheries of the State.

PRINTING COMMISSION
Art. 1, Ch. 120, C. S.; Chs. 134, 247, P. L. 1925

Composition (7)—Governor, Council of State, Commissioner of Labor and Printing, Attorney-General, *ex officio* members.

Function

To contract for all printing and binding done for the State defined as "public printing," which is construed to mean all printing done directly for the State and paid for out of the General Fund, and included in all annual or biennial reports required under the law, all blanks and blank books and office stationery required and no more.

The Commissioner of Labor and Printing is directed to superintend letting of contracts, and the person with whom such contract is made is designated as the public printer who shall give bond for $5,000. The Commission regulates the size of books and publications, general style of publication, style of type and paper to be used; determines what details of Department activities shall be included in Department reports, and also determines the number of laws and resolutions to be printed. The Commissioner of Labor and Printing purchases for the use of the State the paper and stationery used for public printing. He and the Budget Bureau allocate to the several departments the public printing appropriation which is made by the General Assembly in one lump sum to the Commissioner of Labor and Printing.

Historical Note

Created by act of the General Assembly of 1919.

SALARY AND WAGE COMMISSION
Ch. 125, P. L. 1925.
H HOYLE SINK, *Executive Secretary*, Raleigh

Composition—Five members.

Personnel—Julian Price, *Chairman*, Greensboro; Ernest V. Webb, Kinston; R. N. Page, Aberdeen; P. H. Hanes, Jr., Winston-Salem; Frank Tate, Morganton.

Appointment—By the Governor. Executive Secretary and clerical force to be appointed by the Commission and paid at its discretion.

Term—At the will of the Governor.

Compensation—$5 per day and expenses.

Function

To adopt necessary rules and regulations for carrying out the provisions of the law. To report to the Governor as to salaries, working hours and conditions of employment within the state service and upon his approval the report becomes the standard for salaries and wages of state employees; to reassemble at the discretion of the Governor to reconsider and readjust the salary classification and schedule, subject to the approval of the Governor.

Historical Note

Created by act of the General Assembly of North Carolina of 1925.

JUDICIAL CONFERENCE
Ch. 244, P. L. 1925

Composition—Forty-six members: Judges of the Supreme and Superior Courts and the Attorney-General, *ex officio*; one practicing attorney from each judicial district.

Personnel—The attorneys: J. C. B. Ehringhaus, Elizabeth City; H. G. Connor, Jr., Wilson; R. C. Dunn, Enfield; G. K. Freeman, Goldsboro; J. B. James, Greenville; G. V. Cowper, Kinston; J. C. Biggs, Raleigh; J. O. Carr, Wilmington; J. B. Clark, Fayetteville;

B. S. Womble, Winston-Salem; H. F. Seawell, Carthage; C. W. Tillett, Jr., Charlotte; A. H. Price, Salisbury; C. R. Hoey, Shelby; J. J. Hayes, North Wilkesboro; J. S. Ferguson, Waynesville; D. E. Hudgins, Marion; J. G. Merrimon, Asheville; A. L. Brooks, Greensboro.

Appointment—By Governor.

Term—Two years.

Compensation—None. Expenses not exceeding $250 per year allowed the Conference for clerical help.

Function

To report annually to the Governor the work of the various parts of the judicial system, with recommendations of reforms in the system and in the practice and procedure of the courts; to submit suggestions relating to rules of practice and procedure for the consideration of the judges of the various courts.

The Chief Justice and the Clerk of the Supreme Court are, respectively, president and secretary of the Conference. Two meetings yearly are required, at which a quorum is to consist of two justices of the Supreme Court, six judges of the Superior Court, and six attorneys. The Conference may hold public meetings and has power to administer oaths and to require the attendance of witnesses and the production of books and papers.

Historical Note

Created by act of the General Assembly of 1925.

STATE PRISON (Raleigh)
Ch. 130, C. S.; Ch. 163, P. L. 1925
GEO. ROSS POU, *Superintendent*, Raleigh

Board of Directors—One Chairman; six other members; State Treasurer, Treasurer, *ex officio*.

Personnel—J. A. Leake, *chairman*, Wadesboro; H. K. Burgwyn, Jackson; A. E. White, Lumberton; R. M. Chatham, Elkin; J. M. Brewer, Wake Forest; B. B. Everett, Palmyra; J. P. Wilson, Warsaw.

Appointment—By Governor, with consent of Senate.
Term—Four years.
Compensation—$4 per diem and 5 cents mileage.

Function

To direct and manage the affairs of the State Prison and State Hospital for the Dangerous Insane; to provide for the accommodation, maintenance, training, regulation, discipline, classification and employment of all persons committed to the State Prison and for the accommodation, maintenance, regulation and treatment of the criminally insane committed to its custody or transferred from the State Prison.

To employ such officers and employees as it deems necessary and to fix their compensation and prescribe their duties; to adopt and enforce such rules and regulations for the government of the institutions, its agents and employees and the inmates confined therein as they may deem just and proper; to provide for the employment of inmates of the State Prison as prescribed by law and to maintain and operate a State farm and prison camps in which inmates may be quartered and worked.

To have charge of all construction work, enlargements and permanent improvements; to purchase necessary supplies, equipment and materials; to carry out the purpose of the law, to make the State Prison self-supporting.

CHAIRMAN OF BOARD. The Board may allow its chairman a salary in lieu of per diem and mileage, and confer such authority, and impose such duties upon him in reference to the management of the institution as it may think proper; to act as member of Advisory Board of Control.

TREASURER. The State Treasurer is the *ex officio* Treasurer of the State Prison and State Hospital for the Dangerous Insane, and as such shall keep all accounts of the institutions and shall pay out all moneys upon the warrant of the respective chief officers, countersigned by the chairman of the Board of Directors. He shall perform his duties under such regulations as prescribed by the Board with the approval of the Governor. Canceled vouchers to be deposited with the institutions annually.

INSPECTION. Construction of State camps must be in accordance with plans approved by the State Highway Commission and the State Board of Health. The sanitary and hygienic care of prisoners shall be under the direction, supervision and regulation of the State Board of Health, same applying to the State Prison, State farm, and State and county camps, and such regulations regarding clothes, bedding, tableware and bathing for the prisoners shall be carried out by the Board of Directors.

REPORTS. Board of Directors shall make to the Governor or the Budget Bureau, a full report of the financial and physical condition of the State Prison on the first day of July of each year and at such other times as the Governor or director of the budget may require.

OBJECT AND PURPOSE. To execute the law with reference to persons confined in the State Prison; to provide for their maintenance, care, and for their moral betterment as far as practicable; to regulate their conduct, employment and activities; to direct the classification of all prisoners according to the provisions of the law.

Established	1869
Assets in excess of liabilities	$2,117,657.26
Acreage	7,300
Inmates	1,500
Employees	233
Earnings in excess of expenditures (year ending June 30, 1926)	$ 40,000.00

STATE BUREAU OF IDENTIFICATION
Ch. 228, P. L. 1925
H. H. HONEYCUTT, *Director*, Raleigh

Title—Director.

Appointment—A Deputy Warden of the State Prison is designated Director by the Act.

Qualification—Finger-print expert and familiar with other means of identifying criminals.

Term—Not specified.

Function

To receive and collect police information; to assist in locating, identifying, and keeping records of criminals in this State and from other States; to compile, classify and publish all such information for the use of all officials of the State requiring it; to conduct surveys; and to determine the source of crime.

Every chief of police and sheriff in the State is required to furnish the bureau, on special forms supplied by the bureau, the finger prints of every person convicted of a felony and of any person arrested for a crime when deemed advisable by any chief of police or sheriff, and to advise the bureau of the final disposition of all persons finger-printed.

The bureau is maintained by the Board of Trustees of the penitentiary out of the general appropriation to the State Prison.

The director is required to use the Henry system; to submit to the Governor in his annual report for each year ending February 1, a full account of all funds received and expended; and to provide a seal for the bureau.

Historical Note

Created by act of the General Assembly of 1925.

COMMISSIONER OF PARDONS

Ch. 29, P. L. 1925.

H HOYLE SINK, *Commissioner of Pardons*, Raleigh

Appointment—By the Governor.

Term—At the will of the Governor.

Salary—Maximum of $4,000; maximum of $200 per year for traveling expenses.

Function

To assist the Governor in connection with all applications for executive clemency; to perform any other duties assigned by the Governor; to perform his duties under rules and regulations to be prescribed by the Governor; to be assisted by a stenographer at a maximum salary of $150 per month.

Historical Note

Created by an act of the General Assembly of 1925.

EDUCATIONAL COMMISSION
Ch. 203, P. L. 1925

Composition—Twelve members.

Personnel—J. O. Carr, *Chairman*, Wilmington; J. Y. Joyner, *Executive Secretary*, Raleigh; Mrs. E. L. McKee, Sylva; J. K. Norfleet, Winston-Salem; Mrs. J. A. Brown, Chadbourn; C. E. Teague, Sanford; Mrs. J. G. Fearing, Elizabeth City; T. W. Andrews, High Point; S. C. Lattimore, Shelby; E. W. Pharr, Charlotte; Stanley Winborne, Murfreesboro; Nathan O'Berry, Goldsboro.

Appointment—By Governor.

Term—Discretion of the Governor.

Compensation—Expenses, not exceeding $6 per day.

Function

To make a complete survey of the systems of common school and higher education in the State; to investigate the State equalizing fund and its administration in the counties; to investigate the method of determining the cost of the various phases of the operation of the State educational system; to collect and disseminate educational data on the costs and results of the State's educational activities; to perform any other duty which seems proper in reference to the relation of the public to the present educational system; to file a report with the Governor when the purposes of the act shall have been fulfilled.

The commission elects its own officers—a chairman and a secretary.

Historical Note

Created by act of the General Assembly of 1925.

THE EQUALIZING FUND COMMISSION
Sec. 2a, Ch. 275, P. L. 1925

Composition—Five members.

Personnel—E. C. Brooks, Raleigh; C. A. Webb, Asheville; W. C. Femister, Newton; Mrs. W. J. Jones, Salemburg; E. D. Broadhurst, Greensboro.

Appointment—By Governor within 30 days after ratification of the act.

Compensation—$10 per day for not more than 10 days per year.

Function

To apportion the remainder of the equalizing fund for the years 1925-26, 1926-27 (in excess of the amount of the fund, in 1924, which fund shall be apportioned on the same basis as in 1924) so as to result in a more equalized distribution of the fund, provided that no county shall receive any of the remainder until it has levied a tax of at least 44 cents on the $100 of its present valuation for salaries of teachers, principals, and superintendents.

The Commission shall meet and organize within ten days after appointment and shall certify, on or before the first day of June each year, its decision and findings to the State Superintendent of Public Instruction, who shall put the same into effect.

STATE BOARD OF VOCATIONAL EDUCATION
Art. 4, Ch. 95, C. S.; Ch. 172, P. L. 1921

Composition (4)—Superintendent of Public Instruction ex officio chairman and executive officer; three members to represent Agriculture, Home Economics, Trades and Industries, respectively.

Personnel—Leonard Tufts, Pinehurst—Agriculture; W. F. Carr, Durham—Trades and Industries; Miss Mary Arrington, Rocky Mount—Home Economics.

Appointment—By Governor.

Term—Four years.

Compensation—Not specified.

Function

To administer the Federal and State laws in relation to vocational education and funds appropriated therefor; to formulate plans for promotion of vocational education in the public school system and to provide for preparation of teachers in such subjects; to make studies and investigations relating to such subjects and to publish results of same; to promote and aid in establishing by local communities of schools, departments or classes giving instruction in such subjects; to prescribe qualification of teachers, etc., and to provide for certification of such teachers; to coöperate in the maintenance of classes supported or controlled by the public for the preparation of teachers, etc., or to maintain own classes; to coöperate with county boards; to enforce provisions of the law through the State Superintendent of Public Instruction; and to report annually to the Governor the conditions of vocational education in the State, schools benefited and detailed statement of funds received from both State and Federal governments—State appropriation to match Federal appropriation.

To provide for maintenance and vocational rehabilitation and the return to civil employment of persons injured in industry or otherwise, who go into training under provisions of the Federal Industrial Rehabilitation Act, by coöperating with Federal agencies; to administer Federal and State appropriations; to pay not more than $10 for twenty weeks to a single person; to keep record of expenditures and report annually to Governor. ($15,000 appropriated by State.)

The State Treasurer is directed to act as custodian of the funds of the Board and to receive and disburse same.

Historical Note

Created by act of the General Assembly of 1919.

COLLEGE COMMISSION
(For Regulation of Degrees)

Art. 5, Ch. 95, C. S.

Composition (5)—Superintendent of Public Instruction, Chairman *ex officio;* four other members appointed by Governor.

Term—Five years.
Compensation—Not specified.

Function

To prescribe and enforce rules and statutes regulating the conferring of degrees by educational institutions; to investigate financial conditions, equipment and facilities and standards of educational institutions applying for authority to confer degrees, and to grant licenses to same when requirements are met; to revoke licenses in failure to maintain standards, subject to right of review by a judge of the Superior Court.

The Commission has full authority to send an expert to any institution for purpose of examining same. The authority and power of commission are applicable only to educational institutions created or established after enactment of this law, viz., 1919.

STATE COMMITTEE ON HIGH SCHOOL TEXT-BOOKS

Art. 42, Ch. 95, C. S.; Art. 31, Ch. 136, P. L. 1923.

Composition—Five members.

Personnel—R. H. Latham, *chairman*, Winston-Salem; John C. Lockhart, *secretary*, Raleigh; Guy B. Phillips, Salisbury; Edgar W. Knight, Chapel Hill; A. J. Hutchins, Canton.

Appointment—By the Governor and the Superintendent of Public Instruction.

Term—Five years.

Qualifications—None specified.

Compensation—Necessary expenses.

Function

To examine contents, quality and price of each book submitted by the publisher to determine whether or not same is suitable for use in the public high schools; to submit to the Superintendent of Public Instruction every five years a report of its findings with recommendations as to books to be placed on the State approved list, which list constitutes the State adopted list for a period of five years when approved by the State Board of Education. The county is the unit of adoption of High School Textbooks, such adoptions being made from State approved list to be used for a period of five years except for science and history which may be adopted for two years.

Historical Note

Created by act of the General Assembly of 1919, and changed by Chapter 136, Public Laws of 1923.

TEXTBOOK COMMISSION
Ch. 145, P. L. 1921

Composition—Seven members.

Personnel—Supt. Thos. R. Foust, *Chairman*, Greensboro; Supt. T. Wingate Andrews, High Point; Supt. N. F. Steppe, Marion; Supt. C. S. Warren, Lenoir; Miss Jane Sullivan, Asheville; Miss Mary Graham, Charlotte; Miss Celeste Henkel, Statesville.

Appointment—By Governor and Superintendent of Public Instruction.

Term—Five years.

Qualification—Active teacher, supervisor, principal or superintendent.

Compensation—$200 and expenses for each member, and $225 and expenses for chairman for first year; $5 per diem and expenses thereafter.

Function

To prepare subject to the approval of the Superintendent of Public Instruction, an outline course of study indicating subjects to be taught in the elementary schools of the State, outlining basal and supplementary books on each subject used in each grade; to prepare multiple lists of basal books selected in conformity with the outline course of study, from which lists the State Board of Education selects and adopts the basal books for each subject; and upon adoption the State Board may contract with publisher to furnish books for a period of five years or less; to furnish new lists to Board when requested or to recommend substitutions, with approval of State Superintendent, where adopted books prove unsatisfactory.

To elect chairman and secretary and adopt rules and regulations governing its work, subject to approval of State Superintendent, same to be published in the daily papers and copy sent to all publishers submitting bids and samples of books for adoption; to meet on call of State Board of Education or independently.

Subjects to be selected are divided into two classes:

1. Major subjects—readers, arithmetics, language and grammar, history and geography.

2. Minor subjects—all other books on all other subjects. Supplementary books in the outline course of study are for guidance of county and city boards of education which are authorized to adopt necessary supplementary books, but such shall not replace adopted basal books.

OBJECT. To prepare, subject to the approval of the Superintendent of Public Instruction, an outline course of study covering subjects to be taught in the elementary public schools; and to submit to the State Board of Education multiple lists of approved books selected in conformity with the outline course of study for its guidance in adopting the books to be used.

Historical Note

Created by act of the General Assembly of 1921.

TRANSPORTATION ADVISORY COMMISSION
Ch. 266, P. L. 1921.

Composition—Twelve members.

Personnel—J. A. Taylor, Wilmington; E. K. Bishop, New Bern; J. A. Gray, Winston-Salem; J. W. House, Wilson; George Marsh, Raleigh; T. J. Purdee, Fayetteville; M. O. Blount, Bethel; D. M. Ausley, Statesville; Fred Kent, Asheville; J. L. Spencer, Charlotte; T. A. Finch, Thomasville; C. G. Yates, Greensboro.

Appointment—By Governor, who also appoints the chairman and vice-chairman.

Term—Not specified.
Qualification—Experience in business and shipping.
Compensation—$4 per day and mileage.

Function

To adopt rules for its administration; to make a complete and thorough survey of freight rates to, from and within North Carolina to ascertain if there is discrimination against receivers and shippers of freight; to determine the probable causes thereof and to recommend a remedy; to ascertain if the State can aid in the development of water transportation to and from North Carolina ports in coöperation with the Federal government or otherwise. To this end it may take testimony, hold meetings within or without the State, and incur necessary expenses not exceeding $25,000 in the succeeding biennium.

To report to the Governor from time to time and to make recommendations as to legislative action or the institution of proceedings by the Corporation Commission before the Interstate Commerce Commission, the Shipping Board or in the courts in respect to freight rates.

Historical Note

Created by act of the General Assembly of 1925.

STATE SINKING FUND COMMISSION
Chapter 62, P. L. 1925

Composition—Governor, chairman; Auditor, Secretary; State Treasurer, Treasurer—*ex officio* members.

Term—Four years.

Function

It is the duty of the commission to see that the provisions of all sinking fund laws are complied with and to provide for the custody, investment and application of all sinking funds. The commission and its members may call upon the Attorney General for legal advice as to their duties, powers and responsibilities hereunder.

The commission shall adopt rules for its organization and government and the conduct of its affairs. The clerks in the office of the Governor, Auditor and Treasurer may be called upon to assist the commission.

The State Treasurer is ex officio treasurer of the commission and the custodian of the sinking fund and the investments thereof. He and the sureties upon his official bond as State Treasurer are liable for any breach of faithful performance of his duties as treasurer of the commission as well as his duties as State Treasurer, and his official bond must comply with this requirement.

The moneys in the sinking fund cannot be loaned to any department of the State but must be invested in:

(a) Bonds of the United States;

(b) Bonds or notes of the State of North Carolina;

(c) Bonds of any other state whose faith and credit are pledged to the payment of the principal and interest thereof;

(d) Bonds of any county in North Carolina having a population of fifteen thousand or more, any city in North Carolina having a population of four thousand or more and any school district in North Carolina having a population of two thousand five hundred or more, provided such bonds are general obligations of the subdivision or municipality issuing the same and provided that there is no limitation of the rate of taxation for the payment of principal and interest of the bonds; such population of cities and towns is to be determined by the last preceding Federal census, that of the school districts by the commission.

Securities cannot be purchased at more than market price thereof and must not be sold for less than the market price. No securities may be purchased by the commission except bonds of the United States or bonds or notes of the State of North Carolina unless the vendor shall deliver with the securities the opinion of an attorney believed by the commission to be competent and to be recognized by investment companies as an authority upon the law of public securities, to the effect that the securities purchased are valid obligations and are securities which the commission is authorized to purchase, it being the intention of this requirement to asure the commission not only that such securities are valid and eligible for purchase under the law but that the same may not be unsalable by the commission because of doubts as to the validity thereof. The commission is empowered to appoint one or more of its members for the purpose of making purchases and sales of securities.

Historical Note

Created by the General Assembly of 1925. The Act of 1925 provides penalties and repeal or amends certain sections of chapter 188, Public Laws 1923, which created the Sinking Fund.

STATE BOARD OF ELECTIONS

Art. 3 et seq., Ch. 97, C. S.; Ch. 111, P. L. 1923

Composition—Five members.

Personnel—Walter H. Neal, *Chairman*, Laurinburg; Clarence Call, Wilkesboro; R. W. Herring, Fayetteville; T. B. Ward, Wilson; W. E. Breese, Brevard.

Appointment—By Governor.

Term—Two years.

Qualification—Not more than three of same party.

Compensation—$5 per diem and expenses.

Function

To enforce State and county election laws; to prepare and distribute to county boards, ballots, poll books, forms of returns; to order elections in accordance with law; to make recounts and to promulgate general regulations and perform such other functions as may be prescribed by law; to appoint for each county, a county board of elections, consisting of three members, whose terms of office shall be two years, not more than two of whom shall belong to the same political party, such appointments being made on the recommendation of the State Chairman of each political party but power of removal on cause rests with the State Board and such vacancies shall be filled by said board; to appoint county primary election boards; to tabulate returns, declare nominees; and such other functions as may be prescribed by law.

The Board elects its own chairman and secretary.

Historical Note

Created by act of General Assembly of 1901.

STATE BOARD OF CANVASSERS
Art. 13, Ch. 97, C. S.; Ch. 111, P. L. 1923

Composition—Five members: Governor, four members State Board of Elections, *ex officio* members.

Term—Two years.

Qualification—Members of State Board of Elections to be named and selected by said Board.

Function

To ascertain and declare from abstracts of votes cast and prepared by boards of county canvassers and submitted to the Secretary of State by clerks of the Superior Courts, the results of the elections of Governor and all State officers, justices of the Supreme Court, judges of the Superior Court, solicitors, congressmen and United States senators; to cause results to be certified to the Secretary of State; to estimate the votes cast for officers of the Executive Department from the abstracts forwarded to the Secretary of State, and publish a statement of the result of such calculation, but this statement shall be for information of the public only, and shall not have the effect to determine what candidates have been elected to office. Their election shall be ascertained and declared according to Sec. 3, Article III of the Constitution.

Historical Note

Created by act of the General Assembly of 1901.

STATE BOARD OF PENSIONS

Art. 3, Ch. 92, C. S.; Ch. 69, P. L. 1920—Extra Session; Ch. 189, P. L. 1921; Ch. 106, P. L. 1924—Extra Session; Ch. 107, P. L. 1925

Composition (3)—Governor, Attorney-General, Auditor, *ex officio* members.

Function

To examine each applicant for a pension; and to prescribe rules and regulations governing the operation of the pension law.

The Auditor is directed to appoint three reputable ex-Confederate soldiers or sons of ex-Confederate soldiers in each county who, with the Clerk of the Superior Court, shall constitute the County Board of Pensions for their county whose duty is to examine and classify applicants for relief and to certify such applicants as are passed to the Governor, and to perform such other functions as are prescribed by law. The Auditor is further directed to provide form of application, to issue warrants to clerks of the Superior Courts semi-annually, to apportion, distribute and divide the money appropriated by the State for pensions, and to issue warrants to the several pensioners pro rata in their respective grades so that the entire annual appropriation shall be paid each year to the pensioners, notwithstanding the amounts so paid may be in excess of the amounts fixed in this article for the several grades, provided the total appropriation shall not exceed $1,000,000 annually.

In addition to the appropriation made by the General Assembly, there is levied a county tax of 2 cents on each $100 of assessed value of property and 6 cents on each taxable poll. These taxes are collected by a sheriff or other tax collector, and the net proceeds are applied each year to increase pro rata the pensions of persons on the county pension roll. Such funds are disbursed pro rata by the County Commissioners.

Classes and amounts of pensions for Confederate soldiers, their widows and orphans are as follows:

1. Wounded so as to be totally incompetent............$100 per year
2. Blind widows .... 100 per year
3. Loss of leg or arm above knee or elbow............. 90 per year
4. Loss of leg or arm below knee or elbow............. 70 per year

5. Loss of one eye. Widows and all soldiers disabled
   from any cause and unfit to perform manual
   labor .... $ 60 per year

In distributing the $1,000,000 appropriation, the above amounts have been increased pro rata as follows: Classes 1 and 2 receive $150, class 3, $135; class 4, $120; class 5, $105.

In addition all ex-Confederate soldiers and sailors who have become totally blind since the war, or who have lost their sight, or both hands and feet, or one arm and one leg, in the Confederate service, or who have become paralyzed and are totally disabled by reason thereof, shall receive from the public treasury $180 a year, such moneys being paid out of the General Fund and not from the pension appropriation. Applicants for relief under this provision are certified to the Governor by the clerk of the Superior Court of the county in which such applicants reside. Such pensioners are thereupon paid monthly by the State Auditor at the rate of $15 a month.

COMMISSIONER OF THE VETERANS LOAN FUND
Ch. 155, P. L. 1925
JOHN HALL MANNING, Commissioner, Raleigh

Appointment—By Board of Advisers.

Compensation—$3,500.

Board of Advisers—Five members: Secretary of State, chairman, ex officio; Commissioner of Agriculture; Attorney General; Commissioner of Labor and Printing; State Treasurer, Treasurer, ex officio.

Function

Chapter 155, Public Laws of 1925, known as The World War Veterans Loan Act, authorizes the submission to the voters in 1926 of the question of contracting a bonded indebtedness of the State to the amount of two million dollars for the purpose of making loans to any resident of North Carolina who served honorably in the World War. The vote in November, 1926, was favorable.

The administration of the act is under the control of a Board of Advisers who appoint a Commissioner of the Veterans Loan Fund.

The Commissioner, with the approval of the Board of Advisers, may appoint assistants and appraisers. He shall cause each application for a loan to be considered and the property offered as security to be appraised. No loan shall be made unless approved by the commissioner and two members of the Board of Advisers.

Not more than one loan, which shall not exceed $3,000 nor extend for more than 20 years, shall be made to any one person. No loan shall exceed seventy-five per cent of the appraised value of the real property offered as security, and no loan for 20 years shall be made unless application is filed before January 1, 1931. The applicant shall pay in advance the expense of appraisal and shall pay all costs incurred in the investigation of his property.

All loans are repayable in not more than 20 equal annual or 40 equal semi-annual payments and bear interest at six per cent, payable semi-annually. All payments on loans shall be made to the State Treasurer who shall deposit and hold them as a separate fund to be applied to the payment of the bonds when they become due.

The cost of administering the act, including salaries, shall be paid from the difference between the interest received from the loans made hereunder (6 per cent) and the interest on the bonds of the State to be issued (not exceeding 5 per cent), provided that until such time as the income herein provided for shall become sufficient to pay the cost of administration of this act, the expense thereof shall be paid out of the general fund.

BOARD OF PUBLIC BUILDINGS AND GROUNDS

Ch. 117, C. S.; Ch. 315, P. L. 1925.

Composition (4)—Governor, Secretary of State, Treasurer, Attorney-General, *ex officio* members.

Function

To take charge of and keep in repair public buildings of State in city of Raleigh; to procure necessary furniture and equipment for General Assembly and public offices; to certify, through the Secretary of State, all accounts for labor and fuel; to assign rooms and offices where not specified by law; to authorize repair of walks, grounds and trees in and about the Capitol square; to appoint a keeper of the Capitol, a Custodian of the Administration building, and a custodian and a janitor for the State Department Building.

KEEPER OF THE CAPITOL. To have charge of janitorial work and care of trees and grounds of Capitol and Executive Mansion; to appoint and supervise all employees and laborers; to supervise all of the public lots in the city of Raleigh belonging to the State; to contract under supervision of Board for repairs to walks, convict labor to be used where practicable, and accounts for labor and material to be audited. He must execute a bond of at least $250 for the faithful discharge of his duties. The Keeper of the Capitol is also *ex officio* the State Standard Keeper in case of vacancy.

CUSTODIAN OF STATE DEPARTMENT BUILDINGS. Appointed by Board with duties similar to those of the Keeper of the Capitol.

CUSTODIAN OF ADMINISTRATION BUILDING. Appointed by the Board, with duties similar to those of the Keeper of the Capitol.

Historical Note

Created by act of General Assembly of 1871.
W. D. TERRY.................................... *Superintendent*

MUNICIPAL BOARD OF CONTROL
Art. 13, Ch. 56, C. S.

Composition (3)—Attorney-General, Chairman; Secretary of State, Secretary; Chairman Corporation Commission, *ex officio* members.

Function

To hear petitions for incorporation of municipalities; to determine if requirements of law have been fulfilled by the petitioners and that the facts stated are true; to enter orders creating territory into a town, and to provide for holding the first election of mayor and commissioners, the number to be determined by the Board.

Historical Note
Created by act of the General Assembly of 1917.

STATE STANDARD KEEPER
Art. 2, Ch. 133, C. S.
T. F. BROCKWELL, Raleigh

Title—State Standard Keeper.
Appointment—By Governor.
Term—Not specified.
Compensation—$100 per annum.

Function
To take care of the balances, weights and measures and perform the duties relating to weights and measures hitherto imposed on the Governor, and such other duties as the Governor may prescribe; to procure and furnish at prime cost, under direction of the Governor, to any of the counties upon an order from board of county commissioners, any of the standard sealed weights and measures required by law to be kept; to contract for manufacture of plain sealed weights substantially made of iron, steel or brass, as the county ordering may direct, standard yard sticks, gauge sticks, etc., dry and liquid sealed measures; to keep an account of all weights and measures delivered by him, and expenses incurred by him in the purchase of said weights and measures, subject to the inspection of the State Treasurer and the General Assembly.

Historical Note
Created by act of the General Assembly in 1867.

BOARD OF COMMISSIONERS OF NAVIGATION AND PILOTAGE
Ch. 79, P. L. 1921

Composition—Five members.

Personnel—H. C. McQueen, C. W. Worth, D. H. Scott, and J. A. Taylor, Wilmington; and Richard Dosher, Southport.

Appointment—By Governor; vacancies filled by board.

Term—Four years.

Qualification—Four to be residents of New Hanover County; none to be licensed pilots.

Function

To make and enforce rules regulating pilotage service and other matters relating to the navigation of the Cape Fear River from seven miles above Negro-Head Point downwards and out of the bar and inlets.

To appoint annually a harbor master for the Port of Wilmington; to appoint a clerk who shall record all the rules, orders and proceedings of the Board; to examine or cause to be examined applicants as pilots for Cape Fear River and bar, and to license those approved; to renew licenses annually upon payment of fee of $5, and to revoke licenses for cause; to make and enforce rules relating to pilots' apprentices; to organize pilots licensed by Board into a mutual association, each member to pay two per cent of each pilotage fee for expenses of Board, surplus to be placed in fund for benefit of widows and orphans of deceased pilots; to issue permits to run regularly as pilots of steamers plying between Wilmington and other U. S. Ports; to retire pilots and to provide compensation under suitable rules; to exercise jurisdiction over disputes as to pilotage and between pilots; to renew licenses annually upon receipt of a fee of $5.

PILOTAGE. Fees fixed by law—two classes: (1) Sea to Southport or vice versa; (2) Southport to Wilmington or vice versa. Fees are based on ship's draught, 6′ to 30′ and vary in class 1 from $10.46 to $267.66, and in class 2 from $6.46 to $163.36. The first pilot speaking a vessel is entitled to pilotage fees.

LICENSES. Two classes: (1) To Apprentices, of not more than three years service—license covers vessel not exceeding 15′ draught

Age limitations, 21-25 years; (2) Unlimited license—to those who have served at least one year under a license of the first class.

HARBOR MASTER. To keep channel-way clear; to berth vessels at appropriate docks; to collect fees ($3 to $10) from incoming vessels; to arrest violators.

OBJECT. To promote the efficiency of pilotage service and to protect and promote the commerce of the port of Wilmington and the State of North Carolina.

Historical Note

Created by act of the General Assembly of 1921.

CROP PEST COMMISSION
Art. 16, Ch. 84, C. S.

Composition (11)—Board of Agriculture *ex officio*.

Function

To prepare and publish from time to time list of dangerous crop pests, methods of extermination, repression and prevention of spread; to adopt regulations for prevention of introduction of dangerous crop pests from without the State and for governing common carriers in transporting plants liable to harbor such pests to and from the State, such regulations having the force of law; to investigate and inspect premises suspected of being infected, and where found may remove pest or have same removed by owner, costs in either case to be borne by owner.

Historical Note

Created by act of the General Assembly of 1909.

NATIONAL PARK COMMISSION OF NORTH CAROLINA
Resolutions Nos. 16 and 29, Extra Session, 1924

Composition—Eleven members: three chosen by President of the Senate; five by Speaker of the House; the present Speaker of the

House and the presidents of State College and the University, members *ex officio*.

Personnel—Mark Squires, *Chairman*, Lenoir; E. C. Brooks, *Secretary-Treasurer*, Raleigh; D. M. Buck, Bald Mountain; H. W. Chase, Chapel Hill; J. G. Dawson, Kinston; J. H. Dillard, Murphy; Plato Ebbs, Asheville; A. M. Kistler, Morganton; Frank Linney, Boone; E. S. Parker, Jr., Greensboro.

Function

To present the claims of North Carolina to the Commission appointed by the United States for the purpose of effecting the location of a National Park in the Southern Appalachian Mountains; to incur expenses not exceeding $2,500 in gathering information and data.

COMMISSION ON THE REPRODUCTION OF THE CANOVA STATUE OF WASHINGTON
Ch. 253, P. L. 1923; Ch. 303, P. L. 1925

The General Assembly of North Carolina by resolution in 1815 instructed the Governor of the State "to purchase on behalf of this State a full length statue of General Washington." Governor William Miller, under that authority, secured the services of Canova, the Roman sculptor. The statue was received in Raleigh December 24, 1821, and set up in the rotunda of the State House. In 1831 the State House was burned and the statue destroyed. The General Assembly at its next annual session held in 1831 appointed a committee, of which William Gaston was chairman, to provide for the restoration of the statue and appropriated five thousand dollars for that purpose. The services of Ball Hughes, an English sculptor, were secured; but the ruins of the statue were so complete that he was unable to reproduce it, and the matter of reproduction was, therefore, allowed to drop.

In 1908, the Secretary of the North Carolina Historical Commission learned through a former Ambassador to Austria that the original model made by Canova still existed in the Canova Museum at Possagno, Italy. Thereafter Italy, at its own expense, had a plaster replica of the statue made and presented it to the North

Carolina Historical Commission. This replica was received in 1910, and is now preserved in the North Carolina Hall of History.

The General Assembly of North Carolina, at its 1923 session, provided for a Commission on the Reproduction of the Canova Statue of Washington, of which R. D. W. Connor, Walter Woodson, and R. O. Everett were appointed members. The Commission was charged with the duty of collecting data and making recommendations relative to the reproduction of the statue. R. O. Everett made a trip to Possagno, Italy, to view the original model made by Canova, and thereafter a report of the Commission was presented to the General Assembly and ordered printed, in which report recommendations were made that the statue be reproduced. The General Assembly of North Carolina at its session in 1925 provided for the continuation of the Commission and its enlargement by the addition of W. N. Everett and Governor A. W. McLean. The Commission was authorized and directed to have reproduced in Carara marble, from the model now owned by North Carolina, the Canova Statue of Washington, and to have it set up in a suitable place in one of the buildings or on the public grounds of the State of North Carolina. The cost of the reproduction was to be provided for by private subscription.

The services of Gutzon Borglum have been secured to reproduce the statue, but the actual work is being delayed until the committee shall raise a sufficient amount by private subscription. The next General Assembly will be requested to supplement the funds received from private sources, if necessary.

BENNETT PLACE MEMORIAL COMMISSION
Ch. 77, P. L. 1923; Ch. 7, P. L. 1925.

The General Assembly of 1923 appointed a commission consisting of Bennehan Cameron (deceased), J. S. Carr (deceased), R. D. W. Connor, F. C. Brown, W. T. Bost, R. O. Everett, and D. H. Hill (deceased) to arrange for the acceptance in the name of the State from the heirs of Samuel T. Morgan of a memorial to mark the spot where the Confederate War practically ended with the surrender of the army of General Joseph E. Johnston to that of General

W. T. Sherman at the Bennett House near Durham, April 18, 1865. The memorial is a graceful double shaft situated in a park of nearly thirty-one acres of land, all of which is deeded in perpetuity to the State for use as a public park which the board of county commissioners of Durham county is authorized to maintain. The General Assembly of 1925 appointed Mrs. Benjamin N. Duke as successor to J. S. Carr, Mrs. Edward J. Parish as successor to D. H. Hill; and increased the Commission by appointing Miss Lida Carr Vaughan and Samuel Tate Morgan, Jr. The Secretary of State is the custodian of the monument and grounds.

BOARD OF MEDICAL EXAMINERS

Art. 1, Ch. 110, C. S.; Ch. 47, P. L. 1921; Ch. 44, P. L. 1921—Extra Session.

Composition—Seven members.

Personnel—Dr. Foy Roberson, Durham; Dr. Paul H. Ringer, Asheville; Dr. W. Houston Moore, Wilmington; Dr. J. W. MacConnell, Davidson; Dr. T. W. M. Long, Roanoke Rapids; Dr. W. W. Dawson, Grifton; Dr. J. K. Pepper, Charlotte.

Appointment—By North Carolina Medical Society.

Term—Six years.

Qualification—Members of Medical Society.

Compensation—$10 per diem and expenses.

Function

To meet once each year in Raleigh and at such other times and places as may be advisable, five members constituting a quorum; to determine the qualifications of applicant by examination, and to issue a license or diploma upon satisfactory proof as agreed by at least four members of Board; to grant, as conditions warrant, limited or permanent licenses without examination under provisions of the law; to rescind license upon cause; to keep records of applicants and proceedings; to prescribe such rules and regulations as are not inconsistent or in conflict with laws.

Each applicant is required to pay $15 upon application. A fee of $50 is charged if license is issued without examination. This applies to physicians coming into the State. The Board elects its own officers.

REPORTS. No reports are required, but annual reports are made to the Medical Society which publishes them in its annual volume of proceedings.

Historical Note

Created by act of General Assembly of 1858-1859.

BOARD OF CHIROPODY EXAMINERS

Art. 11, Ch. 110, C. S.

Composition—Three members.

Personnel—Dr. L. C. Weathers, Raleigh; Dr. M. P. Buetner, Wilmington; Dr. O. C. MacRae, Greensboro.

Appointment—By North Carolina Pedic Association.

Term—Three years overlapping.

Qualification—One year's practice in North Carolina.

Compensation—$4 per diem and expenses.

Function

To adopt suitable rules and regulations; to examine qualified applicants to practice chiropody upon payment of fee of $15.00 and to issue certificates upon completion of satisfactory examination and payment of additional fee of $10; to issue certificates without examination under certain conditions; to revoke or suspend certificates for cause; to keep record of its transactions and register of applicants and licensees; to hold at least one examination annually.

The Board elects its own officers, and two members constitute a quorum.

REPORTS: No reports are required.

Historical Note

Created by act of the General Assembly of 1919.

THE BOARD OF NURSE EXAMINERS OF NORTH CAROLINA
Art. 7, Ch. 110, C. S.; Ch. 87, P. L. 1925.

Composition—Two physicians, three registered nurses.

Personnel—Mary P. Laxton, *President*, Biltmore; Dorothy Conyers, *Secretary-Treasurer*, Greensboro; E. A. Kelly, Fayetteville; Oren Moore, Charlotte; R. Duval Jones, New Bern.

Appointment—One physican by North Carolina Medical Society, one by the North Carolina State Hospital Association, and three nurses by the North Carolina State Nurses' Association. The President and Secretary-Treasurer are elected by the Board from its nurse members.

Term—Three years overlapping.

Compensation—$5 per diem and expenses; the Secretary-Treasurer, $5 per diem and $300 per year.

Function

To adopt necessary rules and by-laws; to adopt and have custody of a seal; to examine qualified applicants for licenses to register as trained nurses and to practice their profession upon payment of a fee of $10, and to issue licenses upon satisfactory completion of examination; to issue licenses without examination under certain conditions; to revoke licenses for cause; to appoint three members of the Board who together with three members from the North Carolina State Hospital Association, constitutes a joint committee on standardization which advises with the Board in regard to regulations covering applicants for license, admission to examinations, and the standardization of schools of nursing in North Carolina; to fix in coöperation with the standardization board, the duties and compensation of an educational director of schools of nursing, who is appointed annually by the North Carolina State Nurses' Association and who reports annually to the Board of Nurse Examiners and to the North Carolina State Hospital Association; to meet at least annually and oftener as required by law, three members, two of whom must be nurses, constituting a quorum.

Historical Note

The Board of Examiners of Trained Nurses was created by an act of the General Assembly of 1917. The name of the board was changed to The Board of Nurse Examiners of North Carolina and certain new provisions were made by an act of the General Assembly of 1925.

BOARD OF PHARMACY

Art. 3, Ch. 110, C. S.; Ch. 57, P. L. 1921; Ch. 82, P. L. 1923

Composition—Five members.

Personnel—F. W. Hancock, *Secretary-Treasurer*, Oxford; C. P. Greyer, Morganton; E. V. Zoellner, Tarboro; Dr. I. W. Rose, Rocky Mount; J. G. Ballew, Lenoir.

Appointment—Elected by North Carolina Pharmaceutical Association and commissioned by Governor.

Term—Five years overlapping.

Qualification—Licensed pharmacists of North Carolina.

Compensation—Secretary's salary fixed by Board; other members, $10 per diem and expenses.

Function

To adopt rules and regulations not inconsistent with laws for proper discharge of duties as prescribed; to examine at least once annually qualified applicants for licenses to practice pharmacy upon payment of fee of $10, and to issue licenses after applicant has passed satisfactory examination; to issue license without examination under certain conditions; to refuse or revoke a license for cause; to renew licenses annually upon payment of a fee of $5; to keep record of its proceedings, register of all applications, licenses and renewals; and to supervise and enforce law in relation to proprietary medicines, a majority of the Board required for transaction of all business. The Board elects its own officers.

REPORTS. The Board is required to make annually to the Governor written reports of its proceedings and of its receipts and disbursements and of all persons licensed to practice as pharmacists and assistant pharmacists in this State.

Historical Note

Created by act of the General Assembly of 1905.

NORTH CAROLINA BOARD OF VETERINARY MEDICAL EXAMINERS

Art. 10, Ch. 110, C. S.

Composition—Five members.

Personnel—Dr. J. I. Neal, Sanford; Dr. R. H. Parker, Gastonia; Dr. Wm. Moore, Raleigh; Dr. M. J. Ragland, Salisbury; Dr. L. F. Koonce, Raleigh.

Appointment—By Governor.

Term—Five years overlapping.

Qualification—Member of North Carolina Veterinary Medical Association.

Compensation—$4 per diem and expenses.

Function

To adopt suitable rules and regulations; to examine qualified applicants for license to practice veterinary medicine or surgery upon payment of fee of $10 and to issue licenses upon satisfactory completion of examination; to issue temporary licenses under certain conditions and to rescind licenses for cause; to keep records of its proceedings and register of all applicants of licenses; to meet at least once a year, concurrence of majority of Board being necessary before licenses may be issued. The Board elects its own officers.

REPORTS. No reports are required.

Historical Note

Created by act of the General Assembly of 1903.

N. C. STATE BOARD OF DENTAL EXAMINERS

Art. 2, Ch. 110, C. S.

Composition—Six members.

Personnel—Dr. J. S. Betts, *President*, Greensboro; Dr. H. O. Lineberger, *Secretary-Treasurer*, Raleigh; Dr. J. H. Wheeler, Greensboro; Dr. H. L. Keith, Wilmington; Dr. W. T. Martin, Benson; Dr. J. S. Spurgeon, Hillsboro.

Appointment—Elected by North Carolina Dental Society and commissioned by Governor.

Term—Three years overlapping.

Qualification—Members of Society.

Compensation—Fixed by Board, not to exceed $10 per diem and expenses.

Function

To prescribe rules and regulations to carry out the provisions of the law; to receive and record applications and fees for licenses; to hold both written and clinical examinations upon the payment of fee of $20; to issue permanent licenses upon proof of proficiency; to issue temporary or limited licenses; to renew licenses annually upon fee of $1.00; to revoke license upon cause; to keep necessary records and reports; to turn over to State Treasurer for use of the general school fund any sum in excess of $500 remaining after meeting the per diem and other expenses. Four members of Board constitute a quorum, and agreement of quorum is necessary before applicant will be passed.

The Board elects its own officers.

REPORTS. The Board is required to submit to the Governor on or before February 25th of each year a report of its proceedings and all moneys received and disbursed by it.

Historical Note

Created by act of the General Assembly of 1915.

STATE BOARD OF ACCOUNTANCY

Ch. 116, C. S.; Ch. 261, P. L. 1925

Composition—Four members.

Personnel—George Adams, Charlotte; J. B. McCabe, Wilmington; Walter Charnley, Charlotte; Wright Dixon, Raleigh.

Appointment—By Governor.

Term—Three years.

Qualification—Resident public accountant.

Compensation—$10 per diem and traveling expenses.

Function

To formulate rules for the government of the board and for the examination of applicants for certificates; to hold examinations at least once a year; to issue certificates of qualification to such qualified applicants as may have passed an examination in "theory of accounts," "practical accounting," "auditing," "commercial law," and other related subjects; to grant certificates to those who hold certificates issued by other States; to charge a fee of $25 for each examination and certificate; to hold reëxaminations within 18 months from date of application, upon receipt of fee of $15 per applicant; to revoke certificates for cause; to require renewal of all certificates annually on July 1 and to collect a fee not exceeding $5 for each renewal; to submit to the Commissioner of Revenue the names of all persons who have qualified; to keep a complete record of all its proceedings; to elect from its members a president, vice president, and secretary-treasurer; to employ necessary legal and clerical assistance.

REPORTS. The Board is required to submit annually a full report to the Governor and also an account of all fees collected and expenses incurred to the State Treasurer.

Historical Note

Created by act of the General Assembly of 1913, which was superceded by act of General Assembly of 1925.

220 State Departments, Boards, and Commissions

STATE BOARD OF ARCHITECTURAL EXAMINATION AND REGISTRATION
Ch. 86, C. S.

Composition—Five members.

Personnel—Harry Barton, Greensboro; W. G. Rogers, Charlotte; J. B. Lynch, Wilmington; W. C. Northrup, Winston-Salem; W. H. Lord, Asheville.

Appointment—By Governor.

Term—Five years overlapping.

Qualification—Ten years practice, residents of North Carolina.

Compensation—Fixed by Board and paid from fees.

Function

To receive and register applications for examination which shall be accompanied by $25; to hold examinations of such applicants at least once each year and to issue upon satisfactory evidence as to qualification and proficiency, certificates to practice architecture in North Carolina; to reëxamine applicants at regular meeting without payment of additional fee; to refuse, revoke or suspend certificates on cause; to renew annually, for fee of $5, certificates, and to prescribe such regulations as they may deem necessary, provided they are not in conflict with laws of North Carolina.

The Board elects its own officers, and three members constitute a quorum.

Reports. No reports are required.

Historical Note

Created by act of General Assembly of 1915.

STATE BOARD OF CHIROPRACTIC EXAMINERS
Art. 6, Ch. 110, C. S.

Composition—Three members.

Personnel—Dr. C. I. Carlson, Greensboro; Dr. C. C. Cox, Durham; Dr. E. L. Cox, Winston-Salem.

State Board of Embalmers

Appointment—By Governor from list of five recommended by the North Carolina Board of Chiropractors annually.

Term—Three years overlapping.

Qualification—Resident practicing chiropractor.

Compensation—Expenses only, no salary.

Function

To adopt necessary rules and regulations; to examine qualified applicants for license to practice chiropractic upon payment of fee of $25, and to issue licenses upon completion of satisfactory examination; to issue temporary or permanent licenses without examination under certain conditions; to refuse or revoke licenses for cause; to renew licenses annually upon payment of fee of $2; to keep record of its proceedings, register of all applications, licenses and renewals; to meet annually.

The Board elects its own officers and two members constitute a quorum for the transaction of regular business, but agreement of the entire Board is necessary before a license will be issued.

REPORTS. No reports are required.

Historical Note

Created by act of the General Assembly of 1917.

STATE BOARD OF EMBALMERS
Art. 12, Ch. 110, C. S.

Composition—Three members State Board of Health; two practical embalmers.

Personnel—J. Horace Way, M.D., Waynesville; Chas. O'H. Laughinghouse, M.D., Raleigh; Thos. E. Anderson, M.D., Statesville; Wm. Vogler, Winston-Salem; J. M. Harry, Charlotte.

Appointment—Elected by State Board of Health.

Term—Five years overlapping.

Compensation—Per diem and expenses allowed, but amount is not stated.

Function

To adopt suitable rules and by-laws to regulate embalming of dead bodies; to examine qualified applicants upon payment of fee of $5 and to issue license upon satisfactory completion of examination; to renew licenses annually upon payment of fee of $2.00; to revoke licenses for cause; to keep records of its proceedings and register all applicants, licensees, and renewals; to meet at least once each year, majority of the Board constituting a quorum.

The Board elects it own officers annually.

REPORTS. No reports are required.

Historical Note

Created by act of the General Assembly of 1901.

STATE BOARD OF EXAMINERS IN OPTOMETRY
Art. 4, Ch. 110, C. S.; Ch. 42, P. L. 1923

Composition—Five members.

Personnel—Dr. W. L. Best, Greenville; Dr. Sam Levy, Charlotte; Dr. A. P. Staley, High Point; Dr. W. W. Parker, Lumberton; Dr. R. N. Walker, Winston-Salem.

Appointment—By Governor.

Term—Five years overlapping.

Qualification—Five years practice in North Carolina and membership in Optometric Society of North Carolina.

Compensation—$10 per diem and expenses.

Function

To adopt necessary rules and regulations for carrying out provisions of the law; to examine qualified applicants for licenses to practice optometry upon payment of fee of $20 and a further fee of $5 if applicant passes examination, and to issue licenses thereupon; and to renew same annually upon payment of fee of $3; to revoke licenses upon cause; to keep register of licenses; to meet at least twice annually, a majority constituting a quorum, and to keep record of all proceedings. The Board elects its own officers.

REPORTS. The Board is required to make an annual report of its proceedings to the Governor on the first Monday in January of each year which report shall contain an account of moneys received and disbursed by them.

Historical Note

Created by act of the General Assembly of 1909.

STATE BOARD OF OSTEOPATHIC EXAMINATION AND REGISTRATION

Art. 5, Ch. 110, C. S.

Composition—Five members.

Personnel—Dr. Geo. A. Griffiths, Wilmington; Dr. S. W. Hoffman, Statesville; Dr. F. R. Heine, Greensboro; Dr. T. T. Spence, Raleigh; Dr. F. C. Sharp, High Point.

Appointment—By Governor from list of ten recommendations by Society; subsequent appointments, one from list of five.

Term—Five years overlapping.

Qualification—Reputable practitioners.

Salary—$10 per diem and expenses.

Function

To adopt rules for proper discharge of its duties as prescribed; to examine qualified applicants for license to practice osteopathy, and upon payment of fee of $25 to issue certificates after applicants have passed satisfactory examination; to issue certificates without examination under certain conditions; to refuse or revoke a certificate for cause; to keep a record of its proceedings, and a register of all applicants and licenses; to meet annually in July and at such other times as may be necessary. Three members of the Board are necessary to constitute a quorum. The Board elects its own officers.

REPORTS. No reports are required.

Historical Note

Created by act of the General Assembly of 1907.

STATE BOARD OF REGISTRATION FOR ENGINEERS AND LAND SURVEYORS

Ch. 1, P. L. 1921

Composition—Five members.

Personnel—Chas. E. Waddell, Asheville; N. S. Mullican, Walnut Cove; P. H. Daggett, Chapel Hill; Gilbert C. White, Durham; Harry St. George Tucker, Raleigh.

Appointment—By Governor.

Term—Four years overlapping.

Qualification—Two from engineering faculties of University of N. C. and A. and E. College; not more than three from same branch of engineering. Resident of State, practice or teaching for ten years.

Compensation—$10 per diem and expenses.

Function

To adopt suitable by-laws and regulations necessary to carry out provisions of act; to elect annually a chairman, vice-chairman and secretary, and a quorum of three is required; to meet twice a year or oftener; to examine, upon payment of fee of $25 by engineers, or $10 by land surveyors, qualified applicants to practice engineering or land surveying and to issue a certificate of registration to those successfully completing prescribed examination; to renew certificate annually upon payment of $5; to revoke a certificate for cause; to keep a record of its proceedings and a register of all applicants and registrants; to prepare, publish and distribute annually roster of registrants.

REPORTS. The Board is required to submit to the Governor annually, before March 1st, a report of its transactions and statement of receipts and expenditures.

SECRETARY. To receive and account for all moneys derived through fees and pay them to the State Treasurer who shall keep such money in a separate fund, which shall be continued from year to year. All certified expenses of Board shall be paid out of this fund on warrant of Auditor issued on requisition signed by chairman and secretary of Board, provided, however, that at no time shall the total of warrants issued exceed the total amount of funds accumulated under this act. The secretary is required to give bond satisfactory to State Treasurer, premium to be paid out of fund.

Historical Note

Created by act of the General Assembly of 1921.

STATE LICENSING BOARD FOR CONTRACTORS

Ch. 318, P. L. 1925

Membership—Five members.

Personnel—C. D. Riggsbee, Durham; H. C. Caldwell, Asheville; U. O. Underwood, Wilmington; H. P. Grier, Jr., Statesville; F. M. Laxton, Charlotte.

Appointment—By Governor.

Term—Five years overlapping.

Qualification—At least one member to be engaged primarily in highway construction, one in construction of public utilities, and one in construction of buildings.

Compensation—Expenses.

Function

To select a chairman, a vice chairman, and a secretary-treasurer and to make by-laws and regulations; to adopt a seal; to meet in April and in October and at such special times as it may decide upon, three members constituting a quorum; to receive applications for examination, when accompanied by $20; to give examination to any acceptable applicant and to issue certificate of license for practice as a general contractor, if the result of the examination is satisfactory; to give reexamination without extra charge; to revoke licenses for cause; to hear and act on charges made against any licensed general contractor; to turn over for equal division between the engineering departments of the State University and the State College of Agriculture and Engineering all funds above the expenses of the board for the current year; to submit to the Governor by March 1 of each year a report of its transactions for the preceding year.

The secretary-treasurer shall keep a roster of all licensed general contractors in the State, a register of all applicants for license, and a record of the proceedings and finances of the board.

Historical Note

Created by act of the General Assembly of 1925.

PART V

STATE EDUCATIONAL INSTITUTIONS

1. UNIVERSITY OF NORTH CAROLINA.
2. NORTH CAROLINA STATE COLLEGE OF AGRICULTURE AND ENGINEERING.
3. NORTH CAROLINA COLLEGE FOR WOMEN.
4. CULLOWHEE STATE NORMAL SCHOOL.
5. APPALACHIAN STATE NORMAL SCHOOL.
6. EAST CAROLINA TEACHERS COLLEGE.
7. NORTH CAROLINA SCHOOL FOR THE WHITE BLIND AND FOR THE COLORED BLIND AND DEAF.
8. NORTH CAROLINA SCHOOL FOR THE DEAF (Morganton).
9. STONEWALL JACKSON MANUAL TRAINING AND INDUSTRIAL SCHOOL.
10. NORTH CAROLINA NORMAL SCHOOLS AND COLLEGES FOR THE COLORED RACE AND FOR THE CHEROKEE INDIANS OF ROBESON COUNTY.
11. FAYETTEVILLE COLORED NORMAL SCHOOL.
12. ELIZABETH CITY COLORED NORMAL SCHOOL.
13. WINSTON-SALEM TEACHERS COLLEGE AT WINSTON-SALEM.
14. NORTH CAROLINA COLLEGE FOR NEGROES.
15. CHEROKEE INDIAN NORMAL SCHOOL OF ROBESON COUNTY.
16. NEGRO AGRICULTURAL AND TECHNICAL COLLEGE OF NORTH CAROLINA.
17. CASWELL TRAINING SCHOOL.
18. EAST CAROLINA INDUSTRIAL TRAINING SCHOOL FOR BOYS.
19. STATE TRAINING SCHOOL FOR NEGRO BOYS.
20. STATE HOME AND INDUSTRIAL SCHOOL FOR GIRLS AND WOMEN.

UNIVERSITY OF NORTH CAROLINA (Chapel Hill)
Secs. 6, 7, 14, Art. IX, Constitution; Art. 1, Ch. 96, C. S.

H. W. CHASE, *President*

Board of Trustees (102)—One hundred elected by joint ballot of the General Assembly; Governor, President *ex officio;* Superintendent of Public Instruction *ex-officio;* Treasurer, Secretary, elected by Board.

Term—Eight years.

Compensation—Not stated.

Qualification—Sixteen must reside near University or capital.

Function

TRUSTEES. To meet annually at such time and place as prescribed by law or by the Governor, ten trustees constituting a quorum competent to exercise full power and authority of the Board; to remove trustees for cause; to make suitable rules and regulations for the management of the University, not inconsistent with the laws and Constitution; to appoint an executive committee from their own number with such powers as they may grant; to appoint the president, professors, tutors and other officers as they deem necessary, and to remove same for cause; to exercise such financial control and powers as prescribed by law and are vested in a body politic and corporate. The trustees may appoint special meetings as necessary, subject to statutory limits thereon.

To have charge of all construction, enlargement and permanent improvements; to purchase all supplies, materials and equipment.

GOVERNOR. To preside over meetings of Trustees or to appoint some member to act for him; to appoint special meetings of board, but no special meeting shall have power to revoke or alter any order, resolution or vote of an annual meeting; to fill temporarily vacancies in office of Secretary and Treasurer.

PRESIDENT AND FACULTY. To have the power, by and with the consent of the Trustees, of conferring all such degrees or marks of literary distinction as are usually conferred by colleges or universities; to make suitable laws and regulations for the government of the University and preservation of order and good morals therein.

REPORTS. To have annual reports made to the Governor, to be transmitted by him to the General Assembly, showing the receipts of the corporation from all sources and expenditures of same.

OBJECTS AND PURPOSES. To instruct the youth of the State in the arts, sciences, professions, and higher branches of learning; to inculcate the principles of good citizenship, and to advance knowledge and standards of education.

DEPARTMENTS. Collegiate, Applied Science, Teacher Training, Graduate, Law, Medicine, Pharmacy, Bureau of Extension.

Established	1789
Acreage	598
Value of buildings, equipment and land	$6,492,413.64
Invested funds	$2,132,575.69
Students, regular, 1925-26	2,480
Students, Summer School, 1926	2,312
Faculty, 1925-26	178
Appropriation, 1925-26	$712,500.00

Historical Note

The University of North Carolina is at Chapel Hill, Orange County, near the middle of the State. Its charter was granted in 1789; the cornerstone of the first building was laid in 1793 and students were admitted in 1795. The campus of 48 acres and about 550 acres of forest contiguous to it were given by the citizens of the county. All the buildings put up for 112 years were given by friends of the University, the first direct appropriation from the Legislature for construction being $50,000 for a chemistry building in 1905. Of the total amount received by the institution from all sources, since its foundation, one-half has been contributed by alumni and other friends.

During the Reconstruction period after the Civil War the University was stripped of its funds, and much of its property and equipment was destroyed. From 1870 to 1875 its doors were closed.

For the first eighty years of its existence, the University received no money from the State for maintenance. When it was reopened in 1875, with practically nothing but empty halls and meagre contributions from friends, the interest from the Land-Script Fund ($7,500) was turned over to it, but this was later withdrawn. In 1881, the Legislature made its first direct appropriation for maintenance, granting $5,000 to cover one year.

The annual upkeep fund voted by the State was increased little by little, but for a score of years the University was barely able to exist. Toward the end of the century, when the movement for public education was carried to a definite triumph through the efforts of Governor Aycock and others, the institution at Chapel Hill came upon better days. Maintenance appropriations were augmented until now the yearly allowance from the Legislature is $750,000 and a number of new buildings have been erected on the campus since the support of higher education was accepted as a fixed policy of the State.

The University property now consists of:

Campus 48 acres, and woodland 550 acres	$ 327,548.66
Equipment, books, apparatus, furniture, etc.	987,234.69
Buildings and faculty houses	5,177,630.49
	$6,492,413.64
Endowment, including loan funds	$2,132,575.69
Total	$8,624,989.33

The income of the University was derived from the following sources for the year 1925-26.

MAINTENANCE

State appropriation	$712,500.00
Student fees	278,049.10
Invested funds	84,256.03
Other sources	21,998.22
Total	$1,096,803.35

BUILDINGS AND IMPROVEMENTS

State appropriation	$547,102.41
Escheats	150.00
Special Funds	140,998.94
Total	$688,251.35

The University comprises the following divisions: collegiate, applied science, commerce, engineering, teachers' training, graduate, public welfare, law, medicine, pharmacy, the division of extension, the Library, and the University Press.

The University of North Carolina is a member of the Association of American Universities and is on the accredited list of Cambridge University. This means that its standing as a graduate and undergraduate institution is on a par with the highest standards of the University world. Likewise, the professional schools are recognized as of first grade by admission to membership in the associations of "A" grade professional schools of America.

Instruction was given by the University for the years 1921-1926 as follows:

	Resident Students	Summer School	Extension	Total
1921-1922	1679	1096	157	2926
1922-1923	1975	1348	401	3724
1923-1924	2307	1492	1277	5076
1924-1925	2480	1703	2092	6275
1925-1926	2505	1733	2823	7061

The parents of the students represent all professions, creeds, and parties in the State. The leading professions represented are farmers, merchants, lawyers, physicians, manufacturers, ministers, teachers. The leading churches are: Methodist, Baptist, Presbyterian, Episcopal.

Over one-half of the students earn or borrow, in part or in whole, the money for their education. Some 87 of them earn their board by waiting at the table. Few of the families from which these students come are able to stand the strain of the support of a son at college without stringent economy or even many sacrifices. About one-half of the graduates start out as teachers.

There is a splendid spirit of democracy about the institution, which opens the doors of achievement to all alike and places attainment upon merit alone. It is emphatically a place "where wealth is no prejudice and poverty is no shame."

SUMMARY

Charter granted	1789
Opened	1795
Acres of land owned	598
Value of buildings, equipment and land	$6,492,413.64
Invested funds	$2,132,575.69
Number of volumes in library, 1925	147,500.00
Number of students, 1925-26	7,013
Number of faculty, 1925-26	178
Income from State, 1925-26	$ 712,500.00
Income from students	$ 278,049.10
Invested funds	$ 84,256.03

PRESIDENTS OF THE UNIVERSITY

No president	1795-1804
Joseph Caldwell	1804-1835
David L. Swain	1835-1868
Solomon Pool	1869-1870
University closed	1870-1876
Kemp P. Battle	1876-1891
George T. Winston	1891-1896
Edwin A. Alderman	1896-1900
Francis P. Venable	1900-1914
Edward K. Graham	1914-1918
Harry W. Chase	1919-

NORTH CAROLINA STATE COLLEGE OF AGRICULTURE AND ENGINEERING (Raleigh)

Public Laws of North Carolina, Session 1923, Chapter 47

EUGENE CLYDE BROOKS, *President*

Board of Trustees (62)—Sixty, elected by joint ballot of both Houses of the General Assembly; Governor, President *ex officio;* State Superintendent of Public Instruction, *ex officio.*

Term—Eight years, overlapping.

Function

TRUSTEES. There shall be an annual meeting of the Board of Trustees in the city of Raleigh. At any of the annual meetings of the Board any number of trustees, not less than twenty, shall constitute a quorum and be competent to exercise full power and authority to transact any of the business of the corporation, and the Board or the Governor shall have power to appoint special meetings of the trustees at such time and place as, in their opinion, the interest of the corporation may require.

The Board of Trustees shall have power to vacate the appointment and remove a trustee for improper conduct, stating the cause of such removal on their journal; but this shall not be done except at an annual meeting of the Board, and there shall be present at the doing thereof at least twenty members of the Board.

Whenever any vacancy shall happen in the Board of Trustees it shall be the duty of the Secretary of the Board of Trustees to communicate to the General Assembly the existence of such vacancy, and thereupon there shall be elected by joint ballot of both Houses a suitable person to fill the same.

The trustees shall have power to make such rules and regulations for the management of the North Carolina State College of Agriculture and Engineering as they may deem necessary and expedient, not inconsistent with the constitution and laws of the State.

The trustees shall have power to appoint from their own number an executive committee of seven members, which shall meet at the call of the Governor or president of the Board of Trustees.

The trustees shall have the power of appointing a president of the North Carolina State College of Agriculture and Engineering and such professors, tutors, and other officers as to them shall appear necessary and proper, whom they may remove for misbehavior, inability, or neglect of duty.

GOVERNOR. The Governor shall preside at all the meetings of the Board at which he may be present.

PRESIDENT AND FACULTY. The Faculty of the North Carolina State College of Agriculture and Engineering, that is to say, the President and professors, by and with consent of the trustees, shall have the power of conferring all such degrees or marks of literary distinction as are usually conferred by colleges.

REPORTS. It shall be the duty of the trustees to cause annual reports to be made to the Governor, to be transmitted by him to the General Assembly, showing the receipts of the corporation from all sources, and the expenditures thereof, with the objects for which such expenditures were made.

Historical Note

The North Carolina State College of Agriculture and Engineering is the outgrowth of an idea fostered by two distinct movements, each somewhat different in its original aims. One movement, represented by a group of progressive young North Carolinians, banded together in Raleigh as the Watauga Club, sought to bring about the organization of an industrial school for the teaching of "woodwork, mining, metallurgy, and practical agriculture." The other movement, originating among the farmers in North Carolina, and actively sponsored by Colonel L. L. Polk, then editor of the *Progressive Farmer*, had as its object the establishment of an agricultural college supported by State appropriations and by the Land Script Fund of the Federal Government.

On March 7, 1885, a bill introduced by the Honorable Augustus Leazar of Iredell County looking to the founding of an "industrial school" was passed. The Board of Agriculture, by authority of this bill, accepted as the best offer for the location of the "school" the proposal of the City of Raleigh. As the idea of the "school" matured, it broadened; and with the prospect of an appropriation by Congress, supplementing the first Morrill Land Grant Act, for the support of agricultural and mechanical colleges, the "school" was, by Act of the General Assembly of 1887, changed into The North Carolina College of Agriculture and Mechanic Arts.

The newly created College was allotted the Congressional Land Script Fund and "any surplus from the Department of Agriculture." Mr. R. Stanhope Pullen, a broadminded, generous citizen of Raleigh, gave a beautiful site for the College in a tract of eighty-three acres of land adjacent to the city on the west. Appropriations by the State, which have been continued and enlarged as needs increased, were made for buildings and maintenance.

The first building was completed in 1889, and in October of that year the doors of the College were first opened for students. Seventy-two, representing thirty-seven counties, enrolled. The faculty consisted of six professors and two assistants.

Congressional appropriation for immediate college use made in the Morrill Land Grant Act of 1862 was increased by the Second Morrill Act of 1890 and by the Nelson Act of 1907. The College also receives from the Federal Government under Acts of 1887 and 1906 funds for the Agricultural Experiment Station, and under an Act of 1914 funds for Extension Work in Agriculture. Since July 1, 1925, the College receives an annual Federal appropriation under the Purnell Act. The War Department maintains at the College a Unit of the Reserve Officers' Training Corps.

Acting on the suggestion from the alumni and other friends of the College, the General Assembly in 1917 changed the name of the College from the North Carolina College of Agriculture and Mechanic Arts to North Carolina State College of Agriculture and Engineering.

During the history of the College, covering a period now approaching thirty-eight years, five presidents have directed its progress, namely:

ALEXANDER Q. HOLLADAY	1889-1899
GEORGE TAYLOE WINSTON	1899-1908
DANIEL HARVEY HILL	1908-1916
WALLACE CARL RIDDICK	1916-1923
EUGENE CLYDE BROOKS	(June) 1923-

The Organization of State College

THE SCHOOLS AND THEIR PROFESSIONAL OBJECTIVES

The College is divided into five closely related schools: (1) The School of Agriculture, (2) The School of Engineering, (3) The School of Science and Business, (4) The Textile School, and (5) The Graduate School. The courses offered in each are grouped according to definite vocational aims, and students entering will be directed first to elect a vocation.

There are thirty-six major vocations open to young men in the State, for which State College offers from four to seven years training in technical, scientific, and professional service.

PURPOSES OF THE SCHOOLS

The purpose of the School of Agriculture is threefold: (1) To secure through scientific research, experimentation, or demonstration, accurate and reliable information relating to soils, plants, and animals, and to secure from every available source reliable statistical, technical, and scientific data relating to every phase of agriculture that might be of advantage to our State; (2) to provide instruction in College for young men who desire to enter the field of general agriculture, or who wish to become professionals in agricultural education, or specialists in any field of science related to agriculture; and (3) to disseminate reliable information through publications and through extension agents, and through a wise use of this information to give instruction to the agricultural workers of the State in the scientific, experimental, and practical progress in the various lines of agriculture.

The purpose of the School of Engineering is threefold: (1) to educate men for professional service in Architectural, Chemical, Ceramic, Civil, Electrical, Highway, and Mechanical Engineering, and at the same time to equip them to participate in public affairs and to develop their capacities for intelligent leadership; (2) to aid in the development of our commerce and industry through research and experimentation, to open up our undeveloped natural resources and demonstrate their value to the people of the State; (3) to coöperate with private and municipal corporations for the purpose of improving our public utilities, and with commercial and industrial organizations through scientific research for increasing technical skill, improving the value of manufactured products, and eliminating waste.

In order to make effective these purposes, the School of Engineering is organized into five departments: Civil (including Architecture and Highway Engineering), Electrical, Mechanical, Ceramic, and Chemical Engineering, and in addition The Engineering Experiment Station and Extension Service.

The purpose of the School of Science and Business is: (1) To provide systematic instruction for young men desiring to enter managerial positions in business or industry, the technical training being secured in the Schools of Agriculture, Engineering and Textiles; (2) To train teachers of Science, of Agriculture, and of the Trades and Industries, and so to organize their technical or professional courses that the modern pedagogical principles of teaching may be applied; (3) To supply those broadening courses required of students in each of the five Schools of the College, and to supplement the technical training in Agriculture and Engineering by systematic instruction in Language, Literature, History, Citizenship, Economics, and the other Social Sciences, in order to give the young men trained for technical service a higher conception of their duties and obligations as citizens and leaders in our State and Nation; (4) To secure through economic research, reliable data pertaining to social and industrial organizations and the business of agriculture, and to collect from all available sources useful information concerning farm statistics, marketing, industrial management, and social coöperation, that this information may be available for the students and be disseminated through publications and Extension Agents in order to increase wholesome instruction in proper human relationships, that our people may learn how to coöperate as the demands for coöperation increase.

The purpose of the Textile School is: (1) To promote the textile industries of the State by giving instruction in the theory and practice of all branches of the textile industry; (2) To coöperate with the textile mills of the State in securing, through scientific research and experimentation, reliable data pertaining to the textile industry; (3) To educate men for professional service in Textile Manufacturing, Textile Design, Textile Chemistry and Dyeing, and at the same time to develop their capacities for intelligent leadership, so they may participate in public affairs; (4) To demonstrate the value of economic diversification and to aid in the development of the textile industry through research and experimentation.

The purpose of the Graduate School is to provide advanced study and research for college graduates desiring to specialize in the following subjects: Agricultural Economics, Agronomy, Animal Husbandry, Horticulture, Poultry Science, the Biological Sciences, Rural Sociology, Chemistry, Physics, Business Administration, Industrial Management, Agricultural Engineering, Chemical Engineering, Civil Engineering, Electrical Engineering, Mechanical Engineering, Textile Manufacturing, Textile Engineering, Textile Chemistry and Dyeing, and Vocational Education. In addition to the above specialization, it offers courses for those desiring to become teachers in colleges.

A six weeks Summer School is conducted at the College each year. The purpose of the Summer School is to serve farmers and farm women of the State, teachers of agriculture, extension workers, teachers of industrial arts and of industrial education, principals and teachers of high schools, especially teachers of science, and persons interested in executive and administrative positions in industry—a service State College is well equipped to render.

SUMMARY

Established	1887
Number of buildings	33
Number of acres of land	490
Value of buildings, equipment and land	$3,903,709.72
Number of students	1444
Number of teaching faculty	133
Income from State	$ 361,000.00
Income from Students	$ 154,146.47
Other income for instruction (Federal Government)	$ 41,000.00

SHORT COURSES AND CORRESPONDENCE COURSES

Summer School Enrollment	750
Short Courses and Correspondence Courses:	
In Agriculture	2171
In Engineering	489
In Science and Business	123
In Textiles	1
Total	3534

AGRICULTURAL COÖPERATIVE EXTENSION SERVICE

No. Extension Specialists	39
Income from State	$175,000.00
Income from Federal Government	$227,356.06
No. County Farm Agents (White)	76
No. County Farm Agents (Colored)	18
No. County Home Agents (White)	48
No. County Home Agents (Colored)	6

AGRICULTURAL RESEARCH

No. Research Specialists	23
Income from State Department of Agriculture	$ 60,000.00
Income from Federal Government	$ 60,000.00

NORTH CAROLINA COLLEGE FOR WOMEN (Greensboro)
Art. 4, Ch. 96, C. S.
JULIUS I. FOUST, *President*

Board of Directors (11)—Ten members; Superintendent of Public Instruction, Chairman *ex officio*.

Personnel—A. J. Conner, Rich Square; Mrs. Cameron Morrison, Charlotte; C. H. Mebane, Newton; T. D. Murphy, Asheville; J. L. Nelson, Lenoir; Joe Rosenthal, Goldsboro; Mrs. J. A. Brown, Chadbourn; Miss Easdale Shaw, Rockingham; J. D. Grimes, Washington; Mrs. W. T. Bost, Raleigh.

Appointment—State Board of Education, with consent of Senate.

Term—Six years, overlapping.
Qualification—No two from same Congressional District.

Function

BOARD OF DIRECTORS. To make rules and regulations for the government of the corporation and the admission of students, but shall not discriminate against any county in the number of students allowed it in case all applicants cannot be accommodated; each county to have representation in proportion to its white school population.

To appoint a president, professors, tutors and other officers as necessary for such terms and conditions as they may prescribe; to make such regulations for the government of the college as shall not conflict with the laws of the State; to have charge of all construction, enlargement and permanent improvements; to purchase necessary supplies, materials and equipment. Vacancies on the Board are filled by appointment by the Board of Education with the consent of the Senate.

FACULTY. To confer degrees by and with consent of the Board; to extend the influence and usefulness of the college to the persons of the State who are unable to avail themselves of its advantages as resident students, by extension courses, by lectures and by other suitable means.

REPORTS. To report biennially, before the meeting of each General Assembly to the Governor the operations of the corporation.

OBJECTS AND PURPOSE. To teach young white women all branches of knowledge essential to a liberal education; to make special provision for training in the science and art of teaching, school management and school supervision; to provide women with such training in the arts, sciences and industries as may be conducive to their self-support and community usefulness; to render to the people of the State such aid and encouragement as will tend to disseminate knowledge, foster loyalty and patriotism and promote the general welfare; to provide free tuition to those who are to teach in the schools of North Carolina or enter other fields of public service.

The chief mission of the institution lies in furnishing the public school system of the State well-equipped teachers; more than 15,000 students have been enrolled during the thirty-four years of its life.

two-thirds of whom and nine-tenths of the graduates of which become teachers in North Carolina.

Historical Note

The State Normal and Industrial College was established by an act of the General Assembly of 1891. The General Assembly of 1919 changed the name of this institution to The North Carolina College for Women. The purpose of the College, as stated in chapter 199 of the Public Laws of North Carolina, session 1919, amending the charter is as follows:

The objects of the institution shall be (1) to teach young white women all branches of knowledge recognized as essential to a liberal education, such as will familiarize them with the world's best thought and achievement and prepare them for intelligent and useful citizenship; (2) to make special provision for training in the science and art of teaching, school management, and school supervision; (3) to provide women with such training in the arts, sciences, and industries as may be conducive to their self-support and community usefulness; (4) to render to the people of the State such aid and encouragement as will tend to the dissemination of knowledge, the fostering of loyalty and patriotism, and the promotion of the general welfare. Tuition shall be free, upon such conditions as may be prescribed by the Board of Directors, to those who signify their intention to teach in the schools of North Carolina; and also, in the discretion of said board, to those who signify their intention to enter other fields of public service.

. . . That it shall be the duty of the faculty of the North Carolina College for Women to extend its influence and usefulness as far as possible to the persons of the State who are unable to avail themselves of its advantages as resident students, by extension courses, by lectures, and by such other means as may seem to them most effective.

In 1892 the institution began with $30,000 donated by the city of Greensboro; ten acres of land, the gift of R. S. Pullen, R. T. Gray, E. P. Wharton, and others; and an annual appropriation of $10,000 from the State. In addition to the State appropriation and tuition fees, the institution received during the first few years about $3,000 annually from the Peabody Fund and for three years received $2,500 annually from the General Education Board. It also received about $11,000 from the faculty and students, a small amount from Mr. George Foster Peabody, and a library building from Andrew Carnegie. The plant is now worth about $5,800,000 according to the audited reports of state experts; the annual State appropriation is $425,000 and the loan, fellowship and scholarship funds received from various sources in the State and out of it now amount to $62,833.70. The faculty numbers 168. There have been enrolled during the present session (1925-26,) 1,668 students, and during the summer session (1926) 1,909 students; total 3,769, including extension students.

The chief mission of the institution lies in furnishing the public school system of the State well-equipped teachers who are capable of rendering the State intelligent and useful service. It provides regular degree courses, whose admission requirements, curricula of instruction, and standards of scholarship are in keeping with the requirements of our best Southern colleges for men and women.

Special industrial and commercial courses are open to those who do not have free tuition and are not under contract to teach. Provision is also made for teachers who may wish to take brief courses in pedagogy and in the subjects taught in the public schools. For those who cannot remain longer, a two-year course is offered. For various reasons a number of ambitious teachers are not able to avail themselves of the two-year course, and to meet the demands of these a regular summer session has been inaugurated. The advantages of the institution are thus open to every worthy young white woman who has availed herself of the opportunities offered in the public schools of the State.

The patronage of the institution has justified the wisdom of the founders. During the thirty-four years of its life, beginning October, 1892, and closing with the session of June, 1926, there have been enrolled more than 15,000 young women as students. These students have come from all of the 100 counties of the State, and in their political and religious faith, their financial condition, their professional and social life, their intellectual ability and previous educational opportunities, are representative of the people of North Carolina. Of the more than 15,000 young women who have sought the help and strength thus provided, more than 80 per cent received their training in the rural public schools, one-third defrayed their own expenses, and two-thirds, according to their own written statement would not have attended any other North Carolina college. In brief, one of the strongest forces of the college, and a prime source of its usefulness, has been the representative character of its patronage. This coming together of all classes from all sections of the State necessarily creates an atmosphere of wholesome democracy and equal opportunity. The spirit of the State College for Women is, therefore, what the spirit of every state college should be, and, as a result, its representatives acquire that larger sympathy, that breadth of vision, and that intelligent insight into the needs of their State that no textbooks or lectures or mere academic training can ever hope to give.

Some indication of the serviceableness of the college is suggested by what has been said of the scope and character of its patronage. It has, since its establishment, been an open door of opportunity for the white women of North Carolina. Through it the State has added to its resources over 15,000 educated women, who have taught lessons of patriotism and right living to at least 650,000 North Carolina children. Two-thirds of all the students enrolled and nine-tenths of all who graduate become teachers in North Carolina. No large movement for the uplift of the State has failed to have support from its faculty and students, and today there is not a county in the State where representatives of the college are not to be found actively engaged in public service.

SUMMER SESSION

The special purpose of the North Carolina College for Women in organizing the Summer Session was to offer the advantages of its instruction to those women in the State whose occupation during other months of the year prevents their attendance upon the regular session. In the selection and arrangement of its summer courses the college has in view the needs of the following classes:

First. Teachers wishing special work in the principles and methods of teaching (Primary, Grammar, and High School), with opportunities for practice and observation work under experienced supervisors.

Second. Teachers desiring advanced or collegiate courses in Philosophy, Science, Psychology, and the History of Education.

Third. Teachers of special subjects, such as Domestic Science, Vocal Music, Drawing, and Manual Arts.

Fourth. High school teachers who desire advanced or extra work along the line of their specialties with free use of good department libraries and well-equipped laboratories.

Fifth. College students who wish to earn advanced credit or to remove conditions.

Sixth. Students preparing for college.

Seventh. Mothers, wives, and home-makers who feel the need of practical help in such subjects as food and food values, cookery, kitchen conveniences, home nursing, sanitation, and household decoration.

SUMMARY OF ENROLLMENT DURING THE SESSION 1925-1926

Enrolled during the regular session 1668
Enrolled during the summer session 1909

Total number taught at the college during the session 1925-26 3577

SUMMARY

Established	1891
Buildings (including 7 faculty residences)	40
Acreage	350
Value	$5,800,000
Students, regular session	1668
Students, Summer School	1909
Faculty (including officers, physicians and clerks)	168
Appropriation, 1925-1926	$ 425,000

CULLOWHEE STATE NORMAL SCHOOL (Cullowhee)
Art. 5, Ch. 96, C. S.; Ch. 61, P. L. 1921; Ch. 270, P. L. 1925
H. T. HUNTER, *President*

Board of Trustees—Nine members.

Personnel—Reuben Robertson, Canton; Mrs. Giles Cover, Andrews; J. E. Coburn, Bryson City; T. H. Shipman, Brevard; Mrs. J. W. Pless, Sr., Marion; Alex Moore, Franklin; Dr. J. N. Hill, Murphy; Don Elias, Asheville.

Appointment—By Governor and Senate.

Term—Four years.

Qualifications—None specified.

Compensation—Actual expenses.

Function of School

Section 8 of the new charter for Cullowhee states the purpose of the school as follows:

"That the central purpose of the Cullowhee State Normal School shall be to prepare teachers for the public schools of North Carolina. To that end the President shall prepare courses of study, subject to the approval of the State Superintendent of Public Instruction. It shall be the duty of the State Superintendent to visit the Cullowhee State Normal School from time to time, and to advise with the President about standards, equipment and organization, to the end that a normal school of high grade shall be maintained. The standards shall not be lower, in the main, than the average standard of normal schools of like rank in the United States."

Cullowhee is thus committed in its charter to the training of teachers as its *central* purpose. At present, it is devoting its energies to the training of elementary teachers. It is possible that, a little later, it may undertake to prepare teachers for the high schools as well as for the elementary schools. But, with the present limitations as to plant, it is not thought that any considerable extension of the program could be justified.

The Board of Trustees meets annually, elects its own officers, holds the property of the school in trust for the State, selects the President and fixes his salary, and, upon recommendation of the President, elects all teachers and employees and fixes their duties, tenure of office, and salaries.

Reports—The Secretary of the Board (President of the School) shall submit annually a detailed report of the school for the preceding year to the Board and to the State Superintendent of Public Instruction.

For a quarter of a century The Cullowhee Normal was a four-year high school, and in addition offered certain academic and educational courses. Up to 1923-24, the high school students constituted a majority of the student body. The past three years have witnessed the elimination of the high school department, so that after 1927, there will be no high school students under the control of the Normal at Cullowhee. The school will, therefore, be free to devote its energies and its resources to the training of teachers. The authorities at Cullowhee feel that the legislative appropriation to Cullowhee State Normal School was made solely for the purpose of guaranteeing more and better teachers for the Public Schools of North Carolina.

SUMMARY

Founded	1889
Buildings—For school purposes	5
Buildings—Faculty residences, etc.	6
Acreage	385
Instructors	20
Normal Students, Regular Session	157
Normal Students, Summer	388
Value of Plant	$600,000
Annual Appropriation for Maintenance	$ 50,000

APPALACHIAN STATE NORMAL SCHOOL (Boone)

Art. 8, Ch. 96, C. S.; Ch. 61, P. L. 1921; Ch. 204, Priv. Laws, 1925

B. B. DOUGHERTY, *President*

Board of Trustees—Nine members.

Personnel—J. M. Barnhardt, Lenoir; W. C. Newland, Lenoir; Eugene Transou, Sparta; G. H. Geitner, Hickory; T. C. Bowie, Jefferson; T. H. Coffey, Blowing Rock; Miss Celeste Henkle, Statesville; H. H. Sullivan, Asheville.

Appointment—By Governor with confirmation of the Senate.

Term—Four years overlapping.

Compensation—Expenses only.

Function

To give a two-year normal college course based upon high school graduation to teachers of elementary schools in North Carolina.

SUMMARY

Established	1903
Buildings	16
Acreage	435
Value of buildings and equipment	$730,500
Value of land	$ 81,000
Students	1,496
Faculty	22
Appropriation, 1926-27	$ 50,000

EAST CAROLINA TEACHERS COLLEGE (Greenville)

Art. 9. Ch. 96, C. S.; Ch. 68, P. L. 1920—Extra Session; Ch. 27, P. L. 1921, Extra Session; Ch. 306, P. L. 1925.

ROBERT H. WRIGHT, *President*

Board of Trustees (10)—Nine members appointed by the Governor; Superintendent of Public Instruction, chairman *ex officio*.

Personnel—F. C. Harding, Greenville; L. W. Tucker, Greenville; D. S. Boyken, Wilson; Mrs. H. G. Connor, Jr., Wilson; J. S. Hargett, Trenton; J. L. Griffin, Pittsboro; H. C. Bridges, Tarboro; Wayne Mitchell, Kinston.

Term—Four years.

Function

To prescribe course of study, laying emphasis on subjects taught in public schools of the State, and on the art and science of teaching; to waive tuition charges to those who agree to teach; to make no rules that discriminate against one county in favor of another in the admission of pupils into said school; to present diplomas of graduation and certificates of proficiency upon the recommendation of the faculty, and to confer degrees.

To have charge of all construction, enlargement and permanent repairs; to purchase necessary supplies, material and equipment.

REPORTS. The trustees report biennially to the Governor before the meeting of each General Assembly, the operation, condition and needs of the school.

Historical Note

East Carolina Teachers College was established by act of the General Assembly of 1907. The school is located at Greenville. The site contains 91 acres of land, a large part of which is a natural forest.

Twenty-one buildings have been erected: five dormitories with a capacity for 820 students; an administration building containing the offices, auditorium, and class rooms; a building for the kitchen and dining-room (this building contains store rooms for supplies and a refrigerating plant); an infirmary, a building containing the power plant and laundry, an eight-room model school and a residence for the president, a library, auxiliary power plant, four residences for the faculty, and a social-religious building.

The buildings and equipment are modern in every sense and are valued at $2,500,000. The town of Greenville and county of Pitt voted $100,000 in bonds for this school, and the State has made an appropriation of $1,954,325.57 for buildings and equipment. These buildings have not yet been thoroughly equipped, but enough equipment has been installed to enable the school to do efficient work. The equipment installed is of the best type procurable.

Section 5864 of the charter reads: "That the said college shall be maintained by the State for the purpose of giving to young white men and women such education and training as shall fit and qualify them to teach in the public schools of North Carolina."

This clearly sets forth the purpose of the college. To those students who agree to teach there is no charge for tuition. Practically all of the students sign this agreement. This shows that the management is adhering to the purpose of the college as stated in its charter.

The school was first opened for students on October 5, 1909. During the past seventeen years, including the summer terms, there have been enrolled 11,743 students. Number of graduates, 1909 to 1926, 1,391.

SUMMARY

Founded	1907
Number of buildings	21
Number of acres of land	91

Value of buildings and grounds $2,500,000
Number of students, 1909-1926 11,743
Annual appropriation (1926-27) .... $ 160,000
Number of graduates 1,391

PRESIDENT

Robert H. Wright 1907-

NORTH CAROLINA SCHOOL FOR THE WHITE BLIND AND FOR THE COLORED BLIND AND DEAF

Art. 10, Ch. 96, C. S.; Chs. 120, 306, P. L. 1925

G. E. LINEBERRY, *Superintendent*, Raleigh

Board of Directors—Eleven members: State Treasurer, Treasurer *ex officio*.

Personnel—R. L. McMillan, Raleigh; C. M. Wilson, Wilsons Mills; J. R. Baggett, Lillington; W. N. Keener, Durham; R. H. Crichton, Lumberton; J. T. Alderman, Henderson; A. L. McNeill, Sanford; J. A. Oates, Fayetteville; Dr. W. A. Rogers, Franklin; Miss Beatrice Cobb, Morganton; K. M. Barnes, Lumberton.

Appointment—By Governor with consent of Senate.

Term—Four years.

Compensation—Traveling expenses.

Function

The trustees make by-laws regulating the government of the institution; they elect a president, executive committee, superintendent and other officers and fix their compensation; they erect necessary buildings, make improvements, regulate admission of pupils from this and other states, and confer upon the recommendation of the superintendent and faculty such degrees or marks of literary distinction as may be necessary to encourage merit; they meet at stated times and also at such other times as may be necessary.

The treasurer reports to the Board showing receipts, expenditures and balance.

School for the Blind and the Deaf   251

The superintendent has charge of the institution in all of its departments and performs such duties as are incumbent upon such an officer; he employs all employees and fixes their compensation, subject to the approval of the Board; his term of office is three years; he is secretary *ex officio* of the Board of Trustees.

BRANCHES OF THE INSTITUTION

The main department cares for all white blind children of the State. It is located in West Raleigh at the end of Ashe Avenue, next to Pullen Park, and consists of 16 buildings (not including 6 farm buildings) on a plot of 85 acres. Value of buildings and equipment is placed at $950,000; value of land at $80,000. There are at present 142 students and a faculty of 25. This department has a library of 1,900 volumes in ink print and 5,600 in tactile print.

The colored department is situated in East Raleigh. It has four buildings valued at $75,000; 172 students and a faculty of 18. It has a library of 500 volumes in ink print and 1,700 volumes in tactile print.

The white department was founded in January 12, 1845, on Caswell Square in Raleigh, but in 1923 buildings on the new site were completed and the school was moved. The colored department was founded in 1869 on its present location.

Both the white and colored departments operate a kindergarten and a standard school through the high school courses. In addition it gives courses in music, fancy work and sewing, broom and mattress making and piano tuning, shoemaking, carpentry and agriculture.

NAMES AND TERMS OF SERVICE OF ALL PRINCIPALS

W. D. Cooke	1845-1860
Wiley J. Palmer	1860-1869
John Nichols	1869-1871
S. F. Tomlinson	1871-1873

JOHN NICHOLS	1873-1877
HEZEKIAH A. GUDGER	1877-1883
WILLIAM J. YOUNG	1883-1896
FREDERICK R. PLACE, June 1896-September	1896
JOHN E. RAY	1896-1918
JOHN T. ALDERMAN, January, 1918-August	1918
G. E. LINEBERRY	1918-

NORTH CAROLINA SCHOOL FOR THE DEAF (Morganton)
Art. 11, Ch. 96, C. S.; Chs. 120, 306, P. L. 1925
E. McK. GOODWIN, *Superintendent*
MISS ENFIELD JOINER, *Principal*

Board of Directors—Seven members; State Treasurer, Treasurer *ex officio*.

Personnel—Dr. Howard Rondthaler, Winston-Salem; W. W. Neal, Marion; W. C. Dowd, Sr., Charlotte; Mrs. I. P. Jeter, Morganton; J. F. Barrett, Charlotte; Dr. James Morrell, Falkland; A. A. Shuford, Jr., Hickory.

Appointment—By Governor with consent of Senate.

Term—Four years.

Qualification—Not more than two shall be from same county.

Function

To make suitable by-laws for the proper management of the school and its officers; to conduct school on self-sustaining basis as far as possible; to appoint a president and an executive committee whose terms shall be for two years; to elect a superintendent and other officers, teachers and agents as deemed necessary, and fix their compensation, to fix charges and prescribe rules whereby non-resident deaf children may be admitted; to provide for the instruction of all pupils in courses of study as prescribed by law for public schools, and in such other branches as may be of especial benefit to the deaf.

To have charge of all construction, permanent improvements, and repairs; to purchase necessary supplies, materials, and equipment.

SUPERINTENDENT: Term of three years, ex officio secretary of the Board. Teacher of knowledge, skill and ability in his profession and experience in the management and instruction of the deaf; chief executive officer; to devote whole time to supervision of the institution; to see that pupils are instructed in various branches of learning and industrial pursuits as prescribed by law and board; to recommend to Board teachers and subordinate officers.

BRANCHES: 1. Literary Department, Methods—(1) Oral; (2) Manual.

2. Vocational and Industrial Departments.

Boys: Farming and Gardening, Woodwork and Carpentry, Printing, Shoemaking and Tailoring.

Girls: General Domestic work, including cooking, plain sewing and dressmaking.

INSPECTIONS: State Board of Charities and Public Welfare.

REPORTS: None specified.

OBJECT AND PURPOSE: "To receive into the school for purpose of education all white deaf children resident of the State, not of confirmed immoral character nor imbecile or unsound in mind or incapacitated by physical infirmity for useful instruction who are between the ages of seven and twenty-one years." Only bona fide residents of two years standing eligible for free tuition and maintenance.

Established	1894
Buildings	5
Acreage	327
Value of buildings and equipment	$1,060,000
Value of land	$ 90,000
Students	310
Teachers	38
Appropriation, 1926-1927	$ 130,000

STONEWALL JACKSON MANUAL TRAINING AND INDUSTRIAL SCHOOL (Concord)

Art. 1, Ch. 121, C. S.; Chs. 120, 306, P. L. 1925.

CHARLES E. BOGER, *Superintendent*

Board of Trustees—Eleven.

Personnel—Mrs. I. W. Faison, Charlotte; Mrs. Cameron Morrison, Charlotte; Mrs. W. N. Reynolds, Winston-Salem; Miss Easdale Shaw, Rockingham; Miss Katherine McD. Robinson, Fayetteville; J. S. Efird, Albemarle; C. A. Cannon, Concord; D. B. Coltrane, Concord; Herman Cone, Greensboro; J. P. Cook, Concord; P. C. Whitlock, Charlotte.

Appointment—By Governor.

Term—Four years.

Compensation—Expenses.

Function

To have management and control of school; to employ superintendent and other assistants, prescribe their duties and fix their salaries; to establish and conduct such workshops, agricultural, horticultural and other pursuits as they may deem expedient so as to keep regularly at work all able-bodied inmates; to make suitable rules and regulations necessary to the proper government of the school; to receive gifts, donations, etc.; to secure homes for inmates.

To have charge of all construction, enlargement and permanent improvements; to purchase necessary supplies, materials and equipment.

SUPERINTENDENT. To receive all children under the age of 16 years, committed to the institution by competent authority; to cause them to be instructed in rudimentary branches of useful knowledge, and taught useful trades and given manual training subject to discretion of Board; to maintain discipline. The Governor may transfer prisoners under 16, from jail, chain-gang or penitentiary to the reformatory and vice versa.

INSPECTION. State Board of Charities. Governor to visit once a year or oftener, to make suggestions to the Board of Trustees.

REPORTS. To report receipts and expenditures. Time and manner of report not specified, nor to whom report shall be made.

OBJECTS AND PURPOSE. To establish and operate a school for the training, and moral and industrial development of the criminally delinquent children of the State under 16 years.

Established	1907
Buildings	38
Acreage	423.32
Value of buildings and equipment	$675,827
Value of land	$ 85,000
Pupils	398
Appropriation, 1926-27	$140,000

NORTH CAROLINA NORMAL SCHOOLS AND COLLEGES FOR THE COLORED RACE AND FOR THE CHEROKEE INDIANS OF ROBESON COUNTY

N. C. NEWBOLD, *Director*, Raleigh

The State maintains three colleges and two standard normal schools for the training of Negro teachers and one for the training of the Cherokee Indians of Robeson County. The Agricultural and Technical College, at Greensboro, trains teachers in Vocational Agriculture, Trades and Industries; Winston-Salem Teachers' College, at Winston-Salem, emphasizes the training of elementary school teachers, supervisors and principals; North Carolina College for Negroes, at Durham, is offering courses for the training of high school teachers, and liberal arts and pre-medical courses. The normal schools for Negroes are located at Fayetteville and Elizabeth City. The school for the Cherokee Indians of Robeson County is located at Pembroke.

The first superintendent of these schools was Charles L. Coon, elected in 1904. In January, 1907, he was succeeded by John Duckett, who died, November 16, 1908. J. A. Bivens was superintendent from January, 1909, until his death, March 2, 1913. E. E. Sams was superintendent from March, 1913, to June 1, 1919. A. T. Allen was superintendent from June 1, 1919, to June 30, 1921. The Legislature of 1921 created a Division of Negro Education in the Department of Public Instruction with the following personnel:

N. C. Newbold, director; G. H. Ferguson, assistant director; W. A. Robinson, supervisor of Teacher-Training and High Schools; W. F. Credle, supervisor of The Julius Rosenwald Fund; G. E. Davis, supervisor of Rosenwald Buildings; Mrs. Annie W. Holland, supervisor of Elementary Schools; Frank R. Hufty, supervisor of Construction; Miss Annabel Pratt, secretary; Miss Margaret N. Little, clerk for Jeanes and Rosenwald Funds; S. A. Dickerson, stenographer. The director of this division is an *ex officio* member of the Boards of Trustees of these schools (except the colleges in Durham and Greensboro), and this division has general supervision of the schools.

In 1921 the Legislature made available appropriations for improvement and maintenance for Negro education to the amount of $829,000.

In 1921 the Legislature made available appropriations for improvement and maintenance for the Indian Normal School to the amount of $84,200.

In 1923 the General Assembly made available the following appropriations for the purposes indicated:

For building and improvements at the Negro State Normal schools	$469,000
For a similar purpose at the Agriculture and Technical College	455,000
For the establishement of a reformatory for delinquent Negro boys	50,000
Total for building (two year period)	$974,000
Maintenance appropriation for the Indian Normal schools, Agricultural and Technical College, Division of Negro Education, Teacher Training in private schools, summer schools, high schools	316,000
Grand total	$1,290,000

Maintenance appropriation for the Indian Normal
  School (annual) .... $ 18,000
Buildings and improvements .... $ 37,000

Total .... $ 55,000

In 1925 the General Assembly made available appropriations for the purposes indicated:

For building and improvements at the Negro State
  colleges $100,000
For building and improvements at the Negro State
  Normal schools 60,000
For a similar purpose at the Cherokee Indian
  Normal School 50,000

Total for building (two year period) $210,000

Maintenance appropriation for the Cherokee Indian
  Normal School, Negro colleges, Negro normals,
  Morrison Training School, Division of Negro
  Education, Teacher Training in private schools,
  summer schools and rural school supervision.... $554,530

Grand total $764,530

All of the property of these normal schools is held by the State Board of Education.

FAYETTEVILLE COLORED NORMAL SCHOOL

Art. 7, Ch. 96, C. S.; Ch. 61, P. L. 1921; Ch. 306, P. L. 1925

E. E. SMITH, *Principal*, J. W. SEABROOK, *Vice Principal*
N. C. NEWBOLD, *Director*, Raleigh

Board of Trustees—Nine members.

Personnel—G. K. Grantham, Dunn; Archie Graham, Clinton; M. B. Glover, Bailey; Dr. Allen McLean, Wagram; Dr. J. C. Grady,

Kenly; H. L. Cook, Fayetteville; Dr. H. W. Lilly, Fayetteville; V. C. Bullard, Fayetteville; Henderson Steele, Lillington.

Appointment—By the Governor with confirmation of the Senate.

Term—Four years.

Qualification—Genuine interest in Negro Education.

Compensation—Actual expenses.

Function

To elect its own president, secretary and treasurer; to have general management of the school; to elect teachers and to have such other powers of management as are not vested in the State Board of Education. For additional powers of State Board, see Cherokee Normal.

SEC. 17, CH. 146, P. L. 1921. This statute creates a Director of Negro Education, appointed by State Board of Education upon the recommendation of Superintendent of Public Instruction, who shall have supervision of the Negro Normal Schools.

OBJECT AND PURPOSE. To teach and train young men and women of the colored race, from the ages of 15 to 25 years, for teachers in the common schools of the State for the colored race, provided students, who are educated at State expense, agree to teach for not less than three years.

Most of the Negro teachers in the section where the school is located received training at this school. Industrial training, especially in domestic science, is required of all. The law provides that a preparatory department may be established.

SUMMARY

Founded	1877
Number of buildings	11
Number of acres of land	50
Value of buildings	$330,964
Value of land	$ 35,000
Value of furniture and equipment	$ 67,000
Number of students below seventh grade	123

Number of students above seventh grade 584
State appropriation (maintenance), 1926-27 $ 36,000
State appropriation (buildings and permanent improvements), 1926-27 $ 30,000

ELIZABETH CITY COLORED NORMAL SCHOOL

Art. 7, Ch. 96, C. S.; Ch. 61, P. L. 1921; Ch. 306, P. L. 1925

P. W. MOORE, *Principal*; J. H. BIAS, *Vice Principal*

N. C. NEWBOLD, *Director*, Raleigh

Board of Trustees—Nine Members.

Personnel—H. G. Kramer, Elizabeth City; C. A. Cook, Elizabeth City; Clyde McCallum, Hertford; Rev. S. A. Cotton, Washington; T. W. Costen, Gatesville; W. G. Gaither, Elizabeth City; T. S. White, Hertford; H. R. Leary, Edenton; Mrs. J. G. Fearing, Elizabeth City.

Appointment—By the Governor with confirmation of the Senate.

Term—Four years.

Qualification—Genuine interest in Negro Education.

Compensation—Actual expenses.

Function

Separate Board of Directors. Method of appointment, function, object and purpose of school same as at Fayetteville Negro Normal School.

SUMMARY

Founded	1892
Number of buildings	15
Number of acres of land	43
Value of buildings	$433,820
Value of land	$ 25,000
Value of furniture and equipment	$141,650
Number of students below seventh grade	98

Number of students above seventh grade	364
State appropriation (maintenance), 1926-27	$ 38,000
State appropriation (building and improvements used in new buildings), 1926-27	$ 30,000

WINSTON-SALEM TEACHERS' COLLEGE AT WINSTON-SALEM
Art. 7, Ch. 96, C. S.; Ch. 61, P. L. 1921; Ch. 306, P. L. 1925

S. G. ATKINS, *President;* H. LISTON, *Vice President*
N. C. NEWBOLD, *Director*, Raleigh

Board of Trustees—Nine members.

Personnel—Mrs. Lindsay Patterson, Winston-Salem; J. D. Humphreys, Danbury; A. D. Folger, Dobson; N. C. Newbold, Raleigh; H. E. Fries, Winston-Salem; W. A. Blair, Winston-Salem; H. G. Chatham, Winston-Salem; A. H. Eller, Winston-Salem; R. S. Montgomery, Reidsville.

Appointment—By the Governor with confirmation of the Senate.

Term—Four years.

Qualification—Genuine interest in Negro Education.

Compensation—Actual expenses.

Function

Separate Board of Directors. Method of appointment, function, object and purpose of school same as at Elizabeth City, except that this school gives a four-year course leading to the B.S. Degree in Education for the training of elementary school teachers, supervisors and principals; also special courses are offered for the training of Home Economics teachers.

SUMMARY

Founded	1895
Number of acres of land	52
Number of buildings	18
Value of buildings	$108,317

Value of land... $137,500
Other property, including furniture and fixtures $ 83,000
Number students below seventh grade.................. none
Number students above seventh grade 792
State appropriation (maintenance), 1926-27........... $ 44,000
State appropriation (buildings and improvements
 used in new building), 1926-27................................$ 30,000

NORTH CAROLINA COLLEGE FOR NEGROES
(Durham)

JAMES E. SHEPARD, *President*

Board of Trustees—Twelve members.

Personnel—N. W. Walker, Chapel Hill; L. M. Carlton, Roxboro; E. P. Wharton, Greensboro; W. P. Lawrence, Elon College; J. C. Clifford, Dunn; S. E. Douglas, Raleigh; J. A. McMillan, Wake Forest; R. L. Flowers, Durham; J. B. Mason, Durham; W. A. Erwin, Durham; E. A. Muse, Hamlet.

Appointment—By the Governor with confirmation of the Senate.

Term—Four years.

Qualification—Genuine interest in Negro Education.

Compensation—Actual expenses.

Function

Separate Board of Directors. This school is offering courses for the training of high school teachers and liberal arts and pre-medical courses.

SUMMARY

Founded—Under private control until 1923
Number of buildings 10
Number of acres of land.. 33
Value of buildings $90,000
Value of land... $40,000
Value of equipment... $10,000

Number of students below seventh grade .... none
Number of students above seventh grade................ 172
State appropriation (maintenance) 1926-27............ $30,000
State appropriation (buildings and improvements).
1926-27 .... $30,000

CHEROKEE INDIAN NORMAL SCHOOL OF ROBESON COUNTY
(Pembroke)

Art. 6, Ch. 96, C. S.; Ch. 61, P. L. 1921; Ch. 306, P. L. 1925

S. B. SMITHEY, *Principal*
N. C. NEWBOLD, *Director*, Raleigh

Board of Trustees—Nine members.

Personnel—N. C. Newbold, Chairman *ex officio*, Raleigh; James Deal, Lumberton; Ralph Lowry, Pembroke; O. R. Sampson, Pembroke; W. D. Oxendine, Buies; Henry Godwin, Pembroke; C. B. Brayboy, Pembroke; G. G. Locklear, Pembroke; Edmund Lowery, Pembroke; A. A. Locklear, Pembroke.

Appointment—By the Governor with confirmation of the Senate.

Term—Four years.

Qualification—Cherokee Indians.

Compensation—Expenses and $2.50 per diem.

Function

To elect the president of Board and define duties; to employ and discharge teachers; to exercise the usual functions of control and management of said school, action being subject to the approval of State Board of Education. The State Board shall make all needful rules and regulations concerning expenditure of funds, selection of principal, teachers and employees and concerning selection of Board of Trustees. In the fall of 1926 a Junior Normal class was organized, taking work similar to courses offered at Cullowhee and Appalachian Training Schools.

REPORTS. Monthly to Division of Negro Education, Raleigh.

OBJECT AND PURPOSE. To establish and maintain a school of high grade for teachers of Cherokee Indians in Robeson County.

ADMISSION AND QUALIFICATIONS. Cherokee Indians of either sex, of Robeson County, not under 11 years of age, who can pass an approved examination in spelling, reading, writing, primary geography, and fundamental rules of arithmetic, and who agree to teach the youth of the race of Cherokee Indians of Robeson County, may be admitted.

SUMMARY

Founded	1887
Number of buildings	11
Number of acres of land	16
Value of buildings	$178,700
Value of land	$ 13,500
Value of furniture and equipment	$ 71,550
Number of students below seventh grade	96
Number of students above seventh grade	132
State appropriation (maintenance), 1926-27	$ 25,000
State appropriation (buildings and improvements used in new buildings), 1926-27	$ 50,000

NEGRO AGRICULTURAL AND TECHNICAL COLLEGE OF NORTH CAROLINA (Greensboro)

Art. 3, Ch. 96, C. S.

F. D. BLUFORD, *President*

Board of Trustees—Fifteen.

Personnel—F. W. Dunlap, Wadesboro; S. P. Collier, Winston-Salem; J. H. Coward, Ayden; E. H. Bellamy, Wilmington; L. S. Covington, Rockingham; S. W. Finch, Lexington; O. F. Crowson, Burlington; R. F. Beasley, Monroe; D. Alexander Graham, Charlotte; M. C. S. Noble, Chapel Hill; A. M. Scales, Greensboro; C. M. Vanstory, Greensboro; W. L. Poteat, Wake Forest; W. R. Vaughan, Henderson; Dr. Archibald Johnson, Thomasville.

Appointment—Elected by General Assembly.

Term—Six years, each group of five overlapping.

Compensation—Traveling expenses only, not exceeding four times a year.

Function

To prescribe rules for the management of the institution and preservation of good order and morals; to appoint the president, instructors and other officers and servants and fix their salaries; to have general and entire supervision of the establishment and maintenance of the college; to regulate admission of pupils with respect to representation from the several congressional districts; to have charge of the disbursement of funds; to receive any donation of property or funds made to the college, and invest or expend same for benefit of college; to elect an executive board; to elect a chairman of the Board annually.

To have charge of all construction, permanent enlargement and repairs; to purchase necessary supplies, material and equipment.

EXECUTIVE BOARD. Consists of three trustee members elected by Board of Trustees, who shall have the immediate management of the institution when the full board is not in session.

PRESIDENT AND INSTRUCTORS. By and with consent of Board, to have power to confer certificates of proficiency or marks of merit and diplomas.

REPORTS. None specified.

OBJECT AND PURPOSE. To teach practical agriculture and the mechanic arts and such branches of learning as relate thereto, not excluding academical and classical instruction, to the Negro boys of this State.

The college confines its courses of study entirely to agriculture and mechanical education and related subjects. No purely academic courses are offered. The purpose of the Agricultural Department is to train practical farmers and teachers of agriculture, of the Mechanical Arts Department, to give a thorough knowledge of the trades offered.

Established	1891
Buildings	18
Acreage	130

Value of Buildings and Equipment	$850,000
Value of land	$ 64,000
Number of students, regular session	434
Number of students, summer session	369
Faculty	34
Appropriation, 1925-26	$ 59,675

CASWELL TRAINING SCHOOL (Kinston)

Art. 12, Ch. 96, C. S. (except Sec. 5896, which is repealed); Ch. 183, P. L. 1921; Ch. 193, P. L. 1921.

W. H. DIXON, M.D., *Superintendent*

Board of Directors—Nine; State Treasurer, Treasurer *ex officio*.

Personnel—Dr. Gideon H. Macon, Warrenton; C. W. Lassiter, Spring Hope; L. A. Bethune, Clinton; L. P. Tapp, Kinston; T. E. Whitaker, Oak Ridge; S. F. McCotter, Vandemere; Dr. W. W. Dawson, Grifton; V. O. Parker, Raleigh.

Appointment—By Governor with consent of Senate.

Term—Four Years.

Qualification—No two shall be residents of same county.

Function

See State Hospital at Raleigh. Function and powers of the Board are the same.

OBJECT AND PURPOSE. (Sec., 5895 C.S.) To segregate, care for, train and educate as their mentality will permit, the State's mental defectives; to disseminate knowledge concerning the extent, nature and menace of mental deficiency; to suggest and initiate methods for its control, reduction and ultimate eradication; to maintain an extension bureau for instructing the public in the care of the mental defectives who remain in their homes and for the after-care of discharged inmates; to create and maintain a psychological clinic for the study and observation of mental defectives charged with crime, and to give expert advice in all cases of mental defect.

SUMMARY

Established	1911
Buildings	38
Acreage	1016
Value of buildings and equipment	$1,500,000
Value of land	$ 115,000
Pupils	412
Employees	65
Appropriation 1924	$ 125,000

EAST CAROLINA INDUSTRIAL TRAINING SCHOOL FOR BOYS
(Rocky Mount)
Ch. 254, P. L. 1923; Chs. 120, 306, P. L. 1925

SAMUEL E. LEONARD, *Superintendent*

Board of Trustees—Five.

Personnel—J. C. Braswell, Rocky Mount; R. T. Fountain, Rocky Mount; Wilson Lamb, Williamston; S. C. Sitterson, Kinston; Dr. C. F. Strosnider, Goldsboro.

Appointment—By Governor with consent of Senate.

Term—Four years.

Compensation—Expenses.

Function

The trustees are empowered to establish and operate a school in Eastern North Carolina for the training and moral and industrial development of the criminally delinquent white boys of the State; to receive therein such persons under 18 years of age as may be sent thereto by order of Superior Court judges, judges of juvenile courts, or the recorders or other presiding officers of city or criminal courts; to keep and control them during their minority or until such time as the board shall deem proper for their discharge; to employ a superintendent and assistants and to make all regulations necessary for the management of the school; to expend all moneys received in the operation of the school and to account for the same.

All boys committed to the school shall be instructed in useful trades and manual labor and "shall, if possible, be taught the precepts of the Holy Bible, good moral conduct, how to work and to be industrious."

The school was opened in January, 1926.

SUMMARY

Established	1923
Buildings	2
Acreage	130
Value of buildings	$40,000
Value of land	$13,000
Present capacity	30
Appropriation, 1926-27	$12,500

STATE TRAINING SCHOOL FOR NEGRO BOYS
(Hoffman, Richmond County)

Ch. 190, P. L. 1921; Chs. 120, 306, P. L. 1925

LEONARD L. BOYD, *Superintendent*

Board of Trustees—Five.

Personnel—W. L. Parsons, Rockingham; Fred Tate, Charlotte; C. C. Spaulding, Durham; R. D. Phillips, Laurinburg; T. C. Coxe, Wadesboro.

Appointment—By Governor with confirmation of Senate.

Term—Four years.

Compensation—Expenses.

Function

To select a location and prepare for the opening of the school; to have general superintendence and control of the institution, grounds and buildings, officers, employees, inmates; to appoint and dismiss at will a superintendent and other employees; to control the inmates and to determine the time of their discharge; to act as a board of parole of the institution; to determine the actual cost per capita of the training and maintenance.

Delinquent negro boys under sixteen years of age may be committed to the institution by any juvenile, State, or other court having jurisdiction over such boys, but no boy can be sent until the agency desiring to commit him has secured permission from the superintendent of the school. The cost of sending inmates shall be paid by the agency which sends them.

The school was opened January 1, 1925.

SUMMARY

Established	1921
Buildings	4
Acreage	400
Value of buildings and equipment	$40,000
Value of land	$10,000
Number of inmates enrolled	106
Faculty	5
Appropriation, 1926-27	$11,000

STATE HOME AND INDUSTRIAL SCHOOL FOR GIRLS AND WOMEN (Samarcand)

Art. 2, Ch. 121, C.S.; Ch. 69, P. L. 1921—Extra Session; Chs. 120, 306, P. L. 1925

AGNES MACNAUGHTON, *Superintendent*

Board of Managers—Five.

Personnel—Rev. A. A. McGeachy, President, Charlotte; Dr. Elizabeth Delia Dixon-Carroll, Vice President, Raleigh; Mrs. J. R. Page, Secretary-Treasurer, Aberdeen; Mrs. W. N. Everett, Rockingham; Leonard Tufts, Pinehurst.

Appointment—By Governor with consent of Senate.

Term—Four years.

Qualifications—Three women and two men.

Compensation—Necessary expenses.

Function

To have general superintendence, management and control of the institution; of the grounds and buildings and officers and employees thereof; of the inmates therein and all matters relating to the government, discipline, contracts and fiscal concerns thereof; and may make suitable rules and regulations to carry out the purpose of the institution; to receive in its discretion all persons committed by competent authority or voluntarily; to act as the Board of Parole and to discharge or parole any inmate at any time, provided that period of detention shall in no case exceed three years, and that girls committed under 21 may be kept until they are 21 years old; to make suitable provision for care and maintenance of children born in the institution or infants of inmates; to provide industrial training for each inmate.

To appoint from its members a president, secretary and a treasurer whose term shall be for one year; to appoint a woman superintendent; to fix the compensation of the superintendent, all officers and employees and prescribe duties of each; to adopt by-laws, fixing time and place of board meetings, and making such other provisions as may be necessary for the proper management of the institution; to accept gifts, bequests, etc., made to the institution.

To have charge of all construction, enlargement and permanent improvements; to purchase all supplies, material and equipment.

SUPERINTENDENT. Woman of experience and training. Term and duties not specified. To secure the safe-keeping, obedience and good order of inmates, the superintendent has same power as given to keepers of jails and other penal institutions.

REPORTS. None specified.

INSPECTION. State Board of Charities.

OBJECT AND PURPOSE. To establish and maintain a detention home and industrial school for immoral, neglected, and wayward girls, and to provide for their safe-keeping, employment and rehabilitation. The school was established in 1917.

SUMMARY

Established	1917
Opened	July, 1918
Buildings	18
Acreage	352
Value of buildings and equipment	$244,779.12
Value of land	$ 40,000
Average attendance, 1926-27	204
Appropriation, 1926-27	$107,500.00

PART VI

STATE CHARITABLE INSTITUTIONS

1. State Hospital at Raleigh.
2. State Hospital at Morganton.
3. State Hospital at Goldsboro.
4. North Carolina Sanatorium for the Treatment of Tuberculosis.
5. North Carolina Orthopædic Hospital.
6. Oxford Orphanage.
7. North Carolina Orphanage for the Colored Race.
8. The Soldiers' Home.
9. Confederate Women's Home.

STATE HOSPITAL AT RALEIGH

Ch. 103, C. S. (except Secs. 6156-7-8-9, which are repealed); Ch. 183, P. L. 1921; Ch. 193, P. L. 1921; Chs. 120, 306, P. L. 1925

ALBERT ANDERSON, M.D., *Superintendent*

Board of Directors—Nine; State Treasurer, Treasurer *ex officio*.

Personnel—Dr. L. B. Evans, Windsor; Felix Harvey, Kinston; A. L. James, Laurinburg; H. R. Dwire, Winston-Salem; Dr. J. C Baum, Poplar Branch; W. S. O'B. Robinson, Goldsboro; Joseph G. Brown, Raleigh; Mrs. M. F. Williams, Faison; Dr. T. D. Kitchin, Wake Forest.

Appointment—By Governor with consent of Senate.

Term—Four years.

Qualification—No two shall be residents of same county.

Function

To direct and manage affairs of State Hospital at Raleigh and to adopt rules and regulations governing same; to provide for the accommodation, maintenance, care, training and treatment of legally committed white insane patients from the district served, white epileptics, inebriates and drug addicts from all parts of the State; insane and inebriate Indians and epileptics from the entire State and to care for criminal insane of white race from the entire State.

To appoint from its own members a building committee of three who shall have charge of all construction work, enlargements and all permanent improvements.

To appoint a superintendent; to fix the number of assistant physicians and compensation of all officers and employees; to be responsible for the disbursements of appropriations for maintenance and permanent enlargements and repairs; to purchase necessary supplies, equipment and materials.

SUPERINTENDENT. Appointed by the Board for a term of six years; must be a skilled physician. Duties are to appoint the assistant physicians, matrons, steward and all other employees; to have exclusive direction and control over all subordinate officers and employees, and to direct generally, the internal administration of the hospital.

TREASURER. To keep all accounts and pay out all moneys upon warrant of the Superintendent and countersigned by two members of the Board, under rules and regulations prescribed by the Board.

INSPECTIONS. By Board of Directors, General Assembly, State Board of Charities and Public Welfare, and the State Board of Health.

REPORTS. To file with Governor bi-monthly statement showing prices paid for all classes of articles purchased and from whom purchased. To report annually to the Governor on the condition of the institution and biennially to the General Assembly as to its receipts and disbursements.

OBJECT AND PURPOSE. To provide for the accommodation, maintenance, care and treatment of legally committed white insane patients and inebriates in the district served, inebriates and insane Indians and epileptics of the entire State, and criminal insane of white race of entire State.

Established	1856
Buildings	25
Acreage	1500
Patients (June 30th, 1926)	1504
Attendants and nurses	135
Appropriations, 1926	$444,000

STATISTICAL SUMMARY

	Male	Female	Total
Patients remaining June 30th, 1924	651	671	1322
Admitted during last two years (insane)	565	471	1036
Admitted during last two years (criminal insane)	78	6	84
Total number under treatment	1294	1148	2442
Average daily population			1474
Total number discharged and dead (insane)	526	391	917
Total number discharged and dead (criminal insane)	18	3	21
Remaining June 30th, 1926	750	754	1504

STATE HOSPITAL AT MORGANTON
(Western Hospital for the Insane)

Ch. 103, C. S. (except Secs. 6156-7-8-9 which are repealed) ; Chs. 183, 193, P. L. 1921; Chs. 120, 306, P. L. 1925

JOHN McCAMPBELL, M.D., *Superintendent*

Board of Directors—Nine; State Treasurer, Treasurer *ex officio*.

Personnel—J. H. Beall, Lenoir; R. R. Clark, Statesville; J. R. Boyd, Waynesville; J. M. Scott, Charlotte; O. M. Mull, Shelby; C. E. Brooks, Hendersonville; J. H. Giles, Glen Alpine; Dr. G. S. Kirby, Marion; S. M. Robinson, Gastonia.

Appointment—By Governor with consent of Senate.

Term—Four years.

Qualification—No two shall be residents of same county.

Function

See State Hospital at Raleigh. Morganton differs in that it does not receive Indian patients or epileptics.

OBJECT AND PURPOSE: To provide for the accommodation, maintenance, care and treatment of legally committed white insane and inebriates from within the western hospital district.

Established	1875
Open for Patients	1883
Buildings	23
Acreage	1,130
Patients, June 30, 1926	1,986
Appropriation, 1926-27	$450,000

STATE HOSPITAL AT GOLDSBORO
(Eastern Hospital for the Colored Insane)

Ch. 103, C. S. (except Secs. 6156-7-8-9, which are repealed); Ch. 183, P. L. 1921; Ch. 193, P. L. 1921; Chs. 120 and 306, P. L. 1925

W. W. FAISON, M.D., *Superintendent*

Board of Directors—Nine; State Treasurer, Treasurer *ex officio*.

Personnel—Nathan O'Berry, Goldsboro; Dr. J. E. Hart, Wadesboro; Jno. D. Robinson, Wallace; E. W. Timberlake, Wake Forest; W. P

Anderson, Wilson; C. P. Aycock, Pantego; L. M. Blue, Gibson; R. T. Wade, Morehead City.

Appointment—By Governor with consent of Senate.

Term—Four years.

Qualification—No two shall be residents of same county.

Function

See State Hospital at Raleigh. Goldsboro differs in that it receives only colored insane.

OBJECT AND PURPOSES. To provide for the accommodation, maintenance, care and treatment of legally committed colored insane patients and inebriates, resident in the State of North Carolina.

Established	1880
Buildings, (not including employees residences, 27)	25
Acreage	741
Value of buildings and equipment	$1,971,390
Value of land	$ 130,000
Patients	1,535
Attendants	75
Appropriation, 1926-27	$ 267,300

NORTH CAROLINA SANATORIUM FOR THE TREATMENT OF TUBERCULOSIS

Ch. 964, P. L. 1907; Ch. 96, P. L. 1923; Chs. 120, 306, P. L. 1925

P. P. McCAIN, M.D., *Superintendent*, Sanatorium

Board of Directors—Nine.

Personnel—J. R. Jones, Sanford; Jonas Oettinger, Wilson; Dr. J. C. Braswell, Whitakers; W. E. Harrison, Rockingham; A. B. Croom, Winston-Salem; Dr. T. W. M. Long, Roanoke Rapids; U. L. Spence, Carthage; Mrs. Max Payne, Greensboro; J. R. McQueen, Lakeview.

Appointment—By Governor with consent of Senate.

Term—Four years.

Compensation—$2 per diem and expenses.

The North Carolina Sanatorium for the Treatment of Tuberculosis was established by an act of the General Assembly in 1907, which appropriated for the purpose $15,000 for construction and $5,000 for annual maintenance.

The control of the Sanatorium was at first vested in a board of directors composed of twelve members appointed by the Governor and the Secretary of the State Board of Health, who was ex officio a member of the board. The special session of the General Assembly in 1913 transferred the control of the Sanatorium from the board of directors to the State Board of Health.

At the same session the General Assembly provided for the establishment of the Bureau of Tuberculosis, the purpose of which should be to receive reports of cases of tuberculosis from physicians and the executive officers of every private or public hospital, institution for the treatment of disease or dispensary, on forms provided for the purpose; to keep a record of all persons in the State known to be afflicted with tuberculosis; to develop and maintain a correspondence school with those of the State's tuberculous population to the end that they shall be properly advised and directed both as to the methods for obtaining cures and as to the methods of preventing the spread of the disease to other persons.

During the session of 1923 the General Assembly transferred the control of the institution from the State Board of Health to a board of nine directors, whose appointment should be made by the Governor and confirmed by the Senate and whose term of office should be four years.

The institution has steadily grown and is now modern in every respect. It has a white unit which will accommodate 185 patients, a colored unit which will accommodate 64 patients, a prison unit which will accommodate 48 patients, and is almost ready to open the children's building which will accommodate 50 patients. There is a central power house and laundry, and dining room and kitchen facilities in each unit are large enough to take care of twice the number of patients for which there is now hospital space. The need of more room for patients is great, since there are almost as many on the waiting list as there are patients in the institution.

The work previously done by the Bureau of Tuberculosis is now carried on by the Extension Department of the Sanatorium. Last year there was established a monthly tuberculosis periodical, *The Sanatorium Sun*. Teaching and diagnostic clinics are held in the State wherever they may be desired, and special clinics are held for children. For these purposes, two whole-time physicians are employed. Efforts are made constantly to interest and to assist counties in the establishment of local sanatoria.

SUMMARY

Established	1907
Buildings	39
Value	$1,021,019
Acreage	2,000
Value	$ 113,351
Patients	350
Appropriation, 1926-1927	$ 165,000
Sanatorium	$ 165,000
Extension Department	$ 20,000

SUPERINTENDENTS

J. E. Brooks, M.D.	1907-1912
M. E. Street, M.D.	1912-1914
L. B. McBrayer, M.D.	1914-1924
P. P. McCain, M.D.	1924-

NORTH CAROLINA ORTHOPAEDIC HOSPITAL (Gastonia)
Art. 1, Ch. 119, C. S.
Robert B. Babington, *Founder—President*

Board of Trustees—Nine.

Personnel—Miss Evelyn K. Nimrocks, Fayetteville; J. G. Hackett, North Wilkesboro; W. C. Bivens, Gastonia; Geo. Blanton, Shelby; R. R. Ray, McAdenville; J. L. Robinson, Gastonia; R. B. Babington, Gastonia; M. B. Spier, Charlotte; P. C. Whitlock, Charlotte.

Appointment—By Governor.

Term—Six years, three classes with overlapping terms.

Compensation—None.

Function

To direct and manage the affairs of the institution; to provide for the accommodation, maintenance and treatment of crippled children committed to its care; to elect from its members a president, secretary, treasurer and an executive committee of three; to prescribe the duties of the executive committee; to appoint a superintendent, and to perform such other functions as are necessary to the proper administration of the hospital.

To have charge of all construction, enlargement and permanent improvements; to purchase necessary supplies, materials and equipment.

A complete unit was built, dedicated and opened for the treatment of colored children March 1, 1926. This unit has twenty beds for colored children and is located several hundred yards, on the estate, from the white units.

OBJECT AND PURPOSE. To treat, heal and teach scientifically the orphaned poor and neglected crippled and deformed children of sound mind of North Carolina.

Founded	1909
Opened	1921
Acreage	34½
Value of land	$ 35,000
Value of buildings	$220,000
Maintenance appropriation, 1925-26	$ 70,000

OXFORD ORPHANAGE (Oxford)

No Statutory reference. A semi-private Institution subsidized by State funds.

R. L. BROWN, *Superintendent*

Board of Directors—

Appointment—Three by Governor. Other members appointed by Grand Lodge A. F. and A. M.

Function

To provide adequate quarters, maintenance and educational facilities for homeless children.

"The institution is providing the necessities of life for homeless children, the opportunity to acquire an English education, industrial training in cottages, kitchen, sewing room, domestic science, laundry, shoe shop, printing office, electric repair, telegraphy and typewriting, commercial course, dairy and on farm. Each child is in school at least the half of each school day during the school term of nine and a half months, but higher grades in school for eleven months. Moral and religious instruction is prominent in the work." (Red Book, 1921, page 197.)

REPORTS. Annual report of operations made to Governor, State Board of Public Charities and to the Grand Lodge A. F. and A. M. of North Carolina. Monthly report of disbursements to the State Auditor.

INSPECTION. By State Board of Charities.

OBJECT AND PURPOSE. To provide a home and training school for the education, industrial and moral instruction of destitute and homeless white children of the State, not over twelve years of age, who are of sound mind and body.

SUMMARY

Established	1872
Buildings	28
Acreage	276
Value of buildings and lands	$750,000.00
Children	400
Officers and teachers	59
State appropriation, 1926-27	$ 30,000.00
Income, other sources	$129,784.29

NORTH CAROLINA ORPHANAGE FOR THE COLORED RACE (Oxford)

HENRY P. CHEATHAM, *Superintendent*

The North Carolina Orphanage for the Colored Race was founded in 1883 as the result of the joint efforts of Rev. Augustus Shepard, then pastor of the colored Baptist Church in Henderson, and Henry P. Cheatham, then a teacher in the Henderson public schools. Their plans contemplated the establishment of an orphanage in North Carolina for the fatherless and homeless children of the colored race without regard to religious sects. Calling together certain leaders of the colored race, they laid their plans before them. The plans were adopted, a board of directors elected, and a site purchased for the orphanage about a mile and a half south of the town of Oxford. Upon this site were two old and dilapidated buildings, which were repaired and put into immediate use. During the first ten years of its existence the Orphanage was entirely dependent upon the churches, Sunday schools, and sympathetic individuals for support together with what the children could earn by cultivating the six acres of land then belonging to the Orphanage. In 1892 the Grand Lodge of Masons of North Carolina adopted a provision allowing the Orphanage annually ten per cent of its gross receipts, and in 1893 the General Assembly began to make a small annual appropriation which now amounts to $20,000.

SUMMARY

Founded	1883
Number of buildings	16
Number of acres of land	245
Value of land, buildings and equipment	$160,000
Number of children in institution	287
Number of officers, teachers and helpers	13
Annual appropriation from State	$ 20,000
Other sources (1926)	$ 5,000
Farm, garden and dairy (estimated)	$ 4,500
Annual per capita cost	$103.86

SUPERINTENDENTS

Rev. Joshua Perry	1883-1884
Miss Bessie Hackins	1884-
Rev. Walter A. Patillo	1886-1887
Rev. Robert Shepherd	1887-1907
Henry P. Cheatham	1907-

SOLDIERS' HOME
Art. 1, Ch. 92, C. S.

W. T. MANGUM, *Superintendent*, Raleigh

Board of Directors—Seven.

Personnel—Miss Martha Haywood, Raleigh; W. B. Jones, Raleigh; Mrs. R. E. Little, Wadesboro; W. J. Andrews, Raleigh; C. B. Barbee, Raleigh; Baxter Durham, Raleigh; Mrs. H. M. London, Raleigh.

Appointment—Four by the Governor and three by the Soldiers' Home Association.

Term—One year.

So far as can be ascertained from the records on file in the office of the Soldiers' Home, a home for indigent Confederate soldiers was first established in a rented house at the corner of Polk and Bloodworth streets, in the city of Raleigh, and declared to be open on October 15, 1890, with five inmates. W. C. Stronach, under the auspices of the Daughters of the Confederacy, acted as superintendent and looked after the personal comforts of the men.

The General Assembly of 1891, chapter 60, Private Laws, incorporated Gen. Robert F. Hoke, Col. William L. Saunders, Col. A. B. Andrews, Capt. S. A. Ashe, Gen. Rufus Barringer, Gen. A. M. Scales, Gen. Robert B. Vance, Gen. Thomas Clingman, Gen. W. P. Roberts, Gen. Julian S. Carr, Capt. Thomas J. Jarvis, Col. W. P. Wood, Gen. Matt. W. Ransom and other members of the Confederate Veterans' Association, under the name and style of "The Soldiers' Home Association," and conferred upon this association the usual corporate powers. The act gave to the Soldiers' Home Association a tract of land near the eastern section of the city of Raleigh, known as Camp Russell, to be used for the purpose of a soldiers' home, and, if it should cease to be so used, to revert to and belong to the State. The same act appropriated $3,000 for the maintenance of the Soldiers' Home and the support of its inmates. Section 6 of the act is as follows:

"The directors shall cause to be kept a minute-book of the Home, in which full entries shall be kept concerning memorable incidents in the lives of its inmates. They shall also take steps to form a museum of Confederate relics and to perpetuate such historical records of the Confederate soldiers of North Carolina as they shall find it practicable to do."

The act was ratified February 4, 1901.

On April 27, 1891, the number of inmates of the Soldiers' Home having increased to nine, they were removed to an old building at Camp Russell which had been fitted up for the purposes of the Home. Miss Mary Williams was appointed matron, and served in that capacity until February 15, 1893, when Capt. J. H. Fuller was made resident superintendent. On February 1, 1898, Superintendent Fuller resigned. Feebleness of age and the increase in number of inmates had made the duties too arduous for one of his strength.

Capt. R. H. Brooks was elected to succeed Captain Fuller, and served until his death on June 14, 1910. The number of inmates continued to increase during his term, and the necessity for new and larger buildings became urgent. A dormitory was built to accommodate 70 inmates, and furnished by liberal donations from the Daughters of the Confederacy and others. A large hospital was built, medical attention given, nurses employed, water, sewerage, and electric lights provided, and the grounds made attractive. Such heavy expenses exceeded the appropriation made by the State, and at the close of Captain Brooks's term the books showed the Home to be in arrears to the extent of $6,000; but all felt confident that the Legislature would provide for the deficiency.

Capt. W. S. Lineberry was elected to succeed Captain Brooks, and entered upon his duties July 20, 1910.

Colonel D. H. Milton, who was elected to succeed Capt. W. S. Lineberry, September 26, 1916, took charge October 1, 1916. Colonel Milton resigned October 1, 1920, and was succeeded by J. A. Wiggs. Mr. Wiggs resigned in February, 1924, and was succeeded by W. T. Mangum, February 9, 1924.

An appropriation of $35,000 was made by the Legislature of 1915 for the support of the Home. The Home is now out of debt; the buildings bright with new paint; the grounds ornamented with trees and shrubbery, and walks clean. The comrades are, as a rule, contented. The fare is good, the rooms comfortable, the regulations reasonable, and an air of cheerfulness pervades. All this has come from the humble beginning of October, 1890.

SUPERINTENDENTS

Miss Mary Williams	1891-1893
Capt. J. H. Fuller	1893-1898
Capt. R. H. Brooks	1898-1910
Capt. W. S. Lineberry	1910-1916
Col. D. H. Milton	1916-1920
J. A. Wiggs	1920-1924
W. T. Mangum	1924-

CONFEDERATE WOMEN'S HOME (Fayetteville)
Art. 2, Ch. 92, C. S.; Corporate name "Confederate Women's Home Association."

Mrs. M. B. Beaman, *Superintendent*

Board of Directors—Seven. Board elects own president and secretary. State Treasurer, Treasurer *ex officio*.

Personnel—Charles G. Rose, *chairman*, Fayetteville; Mrs. Hunter G. Smith, Fayetteville; Mrs. N. A. Townsend, Dunn; A. H. Boyden, Salisbury; W. H. White, Oxford; J. W. McLaughlin, Raeford; Spencer T. Thorne, Rocky Mount.

Appointment—By Governor.

Term—Two years.

Compensation—Actual expenses.

Function

To appoint all officers and employees and prescribe their duties; to establish rules and regulations for the government and maintenance of the Home and to have entire control and management of it; to prescribe rules for admission and discharge; to take necessary action in reference to the collection and disbursement of subscriptions to the Home or to needy Confederate women elsewhere in the State; to have their accounts duly audited and published; to appoint an advisory board of lady managers.

Advisory Board of Lady Managers. Appointed by the Board of Directors, one from each congressional district, for a term of two years; to assist the Board in the management of the Home and solicit contributions.

Confederate Woman's Home

TREASURER. For duties see Board of Directors Central Hospital for the Insane (Raleigh).

REPORTS. Reports of receipts and disbursements and the general affairs of the Home shall be made annually to the Governor to be by him laid before the General Assembly at its biennial session. To report on the 15th of each month to the State Auditor, disbursements of month preceding.

OBJECT AND PURPOSE. To establish, maintain and govern a Home for the deserving wives and widows of North Carolina Confederate soldiers and other worthy dependent women of the Confederacy who are bona fide residents of North Carolina. The Home was established in 1913. The State appropriation for 1925-26 by the State was $10,000, and for 1926-27, $14,000. The General Assembly of 1925 authorized the issuance of bonds of the State to the amount of $26,500 for permanent improvements (ch. 192, P.L. 1925.)

PART VII

MISCELLANEOUS

1. The North Carolina Railroad Company.
2. The Atlantic and North Carolina Railroad Company.
3. The Appalachian and Western North Carolina Railroad Company.
4. The North Carolina Agricultural Society.
5. The North Carolina State Capitol.
6. State Administration Building.
7. North Carolina Day.
8. Legal Holidays in North Carolina.
9. The State Flag.
10. The Great Seal.
11. State Motto and Its Origin.
12. The Confederate Museum at Richmond.

THE NORTH CAROLINA RAILROAD COMPANY
WILEY G. BARNES, *Secretary and Treasurer*

One of the greatest enterprises so far attempted by the State of North Carolina in the nature of a public or internal improvement was the building of the North Carolina Railroad from Goldsboro by way of Raleigh, Greensboro and Salisbury, to Charlotte.

Considering the experimental state of railroading at that time, the dread of public or private indebtedness, and the limited resources, the movement was a monumental enterprise—and one in advance of anything attempted by almost any other state in the Union. The success, however, which has crowned the labors and sacrifices of our fathers has established beyond all question that their wisdom was equal to, or superior to, any displayed before or since their day.

In 1833 the Raleigh and Gaston Railroad Company and the Wilmington and Raleigh, afterwards known as the Wilmington and Weldon Railroad Company, were chartered, and later these roads were built. In 1848 the former was in the hands of the State, and was in a bankrupt condition for the want of patronage. It was necessary to give it some connection, or to extend it. At the session of November, 1848, the western counties urged a charter for a road from Charlotte to Danville, asking no State aid; but the eastern members opposed that project. The finances of the State were in such an impoverished condition that it was generally deemed impracticable for the State to give any considerable aid to any railroad; but William S. Ashe, the Democratic Senator from New Hanover, introduced a bill to construct a road from Goldsboro to Charlotte, under the name of the North Carolina Railroad, and appropriating two millions of dollars for that purpose, on condition, however, that private parties would subscribe one million, and to secure the payment of the State bonds when issued, a lien was given on the State's stock.

When the western men brought up the Charlotte and Danville bill in the House, Stanly and other eastern men opposed it so bitterly that it could not pass, and then in a dramatic scene, the friends of internal improvement agreed to send to the Senate and take the Ashe bill from the files and offer it as a substitute. After a great

---
*This article is brought forward with some revision, from the MANUAL of 1913, in which acknowledgment is made to Capt. S. A. Ashe for the historical data contained in this sketch.

and prolonged struggle the bill passed the House of Commons. In the Senate it failed by an adverse majority of one; but the Senator from Cumberland was led to support it by passing the bill for the State to build the plank road from Fayetteville to Salem; and then the vote in the Senate was a tie. Speaker Graves, who had up to that moment maintained an impenetrable silence as to the measure, broke the tie in favor of building the road by State aid; and the measure was passed. Speaker Graves was never again elected to any office by the vote of his people.

To secure the needed one million of private stock, Speaker Graves, Governor Morehead and Mr. William Boylan made great exertions, and by their efforts, aided by Joseph Caldwell, Governor W. A. Graham, Paul C. Cameron and others, the necessary stock was eventually raised. On January 29, 1856, the railroad was ready for passage of trains from Goldsboro to Charlotte, and charters had been granted for two other roads—from Goldsboro to Morehead City and from Salisbury to the Tennessee line.

By act ratified 14th of February, 1855, the General Assembly increased the capital stock to $4,000,000, and subscribed for the State the whole of the added capital. From that time till now the State has owned three-fourths and individuals one-fourth of this road.

The first president of the company was Governor John M. Morehead, to whom so much was due for securing the subscription of the private stock, and under his direction the road was constructed. His successors were Charles F. Fisher, of Rowan; Paul C. Cameron, Josiah Turner, Jr., of Orange, and William A. Smith, of Johnston. During the administration of Mr. Smith the road was, on the 11th day of September, 1871, leased to the Richmond and Danville Railroad Company for thirty years, at a rental of 6 per cent per annum. The subsequent presidents of the company have been: Thomas M. Holt, Lee S. Overman, S. B. Alexander, J. F. Kornegay, R. M. Norment, J. L. Armstrong, H. G. Chatham, Charles M. Stedman, Bennehan Cameron, and Word H. Wood.

On the 16th day of August, 1895, in view of the approaching termination of the lease, the property was leased to the Southern Railway Company for a term of ninety-nine years at an annual rental of $6\frac{1}{2}$ per cent for six years and 7 per cent for the remaining ninety-three years, and the stock of the company was selling at $186 per share until the panic of 1907.

On the readjustment of the debt of the State, the State renewed the bonds issued for the purchase of the North Carolina Railroad stock, pledging the original lien on the stock for the payment of the debt.

Col. Peter B. Ruffin for more than thirty years was the faithful and efficient secretary and treasurer of the company.

The secretaries of the company in the order of their election and service are as follows: Cyrus P. Mendenhall, Julius B. Ramsey, R. M. Mills, F. A. Stagg, J. A. McCauley, W. F. Thornburg, P. B. Ruffin, H. B. Worth, Spencer B. Adams, D. H. McLean, A. H. Eller, J. P. Cook, R. B. White, and Wiley G. Barnes.

The State, as is well known, has continued to own its $3,000,000 of the original capital stock, and has acquired two (2) additional shares, thus giving it 30,002 shares, at par value amounting to $3,000,200, which, however, at the recent market value aggregates $5,580,372. And it is confidently believed that if the State desired to part with a controlling interest in the company, its stock would command a much greater price, and those who have watched the constant advance in the price of this stock expect it to go to $200 per share at an early day.

Under the lease of 1871 to the Richmond and Danville Railroad Company, the company could not have claimed the betterments made by the lessee; but under the present lease the company is not only amply secured by bond for the prompt payment of its lease money and organization expenses, to wit, $143,000, on the first day of January and July of each year, but upon the termination of said lease for any cause the company acquires the betterments made thereon.

In addition to the railroad and rolling stock leased to the Southern Railway Company, the company still owns valuable land in and about company shops, now known as the city of Burlington.

When the board of directors appointed by Governor Aycock took charge of the company's affairs, there was a floating indebtedness of $10,000. The May balance, 1912, of the secretary and treasurer showed that said indebtedness had been paid and a special dividend of one-half of one per cent, amounting to $20,000, and the company had to its credit in the bank the sum of $21,128.64, all of which except a small balance, was drawing 4 per cent interest. Again, on August 1, 1912, an extra one-half of one per cent dividend, amounting to $20,000, was paid. Since then the regular 7 per cent dividend on the stock has been paid and occasional dividends of ½ per cent out of cash received from the sale of property. Promptly upon the payment of the lease money on the first of January and July in each year, the directors declare a dividend, and the secretary and treasurer pays to the State Treasurer immediately $105,000, and a like dividend is paid to the private stockholders on the first day of February and August of each year.

A true sketch of this company would be incomplete without calling attention to the long and invaluable service of Gen. R. F. Hoke as director and Mr. Word H. Wood as president. Gen. Hoke's experience and great knowledge of affairs, and life-long devotion to the best interest of the company, entitle him to the gratitude of the State, as well as the private stockholders. His death on July 3, 1912, was deeply and universally lamented. President Wood's long and valuable service is unique in the history of the company. He has been elected by the Board of Directors at the requests of four successive governors of North Carolina: Locke Craig, Thomas W. Bickett, Cameron Morrison and Angus W. McLean.

The question is sometimes asked why the organization of the North Carolina Railroad Company is kept up, and what particular functions it performs.

This company does not, as some people think, belong to the State of North Carolina. It is a quasi-public corporation like all other railroad companies, in which the State owns three-fourths of the stock. It is managed practically as any private corporation would be managed, the principal difference being that the Governor has the appointment of eight of the directors, while the private stockholders have the election of four of the directors.

The organization is maintained for the purpose of enforcing the terms of the lease to the Southern Railway Company, and, in case of the termination of that lease for any cause, to resume the operation of the road.

It is required to see that the bonds given for the prompt payment of the rent, and also the bond to maintain the rolling stock in good condition, are kept in force. It receives the rent money of $280,000 per year, payable semi-annually, and declares a dividend and pays the same to the stockholders of record. It transfers stock like other corporations.

In leasing its property to the Southern Railway Company it reserved its office building, which is the residence of the secretary and treasurer, containing its vault and records, at Burlington, N. C. It owns certain real estate in and about the city of Burlington, which is sold by its land committee from time to time.

The secretary and treasurer is required to give a bond in the sum of $50,000 and his books and accounts are audited by a finance committee at stated times. It is required to file a report annually with the State Corporation Commission and one with the Interstate Commerce Commission, as other railroad companies must do. It also reports its income for Federal taxation like other corporations. Its stock is the most valuable holding that the State of North Carolina has amongst its assets, and whether it will be the policy of the State to hold its stock perpetually or to dispose of the same is a matter for the Legislature of the future.

The present officers and directors of the road are as follows:

WORD H. WOOD, *President*	Charlotte
ALEXANDER WEBB, *Vice President*	Raleigh
WILEY G. BARNES, *Secretary and Treasurer*	Raleigh
J. BAYARD CLARK, *Counsel*	Fayetteville

DIRECTORS

W. H. WOOD	ROBERT W. LASSITER
JOHN F. BOWLES	ALEXANDER WEBB
GILBERT C. WHITE	HUGH MACRAE
A. M. DIXON	W. E. HOLT
M. O. DICKERSON	G. W. MONTCASTLE
G. A. HUNT, JR.	JULIUS CONE

THE ATLANTIC AND NORTH CAROLINA RAILROAD COMPANY

The Atlantic and North Carolina Railroad was chartered by the General Assembly of North Carolina in 1852, duration of the charter being ninety-nine years. The charter was amended in 1854 and 1855,

---

* Reprinted from the *North Carolina Manual*, 1915. The editor regrets that he has not been able to secure from the company data necessary to bring the article up to date.

Work on the railroad was begun shortly afterwards, and pushed to completion from Goldsboro to a point on the seacoast now known as Morehead City, a distance of 95 miles, in 1858.

Not having the necessary data at hand, I state from memory, and from information gained from other sources, the names of the different presidents of the railroad company, in the order of their service from the beginning up to the time when the railroad was leased to the Howland Improvement Company, during the administration of Hon. C. B. Aycock as Governor of North Carolina, on September 1, 1904, as follows: John D. Whitford, Charles R. Thomas, John D. Whitford, E. R. Stanly, R. W. King, L. W. Humphrey, John Hughes, John D. Whitford, Washington Bryan, W. S. Chadwick, Robert Hancock, D. W. Patrick, James A. Bryan.

The road was capitalized at $1,800,000; the par value of the stock was fixed at $100 per share. The State of North Carolina owns 12,666 shares of the stock. The county of Craven owns 1,293 shares, the county of Lenoir owns 500 shares,* the county of Pamlico owns 202 shares. The balance of the stock of the road is owned by private individuals. The equipment of the road was by no means complete when the War Between the States began (1861), and by reason of the fact that a good portion of the road was under the control of the Federal arms from the fall of New Bern in 1862 to the close of the war in 1865, the road when turned over to its rightful owners was little more, if any, than a burden to carry, which was in part the cause of no returns to the stockholders on their investments for thirty-four years after the road was constructed.

During the administration of Hon. T. J. Jarvis, Governor of North Carolina, the railroad was leased to W. J. Best, who had control and operated same for a short time only, and then returned it to its owner.

There is an outstanding bonded indebtedness against the road of $325,000, bearing interest at 6 per cent per annum, the interest payable semi-annually.† During the last year of the presidency of James A. Bryan two suits were instituted in the Federal Court for the Eastern District of North Carolina for the appointment of receivers of the road—first by K. S. Finch of New York, and the

---
* Sold to private individuals.
† Written in 1914.

second by John P. Cuyler of New Jersey. Receivers were appointed in both cases, but relief was granted by higher courts.

The vast amount of unsettled business in which the Atlantic and North Carolina Railroad Company was in any way interested at the time the Howland Improvement Company, "lessees," assumed control of the railroad, was very largely adjusted during the first two years. The expiration of the third year of the lease found only a small amount of difference to be looked after, which in time was settled. Suit was brought in the Superior Court of Craven County, in 1906, to annul the lease to the Howland Improvement Company, resulting in a decision upholding the lease, which decision was affirmed by the Supreme Court.

The contract for lease with the Howland Improvement Company terminates in ninety-one years and four months from the date of its execution, and the stipulations contained in same have, up to the last meeting of the stockholders of the Atlantic and North Carolina Railroad Company, in 1912, been largely complied with, as will be seen from the annual reports to the stockholders' meeting of the president, treasurer and expert of the lessor company. The Atlantic and North Carolina Railroad has, with some other short lines in Eastern North Carolina, been merged into and now forms part of the Norfolk-Southern Railway system.

The following have been presidents of the company: James A. Bryan, J. W. Grainger, S. W. Ferrebee, L. P. Tapp, H. H. Grainger and Thomas D. Warren.

THE APPALACHIAN AND WESTERN NORTH CAROLINA RAILROAD COMPANY

Chapter 148, Public Laws of 1921, authorized the Governor to appoint a special commission of five to investigate the advisability of selling the stock owned by the State in the North Carolina and Atlantic and North Carolina railroads and investing the proceeds in certain railroads in Western North Carolina. The Commission in its report recommended the construction of such roads as would result in a trunk line of railroads from the northwestern part of the State to the seacoast. Wherefore by chapter 116, Public Laws of 1923, the General Assembly authorized A. A. Woodruff of Alleghany County, J. D. Thomas of Ashe County, B. B. Daugherty of Watauga County,

Charles Cowles of Wilkes County, J. H. Burke of Alexander County, Mark Squires of Caldwell County, D. M. Ansley of Iredell County, A. H. Wolf of Surry County, G. T. White of Yadkin County, and others to incorporate as the Appalachian and Western North Carolina Railroad Company. The law provides in general that when fifty-one per cent of the stock shall have been subscribed in good faith to construct the whole road or any particular division of it, the State shall subscribe forty-nine per cent of the stock.

The Special Commission appointed Bennehan Cameron, T. C. Bowie, and W. C. Heath as an executive committee to make surveys of proposed routes. Three routes were surveyed and a petition was filed with the Interstate Commerce Commission requesting a certificate of public convenience and necessity. The petition was dismissed without prejudice. The Interstate Commerce Commission stated that, if a particular and specific route was designated, it would not stand in the way of the construction of the road. The amended petition has not yet been filed with the Interstate Commerce Commission.

THE NORTH CAROLINA AGRICULTURAL SOCIETY
H. M. LONDON, *Secretary*, Raleigh

The North Carolina Agricultural Society, which operates the State Fair annually in Raleigh during the month of October, was chartered by special act of the Legislature in 1852 "to provide a place for the holding of annual fairs, that the citizens may be encouraged by exhibitions, premiums and other means to develop and improve the productions of agriculture and every species of native industry; and to this end, and for these great and valuable purposes, and to no other, shall the corporation apply all the funds which by any means it may acquire."

No capital stock was provided for in that charter. Various public-spirited citizens loaned to the Society a sum of money sufficient to purchase grounds and erect buildings for the purposes of an annual fair, taking therefor the bonds of the Society.

By an amendment to the charter enacted by the 1925 General Assembly it was provided that "the board of directors shall consist of seventeen members, five of whom shall be ex officio as follows:

The Governor of North Carolina, the president of the North Carolina State College of Agriculture and Engineering, the Commissioner of Agriculture, the Mayor of the City of Raleigh, and the president of the North Carolina Agricultural Society; the remaining members of the board of directors shall be appointed as follows: two by the Governor of North Carolina; two by the president of the North Carolina State College of Agriculture and Engineering; two by the Commissioner of Agriculture; four by the members of the North Carolina Agricultural Society and two by the Mayor of the city of Raleigh. The directors shall hold office for one year and until their successors are elected and qualified, and shall have the usual powers with reference to the affairs of the society as do directors of other corporations, and shall elect officers of the society in such manner as the by-laws of the society may prescribe."

On account of the inadequacy of the old buildings and grounds, it was deemed advisable in 1926 to sell the old Fair grounds, located within the limits of the city of Raleigh, and secure another and larger site on which to erect new buildings of a more permanent nature looking toward an expansion of the State Fairs held annually.

THE NORTH CAROLINA STATE CAPITOL

On the morning of June 21, 1831, the State Capitol of North Carolina was destroyed by fire. Though the public records of the State were saved, the State Library, containing many valuable books and manuscripts, was lost.

The citizens of Raleigh naturally bemoaned the destruction of the building but Governor Stokes did not regard it as a great loss. In his opinion there were some mitigating circumstances. In his message to the General Assembly, when it met the following November, he said that the calamity was not so great, because the old State house, built in 1794, was almost ready to tumble down of its own accord, and that perhaps many valuable lives had been saved by its being destroyed by fire instead of tumbling down on the Legislature while in session.

At once Senator Seawell of Wake brought forward a bill providing for the erection of a new Capitol on the site of the old one. At the same time a similar bill was introduced in the House of Commous. As there was a strong sentiment in the State favorable to the removal of the capital from Raleigh to Fayetteville, these two bills to rebuild at Raleigh met with vigorous opposition. Accordingly, Senator Seawell's bill was quickly disposed of. Senator Wilson of Edgecombe moved to table it, and it was tabled. The House bill was longer discussed. The discussion was prolonged for two days, but on a yea and nay vote the bill failed, 65 to 68. The Assembly of 1831 refused to rebuild.

A year passed, and the ruins of the old Statehouse still marked the site of the former Capitol. But the Constitution, or rather the Ordinance, of 1789, located the capital at Raleigh, and the Legislature had no power to move it. It was even questioned with great seriousness whether the Assembly could hold its sessions in the Governor's Mansion, at the end of Fayetteville Street, as that was outside of the limits of the town. To move the capital a convention was necessary, and a majority of the Legislature was not favorable to a convention.

At the session of November, 1832, the Assembly, by a vote of 35 to 28 in the Senate and 73 to 60 in the House, resolved to rebuild on the old site, and $50,000 was appropriated for the purpose.

William Boylan, Duncan Cameron, Henry Seawell, Romulus M. Saunders and William S. Mhoon were appointed commissioners to have the work done. The commissioners, with $50,000 at their command, did not dally. The rubbish was cleared away, the excavations made and the foundations were laid. On July 4, 1833, the cornerstone was set in place. Up to that time W. S. Drummond was the superintendent and chief architect, and he was one of the principal persons in the ceremony of laying the cornerstone.

After the foundation was laid the work progressed more slowly, and it was so expensive that the appropriation was exhausted. The Legislature at its next session appropriated $75,000 more. To do the stone and finer work many skilled artisans had been brought from Scotland and other countries. Part of the work was conducted under the supervision of W. S. Drummond and another part under Colonel Thomas Bragg, but these arrangements did not prove satisfactory, and a year later, in September, 1834, Mr. I. Theil Town of New York, acting for the commissioners, contracted with David Paton to come to Raleigh and superintend the work.

Mr. Paton was an architect who had come from Scotland the year before. He was then thirty-three years of age. He was the son of John Paton, of Edinburgh, who was an extensive builder in that city and vicinity and who had built the greater part of the new town and constructed the famous Dean Bridge across the water of Leith, and he ranked high in his profession. Having received a liberal education at the University of Edinburgh, David Paton took up the profession of his father and was regularly bred as an architect and builder under his father and under Sir John Sloan, R. A., professor of architecture to the Royal Academy of London. He soon demonstrated his capacity. When he first came to Raleigh the cost of overseeing the work on the Capitol was $25 a day. He reduced that cost to $9. Twenty-eight stonecutters were paid $81 a day. This he reduced to $56. He made a saving in these two items alone of $42 a day. He found himself to be not merely supervisor of the work, but the superintendent; not merely the superintendent, but the bookkeeper and paymaster. He had every detail of the work on his shoulders. And then he had to make the working drawings. He was the builder, the architect, the designer.

Both the commissioners and the architect had large ideas. The former were wise enough to expend the original $50,000, which the General Assembly expected would complete the structure, *on its foundation*. Their work being severely critized, they resigned January 1, 1835. Their successors were Beverly Daniel, chairman, Samuel F. Patterson, Charles Manly and Alfred Jones. The Legislature was compelled to make appropriations for the work from time to time. The following is a table of the several appropriations made:

Session of 1832-33	$ 50,000.00
Session of 1833-34	75,000.00
Session of 1834-35	75,000.00
Session of 1835	75,000.00
Session of 1836-37	120,000.00
Session of 1838-39	105,300.00
Session of 1840-41	31,374.46
Total	$531,674.46

It must be remembered that the stone with which the building was erected was the property of the State. Had the State been compelled to purchase this material the cost of the Capitol would have been considerably increased.

The following is a description of the Capitol, written by David Paton, the architect:

"The State Capitol is 160 feet in length from north to south by 140 feet from east to west. The whole height is 97½ feet in the center. The apex of pediment is 64 feet in height. The stylobate is 18 feet in height. The columns of the east and west porticoes are 5 feet 2½ inches in diameter. An entablature, including blocking course is continued around the building, 12 feet high.

"The columns and entablature are Grecian Doric, and copied from the Temple of Minerva, commonly called the Parthenon, which was erected in Athens about 500 years before Christ. An octagon tower surrounds the rotunda, which is ornamented with Grecian cornices, etc., and its dome is decorated at top with a similar ornament to that of the Choragic Monument of Lysicrates, commonly called the Lanthorn of Demosthenes.

"The interior of the Capitol is divided into three stories: First, the lower story, consisting of ten rooms, eight of which are appropriated as offices to the Governor, Secretary, Treasurer, and Comptroller, each having two rooms of the same size—the one containing an area of 649 square feet, the other 528 square feet—the two committee rooms, each containing 200 square feet, and four closets; also the rotunda, corridors, vestibules, and plazas, contain an area of 4,370 square feet. The vestibules are decorated with columns and antae, similar to those of the Ionic Temple on the Ilissus, near the Acropolis of Athens. The remainder is groined with stone and brick, springing from columns and pilasters of the Roman Doric.

"The second story consists of Senatorial and Representatives' chambers, the former containing an area of 2,545 and the latter 2,849 square feet. Four apartments enter from Senate Chamber, two of which contain each an area of 169 square feet; and the other two contain each an area of 154 square feet; also, two rooms enter from Representatives' Chamber, each containing an area of 170 square feet; of two committee rooms, each containing an area of 231 feet; of four presses and the passages, stairs, lobbies, and colonnades, containing an area of 3,204 square feet.

"The lobbies and Hall of Representatives have their columns and antæe of the Octagon Tower of Andronicus Cyrrhestes and the plan of the hall is of the formation of the Greek theater and the columns and antæe in the Senatorial Chamber and rotunda are of the Temple of Erechetus, Minerva Polias, and Pandrosus, the Acropolis of Athens, near the above-named Parthenon.

"Third, or attic story, consists of rooms appropriated to the Supreme Court and Library, each containing an area of 693 square feet. Galleries of both houses have an area of 1,300 square feet; also, two apartments entering from Senate gallery, each 169 square feet, of four presses and the lobbies' stairs, 988 square feet. These lobbies, as well as rotunda, are lit with cupolas, and it is proposed to finish the court and library in the florid Gothic style."

In the summer of 1840 the work was finished. The Assembly had, in December, 1832, appropriated $50,000 for the building. Mr. Boylan, Judge Cameron and State Treasurer Mhoon and their associates spent that sum in the foundation. They proposed to have a Capitol worthy of the State. At every subsequent session the Assembly made additional appropriations. There was some caviling, and the commissioners resigned; but the Legislature and the new commissioners took no step backwards. Year by year they pressed on the work as it had been begun, until at last, after more than seven years, the sum of $531,674.46 was expended. As large as that sum was for the time, when the State was so poor and when the entire taxes for all State purposes reached less than $100,000, yet the people were satisfied. The building had been erected with rigorous economy, and it was an object of great pride to the people. Indeed, never was money better expended than in the erection of this noble Capitol.

Speaking of this structure, Samuel A. Ashe, in an address on David Paton, delivered in 1909, says:

"Not seventy years have passed since the completion of this building, yet it has undying memories. It was finished the year Henry Clay was set aside and his place as the Whig leader given to General Harrison. Four years later Clay spoke from the western portico; but, like Webster and Calhoun, the prize of presidency was denied him. The voices of other men of large mould also have been heard within this Capitol. Here, too, our great jurists—Gaston, Ruffin, Pearson and their associates—held their sessions and brought renown to North Carolina. Here, Badger, Mangum, Dobbin and scores of men known to fame held high debates. Here was brought forth in great travail our system of internal improvements, and of education, ramifying the State, disseminating enlightenment and opening the pathways to prosperous, contented and happy homes for our people.

"Here Ellis and Clark and the mighty Vance directed the affairs of State in trying days of war and suffering and desolation, the glories mingled with pain and sorrow, and fading away in heartrending defeat; but through it all the women and men, alike heroes, worthy the poets' loftiest strains. Then, when the people were still bowed in anguish, Carolinians turned their faces to the future, and, with resolution and intelligence, themselves modified their laws and institutions to meet the new conditions; but in vain, for these mute walls are witnesses of the saturnalia of Reconstruction, still awaiting some Dante to portray the scenes with realistic power. Yet the dark cloud had its silver lining, and the courageous devotion of Jarvis, John Graham and their Spartan band adds historic interest to that time of fearful storm.

"Later, here was the scene of the great State trial, the impeachment of the Chief Magistrate of the Commonwealth and the contest between the intellectual giants of that generation, Governor Graham and Bragg and Merrimon, contesting with Smith and Coningland and Richard Badger.

"And these walls have witnessed the reversal of that State policy forced on an unwilling people by the mailed hand of the conquering power, and the full restoration of Anglo-Saxon control. Never in history has a people been so clearly and effectually vindicated as those gallant souls of North Carolina, who, emulating the constancy of Hamilcar, swore their children to undying opposition to those who would destroy their civilization. Let the oppressed of future ages gaze on the scene and take courage. Already hallowed are the memories that these chambers evoke. What grand occasions yet await them. We may not lift the veil of the future, but experience warns us that history constantly repeats itself, and as the web woven by destiny unrolls itself there will yet occur within these enduring walls occasions of surpassing magnitude affecting the weal and woe of our posterity."

STATE ADMINISTRATION BUILDING

Mindful of the fact that only a little more than a generation ago the State Capitol of North Carolina was destroyed by fire, entailing the loss of many valuable records and papers, for some years prior to the convening of the 1911 session of the General Assembly the demand had been insistent for a safer housing of several departments of the State Government at Raleigh, notably the books and records of the North Carolina Historical Commission, which has now grown to be one of the most important branches of the work at the seat of government.

Early in the session a movement was started for the building of a State administration building at the capital, and after numerous conferences and compromises of differences as to the amount that should be appropriated for that purpose, a bill was at length unanimously passed by both houses, appropriating the sum of $250,000 for this purpose and conferring upon the government the appointment of a State Building Commission for the consummation of this worthy undertaking. Soon after the adjournment of the Legislature Governor W. W. Kitchin named as the members of the Commission Ashley Horne of Clayton, William E. Springer of Wilmington, Julian S. Carr of Durham, W. L. Parsons of Rockingham, A. S. Rascoe of Windsor, J. A. Long of Roxboro, and J. Elwood Cox of High Point, men of affairs and recognized business ability in the State.

The State Building Commission held its first meeting in the office of the State Auditor at 12:30 p. m., May 9, 1911, and organized by the election of Ashley Horne of Clayton, as chairman, and William E. Springer of Wilmington, as secretary. Following organization, a conference was held with the Board of Public Buildings and Grounds, composed of the Governor, Secretary of State, Treasurer, and Attorney-General. It was stated as the purpose of the General Assembly to provide ample room for the Supreme Court, all valuable State records, the State Library, offices for the Attorney-General, and several of the other State departments. The grounds were carefully gone over, the situation canvassed, and a subcommittee composed of Chairman Horne, Secretary Springer, and Commissioner Cox was appointed to go further into the matter of a building and site.

At a subsequent meeting, on May 19, 1911, the committee reported that it had secured an option on three sites, and recommended the purchase of the Grimes tract for $45,000. This recommendation was accepted by the Commission as a whole, and on June 6, 1911, plans as prepared by P. Thornton Marye of Atlanta, were accepted after hearing a number of others and after several conferences. These plans were later reviewed by Glenn Brown of Washington, D. C., another expert in building construction, and were declared eminently proper and in order in every respect. The plans called for a modern fireproof building four stories in height and admirably adapted to the purpose to which it would be put.

On November 1, 1911, the Commission met again in Raleigh, after proposals had been invited for the building, and after considering a number of bids for the construction, the contract was at length awarded to the John T. Wilson Company, of Richmond, Va., at a cost of $188,000, the building to be completed and ready for occupancy by January 19, 1913.

How well the State Building Commission wrought is attested by the splendid building which now stands opposite the Capitol grounds and which was occupied in January, 1914, by the several departments of government as agreed upon after the numerous conferences of the Commission. The departments occupying the building are as follows: First floor, State Library; second floor, North Carolina Historical Commission; third floor, the Supreme Court and Attorney-General; fourth floor, Supreme Court Library.

NORTH CAROLINA DAY

The following act entitled "An Act to Provide for the Celebration of North Carolina Day in the Public Schools," is chapter 164 of the Public Laws of 1901:

The General Assembly of North Carolina do enact:

SECTION 1. That the 12th day of October in each and every year, to be called "North Carolina Day" may be devoted, by appropriate exercises in the public schools of the State, to the consideration of some topic or topics of our State history, to be selected by the Superintendent of Public Instruction. *Provided*, that if the said day shall fall on Saturday or Sunday, then, the celebration shall occur on the

Monday next following: *Provided, further*, that if the said day shall fall at a time when any such schools may not be in session, the celebration may be held within one month from the beginning of the term, unless the Superintendent of Public Instruction shall designate some other time.

SEC. 2. This act shall be in force from and after its ratification.

In the General Assembly read three times and ratified this the 9th day of February, A.D. 1901.

October 12th, the date selected for North Carolina Day, is the anniversary of the laying of the cornerstone of the University of North Carolina, October 12, 1793. In accordance with the provisions of this act, the Superintendent of Public Instruction has had prepared and distributed to the schools of the State each year a program of exercises devoted to the study of some phase of North Carolina history.

Since the creation of North Carolina Day the following subjects have been studied each year (back numbers of the programs can be secured from the State Superintendent of Public Instruction, Raleigh, N. C.):

1901. The Roanoke Island Colonies. Prepared by Fred A. Olds.
1902. The Albemarle Section. Prepared by a Committee.
1903. The Lower Cape Fear Section. Prepared by R. D. W. Connor.
1904. The Pamlico-Neuse Section. Prepared by Charles L. Coon.
1905. The Scotch Highlanders in North Carolina. Prepared by R. D. W. Connor.
1906. Charles D. McIver Memorial Day. Prepared by R. D. W. Connor.
1907. The Scotch-Irish in North Carolina. Prepared by Charles H. Mebane.
1908. The German Settlements in North Carolina. ⎫
1909. Western North Carolina.   ⎪ Each prepared by
1910. North Carolina Poets and Poetry.   ⎬ R. D. W. Connor.
1911. Local and County History.   ⎪
1912. Charles B. Aycock Memorial Day.   ⎭
1913. North Carolina Rural Life and Knapp Memorial Day. Edited by N. C. Newbold.
1914. Community Service.
1915. School and Neighborhood Improvement Day.
1916. Murphey Day: Archibald DeBow Murphey. Prepared by Edgar W. Knight.
1917. Thrift, Conservatism, Patriotism.
1919. Aycock School Improvement Day. Prepared by the State Superintendent of Public Instruction.
1921. Armistice Day. Prepared by R. B. House.
1924. American Education Week.
1925. The State Flag of North Carolina and "Some Makers of the Flag." Prepared by Miss Susan Fulghum and J. Henry Highsmith.

LEGAL HOLIDAYS IN NORTH CAROLINA

Although certain great days in each year—such as New Year's Day, Fourth of July, Thanksgiving Day, and Christmas Day—have long been observed as general holidays, there were no "legal" holidays, in North Carolina prior to 1881. The Legislature of that year, in the interest of commercial transactions, passed an act to make these customary holidays "legal" holidays. It is in chapter 294, Public Laws of 1881, and was brought forward in The Code of 1883 as sections 3784-3786 of chapter 61. It provides:

"That the first day of January, twenty-second day of February, tenth day of May, twentieth day of May, fourth day of July, and a day appointed by the Governor of North Carolina as a thanksgiving day, and the twenty-fifth day of December of each and every year be, and the same are hereby declared to be public holidays; and that whenever any such holiday shall fall upon Sunday, the Monday next following shall be deemed a public holiday, and papers due on such Sunday shall be payable on the Saturday next preceding, and papers which would otherwise be payable on said Monday shall be payable on the Tuesday next thereafter.

"SEC. 2. *Be it further enacted,* That whenever either of the above named days shall fall on Saturday, the papers due on the Sunday following shall be payable on the Monday next succeeding.

"SEC. 3. *Be it further enacted,* That whenever the above named days shall fall on Monday, the papers which should otherwise be payable on that day shall be payable on Tuesday next succeeding."

Ten years later, the nineteenth of January was made a "legal" holiday, by chapter 58, Public Laws of 1891, which provides:

"That the nineteenth day of January, the birthday of the peerless Robert E. Lee, in each and every year hereafter, shall be a public holiday."

In 1899, the first Thursday in September was designated as Labor Day and made a "legal" holiday. The Legislature of 1901 amended this Act by changing the holiday from the first Thursday to the first Monday in September. The reason for this change was recited in the preamble of the act as follows:

"Whereas it is desirable that the same date should be set aside by both State and Federal statutes for the observance of the same holiday;

"And whereas the first Monday in September is designated by statutes in various states and also by Federal Statutes as Labor Day, while the first Thursday in September is designated as Labor Day by statute of this State, thereby causing confusion and annoyance in mercantile transactions, therefore," etc.

These several acts were all brought forward in the Revisal of 1905 as section 2838.

The Legislature of 1907 added another legal holiday to the list by setting aside as a holiday "Tuesday after the first Monday in November, when a general election is held." This is chapter 996, Public Laws of 1907.

The twelfth day of April was made a legal holiday by chapter 888, Public Laws of 1909, which is as follows:

"Whereas the Provincial Congress which met at Halifax, in this State, in April, one thousand seven hundred and seventy-six, after providing for the military organization of the State, did, on the twelfth day of April, one thousand seven hundred and seventy-six, adopt the following resolution, generally known as the 'Halifax Resolutions,' to wit:

"'*Resolved*, That the delegates for this colony in the Continental Congress be empowered to concur with the delegates of the other colonies in declaring independency, and forming foreign alliances, reserving to this colony the sole and exclusive right of forming a constitution and laws for this colony.'

"And whereas said resolution is the first declaration in favor of independence by the people of the whole State, through their duly authorized representatives and was adopted more than two months before the Declaration of Independence by the Continental Congress; and whereas an occurrence so momentous in the history of our State and Nation, and so illustrative of the patriotism and wisdom of the whole people of North Carolina, should be commemorated, therefore,

The General Assembly of North Carolina do enact:
"SECTION 1. That the twelfth day of April in each and every year be, and the same is hereby made a legal holiday in North Carolina."

The latest of our legal holidays is the eleventh of November, designated by chapter 287, Public Laws of 1919, which provides:

"SECTION 1. That the eleventh day of each and every November be, and the same is hereby designated, declared and set apart as a legal holiday for all the citizens of North Carolina.

"SEC. 2. That the Governor shall annually issue his proclamation proclaiming the eleventh day of November as a legal holiday and calling upon the people to appropriately celebrate and observe the same."

Legal Holidays in North Carolina, therefore, are as follows:

January 1.—New Year's Day.

January 19—Birthday of General Robert E. Lee.

February 22—Birthday of George Washington.

April 12—Anniversary of the Resolutions adopted by the Provincial Congress of North Carolina, at Halifax, April 12, 1776, empowering the delegates from North Carolina to the Continental Congress to vote for a Declaration of Independence.

May 10—Confederate Memorial Day.

May 20—Anniversary of the "Mecklenburg Declaration of Independence."

July 4—Independence Day.

September, first Monday—Labor Day.

November, Tuesday after first Monday—General Election Day.

November 11—Armistice Day.

November, last Thursday—Thanksgiving Day.

December 25—Christmas Day.

THE STATE FLAG

The first legislation on the subject of a State flag was enacted by the Convention of 1861. May 20, 1861, the Convention adopted the Ordinance of Secession.

On that same day Col. John D. Whitford, a member of the Convention from Craven County, introduced the following ordinance, which was passed and referred to a select committee of seven:

"Be it ordained that the flag of this State shall be a blue field with a white V thereon, and a star, encircling which shall be the words 'Surgit astrum, May 20th, 1775.'"

Colonel Whitford was made chairman of the committee to which this ordinance was referred. The committee secured the aid and advice of William Garl Brown, an artist of Raleigh. Brown prepared and submitted a model to this committee. And this model was adopted by the Convention on the 22d day of June, 1861. It will be observed that the Brown model, to be hereafter explained, was vastly different from the one originally proposed by Colonel Whitford. Here is the ordinance as it appears on the Journal of the Convention:

"AN ORDINANCE IN RELATION TO A STATE FLAG."

"Be it ordained by this Convention, and it is hereby ordained by the authority of the same, That the flag of North Carolina shall consist of a red field with a white star in the center, and with the inscription, above the star, in a semi-circular form of 'May 20, 1775,' and below the star, in a semi-circular form of 'May 20, 1861.' That there shall be two bars of equal width, and the length of the field shall be equal to the bar, the width of the field being equal to both bars; the first bar shall be blue, and the second shall be white; and the length of the flag shall be one-third more than its width." (Ratified the 22d day of June, 1861.)

This State flag, adopted in 1861, is said to have been issued to the first ten regiments of State troops during the summer of that year, and was borne by them throughout the war, being the only flag, except the National and Confederate colors, used by the North Carolina troops during the Civil War. This flag existed until 1885, when the Legislature of that year adopted a new model.

The bill, which was introduced by General Johnstone Jones on the 5th of February, 1885, passed its final reading one month later after little or no debate. This act reads as follows:

AN ACT TO ESTABLISH A STATE FLAG.

The General Assembly of North Carolina do enact:

SECTION 1. That the flag of North Carolina shall consist of a blue union, containing in the center thereof a white star with the letter N in gilt on the left and the letter C in gilt on the right of said star, the circle containing the same to be one-third the width of the union.

SEC. 2. That the fly of the flag shall consist of two equally proportioned bars; the upper bar to be red, the lower bar to be white; that the length of the bars horizontally shall be equal to the perpendicular length of the union, and the total length of the flag shall be one-third more than its width.

SEC. 3. That above the star in the center of the union there shall be a gilt scroll in semi-circular form, containing in black letters this inscription: "May 20th 1775," and that below the star there shall be a similar scroll containing in black letters the inscription: "April 12, 1776."

In the General Assembly read three times and ratified this 9th day of March, A.D., 1885.

No change has been made in the flag since the passage of this act. By an act of 1907 it is provided:

"That the board of trustees or managers of the several State institutions and public buildings shall provide a North Carolina flag, of such dimensions and material as they may deem best, and the same shall be displayed from a staff upon the top of each and every such building at all times except during inclement weather, and upon the death of any State officer or any prominent citizen the flag shall be put at half-mast until the burial of such person shall have taken place.

"That the Board of County Commissioners of the several counties in this State shall likewise authorize the procuring of a North Carolina flag, to be displayed either on a staff upon the top, or draped behind the judges' stand, in each and every courthouse in the State, and that the State flag shall be displayed at each and every term of court held, and on such other public occasions as the Commissioners may deem proper."

THE GREAT SEAL*

The Constitution of North Carolina, Article III, section 16, requires that

"There shall be a seal of the State which shall be kept by the Governor, and used by him as occasion may require, and shall be called 'The Great Seal of the State of North Carolina.' All grants and commissions shall be issued in the name and by the authority of the State of North Carolina, sealed with 'The Great Seal of the State,' signed by the Governor and countersigned by the Secretary of State."

The use of a Great Seal for the attestation of important documents began with the institution of government in North Carolina. There have been at various times nine different seals in use in the colony and State. The first seal was adopted by the Lords Proprietors of Carolina soon after receiving their charters from the Crown in 1665. This seal is to be seen in the Public Record Office in London. It is described as follows:

---

*Abridged from "The Great Seal of North Carolina," by J. Bryan Grimes; Publications of the the North Carolina Historical Commission, Bulletin No. 5.

"The obverse side has a shield bearing on its face two cornucopias crossed, filled with products and having for supporters, on the sinister side, an Indian chief holding an arrow. On the dexter is an Indian squaw with a papoose by her side and one in her arms. These natives, I imagine, are supposed to be bringing tribute. The crest is a stag upon a wreath above a helmet from which there is a mantling. On the scroll below the shield is the motto, *Domitus Cultoribus Orbis.* Around the shield are the words MAGNUM SIGILLUM CAROLINAE DOMINORUM. On the reverse side is a disc bearing a cross, around which are arranged the coats-of-arms of the Lords Proprietors in the following order: Clarendon, Albemarle, Craven, John Berkeley, Cooper, Carteret, William Berkeley, and Colleton. The size of this seal is 3⅜ inches in diameter, and was made by placing together two wax cakes with tape between before being impressed, and was about ¼ inch thick. This seal was used on all the official papers of the Lords Proprietors for Carolina, embracing North and South Carolina."

About 1665 the government of Albemarle County was organized, and for a seal the reverse side of the seal of the Lords Proprietors was adopted. It bore the word A-L-B-E-M-A-R-L-E, beginning with the letter A between the names of Clarendon and Albemarle, L between the arms of Albemarle and Craven, BE between the arms of Craven, Lord John Berkley, etc.

This was a small seal $1\frac{7}{16}$ inches in diameter, with one face only, and is now frequently to be found attached to colonial papers. It was first used for the government of the county of Albemarle, and then became the seal of the Province of North Carolina, being used until just after the purchase by the Crown.

In 1730, after the purchase of the colony by the Crown, the Lords of Trade proposed to the King a new seal "whereon Liberty is represented introducing Plenty to your Majesty with this motto, *Quae sera tamen respexit,* and this inscription around the circumference, *Sigillum Provinee Nostrae Carolinae, Septentrionalis."* The background on which the King and these figures stand is a map of the coast of North Carolina, and in the offing is a ship. On the reverse of this seal are the Royal Arms, Crown, Garter, Supporters, and Motto, with this inscription around the circumference, *Georgius Secundus Dei Gratia Magnae Britaniae, Franciae, et Hiberniae, Rex, Fidei Defensor, Brunsvici et Lunenbergi Dux, Sacri Romani Imperii Archi Thesaurarius, et Elector.*

This seal was made by placing two cakes or layers of wax together, between which was the ribbon or tape with which the instrument was interlaced and by which the seal was appended. It was customary to put a piece of paper on the outside of these cakes before they were impressed. The seal complete was 4⅜ inches in diameter and from ½ to ⅝ inch thick and weighed about 5½ ounces.

In 1767 Governor Tryon received from the King a new Great Seal for the Province. The new seal was engraved on the one side with the Royal Arms, Garter, Crown, Supporters, and Motto, and this inscription around the circumference "*Georgius III D: G: Mag. Bri. Fr. et Hib. Rex, F. D. Brun, et Lun. Dux, S. R. I. ar Thes. et El.*" On the other side are figures of the King and Liberty who is introducing Plenty to the King with this motto, *Quae Sera Tamen Respexit*. Around the circumference is the following legend: *Sigillium. Provinciae Nostrae Carolinae, Septentrionalis*. This seal was 4 inches in diameter, ½ to ⅝ inches thick, and weight 4½ ounces.

Sometimes a smaller seal than the Great Seal was used, as commissions and grants are often found with a small heart-shaped seal about one inch wide and a quarter of an inch thick which was impressed with a crown. Also a seal was occasionally used about three inches long and two inches wide and a half an inch thick, in the shape of an ellipse. These impressions were evidently made by putting the wax far enough under the edge of the Great Seal to take the impression of the crown. The royal governors also sometimes used their private seals.

When the government of the independent State of North Carolina was organized, the Constitution adopted at Halifax, December 18, 1776, provided, Section XVII, "That there shall be a seal of this State, which shall be kept by the Governor, and used by him as occasion may require; and shall be called the Great Seal of the State of North Carolina and be affixed to all grants and commissions."

The Convention of 1868 changed the section of the Constitution, with reference to the seal, to read as it now stands.

The Assembly of 1778 appointed William Tisdale to cut and engrave the first State seal, under the direction of the Governor. This seal was used until 1794. Its actual size was three inches in diameter and ¼ inch thick. It was made by putting two cakes of wax together with paper wafers on the outside and pressed between the dies forming the obverse and reverse sides of this seal.

The seal of 1778 is described as follows:

"On one side is the figure of Minerva or Liberty holding in the right hand the pole with cap and in the left hand with arm extended is held a large scroll on which appears in large capital letters the word 'Constitution.' Under the figure the words, IN LEGIBUS SALUS. Around the circumference are the words, THE GREAT SEAL OF THE STATE OF NORTH CAROLINA. On the other side of the shield is the figure of a woman, probably Plenty. The right arm is folded across her breast and in her right hand inclining toward her left shoulder is held a distaff. In the left hand with arm extended is held an ear of corn. In the distance beyond a tree browses a cow. Under these figures appear the word and letters INDEPENDENCE—MDCCLXXVI.' Around the circumference appear the words O. FORTUNATOS, NIMIUM, SUA. SI. BONA. NORINT, COLONOS."

In December, 1781, the General Assembly authorized the Governor to procure a seal that should "be prepared with one side only, and calculated to make the impression on the face of such grant, commission, record, or other public act," etc. An artist in Philadelphia submitted a sketch to the Governor as follows: Minerva is represented in the act of introducing Ceres with her horn of plenty to Liberty, who is seated on a pedestal holding in her right hand a book on which is inscribed the word "Constitution." In the background are introduced a pyramid, denoting strength and durability, and a pine tree which relates immediately to the products of the State.

This sketch, omitting Minerva and with some minor charges, was accepted by Governor Spaight. The new seal was very much like the present one. It has two figures, Liberty and Plenty. Liberty is seated on a pedestal with her pole in her right hand, and her cap on the pole; in her left hand is a scroll with the word "Constitution" upon it. Plenty is standing to the left and front of Liberty; around her head is a circlet of flowers; in her right hand, leaning against her shoulder, is her cornucopia, mouth upwards, overflowing with fruits and produce. In her left is an ear of corn. Around the circumference are the words THE GREAT SEAL OF THE STATE OF NORTH CAROLINA.

This seal was $2\frac{1}{2}$ inches in diameter, slightly larger than the present one, and was used until about 1835.

In 1834 the Legislature authorized the Governor to procure a new seal. The preamble to the act states that the old seal had been in use since the first day of March, 1793. The seal adopted in 1835, which was used until 1883, was very similar to its predecessor. On it Liberty and Plenty faced each other. Liberty was standing, her pole with cap on it in her left hand, and a scroll with the word "Constitution" inscribed thereon in her right hand. Plenty is sitting down, her right arm half extended towards Liberty, three heads of wheat in her right hand, and in her left the small end of her horn, the mouth of which is resting at her feet, and the contents of her horn rolling out. Around the circumference were the words THE GREAT SEAL OF THE STATE OF NORTH CAROLINA. This seal was 2¼ inches in diameter.

In 1883 an act was passed relative to the seal, which was incorporated in the Code as section 3329. The seal therein provided for is described as follows:

"The Great Seal of the State of North Carolina shall be two and one-quarter inches in diameter, and its design shall be a representation of the figures of Liberty and Plenty, looking toward each other, but not more that half fronting each other, and otherwise disposed as follows: Liberty, the first figure, standing, her pole with cap on it in her left hand and a scroll with the word 'Constitution' inscribed thereon in her right hand. Plenty, the second figure, sitting down, her right arm half extended towards Liberty, three heads of wheat in her right hand, and in her left the small end of her horn, the mouth of which is resting at her feet, and the contents of the horn rolling out."

In 1893 an act, introduced by Jacob Battle, added at the foot of the coat of arms of the State as a part thereof the motto "Esse Quam Videri," and required that the words, "May 20, 1775," be inscribed at the top of the coat of arms.

The present Great Seal of the State of North Carolina is described as follows:

"The Great Seal of the State of North Carolina is two and one-quarter inches in diameter, and its design is a representation of the figures of Liberty and Plenty, looking towards each other, but not more that half fronting each other, and otherwise disposed as follows: Liberty, the first figure standing, her pole with cap on it in her left hand and a scroll with the word 'Constitution' inscribed thereon in her right hand. Plenty, the second figure, sitting down, her right arm half extended toward Liberty, three heads of wheat in her right hand, and in her left the small end of her horn, the mouth of which is resting at her feet, and the contents of horn rolling out. In the exergue is inserted the words May 20, 1775, above the coat of arms. Around the circumference is the legend, "The Great Seal of the State of North Carolina,' and the motto, 'Esse Quam Videri.'"

STATE MOTTO AND ITS ORIGIN*

The General Assembly of 1893 (chapter 145) adopted the words "Esse Quam Videri" as the State's motto and directed that these words with the date, "20 May, 1775," should be placed with our Coat of Arms upon the Great Seal of the State.

The words "Esse Quam Videri" mean "to be rather than to seem." Nearly every state has adopted a motto, generally in Latin. The reason for their mottoes being in Latin is that the Latin tongue is far more condensed and terse than the English. The three words, "Esse Quam Videri," require at least six English words to express the same idea.

Curiosity has been aroused to learn the origin of our State motto. It is found in Cicero in his essay on Friendship (Cicero De Amicitia, chap. 26). He says, "Virtute enim ipsa non tam multi prediti esse quam videri," i.e, "Virtue is a quality which not so many desire to possess as desire to seem to possess," or, translated literally, "For indeed not so many wish *to be* endowed with virtue *as* wish *to seem to be*."

The phrase is a striking one, and Cicero's version of it has been caught up and often used as a motto. No less than three houses of British nobility have adopted it, to wit: the Earl of Winterton, Earl Brownlow, and Lord Lurgan.

It has been adopted by many associations, especially literary societies. In this State it is the motto of Wilson Collegiate Institute and, and with some modifications of one of the societies at Wake Forest College.

The figures on our State Coat of Arms are Liberty and Plenty. It has been objected that the motto has no reference or application to the figures on the coat of arms. It is very rarely that such

---

*Adapted from an article by Chief Justice Walter Clark in *The North Carolina Booklet*, Vol. IX, No. 3.

is the case. The national motto, "E Pluribus Unum," has no reference to the Eagle and Shield and the Thunderbolts on the national coat of arms. Nor have the "Excelsior" of New York, the "Dirigo" of Maine, the "Qui Transtulet, Sustinet" of Connecticut any application to the figures above them. Indeed, Virginia's "Sic Semper Tyrannis" is one of the very few instances in which the motto bears such reference. But, in fact, is our motto so entirely without reference to the coat of arms as is usually the case? The figures are, as just stated, Liberty and Plenty. Is it inappropriate to say we prefer *to be* free and prosperous than seem *to be so?* There have been states that had all the appearance of liberty and prosperity, when in truth having lost the reality of both, they were tottering to their fall.

It is a little singular that until the act of 1893 the sovereign State of North Carolina had no motto since its declaration of independence. It was one of the very few states which did not have a motto, and the only one of the original thirteen without one.

It may be noted that up to the time it became a "sovereign and independent state" the Colony or Province of North Carolina bore on its great seal "Quae sera tamen respexit." This was taken from the first Eclogue of Virgil (line 27) and, referring to the figure of Liberty, meant "Which, though late, looked upon me"—the full line in Virgil being "Liberty which, though late, looked upon me indolent." No wonder that this was dropped by the new State. Nothing could possibly have been more inappropriate. Liberty came not to her late; and it came not to a people inert or unseeking her rewards. To such, liberty never comes.

It may be mentioned, to prevent any misunderstanding as to the scope of the act of 1893 (now Revisal, sec. 5320), that it does not apply to county seals. Each county is authorized to adopt its own seal. Revisal, sec. 1318 (24). Many counties now have on their county seals the appropriate phrase, "Leges Juraque Vindicamus." Some have adopted the State motto. But this is a matter left to the discretion of the county commissioners in each county.

NOTE BY THE EDITORS (of *The Booklet*). The bill which was passed in 1893 to adopt our State motto was introduced by Senator Jacob Battle, of Nash, afterwards Judge of the Superior Court. We have before us a letter from him in which he states that the motto was selected by Judge—since Chief Justice—Walter Clark, who also drew the bill and requested him to present it. He adds that the words "20 May 1775," secured the hearty coöperation of Senator Brevard McDowell of Mecklenburg, and by their joint efforts the bill passed by the unanimous vote of both houses of the General Assembly, and without amendment.

THE CONFEDERATE MUSEUM AT RICHMOND

In the house in Richmond, Virginia, which was the Executive Mansion of the Confederate States, and as such was occupied by President Davis from 1861 to 1865, is in charge of the Confederate Memorial Literary Society, and is filled with relics of the Confederacy. Each Southern state has a room, to which the Daughters of the Confederacy contribute to the endowment fund. To the support of the North Carolina Room, the General Assembly appropriates $200 annually. About eight years ago it was decided that each room would raise an endowment of $2,000. This amount was not sufficient so it was increased to $3,000. North Carolina, South Carolina, and Virginia have gone over the top and most of the rooms have reached their goal. The North Carolina Room contains a large collection of relics and the largest collection of portraits in the museum. About 15,000 persons visit the Museum annually. Each Confederate State has a regent who is expected to collect relics, etc., and funds for its room and a vice regent who gives personal supervision to the room and its needs. Mrs. Latta C. Johnson is the Regent and Mrs. J. A. Hodges, the Vice Regent for North Carolina.

PART VIII

PLATFORMS OF POLITICAL PARTIES, 1926

1. STATE DEMOCRATIC PLATFORM.
2. STATE REPUBLICAN PLATFORM.

STATE DEMOCRATIC PLATFORM, 1926

We, the representatives of the Democratic Party of North Carolina, in convention assembled, rededicate our allegiance to the fundamental principles which have given strength and power of service to our Party from the beginning of the Republic, and welcome the opportunity to give account of its stewardship, to renew its solemn pledges of fidelity to the public welfare, and to those causes which most surely promote the happiness and prosperity of all the people.

For an unbroken period of a quarter of a century this Party has held responsibility for the administration of the executive, legislative and judical departments of the State government. In all this time it has assumed and exercised responsibility of leadership in constructive policies designed to build a great commonwealth.

For the intelligence and wisdom with which these policies have been conceived, and the faithfulness with which they have been executed, we submit our cause with confidence to the whole people of North Carolina—a State which enjoys, by reason of successful promotion of these policies, distinction of leadership in educational progress, in humane consideration of its unfortunate classes, in agricultural and industrial development and in construction and maintenance of public highways—an achievement which could not have been attained without a substantial measure of unanimity of support of the liberal thought and forward-minded people of the State. These achievements give honor to every administration which has furnished the leadership and to all our people who have coöperated to achieve these great results.

It is not a finished task, but a continuing obligation and opportunity to all our people to work out with continuing wisdom and devotion to the public good a destiny that may not be surpassed by any people.

We pledge the Party to a continuation of this constructive program until every reasonable demand of these causes has been met and as rapidly as by the exercise of rigid economy it may be done within the limits of a sound fiscal policy and by taxation that is not oppressive to any class of taxpayers.

ENDORSEMENT OF STATE ADMINISTRATION

We heartily endorse and commend the administration of Governor McLean and the other Democratic State officials, and the measures enacted by the General Assembly of 1925. The progressive program of development and service inaugurated under previous administrations has not only been continued but has been greatly strengthened by the Executive Budget System and other measures recommended by Governor McLean and enacted by the General Assembly of 1925, for improving and systematizing the administration of State affairs and to provide against waste or extravagance in any department or institution of the State.

We approve and commend all the acts of the General Assembly of 1925, tending to apply methods of sound business economy within all departments of the State government and its institutions.

We commend the careful manner in which the last General Assembly revised our revenue laws to meet the necessities of State revenue without resort to any tax on property or by placing upon the farmers and working people of North Carolina the sales tax, which is based upon consumption instead of ability to pay, and which the Democratic Party has always opposed and which we still oppose. We reaffirm our opposition to the ad valorem property tax for State purposes.

We observe with deep satisfaction and we heartily commend the adoption in many counties of improved methods of administering county affairs. This policy is becoming more and more necessary by reason of the expanding functions of county government in order that there may be at all times an economical and businesslike expenditure of the funds raised by taxation to carry on the constantly enlarging activities of the counties.

While we believe in the time-honored principle of local self-government, we are convinced that the State can and should coöperate with the counties in devising general methods of improving county government. In this connection we observe with interest that the Association, composed of the Commissioners of the various counties in the State, have requested the Governor to appoint, and he has appointed, a commission to study and report to the next meeting of that association for their consideration and action, a plan of simplifying and improving the methods of county administration.

THE PUBLIC SCHOOLS

Believing that a democracy must rely upon an adequate system of public education for the perpetuation of its free institutions and for the preservation of liberty to its citizens against the encroachment of selfish and dominant interests, the Democratic Party has always fostered a system of free schools for all the people. Our public school system is at the foundation of our material progress. From year to year, it has been expanded to meet the widening needs of the people.

Progress in education, like every other kind of progress, is a matter of growth. The principal requisite in our present educational system is to equalize the school facilities of the rural children, particularly those who live in the less wealthy counties, so that we may provide as nearly as possible equality of opportunity in educational advantages for all the children of the State, as fast as our resources will permit. We must constantly strive to reach this goal. The last General Assembly, realizing the need for further progress in education, provided for an Educational Commission to make a complete investigation of the cost of our present system and the means of collecting and disseminating accurate information as to the educational needs of the State, in respect to its system of public schools as well as its institutions of higher learning. In accordance with this act, the Governor has appointed a commission composed of able and conscientious men and women to make the investigation and survey authorized by the act and report their findings of fact and recommendations thereon to the session of the General Assembly which convenes in January next. We believe that the report of said commission will be of great value to the next General Assembly when it comes to determine what shall be the future policy of the State in respect to our entire system of public education.

GOOD ROADS

We rejoice in the remarkable progress that has been made toward the fulfillment of the promise of our platform of 1920, for the establishment and maintenance of a State system of highways. This great achievement is being carried on and will be completed without levying any taxes on property by the State for this or any other purpose, and with a system of financing that will adequately maintain all roads in the State system, pay interest on indebtedness contracted, provide for the full payment of all bonds as they become due and payable, and a substantial additional sum for new construction. It illustrates anew the capacity of the Democratic Party to provide for the State's large needs as well as small, honestly, economically and efficiently, and free from narrow partisanship. We pledge the party to a continuance of the present highway construction program as rapidly as practical from the sources of revenue heretofore set aside and dedicated to that purpose. The State should render every assistance possible, after providing for the completion and maintenance of the State system, to aid the counties in organizing efficient systems of connecting county roads.

FISHING INDUSTRY

We endorse the program commenced several years ago of conserving and building up a great fishing industry. The commercial fisheries of our State are very important and destined to become one of the State's chief assets.

The work of stocking and restocking the numerous fine streams, ponds and lakes of the State by artificial propagation of fish through our State-owned and operated hatcheries is very important, and fast becoming popular throughout the entire State.

We recommend and urge the next General Assembly to work out a plan by which the work of conserving and devolping our commercial fisheries, as well as continuing on a larger scale the work now being done by the State fish hatcheries may be continued.

RAIL AND WATER TRANSPORTATION

Our State should have the benefit of fair, just and equitable freight rates, and any discrimination against our people in this respect must be removed at any cost. We endorse and commend the efforts of the Legislative, Executive and Administrative departments of the State government under Democratic control that have for many years labored in coöperation with shippers of this State to remove discriminations that have existed in interstate rates to the detriment and prejudice of our commerce. We rejoice that substantial measures of relief have been obtained and pledge our unrelenting efforts to this cause until all discriminations are removed. The Democratic Party is likewise committed to the policy of the State's encouraging the development of our water transportation. One of the most important considerations in connection with our rate situation is to do whatever we can without violating sound business principles toward establishing rate basing ports and developing a system of water transportation. The Inland Waterway is a great and constructive project for which the vision and leadership of North Carolina Senators and Representatives in Congress have constantly labored. This great national undertaking is only partially completed and will not develop the volume of water-borne commerce which should be transported through it until it is completed. The completion of the Inland Waterway to Wilmington would add a volume of commerce over this route that would make available regular, frequent and dependable service to all intermediate points. We commend this great enterprise and call upon our Senators and Representatives in Congress to use their best efforts to bring about its completion at the earliest possible moment.

We commend the last General Assembly for its action in providing for a commission charged with the duty of making a complete survey and investigation of the entire rate situation in North Carolina and reporting to the General Assembly the facts which they may find to exist with respect to existing discrimination in rates, the probable causes thereof, the action which in the judgment of the commission will afford a remedy and particularly what action, if any, the State should take in coöperation with the Federal government or otherwise to aid in the development of water transportation to and from North Carolina ports.

PRIMARIES AND ELECTIONS

The Democratic Party believes that all government should be controlled by the people themselves. Every member of our party has a right freely to participate in the choice of our candidates for public office. Every voter has the right freely to participate in the selection of those who fill our offices. The Democratic Party favors all necessary laws to preserve and insure these rights to the increased and increasing number of voters.

No other political party in North Carolina permits its membership to have any part in the choice of candidates, but reserves such selection to a small coterie of selfish politicians, usually Federal office holders.

More than thirty years ago the National Republican Party sought to subject North Carolina to the infamous Force Bill. Today again the threat of that comes from the enemy within our gates, the State organization of that party, in its recently adopted platform. We meet that challenge. We renew our pledge to preserve within the State itself control of all elections. So long as the Democratic Party remains in control of government in this State it will protect the right of every legally qualified voter to exercise the elective franchise uncontrolled and unawed by any centralized authority from without the State.

CAPITAL AND LABOR

Capital and labor are partners in the joint enterprise of production, industry and commerce. Each has rights and the rights of each should be safeguarded and protected. We rejoice that this relationship is generally so cordially recognized and acted upon by these two great forces in the economic life of our State.

The State needs the impetus which comes from the investment of capital in its industries and the development of its natural resources. Every honest business enterprise should be encouraged and justly treated by the government in the enactment and administration of law, and the imposition of taxes. The policy of our party has been to aid and protect all men in the enjoyment of the fruits of their industry and to restrain and prevent any unjust or illegal practices in the conduct of business. Equal and exact justice to all men has been the cardinal tenet of the Democratic Party since the days of its founder. That policy will continue under Democratic administration in North Carolina.

The Democratic Party has always been the firm friend of the toiler. The effective labor legislation on our statute books in both State and Nation came from Democratic leadership. Our party established the Departments of Labor both here and in Washington. It has stood for the inherent right of the laborer to organize and has protected that right by just laws in harmony with the advancing social thought of the time. It has written indelibly into the structure of our law the great principle that labor is not a commodity.

The party will continue to stand for these fundamental principles and for such legislation as will protect and promote the interests of the laborer.

SMOKY MOUNTAIN NATIONAL PARK

The preservation of the natural and distinctive objects of beauty of a State should be one of the prime objects of its people.

We commend the North Carolina Park Commission in its efforts to assist in the establishment of a National Park in North Carolina and thus in some measure to preserve a part of the State's scenic beauty. The efforts of the State should be further exerted toward making The Smoky Mountain National Park an accomplishment.

ENDORSEMENT OF SENATORS AND REPRESENTATIVES IN CONGRESS

We endorse the record of our Senators and Representatives in Congress and express our pride and gratification in the outstanding part played by them in the passage of the recent tax reduction bill, relieving the overburdened taxpayers of the country of $387,000,000 of taxes, not required to meet the needs of the government.

THE TARIFF

We re-declare our firm faith in the time-honored position of the Democratic Party upon the tariff question—in favor of a tax on commodities entering the customs houses that will promote effective competition, protect against monopoly and at the same time produce a fair revenue to support the government.

The abundant benefits of this policy translated into law were strikingly evidenced under the Underwood-Simmons Tariff Act of the Woodrow Wilson administration. Under that act, American business flourished and unprecedented prosperity blessed our people in every walk of life. Our export trade steadily expanded and the products of American farms and factories found ready and profitable markets in every quarter of the world and under every flag.

We denounce and condemn the Fordney-McCumber Tariff Act, which was enacted by the Republican administration to redeem that party's secret campaign obligations to the great favor-seeking interests that have so completely dominated the government throughout the Harding-Coolidge administrations. This iniquitous tariff act, in coördination with trust combinations, enables the beneficiaries of Republican legislation and administration to penalize the American consumers without interference, maintaining at home abnormally high prices on the products of trust and favored interests, which our people must buy, while impairing our foreign markets in which the exportable surplus products of our farms and factories must be sold.

This is strikingly evidenced by the fact that for the first quarter of 1926 the value of our exports for the first time in more than a decade, fell below the value of our imports, turning the balance of trade against the United States, according to the official reports of the United States Department of Commerce, in the sum of $125,143,976.

AGRICULTURE

Agriculture is the basic industry in all civilized lands. Out of its fruits a people are fed and clothed. It furnishes the raw material from which others gather their gains. Above all other industries, this should receive the fostering care of government.

The American farmer enjoyed his greatest period of prosperity under the just and beneficent measures of the Wilson administration. During those eight years the purchasing power of the farmer's dollar averaged $1.04. With the coming of a Republican administration that value began to fall, has steadily decreased, and is now only 60 cents. Since 1921 the farm lands of America have decreased in value in an amount equal to the national debt. These conditions have resulted in such an increase of farm mortgages as to constitute a menace to the whole structure of our rural civilization.

During these five years Republican administrations have made no effort to meet this national problem. They have been responsive to the demands of predatory wealth and the favored few, but have been callously indifferent to the bitter distress of the farmer.

National legislation and action must be had if the farmer is to be given any adequate relief. It is the duty of the National government to exercise its every constitutional power to furnish aid in marketing the surplus of our staple crops. We demand that action to this end be taken by the Congress before it adjourns its present session.

FEDERAL CENTRALIZATION

We believe the powers not granted to the general government by the constitution are reserved to the States. Our dual form of government, founded by our fathers upon this principle in order to secure liberty, must be maintained. State's sovereignty, State's rights and the right of the State in the administration of local affairs should be observed.

There are too many bureaus, boards and commissions—some of them dealing with purely local matters. In Washington we have an almost unlimited number of administrative boards that seem to be functioning as governments—governments within governments—those that are necessary have an almost unlimited number of employees and are answerable to no one in particular and are maintained at an unnecessarily enormous expense to the taxpayers.

Many of these boards and commissions can and should be abolished and the control of the life of our people more largely left to the States and communities.

CONCLUSION

For twenty-five years we have striven to serve the great people who have trusted us with the administration of their public affairs. We have kept the faith. We go on with the great task. We do not make our appeal for continued confidence upon empty pledges not expected to be redeemed, but upon the actual performances of these fruitful years. In all confidence, we submit this platform to a just people, content that it be appraised in the light of our party's record.

We rejoice that in recent elections many members of the opposite party have joined us in the support of the principles and policies here enunciated. We welcome these and all other forward looking men and women to the task of promoting the social, economic and material development of our State.

STATE REPUBLICAN PLATFORM, 1926

Feeling just pride in the achievements of the party in the past, and looking forward to equally great accomplishments in the future, we, the Republican Party of North Carolina, adopt as the basis of our appeal for the support of the people of North Carolina in the coming election the following declaration of principles and policies:

NATIONAL ADMINISTRATION

At the close of the world's greatest war, when the national debt had reached its highest peak and when business was unstable, depressed and chaotic, the people of the United States again turned to the Republican Party with just confidence in its ability to restore business to a normal condition and lift from the people the heavy burden of a national taxation.

At the close of the first administration, public credit had been reestablished, the public debt had been reduced from six to three billion dollars per annum. Taxation had been reduced eight hundred million dollars per annum. Business had been restored, and by the International Agreement for the Limitation of Armaments, America first led the way for universal peace and the fanciful dream of a League of Nations no longer threatened the peace and national independence of our country.

The second Republican administration since the war has also proved the party true to its traditions. The strictest economy has been enforced in every department of the Government. The highest standard of efficiency has been established and by the application of sound business principles to every branch of the Government, every dollar of taxes has paid a dollar of indebtedness. Taxation has decreased and liquidation has increased. The Government debt is no longer a burden and taxation no longer a menace.

With the continuance of the Republican Party in power, we confidently expect the final repeal of all direct taxation. The business of the country is again content with fair and reasonable profits, and labor is satisfied with constant employment at gratifying wages. The people are prosperous and happy, and at no period in our history have they had more faith in their Government and greater confidence in their President than today. By thoughtful, far-sighted, wise decisions in five years of successful administration, our President leaves the Democratic Party without an issue and without a leader. Issues are not developed, nor leaders made battling against success. Three words are expressive of the present administration: Economy, Efficiency and Prosperity.

PROTECTION

We believe that the great industrial development of our State is in a great measure the result of the protective tariff laws enacted by the Republican Party. Our continued prosperity depends on the continuance of this policy. While our people vote for free trade, they have grown rich as the result of the protective tariff laws that are national in scope and effect. Political conditions now confront us that make it necessary for the continuation of this great policy—that our State should vote its real convictions. The South is not now, nor will it ever be again, a free trade section. The party that has made the State rich should receive an expression of gratitude at the coming election. It is no longer safe for North Carolina to vote for free trade and pray for protection. The dormant Whig sentiment should assert itself and the protective tariff sentiment in this State should be represented in Congress and the Senate.

STATE AFFAIRS

We favor the progressive administration of the affairs of the State. We do not believe in extravagance nor in unnecessarily burdening the people with debt, but the growing life of North Carolina demands a progressive administration of State affairs. We believe in encouraging the activities of the State to meet the expanding life of the people.

NATURAL RESOURCES

For the development of our State's abundant natural resources, we need to invite into the State more abundant capital, and in order to do this, we must extend to them every legal advantage offered by the other progressive states of the Nation.

The development of the waterpower of our State in the last few years has added millions of wealth and multiplied our industries until we are fast becoming one of the greatest industrial states of the Union. We believe that every reasonable effort should be made to encourage the further development of our water power and other natural resources, and that the aim of State legislation should be to benefit and encourage, not to destroy.

STATE HIGHWAYS

We favor the early completion of the State system of hard surface highways, and the extension of this system so as to serve equitably and fairly every section of the State. The Republican party has consistently favored the construction of State highways, and on the hustings and in the legislature has consistently supported the legislation directed to that end. Much credit is due the Republican party for its efforts in the legislature to eliminate the highway question from politics. While the Democratic party was timidly advocating a small bond issue for State highways, Republican members of the legislature introduced a bill providing for the sale of $100,000,000 in bonds to be expended in the construction and maintenance of State highways. Although the McGuire bill was defeated by a small vote in the House the State has since recognized the wisdom of this measure and has expended the sum provided for in this bill in the building of highways. The increased income derived from taxes on gasoline and automobiles will justify the State's extending its systems into every rural community of the State and we favor the continuation of this until every section of North Carolina is put in easy touch with an improved highway.

SCHOOLS

We favor a liberal policy in the matter of public education. The Republican party in North Carolina has always favored the education of the people of the State and has consistently advocated the extension and betterment of the public school system. The constitution of the State provides for a State system of public schools. We favor such a system supported by a State system of taxation. There is no defensible reason why a $100 worth of property in one county should pay in taxes 94c for public schools, while $100 worth of property in an adjoining county pays 29c. Equal taxation means equal opportunity. Under the present system an eight-months school term would bankrupt the poorer counties. With a uniform State system of taxation, an eight-months term could be maintained in every school district in the State without being a burden to any of the counties, and we pledge our best efforts to the adoption of a uniform system that will give to all the children of the State an equal opportunity to secure an equal education. Under the present system, extrava gance prevails in the rich counties, with long terms of school, while the weaker counties are struggling with a burden too great to bear in their efforts to maintain their short-term schools. Taxes from all the people in the State should be used to educate all the children in the State. We demand a school system not as weak as the poorest county but as strong as the richest county in the State.

TAXATION

The present Democratic State government boasts that the State is now operating without the levy of any ad valorem tax for State purposes. This is a deception. The public school tax is a tax levied under State laws and under the State Constitution and is a State tax pure and simple, and this tax now higher than for the support of all other departments of the State and County governments combined, is shifted to the counties and ingeniously called a County tax, and all the odium of high taxes is thereby charged to the counties. The school tax should be levied and collected as a State tax apportioned equitably and rateably and justly to the counties according to the school population to maintain a six months school term over the State. This will insure a lower tax rate in a majority of the counties, enforce uniformity, abolish the equalizing fund, stop the borrowing of money by the State Treasury for school purposes, stop the issuance and sale of more State bonds for this purpose, stimulate more interest in popular education in the State and hasten the day when the people will welcome and support an amendment to our State Constitution providing for an eight months school term over the State, now so much desired by the educational leaders of the State.

AGRICULTURE

Agriculture is one of our chief industries, and the basis of our economic life. It has not, and is not, receiving the aid and encouragement from the State that its importance demands. Notwithstanding the fact that the Democratic party has been in complete control of the government for a third of a century, not one act has been placed on the statute books for the benefit of the farmer. Our lands are fertile and our farmers industrious, but the increased cost of farm labor and the annual increase of the State tax burden so diminishes the returns that farming is unprofitable. The only laws the Democratic party has enacted for the farmer's relief are those that annually increase his tax burden, and we presume that it thereby intends to stimulate his industry. Taxation does not stimulate but destroys. The great need of the farmer today is not increased production, but better marketing facilities. With farm products high to the consumer, the producer is not receiving a fair return for labor. The State should, by appropriate legislation, convert the agricultural department into a direct agency for aiding the farmer in finding a market for his products. The effort the farmer is making by attempted coöperative marketing is evidence of the lack of effort on the part of the state in his behalf. Under the present system, the state through its agricultural department is encouraging production, and then leaving the producer to the mercy of the speculator. The farmer must receive from his products the necessary 90 per cent of the consumer's price if agriculture is to prosper.

LABOR

We regard it as shameful that North Carolina, one of the greatest industrial states of the nation, should have done so little to better the condition of the great laboring classes of our people. We favor legislation limiting the hours of labor and properly safe-guarding employees and laborers engaged in dangerous occupations.

Almost all of the great industrial states have adopted a workmen's compensation law. The wisdom of such laws has appealed to both the employer and the employees. Repeated efforts have been made before the North Carolina legislature to secure such legislation for this State. The labor organizations have demanded such legislation, the employers have favored it, but our legislature has persistently refused these demands. We call upon the people of the State in the next election to demand of their prospective representatives pledge that they pass a just workmen's compensation law for this State.

WOMAN SUFFRAGE

Woman suffrage was first endorsed and has been consistently supported in North Carolina by the Republican party. We rejoice that the women of the State have been given the franchise by the Federal Government, and regret that North Carolina did not join in extending to them this right. We recognize in the women voters of the State a power for progress and an uplifting influence in our political life, and see evidences of this in their present demands for a just and fair election law in the State.

ELECTION LAWS

No Republican form of government can long endure that does not provide for the free expression of the will of the people at the ballot box. Fraud in elections and unfair election laws strike at the very heart of a free state. Nothing can be done that will increase crime and encourage criminals more than to give to the official whose duty it is to enforce the law, a tainted commission. The election laws of North Carolina should no longer be tolerated by a free people. The general law makes registration a prerequisite to voting. It gives to the registrar the right to judicially pass upon the qualifications of every citizen. The registrar is made the most important official connected with the election, and the registrar is always a Democract, and no other party is given representation in registering voters.

In practice the registrar is a law unto himself, exercising his judicial discretion arbitrarily, and often giving to those of his political party opportunities to register that are not accorded others. Often he places upon the registration books the names of prospective voters who never appear before him, and strikes from the poll books the names of those he does not desire to vote. If the registrar acts arbitrarily, and if a citizen vigorously protests, he is liable to indictment for felony and for disturbing this high judicial official. Drastic laws are passed to protect him, and little if any law is provided for the citizen who is deprived of franchise.

A wide-open door for fraud is provided by what is known as the Absentee Voters Law. This law was passed primarily for the benefit of the soldiers fighting in the field. Many of them never saw the ballots which were cast for them. Under this law thousands of voters are caused to vote without either their knowledge or consent, and in many instances the dead are voted.

In recent years, many of the Republican counties have been singled out and private election laws have been passed for them. These laws are falsely denominated the Australian Ballot Law. In the name of the Australian Ballot, the most infamous laws ever forced on a free people have been given many of the Republican counties. Under these laws the registrars are all Democrats, and all markers provided to aid electors in voting are Democrats, and all ballots are permitted to be handled only by democratic officials, and the least mark or scratch on a ballot vitiates it. Under these laws, at the first election Republican counties are made Democratic, not by the vote of the people but by the fraud permitted by these laws. One such act was passed designed for two certain counties, and after its passage in the House the names of six other counties by forgery were placed in the act. We as a party have long tolerated these unfair laws. We have often appealed to the Legislature to give us a fair law with equal representation on all election boards. Our petitions are answered by special, infamous laws designed for Republican counties.

We again request and demand the enactment of a just and fair election law that will give representation on all election boards to each of the political parties. If we can not be given this relief by a just law, it shall become our duty to petition the Congress of the United States to enact a National Election Law that will give to each political party equal representation on all election boards and guarantee to each citizen qualified under the law the right to vote and have that vote counted as cast by the elector, in all National elections.

PART IX

ELECTION RETURNS

1. VOTE FOR PRESIDENT BY STATES, 1912-1924.
2. VOTE FOR PRESIDENT BY COUNTIES, 1916-1924.
3. VOTE BY COUNTIES FOR GOVERNOR IN DEMOCRATIC PRIMARIES, 1920-1924.
4. VOTE FOR STATE OFFICERS IN DEMOCRATIC PRIMARIES, 1924.
5. DEMOCRATIC PRIMARY VOTE, JUNE 5, 1926, FOR UNITED STATES SENATOR.
6. VOTE FOR GOVERNOR BY COUNTIES, 1920-1924.
7. VOTE FOR UNITED STATES SENATOR, 1920-1926.
8. VOTE FOR MEMBERS OF CONGRESS, 1922-1926.
9. VOTE FOR CONSTITUTIONAL AMENDMENT AND REFERENDUM BY COUNTIES, 1926.
10. VOTE FOR SOLICITORS, 1926.

VOTE FOR PRESIDENT   339

POPULAR AND ELECTORAL VOTE FOR PRESIDENT BY STATES, 1924

State	Coolidge	Davis	La Follette	Coolidge Plurality	Davis Plurality	Coolidge Republican	Davis Democrat	La Follette Progressive
Alabama	45,066	112,966	8,084		67,960		3	6
Arizona	30,484	26,234	17,148	4,250				
Arkansas	40,394	84,823	13,169		44,429			
California	733,250	105,514	424,649	308,601		13		
Colorado	193,956	75,238	69,903	118,718		6		
Connecticut	246,322	110,184	42,416	136,138		7		
Delaware	52,441	33,445	4,917	18,996		3		
Florida	30,633	62,083	8,625		31,450		6	
Georgia	30,300	123,200	12,691		92,900		14	
Idaho	69,789	24,256	54,160	15,629		4		
Illinois	1,453,321	576,975	432,027	876,346		29		
Indiana	703,042	492,247	71,678	210,795		15		
Iowa	537,635	162,600	272,242	265,392		13		
Kansas	407,671	156,319	98,461	251,352		10		
Kentucky	298,966	274,855	38,159	24,111		13		
Louisiana	24,670	93,218	*		68,540		10	
Maine	138,440	41,964	11,382	96,476		6		
Maryland	162,414	148,072	46,157	14,342		8		
Massachusetts	703,476	280,834	141,225	422,645		18		
Michigan	871,400	151,600	121,200	719,800		15		
Minnesota	420,759	55,913	339,192	81,567		12		
Mississippi	8,370	100,475	3,494		92,105		10	
Missouri	650,283	572,753	84,160	77,530		18		
Montana	74,138	33,805	64,105	13,033		4		
Nebraska	218,585	137,289	106,701	81,296		8		
Nevada	11,243	5,909	9,569	1,674		3		
New Hampshire	100,078	57,576	9,200	42,502		4		
New Jersey	675,162	297,743	108,901	377,419		14		
New Mexico	54,470	48,473	9,248	5,997		3		
New York	1,820,058	950,796	474,905	869,262		45		
North Carolina	191,753	284,270	6,651		92,517		12	
North Dakota	94,931	13,856	89,865	5,066		5		
Ohio	1,176,100	477,888	357,948	698,212		24		
Oklahoma	225,947	255,845	45,841		29,868		10	
Oregon	142,579	67,589	68,463	74,116		5		
Pennsylvania	1,401,481	409,192	307,567	992,289		38		
Rhode Island	125,286	76,606	7,628	48,680		5		
South Carolina	1,123	49,008	620		47,885		9	
South Dakota	100,420	26,484	74,668	25,752		5		
Tennessee	131,064	158,537	10,473		27,473		12	
Texas	128,240	478,425	42,541		350,185		20	
Utah	77,381	47,064	32,671	30,320		4		
Vermont	80,498	16,124	5,943	64,374		4		
Virginia	72,902	139,717	10,369		66,815		12	
Washington	220,224	42,842	150,727	69,497		7		
West Virginia	288,635	257,232	36,723	31,403		8		
Wisconsin	311,614	68,096	453,678	**				13
Wyoming	41,858	12,868	25,174	16,684		3		
Totals	15,718,789	8,387,962	4,822,319	7,339,827		392	136	13

*Louisiana, 4063 (scattering) most of which intended for LaFollette
**Wisconsin, LaFollette's plurality 142,064.

POPULAR AND ELECTORAL VOTE FOR PRESIDENT BY STATES

States	Popular Vote, 1912			Popular Vote, 1916		Popular Vote, 1920		Electoral Vote, 1920	
	Wilson	Taft	Roosevelt	Wilson	Hughes	Harding, Republican	Cox, Democrat	Harding, Republican	Cox, Democrat
Alabama	82,439	9,731	22,689	97,776	28,662	7,121	81,982		12
Arizona	10,324	3,021	6,949	33,170	1,524	37,016	29,546	3	
Arkansas	68,838	24,297	21,653	112,186	49,527	71,117	107,409		9
California	283,436	3,914	283,306	465,836	462,516	624,992	229,191	13	
Colorado	114,223	58,386	72,306	178,816	102,308	173,248	104,936	6	
Connecticut	74,561	68,324	34,126	99,786	106,514	229,238	120,721	7	
Delaware	22,631	15,988	8,886	24,753	25,794	52,858	39,911	3	
Florida	36,417	4,279	4,535	56,158	14,611	44,853	90,515		6
Georgia	93,171	5,140	22,010	125,831	11,225		46,552		14
Idaho	33,921	32,810	25,527	70,021	56,368	88,972	533,385	4	
Illinois	405,048	253,593	386,478	950,081	1,152,316	1,424,430	511,361	29	
Indiana	281,890	151,265	162,007	324,063	341,005	696,370	225,521	15	
Iowa	185,325	119,805	161,819	221,699	280,419	634,671	85,142	13	
Kansas	143,650	74,844	120,766	314,588	277,656	369,195	456,967	10	
Kentucky	219,484	115,512	102,766	269,990	241,854	452,480	87,509		13
Louisiana	60,966	3,833	9,323	79,875	6,644	38,538	58,961		10
Maine	51,113	26,545	48,495	64,116	69,506	136,355	89,626	6	
Maryland	112,674	51,956	57,789	138,359	117,341	236,117	276,094	8	
Massachusetts	173,408	155,948	142,228	247,885	268,812	681,153	283,430	18	
Michigan	150,751	152,244	211,451	286,773	339,097	762,865	233,450	15	
Minnesota	106,426	64,334	125,856	179,152	179,544	519,421	142,994	12	
Mississippi	57,164	1,511	3,627	80,382	4,253	11,576	69,277		10
Missouri	330,746	207,821	124,371	398,032	369,339	727,162	574,799	18	
Montana	27,941	18,512	22,456	101,063	66,750	109,430	57,372	4	
Nebraska	109,008	54,216	72,681	158,827	117,771	247,498	119,608	8	
Nevada	7,986	3,196	5,620	17,776	12,127	15,479	9,851	3	
New Hampshire	34,724	32,927	17,794	43,779	43,725	95,196	62,662	4	
New Jersey	178,289	88,568	145,410	211,018	268,982	611,541	256,668	14	
New Mexico	20,437	17,733	347	33,553	31,164	57,634	16,668	3	
New York	655,475	455,428	390,021	768,880	875,540	1,829,862	778,706	45	

VOTE FOR PRESIDENT 341

North Carolina	144,507	29,120	69,130	168,383	120,880	252,48	305,447		12
North Dakota	29,555	23,090	25,726	55,271	32,651	160,072	37,122	5	
Ohio	423,152	277,066	229,807	604,916	514,886	1,182,022	789,637	20	
Oklahoma	119,156	90,786		148,123	97,233	214,320	216,389	9	
Oregon	47,064	34,673	37,600	129,687	126,813	143,592	80,019	3	
Pennsylvania	395,619	273,315	47,426	521,784	708,711	1,126,215	503,202	42	
Rhode Island	30,142	27,586	16,878	40,394	41,588	107,463	55,062	5	
South Carolina	48,355		1,293	61,916	1,809	2,610	61,170		9
South Dakota	48,942	59,144	58,811	56,591	24,621	110,692	45,958	5	
Tennessee	130,335	28,858	53,225	163,334	116,114	219,829	206,558	12	
Texas	221,589	42,100	26,173	285,909	64,199	115,640	289,688		20
Utah	36,579		24,174	83,400	54,193	81,555	36,639	4	
Vermont	15,350	42,305	21,620	22,708	40,250	68,212	30,919	4	
Virginia	90,332	28,285	21,777	102,824	49,350	57,456	141,670	12	
Washington	86,840	20,415	113,698	183,388	167,244	223,137	84,298	7	
West Virginia	113,197	36,734	79,112	110,403	143,124	282,007	220,789	7	
Wisconsin	161,109	130,872	58,661	193,042	221,323	498,576	113,422	13	
Wyoming	15,310	11,500	9,232	28,348	21,698	35,091	17,429	3	
Totals	6,203,039	3,481,956	1,119,507	9,116,298	8,547,474	15,999,781	8,804,580	404	125

VOTE FOR PRESIDENT BY COUNTIES, 1916-1924

Counties	1916				1920		1924		
	Wilson	Hughes	Benson	Hanley	Cox	Harding	Davis Electors	Coolidge Electors	La Follette Electors
Alamance	2,476	2,278	5	...	5,255	4,619	4,859	3,217	93
Alexander	954	1,187	...	...	2,045	2,643	2,291	2,437	20
Alleghany	796	641	...	...	1,409	1,201	1,643	1,234	6
Anson	2,046	301	...	...	3,175	433	2,372	225	25
Ashe	1,898	1,930	...	...	3,431	3,808	4,333	3,952	3
Avery	360	1,158	...	2	397	2,503	357	2,189	14
Beaufort	1,957	1,274	...	1	3,522	2,266	3,048	1,502	93
Bertie	1,461	116	...	...	1,840	212	1,785	159	5
Bladen	1,261	651	...	...	1,939	1,064	1,551	786	23
Brunswick	810	989	1	...	1,253	1,362	1,118	1,296	41
Buncombe	4,229	3,830	...	...	10,167	8,917	10,098	6,285	467
Burke	1,621	1,474	...	...	3,262	3,592	4,137	3,190	...
Cabarrus	2,080	2,314	22	...	4,418	5,148	4,449	3,510	189
Caldwell	1,725	1,659	...	...	2,931	3,298	3,348	2,503	26
Camden	368	86	...	2	540	142	436	132	9
Carteret	1,165	1,246	...	...	2,070	2,315	2,261	1,854	15
Caswell	849	338	...	...	1,239	505	1,075	467	4
Catawba	2,569	2,614	4	10	5,404	5,935	5,754	5,998	167
Chatham	1,839	1,501	14	...	3,186	2,909	3,446	2,755	15
Cherokee	1,362	1,362	...	...	1,761	2,506	1,742	2,314	23
Chowan	610	91	...	1	1,091	209	714	98	5
Clay	400	453	...	...	755	911	953	1,090	18
Cleveland	2,764	1,497	...	...	5,181	2,953	3,749	1,743	37
Columbus	2,143	1,327	...	2	3,411	1,783	2,757	1,629	26
Craven	1,780	542	...	...	3,413	731	2,942	325	44
Cumberland	1,971	1,217	...	...	3,233	1,972	2,923	1,372	37
Currituck	945	87	...	1	1,000	86	670	52	13
Dare	470	363	...	...	825	632	826	629	2
Davidson	2,675	2,801	12	...	4,797	590	6,507	6,227	56
Davie	910	1,245	6	...	1,624	2,594	1,795	2,672	13
Duplin	1,824	1,527	...	...	3,398	2,697	2,924	1,542	37
Durham	2,463	1,837	...	...	4,646	3,550	4,837	3,093	221
Edgecombe	2,028	135	24	1	3,343	24	2,274	171	109
Forsyth	4,115	3,585	238	...	8,123	6,792	7,404	5,315	459
Franklin	2,057	396	...	...	2,742	589	1,991	302	13
Gaston	3,019	2,542	...	11	7,148	5,803	6,554	3,566	82
Gates	826	309	...	...	796	327	679	215	1
Graham	476	460	...	...	644	915	841	907	11
Granville	1,713	648	...	...	2,622	833	2,220	461	14
Greene	1,066	294	...	...	1,649	439	1,119	182	7
Guilford	4,616	3,670	44	...	9,615	7,920	8,804	6,822	317
Halifax	2,312	299	1	...	3,429	524	3,232	268	83
Harnett	1,992	1,603	8	...	3,919	3,311	3,296	2,895	11
Haywood	2,403	1,523	...	...	4,229	3,000	4,582	2,440	8
Henderson	1,166	1,795	...	...	2,496	3,337	3,007	3,548	48
Hertford	977	209	...	1	1,104	221	932	164	3
Hoke	780	110	...	...	1,266	166	1,146	141	1
Hyde	840	277	4	3	1,134	530	653	305	16
Iredell	3,335	2,073	...	...	6,470	4,402	6,449	3,565	136
Jackson	1,306	1,288	...	...	2,385	2,355	3,100	2,788	17
Johnston	3,468	2,857	...	...	6,030	5,588	4,656	4,910	23
Jones	712	233	...	...	964	385	692	179	2
Lee	1,054	573	...	...	2,327	1,143	1,834	710	10

VOTE FOR PRESIDENT—Continued

Counties	1916				1920		1924		
	Wilson	Hughes	Berger	Hanley	Cox	Harding	Davis Electors	Coolidge Electors	La Follette Electors
Lenoir	1,666	667	2		2,560	1,155	2,191	514	25
Lincoln	1,521	1,369	8	1	3,331	3,137	2,909	2,658	42
Macon	1,146	1,069			2,177	2,050	2,178	2,015	18
Madison	972	1,965			1,340	3,616	1,471	3,252	74
Martin	1,472	281			2,561	530	1,999	216	9
McDowell	1,274	1,218		2	2,809	2,561	3,023	2,590	25
Mecklenburg	4,508	1,257	6		11,313	3,421	8,443	2,572	437
Mitchell	462	1,298			697	2,153	689	1,540	8
Montgomery	1,222	1,196			2,321	2,304	2,483	2,077	5
Moore	1,337	1,047	22		2,679	2,279	2,771	1,974	38
Nash	2,189	826	19		4,031	1,556	3,129	823	131
New Hanover	2,355	492			4,102	712	4,735	1,190	405
Northampton	1,518	45			2,305	165	1,662	144	17
Onslow	1,197	785		1	1,557	853	1,122	423	31
Orange	1,230	1,158			1,993	1,737	1,879	1,065	66
Pamlico	710	527	18		1,286	1,008	798	459	
Pasquotank	1,177	270		1	1,736	507	1,236	305	12
Pender	970	400			1,580	699	1,175	253	17
Perquimans	645	288		1	1,042	487	550	205	8
Person	953	914			1,646	1,566	1,576	1,025	3
Pitt	2,839	719			4,196	864	3,197	512	56
Polk	679	750	1		1,361	1,326	1,613	1,445	13
Randolph	2,747	3,031		3	5,110	6,297	5,397	6,336	24
Richmond	1,553	650			3,341	1,124	2,475	599	163
Robeson	2,894	1,453			6,183	2,220	4,064	311	14
Rockingham	2,316	1,957			4,507	3,605	4,467	2,566	89
Rowan	3,053	2,320			6,421	4,888	4,816	3,560	738
Rutherford	2,445	1,871			5,101	4,015	5,101	3,867	29
Sampson	1,369	2,727			2,426	5,353	2,021	3,188	35
Scotland	938	137			1,705	306	1,469	205	11
Stanly	2,110	1,941	5	4	3,843	4,312	3,832	3,594	50
Stokes	1,569	1,852	21		1,999	2,926	2,309	2,482	44
Surry	2,029	2,977	12		3,547	5,170	4,118	4,990	66
Swain	829	1,128			1,434	2,239	1,769	2,178	24
Transylvania	821	841			1,542	1,680	1,776	1,814	22
Tyrrell	416	392			718	532	638	442	1
Union	2,662	702	1		4,168	1,404	2,724	672	32
Vance	1,451	558			2,461	816	2,013	470	21
Wake	4,627	2,461	5		8,020	3,653	8,376	2,975	185
Warren	1,217	227			1,865	295	1,712	166	62
Washington	651	486			1,116	971	883	831	6
Watauga	1,141	1,352			1,721	2,634	2,365	2,665	8
Wayne	2,625	1,446	3	2	4,794	2,822	3,366	1,579	42
Wilkes	1,632	3,470			2,843	6,451	3,586	6,431	11
Wilson	2,052	730			3,496	1,371	2,649	571	81
Yadkin	879	1,724			1,350	3,391	1,381	2,889	11
Yancey	1,273	1,082			2,280	2,596	2,592	2,456	21
Totals	168,383	120,890	509	53	305,447	232,848	284,270	191,753	6,651

VOTE BY COUNTIES FOR GOVERNOR IN DEMOCRATIC PRIMARIES,* 1920-1924

Counties	1920 First Primary			1920 Second Primary		1924	
	Morrison	Gardner	Page	Morrison	Gardner	McLean	Bailey
Alamance	434	488	482	558	488	1,349	194
Alexander	187	183	14	375	203	375	81
Alleghany	131	60	60	320	200	1,002	162
Anson	590	834	569	986	1,082	1,883	1,516
Ashe	214	107	45	429	173	2,153	202
Avery	18	457	9	41	308	216	193
Beaufort	438	1,086	73	579	1,220	2,153	1,167
Bertie	694	229	350	627	517	1,069	1,134
Bladen	694	229	316	1,037	334	2,623	904
Brunswick	91	306	172	209	445	295	146
Buncombe	1,873	1,443	217	2,052	1,967	5,297	2,007
Burke	633	116	55	737	359	1,492	194
Cabarrus	303	149	284	532	324	1,172	123
Caldwell	270	262	34	361	443	1,663	464
Camden	161	277	106	142	158	334	615
Carteret	419	427	136	382	273	987	337
Caswell	89	219	375	292	433	505	637
Catawba	891	292	343	1,063	401	980	418
Chatham	535	349	319	689	398	1,400	1,375
Cherokee	117	195	17	315	106	298	78
Chowan	282	247	137	232	186	590	593
Clay	101	43	26	103	26	100	42
Cleveland	46	2,219	524	390	3,248	3,344	1,204
Columbus	806	699	420	1,014	1,322	2,964	1,117
Craven	1,263	718	124	1,454	954	1,758	1,728
Cumberland	443	957	443	840	1,323	1,908	1,128
Currituck	408	99	184	450	135	863	416
Dare	202	68	30	189	43	501	188
Davidson	553	284	833	886	752	1,834	538
Davie	160	50	237	277	214	102	145
Duplin	265	697	133	741	757	2,036	817
Durham	752	608	410	1,106	584	3,609	924
Edgecombe	1,254	713	457	1,604	767	1,798	1,402
Forsyth	514	1,094	540	936	1,410	2,802	504
Franklin	1,323	715	547	1,349	632	1,354	1,860
Gaston	956	1,258	279	1,375	1,494	3,080	369
Gates	128	196	120	189	145	448	314
Graham	53		2	180		353	77
Granville	518	627	282	847	713	1,314	1,303
Greene	209	373	70	284	576	518	1,266
Guilford	497	692	1,298	1,031	1,307	2,222	1,616
Halifax	359	1,177	617	915	999	2,721	1,840
Harnett	368	595	542	783	682	1,285	1,834
Haywood	1,674	395	143	1,162	553	3,222	1,321
Henderson	378	228	22	478	257	869	474
Hertford	250	576	243	406	592	512	926
Hoke	450	177	233	469	189	745	448
Hyde	92	254	201	492	444	421	812
Iredell	1,578	478	313	1,959	1,011	4,082	930

PRIMARY VOTE FOR GOVERNOR

VOTE BY COUNTIES FOR GOVERNOR IN DEMOCRATIC PRIMARIES*
1920-1924—Continued

Counties	1920 First Primary			1920 Second Primary			1924
	Morrison	Gardner	Page	Morrison	Gardner	McLean	Bailey
Jackson	397	297	30	266	339	1,568	350
Johnston	1,154	577	178	1,924	1,240	2,725	1,927
Jones	164	254	32	453	378	455	304
Lee	458	230	346	788	368	1,113	532
Lenoir	240	900	290	530	1,050	2,049	1,480
Lincoln	227	543	398	364	595	1,429	430
Macon	175	73	21	350	224	678	382
Madison	215	226	22	269	147	496	186
Martin	537	274	118	632	364	1,598	783
McDowell	309	421	21	422	507	1,449	653
Mecklenburg	3,022	496	2,048	3,443	1,506	5,958	2,449
Mitchell	108	160	14	62	182	202	189
Montgomery	205	49	615	474	304	881	436
Moore	298	69	697	695	202	1,434	622
Nash	953	521	521	1,395	873	1,593	1,712
New Hanover	615	1,097	482	1,167	735	2,393	1,463
Northampton	398	1,023	399	957	835	1,523	1,455
Onslow	118	317	96	131	298	833	402
Orange	85	358	256	181	140	701	770
Pamlico	204	327	28	246	220	645	171
Pasquotank	188	332	350	420	279	1,261	736
Pender	245	208	430	694	235	874	686
Perquimans	69	435	141	112	219	354	320
Person	62	170	164	180	277	556	954
Pitt	896	1,392	792	1,457	1,480	2,795	2,492
Polk	177	138	1	256	177	1,024	125
Randolph	1,034	117	844	1,373	512	1,408	594
Richmond	853	274	986	1,077	785	2,731	960
Robeson	1,974	2,536	615	1,864	2,472	5,556	1,314
Rockingham	76	516	290	447	718	1,212	1,055
Rowan	733	1,104	535	856	878	2,984	1,248
Rutherford	453	1,458	88	643	1,029	2,699	1,682
Sampson	194	183	162	334	206	634	722
Scotland	401	205	276	557	424	1,871	633
Stanly	316	333	168	724	464	964	234
Stokes	154	103	100	384	197	348	156
Surry	345	291	877	580	745	1,542	576
Swain	210	98	16	289	78	327	23
Transylvania	245	94	17	345	256	284	633
Tyrrell	11	146	31	51	107	182	310
Union	528	1,452	898	794	1,463	2,858	1,359
Vance	245	500	398	376	412	939	1,418
Wake	1,060	2,281	1,593	2,434	2,585	4,596	1,854
Warren	485	544	345	678	542	857	873
Washington	36	217	137	154	124	534	255
Watauga	92	25	43	271	24	711	84
Wayne	600	917	162	1,106	955	2,469	1,554
Wilkes	915	117	61	1,435	186	1,772	822
Wilson	1,164	292	354	1,640	823	1,962	1,575
Yadkin	130	130	140	264	195	339	123
Yancey	386	164	11	285	392	856	515
Totals	49,070	48,983	30,480	70,332	61,073	151,197	83,373

*The Republican party held no gubernatorial primary

VOTE FOR STATE OFFICERS IN DEMOCRATIC PRIMARIES, 1924

FOR GOVERNOR—
  Angus Wilton McLean 151,197
  Josiah William Bailey 83,574
FOR LIEUTENANT-GOVERNOR—
  J. Elmer Long 80,231
  R. R. Reynolds 68,676
  T. C. Bowie 62,086
FOR ATTORNEY-GENERAL—
  Dennis G. Brummitt 78,411
  Charles Ross 70,448
  Frank Nash 53,167
FOR COMMISSIONER OF LABOR AND PRINTING—
  First Primary:
  M. L. Shipman 81,011
  Frank D. Grist 69,158
  O. J. Peterson 31,556
  L. M. Nash 19,180
  Second Primary:
  M. L. Shipman 36,847
  Frank D. Grist 69,382
FOR CORPORATION COMMISSION—
  George P. Pell 123,558
  Oscar B. Carpenter 78,240
FOR STATE AUDITOR—
  Baxter Durham 119,900
  James P. Cook 83,162
FOR COMMISSIONER OF AGRICULTURE—
  W. A. Graham 92,561
  Fred P. Latham 76,808
  T. B. Parker 37,776
FOR INSURANCE COMMISSIONER—
  Stacey W. Wade 61,163
  J. Frank Flowers 41,340

DEMOCRATIC PRIMARY VOTE, JUNE 5, 1926 FOR UNITED STATES SENATOR

Counties	L. S. Overman	R. R. Reynolds	Counties	L. S. Overman	R. R. Reynolds
Alamance	633	135	Jones	641	369
Alexander	58	107	Lee	1,107	1,187
Alleghany	632	341	Lenoir	2,330	1,467
Anson	1,918	1,040	Lincoln	989	507
Ashe	111	232	McDowell	253	368
Avery	285	614	Macon	499	890
Beaufort	1,484	437	Madison	226	388
Bertie	781	1,081	Martin	1,306	981
Bladen	1,506	972	Mecklenburg	6,708	2,645
Brunswick	350	68	Mitchell	381	336
Buncombe	2,911	6,973	Montgomery	761	324
Burke	1,313	524	Moore	1,187	1,141
Cabarrus	806	143	Nash	2,125	1,778
Caldwell	2,096	365	New Hanover	2,117	1,564
Camden	602	331	Northampton	1,767	1,050
Carteret	1,129	852	Onslow	911	463
Caswell	867	272	Orange	1,249	586
Catawba	973	519	Pamlico	527	400
Chatham	2,589	1,179	Pasquotank	756	154
Cherokee	700	419	Pender	811	478
Chowan	536	505	Perquimans	174	821
Clay	322	169	Person	1,127	361
Cleveland	2,725	2,191	Pitt	3,198	2,379
Columbus	1,676	1,780	Polk	290	109
Craven	1,863	1,171	Randolph	1,106	91
Cumberland	2,183	913	Richmond	3,033	1,652
Currituck	474	883	Robeson	1,864	1,689
Dare	185	407	Rockingham	2,251	242
Davidson	725	518	Rowan	3,234	628
Davie	310	77	Rutherford	2,260	1,263
Duplin	1,796	716	Sampson	559	195
Durham	3,212	1,900	Scotland	1,511	663
Edgecombe	1,562	638	Stanly	1,309	115
Forsyth	2,962	1,196	Stokes	625	290
Franklin	1,959	1,239	Surry	481	192
Gaston	3,385	1,019	Swain	628	702
Gates	281	389	Transylvania	431	711
Graham	162	151	Tyrrell	178	324
Granville	1,495	877	Union	2,180	1,114
Greene	1,059	461	Vance	1,217	1,309
Guilford	2,117	857	Wake	5,586	6,782
Halifax	3,455	1,100	Warren	1,257	1,251
Harnett	1,473	1,115	Washington	228	223
Haywood	2,360	3,278	Watauga	185	45
Henderson	684	1,199	Wayne	3,584	1,583
Hertford	568	955	Wilkes	481	226
Hoke	466	111	Wilson	1,312	582
Hyde	517	512	Yadkin	163	55
Iredell	4,567	887	Yancey	948	839
Jackson	743	1,761			
Johnston	2,254	1,255	Totals	110,260	91,914

VOTE FOR GOVERNOR BY COUNTIES, 1920-1924

Counties	1920		1924	
	Cameron Morrison	John J. Parker	A. W. McLean	I. M. Meekins
Alamance	5,274	4,624	4,934	3,168
Alexander	2,000	2,613	2,292	2,429
Alleghany	1,417	1,187	1,648	1,242
Anson	3,340	422	2,391	209
Ashe	3,628	3,800	4,350	3,894
Avery	403	2,497	460	2,451
Beaufort	3,559	2,212	3,081	1,283
Bertie	1,886	147	1,836	85
Bladen	1,994	1,010	1,691	600
Brunswick	1,311	1,381	1,123	1,247
Buncombe	10,412	8,005	10,826	6,011
Burke	3,314	3,566	4,089	3,227
Cabarrus	4,394	5,226	4,539	3,604
Caldwell	2,953	3,222	3,371	2,466
Camden	565	116	396	161
Carteret	2,094	2,292	2,313	1,832
Caswell	1,250	496	1,074	443
Catawba	5,124	5,912	5,831	6,028
Chatham	3,249	2,895	3,271	2,752
Cherokee	1,762	2,474	1,767	2,317
Chowan	1,129	162	733	80
Clay	763	913	1,004	1,124
Cleveland	5,116	2,978	3,789	1,796
Columbus	3,313	1,655	2,855	1,428
Craven	3,464	604	3,081	224
Cumberland	3,316	1,849	3,304	1,093
Currituck	974	69	639	82
Dare	846	624	823	638
Davidson	4,907	5,844	6,358	6,202
Davie	1,654	2,583	1,807	2,680
Duplin	3,432	2,704	2,981	1,502
Durham	4,706	3,494	5,233	2,752
Edgecombe	3,395	292	2,437	92
Forsyth	8,250	6,759	7,875	5,256
Franklin	2,786	552	1,987	270
Gaston	7,220	5,749	6,694	3,467
Gates	812	294	664	95
Graham	655	916	871	906
Granville	2,602	793	2,218	433
Greene	1,664	427	1,132	151
Guilford	9,594	7,788	9,236	6,455
Halifax	3,540	443	3,329	185
Harnett	3,902	3,318	3,336	2,824
Haywood	4,227	2,962	4,569	2,375
Henderson	2,525	3,604	3,066	3,406
Hertford	1,165	210	986	108
Hoke	1,266	156	1,160	112
Hyde	1,170	475	657	352
Iredell	6,351	4,494	6,505	3,608

VOTE FOR GOVERNOR, 1920-1924—Continued

Counties	1920		1924	
	Cameron Morrison	John J. Parker	A. W. McLean	I. M. Meekins
Jackson	2,398	2,354	3,170	2,779
Johnston	6,076	5,336	4,727	4,842
Jones	999	328	711	159
Lee	2,319	1,155	1,862	677
Lenoir	2,882	1,024	2,294	395
Lincoln	3,326	3,127	2,948	2,679
Macon	2,404	2,037	2,654	2,248
Madison	1,330	3,609	1,430	3,110
Martin	2,577	496	2,012	193
McDowell	2,824	2,563	3,084	2,557
Mecklenburg	11,224	3,360	8,978	2,128
Mitchell	736	2,235	747	1,604
Montgomery	2,505	2,309	2,510	2,060
Moore	2,708	2,242	2,872	1,848
Nash	4,072	1,518	3,253	765
New Hanover	4,342	472	5,295	558
Northampton	2,329	126	1,705	101
Onslow	1,578	822	1,163	364
Orange	2,081	1,786	2,015	1,193
Pamlico	1,294	1,011	909	393
Pasquotank	1,849	117	1,020	518
Pender	1,611	672	1,219	208
Perquimans	1,057	480	557	283
Person	1,629	1,582	1,603	1,604
Pitt	4,156	834	3,562	433
Polk	1,387	1,349	1,659	1,407
Randolph	5,066	6,243	5,395	6,286
Richmond	3,219	1,134	2,719	504
Robeson	6,185	2,111	4,778	610
Rockingham	4,169	3,592	4,481	2,569
Rowan	6,427	4,853	5,335	3,638
Rutherford	5,092	4,002	5,170	3,842
Sampson	2,428	5,333	2,089	3,346
Scotland	1,674	296	1,511	138
Stanly	2,904	4,273	3,968	3,529
Stokes	2,004	2,899	2,298	2,190
Surry	3,569	5,173	4,591	4,979
Swain	1,448	2,252	1,795	2,177
Transylvania	1,549	1,659	1,842	1,775
Tyrrell	717	535	493	599
Union	4,025	1,499	2,782	613
Vance	2,459	804	2,274	357
Wake	8,115	3,349	9,300	2,267
Warren	1,894	211	1,827	94
Washington	1,115	971	846	834
Watauga	1,753	2,600	2,105	2,717
Wayne	4,847	2,776	3,804	1,205
Wilkes	2,884	6,453	3,563	6,148
Wilson	3,550	1,296	2,659	467
Yadkin	1,355	3,295	1,389	2,880
Yancey	2,506	2,574	2,649	2,132
Totals	308,454	230,175	294,441	185,627

W. B. Taylor, Socialist, 456.

VOTE FOR UNITED STATES SENATOR, 1920-1926

Counties	1920		1924		1926	
	Lee S. Overman	A. E. Holton	F. M. Simmons	A. A. Whitener	L. S. Overman	Johnson Hayes
Alamance	5,289	4,604	4,955	3,180	4,360	3,304
Alexander	2,045	2,639	2,297	2,424	2,320	2,203
Alleghany	1,426	1,182	1,658	1,220	1,412	1,073
Anson	3,575	423	2,404	209	1,694	64
Ashe	3,630	3,793	4,350	3,891	3,908	3,404
Avery	404	2,496	461	2,150	416	1,499
Beaufort	3,564	2,214	3,084	1,276	1,242	197
Bertie	1,887	145	1,836	83	729	21
Bladen	2,000	1,003	1,703	584	1,457	439
Brunswick	1,317	1,378	1,130	1,227	1,173	1,026
Buncombe	10,413	7,914	10,536	5,982	8,699	4,411
Burke	3,311	3,562	4,097	3,199	3,550	3,185
Cabarrus	4,429	5,208	4,533	3,596	4,804	3,997
Caldwell	2,996	3,208	3,383	2,464	2,893	1,580
Camden	563	118	433	136	152	14
Carteret	2,094	2,289	2,311	1,822	2,389	1,112
Caswell	1,253	493	1,085	439	817	273
Catawba	5,436	5,907	5,845	6,173	5,171	4,688
Chatham	3,229	2,894	3,430	2,731	3,133	2,002
Cherokee	1,753	2,473	1,765	2,308	1,842	2,063
Chowan	1,133	172	735	79	228	11
Clay	763	913	1,008	1,122	845	952
Cleveland	5,202	2,945	3,795	1,789	3,040	797
Columbus	3,337	1,639	2,848	1,425	3,126	1,002
Craven	3,463	603	3,084	221	1,237	81
Cumberland	3,341	1,836	3,316	1,085	1,835	902
Currituck	974	67	590	36	346	12
Dare	845	624	837	625	713	508
Davidson	4,933	5,819	6,434	6,191	6,144	5,971
Davie	1,636	2,579	1,813	2,676	1,953	2,450
Duplin	3,442	2,699	2,995	1,498	2,400	650
Durham	4,772	3,472	5,200	2,793	3,228	1,213
Edgecombe	3,413	247	2,452	87	794	16
Forsyth	8,509	6,717	7,871	5,243	4,790	2,849
Franklin	2,799	540	1,998	268	843	138
Gaston	7,236	5,743	6,693	3,484	4,443	2,654
Gates	812	294	672	194	950	175
Graham	653	914	865	909	858	976
Granville	2,671	795	2,245	430	1,006	109
Greene	1,662	427	1,136	151	503	31
Guilford	9,808	7,733	9,373	6,435	6,589	4,445
Halifax	3,547	404	3,342	184	1,139	109
Harnett	3,018	3,312	3,349	2,823	3,278	2,705
Haywood	4,225	2,962	4,560	2,476	3,672	1,568
Henderson	2,522	3,498	3,084	3,252	3,273	3,683
Hertford	1,168	210	985	106	472	31
Hoke	1,274	154	1,165	112	753	35
Hyde	1,169	476	676	320	307	54
Iredell	6,493	4,384	6,512	3,600	4,774	2,423

VOTE FOR UNITED STATES SENATOR, 1920-1926—Continued

Counties	1920		1924		1926	
	Lee S. Overman	A. E. Holton	F. M. Simmons	A. A. Whitener	L. S. Overman	Johnson J. Hayes
Jackson	2,399	2,354	3,138	2,800	2,550	2,624
Johnston	6,081	5,332	4,787	4,826	6,079	4,946
Jones	1,000	337	717	146	425	30
Lee	2,364	1,124	1,874	675	1,374	291
Lenoir	2,881	1,021	2,285	396	1,375	277
Lincoln	3,337	3,125	2,948	2,673	3,115	2,847
Macon	2,166	2,033	2,648	2,212	2,542	2,079
Madison	1,335	3,610	1,414	3,045	955	1,789
Martin	2,574	498	2,022	190	910	38
McDowell	2,817	2,568	3,082	2,543	2,934	2,815
Mecklenburg	11,542	3,253	8,970	2,110	2,877	424
Mitchell	737	2,554	745	1,604	429	925
Montgomery	2,337	2,294	2,517	2,059	2,266	1,465
Moore	2,747	2,323	2,878	1,849	2,091	1,170
Nash	4,084	1,511	3,281	757	1,833	242
New Hanover	4,342	472	5,268	501	1,050	103
Northampton	2,330	127	1,713	96	941	118
Onslow	1,374	821	1,172	364	744	104
Orange	2,127	1,727	2,036	1,185	1,547	741
Pamlico	1,294	1,010	909	393	436	103
Pasquotank	1,817	416	1,517	236	609	84
Pender	1,606	672	1,229	209	681	98
Perquimans	1,060	478	570	270	476	72
Person	1,656	1,565	1,639	982	1,124	408
Pitt	4,204	824	3,405	416	1,617	127
Polk	1,390	1,350	1,656	1,408	1,711	1,366
Randolph	5,078	6,239	5,452	6,285	5,440	5,487
Richmond	3,368	1,098	2,724	503	2,414	265
Robeson	6,297	2,055	4,777	614	2,352	252
Rockingham	4,512	3,587	4,489	2,573	3,488	1,944
Rowan	6,438	4,888	5,350	3,696	3,372	1,561
Rutherford	5,114	3,993	5,171	3,847	3,909	2,861
Sampson	2,433	5,289	2,097	3,279	2,561	2,620
Scotland	1,702	286	1,498	115	716	64
Stanly	3,511	1,275	3,959	3,520	3,263	2,879
Stokes	2,009	2,988	2,314	2,485	2,137	2,607
Surry	3,584	5,153	1,511	4,970	4,623	4,607
Swain	1,419	2,252	1,795	2,177	1,876	1,840
Transylvania	1,549	1,664	1,837	1,770	1,949	1,908
Tyrrell	747	535	618	418	500	278
Union	4,203	1,365	2,782	607	1,359	228
Vance	2,508	768	2,263	354	1,382	165
Wake	8,307	3,278	9,348	2,084	4,554	493
Warren	1,894	240	1,829	94	1,033	20
Washington	1,115	970	862	812	988	618
Watauga	1,757	2,598	2,105	2,659	2,925	2,895
Wayne	4,867	2,766	3,797	1,203	2,731	997
Wilkes	2,884	6,458	3,573	6,147	3,550	6,014
Wilson	3,539	1,319	2,777	468	896	110
Yadkin	1,760	3,290	1,593	2,874	935	2,131
Yancey	2,306	2,574	2,635	2,126	2,219	2,259
Totals	340,594	229,345	295,404	184,393	218,934	142,894

VOTE FOR MEMBERS OF CONGRESS, 1922-1926

FIRST CONGRESSIONAL DISTRICT

Counties	1922		1924		1926
	Hallett S. Ward	C. E. Kramer	Lindsay C. Warren	Peter D. Burgess	Lindsay C. Warren
Beaufort	1,854	557	3,097	1,193	1,235
Camden	223	6	443	125	167
Chowan	312	2	708	69	232
Currituck	368	10	606	18	348
Dare	648	173	809	559	785
Gates	708	141	668	176	940
Hertford	438	28	971	81	471
Hyde	470	79	712	202	339
Martin	1,030	39	1,927	173	880
Pasquotank	607	150	1,178	172	611
Perquimans	455	108	550	235	478
Pitt	1,653	89	3,285	354	1,622
Tyrrell	611	307	584	380	496
Washington	824	432	849	741	897
Totals	10,201	3,101	16,387	4,478	9,501

SECOND CONGRESSIONAL DISTRICT

Counties	1922	1924		1926
	Claud Kitchin	John H. Kerr	M. R. Nick	John H. Kerr
Bertie	765	1,844	45	736
Edgecombe	1,228	2,098	30	806
Greene	826	1,080	113	498
Halifax	1,311	3,219	188	1,161
Lenoir	1,402	2,092	292	1,374
Northampton	806	1,734	74	1,033
Warren	978	1,761	37	987
Wilson	1,211	2,484	370	889
Totals	8,533	16,312	1,109	7,484

VOTE FOR MEMBERS OF CONGRESS, 1922-1926—Continued
THIRD CONGRESSIONAL DISTRICT

Counties	1922		1924		1926	
	C. L. Abernethy (D.)	Thomas J. Hood (R.)	C. L. Abernethy	William H. Fisher	C. L. Abernethy	Roscoe Butler
Carteret	2,583	1,563	2,213	1,556	2,597	976
Craven	1,867	57	3,112	151	2,225	61
Duplin	2,621	669	2,931	1,367	2,091	624
Jones	494	53	662	132	420	28
Onslow	833	161	1,044	312	743	93
Pamlico	838	280	843	283	436	95
Pender	900	242	1,126	173	674	44
Sampson	1,494	3,117	2,067	3,325	2,595	2,608
Wayne	2,471	782	3,687	1,132	2,739	969
Totals	14,101	6,925	17,685	8,431	13,520	5,498

FOURTH CONGRESSIONAL DISTRICT

Counties	1922		1924		1926	
	Edward W. Pou (D.)	F. Eugene Hester (R.)	Edward W. Pou	Young Z. Parker	Edward W. Pou	Hobart Brantley
Chatham	3,326	2,814	5,336	2,637	3,105	1,959
Franklin	1,435	141	1,864	245	844	128
Johnston	5,271	4,210	4,847	4,643	6,110	4,931
Nash	2,277	104	3,125	682	1,775	238
Vance	921	155	2,072	327	1,361	152
Wake	4,275	662	8,813	1,971	4,775	473
Totals	16,205	8,086	24,057	10,505	17,700	7,881

VOTE FOR MEMBERS OF CONGRESS, 1922-1926—Continued
FIFTH CONGRESSIONAL DISTRICT

Counties	1922		1924		1926	
	Charles M. Stedman (D.)	Lucy B. Patterson	Charles M. Stedman	Thomas C. Carter	Charles M. Stedman	O. C. Durland
Alamance	3,851	1,579	4,766	3,270	4,375	3,292
Caswell	860	191	1,036	440	809	331
Durham	3,194	1,478	4,590	2,738	2,906	1,066
Forsyth	5,718	3,479	7,689	5,232	4,798	2,811
Granville			2,075	412	999	107
Guilford	5,553	3,598	9,384	6,171	6,540	4,408
Orange	1,697	868	1,849	1,149	1,378	648
Person	1,647	827	1,438	871	993	336
Rockingham	4,155	2,071	4,419	2,556	3,168	1,912
Stokes	1,818	2,067	2,256	2,435	2,142	2,517
Surry	3,755	4,020	4,546	4,981	4,619	4,588
Totals	33,694	20,380	44,048	30,255	32,727	22,014

SIXTH CONGRESSIONAL DISTRICT

Counties	1922		1924		1926	
	Homer L. Lyon (D.)	William J. McDonald	Homer L. Lyon	William J. McDonald	Homer L. Lyon	Leaman Baggett
Bladen	2,325	569	1,602	534	1,210	703
Brunswick	1,138	1,109	1,126	1,238	1,179	1,04
Columbus	2,241	466	2,847	1,369	2,426	1,704
Cumberland	1,163	373	3,305	1,151	1,904	973
Harnett	3,529	2,098	3,301	2,643	3,030	2,750
New Hanover	1,871	85	5,176	501	1,052	84
Robeson	2,729	566	4,325	717	2,087	592
Totals	14,996	5,266	21,682	8,153	12,888	7,846

VOTE FOR MEMBERS OF CONGRESS, 1922-1926 — Continued
SEVENTH CONGRESSIONAL DISTRICT

Counties	1922		1924		1926	
	William C. Hammer (D.)	W. B. Love (R.)	William C. Hammer	Z. Carter Williams	William C. Hammer	Z. Carter Williams
Anson	1,753	70	2,407	206	1,707	59
Davidson	5,753	5,100	6,542	6,439	6,217	5,930
Davie	1,617	1,989	1,805	2,464	1,963	2,426
Hoke	627	20	1,172	104	758	32
Lee	1,363	348	1,808	670	1,373	274
Montgomery	2,491	2,119	2,489	2,044	2,217	1,466
Moore	2,468	1,708	2,889	1,812	2,127	1,112
Randolph	5,691	5,558	5,516	6,165	5,486	5,410
Richmond	2,440	218	2,737	481	2,466	227
Scotland	858	30	1,191	160	715	58
Union	1,362	234	2,746	582	1,370	233
Wilkes	3,051	4,354	3,463	6,035	3,888	5,610
Yadkin	1,455	1,883	1,426	2,760	1,015	1,902
Totals	30,629	23,592	36,491	29,050	31,552	24,469

EIGHTH CONGRESSIONAL DISTRICT

Counties	1922		1924		1926	
	Robert L. Doughton (D.)	J. Ike Campbell (R.)	Robert L. Doughton	J. D. Dorsett	Robert L. Doughton	O. F. Pool
Alexander	2,192	2,221	2,316	2,419	2,373	2,197
Alleghany	1,584	1,105	1,756	1,046	1,733	892
Ashe	4,089	3,629	4,436	3,846	4,106	3,267
Cabarrus	4,236	3,929	4,516	3,552	4,817	3,996
Caldwell	3,396	2,782	3,392	2,475	2,944	1,555
Iredell	5,484	2,468	6,568	3,562	4,941	2,362
Rowan	4,633	2,620	5,225	3,756	3,364	1,539
Stanly	3,673	3,620	3,963	3,520	3,284	2,875
Watauga	2,056	2,119	2,520	2,520	2,988	2,860
Totals	31,340	24,235	34,692	26,675	30,520	21,543

VOTE FOR MEMBERS OF CONGRESS, 1922-1926—Continued
NINTH CONGRESSIONAL DISTRICT

Counties	1922		1924		1926	
	A. L. Bulwinkle (D.)	R. H. Shuford (R.)	A. L. Bulwinkle	John A. Hendricks	Alfred L. Bulwinkle	Garrett D. Bailey
Avery	552	1,605	527	1,735	578	1,201
Burke	3,963	2,881	4,137	3,190	3,521	3,122
Catawba	5,595	4,923	5,795	5,900	4,999	4,664
Cleveland	2,532	981	3,767	1,723	3,017	800
Gaston	4,212	1,147	6,592	3,388	4,510	1,952
Lincoln	3,014	2,255	2,917	2,637	3,120	2,833
Madison	1,390	1,919	1,470	3,114	1,026	1,743
Mecklenburg	3,976	677	8,657	2,153	2,970	395
Mitchell	634	1,191	781	1,458	481	911
Yancey	2,728	1,589	2,727	2,129	2,102	2,424
Totals	28,596	19,168	37,370	27,427	26,354	20,045

TENTH CONGRESSIONAL DISTRICT

Counties	1922		1924		1926	
	Zebulon Weaver (D.)	Ralph A. Fisher (R.)	Zebulon Weaver	Lewis P. Hamlin	Zebulon Weaver	R. Kenneth Smathers
Buncombe	9,556	5,331	10,816	6,086	8,765	4,540
Cherokee	1,994	2,019	1,789	2,274	2,077	2,028
Clay	950	935	1,005	1,120	860	960
Graham	785	931	870	893	871	970
Haywood	4,224	1,728	4,572	2,357	3,635	1,605
Henderson	2,874	2,580	3,098	3,421	3,184	3,716
Jackson	2,798	2,533	3,129	2,791	2,576	2,624
McDowell	3,231	2,522	3,080	2,557	2,922	2,830
Macon	2,539	1,982	2,644	2,216	2,488	2,099
Polk	1,361	1,384	1,610	1,403	1,713	1,359
Rutherford	4,194	2,838	4,932	3,800	3,928	2,767
Swain	1,572	1,497	1,705	2,113	1,883	1,855
Transylvania	1,745	1,912	1,780	1,840	1,927	1,850
Totals	37,626	28,192	41,030	32,871	36,829	29,200

VOTE ON CONSTITUTIONAL AMENDMENT AND REFERENDUM BY COUNTIES, 1926

Proposed Amendment to the Constitution of North Carolina Submitted to a Vote of the People at the General Election November 2, 1926

CONSTITUTIONAL AMENDMENT ADOPTED:

Amendment to section 3, Article III—Relating to election returns for officers of the executive department.

Chapter 88, Public Laws 1925

AN ACT TO AMEND THE CONSTITUTION OF NORTH CAROLINA, RELATING TO ELECTION RETURNS FOR OFFICERS OF THE EXECUTIVE DEPARTMENT

The General Assembly of North Carolina do enact:

SECTION 1. That section three of article three of the Constitution of North Carolina be and the same is hereby amended by striking out all of section three and inserting in lieu thereof the following: "Section three. The return of every election for officers of the executive department shall be sealed up and transmitted to the seat of government by the returning officer, directed to the Secretary of State. The return shall be canvassed and the result declared in such manner as may be prescribed by law. Contested elections shall be determined by a joint ballot of both Houses of the General Assembly in such manner as shall be prescribed by law."

SEC. 2. That this amendment shall be submitted at the next general election to the qualified voters of the State, in the same manner and under the same rules and regulations as provided in the law regulating general elections in this State.

SEC. 3. That at said election, into a ballot box labeled "Ballot Box for Constitutional Amendment" or "Ballot Box for Constitutional Amendments," those persons desiring to vote for such amendment shall cast a separate printed ballot with the words "For Constitutional Amendment Relating to Election Returns for Officers of the Executive Department"; and those with a contrary opinion may cast a separate ballot with the words "Against Constitutional

Amendment Relating to Election Returns for Officers of the Executive Department" thereon.

Sec. 4. That the said election shall be held and the votes returned, compared, counted and canvassed, and the result announced under the same rules and regulations as are in force at the general election in the year one thousand nine hundred and twenty-six for returning, comparing, counting and canvassing the votes for Governor; and if a majority of the votes cast be in favor of the amendment, it shall be the duty of the Governor of the State to certify said amendment under the seal of the State to the Secretary of State, who shall enroll the said amendment so certified among the permanent records of his office.

Sec. 5. All laws and clauses of laws in conflict with the provisions of this act are hereby repealed.

Sec. 6. That this act shall be in force from and after its ratification.

Ratified this the 28th day of February, A.D. 1925.

REFERENDUM

World War Veterans Loan Fund—Providing for a bond issue of two million dollars to be loaned to World War veterans for the purchase of homes.

An Act to Provide a World War Veterans Loan Fund

To authorize a bond issue of two million dollars at an interest rate of not exceeding 5 per cent, the proceeds to be loaned World War Veterans in amounts not in excess of three thousand dollars at six per cent to each veteran and not exceeding 75 per cent of the appraised value of the real property offered as security, the loan to be used in the purchase of homes. The fund is to be administered by a Board of Advisers consisiting of the Secretary of State, the Commissioner of Agriculture, the Attorney-General, the Commissioner of Labor and Printing and the State Treasurer who shall appoint a person known as the "Commissioner of the Veterans Loan Fund" drawing an annual salary of $3,500. (Ch. 155, P.L. 1925.)

VOTE ON FOREGOING AMENDMENT
Relating to Election Returns

Counties	For	Against	Counties	For	Against
Alamance	125	75	Jones	170	56
Alexander	6	2	Lee	518	199
Alleghany	46	56	Lenoir	331	130
Anson	700	459	Lincoln	488	576
Ashe	5	13	Macon	101	32
Avery	18	20	Madison	166	135
Beaufort	685	119	Martin	379	95
Bertie	278	80	McDowell	173	45
Bladen	170	371	Mecklenburg	880	355
Brunswick	56	126	Mitchell	9	5
Buncombe	6,943	981	Montgomery	41	245
Burke	179	128	Moore	852	406
Cabarrus	1,007	173	Nash	578	159
Caldwell	31	58	New Hanover	224	98
Camden	115	12	Northampton	421	193
Carteret	149	56	Onslow	115	139
Caswell	144	173	Orange	391	191
Catawba	55	16	Pamlico	110	50
Chatham	882	1,034	Pasquotank	229	174
Cherokee	209	18	Pender	106	206
Chowan	93	15	Perquimans	262	44
Clay	78	8	Person	90	143
Cleveland	412	207	Pitt	650	420
Columbus	109	579	Polk	161	30
Craven	1,017	74	Randolph	53	613
Cumberland	851	818	Richmond	831	324
Currituck	126	27	Robeson	1,365	434
Dare	143	36	Rockingham	558	195
Davidson	86	58	Rowan	547	447
Davie	140	53	Rutherford	969	648
Duplin	903	504	Sampson	348	80
Durham	755	293	Scotland	48	32
Edgecombe	335	125	Stanly	639	1,011
Forsyth	1,702	258	Stokes	115	341
Franklin	425	136	Surry	12	46
Gaston	1,860	275	Swain	132	21
Gates	70	114	Transylvania	9	201
Graham			Tyrrell	320	59
Granville	307	314	Union	391	150
Greene	153	145	Vance	275	99
Guilford	1,460	720	Wake	1,921	723
Halifax	521	294	Warren	248	348
Harnett	1,794	1,351	Washington	350	124
Haywood	626	155	Watauga	23	103
Henderson	237	67	Wayne	620	918
Hertford	171	86	Wilkes	228	449
Hoke	338	164	Wilson	209	111
Hyde	132	11	Yadkin	117	44
Iredell	1,222	612	Yancey	12	2
Jackson					
Johnston	1,925	1,319	Totals	47,648	24,800

VOTE ON REFERENDUM

Counties	For	Against	Counties	For	Against
Alamance	486	141	Jones	147	97
Alexander	67	4	Lee	537	277
Alleghany	147	61	Lenoir	384	288
Anson	866	412	Lincoln	907	720
Ashe	265	13	Macon	267	15
Avery	282	11	Madison	531	154
Beaufort	700	103	Martin	300	211
Bertie	354	88	McDowell	464	106
Bladen	246	367	Mecklenburg	991	457
Brunswick	437	7	Mitchell	126	3
Buncombe	5,512	1,136	Montgomery	518	218
Burke	1,602	447	Moore	1,173	342
Carbarrus	2,435	280	Nash	643	199
Caldwell	120	61	New Hanover	369	125
Camden	48	74	Northampton	374	242
Carteret	1,041	28	Onslow	129	138
Caswell	193	109	Orange	346	248
Catawba	334	40	Pamlico	144	32
Chatham	1,568	995	Pasquotank	143	288
Cherokee	527	24	Pender	160	269
Chowan	49	92	Perquimans	284	72
Clay	93	2	Person	249	194
Cleveland	422	343	Pitt	618	492
Columbus	492	452	Polk	479	47
Craven	1,000	111	Randolph	325	703
Cumberland	958	1,070	Richmond	1,150	300
Currituck	177	35	Robeson	1,199	450
Dare	208	20	Rockingham	1,423	154
Davidson	222	146	Rowan	910	595
Davie	348	115	Rutherford	1,161	743
Duplin	935	744	Sampson	73	188
Durham	765	420	Scotland	109	35
Edgecombe	259	250	Stanly	828	978
Forsyth	1,482	316	Stokes	172	456
Franklin	469	157	Surry	728	61
Gaston	2,417	186	Swain	383	22
Gates	39	166	Transylvania	214	
Graham			Tyrrell	371	38
Granville	428	269	Union	375	282
Greene	139	161	Vance	358	188
Guilford	2,234	537	Wake	2,471	681
Halifax	665	265	Warren	170	459
Harnett	2,055	959	Washington	555	101
Haywood	1,277	140	Watauga	69	
Henderson	30	10	Wayne	806	1,181
Hertford	159	105	Wilkes	1,046	415
Hoke	453	158	Wilson	220	169
Hyde	180	34	Yadkin	204	49
Iredell	1,544	427	Yancey	329	3
Jackson					
Johnston	3,350	538	Totals	65,951	26,084

VOTE FOR SOLICITORS, 1926

FIRST JUDICIAL DISTRICT

Counties	W. L. Small
Camden	168
Gates	1,121
Currituck	314
Chowan	243
Pasquotank	665
Beaufort	1,245
Hyde	304
Dare	876
Perquimans	502
Tyrrell	572
Total	6,034

THIRD JUDICIAL DISTRICT

Counties	R. Hunt Parker
Bertie	737
Hertford	463
Northampton	1,028
Halifax	1,234
Warren	1,038
Vance	1,428
Total	5,928

SECOND JUDICIAL DISTRICT

Counties	Donnell Gilliam	Wheeler Martin
Nash	1,902	
Wilson	926	76
Edgecombe	796	
Martin	902	50
Washington	1,001	687
Total	5,527	813

FOURTH JUDICIAL DISTRICT

Counties	Clawson L. Williams	R. H. Dixon, Jr.
Lee	1,379	277
Chatham	3,095	1,972
Johnston	7,073	5,119
Wayne	2,817	983
Harnett	3,344	2,711
Total	17,708	11,062

VOTE FOR SOLICITORS, 1926—*Continued*

FIFTH JUDICIAL DISTRICT

Counties	D. M. Clark
Pitt	1,636
Craven	1,272
Carteret	2,625
Pamlico	458
Jones	455
Greene	511
Total	6,957

SEVENTH JUDICIAL DISTRICT

Counties	L. S. Brassfield	Y. Z. Parker
Wake	4,571	481
Franklin	855	126
Total	5,426	607

SIXTH JUDICIAL DISTRICT

Counties	James A. Powers	W. H. Fisher
Onslow	830	94
Duplin	2,154	620
Sampson	2,510	2,741
Lenoir	1,481	437
Total	7,005	3,892

EIGHTH JUDICIAL DISTRICT

Counties	Woodus Kellum	Louis Goodman
Brunswick	1,198	1,006
Columbus	3,429	1,026
New Hanover	1,026	104
Pender	464	
Total	6,117	2,136

VOTE FOR SOLICITORS, 1926—Continued

NINTH JUDICIAL DISTRICT

Counties	T. A. McNeill	D. G. Downing
Robeson	2,330	278
Bladen	1,677	478
Hoke	746	29
Cumberland	2,017	950
Total	6,770	1,735

ELEVENTH JUDICIAL DISTRICT

Counties	S. Porter Graves	C. M. Bernard
Ashe	3,979	3,302
Forsyth	4,862	2,790
Rockingham	3,217	1,957
Caswell	879	252
Surry	4,865	4,358
Alleghany	1,589	1,072
Total	19,391	13,731

TENTH JUDICIAL DISTRICT

Counties	W. B. Umstead	Heman Hughes
Granville	1,045	
Person	1,338	
Alamance	4,340	
Durham	3,482	
Orange	1,640	732
Total	11,845	732

TWELFTH JUDICIAL DISTRICT

Counties	J. F. Spruill	J. T. Jackson
Davidson	6,306	5,948
Guilford	6,745	4,370
Stokes	2,268	2,628
Total	15,319	12,946

VOTE FOR SOLICITORS, 1926—Continued

THIRTEENTH JUDICIAL DISTRICT

Counties	E. D. Phillips	G. D. B. Reynolds
Richmond	2,107	230
Stanly	2,926	2,804
Union	1,382	224
Moore	2,153	1,133
Anson	1,701	47
Scotland	718	49
Total	10,986	4,487

FOURTEENTH JUDICIAL DISTRICT

Counties	John G. Carpenter	J. C. Newell
Mecklenburg	2,745	282
Gaston	4,610	1,974
Total	7,355	2,256

FIFTEENTH JUDICIAL DISTRICT

Counties	Zeb. V. Long
Montgomery	2,208
Randolph	5,281
Iredell	4,951
Cabarrus	4,816
Rowan	3,420
Total	20,676

SIXTEENTH JUDICIAL DISTRICT

Counties	L. S. Spurling	Harvey A. Jones
Lincoln	3,135	2,896
Cleveland	3,191	830
Caldwell	3,010	1,501
Burke	3,731	3,225
Catawba	4,961	4,677
Total	18,028	13,129

VOTE FOR SOLICITORS, 1926—Continued

SEVENTEENTH JUDICIAL DISTRICT

Counties	J. A. Rousseau	John R. Jones
Avery	536	1,655
Davie	2,076	2,403
Mitchell	445	1,017
Wilkes	3,986	5,482
Yadkin	992	2,087
Watauga	3,118	2,785
Alexander	2,319	2,198
Total	13,472	17,627

NINETEENTH JUDICIAL DISTRICT

Counties	R. M. Wells	Don C. Young
Buncombe	8,318	4,951
Madison	919	2,112
Total	9,237	7,063

EIGHTEENTH JUDICIAL DISTRICT

Counties	J. W. Pless, Jr.
McDowell	2,944
Transylvania	1,928
Yancey	2,065
Rutherford	3,971
Henderson	3,195
Polk	1,719
Total	15,822

TWENTIETH JUDICIAL DISTRICT

Counties	Grover C. Davis
Haywood	3,696
Swain	1,869
Cherokee	1,981
Macon	2,527
Graham	863
Clay	855
Jackson	2,537
Total	14,328

PART X

1. The Halifax Resolution of April 12, 1776.
2. The Declaration of Independence.

THE HALIFAX RESOLUTION

Adopted by the Provincial Congress of North Carolina in session at Halifax, April 12, 1776

It appears to your committee that pursuant to the plan concerted by the British Ministry for subjugating America, the King and Parliament of Great Britain have usurped a power over the persons and properties of the people unlimited and uncontrolled; and disregarding their humble petitions for peace, liberty and safety, have made divers legislative acts, denouncing war, famine, and every species of calamity, against the Continent in general. The British fleets and armies have been, and still are, daily employed in destroying the people, and committing the most horrid devastations on the country. The Governors in different Colonies have declared protection to slaves who should imbrue their hands in the blood of their masters. That ships belonging to America are declared prizes of war, and many of them have been violently seized and confiscated. In consequence of all of which multitudes of the people have been destroyed, or from easy circumstances reduced to the most lamentable distress.

And whereas the moderation hitherto manifested by the United Colonies and their sincere desire to be reconciled to the mother country on constitutional principles, have procured no mitigation of the aforesaid wrongs and usurpations, and no hopes remain of obtaining redress by those means alone which have been hitherto tried, your committee are of opinion that the House should enter into the following resolve, to wit:

Resolved, That the delegates for this Colony in the Continental Congress be impowered to concur with the delegates of the other Colonies in declaring Independency, and forming foreign alliances, reserving to this Colony the sole and exclusive right of forming a Constitution and laws for this Colony, and of appointing delegates from time to time (under the direction of a general representation thereof), to meet the delegates of the other Colonies for such purposes as shall be hereafter pointed out.

THE DECLARATION OF INDEPENDENCE

In Congress, July 4, 1776

The Unanimous Declaration of the Thirteen United States of America

When, in the course of human events, it becomes necessary for one people to dissolve the political bands which have connected them with another, and to assume among the Powers of the earth, the separate and equal station to which the Laws of Nature and of Nature's God entitle them, a decent respect to the opinions of mankind requires that they should declare the causes which impel them to the separation.

We hold these truths to be self-evident, that all men are created equal, that they are endowed by their Creator with certain unalienable Rights, that among these are Life, Liberty and the pursuit of Happiness. That to secure these rights, Governments are instituted among Men, deriving their just powers from the consent of the governed. That whenever any Form of Government becomes destructive of these ends, it is the Right of the People to alter or to abolish it, and to institute new Government, laying its foundation on such principles and organizing its powers in such form, as to them shall seem most likely to effect their Safety and Happiness. Prudence, indeed, will dictate that Governments long established should not be changed for light and transient causes and accordingly all experience hath shown, that mankind are more disposed to suffer, while evils are sufferable, than to right themselves by abolishing the forms to which they are accustomed. But when a long train of abuses and usurpations, pursuing invariably the same Object evinces a design to reduce them under absolute Despotism, it is their right, it is their duty, to throw off such Government, and to provide new Guards for their future security. Such has been the patient sufferance of these Colonies; and such is now the necessity which constrains them to alter their former Systems of Government. The history of the present King of Great Britain is a history of repeated injuries and usurpations, all having in direct object the establishment of an absolute Tyranny over these States. To provide this, let Facts be submitted to a candid world.

He has refused his Assent to Laws, the most wholesome and necessary for the public good.

He has forbidden his Governors to pass Laws of immediate and pressing importance, unless suspended in their operation till his Assent should be obtained; and when so suspended, he has utterly neglected to attend to them.

He has refused to pass other Laws for the accommodation of large districts of people, unless those people would relinquish the right of Representation in the Legislature, a right inestimable to them and formidable to tyrants only.

He has called together legislative bodies at places unusual, uncomfortable, and distant from the depository of their Public Records, for the sole purpose of fatiguing them into compliance with his measures.

He has dissolved Representative Houses repeatedly, for opposing with manly firmness his invasion on the rights of the people.

He has refused for a long time, after such dissolutions, to cause others to be elected; whereby the Legislative Powers, incapable of annihilation, have returned to the People at large for their exercise; the State remaining in the mean time exposed to all the dangers of invasion from without, and convulsions within.

He has endeavored to prevent the population of these States; for that purpose obstructing the Laws of Naturalization of Foreigners; refusing to pass others to encourage their migration hither, and raising the conditions of new Appropriations of Lands.

He has obstructed the Administration of Justice, by refusing his Assent to Laws for establishing Judiciary Powers.

He has made Judges dependent on his Will alone, for the tenure of their offices, and the amount and payment of their salaries.

He has erected a multitude of New Offices, and sent hither swarms of Officers to harass our People, and eat out their substance.

He has kept among us, in times of peace, Standing Armies without the Consent of our legislature.

He has affected to render the Military independent of and superior to the Civil Power.

He has combined with others to subject us to a jurisdiction foreign to our constitution, and unacknowledged by our laws; giving his Assent to their acts of pretended legislaton:

For quartering large bodies of armed troops among us:

For protecting them, by a mock Trial, from Punishment for any Murders which they should commit on the inhabitants of these States:

For cutting off of Trade with all parts of the world:

For imposing taxes on us without our Consent:

For depriving us in many cases, of the benefits of Trial by Jury:

For transporting us beyond Seas to be tried for pretended offenses:

For abolishing the free System of English Laws in a neighboring Province, establishing therein an Arbitrary government, and enlarging its Boundaries so as to render it at once an example and fit instrument for introducing the same absolute rule into these Colonies:

For taking away our Charters, abolishing our most valuable Laws, and altering fundamentally the Forms of our Governments.

For suspending our own Legislature, and declaring themselves invested with Power to legislate for us in all cases whatsoever.

He has abdicated Government here, by declaring us out of his Protection and waging War against us.

He has plundered our seas, ravaged our Coasts, burnt our towns, and destroyed the lives of our people.

He is at this time transporting large armies of foreign mercenaries to complete the works of death, desolation and tyranny, already begun with circumstances of Cruelty & perfidy scarcely paralleled in the most barbarous ages, and totally unworthy the Head of a civilized nation.

He has constrained our fellow Citizens taken Captive on the high Seas to bear Arms against their Country, to become the executioners of their friends and Brethren, or to fall themselves by their Hands.

He has excited domestic insurrections amongst us, and has endeavoured to bring on the inhabitants of our frontier, the merciless Indian Savages, whose known rule of warfare, is an undistinguished destruction of all ages, sexes and conditions.

In every stage of these Oppressions We have Petitioned for Redress in the most humble terms: Our repeated Petitions have been answered only by repeated injury. A Prince, whose character is thus marked by every act which may define a Tyrant, is unfit to be the ruler of a free People.

Nor have We been wanting in attention to our British brethren. We have warned them from time to time of attempts by their legislature to extend an unwarrantable jurisdiction over us. We have reminded them of the circumstances of our emigration and settlement here. We have appealed to their native justice and magnanimity, and we have conjured them by the ties of our common kindred to disavow these usurpations which would inevitably interrupt our connection and correspondence. They too have been deaf to the voice of justice and of consanguinity. We must, therefore, acquiesce in the necessity, which denounces our Separation, and hold them, as we hold the rest of mankind, Enemies in War, in Peace, Friends.

We, therefore, the Representatives of the United States of America, in General Congress, Assembled, appealing to the Supreme Judge of the world for the rectitude of our intentions, do, in the Name, and by Authority of the good People of these Colonies, solemnly publish and declare, That these United Colonies are, and of Right ought to be Free and Independent States; that they are Absolved from all Allegiance to the British Crown, and that all political connection between them and the State of Great Britain, is and ought to be totally dissolved; and that as Free and Independent States, they have full Power to Levy War, conclude Peace, contract Alliances, establish Commerce, and do all other Acts and Things which Independent States may of right do. And for the support of this Declaration, with a firm reliance on the Protection of Divine Providence, we mutually pledge to each other our Lives, our Fortunes and our sacred Honor. JOHN HANCOCK.

New Hampshire—JOSIAH BARTLETT, WM. WHIPPLE, MATTHEW THORNTON.

Massachusetts Bay—SAML. ADAMS, JOHN ADAMS, ROBT. TREAT PAINE, ELBRIDGE GERRY.

Rhode Island—STEP. HOPKINS, WILLIAM ELLERY.

Connecticut—ROGER SHERMAN, SAM'EL HUNTINGTON, WM. WILLIAMS, OLIVER WOLCOTT.

New York—WM. FLOYD, PHIL. LIVINGSTON, FRANS. LEWIS, LEWIS MORRIS.

New Jersey—Richd. Stockton, Jno. Witherspoon, Fras. Hopkinson, John Hart, Abra. Clark.

Pennsylvania—Robt. Morris, Benjamin Rush, Benja. Franklin, John Morton, Geo. Clymer, Jas. Smith, Geo. Taylor, James Wilson, Geo. Ross.

Delaware—Caesar Rodney, Geo. Read, Tho. M'Kean.

Maryland—Samuel Chase, Wm. Paca, Thos. Stone, Charles Carroll of Carrolton.

Virginia—George Wythe, Richard Henry Lee, Th. Jefferson, Benja. Harrison, Thos. Nelson, Jr., Francis Lightfoot Lee, Carter Braxton.

North Carolina—Wm. Hooper, Joseph Hewes, John Penn.

South Carolina—Edward Rutledge, Thos. Heywood, junr., Thomas Lynch, junr., Arthur Middleton.

Georgia—Button Gwinnett, Lyman Hall, Geo. Walton.*

---

* This arrangement of the names is made for convenience. The States are not mentioned in the original.

PART XI

CONSTITUTIONS

1. Constitution of the United States of America.
2. Constitution of the State of North Carolina.
3. Index to the Constitution of North Carolina.

CONSTITUTION OF THE UNITED STATES OF AMERICA

WE, THE PEOPLE of the United States, in order to form a more perfect Union, establish Justice, insure domestic Tranquility, provide for the common defense, promote the general Welfare, and secure the Blessings of Liberty to ourselves and our Posterity, do ordain and establish this CONSTITUTION for the United States of America.

ARTICLE I

SECTION 1. All legislative Powers herein granted shall be vested in a Congress of the United States, which shall consist of a Senate and House of Representatives.

SEC. 2. The House of Representatives shall be composed of Members chosen every second Year by the People of the several States, and the Electors in each State shall have the Qualifications requisite for Electors of the most numerous Branch of the State Legislature.

No person shall be a Representative who shall not have attained to the Age of twenty five years, and been seven Years a Citizen of the United States, and who shall not, when elected, be an Inhabitant of that State in which he shall be chosen.

Representatives and direct Taxes shall be apportioned among the several States which may be included within the Union, according to their respective Numbers, which shall be determined by adding to the whole Number of free Persons, including those bound to Service for a Term of Years, and excluding Indians not taxed, three-fifths of all other Persons. The actual Enumeration shall be made within three Years after the first Meeting of the Congress of the United States, and within every subsequent Term of ten Years, in such Manner as they shall by Law direct. The number of Representatives shall not exceed one for every thirty Thousand, but each State shall have at Least one Representative; and until such enumeration shall be made, the State of New Hampshire shall be entitled to chuse three, Massachusetts eight, Rhode Island and Providence Plantations one, Connecticut five, New York six, New Jersey four, Pennsylvania eight, Delaware one, Maryland six, Virginia ten, North Carolina five, South Carolina five, and Georgia three.

When vacancies happen in the Representation from any State, the Executive Authority thereof shall issue Writs of Election to fill such vacancies.

The House of Representatives shall chuse their Speaker and other Officers; and shall have the sole Power of Impeachment.

SEC. 3. The Senate of the United States shall be composed of two Senators from each State, chosen by the Legislature thereof, for six Years; and each Senator shall have one Vote.

Immediately after they shall be assembled in Consequence of the first Election, they shall be divided as equally as may be into three Classes. The Seats of the Senators of the first Class shall be vacated at the Expiration of the second Year, of the second Class at the Expiration of the fourth Year, and of the third Class at the Expiration of the sixth Year, so that one-third may be chosen every second Year; and if Vacancies happen by Resignation, or otherwise, during the Recess of the Legislature of any State, the Executive thereof may make temporary Appointments until the next Meeting of the Legislature, which shall then fill such Vacancies.

No Person shall be a Senator who shall not have attained to the Age of thirty Years, and been nine Years a Citizen of the United States, and who shall not, when elected, be an Inhabitant of that State for which he shall be chosen.

The Vice-president of the United States shall be President of the Senate, but shall have no Vote, unless they be equally divided.

The Senate shall chuse their other Officers, and also a President pro tempore, in the absence of the Vice-president, or when he shall exercise the Office of President of the United States.

The Senate shall have the sole Power to try all Impeachments. When sitting for that Purpose, they shall be on Oath or Affirmation. When the President of the United States is tried, the Chief Justice shall preside: And no Person shall be convicted without the Concurrence of two-thirds of the Members present.

Judgment in Cases of Impeachment shall not extend further than to removal from Office, and disqualification to hold and enjoy any Office of honor, Trust or Profit under the United States: but the Party convicted shall nevertheless be liable and subject to Indictment, Trial, Judgment and Punishment, according to Law.

SEC. 4. The Times, Places and Manner of holding Elections for Senator and Representatives, shall be prescribed in each State by the Legislature thereof; but the Congress may at any time by Law make or alter such Regulations, except as to the places of chusing Senators.

The Congress shall assemble at least once in every Year, and such Meeting shall be on the first Monday in December, unless they shall by Law appoint a different Day.

SEC. 5. Each House shall be the Judge of the Elections, Returns and Qualifications of its own Members, and a Majority of each shall constitute a Quorum to do Business; but a smaller Number may adjourn from day to day, and may be authorized to compel the Attendance of absent Members, in such Manner and under such Penalties as each House may provide.

Each House may determine the Rules of the Proceedings, punish its Members for disorderly Behavior, and, with the Concurrence of two-thirds, expel a Member.

Each House shall keep a Journal of its Proceedings, and from time to time publish the same, excepting such Parts as may in their Judgment require Secrecy; and the Yeas and Nays of the Members of either House on any question shall, at the Desire of one-fifth of those Present, be entered on the Journal.

Neither House, during the Session of Congress, shall, without the Consent of the other, adjourn for more than three days, nor to any other Place than that in which the two Houses shall be sitting.

SEC. 6. The Senators and Representatives shall receive a Compensation for their Services, to be ascertained by Law, and paid out of the Treasury of the United States. They shall in all Cases, except Treason, Felony and Breach of the Peace, be privileged from Arrest during their Attendance at the Session of their respective Houses, and in going to and returning from the same; and for any Speech or Debate in either House, they shall not be questioned in any other Place.

No Senator or Representative shall, during the Time for which he was elected, be appointed to any civil Office under the Authority of the United States, which shall have been created, or the Emoluments whereof shall have been encreased during such time; and no Person holding any Office under the United States, shall be a Member of either House during his Continuance in Office.

Sec. 7. All Bills for raising Revenue shall originate in the House of Representatives; but the Senate may propose or concur with Amendments as on other Bills.

Every Bill which shall have passed the House of Representatives and the Senate, shall, before it become a Law, be presented to the President of the United States; If he approve he shall sign it, but if not he shall return it, with his Objections to that House in which it shall have originated, who shall enter the Objections at large on their Journal, and proceed to reconsider it. If after such Reconsideration two-thirds of the House shall agree to pass the Bill, it shall be sent, together with the Objections, to the other House, by which it shall likewise be reconsidered, and if approved by two-thirds of that House, it shall become a law. But in all such Cases the Votes of both Houses shall be determined by Yeas and Nays, and the Names of the Persons voting for and against the Bill shall be entered on the Journal of each House respectively. If any Bill shall not be returned by the President within ten Days (Sundays excepted) after it shall have been presented to him, the Same shall be a Law, in like Manner as if he had signed it, unless the Congress by their Adjournment prevent its Return, in which Case it shall not be a Law.

Every Order, Resolution, or Vote to which Concurrence of the Senate and House of Representatives may be necessary (except on a question of Adjournment) shall be presented to the President of the United States; and before the Same shall take Effect, shall be approved by him, or being disapproved by him, shall be repassed by two-thirds of the Senate and House of Representatives according to the Rules and Limitations prescribed in the Case of a Bill.

Sec. 8. The Congress shall have Power To lay and collect Taxes, Duties, Imposts and Excises, to pay the Debts and provide for the common Defense and General Welfare of the United States; but all Duties, Imposts and Excises shall be uniform throughout the United States;

To borrow Money on the credit of the United States;

To regulate Commerce with foreign Nations, and among the several States, and with the Indian Tribes;

To establish an uniform Rule of Naturalization, and uniform Laws on the subject of Bankruptcies throughout the United States;

To coin Money, regulate the Value thereof, and of foreign Coin, and to fix the Standard of Weights and Measures;

To provide for the Punishment of counterfeiting the Securities and current Coin of the United States;

To establish Post Offices and post Roads;

To promote the Progress of Science and useful Arts, by securing for limited Times to Authors and Inventors the exclusive Right to their respective Writings and Discoveries;

To constitute Tribunals inferior to the supreme Court;

To define and punish Piracies and Felonies committed on the high Seas, and Offences against the Law of Nations;

To declare War, grant Letters of Marque and Reprisal, and make Rules concerning Captures on Land and Water;

To raise and support Armies, but no Appropriation of Money to that Use shall be for a longer Term than two Years;

To provide and maintain a Navy;

To make Rules for the Government and Regulation of the land and naval Forces;

To provide for calling forth the Militia to execute the Laws of the Union, suppress Insurrections and repel Invasions;

To provide for organizing, arming, and disciplining the Militia, and for governing such Part of them as may be employed in the Service of the United States, reserving to the States respectively, the Appointment of the Officers, and the Authority of training the Militia according to the discipline prescribed by Congress;

To exercise exclusive Legislation in all Cases whatsoever, over such District (not exceeding ten Miles square) as may, by Cession of particular States, and the Acceptance of Congress, become the Seat of the Government of the United States, and to exercise like Authority over all Places purchased by the Consent of the Legislature of the State in which the same shall be, for the Erection of Forts, Magazines, Arsenals, dock-Yards, and other needful Buildings;— And

To make all Laws which shall be necessary and proper for carrying into Execution the foregoing Powers, and all other Powers vested by this Constitution in the Government of the United States, or in any Department or Officer thereof.

SEC. 9. The Migration or Importation of such Persons as any of the States now existing shall think proper to admit, shall not be prohibited by the Congress prior to the Year one thousand eight hundred and eight, but a Tax or duty may be imposed on such Importation not exceeding ten dollars for each Person.

The Privilege of the Writ of Habeas Corpus shall not be suspended, unless when in Cases of Rebellion or Invasion the public Safety may require it.

No bill or Attainder or ex post facto Law shall be passed.

No Capitation, or other direct, Tax should be laid, unless in Proportion to the Census or Enumeration hereinbefore directed to be taken.

No Tax or Duty shall be laid on Articles exported from any State.

No Preference shall be given by any Regulation of Commerce or Revenue to the Ports of one State over those of another; nor shall Vessels bound to, or from, one State, be obliged to enter, clear, or pay Duties in another.

No Money shall be drawn from the Treasury, but in Consequence of Appropriations made by Law; and a regular Statement and Account of the Receipts and Expenditures of all public Money shall be published from time to time.

No Title of Nobility shall be granted by the United States: and no Person holding any office of Profit or Trust under them, shall, without the Consent of the Congress, accept of any present, Emolument, Office, or Title, of any kind whatever, from any King, Prince or foreign State.

SEC. 10. No State shall enter into any Treaty, Alliance, or Confederation; grant Letters of Marque and Reprisal; coin Money; emit Bills of Credit; make any Thing but gold and silver Coin a Tender in Payment of Debts; pass any Bill of Attainder, ex post facto Law, or Law impairing the Obligation of Contracts, or grant any Title of Nobility.

No State shall, without the Consent of the Congress, lay any Imposts or Duties on Imports or Exports, except what may be absolutely necessary for executing its inspection Laws: and the net

Produce of all Duties and Imposts, laid by any State on Imports or Exports, shall be for the Use of the Treasury of the United States; and all such Laws shall be subject to the Revision and Control of the Congress.

No State shall, without the Consent of Congress, lay any Duty of Tonnage, keep Troops, or Ships of War in time of Peace, enter into any Agreement or Compact with another State, or with a foreign Power, or engage in War, unless actually invaded, or in such imminent Danger as will not admit of Delay.

Article II

Section 1. The executive Power shall be vested in a President of the United States of America. He shall hold his Office during the Term of four Years, and, together with the Vice-President, chosen for the same Term, be elected, as follows:

Each State shall appoint, in such Manner as the Legislature thereof may direct, a Number of Electors, equal to the whole Number of Senators and Representatives to which the State may be entitled in the Congress; but no Senator or Representative, or Person holding an Office of Trust or Profit under the United States, shall be appointed an Elector.

The Electors shall meet in their respective States, and vote by Ballot for two Persons, of whom one at least shall not be an Inhabitant of the same State with themselves. And they shall make a List of all Persons voted for, and of the Number of votes for each; which List they shall sign and certify, and transmit sealed to the Seat of the Government of the United States, directed to the President of the Senate. The President of the Senate shall, in the Presence of the Senate and House of Representatives, open all the Certificates, and the Votes shall then be counted. The Person having the greatest Number of Votes shall be the President, if such Number be a Majority of the whole Number of Electors appointed; and if there be more than one who have such Majority, and have an equal Number of Votes, then the House of Representatives shall immediately chuse by Ballot one of them for President; and if no Person have a Majority, then from the five highest on the List the said House shall in like manner chuse the President. But in chusing the President, the Votes shall be taken by States, the Representation from each State having one Vote; A quorum for this Purpose shall consist of a Member or Members from two-thirds of the States, and a Majority of all the States shall be necessary to a Choice. In every Case, after the Choice of the President, the Person having the greatest Number of Votes of the Electors shall be the Vice-president. But if there should remain two or more who have equal Votes, the Senate shall chuse from them by Ballot the Vice President.

The Congress may determine the Time of chusing the Electors, and the Day on which they shall give their Votes; which Day shall be the same throughout the United States.

No person except a natural born Citizen, or a Citizen of the United States, at the time of the Adoption of the Constitution, shall be eligible to the Office of President; neither shall any Person be eligible to that Office who shall not have attained to the Age of thirty-five Years, and been fourteen Years a Resident within the United States.

In Case of the Removal of the President from Office, or of his Death, Resignation, or Inability to Discharge the Powers and Duties of the said Office, the Same shall devolve on the Vice President, and the Congress may by law provide for the Case of Removal, Death, Resignation or Inability, both of the President and Vice President, declaring what Officer shall then act as President and such Officer shall act accordingly, until the Disability be removed, or a President shall be elected.

The President shall, at stated Times, receive for his Services, a Compensation, which shall neither be encreased nor diminished during the Period for which he shall have been elected, and he shall not receive within that Period any other Emoluments from the United States, or any of them.

Before he enters on the Execution of his office, he shall take the following Oath or Affirmation:—

"I do solemnly swear (or affirm) that I will faithfully execute the Office of President of the United States, and will to the best of my Ability, preserve, protect, and defend the Constitution of the United States."

SEC. 2. The President shall be Commander in Chief of the Army and Navy of the United States, and of the Militia of the several States, when called into the actual Service of the United States;

he may require the Opinion, in writing, of the principal Officer in each of the executive Departments, upon any Subject relating to the Duties of their respective Offices, and he shall have Power to grant Reprieves and Pardons for Offences against the United States, except in Cases of Impeachment.

He shall have Power, by and with the Advice and Consent of the Senate, to make Treaties, provided two-thirds of the Senators present concur; and he shall nominate, and by and with the Advice and Consent of the Senate, shall appoint Ambassadors, other public Ministers and Consuls, Judges of the supreme Court, and all other Officers of the United States, whose Appointments are not herein otherwise provided for, and which shall be established by Law: but the Congress may by Law vest the Appointment of such inferior Officers, as they think proper, in the President alone, in the Courts of Law, or in the Heads of Departments.

The President shall have Power to fill up all Vacancies that may happen during the Recess of the Senate, by granting Commissions which shall expire at the End of their next Session.

Sec. 3. He shall from time to time give to the Congress Information of the State of the Union, and recommend to their Consideration such Measures as he shall judge necessary and expedient; he may, on extraordinary Occasions, convene both Houses, or either of them, and in Case of Disagreement between them, with Respect to the Time of Adjournment, he may adjourn them to such Time as he shall think proper; he shall receive Ambassadors and other public Ministers; he shall take Care that the Laws be faithfully executed and shall Commission all the Officers of the United States.

Sec. 4. The President, Vice President and all civil Officers of the United States, shall be removed from Office on Impeachment for, and Conviction of, Treason, Bribery, or other high Crimes and Misdemeanors.

ARTICLE III

Section 1. The judicial Power of the United States, shall be vested in one supreme Court, and such inferior Courts as the Congress may from time to time ordain and establish. The Judges, both of the supreme and inferior Courts, shall hold their Offices during good Behaviour, and shall, at stated Times, receive for their

Services a Compensation, which shall not be diminished during their Continuance in Office.

SEC. 2. The judicial Power shall extend to all Cases, in Law and Equity, arising under this Constitution, the Laws of the United States, and Treaties made, or which shall be made, under their Authority;—to all Cases affecting Ambassadors, other public Ministers and Consuls;—to all Cases of admiralty and maritime Jurisdiction;—to Controversies to which the United States shall be a Party;—to Controversies between two or more States;—between a State and Citizens of another State;—between Citizens of different States;—between Citizens of the same State claiming Lands under Grants of different States, and between a State, or the Citizens thereof, and foreign States, Citizens, or Subjects.

In all Cases affecting Ambassadors, other public Ministers and Consuls, and those in which a State shall be a Party, the supreme Court shall have original Jurisdiction. In all the other Cases before mentioned, the supreme Court shall have appellate Jurisdiction, both as to Law and Fact, with such Exceptions, and under such Regulation as the Congress shall make.

The Trial of all Crimes, except in Cases of Impeachment, shall be by Jury; and such Trial shall be held in the State where the said Crimes shall have been committed; but when not committed within any State, the Trial shall be at such Place or Places as the Congress may by Law have directed.

SEC. 3. Treason against the United States, shall consist only in levying War against them, or in adhering to their Enemies, giving them Aid and Comfort. No Person shall be convicted of Treason unless on the Testimony of two Witnesses to the same overt Act, or on Confession in open Court.

The Congress shall have Power to declare the Punishhment of Treason, but no Attainder of Treason shall work Corruption of Blood, or Forfeiture except during the Life of the Person attainted.

ARTICLE IV

SECTION 1. Full Faith and Credit shall be given in each State to the public Acts, Records, and judicial Proceedings of every other State. And the Congress may by general Laws prescribe the Manner in which such Acts, Records and Proceedings shall be proved, and the Effect thereof.

SEC. 2. The Citizens of each State shall be entitled to all Privileges and Immunities of Citizens in the several States.

A person charged in any State with Treason, Felony, or other Crime, who shall flee from Justice, and be found in another State, shall on Demand of the executive Authority of the State from which he fled, be delivered up, to be removed to the State having Jurisdiction of the Crime.

No Person held to Service or Labour in one State, under the Laws thereof, escaping into another, shall, in Consequence of any Law, or Regulation therein, be discharged from such Service or Labour, but shall be delivered up on Claim of the Party to whom such Service or Labour may be due.

SEC. 3. New States may be admitted by the Congress into this Union; but no new State shall be formed or erected within the Jurisdiction of any other State; nor any State be formed by the Junction of two or more States, or Parts of States, without the Consent of the Legislatures of the States concerned as well as of the Congress.

The Congress shall have Power to dispose of and make all needful Rules and Regulations respecting the Territory or other Property belonging to the United States; and nothing in this Constitution shall be so construed as to Prejudice any Claims of the United States, or any particular State.

SEC. 4. The United States shall guarantee to every State in this Union a Republican Form of Government, and shall protect each of them against Invasion; and on Application of the Legislature, or of the Executive (when the Legislature cannot be convened) against domestic Violence.

ARTICLE V

The Congress, whenever two-thirds of both Houses shall deem it necessary, shall propose Amendments to this Constitution, or, on the Application of the Legislatures of two-thirds of the several States, shall call a Convention for proposing Amendments, which in either Case, shall be valid to all Intents and Purposes as part of this Constitution, when ratified by the Legislatures of three-fourths of the several States, or by Conventions in three-fourths thereof, as the one or the other Mode of Ratification may be proposed by the Congress; Provided that no Amendment which may be made prior to the Year One thousand eight hundred and eight shall in any Manner affect the first and fourth Clauses in the Ninth Section of the first Article; and that no State, without its Consent, shall be deprived of its equal Suffrage in the Senate.

ARTICLE VI

All Debts contracted and Engagements entered into, before the Adoption of this Constitution, shall be as valid against the United States under this Constitution, as under the Confederation.

This Constitution, and the Laws of the United States which shall be made in Pursuance thereof; and all Treaties made, or which shall be made, under the Authority of the United States, shall be the supreme Law of the Land; and the Judges in every State shall be bound thereby, any Thing in the Constitution or Laws of any State to the Contrary notwithstanding.

The Senators and Representatives before mentioned, and the Members of the several State Legislatures, and all executive and judicial Officers, both of the United States and of the several States, shall be bound by Oath or Affirmation, to support this Constitution; but no religious Test shall ever be required as a Qualification to any Office or public Trust under the United States.

ARTICLE VII

The Ratification of the Conventions of nine States shall be sufficient for the Establishment of this Constitution between the States so ratifying the Same.

THE AMENDMENTS

I

Congress shall make no law respecting an establishment of religion, or prohibiting the free exercise thereof; or abridging the freedom of speech, or of the press; or the right of the people peaceably to assemble, and to petition the Government for redress of grievances.

II

A well-regulated Militia, being necessary to the security of a free State, the right of the people to keep and bear Arms, shall not be infringed.

III

No Soldier shall, in time of peace, be quartered in any house, without the consent of the Owner, nor in time of war, but in a manner to be prescribed by law.

IV

The right of the people to be secure in their persons, houses, papers, and effects, against unreasonable searches and seizures, shall not be violated, and no Warrants shall issue, but upon probable cause, supported by Oath or affirmation, and particularly describing the place to be searched, and the persons or things to be seized.

V

No person shall be held to answer for a capital, or otherwise infamous crime, unless on a presentment or indictment of a Grand Jury, except in cases arising in the land or naval forces, or in the Militia, when in actual service in time of War or public danger; nor shall any person be subject for the same offence to be twice put in jeopardy of life or limb; nor shall be compelled in any Criminal Case to be witness against himself, nor be deprived of life, liberty, or property, without due process of law; nor shall private property be taken for public use, without just compensation.

VI

In all criminal prosecutions, the accused shall enjoy the right to a speedy and public trial, by an impartial jury of the State and district wherein the crime shall have been committed, which district shall have been previously ascertained by law, and to be informed of the nature and cause of the accusation; to be confronted with the witnesses against him; to have compulsory process for obtaining Witnesses in his favor, and to have the Assistance of Counsel for his defence.

VII

In suits at common law, where the value in controversy shall exceed twenty dollars, the right of trial by jury shall be preserved, and no fact tried by a jury shall be otherwise re-examined in any Court of the United States, than according to the rules of the common law.

VIII

Excessive bail shall not be required, nor excessive fines imposed, nor cruel and unusual punishments inflicted.

IX

The enumeration in the Constitution, of certain rights, shall not be construed to deny or disparage others retained by the people.

X

The powers not delegated to the United States by the Constitution, nor prohibited by it to the States, are reserved to the States respectively, or to the people.

XI

The Judicial power of the United States shall not be construed to extend to any suit in law or equity, commenced or prosecuted against one of the United States by Citizens of another State, or by Citizens or Subjects of any Foreign State.

XII

The Electors shall meet in their respective States and vote by ballot for President and Vice President, one of whom, at least, shall not be an inhabitant of the same State with themselves; they shall name in their ballots the person voted for as President, and in distinct ballots the person voted for as Vice President, and they shall make distinct lists of all persons voted for as President, and of all persons voted for as Vice President, and of the number of votes for each, which lists they shall sign and certify, and transmit sealed to the seat of the government of the United States, directed to the President of the Senate;—The President of the Senate shall, in the presence of the Senate and House of Representatives, open all the certificates and the votes shall then be counted;—The person having the greatest number of votes for Presidest shall be the President, if such number be a majority of the whole number of Electors appointed; and if no person have such majority, then from the persons having the highest numbers not exceeding three on the list of those voted for as President, the House of Representatives shall choose immediately, by ballot, the President. But in choosing the President, the vote shall be taken by States, the representation from each State having one vote; a quorum for this purpose shall consist of a member or members from two-thirds of the States, and a majority of all the States shall be necessary to a choice. And if the House of Representatives shall not choose a President whenever the right of choice shall devolve upon them, before the fourth day of March next following, then the Vice President shall act as President, as in the case of the death or other constitutional disability of the President. The person having the greatest number of votes as Vice President shall be Vice President, if such number be a majority of the whole number of Electors appointed, and if no person have a majority, then from the two highest numbers on the list, the Senate shall choose the Vice President; a quorum for the purpose shall consist of two-thirds of the whole number of Senators, and a majority of the whole number shall be necessary to a choice. But no person constitutionally ineligible to the office of President shall be eligible to that of Vice President of the United States.

XIII

SECTION 1. Neither slavery nor involuntary servitude, except as a punishment for crime whereof the party shall have been duly convicted, shall exist within the United States, or any place subject to their jurisdiction.

SEC. 2. Congress shall have power to enforce this article by appropriate legislation.

XIV

SECTION 1. All persons born or naturalized in the United States, and subject to the jurisdiction thereof, are citizens of the United States and of the State wherein they reside. No State shall make or enforce any law which shall abridge the privileges or immunities of citizens of the United States, nor shall any State deprive any person of life, liberty, or property, without due process of law; nor deny to any person within its jurisdiction the equal protection of the laws.

SEC. 2. Representatives shall be apportioned among the several States according to their respective numbers, counting the whole number of persons in each State, excluding Indians not taxed. But when the right to vote at any election for the choice of electors for President and Vice President of the United States, Representatives in Congress, the Executive and Judicial officers of a State, or the members of the Legislature thereof, is denied to any of the male inhabitants of such State, being twenty-one years of age, and citizens of the United States, or in any way abridged except for participation in rebellion, or other crime, the basis of representation therein shall be reduced in the proportion which the number of such male citizens shall bear to the whole number of male citizens twenty-one years of age in such State.

Sec. 3. No person shall be a Senator or Representative in Congress, or elector of President and Vice President, or hold any office, civil or military, under the United States, or under any State, who, having previously taken an oath, as a member of Congress, or as an officer of the United States, or as a member of any State Legislature, or as an executive or judicial officer of any State, to support the Constitution of the United States, shall have engaged in insurrection or rebellion against the same, or given aid or comfort to the enemies thereof. But Congress may by a vote of two-thirds of each House, remove such disability.

Sec. 4. The validity of the public debt of the United States, authorized by law, including debts incurred for payment of pensions and bounties for services in supressing insurrection or rebellion, shall not be questioned. But neither the United States nor any State shall assume or pay any debt or obligation incurred in aid of insurrection or rebellion against the United States, or any claim for the loss or emancipation of any slave; but all such debts, obligations and claims shall be held illegal and void.

Sec. 5. The Congress shall have power to enforce, by appropriate legislation, the provisions of this article.

XV

Section 1. The right of the citizens of the United States to vote shall not be denied or abridged by the United States or by any State on account of race, color, or previous condition of servitude.

Sec. 2. The Congress shall have power to enforce this article by appropriate legislation.

XVI

The Congress shall have power to lay and collect taxes on incomes, from whatever source derived, without apportionment among the several States, and without regard to any census or enumeration.

XVII

SECTION 1. The Senate of the United States shall be composed of two Senators from each State, elected by the people thereof, for six years; and each Senator shall have one vote. The electors in each State shall have the qualifications requisite for electors of the most numerous branch of the State legislatures.

SEC. 2. When vacancies happen in the representation of any State in the Senate, the executive authority of such State shall issue writs of election to fill such vacancies: *Provided*, That the legislature of any State may empower the executive thereof to make temporary appointment until the people fill the vacancies by election as the legislature may direct.

SEC. 3. This amendment shall not be so construed as to affect the election or term of any Senator chosen before it becomes valid as part of the Constitution.

XVIII

SECTION 1. After one year from the ratification of this article the manufacture, sale, or transportation of intoxicating liquors within, the importation thereof into, the exportation thereof from the United States and all territory subject to the jurisdiction thereof, for beverage purposes is hereby prohibited.

SEC. 2. The Congress and the several States shall have concurrent power to enforce this article by appropriate legislation.

XIX

SECTION 1. The right of citizens of the United States to vote shall not be denied or abridged by the United States or by any State on account of sex.

SEC. 2. Congress shall have power by appropriate legislation, to enforce the provisions of this Article.

RATIFICATION OF THE CONSTITUTION

The Constitution was ratified by the thirteen original States in the following order:

Delaware, December 7, 1787; Pennsylvania, December 12, 1787; New Jersey, December 18, 1787; Georgia, January 2, 1788; Connecticut, January 9, 1788; Massachusetts, February 6, 1788; Maryland, April 28, 1788; South Carolina, May 23, 1788; New Hampshire, June 21, 1788; Virginia, June 25, 1788; New York, July 26, 1788; North Carolina, November 21, 1789; Rhode Island, May 29, 1790.

RATIFICATION OF THE AMENDMENTS

The First to Tenth, inclusive, were declared in force December 15, 1791; the Eleventh, January 8, 1798; the Twelfth, September 25, 1804; the Thirteenth was proclaimed December 18, 1865; the Fourteenth, July 28, 1868; the Fifteenth, March 30, 1870; the Sixteenth, February 25, 1913; the Seventeenth, May 31, 1913; the Eighteenth, January 29, 1919; the Nineteenth, August 26, 1920.

CONSTITUTION OF THE STATE OF NORTH CAROLINA

Adopted April 24, 1868, With Amendments to 1927

(See Freeman v. Lide, 176-434.)

PREAMBLE

We, the people of the State of North Carolina, grateful to Almighty God, the Sovereign Ruler of nations, for the preservation of the American Union and the existence of our civil, political and religious liberties, and acknowledging our dependence upon Him for the continuance of those blessings to us and our posterity, do, for the more certain security thereof, and for the better government of this State, ordain and establish this Constitution.

Const. 1868.

ARTICLE I

DECLARATION OF RIGHTS

That the great, general and essential principles of liberty and free government may be recognized and established, and that the

relations of this State to the Union and Government of the United States, and those of the people of this State to the rest of the American people may be defined and affirmed, we do declare:
Const. 1868.

SECTION 1. *The equality and rights of men.* That we hold it to be self-evident that all men are created equal; that they are endowed by their Creator with certain unalienable rights; that among these are life, liberty, the enjoyment of the fruits of their own labor, and the pursuit of happiness.
Const. 1868; Decl. Independence.
State v. Hay, 126-1006; State v. Hill, 126-139.

SEC. 2. *Political power and government.* That all political power is vested in, and derived from, the people; all government of right originates from the people, is founded upon their will only, and is instituted solely for the good of the whole.
Const. 1868; Const. 1776, Decl. Rights, s. 1.
Quinn v. Lattimore, 120-428; Nichols v. McKee, 68-430.

SEC. 3. *Internal government of the State.* That the people of this State have the inherent, sole and exclusive right of regulating the internal government and police thereof, and of altering and abolishing their Constitution and form of government whenever it may be necessary for their safety and happiness; but every such right should be exercised in pursuance of the law, and consistently with the Constitution of the United States.
Const. 1868; Const. 1776, Decl. Rights, s. 2.
State v. Railway, 145-496; State v. Herring, 145-418; State v. Hicks, 143-689; State v. Lewis, 142-626; Durham v. Cotton Mills, 141-616; State v. Sutton, 139-574; State v. Holoman, 139-642; State v. Patterson, 134-612; State v. Gallop, 126-979; Humphrey v. Church, 109-132; Winslow v. Winslow, 95-24.

SEC. 4. *That there is no right to secede.* That this State shall ever remain a member of the American Union; that the people thereof are part of the American nation; that there is no right on the part of the State to secede, and that all attempts, from whatever source or upon whatever pretext, to dissolve said Union, or to sever said nation, ought to be resisted with the whole power of the State.
Const. 1868.

SEC. 5. *Of allegiance to the United States Government.* That every citizen of this State owes paramount allegiance to the Constitution and Government of the United States, and that no law or ordinance of the State in contravention or subversion thereof can have any binding force.

Const. 1868.

SEC. 6. *Public debt; bonds issued under ordinance of Convention of 1868, 68-69, 69-70, declared invalid; exception.* The State shall never assume or pay, or authorize the collection of any debt or obligation, express or implied, incurred in aid of insurrection or rebellion against the United States, or any claim for the loss or emancipation of any slave; nor shall the General Assembly assume or pay, or authorize the collection of any tax to pay, either directly or indirectly, expressed or implied, any debt or bond incurred, or issued, by authority of the Convention of the year one thousand eight hundred and sixty-eight, nor any debt or bond incurred or issued by the Legislature of the year one thousand eight hundred and sixty-eight, either at its special session of the year one thousand eight hundred and sixty-eight or at its regular sessions of the years one thousand eight hundred and sixty-eight and one thousand eight hundred and sixty-nine, and one thousand eight hundred and seventy except the bonds issued to fund the interest on the old debt of the State, unless the proposing to pay the same shall have first been submitted to the people and by them ratified by the vote of a majority of all the qualified voters of the State, at a regular election held for that purpose.

Const. 1868; 1872-3, c. 85; 1879, c. 268.
Const. 1, s. 6—Annot.
Comrs. v. Snuggs, 121-409; Beltzer v. State, 104-265; Horne v. State, 84-362; Brickell v. Comrs., 81-240; Davis v. Comrs., 72-441; Lance v. Hunter, 72-178; Logan v. Plummer, 70-388; Rand v. State, 65-197; R. R. v. Holden, 63-411; Galloway v. Jenkins, 63-152.
Const. 1, s. 7.

SEC. 7. *Exclusive emoluments, etc.* No man or set of men are entitled to exclusive or separate emoluments or privileges from the community but in consideration of public services.

Const. 1868; Const. 1776, Decl. Rights, s. 3.
Power Co. v. Power Co., 175-668, 171-248; Reid v. R. R., 162-355; State v. Perry, 151-661; St. George v. Hardie, 147-88; State v. Cantwell, 142-604; In re Spease Ferry, 138-219; Bray v. Williams, 137-391; Mial v. Ellington, 134-131; Ewbank v. Turner, 134-82; State v. Biggs, 133-729; Jones v. Comrs., 130-451; Hancock v. R. R., 124-255; Motley v. Warehouse Co., 122-350, 124-232; State v. Call, 121-645; Broadfoot v. Fayetteville, 121-418; Rowland v. Loan Assn., 116-879; R. R. Comrs. v. Tel. Co., 113-213; State v. Van Doran, 109-864; State v. Stovall, 103-416; Gregory v. Forbes, 96-77; Bridge Co. v. Comrs., 81-491; State v. Morris, 77-512; Simonton v. Lanier, 71-503; Barrington v. Ferry Co., 69-165; Kingsbury v. R. R., 66-284; Long v. Beard, 7-57; Bank v. Taylor, 6-266,

Constitution of the State of North Carolina

Sec. 8. *The legislative, executive and judicial powers distinct.* The legislative, executive and supreme judicial powers of the government ought to be forever separate and distinct from each other.

Const. 1868; Const. 1776, Decl. Rights, s. 4.
Lee v. Beard, 146-361; State v. Turner, 143-641; White v. Auditor, 126-605; Bird v. Gilliam, 125-79; Wilson v. Jordan, 124-705; Miller v. Alexander, 122-718; Garner v. Worth, 122-257; Caldwell v. Wilson, 121-476; Carr v. Coke, 116-236; Goodwin v. Fertilizer Works, 119-120; In re Suitan, 115-62; Herndon v. Ins. Co., 111-386; Horton v. Green, 104-401; Reucher v. Anderson, 93-105; Burton v. Spiers, 92-503; In re Oldham, 89-23; Brown v. Turner, 70-93; Railroad v. Jenkins, 68-593; Barnes v. Barnes, 53-372; Houston v. Bogle, 32-504; Hoke v. Henderson, 15-1; Robinson v. Barfield, 6-391.

Sec. 9. *Of the power of suspending laws.* All power of suspending laws, or the execution of laws, by any authority, without the consent of the representatives of the people, is injurious to their rights and ought not to be exercised.

Const. 1868; Const. 1776, Decl. Rights, s. 5.
Jones v. Comrs., 130-470; Abbott v. Beddingfield, 125-268 (dissenting opinion); White v. Auditor, 126-605.

Sec. 10. *Elections free.* All elections ought to be free.

Const. 1868; Const. 1776, Decl. Rights, s. 6.

Sec. 11. *In criminal prosecutions.* In all criminal prosecutions every man has the right to be informed of the accusation against him and to confront the accusers and witnesses with other testimony, and to have counsel for his defense, and not be compelled to give evidence against himself, or to pay costs, jail fees, or necessary witness fees of the defense, unless found guilty.

Const. 1868; Const. 1776, Decl. Rights, s. 7.
State v. Neville, 175-731; State v. Fowler, 172-905; State v. Cherry, 154-624; State v. Dry, 152-813; State v. Whedbee, 152-770; State v. Leeper, 146-655; State v. Cline, 146-640; State v. Railway, 145-495; State v. Dowdy, 145-433; State v. Harris, 145-456; State v. Hodge, 142-683; State v. Cole 132-1073; In re Briggs, 135-118; Sheek v. Sain, 127-266; State v. Mitchell, 119-785; Smith v. Smith, 116-386; Holt v. Warehouse Co., 116-488; State v. Shade, 115-759; State v. Massey, 104-880; State v. Cannady, 78-540; State v. Morris, 84-756; State v. Hodson, 74-153; State v. Collins, 70-247; State v. Aboan, 64-366; State v. Thomas, 64-76; State v. Tilghman, 33-513.

Sec. 12. *Answers to criminal charges.* No person shall be put to answer any criminal charge, except as hereinafter allowed, but by indictment, presentment or impeachment.

Const. 1868; Const. 1776, Decl. Rights, s. 8.
State v. Newell, 172-933; State v. Hyman, 164-411; State v. Harris, 145-456; Ex parte McCown, 139-95; State v. Lytle, 138-742; State v. Hunter, 106-806; State v. Dunn, 95-699; State v. Powell, 86-642; State v. Moore, 104-750; State v. Cannady, 78-540; Kane v. Haywood, 66-31; State v. Simons, 68-379; State v. Moss, 47-68.

SEC. 13. *Right of jury.* No person shall be convicted of any crime but by the unanimous verdict of a jury of good and lawful men in open court. The Legislature may, however, provide other means of trial for petty misdemeanors, with the right of appeal.

Const. 1868; Const. 1776, Decl. Rights, s. 9.
Jones v. Brinkley, 174-23; State v. Newell, 172-933; State v. Hyman, 164-411; State v. Rogers, 162-656; State v. Brittain, 143-668; Ex parte McCown, 139-95; State v. Lytle, 138-742; State v. Thornton, 136-616; Hargett v. Bell, 134-396; Smith v. Paul, 133-68; State v. Ostwalt, 118-1211; State v. Gadberry, 117-818; State v. Whitaker, 114-819; State v. Best, 111-646; State v. Cutshall, 110-543; State v. Hunter, 106-800; State v. Dunn, 95-698; State v. Powell, 97-417; State v. Divine, 98-784; State v. Powell, 86-642; State v. Dudley, 83-661; State v. Cannady, 78-541; State v. Dixon, 75-275; Barnes v. Barnes, 53-366; State v. Moss, 47-68.

SEC. 14. *Excessive bail.* Excessive bail should not be required, nor excessive fines imposed, nor cruel or unusual punishment inflicted.

Const. 1868; Const. 1776, Decl. Rights, s. 10. See English Bill of Rights (1689), c. 1, s. 10.
State v. Smith, 174-804; State v. Woodlief, 172-885; State v. Blake, 157-608; State v. Lance, 149-551; State v. Farrington, 141-844; State v. Hanby, 126-1066; Bryan v. Patrick, 124-661; State v. Ballard, 122-1025; State v. Apple, 121-585; State v. Reid, 106-716; State v. Pettie, 80-360; State v. Cannady, 78-543; State v. Driver, 78-423; State v. Reid, 18-377.

SEC. 15. *General warrants.* General warrants, whereby any officer or messenger may be commanded to search suspected places, without evidence of the act committed, or to seize any person or persons not named, whose offense is not particularly described and supported by evidence, are dangerous to liberty and ought not to be granted.

Const. 1868; Const. 1776, Decl. Rights, s. 11.
Brewer v. Wynne, 163-319; State v. Fowler, 172-905.

SEC. 16. *Imprisonment for debt.* There shall be no imprisonment for debt in this State, except in cases of fraud.

Const. 1868; Const. 1776, Decl. Rights, s. 39.
State v. Williams, 150-802; Ledford v. Emerson, 143-527; State v. Morgan, 141-726; State v. Torrence, 127-550; Stewart v. Bryan, 121-49; Lockhart v. Bear, 117-301; Preiss v. Cohen, 117-59; Fertilizer Co. v. Grubbs, 114-471; Burgwyn v. Hall, 108-490; State v. Earnhardt, 107-789; State v. Norman, 110-489; Winslow v. Winslow, 95-24; Kiney v. Longenour, 97-325; Long v. McLean, 88-3; State v. Beasley, 75-212; Melvin v. Melvin, 72-384; Daniel v. Owen, 72-340; State v. Davis, 82-610; State v. Wallin, 89-578; State v. Cannady, 78-539; Pain v. Pain, 80-322; Moore v. Mullen, 77-327; Moore v. Green, 73-394; State v. Green, 71-173; State v. Palin, 63-471; Bunting v. Wright, 61-295; Burton v. Dickens, 7-103.

SEC. 17. *No person taken, etc., but by law of land.* No person ought to be taken, imprisoned, or disseized of his freehold, liberties or privileges, or outlawed or exiled, or in any manner deprived of his life, liberty or property, but by the law of the land.

Const. 1868; Const. 1776, Decl. Rights, s. 12; Mag. Carta, (1215) c. 39, (1225), c. 29.

Bradshaw v. Lumber Co., 179-501; State v. Kirkpatrick, 179-747; Parker v. Comrs., 178-92; Comrs. v. Boring, 175-105; Comrs. v. State Treasurer, 174-141; Lang v. Development Co., 169-662; State v. Collins, 169-323; State v. Bullock, 161-223; Dalton v. Brown, 159-175; Lawrence v. Hardy, 151-123; Starnes v. Mfg. Co., 147-556; Caldwell Land, etc., Co. v. Smith, 146-199; State v. Williams, 146-618; Dewey v. R. R., 142-392; Anderson v. Wilkins, 142-154; State v. Morgan, 141-726; Daniels v. Home, 139-237; State v. Jones, 139-613; Cozard v. Hardware Co., 139-296; Porter v. Armstrong, 139-179; Ex parte McCown, 139-95; Mial v. Ellington, 134-172; Lumber Co. v. Lumber Co., 135-742; Parish v. Cedar Co., 133-478; Jones v. Comrs., 130-461; Dyer v. Ellington, 126-941; State v. Dill, 126-1139; Herring v. Pugh, 126-852; Hutton v. Webb, 124-179, 126-897; Southport v. Stanly, 125-464; Hogan v. Brown, 125-251; Morris v. House, 125-559; Day's Case, 124-362; Caldwell v. Wilson, 124-477; Wood v. Bellamy, 120-212; Hilliard v Asheville, 118-845; Call v. Wilkesboro, 115-337; State v. Warren, 113-683; Lance v. Harris, 112-489; Williams v. Johnson, 112-435; Bass v. Navigation Co., 111-439; Staton v. R. R., 111-278; State v. Cutshall, 110-543; State v. Hunter, 106-800; Moose v. Carson, 104-431; London v. Headen, 76-72; Rhea v. Hampton, 101-53; State v. Wilson, 107-865; Woodard v. Blue, 103-109; Railroad v. Ely, 95-77; Winslow v. Winslow, 95-24; Worth v. Cox, 89-44; Whitehead v. Latham, 83-232; Vann v. Pipkin, 77-410; State v Morris, 77-512; Whitehead v. R. R., 87-255; Bridge Co. v. Comrs., 81-491; Pool v. Trexler, 76-297; Privett v. Whitaker, 73-554; State v. Dixon, 75-275; Wilson v. Charlotte, 74-756; State v. Mooney, 74-100; Brown v. Turner, 70-93; King v. Hunter, 65-603; Bank v. Jenkins, 64-719; Norfleet v. Cromwell, 70-634; Johnson v. Rankin, 70-550; Franklin v. Vannoy, 66-151; Sedberry v. Comrs., 66-486; Miller v. Gibbon, 63-635; Schenck Ex parte, 65-353; Keener v. Wallace, 52-494; Barner v. Barner, 53-372; Cotten v. Ellis, 52-545; Cornelius v. Glen, 52-512; State v. Glen, 52-324; Stanmire v. Taylor, 48-207; State v. Matthews, 48-452; McNamara v. Kearns, 24-66; Houston v. Bogle, 32-496; State v. Allen, 23-183; Mills v. Williams, 33-558; State v. Johnson, 33-647; R. R. v. Davis, 19-451; Hoke v. Henderson, 15-1; Pipkin v. Wynne, 13-402; Hamilton v. Adams, 6-161; Oats v. Darden, 5-500; University v. Foy, 5-58, 3-310.

See, also, section 19 of this article.

SEC. 18. *Persons restrained of liberty.* Every person restrained of his liberty is entitled to a remedy to inquire into the lawfulness thereof, and to remove the same, if unlawful; and such remedy ought not to be denied or delayed.

Const. 1868; Const. 1776, Decl. Rights, s. 13.
Harkins v. Cathey, 119-663; State v. Herndon, 107-935; In re Schenck, 74-607

SEC. 19. *Controversies at law respecting property.* In all controversies at law respecting property, the ancient mode of trial by jury is one of the best securities of the rights of the people, and ought to remain sacred and inviolable.

Const. 1868; Const. 1776, Decl. Rights, s. 14.
In re Stone, 176-336; Crews v. Crews, 175-168; Walls v. Strickland, 174-298; Silvey v. R. R., 172-110; State v. Rogers, 162-656; Williams v. R. R., 140-623; Kearns v. R. R., 139-482; Smith v. Paul, 133-66; Boutten v. R. R. 128-310; Caldwell v. Wilson, 121-465; Wilson v. Featherstone, 120-147; Harkins v. Cathey, 119-662; State v. Mitchell, 119-786; Driller Co. v. Worth, 117-517; McQueen v. Bank, 111-515; Smith v. Hicks, 108-218; Lassiter v. Upchurch, 107

411; Railroad v. Parker, 105-246; Stevenson v. Felton, 99-58; Harris v. Shaffer, 92-30; Grant v. Hughes, 96-177; Pasour v. Lineberger, 90-159; Worthy v. Shields, 90-192; Wessel v. Rathjohn, 89-377; Grant v. Reese, 82-72; Chasteen v. Martin, 84-51; Overby v. Association, 84-62; Bernheim v. Waring, 79-56; Atkinson v. Whitehead, 77-418; Perry v. Tupper, 77-413; Womble v. Fraps, 77-198; Wilson v. Charlotte, 74-756; Armfield v. Brown, 72-81; Lippard v. Troutman, 72-551; Isler v. Murphy, 71-436; Witkowsky v. Wasson, 71-460; Pearson v. Caldwell, 70-294; Armfield v. Brown, 70-27; Green v. Castlebury, 70-20; Maxwell v. Maxwell, 70-267; Klutts v. McKenzie, 65-402; Andrews v. Pritchett, 66-387; White v. White, 15-257; Smith v. Campbell, 10-590; Bayard v. Singleton, 1-5.

Sec. 20. *Freedom of the press.* The freedom of the press is one of the great bulwarks of liberty, and therefore ought never to be restrained, but every individual shall be held responsible for the abuse of the same.

Const. 1868; Const. 1776, Decl. Rights, s. 15.
Osborn v. Leach, 135-628; Cowan v. Fairbrother, 118-406.

Sec. 21. *Habeas corpus.* The privileges of the writ of habeas corpus shall not be suspended.

Const. 1868.
Ex parte Moore, 64-802.

Sec. 22. *Property qualification.* As political rights and privileges are not dependent up. or modified by, property, therefore no property qualification ought to affect the right to vote or hold office.

Const. 1868.
Wilson v. Charlotte, 74-756.

Sec. 23. *Representation and taxation.* The people of the State ought not to be taxed or made subject to the payment of any impost or duty, without the consent of themselves, or their representatives in General Assembly, freely given.

Const. 1868; Const. 1776, Decl. Rights, s. 16.
State v. Wheeler, 141-773; Winston v. Taylor, 99-210; Moore v. Fayetteville, 80-154; Worth v. Comrs., 60-617.

Sec. 24. *Militia and the right to bear arms.* A well-regulated militia being necessary to the security of a free state, the right of the people to keep and bear arms shall not be infringed; and, as standing armies in time of peace are dangerous to liberty, they ought not to be kept up, and the military should be kept under strict subordination to, and governed by, the civil power. Nothing herein contained shall justify the practice of carrying concealed weapons, or prevent the Legislature from enacting penal statutes against said practice.

Const. 1868; Const. 1776, Decl. Rights, s. 17; Convention 1875.
State v. Barrett, 138-637; State v. Boone, 132-1107; State v. Reams, 121-556; State v. Speller, 86-697.

SEC. 25. *Right of the people to assemble together.* The people have a right to assemble together to consult for their common good, to instruct their representatives, and to apply to the Legislature for redress or grievances. But secret political societies are dangerous to the liberties of a free people and should not be tolerated.
Const. 1868; Const. 1776, Decl. Rights, s. 18; Convention 1875.

SEC. 26. *Religious liberty.* All men have a natural and unalienable right to worship Almighty God according to the dictates of their own consciences, and no human authority should, in any case whatever, control or interfere with the rights of conscience.
Const. 1868; Const. 1776, Decl. Rights, s. 19.
Rodman v. Robinson, 134-503; Lord v. Hardie, 82-241; Melvin v. Easley, 52-356.

SEC. 27. *Education.* The people have the right to the privilege of education, and it is the duty of the State to guard and maintain that right.
Const. 1868.
Collie v. Comrs., 145-170, overruling Barksdale v. Comrs., 93-483; Lowery v. School Trustees, 140-33; Bear v. Comrs., 124-212.

SEC. 28. *Elections should be frequent.* For redress of grievances, and for amending and strengthening the laws, elections should be often held.
Const. 1868; Const. 1776, Decl. Rights, s. 20.

SEC. 29. *Recurrence to fundamental principles.* A frequent recurrence to fundamental principles is absolutely necessary to preserve the blessings of liberty.
Const. 1868; Const. 1776, Decl. Rights, s. 21.

SEC. 30. *Hereditary emoluments, etc.* No hereditary emoluments, privileges, or honors ought to be granted or conferred in this State.
Const. 1868; Const. 1776, Decl. Rights, s. 22.
State v. Cantwell, 112-611; Bryan v. Patrick, 124-661; Bridge Co. v. Comrs, 81-504.

SEC. 31. *Perpetuities, etc.* Perpetuities and monopolies are contrary to the genius of a free state, and ought not to be allowed.
Const. 1868; Const. 1776, Decl. Rights, s. 23.
State v. Kirkpatrick, 179-747; Allen v. Reidsville, 178-513; State v. Perry, 154-664; St. George v. Hardie, 147-88; State v. Cantwell, 112-611; In re Spease Ferry, 138-259; State v. Biggs, 133-729; Robinson v. Lamb, 126-492; Garsed v. Greensboro, 126-160; Bennett v. Comrs., 125-468; Bryan v. Patrick, 124-661;

Guy v. Comrs., 122-471; Thrift v. Elizabeth City, 122-31; Railway v. Railway, 114-725; State v. Moore, 104-718; Hughes v. Hodges, 102-236; Bridge Co. v. Comrs., 81-504; Railroad v. Reid, 64-155; Simonton v. Lanier, 71-503; State v. McGowen, 37-9; State v. Gerrard, 37-210; Griffin v. Graham, 8-96; Bank v. Taylor, 6-266.

SEC. 32. *Ex post facto laws.* Retrospective laws, punishing acts committed before the existence of such laws, and by them only declared criminal, are oppressive, unjust and incompatible with liberty; wherefore no ex post facto law ought to be made. No law taxing retrospectively sales, purchases, or other acts previously done ought to be passed.

Const. 1868; Const. 1776, Decl. Rights, s. 24.
State v. Broadway, 157-598; Penland v. Barnard, 146-378; Anderson v. Wilkins, 142-154; Robinson v. Lamb, 129-16; City of Wilmington v. Cronly, 122-383; Culbreth v. Downing, 121-205; Morrison v. McDonald, 113-327; Kelly v. Fleming, 113-133; Lowe v. Harris, 112-472; State v. Ramsour, 113-642; Gilchrist v. Middleton, 108-705; Leak v. Gay, 107-468; Williams v. Weaver, 94-134; State v. Littlefield, 93-614; Burton v. Speers and Clark, 92-503; King v. Foscue, 91-116; Strickland v. Draughan, 91-103; Wilkerson v. Buchanan, 83-296; Whitehead v. Latham, 83-232; Tabor v. Ward, 83-291; Pearsall v. Kenan, 79-472; Lilly v. Purcell, 78-82; Young v. Henderson, 76-420; Libbett v. Maultsby, 71-345; Etheridge v. Vernoy, 71-184; Franklin v. Vannoy, 66-145; Johnson v. Winslow, 64-27; Jacobs v. Smallwood, 63-112; State v. Keith, 63-144; Robeson v. Brown, 63-554; State v. Bell, 61-76; Hinton v. Hinton, 61-410; Cooke v. Cooke, 61-583; Parker v. Shannonhouse, 61-209; Barnes v. Barnes, 53-366; State v. Bond 49-9; Phillips v. Cameron, 48-391; Salter v. Bryan, 26-494; Taylor v. Harrison, 13-374; Oats v. Darden, 5-500.

SEC. 33. *Slavery prohibited.* Slavery and involuntary servitude, otherwise than for crime, whereof the parties shall have been duly convicted, shall be, and are hereby, forever prohibited within the State.

Const. 1868.
State v. Hairston, 63-451.

SEC. 34. *State boundaries.* The limits and boundaries of the State shall be and remain as they now are.

Const. 1868; Const. 1776, Decl. Rights, s. 25.

SEC. 35. *Courts shall be open.* All courts shall be open; and every person for an injury done him in his lands, goods, person, or reputation, shall have remedy by due course of law, and right and justice administered without sale, denial or delay.

Const. 1868.
Osborn v. Leach, 135-628; Jones v. Comrs., 130-461; Driller Co. v. Worth, 118-746; Dunn v. Underwood, 116-526; Hewlett v. Nutt, 79-263.

SEC. 36. *Soldiers in time of peace.* No soldier shall in time of peace be quartered in any house without the consent of the owner; nor in time of war but in a manner prescribed by law.

Const. 1868.

SEC. 37. *Other rights of the people.* This enumeration of rights shall not be construed to impair or deny others retained by the people; and all powers not herein delegated remain with the people.

Const. 1868.
State v. Williams, 146-618; Daniels v. Homer, 139-237; Thrift v. Elizabeth City, 122-38; Railroad v. Holden, 63-410; Nichols v. McKee, 68-430; State v. Keith, 63-144; Railroad v. Reid, 64-155.

ARTICLE II

LEGISLATIVE DEPARTMENT

SECTION 1. *Two branches.* The legislative authority shall be vested in two distinct branches, both dependent on the people, to wit: a Senate and House of Representatives.

Const. 1868; Const. 1776, s. 1.
Wilson v. Jordon, 124-719; Comrs. v. Call, 123-323.

SEC. 2. *Time of assembly.* The Senate and House of Representatives shall meet biennially on the first Wednesday after the first Monday in January next after their election; and when assembled shall be denominated the General Assembly. Neither house shall proceed upon public business unless a majority of all the members are actually present.

Const. 1868; 1872-3, c. 82; Convention 1875; Const. 1776, ss. 4, 46; Convention 1835, art. 1, s. 4, cl. 7.
Herring v. Pugh, 126-862.

SEC. 3. *Number of senators.* The Senate shall be composed of fifty senators, biennially chosen by ballot.

Const. 1868; Convention 1835, art. 1, s. 1, cl. 1.

SEC. 4. *Regulations in relation to districting the State for senators.* The Senate districts shall be so altered by the General Assembly, at the first session after the return of every enumeration by order of Congress, that each Senate district shall contain, as near as may be, an equal number of inhabitants, excluding aliens and Indians not taxed, and shall remain unaltered until the return of another enumeration, and shall at all times consist of contiguous territory; and no county shall be divided in the formation of a Senate district, unless such county shall be equitably entitled to two or more senators.

Const. 1868; 1872-3, c. 81.

SEC. 5. *Regulations in relation to apportionment of representatives.* The House of Representatives shall be composed of one hundred and twenty representatives, biennially chosen by ballot, to be elected by the counties respectively, according to their population, and each county shall have at least one representative in the House of Representatives, although it may not contain the requisite ratio of representation; this apportionment shall be made by the General Assembly at the respective times and periods when the districts of the Senate are hereinbefore directed to be laid off.

Const. 1868; 1872-3, c. 82; Convention 1835, art. 1. s. 1, cls. 2, 3.
Comrs. v. Ballard, 69-18; Mills v. Williams, 33-563.

SEC. 6. *Ratio of representation.* In making the apportionment in the House of Representatives the ratio of representation shall be ascertained by dividing the amount of the population of the State, exclusive of that comprehended within those counties which do not severally contain the one hundred and twentieth part of the population of the State, by the number of representatives, less the number assigned to such counties; and in ascertaining the number of the population of the State, aliens and Indians not taxed shall not be included. To each county containing the said ratio and not twice the said ratio there shall be assigned one representative; to each county containing two but not three times the said ratio there shall be assigned two representatives, and so on progressively, and then the remaining representatives shall be assigned severally to the counties having the largest fractions.

Const. 1868; Convention 1835, art. 1, s. 1, cl. 4.
Moffitt v. Asheville, 103-237; Comrs. v. Ballard, 69-18.

SEC. 7. *Qualifications for Senators.* Each member of the Senate shall not be less than twenty-five years of age, shall have resided in this State as a citizen two years, and shall have usually resided in the district for which he was chosen one year immediately preceding his election.

Const. 1868.

SEC. 8. *Qualifications for representatives.* Each member of the House of Representatives shall be a qualified elector of the State, and shall have resided in the county for which he is chosen for one year immediately preceding his election.

Const. 1868.

SEC. 9. *Election of officers.* In the election of all officers, whose appointment shall be conferred upon the General Assembly by the Constitution, the vote shall be viva voce.

Const. 1868; Convention 1835, art. 1, s. 4, cl. 1.
Cherry v. Burns, 124-766; Stanford v. Ellington, 117-161.

SEC. 10. *Powers in relation to divorce and alimony.* The General Assembly shall have power to pass general laws regulating divorce and alimony, but shall not have power to grant a divorce or secure alimony in any individual case.

Const. 1868; Convention 1835, art. 4, s. 4, cl. 3.
Cooke v. Cooke, 164-272; In re Boyett, 136-415; Ladd v. Ladd, 121-118; Baily v. Cranfill, 91-293.

SEC. 11. *Private laws in relation to names of persons, etc.* The General Assembly shall not have power to pass any private law, to alter the name of any person, or to legitimate any person not born in lawful wedlock, or to restore to the rights of citizenship any person convicted of any infamous crime, but shall have power to pass general laws regulating the same.

Const. 1868; Convention 1835, art. 1, s. 4, cl. 4.

SEC. 12. *Thirty days notice shall be given anterior to passage of private laws.* The General Assembly shall not pass any private law, unless it shall be made to appear that thirty days' notice of application to pass such a law shall have been given, under such direction and in such manner as shall be provided by law.

Const. 1868; Convention 1835, art. 1, s. 4, cl. 5.
Power Co. v. Power Co., 175-668; Cox v. Comrs., 146-584; Bray v. Williams, 137-390; Comrs. v. Coke, 116-235; Gatlin v. Tarboro, 78-119; Broadnax v. Comrs., 64-244.

SEC. 13. *Vacancies.* If vacancies shall occur in the General Assembly by death, resignation or otherwise, writs of elections shall be issued by the Governor under such regulations as may be prescribed by law.

Const. 1868; Convention 1835, art. 1, s. 4, cl. 6.

SEC. 14. *Revenue.* No law shall be passed to raise money on the credit of the State, or to pledge the faith of the State, directly or indirectly, for the payment of any debt, or to impose any tax upon the people of the State, or allow the counties, cities or towns to do so, unless the bill for the purpose shall have been read three several times in each house of the General Assembly and passed three several readings, which readings shall have been on three different days, and agreed to by each house respectively, and unless the yeas and nays on the second and third readings of the bill shall have been entered on the journal.

Const. 1868.
Road Com. v. Comrs., 178-61; Guire v. Comrs., 177-516; Wagstaff v. Highway Com., 177-354; Woodall v. Highway Com., 176-377; Wagstaff v. Highway Com., 174-377; Claywell v. Comrs., 173-657; Brown v. Comrs., 173-598; Cottrell v. Lenoir, 173-138; Hargrave v. Comrs., 168-626; Gregg v. Comrs., 162-479; Pritchard v. Comrs., 160-476, 159-636; Russell v. Troy, 159-366; Comrs., v. Comrs., 157-515; Comrs. v. Bank, 152-387; Tyson v. Salisbury, 151-468; Bank v. Lacy, 151-3; Battle v. Lacy, 150-573; Wittowsky v. Comrs., 150-90; Lutterloh v. Fayetteville, 149-65; Cox v. Comrs., 146-584; Improvement Co. v. Comrs., 146-353; Comrs. v. Trust Co., 143-110; Fortune v. Comrs., 140-329; Comrs. v. Stafford, 138-453; Bray v. Williams, 137-390; Graves v. Comrs., 135-49; Brown v. Stewart, 134-357; Wilson v. Markley, 133-616; Debnam v. Chitty, 131-657; Hooker v. Greenville, 130-293; Cotton Mills v. Waxhaw, 130-293; Armstrong v. Stedman, 130-219; Comrs. v. DeRossett, 129-275; Black v. Comrs., 129-122; Glenn v. Wray, 126-730; Edgerton v. Water Co., 126-96; Smathers v. Comrs., 125-480; Slocumb v. Fayetteville, 125-362; Comrs. v. Payne, 123-486, 123-432; McGuire v. Williams, 123-349; Comrs. v. Call, 123-308; Charlotte v. Shepard, 122-602; Robinson v. Goldsboro, 122-211; Rodman v. Washington, 122-39; Mayo v. Comrs., 122-5; Comrs. v. Snuggs, 121-394; Bank v. Comrs., 119-214; Bank v. Comrs., 116-339; Jones v. Comrs., 107-265; Wood v. Oxford, 97-227; Galloway v. Jenkins, 63-147.

SEC. 15. *Entails.* The General Assembly shall regulate entails in such manner as to prevent perpetuities.

Const. 1868; Const. 1776, s. 43.

SEC. 16. *Journals.* Each house shall keep a journal of its proceedings, which shall be printed and made public immediately after the adjournment of the General Assembly.

Const. 1868; Const. 1776, s. 46.
Wilson v. Markley, 133-616; Carr v. Coke, 116-234.

SEC. 17. *Protest.* Any member of either house my dissent from, and protest against, any act or resolve which he may think injurious to the public, or any individual, and have the reason of his dissent entered on the journal.

Const. 1868; Const. 1776, s. 45.

SEC. 18. *Officers of the House.* The House of Representatives shall choose their own speaker and other officers.

Const. 1868; Const. 1776, s. 10.
Nichols v. McKee, 68-432.

SEC. 19. *President of the Senate.* The Lieutenant-Governor shall preside in the Senate, but shall have no vote unless it may be equally divided.

Const. 1868.

CONSTITUTION OF THE STATE OF NORTH CAROLINA   407

SEC. 20. *Other senatorial officers.* The Senate shall choose its other officers and also a speaker (pro tempore) in the absence of the Lieutenant-Governor, or when he shall exercise the office of Governor.
<small>Const. 1868; Const. 1776, s. 10.
Nichols v. McKee, 68-432.</small>

SEC. 21. *Style of the acts.* The style of the acts shall be: "The General Assembly of North Carolina do enact."
<small>Const. 1868.
State v. Patterson, 98-664.</small>

SEC. 22. *Powers of the General Assembly.* Each house shall be judge of the qualifications and election of its own members, shall sit upon its own adjournment from day to day, prepare bills to be passed into laws; and the two houses may also jointly adjourn to any future day, or other place.
<small>Const. 1868; Const. 1776, s. 10.
State v. Pharr, 179-699.</small>

SEC. 23. *Bills and resolutions to be read three times, etc.* All bills and resolutions of a legislative nature shall be read three times in each house before they pass into laws, and shall be signed by the presiding officers of both houses.
<small>Const. 1868; Const. 1776, s. 11.
State v. Patterson, 134-620; Wilson v. Markley, 133-616; Cotton Mills v. Waxhaw, 130-293; Smathers v. Comrs., 125-486; Comrs. v. Snuggs, 121-400; Russell v. Ayer, 120-211; Bank v. Comrs., 119-222; Cook v. Mears, 116-592; Carr v. Coke, 116-234; Scarborough v. Robinson, 81-409.</small>

SEC. 24. *Oath of members.* Each member of the General Assembly, before taking his seat, shall take an oath or affirmation that he will support the Constitution and laws of the United States, and the Constitution of the State of North Carolina, and will faithfully discharge his duty as a member of the Senate or House of Representatives.
<small>Const. 1868; Const. 1776, s. 12.</small>

SEC. 25. *Terms of office.* The terms of office for Senators and members of the House of Representatives shall commence at the time of their election.
<small>Const. 1868; Convention 1875.
Aderholt v. McKee, 65-259.</small>

SEC. 26. *Yeas and nays.* Upon motion made and seconded in either house by one-fifth of the members present, the yeas and nays upon any question shall be taken and entered upon the journals.
<small>Const. 1868.</small>

SEC. 27. *Election for members of the General Assembly.* The election for members of the General Assembly shall be held for the respective districts and counties, at the places where they are now held, or may be directed hereafter to be held, in such manner as may be prescribed by law, on the first Thursday in August, in the year one thousand eight hundred and seventy, and every two years thereafter. But the General Assembly may change the time of holding the elections.

Const. 1868; Convention 1875.
Aderholt v. McKee, 65-259; Loftin v. Sowers, 65-251.

SEC. 28. *Pay of members and officers of the General Assembly; extra session.* The members of the General Assembly for the term for which they have been elected shall receive as a compensation for their services the sum of four dollars per day for each day of their session, for a period not exceeding sixty days; and should they remain longer in session they shall serve without compensation. They shall also be entitled to receive ten cents per mile, both while coming to the seat of government and while returning home, the said distance to be computed by the nearest line or route of public travel. The compensation of the presiding officers of the two houses shall be six dollars per day and mileage. Should an extra session of the General Assembly be called, the members and presiding officers shall receive a like rate of compensation for a period not exceeding twenty days.

Convention 1875.
Kendall v. Stafford, 178-461; Bank v. Worth, 117-153.

SEC. 29. *Limitations upon power of General Assembly to enact private or special legislation.* The General Assembly shall not pass any local, private, or special act or resolution relating to the establishment of courts inferior to the Superior Court; relating to the appointment of justices of the peace; relating to health, sanitation, and the abatement of nuisances; changing the names of cities, towns and townships; authorizing the laying out, opening, altering, maintaining or discontinuing of highways, streets, or alleys; relating to ferries or bridges; relating to non-navigable streams; relating to cemeteries; relating to the pay of jurors; erecting new townships, or changing township lines, or establishing or changing the lines of school districts; remitting fines, penalties, and forfeitures or refunding moneys legally paid into the public treasury; regulating labor, trade, mining, or manufacturing; extending the time for the assessment or collection of taxes or otherwise relieving any collector of taxes from the due performance of his official duties or his sureties from liability; giving effect to informal wills and deeds; nor shall the General Assembly enact any such local, private or special act by the partial repeal of a general law, but the General Assembly may at any time repeal local, private or special laws enacted by it. Any local, private or special act or resolution passed in violation of the provisions of this section shall be void. The General Assembly shall have power to pass general laws regulating matters set out in this section.

1915, c. 99. In effect Jan. 10, 1917. See Reade v. Durham, 173-668; Mills v. Comrs., 175-215.

Davis v. Lenoir County, 178-668; Comrs. v. Pruden, 178-394; Comrs. v. Trust Co., 178-170; Martin County v. Trust Co., 178-26; Parvin v. Comrs., 177-508; Mills v. Comrs., 175-215; Highway Com. v. Malone, 173-685; Richardson v. Comrs., 173-685; Ranklin v. Gaston County, 173-683; Reade v. Durham, 173-668; Brown v. Comrs., 173-598.

Sec. 30. The General Assembly shall not use nor authorize to be used any part of the amount of any sinking fund for any purpose other than the retirement of the bonds for which said sinking fund has been created.

ARTICLE III

EXECUTIVE DEPARTMENT

SECTION 1. *Officers of the executive department; terms of office.* The executive department shall consist of a Governor, in whom shall be vested the supreme executive power of the State; a Lieutenant-Governor, a Secretary of State, an Auditor, a Treasurer, a Superintendent of Public Instruction, and an Attorney-General, who shall be elected for a term of four years by the qualified electors of the State, at the same time and place and in the same manner as members of the General Assembly are elected. Their term of office shall commence on the first day of January next after their election, and continue until their successors a elected and qualified: Provided, that the officers first elected shall assume the duties of their office ten days after the approval of this Constitution by the Congress of the United States, and shall hold their office four years from and after the first day of January.

Const. 1868; Convention 1835, art. II, s. 1.
Wilson v. Jordan, 124-719; Rhyne v. Lipscombe, 122-652; Caldwell v. Wilson, 121-176; Winslow v. Morton, 118-490; Battle v. McIver, 68-467; Howerton v. Tate, 68-546.

Sec. 2. *Qualifications of Governor and Lieutenant-Governor.* No person shall be eligible as Governor or Lieutenant-Governor unless he shall have attained the age of thirty years, shall have been a citizen of the United States five years, and shall have been a resident of this State for two years next before the election; nor shall the person elected to either of these two offices be eligible to the same office more than four years in any term of eight years, unless the office shall have been cast upon him as Lieutenant-Governor or President of the Senate.

Const. 1868; Const. 1776, s. 15.

Sec. 3. *Returns of elections.* The return of every election for officers of the executive department shall be sealed up and transmitted to the seat of government by the returning officer, directed to the Secretary of State. The return shall be canvassed and the result declared in such manner as may be prescribed by law. Contested elections shall be determined by a joint ballot of both houses of the General Assembly in such manner as shall be prescribed by law.

Const. 1868; Convention 1835, art. II, ss. 3, 4
Winslow v. Morton, 118-486; O'Hara v. Powell, 80-108.

Sec. 4. *Oath of office for Governor.* The Governor, before entering upon the duties of his office, shall, in the presence of the members of both branches of the General Assembly, or before any justice of the Supreme Court, take an oath or affirmation that he will support the Constitution and laws of the United States and of the State of North Carolina, and that he will faithfully perform the duties appertaining to the office of Governor to which he has been elected.

Const. 1868; Convention 1835, art. II, s. 5.

Sec. 5. *Duties of Governor.* The Governor shall reside at the seat of government of this State, and he shall, from time to time, give the General Assembly information of the affairs of the State, and recommend to their consideration such measures as he shall deem expedient.

Const. 1868.

SEC. 6. *Reprieves, commutations, and pardons.* The Governor shall have power to grant reprieves, commutations and pardons, after conviction, for all offenses (except in cases of impeachment), upon such conditions as he may think proper, subject to such regulations as may be provided by law relative to the manner of applying for pardons. He shall biennially communicate to the General Assembly each case of reprieve, commutation or pardon granted, stating the name of each convict, the crime for which he was convicted, the sentence and its date, the date of commutation, pardon or reprieve, and the reasons therefor.

Const. 1868; Const. 1776, s. 19.
In re Williams, 149-436; State v. Bowman, 145-425; Herring v. Pugh, 126-862; In re McMahon, 125-46; State v. Mathis, 109-815; State v. Cardwell, 95-643; State v. Alexander, 76-231; State v. Mooney, 74-98; State v. Blalock, 61-242.

SEC. 7. *Annual reports from officers of executive department and of public institutions.* The officers of the executive department and of the public institutions of the State shall, at least five days previous to each regular session of the General Assembly, severally report to the Governor, who shall transmit such reports, with his message, to the General Assembly; and the Governor may, at any time, require information in writing from the officers in the executive department upon any subject relating to the duties of their respective offices, and shall take care that the laws be faithfully executed.

Const. 1868.
Arendell v. Worth, 125-122; Welker v. Bledsoe, 68-463; Nichols v. McKee, 68-435.

SEC. 8. *Commander-in-Chief.* The Governor shall be Commander-in-Chief of the militia of the State, except when they shall be called into the service of the United States.

Const. 1868; Const. 1776, s. 18.
Winslow v. Morton, 118-486.

SEC. 9. *Extra session of General Assembly.* The Governor shall have power on extraordinary occasions, by and with the advice of the Council of State, to convene the General Assembly in extra session by his proclamation, stating therein the purpose or purposes for which they are thus convened.

Const. 1868.

SEC. 10. *Officers whose appointments are not otherwise provided for.* The Governor shall nominate, and by and with the advice and consent of a majority of the senators-elect, appoint all officers whose offices are established by this Constitution and whose appointments are not otherwise provided for.

Const. 1868; Convention 1875.
Salisbury v. Croom, 167-223; State v. Baskerville, 141-811; Day's Case 124-366; Ewart v. Jones, 116-570; University v. McIver, 72-76; Cloud v. Wilson, 72-155; Battle v. McIver, 68-467; Nichols v. McKee, 68-429; Howerton v. Tate, 68-546; Rogers v. McGowan, 68-520; Badger v. Johnson, 68-471; Welker v. Bledsoe, 68-457; Clark v. Stanley, 66-59; State v. Pender, 66-317; Railroad v. Holden, 63-410.

SEC. 11. *Duties of the Lieutenant-Governor.* The Lieutenant-Governor shall be President of the Senate, but shall have no vote unless the Senate be equally divided. He shall, whilst acting as President of the Senate, receive for his services the same pay which shall, for the same period, be allowed to the Speaker of the House of Representatives; and he shall receive no other compensation except when he is acting as Governor.

Const. 1868.

SEC. 12. *In case of impeachment of Governor, or vacancy caused by death or resignation.* In case of the impeachment of the Governor, his failure to qualify, his absence from the State, his inability to discharge the duties of his office, or in case the office of Governor shall in anywise become vacant, the powers, duties and emoluments of the office shall devolve upon the Lieutenant-Governor until the disabilities shall cease or a new Governor shall be elected and qualified. In every case in which the Lieutenant-Governor shall be unable to preside over the Senate, the senators shall elect one of their own number president of their body; and the powers, duties and emoluments of the office of Governor shall devolve upon him whenever the Lieutenant-Governor shall, for any reason, be prevented from discharging the duties of such office as above provided, and he shall continue as acting Governor until the disabilities are removed or a new Governor or Lieutenant-Governor shall be elected and qualified. Whenever, during the recess of the General Assembly, it shall become necessary for the President of the Senate to administer the government, the Secretary of State shall convene the Senate, and they may elect such president.

Const. 1868.
Rodwell v. Rowland, 137-626; Cadwell v. Wilson, 121-476.

SEC. 13. *Duties of other executive officers.* The respective duties of the Secretary of State, Auditor, Treasurer, Superintendent of

Public Instruction and Attorney-General shall be prescribed by law. If the office of any of said officers shall be vacated by death, resignation, or otherwise, it shall be the duty of the Governor to appoint another until the disability be removed or his successor be elected and qualified. Every such vacancy shall be filled by election at the first general election that occurs more than thirty days after the vacancy has taken place, and the person chosen shall hold the office for the remainder of the unexpired term fixed in the first section of this article.

Const. 1868.
Rodwell v. Rowland, 137-626; Speed v. Bullock, 80-135; Cloud v. Wilson, 72-163; Clark v. Stanley, 66-59; Nichols v. McKee, 68-429; Battle v. McIver, 68-467; Boner v. Adams, 65-639.

SEC. 14. *Council of State.* The Secretary of State, Auditor, Treasurer and Superintendent of Public Instruction shall constitute, ex officio, the Council of State, who shall advise the Governor in the execution of his office, and three of whom shall constitute a quorum; their advice and proceedings in this capacity shall be entered in a journal, to be kept for this purpose exclusively, and signed by the members present, from any part of which any member may enter his dissent; and such journal shall be placed before the General Assembly when called for by either house. The Attorney-General shall be, ex officio, the legal adviser of the executive department.

Const. 1868; Const. 1776, s. 16.

SEC. 15. *Compensation of executive officers.* The officers mentioned in this article shall, at stated periods, receive for their services a compensation to be established by law, which shall neither be increased nor diminished during the time for which they shall have been elected, and the said officers shall receive no other emolument or allowance whatever.

Const. 1868.

SEC. 16. *Seal of State.* There shall be a seal of the State, which shall be kept by the Governor, and used by him, as occasion may require, and shall be called "The Great Seal of the State of North Carolina." All grants and commissions shall be issued in the name and by the authority of the State of North Carolina, sealed with "The Great Seal of the State," signed by the Governor and countersigned by the Secretary of State.

Const. 1868; Const. 1776, ss. 17, 36.
Howell v. Hurley, 170-798; Richards v. Lumber Co., 158-54.

SEC. 17. *Department of Agriculture, Immigration and Statistics.*
The General Assembly shall establish a Department of Agriculture, Immigration and Statistics, under such regulations as may best promote the agricultural interests of the State, and shall enact laws for the adequate protection and encouragement of sheep husbandry.

Const. 1868; Convention 1875.
Cunningham v. Sprinkle, 124-638; Chemical Co. v. Board of Agriculture, 111-136.

ARTICLE IV

JUDICIAL DEPARTMENT

SECTION 1. *Abolishes distinction between actions at law and suits in equity, and feigned issues.* The distinction between actions at law and suits in equity, and the forms of all such actions and suits, shall be abolished; and there shall be in this State but one form of action for the enforcement or protection of private rights or the redress of private wrongs, which shall be denominated a civil action; and every action prosecuted by the people of the State as a party, against a person charged with a public offense, for the punishment of the same, shall be termed a criminal action. Feigned issues shall also be abolished, and the fact at issue tried by order of court before a jury.

Const. 1868.
Tillotson v. Currin, 176-479; Jerome v. Setzer, 175-391; Hardware Co. v. Lewis, 173-290; Makaen v. Elder, 170-510; Fowle v. McLean, 168-537; Wilson v. Ins. Co., 155-173; Hauser v. Morrison, 146-248; Levin v. Gladstein, 142-484; Turner v. McKee, 137-259; Staton v. Webb, 137-38; Boles v. Caudle, 133-528; Parker v. Express Co., 132-131; Harrison v. Hargrove, 116-448; Peebles v. Gay, 115-41; Moore v. Beaman, 112-560; Hood v. Sudderth, 111-219; Markham v. Markham, 110-356; Conley v. R. R., 109-692; Vegelhan v. Smith, 95-254; Lumber Co. v. Wallace, 93-25; Blake v. Askew, 76-326; Abrams v. Cureton, 74-526; Bitting v. Thaxton, 72-541; Tidline v. Hickerson, 72-421; Belmont v. Reilly, 71-262; Froelich v. Express Co., 67-4; Harkey v. Houston, 65-137; Tate v. Towe, 64-647; State v. McIntosh, 64-607; Mitchell v. Henderson, 63-610; State v. Baker, 63-276.
See, also under C. S., section 399.

SEC. 2. *Division of judicial powers.* The judicial power of the State shall be vested in a court for the trial of impeachments, a Supreme Court, Superior Courts, courts of justices of the peace, and such other courts inferior to the Supreme Court as may be established by law.

Const. 1868; Convention 1875.
State v. Burnett, 179-735; State v. Collins, 154-648; Hauser v. Morrison, 146-248; Ex parte McCown, 139-105; State v. Lytle, 138-741; State v. Baskerville, 141-813; Mott v. Comrs., 126-869; State v. Gallop, 126-983; Rhyne v. Lipscombe, 122-650; Caldwell v. Wilson, 121-476; McDonald v. Morrow, 119-670; Ewart v. Jones, 116-572; Express Co. v. R. R., 111-463; Wool v. Saunders, 108-739; State v. Weddington, 103-364; State v. Speaks, 95-689; State v. Spurtin, 80-363; State v. Cherry, 72-123; State v. Ketchey, 70-621; State v. Davis, 69-495; Rowark v. Gaston, 67-292; Froelich v. Express Co., 67-1; State v. Pender, 66-313; Wilmington v. Davis, 63-583; Edenton v. Wool, 65-379; Washington v. Hammons, 76-34; State v. Threadgill, 76-17; State v. Baker, 63-278; McAdoo v. Benbow, 63-461.

SEC. 3. *Trial court of impeachment.* The court for the trial of impeachments shall be the Senate. A majority of the members shall be necessary to a quorum, and the judgment shall not extend beyond removal from and disqualification to hold office in this State; but the party shall be liable to indictment and punishment according to law.

Const. 1868; Convention 1835, art. III, s. 1, cls. 2, 3.
Caldwell v. Wilson, 121-476.

SEC. 4. *Impeachment.* The House of Representatives solely shall have the power of impeaching. No person shall be convicted without the concurrence of two-thirds of the senators present. When the Governor is impeached the Chief Justice shall preside.

Const. 1868; Convention 1835, art. III, s. 1, cl. 3.

SEC. 5. *Treason against the State.* Treason against the State shall consist only in levying war against it, or adhering to its enemies, giving them aid and comfort. No person shall be convicted of treason unless on the testimony of two witnesses to the same overt act, or on confession in open court. No conviction of treason or attainder shall work corruption of blood or forfeiture.

Const. 1868. See Const. U. S., art. III, s. 3.

SEC. 6. *Supreme Court justices.* The Supreme Court shall consist of a Chief Justice and four associate justices.

Const. 1868; Convention 1875; 1887, c. 212.

SEC. 7. *Terms of the Supreme Court.* The terms of the Supreme Court shall be held in the city of Raleigh, as now, until otherwise provided by the General Assembly.

Const. 1868; Convention 1875.
State v. Marsh, 134-197.

SEC. 8. *Jurisdiction of Supreme Court.* The Supreme Court shall have jurisdiction to review, upon appeal, any decision of the courts below, upon any matter of law or legal inference. And the jurisdiction of said court over "issues of fact" and "questions of fact" shall be the same exercised by it before the adoption of the Constitution of one thousand eight hundred and sixty-eight, and the court shall have the power to issue any remedial writs necessary to give it a general supervision and control over the proceedings of the inferior courts.

Convention 1875. See Const. 1868, art. IV, s. 10.

R. R. v. Cherokee County, 177-86; Taylor v. Johnson, 171-84; State v. Tripp, 168-150; State v. Lee, 166-250; Page v. Page, 166-90; In re Wiggins, 165-457; Mott v. R. R., 164-367; Johnson v. R. R., 163-431; Pender v. Ins. Co, 163-98; Overman v. Lanier, 156-537; State v. Webb, 155-426; In re Holley, 154-163; Harvey v. R. R., 153-567; Stokes v. Cogdell, 153-181; In re Applicants for License, 143-1; Hollingsworth v. Skelding, 142-256; Slocumb v. Construction Co., 142-354; State v. Lilliston, 141-867; Brown v. Power Co., 140-348; Barker v. R. R., 137-222; State v. Marsh, 134-185; Mott v. Comrs., 126-869; Wilson v. Jordan, 124-719; State v. Hinson, 123-757; Harkins v. Cathey, 119-658; McDonald v. Morrow, 119-670; Carr v. Coke, 116-242; State v. Whitaker, 114-818; Express Co. v. R. R., 111-463; State v. Herndon, 107-934; Farrar v. Staton, 101-78; Rencher v. Anderson, 93-105; Railroad v. Warren, 92-620; Coats v. Wilkes, 92-381; Murrill v. Murrill, 90-120; Worthy v. Shields, 90-192; Young v. Rollins, 90-123; Wessel v. Rathjohn, 89-377; McMillan v. Baker, 85-291; Greenboro v. Scott, 84-184; Shields v. Whitaker, 82-516; Simmons v. Foscue, 81-86; Jones v. Boyd, 80-258; State v. McGimsey, 80-383; Battle v. Mayo, 102-435; In re Schenck, 74-609; Keener v. Finger, 70-42; Long v. Holt, 68-53; Rush v. Steamboat Co., 68-74; Isler v. Brown, 67-175; State v. Jefferson, 66-309; Rogers v. Goodwin, 64-279; McKimmon v. Faulk, 63-279; Biggs Ex parte, 64-262; Heilig v. Stokes, 63-612; Foushee v. Pattershall, 67-453; Perry v. Shepherd, 78-85; Graham v. Skinner, 57-94.

See, also, C. S. sec. 1411.

Sec. 9. *Claims against the State.* The Supreme Court shall have original jurisdiction to hear claims against the State, but its decisions shall be merely recommendatory; no process in the nature of execution shall issue thereon; they shall be reported to the next session of the General Assembly for its action.

Const. 1868.

Miller v. State, 134-272; Moody v. State Prison, 128-14; White v. Auditor, 126-598; Printing Co. v. Hoey, 124-795; Railroad v. Dortch, 124-675; Pate v. R. R., 122-578; Garner v. Worth, 122-250; Blount v. Simmons, 119-51; Burton v. Furman, 115-171; Cowles v. State, 115-173; Baltzer v. State, 109-187, 104-270; Martin v. Worth, 91-45; Clodfelter v. State, 86-51; Bain v. State, 86-49; Horne v. State, 82-382, 84-362; Sinclair v. State, 69-47; Bayne v. Jenkins, 66-358; Bledsoe v. State, 64-592; Reynolds v. State, 64-460; Rand v. State, 65-194; Battle v. Thompson, 65-408; Boner v. Adams, 65-644.

Sec. 10. *Judicial districts for Superior Courts.* The State shall be divided into nine judicial districts, for each of which a judge shall be chosen; and there shall be held a Superior Court in each county at least twice in each year, to continue for such time in each county as may be prescribed by law. But the General Assembly may reduce or increase the number of districts.

Const. 1868; Convention 1875.
State v. Shuford, 128-588; Wilson v. Jordan, 124-705; Rhyne v. Lipscombe, 122-650; Ewart v. Jones, 116-578; State v. Spurtin, 80-363; State v. Taylor, 76-64; State v. Adair, 66-298.

SEC. 11. *Residences of judges; rotation in judicial districts; special terms.* Every judge of the Superior Court shall reside in the district for which he is elected. The judges shall preside in the courts of the different districts successively, but no judge shall hold the courts in the same district oftener than once in four years; but in case of the protracted illness of the judge assigned to preside in any district, or of any other unavoidable accident to him, by reason of which he shall be unable to preside, the Governor may require any judge to hold one or more specified terms in said district in lieu of the judge assigned to hold the courts of the said district; and the General Assembly may by general laws provide for the selection of special or emergency judges to hold the Superior Courts of any county or district when the judge assigned thereto, by reason of sickness, disability, or other cause, is unable to attend and hold said court, and when no other judge is available to hold the same. Such special or emergency judges shall have the power and authority of regular judges of the Superior Courts, in the courts which they are so appointed to hold; and the General Assembly shall provide for their reasonable compensation.

Const. 1868; Convention 1875; 1915, c. 99. Last part of section, providing for "special or emergency judges," took effect Jan. 10, 1917. See Reade v. Durham, 173-668.
Watson v. R. R., 152-215; State v. Shuford, 128-588; Mott v. Comrs., 126-866; Rhyne v. Lipscombe, 122-650; State v. Turner, 119-841; McDonald v. Morrow, 119-670; Delafield v. Stafford, 114-239; State v. Lewis, 107-967; State v. Speaks, 95-689; State v. Bowman, 80-437; State v. McGimsey, 80-377; State v. Munroe, 80-373; State v. Watson, 75-136; State v. Keichey, 70-622; Howes v. Mauney, 66-222; State v. Adair, 66-298; Myers v. Hamilton, 65-568.

SEC. 12. *Jurisdiction of courts inferior to Supreme Court.* The General Assembly shall have no power to deprive the judicial department of any power or jurisdiction which rightfully pertains to it as a coördinate department of the government; but the General Assembly shall allot and distribute that portion of this power and jurisdiction which does not pertain to the Supreme Court among the other courts prescribed in this Constitution or which may be established by law, in such manner as it may deem best; provide also a proper system of appeals; and regulate by law, when necessary, the method of proceeding, in the exercise of their powers, of all courts below the Supreme Court, so far as the same may be done without conflict with other provisions of this Constitution.

Convention 1875.
State v. Little, 175-743; Cole v. Sanders, 174-112; Jones v. Brinkley, 174-23; Corp. Com. v. R. R., 170-560; Oil Co. v. Grocery Co., 169-521; State v. Brown, 159-467; State v. Collins, 151-648; State v. Shine, 149-480; Lee v. Beard, 146-361; Duckworth v. Mull, 143-469; In re Applicants for License, 143-1; State v. Baskerville, 141-813; Settle v. Settle, 141-564; Corp. Com. v. R. R., 139-126; Ex parte McCowan, 139-105; State v. Lytle, 138-741; State v. Lew, 133-666; Brinkley v. Smith, 130-225; In re Gorham, 129-490; State v. Brown, 127-564; Mott v. Comrs., 126-868; State v. Davis, 126-1007; State v. Battle, 126-1026; McCall v. Webb, 125-243; Wilson v. Jordan, 124-690; State v. Ray, 122-1098; Pate v. R. R., 122-877; Tate v. Comrs., 122-661; Rhyne v. Lipscombe, 122-650; Malloy v. Fayetteville, 122-480; Caldwell v. Wilson, 121-477; McDonald v. Morrow, 119-670; Springer v. Shavender, 118-42; Ewart v. Jones, 116-575; Express Co. v. R. R., 111-463; State v. Flowers, 109-841; In re Deaton 105-62; State v. Moore, 104-751; Walker v. Scott, 102-487; State v. Powell, 97-417; Bynum v. Powe, 97-874; Freight Discrimination Cases, 95-435; Rencher v. Anderson, 93-105; Murrill v. Murrill, 90-120; Cheek v. Watson, 90-302; In re Oldham, 89-23; Simpson v. Jones, 82-324; State v. Munroe, 80-373; State v. Spurtin, 86-362; Walton v. Walton, 80-26; Bratton v. Davidson, 79-423; Washington v. Hammond, 76-35; State v. Upchurch, 72-33; State v. Burk, 73-266; Bryan v. Rousseau, 71-194; Credle v. Gills, 65-192; Wilmington v. Davis, 63-582; Donaldson v. Waldrop, 63-507.

SEC. 13. *In case of waiver of trial by jury.* In all issues of fact, joined in any court, the parties may waive the right to have the same determined by a jury; in which case the finding of the judge upon the facts shall have the force and effect of a verdict by a jury.

Const. 1868.
Lumber Co. v. Lumber Co., 137-439; Wilson v. Featherstone, 120-447; Taylor v. Smith, 118-127; Driller Co. v. Worth, 117-518; Nissen v. Mining Co., 104-309; Battle v. Mayo, 102-134; Passour v. Lineberger, 90-159; Keener v. Finger, 70-42; Armfield v. Brown, 70-29.
See also, C. S., Secs. 568, 1502.

SEC. 14. *Special courts in cities.* The General Assembly shall provide for the establishment of special courts, for the trial of misdemeanors, in cities and towns, where the same may be necessary.

Const. 1868.
Oil Co. v. Grocery Co., 169-521; State v. Brown, 159-467; State v. Doster, 157-634; State v. Collins, 151-648; State v. Baskerville, 141-811; State v. Lytle, 138-741; Mott v. Comrs., 126-878; State v. Higgs, 126-1019; State v. Powell, 97-417; Washington v. Hammond, 76-34; State v. Ketchey, 70-622; State v. Pender, 66-318; State v. Walker, 65-462; Edenton v. Wool, 65-381; Wilmington v. Davis, 63-583.

SEC. 15. *Clerk of the Supreme Court.* The Clerk of the Supreme Court shall be appointed by the Court, and shall hold his office for eight years.

Const. 1868.

SEC. 16. *Election of Superior Court clerk.* A clerk of the Superior Court for each county shall be elected by the qualified voters thereof, at the time and in the manner prescribed by law for the election of members of the General Assembly.
Const. 1868.
Rodwell v. Rowland, 137-620; White v. Murray, 126-157; Clarke v. Carpenter, 81-311; University v. McIver, 72-85.

SEC. 17. *Term of office.* Clerks of the Superior Courts shall hold their offices for four years.
Const. 1868.
Rodwell v. Rowland, 137-620.

SEC. 18. *Fees, salaries and emoluments.* The General Assembly shall prescribe and regulate the fees, salaries and emoluments of all officers provided for in this article; but the salaries of the judges shall not be diminished during their continuance in office.
Const. 1868; Convention, 1835, art. III, s. 2.
In re taxation of judges' salaries, 131-692; Mott v. Comrs., 126-869; In re Walker, 82-94; Burton v. Comrs., 82-91; Bunting v. Gales, 77-151; King v. Hunter, 65-603.

SEC. 19. *What laws are, and shall be, in force.* The laws of North Carolina, not repugnant to this Constitution or the Constitution and laws of the United States, shall be in force until lawfully altered.
Const. 1868.
State v. Baskerville, 141-811; Mott v. Comrs., 126-878; Ewart v. Jones, 116-577; State v. King, 69-422; State v. Hairston, 63-452; State v. Baker, 63-278; State v. Colbert, 75-368; Boyle v. New Bern, 61-661 State v. Underwood, 63-98; State v. Jarvis, 63-556.

SEC. 20. *Disposition of actions at law and suits in equity pending when this Constitution shall go into effect, etc.* Actions at law and suits in equity pending when this Constitution shall go into effect shall be transferred to the courts having jurisdiction thereof, without prejudice by reason of the change; and all such actions and suits commenced before and pending at the adoption by the General Assembly of the rules of practice and procedure herein provided for shall be heard and determined according to the practice now in use, unless otherwise provided for by said rules.
Const. 1868.
Lash v. Thomas, 86-316; Patton v. Shipman, 81-349; Sharpe v. Williams, 76-91; Baldwin v. York, 71-466; Green v. Moore, 66-125; Johnson v. Sedberry, 65-1; Foard v. Alexander, 64-71; Teague v. Jones, 63-91; Gaither v. Gibson, 63-93.

SEC. 21. *Election, terms of office, etc., of justices of the Supreme and judges of the Superior Courts.* The justices of the Supreme Court shall be elected by the qualified voters of the State, as is provided for the election of members of the General Assembly. They shall hold their offices for eight years. The judges of the Superior Courts, elected at the first election under this amendment, shall be elected in like manner as is provided for justices of the Supreme Court, and shall hold their offices for eight years. The General Assembly may from time to time provide by law that the judges of the Superior Courts, chosen at succeeding elections, instead of being elected by the voters of the whole State, as is herein provided for, shall be elected by the voters of their respective districts.

Const. 1868; Convention 1875.
Rodwell v. Rowland, 137-626; Tate v. Comrs., 122-663; Appendix, 114-927; Hargrove v. Hilliard, 72-169; Cloud v. Wilson, 72-155; University v. McIver, 72-76; Loftin v. Sowers, 65-254.

SEC. 22. *Transaction of business in the Superior Courts.* The Superior courts shall be, at all times, open for the transaction of all business within their jurisdiction, except the trial of issues of fact requiring a jury.

Const. 1868.
Mott v. Comrs., 126-869; Delafield v. Construction Co., 115-21; Bynum v. Powe, 97-374; Comrs. v. Cook, 86-19; Harrell v. Peebles, 79-26; Hervey v. Edmunds, 68-243; Hunt v. Sneed, 64-180; Green v. Moore, 66-426; McAdoo v. Benbow, 63-463; Foard v. Alexander, 61-69.

SEC. 23. *Solicitors for each judicial district.* A solicitor shall be elected for each judicial district by the qualified voters thereof, as is prescribed for members of the General Assembly, who shall hold office for the term of four years, and prosecute on behalf of the State in all criminal actions in the Superior Courts, and advise the officers of justice in his district.

Const. 1868.
Rodwell v. Rowland, 137-626; Wilson v. Jordan, 124-690; Tate v. Comrs., 122-663.

SEC. 24. *Sheriffs and Coroners.* In each county a sheriff and coroner shall be elected by the qualified voters thereof, as is prescribed for members of the General Assembly, and shall hold their offices for two years. In each township there shall be a constable elected in like manner by the voters thereof, who shall hold his office for two years. When there is no coroner in a county, the clerk of the Superior Court for the county may appoint one for special cases. In case of a vacancy existing for any cause in any of the offices created by this section, the commissioners of the county may appoint to such office for the unexpired term.

Const. 1868; Const. 1776, s. 38.
Rodwell v. Rowland, 137-620; Rhyne v. Lipscombe, 122-650; State v. Sigman, 106-730; King v. McLure, 84-153; Worley v. Smith, 84-307; Wittkowsky v. Wasson, 69-38.

SEC. 25. *Vacancies.* All vacancies occurring in the offices provided for by this article of the Constitution shall be filled by the appointments of the Governor, unless otherwise provided for, and the appointees shall hold their places, until the next regular election for members of the General Assembly, when elections shall be held to fill such offices. If any person elected or appointed to any of said offices, shall neglect and fail to qualify, such offices shall be appointed to, held and filled as provided in case of vacancies occurring therein. All incumbents of said offices shall hold until their successors are qualified.

Const. 1868; Convention 1875.
State v. Baskerville, 141-811; Rodwell v. Rowland, 137-620; Ewart v. Jones, 116-570; Appendix C. S., 114-927; State v. Lewis, 107-976; Gilmer v. Holton, 98-26; King v. McLure, 84-153; Worley v. Smith, 84-307; Buchanan v. Comrs., 80-126; Hargrove v. Hilliard, 72-169; Cloud v. Wilson, 72-155; Nichols v. McKee, 68-429.

SEC. 26. *Terms of office of first officers.* The officers elected at the first election held under this Constitution shall hold their offices for the terms prescribed for them respectively, next ensuing after the next regular election for members of the General Assembly. But their terms shall begin upon the approval of this Constitution by the Congress of the United States.

Const. 1868.
Opinion of Judges, 114-925; Aderholt v. McKee, 65-258; Loftin v. Sowers, 65-254.

SEC. 27. *Jurisdiction of justices of the peace.* The several justices of the peace shall have jurisdiction, under such regulations as the General Assembly shall prescribe, of civil actions founded on contract, wherein the sum demanded shall not exceed two hundred dollars, and wherein the title to real estate shall not be in controversy; and all of criminal matters arising within their counties where the punishment cannot exceed a fine of fifty dollars or imprisonment for thirty days. And the General Assembly may give to justices of the peace jurisdiction of other civil actions wherein the value of the property in controversy does not exceed fifty dollars. When an issue of fact shall be joined before a justice, on demand of either party thereto he shall cause a jury of six men to be summoned, who shall try the same. The party against whom the judgment shall be rendered in any civil action may appeal to the Superior Court from the same. In all cases of a criminal nature the party against whom the judgment is given may appeal to the Superior Court, where the matter shall be heard anew. In all cases brought before a justice, he shall make a record of the proceedings, and file the same with the Clerk of the Superior Court for his county.

Const. 1868; Convention 1875.
Comrs. v. Sparks, 179-581; Jerome v. Setzer, 175-391; Oil Co. v. Grocery Co., 169-521; State v. Doster, 157-634; Wilson v. Ins. Co., 155-173; Riddle v. Milling Co., 150-689; Hauser v. Morrison, 146-248; State v. Bossee, 145-579; Duckworth v. Mull, 143-461; Brown v. Southerland, 142-614; State v. Baskerville, 141-811; State v. Lytle, 138-745; State v. Moore, 136-582; State v. Giles, 134-735, overruling State v. Ostwalt, 118-1209; Knight v. Taylor, 131-85; Cowell v. Gregory, 130-85; State v. Davis, 129-570; Mott v. Comrs., 126-869; State v. White, 125-674; State v. Ray, 122-1098; Rhyne v. Lipscombe, 122-650; Malloy v. Fayetteville, 122-480; State v. Addington, 121-540; McDonald v. Morrow, 119-674; Harkins v. Cathey, 119-665; State v. Nelson, 119-801; State v. Ivie, 118-1230; Alexander v. Gibbon, 118-805; Gambling v. Dickey, 118-986; State v. Wynne, 116-985; Williams v. Bowling, 111-295; Martin v. Goode, 111-289; Slocumb v. Shingle Co., 110-24; State v. Biggers, 108-762; Henderson v. Davis, 106-91; Durham v. Wilson, 104-598; Peck v. Culberson, 104-428; State v. Powell, 97-417, 86-640; Montague v. Mial, 89-137; Allen v. Jackson, 86-321; Morris v. Saunders, 85-140; Katzenstein v. R. R., 84-694; Boing v. R. R., 87-360; Hannah v. R. R., 87-351; Lutz v. Thompson, 87-334; Love v. Rhyne, 86-576; McLane v. Layton, 76-571; McAdoo v. Callum, 86-419; Allen v. Jackson, 86-321; Coggins v. Harrell, 86-317; Brickell v. Bell, 84-85; Fisher v. Webb, 84-44; State v. Dudley, 83-661; State v. Jones, 83-659; Derr v. Stubbs, 83-559; State v. Moore, 82-659; Dalton v. Webster, 82-282; Murphy v. McNeill, 82-221; McDonald v. Cannon, 82-247; State v. Edney, 80-360; Evans v. Williamson, 79-86; State v. Styles, 76-156; Heyer v. Beatty, 76-29; State v. Threadgill, 76-18; Nance v. R. R., 76-9; Pullen v. Green, 75-218; Hinton v. Davis, 75-18; Forsyth v. Bullock, 74-137; Hendrick v. Mayfield, 74-626; State v. Buck, 73-631; State v. Bailey, 73-70; Latham v. Rollins, 72-455; State v. Quick, 72-214; State v. Presley, 72-205; State v. Upchurch, 72-148; State v. Cherry, 72-123; State v. Perry, 71-523; Templeton v. Summers, 71-270; State v. Vermington, 71-263; Bryan v. Rousseau, 71-194; Bullinger v. Marshall, 71-520; Railroad v. Sharpe, 70-510; State v. Heidelburg, 70-496; State v. Yarborough, 70-250; Fell v. Porter, 69-140; Caldwell v. Beatty, 69-364; Davis v. Baker, 67-388; Froelich v. Express Co., 67-1; State v. Pendleton, 65-618; State v. Deaton, 65-497; Edenton v. Wool, 65-379; Hedgecock v. Davis, 64-650; State v. Johnson, 64-581; Wilmington v. Davis, 63-584; Winslow v. Weith, 66-432; Durlin v. Howard, 66-433; Froniburger v. Lee, 66-333; State v. Pender, 66-313; Creedle v. Gibbs, 65-192; Rives v. Guthrie, 46-84.
See, also, C. S., secs. 1473, 1474, 1481.

Sec. 28. *Vacancies in office of justice.* When the office of justice of the peace shall become vacant otherwise than by expiration of the term, and in case of a failure by the voters of any district to elect, the clerk of the Superior Court for the county shall appoint to fill the vacancy for the unexpired term.

Const. 1868.
Redwell v. Rowland, 137-628; Gilmer v. Holton, 98-26; Cloud v. Wilson, 72-155.

SEC. 29. *Vacancies in office of Superior Court clerk.* In case the office of clerk of a Superior Court for a county shall become vacant otherwise than by expiration of the term, and in case of a failure by the people to elect, the judge of the Superior Court for the county shall appoint to fill the vacancy until an election can be regularly held.

Const. 1868.
Redwell v. Rowland, 137-628; White v. Murray, 126-157; Williams v. Bowling, 111-295; Martin v. Goode, 111-289.

SEC. 30. *Officers of other courts inferior to Supreme Court.* In case the General Assembly shall establish other courts inferior to the Supreme Court, the presiding officers and clerk thereof shall be elected in such manner as the General Assembly may from time to time prescribe, and they shall hold their office for a term not exceeding eight years.

Convention 1875.
White v. Murray, 126-157; Ewart v. Jones, 116-572; State v. Weddington, 103-364.

SEC. 31. *Removal of judges of the various courts for inability.* Any judge of the Supreme Court, or of the Superior Courts, and the presiding officers of such courts inferior to the Supreme Court as may be established by law, may be removed from office for mental or physical inability, upon a concurrent resolution of two-thirds of both houses of the General Assembly. The judge or presiding officer against whom the General Assembly may be about to proceed shall receive notice thereof, accompanied by a copy of the causes alleged for his removal, at least twenty days before the day on which either house of the General Assembly shall act thereon.

Convention 1875. See Convention 1835, art. III, s. 2, cl. 1

SEC. 32. *Removal of clerks of the various courts for inability.* Any clerk of the Supreme Court, or of the Superior courts, or of such courts inferior to the Supreme Court as may be established by law, may be removed from office for mental or physical inability; the clerk of the Supreme Court by the judges of said court, the clerks of the Superior courts by the judge riding the district, and the clerks of such courts inferior to the Supreme Court as may be established by law by the presiding officer of said courts. The clerk against whom proceedings are instituted shall receive notice thereof, accompanied by a copy of the causes alleged for his removal, at least ten days before the day appointed to act thereon, and the clerk shall be entitled to an appeal to the next term of the Superior court, and thence to the Supreme Court, as provided in other cases of appeal.

Convention 1875.

SEC. 33. *Amendments not to vacate existing offices.* The amendments made to the Constitution of North Carolina by this convention shall not have the effect to vacate any office or term of office now existing under the Constitution of the State, and filled, or held, by virtue of any election or appointment under the said Constitution, and the laws of the State made in pursuance thereof.

Convention 1875.
State v. Moore, 136-581; Appendix, 114-928.

ARTICLE V

REVENUE AND TAXATION

SECTION 1. *Capitation tax; exemptions.* The General Assembly may levy a capitation tax on every male inhabitant of the State over twenty-one and under fifty years of age, which said tax shall not exceed two dollars, and cities and towns may levy a capitation tax which shall not exceed one dollar. No other capitation tax shall be levied. The commissioners of the several counties and of the cities and towns may exempt from the capitation tax any special cases on account of poverty or infirmity.

Davis v. Lenoir, 178-668; R. R. v. Comrs., 178-449; Guire v. Comrs., 177-516; Parvin v. Comrs., 177-508; Wagstaff v. Central Highway Com., 177-354; R. R. v. Cherokee County, 177-86; Hill v. Lenoir County, 176-572; Bennett v. Comrs., 173-625; Ingram v. Johnson, 172-676; Moore v. Comrs., 172-419; Hargrave v. Comrs., 168-627; Kitchin v. Wood, 154-565; Bd. of Education v. Comrs., 150-116; Perry v. Comrs., 148-521; R. R. v. Comrs., 148-248; R. R. v. Comrs., 148-220; Collie v. Comrs., 145-172; State v. Wheeler, 141-774; Pace v. Raleigh 140-67; Bd. of Ed. v. Comrs., 137-313; Wingate v. Parker, 136-369; State v. Ballard, 122-1026; Comrs. v. Snugg, 121-409; Russell v. Ayer, 120-180; Williams v. Comrs., 119-520; Bd. of Ed. v. Comrs., 111-578; 107-112; Jones v. Comrs., 107-248; Redmond v. Comrs., 106-137; Parker v. Comrs., 104-168; Barksdale v. Comrs., 93-472; Cromartie v. Comrs., 87-139, 85-217; Clifton v. Wynne, 80-145; French v. Wilmington, 75-477; Griffin v. Comrs, 74-701; French v. Comrs., 74-692; Brown v. Comrs., 72-388; Mauney v. Comrs., 71-486; Brothers v Comrs., 70-726; Street v. Comrs., 70-644; Johnson v. Comrs., 67-101; Sedberry v. Comrs., 66-486; University v. Holden, 63-410; R. R. v. Holden, 63-400; Gardner v. Hall, 61-21.

CONSTITUTION OF THE STATE OF NORTH CAROLINA   425

SEC. 2. *Application of proceeds of State and county capitation tax.* The proceeds of the State and county capitation tax shall be applied to the purposes of education and the support of the poor, but in no one year shall more than twenty-five per cent thereof be appropriated to the latter purpose.

Const. 1868.
Wagstaff v. Central Highway Com., 177-354; Hill v. Lenoir County, 176-572; Moose v. Comrs., 172-419; Board of Ed. v. Comrs., 150-116; Perry v. Comrs., 148-521; R. R. v. Comrs., 148-248; Collie v. Comrs., 145-170; State v. Wheeler, 141-774; Crocker v. Moore, 140-432; Board of Ed. v. Comrs., 137-311; School Directors v. Comrs., 127-263; Bd. of Ed. v. Comrs., 113-379; Redmond v. Comrs., 106-137; Parker v. Comrs., 104-168; Durham v. Bostick, 72-353; Jacobs v. Smallwood, 63-112.

SEC. 3. *Taxation shall be by uniform rule and ad valorem; exemptions.* Laws shall be passed taxing, by a uniform rule, all moneys, credits, investments in bonds, stocks, joint-stock companies, or otherwise; and, also, all real and personal property, according to its true value in money.

Provided, notes, mortgages, and all other evidences of indebtedness or any renewal thereof, given in good faith to build, repair or purchase a home, when said loan does not exceed eight thousand dollars ($8,000), and said notes and mortgages and other evidences of indebtedness, or any renewal thereof, shall be made to run for not less than one nor more than thirty-three years, shall be exempt from taxation of every kind for fifty per cent of the value of the notes and mortgages: *Provided*, the holder of said note or notes must reside in the county where the land lies and there list it for taxation: *Provided further*, that when said notes and mortgages are held and taxed in the county where the home is situated, then the owner of the home shall be exempt from taxation of every kind for fifty per cent of the value of said notes and mortgages. The word 'home' is defined to mean lands, whether consisting of a building lot or a larger tract, together with all the buildings and outbuildings which the owner in good faith intends to use as a dwelling place for himself or herself, which shall be conclusively established by the actual use and occupancy of such premises as a dwelling place of the purchaser or owner for a period of three months.

The General Assembly may also tax trades, professions, franchises, and incomes: Provided, the rate of tax on incomes shall not in any case exceed six per cent (6%), and there shall be allowed the following exemptions, to be deducted from the amount of annual incomes, to wit: for married man with a wife living with him, or to a widow or widower having minor child or children, natural or adopted, not less than $2,000; to all other persons not less than $1,000, and there may be allowed other deductions (not including living expenses) so that only net incomes are taxed.

Const. 1868; 1917, c. 119. Adding provisions 1 and 2, making limited exemption for purchase price of homes.

Brown v. Jackson, 179-363; Motor Corp. v. Flynt, 178-399; Bickett v. Tax Com., 177-433; Smith v. Wilkins, 164-135; State v. Bullock, 161-223; Comrs., v. Webb, 160-594; Dalton v. Brown, 159-175; State v. Williams, 158-610; Guano Co. v. Biddle, 158-212; Pullen v. Corp. Com., 152-548; Wolfenden v. Comrs., 152-83; State v Danenburg, 151-718; Land Co. v. Smith, 151-70; R. R. v. New Bern, 147-165; Lumber Co. v. Smith, 146-198; Collie v. Comrs., 145-170; State v. Wheeler, 141-773; In re Morris Estate, 138-259; State v. Roberson, 136-587; Plymouth v. Cooper, 135-1; Lacy v. Packing Co., 134-567; Jackson v. Comrs., 130-387; State v. Hunt, 129-686; State v. Carter, 129-560; State v. Irvin, 126-989; State v. Sharp, 125-631; Collins v. Pettitt, 124-727; State v. Ballard, 122-1026; Cobb v. Comrs., 122-307; Hilliard v. Asheville, 118-845; Schaul v. Charlotte, 118-733; Rosenbaum v. Newbern, 118-83; State v. Worth, 116-1007; Loan Assn. v. Comrs., 115-410; State v. Moore, 113-697; State v. Georgia Co., 112-34; Wiley v. Comrs., 111-400; Raleigh v. Peace, 110-38; State v. Wessel, 109-735; State v. Stevenson, 109-733; State v. French, 109-722; Jones v. Comrs., 107-257; Redmond v. Comrs., 106-137; Puitt v. Comrs., 94-709; Holton v. Comrs., 93-430; Busbee v. Comrs., 93-143; Wilmington v. Macks, 86-91; Busbee v. Comrs., 93-143; Railroad v. Comrs., 91-454; Jones v. Arrington, 91-125; Cain v. Comrs., 86-8; Railroad v. Comrs., 84-504; Worth v. Comrs., 82-420; Worth v. Railroad, 89-301; Evans v. Comrs., 89-154; Belo v. Comrs., 82-415; Mowery v. Salisbury, 82-175; Hewlett v. Nutt, 79-263; Gatlin v. Tarboro, 78-119; Young v. Henderson, 76-420; Railroad v. Comrs., 75-477; French v. Wilmington, 75-477; Kyle v. Comrs., 75-445; Wilson v. Charlotte, 74-748; Rwy. Co. v. Wilmington, 72-73; R. R. v. Comrs., 72-10; Ruffin v. Comrs., 69-498; Lilly v. Comrs., 69-300; Pullen v. Comrs, 68-451; University v. Holden, 43-410.

SEC. 4. *Restrictions upon the increase of the public debt except in certain contingencies.* Except for the refunding of valid bonded debt, and except to supply a casual deficit, or for suppressing invasions or insurrections, the General Assembly shall have no power to contract any new debt or pecuniary obligation in behalf of the State to an amount exceeding in the aggregate, including the then existing debt recognized by the State, and deducting sinking funds then on hand, and the par value of the stock in the North Carolina Railroad Company and the Atlantic and North Carolina Railroad Company owned by the State, seven and one-half per cent of the assessed valuation of taxable property within the State as last fixed for taxation.

And the General Assembly shall have no power to give or lend the credit of the State in aid of any person, association, or corporation, except to aid in the completion of such railroads as may be unfinished at the time of the adoption of this Constitution, or in which the State has a direct pecuniary interest, unless the subject be submitted to a direct vote of the people of the State, and be approved by a majority of those who shall vote thereon.

Const. 1868.
Comrs. v. State Treasurer, 174-141; Moran v. Comrs., 168-289; Comrs. v. Snuggs, 121-402; Mauney v. Comrs., 71-486; R. R. v. Jenkins, 65-173; University v. Holden, 63-410; Galloway v. R. R., 65-147.

SEC. 5. *Property exempt from taxation.* Property belonging to the State or to municipal corporations shall be exempt from taxation. The General Assembly may exempt cemeteries and property held for educational, scientific, literary, charitable, or religious purposes; also wearing apparel, arms for muster, household and kitchen furniture, the mechanical and agricultural implements of mechanics and farmers; libraries and scientific instruments, or any other personal property, to a value not exceeding three hundred dollars.

Const. 1868; 1872-3, c. 83.
Wagstaff v. Central Highway Com., 177-354; Leary v. Comrs., 172-25; Southern Assembly v. Palmer, 166-75; Davis v. Salisbury, 161-56; Comrs. v. Webb, 160-594; Corp. Com. v. Construction Co., 160-582; Bd. of Ed. v. Comrs., 137-314; United Brethren v. Comrs., 115-489; Loan Assn. v. Comrs., 115-410; State v. Stevenson, 109-730; R. R. v. Comrs., 75-474, 84-504.

SEC. 6. *Taxes levied for counties.* The total of the State and county tax on property shall not exceed fifteen cents on the one hundred dollars value of property except when the county property tax is levied for a special purpose and with the special approval of the General Assembly, which may be done by special or general act: Provided, this limitation shall not apply to taxes levied for the maintenance of the public schools of the State for the term required by article nine, section three, of the Constitution: Provided, further, the State tax shall not exceed five cents on the one hundred dollars value of property.

Comrs. v. Spitzer, 179-436.

SEC. 7. *Acts levying taxes shall state object, etc.* Every act of the General Assembly levying a tax shall state the special object to which it is to be applied, and it shall be applied to no other purpose.

Const. 1868.
Parker v. Comrs., 178-92; Bd. of Ed. v. Comrs., 137-311; McCless v. Meekins, 117-34; Parker v. Comrs., 104-170; Clifton v. Wynne, 80-145; R. R. v. Holden, 63-410.

ARTICLE VI

SUFFRAGE AND ELIGIBILITY TO OFFICE

SECTION 1. *Who may vote.* Every male person born in the United States, and every male person who has been naturalized, twenty-one years of age, and possessing the qualifications set out in this article, shall be entitled to vote at any election by the people in the State, except as herein otherwise provided.

1899, c. 218; 1900, c. 2.
Woodall v. Highway Co., 176-377; Ingram v. Johnson, 172-676; State v. Knight, 169-333; Gill v. Comrs., 160-176; Pace v. Raleigh, 140-68; Clarke v. Statesville, 139-492; Quinn v. Lattimore, 120-428; In re Reid, 119-641; Harris v. Scarborough, 110-232; Hannon v. Grizzard, 89-115; State v. Jones, 82-685; Lee v. Dunn, 73-595; Van Bokkelen v. Canady, 73-198; Railroad v. Comrs., 72-486; University v. McIver, 72-76; Perry v. Whitaker, 71-475; Jacobs v. Smallwood, 63-112; Roberts v. Cannon, 20-256.

SEC. 2. *Qualifications of voters.* He shall reside in the State of North Carolina for one year and in the precinct, ward, or other election district in which he offers to vote four months next preceding the election: Provided, that removal from one precinct, ward or other election district to another in the same county shall not operate to deprive any person of the right to vote in the precinct, ward or other election district from which he has removed until four months after such removal. No person who has been convicted, or who has confessed his guilt in open court upon indictment, of any crime the punishment of which now is, or may hereafter be, imprisonment in the State's Prison shall be permitted to vote, unless the said person shall be first restored to citizenship in the manner prescribed by law.

Convention 1875; 1899, c. 218; 1900, c. 2, s. 2.
State v. Windley, 178-670; Woodall v. Highway Com., 176-377; State v. Smith, 174-804; Watson v. R. R., 152-215; Cox v. Comrs., 146-584; Harris v. Scarborough, 110-232; Pace v. Raleigh, 140-68; Clark v. Statesville, 139-492; Quinn v. Lattimore, 120-428; DeBerry v. Nicholson, 102-465; Van Bokkelen v. Canady, 73-198; Railroad v. Comrs., 72-486; Perry v. Whitaker, 71-475.
See, also, C. S., secs. 5936, 5937.

SEC. 3. *Voter to be registered.* Every person offering to vote shall be at the time a legally registered voter as herein prescribed, and in the manner hereafter provided by law, and the General Assembly of North Carolina shall enact general registration laws to carry into effect the provisions of this article.

1899, c. 218; 1900, c. 2, s. 3.
Cox v. Comrs., 146-584; Pace v. Raleigh, 140-68; Harris v. Scarborough, 110-232.

SEC. 4. *Qualifications for registration.* Every person presenting himself for registration shall be able to read and write any section of the Constitution in the English language. But no male person who was, on January 1, 1867, or at any time prior thereto, entitled to vote under the laws of any State in the United States wherein he then resided, and no lineal descendant of any such person, shall be denied the right to register and vote at any election in this State by reason of his failure to possess the educational qualifications herein prescribed: Provided, he shall have registered in accordance with the terms of this section prior to December 1, 1908. The General Assembly shall provide for the registration of all persons entitled to vote without the educational qualifications herein prescribed, and shall, on or before November 1, 1908, provide for the making of a permanent record of such registration, and all persons so registered shall forever thereafter have the right to vote in all elections by the people in this State, unless disqualified under section two of this article.

Const. 1868; 1899, c. 218; 1900, c. 2, s. 4.
Ingram v. Johnson, 172 676; Moose v. Comrs., 172-419; State v. Knight, 169-333; Perry v. Comrs., 148-521; Cox v. Comrs., 146-584; Collie v. Comrs., 145-475; Pace v. Raleigh, 110-68; Clarke v. Statesville, 139-492; Harris v. Scarborough, 110-232; Hannon v. Grizzard, 89-115

SEC. 5. *Indivisible plan; legislature intent.* That this amendment to the Constitution is presented and adopted as one indivisible plan for the regulation of the suffrage, with the intent and purpose to so connect the different parts, and to make them so dependent upon each other that the whole shall stand or fall together.

1900, c. 2, s. 5.

SEC. 6. *Elections by people and General Assembly.* All elections by the people shall be by ballot, and all elections by the General Assembly shall be viva voce.

Const. 1868; 1899, c. 218.

SEC. 7. *Eligibility to office; official oath.* Every voter in North Carolina, except as in this article disqualified, shall be eligible to office, but before entering upon the duties of the office, he shall take and subscribe the following oath:

"I, ..., do solemnly swear (or affirm) that I will support and maintain the Constitution and laws of the United States, and the Constitution and laws of North Carolina not inconsistent therewith, and that I will faithfully discharge the duties of my office as ....; so help me, God."

1899, c. 218; 1900, c. 2, s. 7.
Cole v. Saunders, 174-112; State v. Knight, 169-333; St. v. Bateman, 162-588.

SEC. 8. *Disqualification for office.* The following classes of persons shall be disqualified for office: First, all persons who shall deny the being of Almighty God. Second, all persons who shall have been convicted, or confessed their guilt on indictment pending, and whether sentenced or not, or under judgment suspended, of any treason or felony, or of any other crime for which the punishment may be imprisonment in the penitentiary, since becoming citizens of the United States, or of corruption or malpractice in office, unless such person shall be restored to the rights of citizenship in a manner prescribed by law.

1899, c. 218; 1900, c. 2, s. 8.
State v. Windley, 178-679; Bank v. Redwine, 171-559; State v. Knight, 169-333.

SEC. 9. *When this chapter operative.* That this amendment to the Constitution shall go into effect on the first day of July, nineteen hundred and two, if a majority of votes cast at the next general election shall be cast in favor of this suffrage amendment.

1899, c. 218; 1900, c. 2, s. 9.

ARTICLE VII

MUNICIPAL CORPORATIONS

SECTION 1. *County officers.* In each county there shall be elected biennially by the qualified voters thereof, as provided for the election of members of the General Assembly, the following officers: A treasurer, register of deeds, surveyor, and five commissioners.

Const. 1868.
Rhodes v. Lewis, 80-136; Van Bokkelen v. Canady, 73-198; Aderholt v. McKee, 65-257.

SEC. 2. *Duty of county commissioners.* It shall be the duty of the commissioners to exercise a general supervision and control of the penal and charitable institutions, schools, roads, bridges, levying of taxes and finances of the county, as may be prescribed by law. The register of deeds shall be, ex officio, clerk of the board of commissioners.

Const. 1868.
Holmes v. Bullock, 178-376; Wilson v. Holding, 170-352; Comrs. v. Comrs., 165-632; Bunch v. Comrs., 159-335; Southern Audit Co. v. McKensie, 147-461;

Crocker v. Moore, 140-433; In re Spease Ferry, 138-219; Barrington v. Ferry Co., 69-165; Canal Co. v. McAllister, 74-163; Lane v. Stanley, 65-156; R. R. v. Holden, 63-434.
See, also, C. S., secs. 1297, 1299, 1300.

SEC. 3. *Counties to be divided into districts.* It shall be the duty of the commissioners first elected in each county to divide the same into convenient districts, to determine the boundaries and prescribe the name of the said districts, and to report the same to the General Assembly before the first day of January, 1869.

Const. 1868.
Road Com. v. Comrs., 178-61; Motor Co. v. Flynt, 178-399; Wittkowsky v. Comrs., 150-90; Wallace v. Trustees, 84-164; Gamble v. McCrady, 75-509; McNeill v. Green, 75-329; Tucker v. Raleigh, 75-267; Wilson v. Charlotte, 74-748; Canal Co. v. McAllister, 74-159; Grady v. Comrs., 74-101; Wade v. Comrs., 74-81; Bladen Co. v. Clarke, 73-255; Mitchell v. Trustees, 71-400; Barrington v. Ferry Co., 69-165; University v. Holden, 63-410; Gooch v. Gregory, 65-142; Lane v. Stanley, 65-153.

SEC. 4. *Townships have corporate powers.* Upon the approval of the reports provided for in the foregoing section by the General Assembly, the said districts shall have corporate powers for the necessary purposes of local government, and shall be known as townships.

Const. 1868.
Road Com. v. Comrs., 178-61; Motor Co. v. Flynt, 178-399; Mann v. Allen, 171-219; Jones v. New Bern, 152-64; Wittkowsky v. Comrs., 150-90; Crocker v. Moore, 140-429; Cotton Mills v. Waxhaw, 130-295; Brown v. Comrs., 100-92; Wallace v. Trustees, 84-164; Mitchell v. Trustees, 71-400; Payne v. Caldwell, 65-488; Lane v. Stanley, 65-153.

SEC. 5. *Officers of townships.* In each township there shall be biennially elected, by the qualified voters thereof, a clerk and two justices of the peace, who shall constitute a board of trustees, and shall, under the supervision of the county commissioners, have control of the taxes and finances, roads and bridges of the townships, as may be prescribed by law. The General Assembly may provide for the election of a larger number of justices of the peace in cities and towns, and in those townships in which cities and towns are situated. In every township there shall also be biennially elected a school committee, consisiting of three persons, whose duty shall be prescribed by law.

Const. 1868.
Road Com. v. Comrs., 178-61; Wallace v. Trustees, 84-164; Simpson v. Comrs., 84-158; Mitchell v. Trustees, 71-400; Haughton v. Comrs., 70-466; Edenton v. Wool, 65-379; Conoley v. Harris, 64-662; Wilmington v. Davis, 63-582.

SEC. 6. *Trustees shall assess property.* The township board of trustees shall assess the taxable property of their townships and make return to the county commissioners for revision, as may be prescribed by law. The clerk shall be, ex officio, treasurer of the township.

Const. 1868.
R. R. v. Comrs., 178-449; Road Com. v. Comrs., 178-62; Guire v. Comrs., 177-516; Parvin v. Comrs., 177-508; Jones v. Comrs., 107-261; R. R. v. Comrs., 84-508; R. R. v. Comrs., 82-261; Cobb v. Elizabeth City, 75-1; R. R. v. Comrs., 72-12.

SEC. 7. *No debt or loan except by a majority of voters.* No county, city, town or other municipal corporation shall contract any debt, pledge its faith or loan its credit, nor shall any tax be levied or collected by any officers of the same except for the necessary expenses thereof, unless by a vote of the majority of the qualified voters therein.

Const. 1868.
Comrs. v. Spitzer, 179-356; Davis v. Lenoir County, 178-668; Guire v. Comrs., 177-516; Parvin v. Comrs., 177-516; Hill v. Lenoir, 176-572; Williams v. Comrs., 176-554; Woodall v. Highway Com., 176-377; Comrs. v. Boring, 175-105; Comrs. v. State Treasurer, 174-141; Comrs. v. Spitzer, 173-147; Cottrell v. Lenoir, 173-138; Archer v. Joyner, 173-75; Swindell v. Belhaven, 173-1; Stephens v. Charlotte, 172-564; Moose v. Comrs., 172-419; Keith v. Lockhart, 171-451; Kinston v. Trust Co., 169-207; Hargrave v. Comrs., 168-626; Moran v. Comrs., 168-289; Comrs. v. Comrs., 165-632; Sprague v. Comrs., 165-603; Withers v. Voters, 163-341; Pritchard v. Comrs., 160-476; Russell v. Troy 159-366; Winston v. Bank, 158-512; Tripp v. Comrs., 158-180; Ellis v. Trustees, 156-10; Board of Trustees v. Webb, 155-379; Sanderlin v. Luken, 152-738; Highway Com. v. Webb, 152-710; Underwood v. Ashboro, 152-641; Ellison v. Williamston, 152-147; Burgin v. Smith, 151-561; Hightower v. Raleigh, 150-569; Smith v. Belhaven, 150-156; Wittkowsky v. Comrs., 150-90; Hendersonville v. Jordan, 150-35; Wharton v. Greensboro, 149-62; Perry v. Comrs., 148-524; Hollowell v. Borden, 148-255; R. R. v. Comrs., 148-248; R. R. v. Comrs., 148-220; Comrs. v. McDonald, 148-125; Comrs. v. Webb, 148-120; McLeod v. Comrs., 148-77; Swinson v. Mount Olive, 147-611; Wharton v. Greensboro, 146-356; Collie v. Comrs., 145-478; Crocker v. Moore, 140-432; Greensboro v. Scott, 138-184; Smith v. Trustees, 144-151; Jones v. Comrs., 137-579; Wingate v. Parker, 136-369; Faucett v. Mount Airy, 134-1; Cotton Mills v. Waxhaw, 130-293; Black v. Comrs., 129-122; Broadfoot v. Fayetteville, 128-529; State v. Irvin, 126-992; Garsed v. Greensboro, 126-164; Edgerton v. Water Co., 126-93; Smathers v. Comrs., 125-488; Slocomb v. Fayetteville, 125-362; Bear v. Comrs., 124-204; Comrs. v. Payne, 123-432; Tate v. Comrs., 122-812; Charlotte v. Shepard, 122-602; Herring v. Dixon, 122-420; Rodman v. Washington, 122-39; Thrift v. Elizabeth City, 122-31; Mayo v. Comrs., 122-5; Comrs. v. Snugg, 121-403; Charlotte v. Shepard, 120-411; Williams v. Comrs., 119-520; Vaughn v. Comrs., 117-435; McCless v. Meekins, 117-34; R. R. v. Comrs, 116-563; Bank v. Comrs., 116-339; Bd. of Ed. v. Comrs., 113-379; Graded School v. Broadhurst, 109-228; R. R. v. Comrs., 109-159; Jones v. Comrs., 107-248; Parker v. Comrs., 104-16*; Brown v. Comrs., 100-92; Rigsbee v. Durham, 99-341, 98-81; Gardner v. New Bern, 98-228; Wood v. Oxford, 97-227; McDowell v. Construction Co., 96-514; Markham v. Manning, 96-133; Duke v. Brown, 96-127; Southerland v. Goldsboro, 96-49; Halcombe v. Comrs., 89-346; Evans v. Comrs., 89-154; Shuford v. Comrs., 86-553; Norment v. Charlotte, 85-387; Simpson v. Comrs., 84-158; Gatlin v. Tarboro, 78-119; Young v. Henderson, 76-420; French v. Wilmington, 75-477; Kyle v. Comrs., 75-445; Tucker v. Raleigh, 75-267; Wilson v. Charlotte, 74-748; French v. Comrs., 74-692; Van Bokkelen v. Canady, 73-198; R. R. v. Comrs. 72-486; Trull v. Comrs.,

72-388; Weinstein v. Comrs., 71-525; Reiger v. Comrs., 70-319; Payne v. Caldwell, 65-488; Lane v. Stanly, 65-153; Broadnax v. Groom, 64-244; Winslow v. Comrs., 64-218; University v. Holden, 63-410.
See, also, C. S., secs. 1297, 2691.

SEC. 8. *No money drawn except by law.* No money shall be drawn from any county or township treasury, except by authority of law.
Const. 1868.
Faison v. Comrs., 171-411; Grady v. Comrs., 74-101.

SEC. 9. *Taxes to be ad valorem.* All taxes levied by any county, city, town or township shall be uniform and ad valorem upon all property in the same, except property exempted by this Constitution.
Const. 1868.
Marshburn v. Jones, 176-516; Keith v. Lockhart, 171-451; Board of Trustees v. Webb, 155-379; Comrs., v. Webb, 160-594; Perry v. Comrs., 148-521; McLeod v. Comrs., 148-77; Smith v. Trustees, 141-151; Jones v. Comrs., 137-600; Wingate v. Parker, 136-369; Harper v. Comrs., 133-106; Winston v. Salem, 131-404; Ins. Co. v. Stedman, 130-223; State v. Irvin, 126-993; Hilliard v. Asheville, 118-845; Loan Assn. v. Comrs., 115-410; Wiley v. Comrs., 111-397; Raleigh v. Peace, 110-32; Redmond v. Comrs., 106-122; Jones v. Comrs., 106-122; Moore v. Comrs., 80-154; Young v. Henderson, 76-420; Cain v. Comrs., 86-15; Kyle v. Comrs., 75-447; Cobb v. Elizabeth City, 75-7; Wilson v. Charlotte, 74-754; Rwy. Co. v. Wilmington, 72-73; Grady v. Comrs. 74-101; Weinstein v. Comrs., 71-535; Pullen v. Raleigh, 68-451.
See, also, C. S., sec. 2678.

SEC. 10. *When officers enter on duty.* The county officers first elected under the provisions of this article shall enter upon their duties ten days after the approval of this Constitution by the Congress of the United States.
Const. 1868.

SEC. 11. *Governor to appoint justices.* The Governor shall appoint a sufficient number of justices of the peace in each county, who shall hold their places until sections four, five and six of this article shall have been carried into effect.
Const. 1868.
Nichols v. McKee, 68-429.
See, also, C. S., secs. 1462-1472.

SEC. 12. *Charters to remain in force until legally changed.* All charters, ordinances and provisions relating to municipal corporations shall remain in force until legally changed, unless inconsistent with the provisions of this Constitution.
Const. 1868.
Ward v. Elizabeth City, 121-1; Dare Co. v. Currituck Co., 95-189.

SEC. 13. *Debts in aid of the rebellion not to be paid.* No county, city, town or other municipal corporation shall assume to pay, nor

shall any tax be levied or collected for the payment of any debt, or
the interest upon any debt, contracted directly or indirectly in aid
or support of the rebellion.

Const. 1868.
Board of Trustees v. Webb, 155-379; R. R. v. Comrs., 148-220; Smith v. School
Trustees, 141-157; Jones v. Comrs., 137-600; Wingate v. Parker, 136-369; Brickell
v. Comrs., 81-242; Weith v. Wilmington, 68-24; Poindexter v. Davis, 67-112;
Davis v. Poindexter, 72-441; Lance v. Hunter, 72-178; Logan v. Plummer, 70-388;
Rand v. State, 65-194; Setzer v. Comrs., 64-516; Winslow v. Comrs., 64-218;
Leak v. Comrs., 64-132.

SEC. 14. *Powers of General Assembly over municipal corporations.* The General Assembly shall have full power by statute to modify, change, or abrogate any and all of the provisions of this article, and substitute others in their place, except sections seven, nine, and thirteen.

Convention 1875.
Motor Co. v. Flynt, 178-399; Road Com. v. Comrs., 178-64; Cole v. Sanders,
174-112; Mann v. Allen, 171-219; Comrs. v. Comrs., 165-632; Bunch v. Comrs;
159-335; Board of Trustees v. Webb, 155-379; Southern Audit Co. v. McKenzie,
147-461; Smith v. School Trustees, 141-157; Crocker v. Moore, 140-433; Jones v.
Comrs., 137-600; Wingate v. Parker, 136-369; In re Spease Ferry, 138-220;
Gattis v. Griffin, 125-334; Harris v. Wright, 121-172; Bd. of Ed. v. Comrs., 111-
578; Sneed v. Bullock, 80-132; Jones v. Jones, 80-127.

ARTICLE VIII

CORPORATIONS OTHER THAN MUNICIPAL

SECTION 1. *Corporations under general laws.* No corporation shall be created nor shall its charter be extended, altered, or amended by special act, except corporations for charitable, educational, penal, or reformatory purposes that are to be and remain under the patronage and control of the State; but the General Assembly shall provide by general laws for the chartering and organization of all corporations and for amending, extending, and forfeiture of all charters, except those above permitted by special act. All such general laws and special acts may be altered from time to time or repealed; and the General Assembly may at any time by special act repeal the charter of any corporation.

1915, c 99. In effect Jan. 10, 1917; see Reade v. Durham, 173-668; Mills v.
Comrs., 175-215; Woodall v. Highway Com., 176-377.
Mills v. Comrs., 175-215; Board of Education v. Comrs., 174-47; Stagg v.
Land Co., 171-583; Mann v. Allen, 171-219; R. R. v. Oates, 164-167; Reid v.
R. R. 162-355; Power Co. v. Whitney Co., 150-31; State v. Cantwell, 142-614;
Coleman v. R. R., 138-354; Debnam v. Tel. Co., 126-843; Gattis v. Griffin, 125-334-
Railroad v. Dortch, 124-673; Griffin v. Water Co., 122-210; Ward v. Elizabeth
City, 121-1; Wilson v. Leary, 120-92; Winslow v. Morton, 118-486; Hanstein v.

Johnson, 112-253; R. R. v. Comrs., 108-60; McGowan v. Railroad, 95-417; R. R. v. Rollins, 82-523; State v. Jones, 67-210; Clark v. Stanley, 66-59; R. R. v. Reid, 64-226, 155; State v. Matthews, 56-451; State v. Petway, 55-396.

SEC. 2. *Debts of corporations, how secured.* Dues from corporations shall be secured by such individual liabilities of the corporations, and other means, as may be prescribed by law.

Const. 1868.
Reade v. Durham, 173-668; Van Bokkelen v. Canady, 73-198.

SEC. 3. *What corporations shall include.* The term "corporation" as used in this article, shall be construed to include all associations and joint-stock companies having any of the powers and privileges of corporations not possessed by individuals or partnerships. And all corporations shall have the right to sue, and shall be subject to be sued, in all courts, in like cases as natural persons.

Const. 1868.
Barker v. R. R., 137-223; Hanstein v. Johnson, 112-253.

SEC. 4. *Legislature to provide for organizing cities, towns, etc.* It shall be the duty of the Legislature to provide by general laws for the organization of cities, towns, and incorporated villages, and to restrict their power of taxation, assessment, borrowing money, contracting debts, and loaning their credit, so as to prevent abuses in assessment and in contracting debts by such municipal corporations.

Const. 1868; 1915, c. 99, which added "by general laws" after "to provide" and before "for the organization," and changed "assessments" to "assessment" after "abuses in" and before "and". In effect Jan. 10, 1917, see under sec. 1 of this article.
Taylor v. Greensboro, 175-423; Mills v. Comrs., 175-215; Reade v. Durham, 173-668; Bramham v. Durham, 171-196; Winston v. Bank, 158-512; Murphy v. Webb, 156-402; Ellison v. Williams, 152-147; Bradshaw v. High Point, 151-517; Perry v. Comrs., 148-521; Cox v. Comrs., 146-584; Wingate v. Parker, 136-369; Robinson v. Goldsboro, 135-382; Brockenbrough v. Comrs., 134-17; Wadsworth v. Concord, 133-587; State v. Green, 126-1032; Cotton Mills v. Waxhaw, 130-293; State v. Irvin, 126-993; Hutton v. Webb, 124-749; Rosenbaum v. Newbern, 118-84; Railway v. Railway, 114-725; Raleigh v. Peace, 110-32; Jones v. Comrs., 107-263; Gatlin v. Tarboro, 78-119; French v. Wilmington, 75-477; Tucker v. Raleigh, 75-267; Wilson v. Charlotte, 74-748; Van Bokkelen v. Canady, 73-198; Pullen v. Raleigh, 68-451; Dellinger v. Tween, 66-206.

ARTICLE IX

EDUCATION

SECTION 1. *Education shall be encouraged.* Religion, morality and knowledge being necessary to good government and the happiness of mankind, schools and the means of education shall forever be encouraged.

436 CONSTITUTIONS

Const. 1868; Const. 1776, sec. 41.
Bd. of Ed. v. Comrs., 178-305; Bd. of Ed. v. Comrs., 174-469; Comrs., v. Bd. of Ed., 163-404; Corp. Com. v. Construction Co., 160-582; Collie v. Comrs., 145-170; Green v. Owen, 125-223; Bd. of Ed. v. Comrs., 111-582; Lane v. Stanley, 65-153; Barksdale v. Comrs., 93-472.

SEC. 2. *General Assembly shall provide for schools; separation of the races.* The General Assembly, at its first session under this Constitution, shall provide by taxation and otherwise for a general and uniform system of public schools, wherein tuition shall be free of charge to all the children of the State between the ages of six and twenty-one years. And the children of the white race and the children of the colored race shall be taught in separate public schools; but there shall be no discrimination in favor of, or to the prejudice of, either race.

Const. 1868; Convention 1875.
Bd. of Ed. v. Comrs., 178-305; Bd. of Ed. v. Comrs., 174-469; Moose v. Comrs., 172-419; School Comrs. v. Bd. of Ed., 169-196; Johnson v. Bd. of Ed., 166-468; Comrs. v. Bd. of Ed., 163-404; Williams v. Bradford, 158-36; Bontiz v. School Trustees, 154-375; State v. Wolf, 145-440; Collie v. Comrs., 145-178; Lowery v. School Trustees, 140-39; Bd. of Ed. v. Comrs., 137-314; Hooker v. Greenville, 130-474; Bear v. Comrs., 124-213; Bd. of Ed. v. State Board, 114-313; Bd. of Ed. v. Comrs., 111-578; Markham v. Manning, 96-132; Puitt v. Comrs., 94-709; Riggsbee v. Durham, 94-800; R. R. v. Holden, 63-436.

SEC. 3. *Counties to be divided into districts.* Each county of the State shall be divided into a convenient number of districts, in which one or more public schools shall be maintained at least six months in every year; and if the commissioners of any county shall fail to comply with the aforesaid requirements of this section, they shall be liable to indictment.

Const. 1868; 1917, c. 192, inserting "six months" for "four months" for annual school term.
Bd. of Ed. v. Comrs., 178-305; Hill v. Lenoir County, 176-572; Bd. of Ed. v. Comrs., 174-469; Bennett v. Comrs., 173-625; Bd. of Ed. v. Comrs., 150-116; R. R. v. Comrs., 148-220; Collie v. Comrs., 145-172; Bd. of Ed. v. Comrs., 111-578; 113-379; Barksdale v. Comrs., 93-172.

SEC. 4. *What property devoted to educational purposes.* The proceeds of all lands that have been or hereafter may be granted by the United States to this State, and not otherwise appropriated by this State or the United States; also all moneys, stocks, bonds, and other property now belonging to any State fund for purposes of education; also the net proceeds of all sales of the swamp lands belonging to the State, and all other grants, gifts or devises that have been or hereafter may be made to the State, and not otherwise appropriated by the State, or by terms of the grant, gift, or devise, shall be paid into the State treasury, and, together with so much of the ordinary revenue of the State as may be by law set apart for that purpose, shall be faithfully appropriated for establishing and maintaining in this State a system of free public schools and for no other uses or purposes whatsoever.

Const. 1868; Convention 1875.
Collie v. Comrs., 145-186; Bear v. Comrs., 124-212; McDonald v. Morrow, 119-674; Sutton v. Phillips, 116-434; Bd. of Ed. v. Comrs., 111-578; University v. Holden, 63-410.
See, also, C. S., sec. 3480.

SEC. 5. *County school fund; proviso.* All moneys, stocks, bonds, and other property belonging to a county school fund; also the net proceeds from the sale of estrays; also the clear proceeds of all penalties and forfeitures and of all fines collected in the several counties for any breach of the penal or military laws of the State; and all moneys which shall be paid by persons as an equivalent for exemption from military duty, shall belong to and remain in the several counties, and shall be faithfully appropriated for establishing and maintaining free public schools in the several counties of this State: Provided, that the amount collected in each county shall be annually reported to the Superintendent of Public Instruction.

Const. 1868; Convention 1875.
In re Wiggins, 171-372; Collie v. Comrs., 145-178; State v. Maultsby, 139-584; School Directors v. Asheville, 137-507; Bearden v. Fullam, 129-479; School Directors v. Asheville, 128-249; Bd. of Ed. v. Henderson, 126-689; Carter v. R. R. 126-437; Godwin v. Fertilizer Works, 119-120; Sutton v. Phillips, 116-502; Burrell v. Hughes, 116-434; Bd. of Ed. v. Comrs., 111-578; Hodge v. R. R., 108-25; Katzenstein v. R. R., 84-688; University v. McIver, 72-76.

SEC. 6. *Election of trustees, and provisions for maintenance, of University.* The General Assembly shall have power to provide for the election of trustees of the University of North Carolina, in whom, when chosen, shall be vested all the privileges, rights, franchises and endowments thereof in anywise granted to or conferred upon the trustees of said University; and the General Assembly may make such provisions, laws and regulations, from time to time, as may be necessary and expedient for the maintenance and management of said University.

1872-3, c. 86. See Const. 1776, sec. 41.
Finger v. Hunter, 130-529; Brewer v. University, 110-26; University v. R. R. 76-103; University v. McIver, 72-76.

SEC. 7. *Benefits of the University.* The General Assembly shall provide that the benefits of the University, as far as practicable, be extended to the youth of the State free of expense for tuition; also, that all the property which has heretofore accrued to the State, or shall hereafter accrue, from escheats, unclaimed dividends, or distributive shares of the estate of deceased persons, shall be appropriated to the use of the University.

Const. 1868.
University v. R. R., 76-103; University v. Maultsby, 43-257.

SEC. 8. *Board of Education.* The Governor, Lieutenant-Governor, Secretary of State, Treasurer, Auditor, Superintendent of Public Instruction, and Attorney-General shall constitute a State Board of Education.

Const. 1868.

SEC. 9. *President and secretary.* The Governor shall be president and the Superintendent of Public Instruction shall be secretary of the Board of Education.

Const. 1868.

SEC. 10. *Powers of the board.* The Board of Education shall succeed to all the powers and trusts of the president and directors of the Literary Fund of North Carolina, and shall have full power to legislate and make all needful rules and regulations in relation to free public schools and the educational fund of the State, but all acts, rules and regulations of said board may be altered, amended or repealed by the General Assembly, and when so altered, amended or repealed they shall not be reënacted by the board.

Const. 1868.
Board v. Makely, 139-34; Dosh v. Lumber Co., 128-85; Bd. of Ed. v. State Board, 114-317.

SEC. 11. *First session of the board.* The first session of the Board of Education shall be held in the capital of the State within fifteen days after the organization of the State government under this Constitution; the time of future meetings may be determined by the board.

Const. 1868.

SEC. 12. *Quorum.* A majority of the board shall constitute a quorum for the transaction of business.

Const. 1868.

SEC. 13. *Expenses.* The contingent expenses of the board shall be provided by the General Assembly.

Const. 1868.
Ewart v. Jones, 116-578.

SEC. 14. *Agricultural department.* As soon as practicable after the adoption of this Constitution, the General Assembly shall establish and maintain, in connection with the University, a department of agriculture, of mechanics, of mining, and of normal instruction.
Const. 1868.
Chemical Co. v. Board of Agriculture, 111-136.

SEC. 15. *Children must attend school.* The General Assembly is hereby empowered to enact that every child, of sufficient mental and physical ability, shall attend the public schools during the period between the ages of six and eighteen years, for a term of not less than sixteen months, unless educated by other means.
Const. 1868.
State v. Wolf, 145-440; Bear v. Comrs., 124-212.

ARTICLE X

HOMESTEADS AND EXEMPTIONS

SECTION 1. *Exceptions of personal property.* The personal property of any resident of this State, to the value of five hundred dollars, to be selected by such resident, shall be and is hereby exempted from sale under execution or other final process of any court, issued for the collection of any debt.
Const. 1868.
Befarrah v. Spell, 178-231; Grocery Co. v. Bails, 177-298; Gardner v. McConnaughey, 157-481; Cromer v. Self, 149-164; McKeithan v. Blue, 142-352; Lynn v. Cotton Mills, 130-621; Chitty v. Chitty, 118-647; Lockhart, v. Bear, 117-301; Jones v. Alsbrook, 115-49; Wilmington v. Sprunt, 114-310; Dickens v. Long, 109-165; Shepherd v. Murrill, 90-208; Slaughter v. Winfrey, 85-159; Smith v. McMillan, 84-583; Durham v. Speeke, 82-87; Gheen v. Summey, 85-187; Gamble v. Rhyne, 80-183; Earle v. Hardie, 80-177; Richardson v. Wicker, 80-172; Welch v. Macy, 78-240; Pemberton v. McRae, 75-497; Vann v. B. & L. Assn., 75-494; Gaster v. Hardie, 75-460; Comrs., v. Riley, 75-144; Curlee v. Thomas, 74-51; Duvall v. Rollins, 71-218; Garrett v. Cheshire, 69-396; Burns v. Harris, 67-140, 66-509; Dellinger v. Tweed, 66-206; Watts v. Leggett, 66-197; Johnson v. Cross, 66-167; Horton v. McCall, 66-159; McKeithan v. Terry, 64-25; Hill v. Kessler, 63-437; Dean v. King, 35-20.
See, also, C. S., sec. 728.

SEC. 2. *Homestead.* Every homestead, and the dwellings and buildings used therewith, not exceeding in value one thousand dollars, to be selected by the owner thereof, or in lieu thereof, at the option of the owner, any lot in a city, town or village, with the dwelling and buildings used thereon, owned and occupied by any resident of this State, and not exceeding the value of one thousand dollars, shall be exempt from sale under execution or other final process obtained on any debt. But no property shall be exempt from sale for taxes, or for payment of obligations contracted for the purchase of said premises.

Const. 1868.
Kirkwood v. Peden, 173-460; Sash Co. v. Parker, 153-130; Simmons v. Respass, 151-5; Carpenter v. Duke, 144-291; McKeithan v. Blue, 142-352; Smith v. Bruton, 137-79; Vann v. Edwards, 135-661; Joyner v. Sugg, 132-580; Cawfield v. Owens, 129-286, 130-643; Lynn v. Cotton Mills, 130-621; Finger v. Hunter, 130-529; Watts ex parte, 130-237; Vann v. Edwards, 128-428; Coffin v. Smith, 128-255; Tiddy v. Graves, 126-620, 127-503; Toms v. Flack, 127-423; Brinkley v. Ballance, 126-396; McLamb v. McPhail, 126-618; Jennings v. Hinton, 126-48; Walton v. Bristol, 125-419; Weathers v. Borders, 124-615; Slocumb v. Ray, 123-571; Moore v. Wolf, 122-716; McGowan v. McGowan, 122-168; Campbell v. Potts, 119-533; Chitty v. Chitty, 118-647; Springer v. Colwell, 116-520; Jones v. Alsbrook, 115-52; Gardner v. Batts, 114-496; Fulton v. Roberts, 113-421; Vanstory v. Thornton, 112-196; Lovick v. Life Assn., 110-93; Tucker v. Tucker, 110-333; Vanstory v. Thornton, 110-40; Dickens v. Long, 109-169; Tucker v. Tucker, 108-237; Long v. Walker, 105-116; Ducker v. Wilson, 104-595; Hardy v. Carr, 104-33; Peck v. Culberson, 104-425; Hughes v. Hodges, 102-252; Jones v. Briton, 102-168; Lee v. Moseley, 101-311; Miller v. Miller, 89-402; Mebane v. Layton, 89-395; Campbell v. White, 95-491; Toms v. Fite, 93-274; Wilson v. Patton, 87-318; Butler v. Stainback, 87-216; Burton v. Spiers, 87-87; Cumming v. Bloodworth, 87-83; Murchison v. Plyler, 87-79; Gill v. Edwards, 87-76; Gregory v. Ellis, 86-579; Grant v. Edwards, 86-513; McDonald v. Dickson, 85-248; Wyche v. Wyche, 85-96; Smith v. High, 85-93; Gamble v. Watterson, 83-573; Watkins v. Overby, 83-165; Adrian v. Shaw, 82-474; Murphy v. McNeill, 82-221; Bruce v. Strickland, 81-267; Gheen v. Summey, 80-169; Richardson v. Wicker, 80-172; Wharton v. Leggett, 80-169; Suit v. Suit, 78-272; Bank v. Green, 78-247; Spoon v. Reid, 78-244; Bunting v. Jones, 78-242; Welsh v. Macy, 78-240; Littlejohn v. Egerton, 77-379; Pemberton v. McRae, 75-497; Edwards v. Kearsey, 75-411; Comrs., v. Riley, 75-144; Brodie v. Batchelor, 75-51; Whitaker v. Elliott, 73-186; Abbott v. Cromartie, 72-292; Branch ex parte, 72-106; McAfee v. Bettis, 72-28; Mayho v. Cotton, 69-289; Hagar v. Nixon, 69-108; Crummen v. Bennett, 68-494; Cheatham v. Jones, 68-453; Martin v. Hughes, 67-293; Dellinger v. Tweed, 66-206; Watts v. Leggett, 66-197; Ladd v. Adams, 66-164; Poe v. Hardie, 65-447; Lute v. Reilly, 65-20; Sluder v. Rogers, 64-289; McKeithan v. Terry, 64-25.
See, also C. S., sec. 728.

SEC. 3. *Homestead exemption from debt.* The homestead, after the death of the owner thereof, shall be exempt from the payment of any debt during the minority of his children, or any of them.

Const. 1868.
Simmons v. Respass, 151-5; Joyner v. Sugg, 132-580; Jackson v. Comrs., 130-387; Spence v. Goodman, 128-273; Bruton v. McRae, 125-201; Chitty, v. Chitty, 118-647; Stern v. Lee, 115-430; Duckers v. Long, 112-317; Vanstory v. Thornton, 112-218; Hughes v. Hodges, 102-252; Jones v. Britton, 102-168; Saylor v. Powell, 90-202; Gregory v. Ellis, 86-597; Gamble v. Watterson, 83-573; Simpson v. Wallace, 83-477; Wharton v. Leggett, 80-169; Welch v. Macy, 78-240; Beavan v. Speed, 74-544; Allen v. Shields, 72-504; Hagar v. Nixon, 69-108; Poe v. Hardie, 65-447; Hill v. Kessler, 63-437.

SEC. 4. *Laborer's lien.* The provisions of sections one and two of this article shall not be so construed as to prevent a laborer's lien for work done and performed for the person claiming such exemption, or a mechanic's lien for work done on the premises.

CONSTITUTION OF THE STATE OF NORTH CAROLINA   441

Const. 1868.
Isler v. Dixon, 140-530; Vann v. Edwards, 128-425; Broyhill v. Gaither, 119-443; Paper Co. v. Chronicle, 115-146; McMillan v. Williams, 109-252; Cumming v. Bloodworth, 87-83.

SEC. 5. *Benefit of widow.* If the owner of a homestead die, leaving a widow but no children, the same shall be exempt from the debts of her husband, and the rents and profits thereof shall inure to her benefit during her widowhood, unless she be the owner of a homestead in her own right.

Const. 1868.
Caudle v. Morris, 160-168; Thomas v. Bunch, 158-175; Fulp v. Brown, 153-531; Simmons v. Respass, 151-5; Joyner v. Suggs, 132-580; Spence v. Goodwin, 128-277; Campbell v. Potts, 119-532; Vanstory v. Thornton, 112-218; Tucker v. Tucker, 108-237; Hughes v. Hodges, 102-252; Jones v. Britton, 102-468; Saylor v. Powell, 90-202; Simpson v. Wallace, 83-477; Richardson v. Wicker, 80-172; Wharton v. Leggett, 80-169; Beaven v. Speed, 74-544; Hagar v. Nixon, 69-108; Watts v. Leggett, 66-197; Johnson v. Cross, 66-167; Poe v. Hardie, 65-447.
See, also, C. S., sec. 748.

SEC. 6. *Property of married women secured to them.* The real and personal property of any female in this State acquired before marriage, and all property, real and personal, to which she may, after marriage, become in any manner entitled, shall be and remain the sole and separate estate and property of such female, and shall not be liable for any debts, obligations or engagements of her husband, and may be devised and bequeathed, and, with the written assent of her husband, conveyed by her as if she were unmarried.

Const. 1868.
Sills v. Bethea, 178-315; Lancaster v. Lancaster, 178-22; Deese v. Deese, 176-527; Freeman v. Lide, 176-434; Stallings v. Walker, 176-321; Gooch v. Bank, 176-213; Kilpatrick v. Kilpatrick, 176-182; Everett v. Ballard, 174-16; Freeman v. Belfer, 173-581; Satterwhite v. Gallagher, 173-525; Graves v. Johnson, 172-176; McCurry v. Purgason, 170-463; Warren v. Dail, 170-406; Butler v. Butler, 169-584; Royal v. Southerland, 168-105; Patterson v. Franklin, 168-75; McKinnon v. Caulk, 167-411; Norwood v. Totten, 166-648; Jackson v. Beard, 162-105; Greenville v. Gornto, 161-341; Sipe v. Herman, 161-107; Flanner v. Flanner, 160-126; Rea v. Rea, 156-529; Council v. Pridgen, 153-443; Richardson v. Richardson, 150-549; Jones v. Smith, 149-317; State v. Robinson, 143-620; Hodgin v. R. R., 143-93; Ball v. Paquin, 140-88; Smith v. Bruton, 137-83; Vann v. Edwards, 135-661; Perkins v. Brinkley, 133-154; State v. Jones, 132-1046; Hallyburton v. Slagle, 132-947; Ray v. Long, 132-891; Finger v. Hunter, 130-529; Watts ex parte, 130-237; Cawfield v. Owens, 129-286; Vann v. Edwards, 128-428; Coffin v. Smith, 128-255; Tiddy v. Graves, 126-620, 127-503; Toms v. Flack, 127-423; Brinkley v. Ballance, 126-396; McLamb v. McPhail, 126-218; Jennings v. Hinton, 126-48; Walton v. Bristol, 125-419; Weathers v. Borders, 124-615; Strather v. R. R., 123-198; Slocumb v. Ray, 123-571; Moore v. Wolf, 122-716; McLeod v. Williams, 122-455; Green v. Bennett, 120-396; Barrett v. Barrett, 120-131; Houck v. Somers, 118-611; Hall v. Walker, 118-380; Bank v. Howell, 118-273; Kirby v. Boyette, 118-258, 116-165; Bates v. Saltor, 117-101; Zimmerman v. Robinson, 114-39; Strouse v. Cohen, 113-349; Jones v.

Coffey, 109-515; Walker v. Long, 109-510; Thompson v. Wiggins, 109-508; Osborne v. Withers, 108-677; Kirkpatrick v. Holmes, 108-209; Ferguson v. Kinsland, 93-337; Southerland v. Hunter, 93-310; Long v. Barnes, 87-329; Cecil v. Smith, 81-285; O'Connor v. Harris, 81-279; Hall v. Short, 81-273; Holliday v. McMillan, 79-315; Manning v. Manning, 79-300; Manning v. Manning, 79-293; Kirkman v. Bank, 77-394; King v. Little, 77-138; Atkinson v. Richardson, 74-455; Rountree v. Gay, 74-447; Pippen v. Wesson, 74-437; Purvis v. Carstaphan, 73-575; Harris v. Jenkins, 72-183; Shuler v. Milsaps, 71-297; Teague v. Downs, 69-280; Woody v. Smith, 65-116; Rowland v. Perry, 64-578.
See, also, C. S., sec. 2506, et seq.

SEC. 7. *Husband may insure his life for the benefit of wife and children.* The husband may insure his own life for the sole use and benefit of his wife and children, and in case of the death of the husband the amount thus insured shall be paid over to the wife and children, or to the guardian, if under age, for her or their own use, free from all the claims of the representatives of her husband, or any of his creditors.

Const. 1868.
Herring v. Sutton, 129-112; Hooker v. Sugg, 102-115; Burton v. Fairinholt, 86-260; Burwell v. Snow, 107-82.

SEC. 8. *How deed for homestead may be made.* Nothing contained in the foregoing sections of this article shall operate to prevent the owner of a homestead from disposing of the same by deed; but no deed made by the owner of a household shall be valid without the voluntary signature and assent of his wife, signified on her private examination according to law.

Const. 1868.
Power Co. v. Power Co., 168-219; Dalrymple v. Cole, 156-353, 170-102; Davenport v. Fleming, 154-291; Sash Co. v. Parker, 153-130; Ball v. Paquin, 140-97; Joyner v. Sugg, 132-580; Cawfield v. Owen, 129-286, 130-644; Spence v. Goodwin, 128-276; Jordan v. Newsome, 126-558; Wittkowsky v. Gidney, 124-437; McLeod v. Williams, 122-455; Bevan v. Ellis, 121-224; Barrett v. Barrett, 120-131; Chitty v. Chitty, 118-648; Thomas v. Fulford, 117-673; Shaffer v. Bledsoe, 117-144; Stern v. Lee, 115-442; Allen v. Volen, 114-564; Vanstory v. Thornton, 112-196; Leak v. Gay, 107-482; Long v. Walker, 105-116; Hughes v. Hodges, 102-252; Adrian v. Shaw, 82-471; Littlejohn v. Egerton, 76-468; Beavan v. Speed, 74-544; Lambert v. Kinnery, 74-348; Mayho v. Cotton, 69-289; Poe v. Hardie, 65-447.
See, also, C. S., sec. 729.

ARTICLE XI

PUNISHMENTS, PENAL INSTITUTIONS AND PUBLIC CHARITIES

SECTION 1. *Punishments; convict labor; proviso.* The following punishments only shall be known to the laws of this State, viz.: Death, imprisonment with or without hard labor, fines, removal from office, and disqualification to hold and enjoy any office of honor.

trust or profit under this State. The foregoing provision for imprisonment with hard labor shall be construed to authorize the employment of such convict labor on public works or highways, or other labor for public benefit, and the farming out thereof, where and in such manner as may be provided by law; but no convict shall be farmed out who has been sentenced on a charge of murder, manslaughter, rape, attempt to commit rape, or arson: Provided, that no convict whose labor may be farmed out shall be punished for any failure of duty as a laborer, except by a responsible officer of the State; but the convict so farmed out shall be at all times under the supervision and control, as to their government and discipline, of the penitentiary board or some officer of this State.

Const. 1868; Convention 1875.
State v. Nipper, 166-272; State v. Young, 138-574; State v. Burke, 73-83; State v. King, 69-419.

SEC. 2. *Death punishment.* The object of punishments being not only to satisfy justice, but also to reform the offender, and thus prevent crime, murder, arson, burglary and rape, and these only, may be punishable with death, if the General Assembly shall so enact.

Const. 1868.
State v. Burnett, 179-735; State v. Lytle, 138-744; State v. Burke, 73-83; State v. King, 69-419.

SEC. 3. *Penitentiary.* The General Assembly shall, at its first meeting, make provision for the erection and conduct of a State's prison or penitentiary, at some central and accessible point within the State.

Const. 1868.
Day's Case, 124-367; Welker v. Bledsoe, 68-457; R. R. v. Holden, 63-436.

SEC. 4. *Houses of correction.* The General Assembly may provide for the erection of houses of correction, where vagrants and persons guilty of misdemeanors shall be restrained and usefully employed.

Const. 1868.
In re Watson, 157-340; Moffitt v. Asheville, 103-237.

SEC. 5. *Houses of refuge.* A house or houses of refuge may be established whenever the public interest may require it, for the correction and instruction of other classes of offenders.

Const. 1868.

SEC. 6. *The sexes to be separated.* It shall be required, by competent legislation, that the structure and superintendence of penal institutions of the State, the county jails, and city police prisons secure the health and comfort of the prisoners, and that male and female prisoners be never confined in the same room or cell.
Const. 1868.
Moffitt v. Asheville, 103-237.

SEC. 7. *Provision for the poor and orphans.* Beneficent provision for the poor, the unfortunate and orphan, being one of the first duties of a civilized and Christian state, the General Assembly shall, at its first session, appoint and define the duties of a Board of Public Charities, to whom shall be entrusted the supervision of all charitable and penal State institutions, and who shall annually report to the Governor upon their condition, with suggestions for their improvement.
Const. 1868.
Comrs. v. Spitzer, 173-147; Bd. of Ed. v. Comrs., 137-314; Miller v. Atkinson, 63-540.

SEC. 8. *Orphan houses.* There shall also, as soon as practicable, be measures devised by the State for the establishment of one or more orphan houses, where destitute orphans may be cared for, educated, and taught some business or trade.
Const. 1868.
Miller v. Atkinson, 63-537.

SEC. 9. *Inebriates and idiots.* It shall be the duty of the Legislature, as soon as practicable, to devise means for the education of idiots and inebriates.
Const. 1868.
Board of Education v. State Board, 114-313.

SEC. 10. *Deaf-mutes, blind and insane.* The General Assembly may provide that the indigent deaf-mute, blind and insane of the State shall be cared for at the charge of the State.
Const. 1868; 1879, cc. 314, 254, 268.
In re Boyette, 136-418; Hospital v. Fountain, 128-25; In re Hybart, 119-359.

SEC. 11. *Self-supporting.* It shall be steadily kept in view by the Legislature and the Board of Public Charities that all penal and charitable institutions should be made as nearly self-supporting as is consistent with the purposes of their creation.
Const. 1868.

ARTICLE XII

MILITIA

SECTION 1. *Who are liable to militia duty.* All able-bodied male citizens of the State of North Carolina, between the ages of twenty-one and forty years, who are citizens of the United States, shall be liable to duty in the militia: Provided, that all persons who may be averse to bearing arms, from religious scruples, shall be exempt therefrom.
Const. 1868.

SEC. 2. *Organizing, etc.* The General Assembly shall provide for the organizing, arming, equipping and discipline of the militia, and for paying the same, when called into active service.
Const. 1868.
Winslow v. Morton, 118-486; Worth v. Comrs. 118-112.

SEC. 3. *Governor Commander-in-Chief.* The Governor shall be Commander-in-Chief, and shall have power to call out the militia to execute the law, suppress riots or insurrection, and to repel invasion.
Const. 1868.
Winslow v. Morton, 118-486; Worth v. Comrs., 118-112.

SEC. 4. *Exemptions.* The General Assembly shall have power to make such exemptions as may be deemed necessary, and to enact laws that may be expedient for the government of the militia.
Const. 1868.

ARTICLE XIII

AMENDMENTS

SECTION 1. *Convention, how called.* No convention of the people of this State shall ever be called by the General Assembly unless by the concurrence of two-thirds of all the members of each house of the General Assembly and except the proposition, convention or no convention, be first submitted to the qualified voters of the whole State, at the next general election, in a manner to be prescribed by law. And should a majority of the votes cast be in favor of said convention, it shall assemble on such day as may be prescribed by the General Assembly.
Const. 1868; Convention 1875; Convention 1835; art. 1, sec. 1.
Moose v. Comrs., 172-461.

SEC. 2. *How the Constitution may be altered.* No part of the Constitution of this State shall be altered unless a bill to alter the same shall have been agreed to by three-fifths of each house of the General Assembly. And the amendment or amendments so agreed to shall be submitted at the next general election to the qualified voters of the whole State, in such manner as may be prescribed by law. And in the event of their adoption by a majority of the votes cast, such amendment or amendments shall become a part of the Constitution of this State.

Const. 1868; Convention 1875; Convention 1835, art. 4, sec. 1.
Reade v. Durham, 173-668; Moose v. Comrs., 172-461; University v. McIver, 72-76.

ARTICLE XIV

MISCELLANEOUS

SECTION 1. *Indictments.* All indictments which shall have been found, or may hereafter be found, for any crime or offense committed before this Constitution takes effect, may be proceeded upon in the proper courts, but no punishment shall be inflicted which is forbidden by this Constitution.

Const. 1868.
Debnam v. Tel. Co., 126-835; Morris v. Hauser, 125-559; Day's Case, 124-365; State v. Moore, 120-567.

SEC. 2. *Penalty for fighting duel.* No person who shall hereafter fight a duel, or assist in the same as a second, or send, accept, or knowingly carry a challenge therefor, or agree to go out of the State to fight a duel, shall hold any office in this State.

Const. 1868.
Cole v. Sanders, 174-112; State v. Lord, 145-479.

SEC. 3. *Drawing money.* No money shall be drawn from the treasury but in consequence of appropriations made by law; and an accurate account of the receipts and expenditures of the public money shall be annually published.

Const. 1868.
Martin v. Clark, 135-180; White v. Auditor, 126-602; White v. Hill, 125-200; Garner v. Worth, 122-252; Cotton Mills v. Comrs., 108-685.

SEC. 4. *Mechanic's lien.* The General Assembly shall provide, by proper legislation, for giving to mechanics and laborers an adequate lien on the subject-matter of their labor.

Const. 1868.
Mfg. Co. v. Andrews, 165-285; Moore v. Industrial Co., 138-306; Finger v. Hunter, 130-529; Tedder v. R. R., 124-344; Lester v. Houston, 101-605; Whitaker v. Smith, 81-341.

SEC. 5. *Governor to make appointments.* In the absence of any contrary provision, all officers of the State, whether heretofore elected or appointed by the Governor, shall hold their positions only until other appointments are made by the Governor, or, if the officers are elective, until their successors shall have been chosen and duly qualified according to the provisions of this Constitution.
Const. 1868.
Markham v. Simpson, 175-135.

SEC. 6. *Seat of government.* The seat of government in this State shall remain at the city of Raleigh.
Const. 1868.

SEC. 7. *Holding office.* No person who shall hold any office or place of trust or profit under the United States, or any department thereof, or under this State, or under any other state or government, shall hold or exercise any other office or place of trust or profit under the authority of this State, or be eligible to a seat in either house of the General Assembly: Provided, that nothing herein contained shall extend to officers in the militia, justices of the peace, commissioners of public charities or commissioners for special purposes.
Const. 1868; 1872-3, c. 88; Convention 1835, art. 4, sec. 4
Kendall v. Stafford, 178-461; Cole v. Sanders, 174-112; Bank v. Redwine, 171-559; State v. Knight, 169-333; Graves v. Barden, 169-8; Whitehead v. Pittman, 165-89; Midgett v. Gray 158-133; McCullers v. Comrs., 158-75; State v. Lord, 145-479; State v. Smith, 145-476; Dunham v. Anders, 128-207; White v. Murray, 126-153; Dowtin v. Beardsley, 126-116; Barnhill v. Thompson, 122-493; Wood v. Bellamy, 120-223; Harkins v. Cathey, 119-659; Bank v. Worth, 117-152; McNeill v. Somers, 96-467; Doyle v. Raleigh, 89-133.
See, also, C. S., sec. 3200.

SEC. 8. *Intermarriage of whites and negroes prohibited.* All marriages between a white person and a negro, or between a white person and a person of negro descent to the third generation inclusive, are hereby forever prohibited.
Convention, 1875.
Johnson v. Bd. of Ed., 166-468; Ashe v. Miz. Co., 154-241; Ferrall v. Ferrall, 153-174; Hopkins v. Bowers, 111-175.

Index to the Constitution of North Carolina

Abuses in assessments and contracting debts by municipal corporations, general assembly to prevent. A. 8, S. 4.
Actions at law and equity suits, no distinction. A. 4, S. 1.
    pending when constitution took effect. A. 4, S. 20.
Acts of general assembly, style of. A. 2, S. 21.
    levying taxes, must state object. A. 5, S. 7.
Agricultural department. A. 3, S. 17.
    in connection with university. A. 9, S. 14.
Alimony, general assembly does not secure. A. 2, S. 10.
Allegiance to United States government. A. 1, S. 5.
Alleys, laws authorizing, etc. A. 2, S. 29.
Amendments. A. 13.
    do not vacate existing office. A. 4, S. 33.
Answer to criminal charge. A. 1, S. 12.
Apportionment of senators and representatives. A. 2, SS. 4, 5, 6.
Arms, right to bear. A. 1, S. 24.
Article seven, general assembly may modify or repeal certain sections. A. 7, S. 14.
Assemblage, right of. A. 1, S. 25.
Assessment or collection of taxes, extending time for. A. 2, S. 29.
Attorney-General advises executive. A. 3, S. 14.
    duties of. A. 3, S. 13.
Auditor, duties of. A. 3, S. 13.
Bail, excessive. A. 1, S. 14.
Ballot, elections to be by. A. 6, S. 6.
Bills of general assembly, read three times. A. 2, S. 23.
Blind provided for. A. 11, S. 10.
Board of charities. A. 11, S. 7.
Boundaries of state. A. 1, S. 34.
Bridges, laws relating to. A. 2, S. 29.
Capital punishment. A. 11, S. 2.
Capitation tax. A. 5, S. 1.
    application of proceeds from. A. 5, S. 2.
    exemptions. A. 5, S. 1.
Cemeteries, laws relating to. A. 2, S. 29.
Charities, public. A. 11.
    deaf-mutes and the blind. A. 11, S. 10.
    idiots and inebriates. A. 11, S. 9.
    provisions for orphans and the poor. A. 11, S. 7.
    self-supporting as far as possible. A. 11, S. 11.
Cities, laws changing names of. A. 2, S. 29.
    organized by legislation. A. 8, S. 4.
Citizenship, restoration to. A. 2, S. 11.
Civil and criminal actions. A. 4, S. 1.
Claims against the state. A. 4, S. 9.
Clerk of superior court, election of. A. 4, S. 16.
    removal for inability. A. 4, S. 32.
    terms of office of. A. 4, S. 17.

Clerk of supreme court. A. 4, S. 15.
    removal of. A. 4, S. 32.
    term of office of. A. 4, S. 15.
Collection of taxes, extending time for. A. 2, S. 29.
Collector of taxes, law relieving. A. 2, S. 29.
Communications. A. 3, S. 6.
Compulsory education, general assembly may provide. A. 9, S. 15.
Concealed weapons, carrying not justified. A. 1, S. 24.
Constitution, how changed. A. 13, S. 2.
Controversies at law about property. A. 1, S. 19.
Convention, how called. A. 13.
Convict labor. A. 11, S. 1.
Coroner and sheriff. A. 4, S. 24.
Corporations, municipal. A. 7.
    charters remain in force till legally changed. A. 7, S. 12.
    power of general assembly over. A. 7, S. 14; A. 8, S. 4.
Corporations other than municipal. A. 8.
    debts of, how secured. A. 8, S. 2.
    special charters prohibited. A. 8, S. 1.
Correction, houses of. A. 11, S. 4.
Council of state. A. 3, S. 14.
Counsel allowed defendant. A. 1, S. 11.
Counties, commissioners divide into districts. A. 7, S. 3.
    districts have corporate powers as townships. A. 7, S. 4.
    majority of voters necessary to levy taxes, etc. A. 7, S. 7.
    money, how drawn from treasury. A. 7, S. 8.
    officers enter on duty, when. A. 7, S. 10.
        of townships. A. 7, S. 5.
    school districts. A. 9, S. 3.
        fund. A. 9, S. 5.
Counties, taxes to be ad valorem. A. 7, S. 9.
    township trustees assess property. A. 7, S. 6.
County treasurer. A. 7, S. 1.
County commissioners, election and duty of. A. 7, SS. 1, 2.
Courts to be open. A. 1, S. 35.
    inferior, laws relating to establishment of. A. 2, S. 29; A. 4, S. 12.
    kinds of. A. 4, S. 2.
Criminal and civil action. A. 4, S. 1.
    courts for cities and towns. A. 4, S. 14.
    prosecutions. A. 1, S. 11.
Criminal charges, answer to. A. 1, S. 12.
Deaf-mutes provided for. A. 11, S. 10.
Death punishment. A. 11, S. 2.
Debt does not affect homestead. A. 10, S. 3.
    county, city or town cannot contract, except by majority of qualified voters. A. 7, S. 7.
    imprisonment for. A. 1, S. 16.
    in aid of rebellion, void. A. 7, S. 13.
    restrictions upon increase of public, etc. A. 5, S. 4.
    what bonds declared invalid. A. 4, S. 6.
Declaration of rights. A. 1.
Deeds, laws giving effect to. A. 2, S. 29.

Department of Agriculture. A. 3, S. 17.
Disqualification for office. A. 6, S. 8; A. 11, S. 7.
 dueling disqualities. A. 14, S. 2.
Divorce, general assembly does not grant. A. 2, S. 10.
Education, board of. A. 9, S. 8.
 county school fund. A. 9, S. 5.
 encouraged. A. 1, S. 27; A. 9, S. 1.
 expenses. A. 9, S. 13.
 first session of. A. 9, S. 11.
 officers. A. 9, S. 9.
 power of. A. 9, S. 10.
 property devoted to. A. 9, SS. 4, 5.
 quorum. A. 9, S. 12.
Election of officers by general assembly, viva voce. A. 2, S. 9.
Elections, by people by ballot and by general assembly, viva voce. A. 6, S. 6.
 contested, returns of. A. 3, S. 3.
 fee. A. 1, S. 19.
 frequent. A. 1, S. 28.
Electors, qualifications of. A. 6, SS. 1, 2, 3.
 registration of. A. 6, SS. 3, 4.
Eligibility to office. A. 6.
Emergency judges. A. 4, S. 11.
Emoluments, exclusive, none. A. 1, S. 7.
 hereditary. A. 1, S. 30.
Entails to be regulated. A. 2, S. 15.
Enumeration of rights not to impair others retained by people. A. 1, S. 37.
Equity suits and actions at law, distinction abolished. A. 4, S. 1.
 pending when constitution took effect. A. 4, S. 20.
Evidence against himself, criminal not compelled to give. A. 1, S. 11.
Executive, attorney-general advises. A. 3, S. 14.
 department of. A. 3.
 distinct. A. 1, S. 8.
 officers. A. 3, S. 1.
  compensation. A. 3, S. 15.
  duties. A. 3, S. 13.
  reports of. A. 3, S. 7.
  terms of office of. A. 3, S. 1.
 seal of state. A. 3, S. 16.
 vacancy in, how filled. A. 3, S. 13.
Exemption, personal property. A. 10, S. 1.
 by reason of military duty, etc. A. 12, S. 4.
 property of *feme covert* not liable for husband's debts. A. 10, S. 6.
Ex post facto laws. A. 1, S. 32.
Extra session of general assembly. A. 3, S. 9.
Feigned issues abolished. A. 4, S. 1.
Ferries, laws relating to. A. 2, S. 29.
Fines, excessive. A. 1, S. 14.
 laws remitting fines, etc. A. 2, S. 29.
Forfeitures, laws remitting. A. 2, S. 29.
Freedom of the press. A. 1, S. 20.
Fundamental principles, frequent recurrence to. A. 1, S. 29.
General assembly, acts, style of. A. 2, S. 21.
 article seven may be modified or repealed by. A. 7, S. 14.
 bills and resolutions read three times. A. 2, S. 23.

compulsory education may be enforced by. A. 9, S. 15.
elections by, to be viva voce. A. 6, S. 6.
entails regulated by. A. 2, S. 15.
extra sessions. A. 2, S. 28; A. 3, S. 9.
journals kept. A. 2, S. 16.
protest entered on. A. 2, S. 17.
General assembly, meetings of, when. A. 2, S. 2.
members, election for, when. A. 2, S. 27.
oath of. A. 2, S. 24.
office a disqualification. A. 14, S. 7.
terms commence with election. A. 2, S. 25.
vacancies, how filled. A. 2, S. 13.
municipal corporations controlled by. A. 7, S. 14.
names, personal, not changed by. A. 2, S. 11.
nonnavigable streams, laws relating to. A. 2, S. 29.
officers of, election, viva voce. A. 2, S. 9.
pay of. A. 2, S. 28.
president of senate. A. 2, S. 19.
speaker of house. A. 2, S. 18.
powers of. A. 2, S. 22.
in relation to divorce and alimony. A. 2, S. 10.
in relation to private or special legislation. A. 2, S. 29
representation apportioned by. A. 2, SS. 4, 5.
revenue. A. 2, S. 14.
schools provided by. A. 9, S. 2.
university to be maintained by. A. 9, SS. 6, 7.
use of sinking fund, by, regulated. A. 2, S. 30.
yeas and nays. A. 2, SS. 14, 26.
Government, allegiance to United States. A. 1, S. 5.
internal, of state. A. 1, S. 3.
origin of. A. 1, S. 2.
seat of, remains at Raleigh. A. 14, S. 6.
Governor, commands militia. A. 3, S. 8.
commutations, pardons, reprieves. A. 3, S. 6.
compensation. A. 3, S. 15.
duties performed by the lieutenant-governor, when. A. 3, S. 12.
extra sessions called by. A. 3, S. 9.
impeachment of. A. 3, S. 12.
justices of peace, appointed by, when. A. 7, S. 11.
lieutenant, qualification of. A. 3, S. 2.
oath of office. A. 3, S. 4.
officers appointed by. A. 3, S. 10; A. 14, S. 5.
qualifications of. A. 3, S. 2.
resident of. A. 3, S. 5.
vacancy in office of. A. 3, S. 12.
Health, laws relating to. A. 2, S. 29.
Habeas Corpus. A. 1, S. 21.
Hereditary emoluments. A. 1, S. 30.
Highways, laws authorizing, etc. A. 2, S. 29.
Homestead and exemption. A. 10, S. 2.
benefit of widow in. A. 10, S. 5.
exempted from debt. A. 10, S. 3.
laborer's lien attaches. A. 10, S. 4.
notes, exempt from tax. A. 5, S. 3.
privy examination of wife to dispose of. A. 10, S. 8.
Houses of correction. A. 11, S. 4.
Houses of refuge. A. 11, S. 5.

House of Representatives, representatives, apportionment. A. 2, S. 5.
    officers of. A. 2, S. 18.
    qualification for. A. 2, S. 8.
    ratio of. A. 2, S. 6.
    term begins when. A. 2, S. 25.
Husband can insure life for benefit of family. A. 10, S. 7.
Idiots provided for. A. 11, S. 9.
Immigration, department of. A. 3, S. 17.
Impeachment. A. 4, S. 4.
    court of. A. 4, S. 3.
    of governor. A. 3, S. 12.
Imprisonment for debt. A. 1, S. 16.
    except by law, wrong. A. 1, S. 17.
    income tax. A. 5, S. 3.
Indictments for crime committed before constitution took effect. A. 14, S. 1.
Inebriates. A. 11, S. 9.
Inferior courts. A. 4, S. 12.
    officers of. A. 4, S. 30.
Insane provided for. A. 11, S. 10.
Institutions, charitable. A. 11.
    penal. A. 11.
    public, annual reports from. A. 3, S. 7.
    self-supporting as far as possible. A. 11, S. 11.
    sexes to be separated. A. 11, S. 6.
Instruction, superintendent of public. A. 3, S. 13.
Intermarriage of whites and negroes prohibited. A. 14, S. 8.
Internal government of state. A. 1, S. 3.
Issues of fact, by whom tried and how waived. A. 4, S. 13.
Judges, election, terms of, etc. A. 4, S. 21.
    fees, salaries, emoluments. A. 4, S. 18.
    removal of, for inability. A. 4, S. 31.
    residence of. A. 4, S. 11.
    special or emergency. A. 4, S. 11.
Judicial department. A. 4.
    districts for superior courts. A. 4, S. 10.
    general assembly not to deprive of jurisdiction. A. 4, S. 12.
    powers, division of. A. 4, S. 2.
    terms of first officers under constitution. A. 4, S. 26.
    vacancies. A. 4, S. 25.
Judicial remedy, allowed all. A. 1, S. 35.
Judiciary distinct. A. 1, S. 8.
Jurisdiction, courts inferior to supreme. A. 4, S. 12.
    justices of the peace. A. 4, S. 27.
    supreme court. A. 4, S. 8.
Jurors, laws relating to pay of. A. 2, S. 29.
Jury, right of. A. 1, S. 13.
    sacred and inviolable. A. 1, S. 19.
    trial by, waived. A. 4, S. 13.
Justices of the peace, governor appoints, when. A. 7, S. 11.
    jurisdiction of. A. 4, S. 27.
    laws relating to appointment of. A. 2, S. 29.
    vacancies in office. A. 4, S. 28.
Labor, etc., laws regulating. A. 2, S. 29.

Laborers' and mechanics' lien. A. 14, S. 4.
   attaches to homestead. A. 10, S. 4.
Law of the land, no person imprisoned, or deprived of life, etc., but by. A. 1, S. 17.
Laws, ex post facto and retrospective. A. 1, S. 32.
   private, thirty days notice before passage. A. 2, S. 12.
   what in force. A. 4, S. 19.
Legislative department, distinct. A. 1, S. 8.
Legislature, two branches of. A. 2, S. 1.
   provide for organizing towns, etc. A. 8, S. 4.
   trials other than jury. A. 1, S. 13.
Legitimation, general assembly can pass general laws for. A. 2, S. 11.
Liberty, deprivation of, except by law. A. 1, S. 17.
   religious. A. 1, S. 26.
   restraint of, remedied. A. 1, S. 18.
   warrants without evidence, dangerous to. A. 1, S. 15.
Lien of laborers and mechanics. A. 14, S. 4.
Lieutenant-governor, president of senate, duties of. A. 3, S. 11.
   when governor. A. 3, S. 12.
Literary fund, board of education to succeed to rights of. A. 9, S. 10.
Local legislation prohibited. A. 2, S. 29.
Manufacturing, laws regulating. A. 2, S. 29.
Marriages between whites and negroes forbidden. A. 14, S. 8.
Married woman, husband can insure life for benefit of. A. 10, S. 7.
   privy examination of to dispose of homestead. A. 10, S. 8.
   property of, not liable for husband's debts. A. 10, S. 6.
Mechanics lien. A. 14, S. 4.
Men, equality, rights of. A. 1, S. 1.
Militia. A. 1, S. 24; A. 12.
   exemptions from duty. A. 12, S. 4.
   governor commands. A. 3, S. 8; A. 12, S. 3.
   organization of. A. 12, S. 2.
   who liable to bear arms. A. 12, S. 1.
Mining, laws regulating. A. 2, S. 29.
Money, how drawn from state treasury. A. 14, S. 3.
   county or township treasury. A. 7, S. 8.
   paid into treasury, refunding. A. 2, S. 29.
Monopolies are injurious. A. 1, S. 31.
Mortgages given for price of home, etc. A. 5, S. 3.
Municipal corporations. A. 7.
   cannot contract debt except by majority of qualified voters. A. 7, S. 7.
   charters remain in force till changed. A. 7, S. 12.
   general assembly to provide for organization of; taxation, etc., by. A. 8, S. 4.
   power of general assembly over. A. 7, S. 14; A. 8, S. 4.
   special charter prohibited. A. 8, S. 4.
Names of cities, towns and townships, laws changing. A. 2, S. 29.
Names, personal, how changed. A. 2, S. 11.
Normal school, to be maintained by general assembly at university. A. 9, S. 14.
Notes given for price of home, not taxable. A. 5, S. 3.
Nuisances, laws relating to abatement of. A. 2, S. 29.
Oath of Governor. A. 3, S. 4.

Oath of members of general assembly. A. 2, S. 24.
Oath of Office. A. 6, S. 7.
Office, cannot hold two. A. 14, S. 7.
   disqualification. A. 6, S. 8.
   dueling disqualifies for. A. 14, S. 2.
   eligibility to. A. 6.
   qualification, property, none. A. 1, S. 22.
Officers, county. A. 7, SS. 1, 10.
   first elected. A. 4, S. 26.
   what, appointed by governor. A. 3, S. 10; A. 14, S. 5.
Orphans, houses for. A. 11, S. 8.
   provisions for. A. 11, S. 7.
Pardons. A. 3, S. 6.
Peace, soldiers quartered in time of. A. 1, S. 36.
Penalties, laws remitting. A. 2, S. 29.
Penitentiary. A. 11, S. 3.
   convict labor. A. 11, S. 1.
   self-supporting as far as possible. A. 11, S. 11.
   sexes separated. A. 11, S. 6.
People, right of, to assemble together. A. 1, S. 25.
Perpetuities, injurious. A. 1, S. 31.
   general assembly shall prevent. A. 2, S. 15.
Political power and government. A. 1, S. 2.
   societies in secret dangerous. A. 1, S. 25.
Poll tax. A. 5, S. 1.
Poor, provision for. A. 11, S. 7.
Power of general assembly. A. 2, S. 22.
   to suspend laws injurious. A. 1, S. 9.
Powers, executive, judicial and legislative, distinct. A. 1, S. 8.
   judicial, division of. A. 4, S. 2.
Press, freedom and abuse of. A. 1, S. 20.
Principles, recurrence to fundamental. A. 1, S. 29.
Prisoners, health and comfort secured. A. 11, S. 6.
Private laws. A. 2, SS. 11, 12.
   local or special legislation. A. 2, S. 29.
Privileges exclusive, none. A. 1, S. 7.
Property, controversies at law about. A. 1, S. 19.
   deprivation of, except by law, wrong. A. 1, S. 17.
   devoted to education. A. 9, S. 4.
   exemptions from taxation. A. 5, S. 5.
   qualifications, none. A. 1, S. 22.
Prosecution, criminal. A. 1, S. 11.
Protest, against act or resolves, by whom and when made. A. 2, S. 17.
Public debt, increase of, restricted, etc. A. 5, S. 4.
   what bonds declared invalid. A. 1, S. 6.
Public money, how drawn. A. 14, S. 3.
Public schools, general assembly to provide for. A. 9, S. 2.
Punishment, penal institutions and public charities. A. 11.
   cruel or unusual. A. 1, S. 14; A. 14, S. 1.
Qualification and election of members of general assembly, each house judge of. A. 2, S. 22.
Rebellion, debt in aid of, not to be paid. A. 7, S. 13.

INDEX TO THE CONSTITUTION OF NORTH CAROLINA   455

Recurrence to fundamental principles. A. 1, S. 29.
Refuge, houses of. A. 11, S. 5.
Register of deeds. A. 7, S. 1.
Registration of electors. A, 6, SS. 3, 4.
Religious liberty. A. 1, S. 26.
    scruples against bearing arms. A. 12, S. 1.
Removal of judges. A. 4, S. 31.
    of clerks. A. 4, S. 32.
Representation and taxation. A. 1, S. 23.
Reprieves. A. 3, S. 6.
Retrospective laws. A. 1, S. 32.
Revenue. A. 2, S. 14; A. 5.
Right of assemblage. A. 1, S. 25.
    of jury. A. 1, S. 13.
    of secession, none. A. 1, S. 4.
        to bear arms. A. 1, S. 24.
    to suspend laws, injurious. A. 1, S. 9.
Rights, declaration of. A. 1.
    of men. A. 1, SS. 1, 37.
Salaries and fees of officers of judicial department, general assembly regulates.
    A. 4, S. 18.
Sanitation, laws relating to. A. 2, S. 29.
School districts, laws establishing or changing lines. A. 2, S. 29.
Schools, attendance of children. A. 9, S. 15.
    county, divided into districts. A. 9, S. 3.
    fund. A. 9, S. 5.
    provided by legislature. A. 9, S. 2.
    races separate. A. 9, S. 2.
    term, six months required. A. 9, S. 3.
Seal of state. A. 3, S. 16.
Search warrants without evidence, wrong. A. 1, S. 15.
Seat of government at Raleigh. A. 14, S. 6.
Secession, no right of. A. 1, S. 4.
Secretary of State, duties of. A. 3, S. 13.
Senate, presiding officer. A. 2, S. 19.
    pro tem, speaker, when elected. A. 2, S. 20.
Senators, number of. A. 2, S. 3.
    president of. A. 2, S. 19.
    qualifications for. A. 2, S. 7.
    regulating senatorial districts. A. 2, S. 4.
    senatorial officers. A. 2, S. 20.
Separation of governmental powers. A. 1, S. 8.
Sexes separated in confinement. A. 11, S. 6.
Sheriff and coroner. A. 4, S. 24.
Sinking funds, regulation of use. A. 2, S. 30.
Slavery prohibited. A. 1, S. 33.
Societies, secret political, dangerous. A. 1, S. 25.
Soldiers, how quartered. A. 1, S. 36.
Solicitor how elected. A. 4, S. 23.
Special courts. A. 4, S. 14.
Special legislation, powers of general assembly as to. A. 2, S. 29.
State boundaries. A. 1, S. 34.
    claims against. A. 4, S. 9.
    internal government. A. 1, S. 3.
Statistics, department of. A. 3, S. 17.
Streets, laws authorizing, etc. A. 2, S. 29.
Suffrage and eligibility to office. A. 6.

Superintendent of Public Instruction. A. 3, S. 13.
    reports of county school fund to be made. A. 9, S. 5.
Superior court, open at all times except for jury trials. A. 4, S. 22.
    clerk, his election. A. 4, S. 16.
        removal from office. A. 4, S. 32.
        term. A. 4, S. 17.
    vacancy. A. 4, SS. 2, 9.
    districts. A. 4, S. 10.
    judges, election and term. A. 4, S. 21.
        residence. A. 4, S. 11.
        rotation. A. 4, S. 11.
    solicitor for each district. A. 4, S. 23.
    special term. A. 4, S. 11.
    terms, annually in counties. A. 4, S. 10.
    transaction of business, to be open for. A. 4, S. 22.
Supreme court, clerk. A. 4, S. 15.
    clerk, removal from office. A. 4, S. 32.
    jurisdiction. A. 4, SS. 8, 9.
    justices. A. 4, S. 6.
        election and terms of. A. 4, S. 21.
    terms of. A. 4, S. 7.
Surveyor, county. A. 7, S. 1.
Suspending laws without consent of representatives, forbidden. A. 1, S. 9.
Taxation, *ad valorem* and uniform. A. 5, S. 3.
    and revenue. A. 1, S. 23; A. 5.
    except for necessary expenses, not levied by county, city or town without
        assent of majority of voters. A. 7, S. 7.
    homestead notes exempt. A. 5, S. 3.
    income. A. 5, S. 3.
    levied by county commissioners. A. 5, S. 6.
    of county to be *ad valorem*. A. 7, S. 9.
    of purchase and sales retrospectively not to be passed. A. 1, S. 32.
    property, exemptions from. A. 5, S. 5.
Taxes, acts to levy, to state object. A. 5, S. 7.
Towns, etc., organized by legislature. A. 8, S. 4.
Towns, laws changing names of. A. 2, S. 29.
Townships, officers of. A. 7, S. 5.
    laws changing names of. A. 2, S. 29.
    laws erecting, changing lines. A. 2, S. 29.
Trade, laws regulating. A. 2, S. 29.
Trials on against state. A. 4, S. 5.
Treasurer, duties of. A. 3, S. 13.
University, agricultural department of, mechanics, mining and normal instruction connected with. A. 9, S. 14.
    benefits of. A. 9, S. 7.
    election of trustees. A. 9, S. 6.
    general assembly shall maintain. A. 9, S. 7.
    maintenance of. A. 9, S. 6.
    property devoted to. A. 9, S. 7.
Vacancies in general assembly. A. 2, S. 13.
    other. A. 3, SS. 12, 13; A. 4, SS. 25, 28, 29.
Vagrants, houses of correction for. A. 11, S. 4.
Warrants without evidence injurious. A. 1, S. 15.
Whites and negroes cannot intermarry. A. 14, S. 8.
    separated in schools. A. 9, S. 2.
Widow, homestead benefits. A. 10, S. 5.
Wills, laws giving effect to. A. 2, S. 29.
Yeas and nays, when entered. A. 2, SS. 14, 26.

PART XII

CENSUS

1. POPULATION AND AREA OF THE SEVERAL STATES AND TERRITORIES, 1910-1920.
2. POPULATION (ESTIMATED) OF NORTH CAROLINA, 1675-1786.
3. CENSUS OF NORTH CAROLINA, 1790-1840.
4. CENSUS OF NORTH CAROLINA, 1850-1920.
5. POPULATION OF NORTH CAROLINA CITIES AND TOWNS, 1900-1920.
6. NORTH CAROLINA COUNTIES AND COUNTY SEATS.
7. ECONOMIC DEVELOPMENT OF NORTH CAROLINA.

POPULATION AND AREA OF THE SEVERAL STATES AND TERRITORIES, 1910-1920

State	Settled	Capital	Area	Population, 1910	Population, 1920	
Virginia	1607	Richmond	42,450	2,061,612	2,309,187	One of original thirteen states.
New York	1613	Albany	49,170	9,113,614	10,385,227	One of original thirteen states.
Massachusetts	1620	Boston	8,315	3,366,416	3,852,356	One of original thirteen states.
New Hampshire	1623	Concord	9,305	430,572	443,083	One of original thirteen states.
Connecticut	1633	Hartford	4,990	1,114,756	1,380,631	One of original thirteen states.
Maryland	1634	Annapolis	12,210	1,295,346	1,449,661	One of original thirteen states.
Rhode Island	1636	Providence	1,250	542,610	604,397	One of original thirteen states.
Delaware	1638	Dover	2,050	202,322	223,003	One of original thirteen states.
North Carolina	1653	Raleigh	52,250	2,206,287	2,559,123	One of original thirteen states.
New Jersey	1664	Trenton	7,815	2,537,167	3,155,900	One of original thirteen states.
South Carolina	1670	Columbia	30,570	1,515,400	1,683,724	One of original thirteen states.
Pennsylvania	1682	Harrisburg	45,215	7,665,111	8,720,017	One of original thirteen states.
Georgia	1733	Atlanta	59,475	2,609,121	2,895,832	One of original thirteen states.
	Admitted to Union					
Vermont	1791	Montpelier	9,565	355,956	352,428	Territory claimed by New York and New Hampshire.
Kentucky	1792	Frankfort	40,400	2,289,905	2,416,630	Ceded by Virginia.
Tennessee	1796	Nashville	41,750	2,184,789	2,337,885	Ceded by North Carolina.
Ohio	1803	Columbus	40,760	4,767,121	5,759,394	Northwest Territory.
Louisiana	1812	Baton Rouge	45,420	1,656,388	1,798,509	Louisiana Territory.
Indiana	1816	Indianapolis	35,910	2,700,876	2,930,390	Northwest Territory.
Mississippi	1817	Jackson	46,340	1,797,114	1,790,618	Ceded by South Carolina and Georgia.
Illinois	1818	Springfield	56,000	5,638,591	6,485,280	Northwest Territory.
Alabama	1819	Montgomery	51,540	2,138,093	2,348,174	Ceded by South Carolina and Georgia.
Maine	1820	Augusta	29,895	742,371	768,014	Ceded by Massachusetts.
Missouri	1821	Jefferson City	68,735	3,293,335	3,404,055	Louisiana Purchase.
Arkansas	1836	Little Rock	53,045	1,574,449	1,752,204	Louisiana Purchase.
Michigan	1837	Lansing	57,450	2,810,173	3,668,412	Northwest Territory.
Florida	1845	Tallahassee	54,240	752,619	968,470	Spanish cession.
Texas	1845	Austin	262,290	3,896,542	4,663,228	By annexation.
Iowa	1846	Des Moines	55,475	2,224,771	2,404,021	Louisiana Purchase.
Wisconsin	1848	Madison	54,450	2,333,860	2,632,067	Northwest Territory.
California	1850	Sacramento	155,980	2,377,549	3,426,861	Mexican cession.
Minnesota	1858	St. Paul	79,205	2,075,708	2,387,125	Northwest Territory and Louisiana Purchase.
Oregon	1859	Salem	94,560	672,765	783,389	Oregon Country.
Kansas	1861	Topeka	81,700	1,690,949	1,769,257	Louisiana Purchase.
West Virginia	1863	Wheeling	24,645	1,221,119	1,463,701	Formed from Virginia.

POPULATION AND AREA OF THE SEVERAL STATES AND TERRITORIES, 1910-1920—Continued

State	Settled	Capital	Area	Population, 1910	Population, 1920	
Nevada	1848	Carson City	109,740	81,875	77,407	Mexican cession
Nebraska	1847	Lincoln	76,840	1,192,214	1,296,372	Louisiana Purchase
Colorado	1858	Denver	103,645	799,024	939,629	Louisiana Purchase and Mexican cession
North Dakota	1829	Bismarck	70,195	577,056	645,680	Louisiana Purchase
South Dakota	1859	Pierre	76,850	583,888	636,547	Louisiana Purchase
Montana	1809	Helena	145,310	376,053	548,889	Louisiana Purchase
Washington	1811	Olympia	66,836	1,141,990	1,356,621	Oregon Country
Idaho	1842	Boise	83,388	325,594	431,866	Oregon Country
Wyoming	1834	Cheyenne	97,548	145,965	194,402	Louisiana Purchase and Mexican cession
Utah	1847	Salt Lake City	82,190	373,351	449,396	Mexican cession
Oklahoma	1889	Guthrie	69,414	1,657,155	2,028,283	Mexican cession
New Mexico	1605	Santa Fe	122,460	327,396	360,350	Mexican cession
Arizona	1580	Phoenix	112,920	204,354	333,903	Mexican cession
District of Columbia			60	331,069	437,571	

Territories	Organ-ized					
Alaska	1884	Juneau	590,884	64,356	55,036	Purchased from Russia
Hawaii	1900	Honolulu	6,449	191,909	255,912	By annexation

Outlying Possessions						
Porto Rico			3,435	1,118,012	1,299,809	Spanish cession
Philippines			115,026	7,635,426	10,350,640	Spanish cession
Guam			210	11,806	13,275	
American Samoa			77	7,251	8,056	
Panama Canal Zone			527	62,810	22,858	
Military and Naval Serv. services abroad					117,238	
Virgin Islands of the United States			132	27,063	26,051	
Continental United States			3,026,789	91,972,266	105,710,620	
U.S. with outlying possessions and territories			3,743,529	101,146,530	117,823,165	

[1] Population in 1903.
[2] Population in 1918.
[3] Population in 1912.
[4] Population in 1912.
[5] Population in 1911.
[6] Population in 1917.

POPULATION (Estimated) OF NORTH CAROLINA, 1675-1786

Year	Population
1675	4,000
1701	5,000
1707	7,000
1715	11,000
1729	35,000
1752	100,000
1765	200,000
1771	250,000
1786	350,000

CENSUS OF NORTH CAROLINA, 1790-1840

Counties	Date of Formation	1790	1800	1810	1820	1830	1840
1 Alamance	1840						
2 Alexander	1847						
3 Alleghany	1859						
4 Anson	1749	5,133	8,146	8,831	12,534	14,095	15,077
5 Ashe	1799		2,783	3,694	4,335	6,987	7,467
6 Avery							
7 Beaufort	1705	5,462	6,242	7,203	9,850	10,969	12,225
8 Bertie	1722	12,606	11,249	11,218	10,805	12,262	12,175
9 Bladen	1734	5,084	7,028	5,671	7,276	7,811	8,022
10 Brunswick	1764	3,071	4,110	4,778	5,480	6,516	5,265
11 Buncombe	1791		5,812	9,277	10,542	16,281	10,084
12 Burke	1777	8,118	9,929	11,007	13,411	17,888	15,799
13 Cabarrus	1792		5,094	6,158	7,248	8,810	9,259
14 Caldwell	1841						
15 Camden	1777	4,033	4,191	5,347	6,347	6,733	5,663
16 Carteret	1722	3,732	4,399	4,823	5,609	6,597	6,592
17 Caswell	1777	10,096	8,701	11,757	13,253	15,785	14,693
18 Catawba	1842						
19 Chatham	1770	9,221	11,861	12,977	12,661	15,405	16,242
20 Cherokee	1839						3,427
21 Chowan	1672	5,011	5,132	5,297	6,464	6,697	6,690
22 Clay	1861						
23 Cleveland	1841						
24 Columbus	1808			3,022	3,912	4,141	3,941
25 Craven	1712	10,469	10,245	12,676	13,394	13,734	13,438
26 Cumberland	1754	8,671	9,264	9,382	14,446	14,834	15,284
27 Currituck	1672	5,219	6,928	6,985	8,098	7,655	6,703
28 Dare	1870						
29 Davidson	1822					13,389	14,606
30 Davie	1836						7,574
31 Duplin	1749	5,662	6,796	7,863	9,744	11,291	11,182
32 Durham	1881						
33 Edgecombe	1732	10,225	10,421	12,423	13,276	14,935	15,708
34 Forsyth	1849						
35 Franklin	1779	7,559	8,529	10,166	9,741	10,665	10,980
36 Gaston	1846						
37 Gates	1779	5,392	5,881	5,965	6,837	7,866	8,161
38 Graham	1872						
39 Granville	1746	10,982	14,015	15,576	18,222	19,355	18,817
40 Greene*	1799	6,983	4,218	4,867	4,533	6,413	6,595
41 Guilford	1770	7,191	9,442	11,420	14,511	18,737	19,175
42 Halifax	1758	13,965	13,945	13,620	17,237	17,739	16,865
43 Harnett	1855						
44 Haywood	1808			2,780	4,073	4,578	4,975
45 Henderson	1838						5,129
46 Hertford	1759	5,828	6,701	6,052	7,712	8,537	4,484
47 Hoke							
48 Hyde	1705	4,120	4,829	6,029	4,967	6,184	6,458
49 Iredell	1788	5,435	8,856	10,972	13,071	14,918	15,685
50 Jackson	1851						
51 Johnston	1746	5,634	6,301	6,867	9,607	10,938	10,599
52 Jones	1779	4,822	4,339	4,968	5,216	5,608	4,945
53 Lee	1907						
54 Lenoir	1791		4,005	5,572	6,799	7,723	7,605
55 Lincoln	1779	9,224	12,660	16,359	18,147	22,455	26,160
56 McDowell	1842						
57 Macon	1828					5,333	4,869
58 Madison	1851						
59 Martin	1774	6,080	5,629	5,987	6,320	8,539	7,637

*In 1758 Dobbs County was formed from part of Johnston. In 1791 Dobbs was divided into Lenoir and Glasgow. In 1799 the name of Glasgow was changed to Greene.

CENSUS OF NORTH CAROLINA, 1850-1920

1850	1860	1870	1880	1890	1900	1910	1920	Land Area in Square Miles	
11,444	11,852	11,874	14,613	18,271	25,665	28,712	32,718	494	1
5,220	6,022	6,868	8,355	9,430	10,960	11,592	12,212	297	2
		3,598	3,691	5,486	6,523	7,759	7,745	7,403	223	3
13,489	13,664	12,428	17,994	20,027	21,870	25,465	28,334	551	4
8,777	7,956	9,573	14,437	15,628	19,581	19,074	21,004	399	5
							10,335		6
13,816	14,766	13,014	17,174	21,072	26,404	30,877	31,024	819	7
12,854	14,310	12,950	16,399	19,176	20,538	23,039	23,993	712	8
9,767	11,995	12,831	16,158	16,763	17,677	18,006	19,761	1,013	9
7,272	8,406	7,754	9,389	10,900	12,657	14,432	11,876	812	10
12,425	12,654	15,412	21,909	35,206	44,288	49,798	61,148	624	11
7,772	9,237	9,777	12,809	14,939	17,699	21,408	23,297	534	12
9,747	10,546	11,954	14,964	18,142	22,456	26,240	33,720	387	13
6,317	7,497	8,476	10,291	12,298	15,694	20,579	19,984	507	14
6,049	5,343	5,361	6,274	5,667	5,474	5,640	5,382	248	15
6,939	8,186	9,010	9,784	10,825	11,811	13,770	15,384	558	16
15,269	16,215	16,081	17,825	16,028	15,028	14,858	15,759	396	17
8,862	10,729	10,984	14,946	18,689	22,125	27,918	33,829	408	18
18,149	19,101	19,723	23,453	25,413	23,912	22,635	23,814	785	19
6,838	9,166	8,080	8,184	9,976	11,860	11,136	15,212	451	20
6,721	6,842	6,450	7,900	9,167	10,258	11,393	10,649	461	21
		2,461	3,316	4,397	4,532	3,909	4,646	185	22
10,396	12,348	12,696	16,571	20,394	25,678	29,494	34,272	485	23
5,909	8,597	8,474	14,430	17,856	21,274	28,020	20,124	937	24
14,709	16,268	20,516	19,729	20,533	24,164	25,594	29,048	685	25
20,610	16,369	17,035	23,836	27,321	29,249	35,284	35,064	1,008	26
7,226	7,415	5,131	6,476	6,717	6,529	7,693	7,268	273	27
		2,778	3,211	3,768	4,757	4,541	5,115	465	28
15,320	16,601	17,414	20,333	21,702	25,403	29,404	35,204	563	29
7,866	8,494	9,620	11,096	14,621	12,115	13,594	13,578	264	30
13,514	15,784	15,542	18,773	18,680	22,405	25,442	30,223	830	31
				18,141	26,233	35,276	42,219	281	32
17,189	17,376	22,970	26,181	24,113	26,591	32,016	37,395	515	33
11,168	12,692	13,050	18,078	28,434	35,261	47,311	77,269	369	34
11,713	11,107	14,135	20,829	21,098	25,116	24,692	26,667	471	35
8,173	9,307	12,602	14,254	17,764	27,903	37,063	51,212	359	36
8,426	8,443	7,724	8,897	10,252	10,413	10,455	10,557	356	37
			2,335	3,313	4,343	4,749	4,872	302	38
21,249	23,396	24,831	31,286	24,840	23,263	25,102	26,846	504	39
6,619	7,925	8,687	10,457	10,639	12,038	13,083	16,212	258	40
19,754	20,056	22,736	23,585	28,052	39,074	60,497	79,272	674	41
16,589	19,442	20,408	30,300	28,908	30,793	37,616	43,766	681	42
		8,039	8,895	10,862	13,700	15,988	22,174	28,343	596	43
7,074	5,081	7,924	10,274	13,346	16,222	21,020	23,496	541	44
6,853	10,418	7,706	10,284	12,589	14,104	16,262	18,248	362	45
8,142	9,504	9,273	11,843	13,854	14,294	15,436	16,294	339	46
							11,722		47
7,636	7,752	6,445	7,765	8,903	9,278	8,840	8,386	596	48
11,719	15,317	16,934	22,675	25,462	29,061	31,915	37,956	592	49
		5,515	6,683	7,315	9,512	11,855	12,998	13,396	494	50
13,726	15,656	16,897	23,461	27,239	32,250	41,401	48,998	688	51
5,058	5,750	5,002	7,194	7,403	8,226	8,721	9,942	465	52
						11,376	13,100		53
7,828	10,220	10,454	15,311	14,879	18,639	22,769	29,555	456	54
7,716	8,195	9,573	11,064	12,586	15,498	17,132	17,862	296	55
6,246	7,120	7,592	9,836	10,939	12,507	13,358	16,763	447	56
6,389	6,004	6,615	8,064	10,102	12,104	12,194	12,887	534	57
		5,908	8,192	12,810	17,805	20,644	20,432	20,083	434	58
8,307	10,195	9,647	13,110	15,221	15,383	17,797	20,826	438	59

CENSUS OF NORTH CAROLINA, 1790-1840—Continued

Counties	Date of Formation	1790	1800	1810	1820	1830	1840
60 Mecklenburg	1762	11,395	10,439	14,272	16,895	20,073	18,273
61 Mitchell	1861						
62 Montgomery	1779	4,725	7,677	8,430	8,603	10,919	10,780
63 Moore	1784	3,770	4,767	6,367	7,128	7,745	7,988
64 Nash	1777	7,393	6,975	7,268	8,125	8,490	9,047
65 New Hanover	1729	6,831	7,060	11,465	10,866	10,959	13,312
66 Northampton	1741	9,981	12,853	13,082	13,242	13,391	13,369
67 Onslow	1734	5,387	5,623	6,669	7,016	7,814	7,527
68 Orange	1752	12,216	16,362	20,135	23,492	23,908	24,356
69 Pamlico	1872						
70 Pasquotank	1672	5,497	5,379	7,674	8,008	8,641	8,544
71 Pender	1875						
72 Perquimans	1672	5,440	5,708	6,052	6,857	7,419	7,346
73 Person	1791		6,102	6,642	9,029	10,027	9,790
74 Pitt	1760	8,275	9,084	9,169	10,001	12,093	11,806
75 Polk	1855						
76 Randolph	1779	7,276	9,234	10,112	11,331	12,406	12,875
77 Richmond	1779	5,055	5,623	6,695	7,537	9,396	8,909
78 Robeson	1786	5,326	6,839	7,528	8,204	9,433	10,370
79 Rockingham	1785	6,187	8,277	10,316	11,474	12,935	13,442
80 Rowan	1753	15,828	20,064	21,543	26,009	20,786	12,109
81 Rutherford	1779	7,808	10,753	13,202	15,351	17,557	19,202
28 Sampson	1784	6,065	6,719	6,620	8,908	11,634	12,157
83 Scotland	1899						
84 Stanly	1841						
85 Stokes	1789	8,528	11,026	11,645	14,033	16,196	16,265
86 Surry	1771	7,191	8,509	10,336	12,330	14,504	15,079
87 Swain	1871						
88 Transylvania	1861						
89 Tyrrell	1729	1,744	3,395	3,364	4,319	4,732	4,657
90 Union	1842						
91 Vance	1881						
92 Wake	1770	10,192	13,437	17,086	20,102	20,398	21,118
93 Warren	1779	9,397	11,284	11,004	11,458	11,877	12,919
94 Washington	1799		2,122	3,464	3,986	4,552	4,525
95 Watauga	1849						
96 Wayne	1779	6,133	6,772	8,687	9,040	10,331	10,893
97 Wilkes	1777	8,143	7,247	9,054	9,967	11,968	12,577
98 Wilson	1855						
99 Yadkin	1850						
100 Yancey	1833						5,962
Totals		393,751	478,103	555,500	638,829	737,987	753,409

CENSUS OF NORTH CAROLINA, 1850-1920—Continued

1850	1860	1870	1880	1890	1900	1910	1920	Land Area in Square Miles	
13,914	17,374	24,299	31,175	42,673	55,268	67,031	80,695	590	60
		4,705	9,425	12,807	15,221	17,245	11,278	362	61
6,872	7,649	7,487	9,374	11,239	14,197	14,967	14,607	189	62
9,342	11,427	12,048	16,821	20,179	23,622	17,010	21,388	798	63
10,657	11,687	11,077	17,734	20,707	25,478	33,727	41,054	584	64
17,668	21,715	27,978	21,376	24,026	25,785	32,037	40,620	499	65
13,335	13,372	14,749	20,032	21,242	21,150	22,323	23,181	523	66
8,283	8,856	7,569	9,829	10,303	11,940	14,125	14,703	645	67
17,055	16,947	17,507	23,698	14,948	14,690	15,064	17,895	386	68
			6,323	7,146	8,045	9,966	9,060	358	69
8,950	8,940	8,131	10,369	10,718	13,060	16,693	17,670	221	70
			12,468	12,514	12,381	15,471	14,788	883	71
7,332	7,238	7,745	9,466	9,293	10,094	11,054	11,137	251	72
10,781	11,224	11,170	13,719	15,151	16,985	17,356	18,373	386	73
13,397	16,080	17,276	21,794	25,519	30,889	36,340	45,569	644	74
		4,043	4,319	5,062	5,902	7,004	7,640	8,832	258	75
15,832	16,793	17,551	20,836	25,195	28,232	29,491	20,856	795	76
9,848	11,009	12,882	18,245	23,948	15,855	19,673	25,567	466	77
12,826	15,489	16,262	23,380	31,483	40,371	51,945	54,674	1,043	78
14,495	16,746	15,718	21,714	25,363	33,163	36,442	44,149	573	79
13,870	14,589	16,810	19,965	24,123	31,066	37,521	44,062	483	80
13,550	14,573	13,121	15,198	18,770	25,104	28,385	31,426	547	81
14,585	16,624	16,436	22,894	25,096	26,380	29,982	36,002	921	82
					12,553	15,363	15,600	387	83
6,922	7,801	8,315	10,505	12,136	15,220	19,909	27,429	413	84
9,206	10,402	11,208	15,353	17,199	19,866	20,151	20,555	472	85
18,443	10,380	11,252	15,302	19,281	25,515	29,705	32,464	531	86
			3,784	6,577	8,401	10,403	15,224	560	87
		3,536	5,340	5,884	6,620	7,194	9,303	371	88
5,133	4,914	4,173	4,515	4,225	4,980	5,219	4,849	397	89
10,151	11,202	12,217	18,056	21,259	27,150	33,277	36,029	561	90
				17,581	16,684	19,425	22,799	276	91
24,888	28,627	35,617	47,939	49,207	54,626	63,229	75,155	811	92
13,912	15,726	17,768	22,619	19,360	19,151	20,296	21,593	432	93
5,664	6,357	6,516	8,928	10,200	10,608	11,062	11,429	354	94
3,400	4,957	5,287	8,460	10,614	13,117	13,556	13,447	330	95
12,486	14,905	18,144	24,951	26,100	31,356	35,698	43,640	597	96
12,899	14,749	15,539	19,181	22,675	26,872	30,282	32,644	718	97
		9,720	12,258	16,064	18,644	23,596	28,269	36,813	392	98
		10,714	10,697	12,420	13,790	14,083	15,428	16,394	334	99
8,204	8,655	5,909	7,694	9,490	11,464	12,072	15,083	302	100
869,039	992,622	1,071,361	1,399,750	1,617,947	1,893,810	2,206,287	2,559,123	48,580	

POPULATION OF NORTH CAROLINA CITIES AND TOWNS
1900-1920

City or Town	County	1920	1910	1900
Abbottsburg	Bladen	78	159	
Aberdeen	Moore	858	794	559
Acme	Columbus	183		
Advance	Davie	280	283	273
Ahoskie	Hertford	1,429	924	302
Albemarle	Stanly	2,691	2,116	1,382
Alexander*	Buncombe		118	
Almond	Swain	146	98	
Andrews	Cherokee	1,634	936	
Angier	Harnett	375	224	
Ansonville*	Anson	486	486	
Apex	Wake	926	684	349
Archdale	Randolph	178	145	182
Arden	Buncombe		154	137
Asheboro	Randolph	2,559	1,865	992
Asheville	Buncombe	28,504	18,762	14,694
Atkinson	Pender	296	115	
Atlantic	Carteret	610	524	
Aulander	Bertie	803	543	342
Aurora	Beaufort	524	440	314
Autryville	Sampson	99	77	61
Ayden	Pitt	1,673	990	557
Bailey	Nash	518	195	
Bakersville	Mitchell	332	416	511
Banner Elk	Avery	264		
Bath	Beaufort	274	283	400
Battleboro	Edgecombe and Nash	309	244	229
Bayboro	Pamlico	349	370	292
Beargrass	Martin	108	59	
Beaufort	Carteret	2,968	2,483	2,195
Belhaven	Beaufort	1,816	2,863	383
Belmont	Gaston	2,941	1,176	145
Bennett	Chatham	190		
Benson	Johnston	1,123	800	384
Benton Heights	Union	324		
Bessemer City	Gaston	2,476	1,529	1,100
Bethel	Pitt	817	569	457
Beulahville	Duplin	354		
Big Lick*	Stanly		192	132
Biltmore	Buncombe	172	173	71
Biscoe	Montgomery	755	697	
Black Creek	Wilson	274	219	196
Black Mountain	Buncombe	531	314	200
Bladenboro	Bladen	459	276	
Blowing Rock	Watauga	338	264	334
Boardman	Columbus	828	796	604
Bolivia	Brunswick	199		
Bolton	Columbus	699		
Bonlee	Chatham	178		
Bonsal*	Chatham and Wake		85	
Boone	Watauga	374	179	155
Boonville	Yadkin	162	28	183
Bostic	Rutherford	206	209	97
Bowdens	Duplin	418		
Brevard	Transylvania	1,658	919	584
Bridgersville*	Wilson		50	42
Bridgeton	Craven	548	348	
Broadway	Lee	250	149	
Brookford	Catawba	709	725	
Bryson	Swain	882	612	417
Buie	Robeson	78	66	
Buie's Creek	Harnett	291	249	
Bunn	Franklin	150		

Towns marked * are not listed in U. S. Census, 1920.

POPULATION OF CITIES AND TOWNS—Continued

City or Town	County	1920	1910	1900
Burgaw	Pender	1,040	956	387
Burlington	Alamance	5,952	4,808	3,692
Burnsville*	Yancey		422	267
Calypso	Duplin	405		
Cameron	Moore	241	259	218
Candor	Montgomery	267	160	
Canton	Haywood	2,584	1,393	250
Carrboro	Orange	1,129		
Carthage	Moore	962	863	665
Cary	Wake	615	383	333
Castalia	Nash	263	219	163
Catawba	Catawba	250	222	169
Cerro Gordo	Columbus	262	323	123
Chadbourn	Columbus	1,121	1,242	243
Chapel Hill	Orange	1,483	1,149	1,099
Charlotte	Mecklenburg	46,338	34,014	18,091
Cherry	Washington	99	76	
Cherryville	Gaston	1,884	1,153	1,008
China Grove	Rowan	1,027	852	887
Chocowinity*	Beaufort		127	
Claremont	Catawba	435	297	160
Clarendon	Columbus	135	147	
Clarkton	Bladen	368	276	
Clayton	Johnston	1,423	1,441	754
Cleveland	Rowan	366	426	198
Clinton	Sampson	2,410	1,401	958
Clyde	Haywood	363	344	244
Coats	Harnett	526	160	
Colerain	Bertie	215	189	207
Collettsville	Caldwell	123	80	57
Columbia	Tyrrell	738	818	382
Columbus	Polk	168	122	334
Concord	Cabarrus	9,903	8,715	7,910
Conetoe	Edgecombe	160	158	132
Conover	Catawba	684	421	443
Contentnea*	Greene		216	
Conway	Northampton	294		
Cornelius	Mecklenburg	1,141	833	
Council	Bladen	92	74	
Cove City	Craven	258	308	
Creedmoor	Granville	392	324	
Creswell	Washington	393	329	224
Crouse	Lincoln	209	175	
Culberson	Cherokee	190		
Cumberland	Cumberland	80	300	343
Dallas	Gaston	1,397	1,065	544
Davidson	Mecklenburg	1,156	1,056	904
Delco	Columbus	210		
Denton	Davidson	559	520	
Denver	Lincoln	243	282	199
Dillsboro	Jackson	228	277	279
Dobson	Surry	368	360	327
Dover	Craven	670	737	
Drexel	Burke	392		
Dublin	Bladen	99		
Dudley	Wayne	210	164	
Dunn	Harnett	2,805	1,823	1,072
Durham	Durham	21,719	18,241	6,679
East Bend	Yadkin	508	522	144
East Kings Mountain	Gaston	835	383	
East Laurinburg	Scotland	511	577	
East Lumberton	Robeson	1,044	884	

Towns marked * are not listed in U. S. Census, 1920.

POPULATION OF CITIES AND TOWNS—Continued

City or Town	County	1920	1910	1900
East Spencer	Rowan	2,239	1,729	
Edenton	Chowan	2,777	2,789	3,046
Edwards	Beaufort	153	171	99
Elizabeth City	Pasquotank	8,925	8,412	6,348
Elizabethtown	Bladen	335	117	144
Elk Park*	Avery	452	377	498
Elkin	Surry	1,195	886	860
Ellenboro	Rutherford	383	293	172
Ellerbee	Richmond	473		
Elon College	Alamance	425	200	638
Enfield	Halifax	1,648	1,167	361
Enochsville*	Rowan		81	93
Eureka	Wayne	187	162	123
Everetts	Martin	230	146	127
Evergreen	Columbus	139	248	
Fair Bluff	Columbus	397	441	328
Fairmont	Robeson	1,000	730	432
Faison	Duplin	477	519	308
Faith	Rowan	348	352	
Falcon	Cumberland	200		
Falkland	Pitt	198	132	139
Farmville	Pitt	1,780	816	262
Fayetteville	Cumberland	8,877	7,045	4,670
Forest City	Rutherford	2,312	1,592	1,090
Forestville*	Wake		137	157
Fountain	Pitt	243	189	
Four Oaks	Johnston	583	329	171
Franklin	Macon	773	379	335
Franklinsville	Randolph	631		
Franklinton	Franklin	1,058	809	761
Fremont	Wayne	1,294	951	435
Fuquay Springs	Wake	555	127	
Garland	Sampson	301		
Garner Springs	Wake	376	281	
Garysburg	Northampton	263	169	269
Gastonia	Gaston	12,871	5,759	4,610
Gatesville*	Gates		203	200
Germantown	Stokes	132	154	129
Gibson	Scotland	264		
Gibsonville	Alamance-Guilford	1,302	1,162	521
Glen Alpine	Burke	346	308	137
Glenwood	McDowell	132	149	
Godwin	Cumberland	90	102	
Gold Hill	Rowan	261	304	514
Gold Point	Martin	130	126	124
Goldsboro	Wayne	11,296	6,107	5,877
Goldston	Chatham	239	240	
Graham	Alamance	2,366	2,504	2,052
Granite Falls	Caldwell	1,101	381	277
Granite Quarry	Rowan	466	363	
Greensboro	Guilford	19,861	15,895	10,035
Greenville	Pitt	5,772	4,101	2,565
Grifton	Pitt	375	294	229
Grimesland	Pitt	463	339	277
Grover	Cleveland	296	209	174
Halifax	Halifax	299	314	306
Hamilton	Martin	474	452	493
Hamlet	Richmond	3,808	2,173	639
Hampton	Rutherford	175	205	
Hardin Mills*	Gaston		230	205
Harrellsville	Hertford	131	140	109
Hassell	Martin	85	90	

Towns marked * not listed in the U. S. Census, 1920

POPULATION OF CITIES AND TOWNS—Continued

City or Town	County	1920	1910	1900
Hayesville	Clay	257		
Haywood	Chatham	141	162	
Hazelwood	Haywood	484	428	
Henderson	Vance	5,222	4,503	3,746
Hendersonville	Henderson	3,720	2,818	1,917
Hertford	Perquimans	1,501	1,844	1,382
Hickory	Catawba	5,076	3,716	2,525
High Point	Guilford	14,302	9,525	4,163
Highland	Catawba	1,062	487	
Highlands	Macon	313	267	249
Hildebrand	Burke	172	440	164
Hillsboro	Orange	1,180	857	707
Hobgood	Halifax	336	165	122
Hoffman	Richmond	385	175	184
Holly Springs	Wake	353	264	249
Hollyville	Pamlico	107	126	
Hookerton	Greene	294	204	139
Hope Mills	Cumberland	783	964	881
Hot Springs	Madison	495	443	445
Hudson	Caldwell	403	411	
Huntersville	Mecklenburg	833	594	543
Icemorlee	Union	447	298	
Indian Trail	Union	224	154	
Ingold*	Sampson		124	86
Iron Station	Lincoln	223	107	
Jackson	Northampton	579	527	444
Jacksonville	Onslow	656	505	309
Jamesville	Martin	389	398	235
Jason*	Greene		60	
Jefferson	Ashe	196	184	230
Jonesboro	Lee	886	799	640
Jonesville	Yadkin	787	624	
Jupiter	Buncombe	87	441	127
Kelford	Bertie	223	316	167
Kenansville	Duplin	302	270	274
Kenly	Johnston	827	726	260
Kernersville	Forsyth	1,219	1,128	652
Keyser	Moore	113	170	180
Kings Mountain	Cleveland-Gaston	2,800	2,218	2,062
Kinston	Lenoir	9,771	6,995	4,106
Kittrell	Vance	223	212	168
LaGrange	Lenoir	1,399	1,007	853
Lake Waccamaw	Columbus	237		
Landis	Rowan	972	137	
Lasker	Northampton	196	203	124
Lattimore	Cleveland	262	297	108
Laurinburg	Scotland	2,643	2,322	1,334
Lawndale	Cleveland	774	568	
Leaksville	Rockingham	1,606	1,127	688
Leechville*	Beaufort		154	100
Leicester*	Buncombe		153	120
Lenoir	Caldwell	3,748	3,364	1,296
Lewarae	Richmond	124	279	
Lewiston	Bertie	214	262	163
Lexington	Davidson	5,254	4,163	1,254
Liberty	Randolph	636	471	301
Lilesville	Anson	440	386	213
Lillington	Harnett	593	380	65
Lincolnton	Lincoln	3,390	2,413	828
Linden	Cumberland	194		
Littleton	Halifax-Warren	1,040	1,152	

Towns marked * are not listed in the U. S. Census, 1920

POPULATION OF CITIES AND TOWNS—Continued

City or Town	County	1920	1910	1900
Locust	Stanly	95		
Longview	Catawba	755	243	
Louisburg	Franklin	1,954	1,775	1,178
Lowell	Gaston	1,151	876	290
Lucama	Wilson	316	266	236
Lumber Bridge	Robeson	202	165	181
Lumberton	Robeson	2,691	2,230	849
McAdenville	Gaston	1,162	983	1,144
McDonalds	Robeson	120		
McFarland	Anson	219	186	112
Maccelsfield	Edgecombe	294		
Macon	Warren	149	189	157
Madison	Rockingham	1,247	1,033	813
Magnolia	Duplin	694	653	454
Maiden	Catawba	1,266	664	614
Manly	Moore	141	220	176
Manteo	Dare	394	408	312
Mapleton	Hertford	99	52	
Marble	Cherokee	166		
Margarettsville	Northampton	147	107	123
Marietta	Robeson	85		
Marion	McDowell	1,784	1,519	1,116
Marlboro*	Pitt		225	111
Mars Hill	Madison	364	301	289
Marshall	Madison	748	802	337
Marshville	Union	828	499	349
Matthews	Mecklenburg	310	396	378
Maupin*	Pitt		141	
Maury	Greene	61		
Maxton	Robeson	1,397	1,321	935
Mayodan	Rockingham	1,886	874	904
Maysville	Jones	536	345	98
Mebane	Alamance-Orange	1,351	693	218
Merry Oaks	Chatham	118	88	
Micro	Johnston	183	74	61
Middleburg	Vance	104	117	169
Middlesex	Nash	697	467	
Milton	Caswell	375	419	490
Milwaukee	Northampton	197		
Mineral Springs	Union	84	86	
Mint Hill*	Mecklenburg		194	192
Mocksville	Davie	1,146	1,063	745
Moncure	Chatham	136	100	
Monroe	Union	4,084	4,082	2,427
Montezuma	Mitchell	167	254	219
Mooresboro	Cleveland	228	198	144
Mooresville	Iredell	4,315	3,400	1,533
Morehead City	Carteret	2,958	2,039	1,379
Morganton	Burke	2,867	2,712	1,928
Morrisville	Wake	166	151	100
Mortimer	Caldwell	88	261	
Morven	Anson	634	498	447
Mount Airy	Surry	4,752	3,844	2,680
Mount Gilead	Montgomery	975	723	395
Mount Holly	Gaston	1,160	526	630
Mount Olive	Wayne	2,297	1,071	617
Mount Pleasant	Cabarrus	770	753	444
Mountain Island*	Gaston		347	450
Murfreesboro	Hertford	621	809	657
Murphy	Cherokee	1,314	977	604
Nashville	Nash	939	750	479
Nebo	McDowell	243	160	

Towns marked * are not listed in the U. S. Census, 1920.

POPULATION OF CITIES AND TOWNS—Continued

City or Town	County	1920	1910	1900
New Hill*	Wake		95	
Newland	Avery	289		
New London	Stanly	228	342	299
New Bern	Craven	12,198	9,961	8,090
Newport	Carteret	401	324	328
Newton	Catawba	3,021	2,316	1,583
Newton Grove	Sampson	125	75	75
Norlina	Warren	673		
North Lumberton	Robeson	367		
North Wilkesboro	Wilkes	2,363	1,902	918
Norwood	Stanly	1,224	928	663
Oakboro	Stanly	282		
Oak City	Martin	397	254	115
Oakley	Pitt	49	57	
Old Fort	McDowell	961	778	253
Ore Hill*	Chatham		94	
Oriental	Pamlico	607	645	300
Orrum	Robeson	86	214	
Oxford	Granville	3,606	3,018	2,059
Pactolus	Pitt	240	154	52
Palmyra	Halifax	103	94	134
Pantego	Beaufort	335	324	253
Parkersburg	Sampson	76	67	57
Parkton	Robeson	382	219	
Parmele	Martin	355	272	336
Patterson	Caldwell	183	86	
Peachland	Anson	196	232	156
Pee Dee	Richmond	858	628	
Pembroke	Robeson	329	258	
Pendleton*	Northampton		62	56
Pikeville	Wayne	353	240	168
Pilot Mountain	Surry	707	652	710
Pine Level	Johnston	373	394	266
Pine Bluff	Moore	165	92	
Pinetops	Edgecombe	465	244	
Pinetown	Beaufort	352	412	
Pineville	Mecklenburg	650	688	585
Pink Hill	Lenoir	166	58	
Pittsboro	Chatham	581	502	424
Plymouth	Washington	1,817	2,165	1,044
Polkton	Anson	575	287	276
Pollocksville	Jones	339	227	198
Powellsville	Bertie	157	75	44
Princeton	Johnston	403	354	284
Princeville	Edgecombe	562	627	552
Proctorville	Robeson	204		
Raeford	Hoke	1,235	580	
Raleigh	Wake	27,076	19,218	13,643
Ramseur	Randolph	1,044	1,022	769
Randleman	Randolph	1,967	1,950	2,190
Red Springs	Robeson	1,048	1,089	858
Reidsville	Rockingham	5,335	4,828	3,262
Rennert	Robeson	292	1,179	133
Rhodhiss	Caldwell	855	370	
Rich Square	Northampton	475	367	232
Richfield	Stanly	177	210	73
Richlands	Onslow	548	115	160
Ringwood*	Halifax		147	98
Roanoke Rapids	Halifax	2,369	1,670	1,009
Robbinsville	Graham	119	122	

Towns marked * are not listed in the U.S. Census, 1920.

POPULATION OF CITIES AND TOWNS—Continued

City or Town	County	1920	1910	1900
Roberdel	Richmond	476	422	
Robersonville	Martin	1,199	646	275
Rockingham	Richmond	2,509	2,155	1,507
Rockwell	Rowan	453	249	
Rocky Mount	Edgecombe-Nash	12,742	8,051	2,937
Rocky Mount Mills	Nash	833	480	605
Rolesville*	Wake		170	155
Roper	Washington	1,043	819	
Rose Hill	Duplin	516	364	
Roseboro	Sampson	719	183	63
Rosman	Transylvania	527	145	
Rowland	Robeson	767	787	357
Roxboro	Person	1,651	1,425	1,021
Roxobel	Bertie	330	494	227
Royall Cotton Mills	Wake	442	437	
Rutherford College	Burke	275	229	
Rutherfordton	Rutherford	1,693	1,062	880
St. Pauls	Robeson	1,147	419	
Salem†	Forsyth		5,533	3,642
Salemburg	Sampson	245		
Salisbury	Rowan	13,884	7,153	6,277
Saluda	Polk	549	235	211
Sanford	Lee	2,977	2,282	1,044
Saratoga*	Wilson		136	123
Scotland Neck	Halifax	2,061	1,726	1,348
Seaboard*	Northampton		280	287
Seagrove	Randolph	189		
Selma	Johnston	1,661	1,331	816
Severn	Northampton	284		
Shallotte	Brunswick	174	139	149
Sharpsburg	Nash	334	121	
Shelby	Cleveland	3,609	3,127	1,874
Shelmerdine	Pitt	93	315	
Shore*	Yadkin		308	
Siler City	Chatham	1,253	895	440
Smithfield	Johnston	1,895	1,347	764
Snow Hill	Greene	700	450	405
South Biltmore	Buncombe	245	238	312
South Creek	Beaufort	326		
South Mills	Camden	373	390	
South Wadesboro	Anson	293	202	154
Southern Pines	Moore	743	542	517
Southport	Brunswick	1,664	1,484	1,336
Sparta	Alleghany	159	199	501
Spencer	Rowan	2,510	1,915	
Spring Hope	Nash	1,221	1,246	666
Spruce Pine	Mitchell	717		
Staley	Randolph	157		
Stanley	Gaston	584	321	441
Stantonsburg	Wilson	424	204	
Star	Montgomery	467	239	211
Statesville	Iredell	7,895	4,599	3,141
Stedman	Cumberland	121		
Stem	Granville	245		
Stokes	Pitt	138	79	
Stokesdale	Guilford	179	159	
Stoneville	Rockingham	472	404	
Stonewall	Pamlico	218	161	168
Stouts*	Union		82	
Stovall	Granville	414	305	
Swan Quarter	Hyde	184	185	
Swansboro	Onslow	420	390	265
Sylva	Jackson	863	698	281
Tabor	Columbus	782	418	
Tarboro	Edgecombe	4,568	4,129	2,499
Taylorsville	Alexander	1,122	662	413

Towns marked * are not listed in the U. S. Census, 1920.
†Reported under Winston-Salem.

POPULATION OF CITIES AND TOWNS—Continued

City or Town	County	1920	1910	1900
Teacheys	Duplin	164	154	
Thomasville	Davidson	5,676	3,877	751
Tillery*	Halifax		269	258
Todd	Ashe	92		
Toisnot‡	Wilson		590	560
Townsville	Vance	206		
Trenton	Jones	488	334	338
Trinity	Randolph	400	332	274
Troutman	Iredell	342	230	
Troy	Montgomery	1,102	1,055	878
Tryon	Polk	1,067	700	324
Tunis	Hertford	142	43	
Turkey	Sampson	146		
Union	Hertford	147	139	176
Union Mills	Rutherford	156	155	
Unionville	Union	135		
Vanceboro	Craven	540	392	294
Vandemere	Pamlico	308	296	169
Vass	Moore	467	273	
Vaughan	Warren	273	420	
Waco	Cleveland	189	185	160
Wade	Cumberland	190		
Wadesboro	Anson	2,648	2,376	1,546
Wagram	Scotland	174		
Wake Forest	Wake	1,425	1,443	823
Wakefield*	Wake		287	112
Wallace	Duplin	648	444	218
Walnut*	Madison		215	
Walnut Cove	Stokes	651	480	336
Walstonburg	Greene	158	127	
Warrenton	Warren	927	807	836
Warsaw	Duplin	1,108	723	579
Washington	Beaufort	6,314	6,211	4,842
Watha	Pender	181	160	
Waxhaw	Union	750	602	752
Waynesville	Haywood	1,942	2,008	1,307
Weaverville	Buncombe	606	442	329
Webster	Jackson	74	227	
Weldon	Halifax	1,872	1,999	1,433
Wendell	Wake	1,239	759	
West Hickory	Catawba	1,296	846	243
West Jefferson	Ashe	462		
West Lumberton*	Robeson		234	
Westray	Nash	48	46	
Whitakers	Edgecombe-Nash	723	755	388
Whitehall	Wayne	164	179	114
Whiteville	Columbus	1,664	1,368	643
Whittier	Jackson-Swain	264	216	
Wilbanks	Wilson		45	46
Wilkesboro	Wilkes	844	799	635
Williams*	Yadkin		53	
Williamston	Martin	1,800	1,574	942
Wilmington	New Hanover	33,372	25,748	20,976
Wilson	Wilson	10,612	6,717	3,525
Windsor	Bertie	1,210	684	597
Winfall	Perquimans	288	289	222
Wingate	Union	470	353	
Winston-Salem	Forsyth	48,395	17,167	10,008
Winterville	Pitt	650	484	243
Winton	Hertford	489	624	688
Wood	Franklin	193		
Woodland	Northampton	400	342	242
Woodleaf*	Rowan		187	
Woodville	Bertie	384		
Worthville	Randolph	397	393	467
Wrightsville Beach	New Hanover	20	54	22
Yadkin College*	Davidson		150	210
Yadkinville	Yadkin	145	132	292
Yanceyville	Caswell		338	
Youngsville	Franklin	414	434	345
Zebulon	Wake	953	483	

Towns marked * are not listed in the U. S. Census, 1920
‡ Reported under Elm City

NORTH CAROLINA COUNTIES AND COUNTY SEATS

Names	Date of formation	Formed from	Named for	County Seats
Alamance	1849	Orange, Caldwell and Wilkes	Indian word	Graham
Alexander	1847	Iredell, Caldwell and Wilkes	Wm. J. Alexander	Taylorsville
Alleghany	1859	Ashe	Indian tribe	Sparta
Anson	1749	Bladen	George, Lord Anson	Wadesboro
Ashe	1799	Wilkes	Samuel Ashe	Jefferson
Avery	1911	Mitchell, Watauga and Caldwell	Waightstill Avery	Newland
Beaufort	1705	Bath	Henry Charles Somerset, Duke of Beaufort	Washington
Bertie	1722	Bath	James and Henry Bertie	Windsor
Bladen	1734	Bath	Martin Bladen	Elizabethtown
Brunswick	1764	New Hanover and Bladen	House of Brunswick	Southport
Buncombe	1791	Burke and Rutherford	Edward Buncombe	Asheville
Burke	1777	Rowan	Dr. Thomas Burke	Morganton
Cabarrus	1792	Mecklenburg	Stephen Cabarrus	Concord
Caldwell	1841	Burke and Wilkes	Joseph Caldwell	Lenoir
Camden	1777	Pasquotank	Charles Pratt, Earl of Camden	Camden Courthouse
Carteret	1723	Bath	Sir John Carteret	Beaufort
Caswell	1777	Orange	Richard Caswell	Yanceyville
Catawba	1842	Lincoln	Indian tribe	Newton
Chatham	1770	Orange	William Pitt, Earl of Chatham	Pittsboro
Cherokee	1839	Macon	Indian tribe	Murphy
Chowan	1672	Albemarle	Indian tribe	Edenton
Clay	1861	Cherokee	Henry Clay	Hayesville
Cleveland	1841	Rutherford and Lincoln	Benjamin Cleveland	Shelby
Columbus	1808	Bladen and Brunswick	Christopher Columbus	Whiteville
Craven	1712	Bath	William, Lord Craven	New Bern
Cumberland	1754	Bladen	William Augustus, Duke of Cumberland	Fayetteville
Currituck	1672	Albemarle	Indian tribe	Currituck Courthouse
Dare	1870	Currituck, Tyrrell and Hyde	Virginia Dare	Manteo
Davidson	1822	Rowan	William Lee Davidson	Lexington
Davie	1836	Rowan	William R. Davie	Mocksville
Duplin	1749	New Hanover	George Henry Hay, Lord Duplin	Kenansville
Durham	1881	Orange and Wake	Town of Durham	Durham
Edgecombe	1735	Bertie	Richard Edgecombe, Baron Edgecombe	Tarboro
Forsyth	1849	Stokes	Benjamin Forsyth, U. S. A.	Winston-Salem
Franklin	1779	Bute	Benjamin Franklin	Louisburg
Gaston	1846	Lincoln	William Gaston	Dallas

Counties and County Seats

County	Date	Formed from	Named for	County Seat
Gates	1778	Chowan, Perquimans and Hertford	Horatio Gates	Gatesville
Graham	1872	Cherokee	William A. Graham	Robbinsville
Granville	1746	Edgecombe	John Carteret, Earl Granville	Oxford
Greene	1799	Glasgow	Nathaniel Greene	Snow Hill
Guilford	1770	Rowan and Orange	Francis North, Earl of Guilford	Greensboro
Halifax	1758	Edgecombe	George Montague Dunk, Earl of Halifax	Halifax
Harnett	1855	Cumberland	Cornelius Harnett	Lillington
Haywood	1808	Buncombe	John Haywood	Waynesville
Henderson	1838	Buncombe	Leonard Henderson	Hendersonville
Hertford	1759	Chowan, Bertie and Northampton	Francis Seymour Conway, Marquis of Hertford	Winton
Hoke	1911	Cumberland and Robeson	Robert F. Hoke	Raeford
Hyde	1705	Bath	Edward Hyde	Swan Quarter
Iredell	1788	Rowan	James Iredell	Statesville
Jackson	1851	Haywood and Macon	Andrew Jackson	Webster
Johnston	1746	Craven	Gabriel Johnston	Smithfield
Jones	1778	Craven	Willie Jones	Trenton
Lee	1907	Chatham and Moore	Robert E. Lee	Sanford
Lenoir	1791	Dobbs and Craven	William Lenoir	Kinston
Lincoln	1779	Tryon	Benjamin Lincoln	Lincolnton
Macon	1828	Haywood	Nathaniel Macon	Franklin
Madison	1851	Buncombe and Yancey	James Madison	Marshall
Martin	1774	Halifax and Tyrrell	Josiah Martin	Williamston
McDowell	1842	Rutherford and Burke	Joseph McDowell	Marion
Mecklenburg	1762	Anson	Princess Charlotte of Mecklenburg	Charlotte
Mitchell	1861	Yancey, Watauga, Caldwell, Burke and McDowell	Dr. Elisha Mitchell	Bakersville
Montgomery	1778	Anson	Richard Montgomery	Troy
Moore	1784	Cumberland	Capt. Alfred Moore	Carthage
Nash	1777	Edgecombe	Francis Nash	Nashville
New Hanover	1729	Bath	Hanover, whence George I of England came	Wilmington
Northampton	1741	Bertie	George, Earl of Northampton	Jackson
Onslow	1734	Bath	Arthur Onslow	Jacksonville
Orange	1752	Granville, Johnston and Bladen	William, of Orange	Hillsboro
Pamlico	1872	Craven and Beaufort	Indian tribe	Bayboro
Pasquotank	1672	Albemarle	Indian tribe	Elizabeth City
Pender	1875	New Hanover	William D. Ponder	Burgaw
Perquimans	1672	Albemarle	Indian tribe	Hertford
Person	1791	Caswell	Thomas Person	Roxboro
Pitt	1760	Beaufort	William Pitt	Greenville
Polk	1855	Rutherford and Henderson	William Polk	Columbus
Randolph	1779	Guilford	Peyton Randolph	Asheboro
Richmond	1779	Anson	Charles Lennox, Duke of Richmond	Rockingham

COUNTIES AND COUNTY SEATS — Continued

Names	Date of Formation	Formed from	Named for	County Seat
Robeson	1786	Bladen	Thomas Robeson	Lumberton
Rockingham	1785	Guilford	Charles Watson Wentworth, Marquis of Rockingham	Wentworth
Rowan	1753	Anson	Matthew Rowan	Salisbury
Rutherford	1779	Tryon and Burke	General Griffith Rutherford	Rutherfordton
Sampson	1784	Duplin and New Hanover	Colonel Sampson	Clinton
Scotland	1899	Richmond	Scotland	Laurinburg
Stanly	1841	Montgomery	John Stanly	Albemarle
Stokes	1789	Surry	Colonel John Stokes	Danbury
Surry	1770	Rowan	Charles Howard, Earl of Surry	Dobson
Swain	1871	Jackson and Macon	David Lowrie Swain	Bryson City
Transylvania	1861	Henderson and Jackson	Derived from two Latin words, "trans" across, "Sylva" woods	Brevard
Tyrrell	1729	Albemarle	Sir John Tyrrell	Columbia
Union	1842	Anson and Mecklenburg		Monroe
Vance	1881	Granville, Warren and Franklin	Zebulon B. Vance	Henderson
Wake	1770	Johnston, Cumberland and Orange	Margaret Wake	Raleigh
Warren	1779	Bute	George Joseph Warren	Warrenton
Washington	1799	Tyrrell	George Washington	Plymouth
Watauga	1849	Ashe, Wilkes, Caldwell and Yancey	Indian tribe	Boone
Wayne	1779	Dobbs and Craven	General Anthony Wayne	Goldsboro
Wilkes	1777	Surry and Burke	John Wilkes	Wilkesboro
Wilson	1855	Edgecombe, Nash, Johnston and Wayne	Louis D. Wilson	Wilson
Yadkin	1850	Surry	Yadkin River	Yadkinville
Yancey	1833	Burke and Buncombe	Bartlett Yancey	Burnsville

ECONOMIC DEVELOPMENT OF NORTH CAROLINA

The following table is copied by permission of the publishers from page 155 of the copyrighted publication: *Blue Book of Southern Progress*, 1924. Published by *Manufacturers Record*, Baltimore, Md.

Land area, 48,740 square miles

	1900	1910	1922	1923
Population	1,803,810	2,206,287		*2,559,123
Manufacturers:				
Capital	$ 68,283,005	$ 217,185,588	$ 669,144,000	
Production	$ 85,274,083	$ 216,656,055	$ *943,808,000	$ †965,148,000
Mines and quarries:				
Capital		$ 5,985,412		$ *2,250,434
Products		$ 1,358,617		$ *2,741,583
Cotton mills:				
Spindles, active	1,134,909	3,163,199	5,281,268	5,424,096
Looms, active	25,469	55,000	74,043	76,974
Cotton used, pounds	190,139,000	317,467,000	581,852,000	646,921,000
Pig iron made, tons	*38,049	‡49,490		
Lumber cut, feet	1,278,399,000	1,824,722,000	936,248,000	
Mineral products, value	$ 1,458,848	$ 2,616,131	$ 45,456,479	$ †††7,268,000
Iron ore mined, tons	**	65,278	17,279	60,000
Farm crops, value	$ 68,625,000	$ 131,072,000	$ 344,812,000	$ 136,800,000
Cotton crop, bales	550,000	706,000	852,000	1,020,000
Tobacco crop, pounds	127,503,000	138,813,163	252,500,000	386,400,000
Grain products:				
Corn, bushels	29,790,000	49,200,000	51,540,000	58,568,000
Wheat, bushels	5,961,000	6,817,000	5,100,000	6,038,000
Oats, bushels	5,046,000	4,022,000	4,620,000	5,082,000
Livestock:				
Cattle	625,000	701,000	639,000	631,000
Sheep	302,000	214,000	81,000	82,000
Swine	1,300,000	1,228,000	1,195,000	1,159,000
Railroad mileage	3,831	4,932	*5,522	†5,388
National banks:				
Resources	$ 15,362,182	$ 55,455,371	$ 170,685,000	$ 192,329,000
Capital	$ 3,043,500	$ 8,010,000	$ 13,310,000	$ 13,557,000
Deposits	$ 7,477,057	$ 26,268,062	$ 125,793,000	$ 125,170,000
Other banks, deposits	$ 9,280,798	$ 41,240,000	$ 182,216,000	$ 219,972,000
Common schools, expenditures	$ 950,300	$ 12,796,000	$ *12,148,000	$ †††22,079,000
Assessed value property	$ 306,579,715	$ 613,000,000	$ 2,576,368,000	

*Census 1920.   **Included with Georgia.   †1921.   ‡1908.   †††1922.   • Includes Missouri.

PART XIII

BIOGRAPHICAL SKETCHES

1. Executive Officials.
2. Justices of the Supreme Court.
3. Senators and Representatives in Congress.
4. Members of the General Assembly.

BIOGRAPHICAL SKETCHES

EXECUTIVE OFFICIALS

ANGUS WILTON McLEAN

GOVERNOR

Angus Wilton McLean, Democrat, of Robeson County, was born in Robeson County, April 20, 1870. Son of Archibald Alexander and Caroline (Purcell) McLean. Educated in McMillan Military School, Laurinburg High School, University of North Carolina (LL.B., 1892). Lawyer, formerly member of firm, McLean, Varser & McLean, Lumberton. President of National Bank of Lumberton, Robeson Development Company, McLean Trust Company, Atlantic Joint Stock Land Bank, Vice President Mansfield Cotton Mills, Jennings Cotton Mills. Chairman Robeson County Democratic Executive Committee, 1892. Member State Democratic Executive Committee, 1910-1921. Delegate to Democratic National Conventions, 1904 and 1912. Chairman Democratic Presidential Committee for North Carolina, 1912 and 1916. Member Democratic National Committee, 1916-1924. Director and Managing Director of War Finance Corporation, 1918-1922. Assistant Secretary of the Treasury of the United States in charge of customs and internal revenue (Wilson Administration). Member selective service Advisory Committee, 1917 and 1918. General Counsel in North Carolina for Alien Property Custodian, 1919. Organized Red Cross and Liberty Loan work in Robeson County. Chairman of the trustees of Flora MacDonald College. Trustee University of North Carolina. Member American Bar Association, North Carolina Bar Association (ex president), Clan McLean Association of Glasgow, American Academy of Political and Social Science, Scottish Society of America (ex president), Sigma Chi. Presbyterian. Married Margaret French of Lumberton, April 14, 1904. Address: Raleigh, N. C.

WILLIAM NASH EVERETT

SECRETARY OF STATE

William Nash Everett, Democrat, Secretary of State, was born in Rockingham, December 29, 1864. Son of William I. and Fannie (LeGrand) Everett. Attended Rockingham High School, 1882; University of North Carolina, 1886. Farmer and merchant. State Senator, 1917. Member House 1919, 1921, 1923. Appointed Secretary of State by Governor Morrison; elected, November 4, 1924. Methodist. Married Miss Lena Payne in 1888. Address: Raleigh, N. C.

BAXTER DURHAM

STATE AUDITOR

Baxter Durham, Democrat, was born in Durham, N. C., August 20, 1878. Son of Columbus and Lila (Walters) Durham. Attended public schools of Durham and Raleigh, 1884-1892; Raleigh Male Academy, 1892-1894; Wake Forest College, 1894-1895. Traveling Auditor, Department of State Auditor. Served as private, sergeant, captain and major in National Guard, 1907-1919. Elected State Auditor, November 2, 1920; reëlected, November 4, 1924. Baptist. Address: Raleigh, N. C.

BENJAMIN RICE LACY

STATE TREASURER

Benjamin R. Lacy, Democrat, of Wake County, was born in Raleigh, N. C., June 19, 1854. Son of Rev. Drury and Mary Rice Lacy, and a grandson of the Revs. Drury Lacy and Benjamin H. Rice. Both his grandfathers, his father, his brother and his son were Presbyterian ministers, and he is an elder in the First Presbyterian Church in the city of Raleigh. He attended the preparatory school of R. H. Graves, Graham, N. C., 1868; Bingham School, Mebane, N. C., 1869. Then served a regular apprenticeship as a machinist in the old Raleigh and Gaston shops, was general foreman of these shops for four years and ran a locomotive engine for fifteen years. He is a member of Division No. 339, Brotherhood of Locomotive Engineers, was a delegate to three Grand Conventions of the B. of L. E.; is a member of Manteo Lodge, Independent Order of Odd Fellows, also of Walnut Creek Council, No. 55, Jr. O. U. A. M. Is Past Worshipful Master of William G. Hill Lodge, No. 218, Raleigh, N. C., and Neuse Lodge, No. 97, Millbrook, N. C., A. F. & A. M., and is Grand Treasurer of the Grand Lodge. Was alderman of the city of Raleigh. State Commissioner of Labor and Printing for six years. Elected State Treasurer in 1900; reëlected in 1904, 1908, 1912, 1916, 1920, and 1924. Term expires 1928. Married, June 27, 1882, to Miss Mary Burwell. They have seven children. Address: Raleigh, N. C.

ARCH TURNER ALLEN

SUPERINTENDENT OF PUBLIC INSTRUCTION

Arch Turner Allen, Democrat, was born in Alexander County on January 10, 1875. Son of George J. and Mary Elizabeth (Campbell) Allen. Attended the one-teacher school at Rocky Springs. For one year was under the tutelage of Dr. Brantley York. Was prepared for college at the Vashti High School and the Patton School at Morganton. Graduated from the University of North Carolina in 1897. Member of the Phi Beta Kappa and Phi Delta Kappa. Spent one term at Columbia University. Principal of the Statesville Public Schools, 1897-1904; principal Washington, N. C., Public Schools, 1904-1905; principal Dilworth School, Charlotte, 1905-1907; superintendent of the Graham City Schools, 1907-1910; superintendent Salisbury City Schools, 1910-1917; member Text Book Commission, 1916; member State Board of Examiners and Institute Conductors, 1917-1919; secretary State Board of Examiners, 1919-1921; director Teacher Training, State Department of Education, 1921-1923; appointed Superintendent of Public Instruction, June 11, 1923, to fill unexpired term of Dr. Brooks; elected Superintendent of Public Instruction on November 4, 1924. Identified with the North Carolina Teachers' Assembly for many years. President of Department of City Superintendents in 1915; President of the N. C. Teachers Assembly in 1917; Secretary, 1919-1922. Married Miss Claribel McDowell, June 19, 1909. Two children, Arch Turner, Jr., and Elizabeth McDowell. Methodist; Jr. O. U. A. M.

DENNIS G. BRUMMITT
ATTORNEY-GENERAL

Dennis G. Brummitt, Democrat, of Granville County, was born on a farm in Granville County, February 7, 1881. Son of Thomas Jefferson and Caroline (Bradford) Brummitt. LL.B. of Wake Forest College, 1907. Secretary of Ganville County Democratic Executive Committee, 1908-1910; chairman, 1910-1914, 1922-1924. Member of State Democratic Executive Committee, 1913-1924. Mayor of Oxford, 1909-1913. Member Board of Town Commissioners, 1913-1915. Representative in General Assembly, 1915, 1917, 1919; speaker of House of Representatives, 1919. Trustee Oxford Graded Schools, 1921-1925. Democratic Elector, 1920. Trustee of State College, 1923-1925. Trustee Wake Forest College, 1925. Elected Attorney-General, 1924. Mason. Odd Fellow. W. O. W., M. W. A., Jr. O. U. A. M. Baptist. Married, June 25, 1912, Miss Kate Hays Fleming. Home address: Oxford, N. C.

WILLIAM A. GRAHAM
COMMISSIONER OF AGRICULTURE

William A. Graham, Democrat, of Lincoln County, was born at old Graham homestead in same county. Son of Major William A. and Julia (Lane) Graham. Attended Piedmont Seminary, Horner Military School, and University of North Carolina. Farmer. President Lincoln County Farmers' Alliance. State Senator from the Twenty-fifth Senatorial District, session 1923, Legislature. Chairman of Committee on Agriculture at that session. Appointed Commissioner of Agriculture by Governor Morrison, December 26, 1923, to fill unexpired term of his father, deceased. Elected, November 4, 1924, to succeed himself for a full term. Has been active in Democratic party all his life; been member of precinct executive committee since becoming twenty-one years of age, now chairman; member executive committee, Lincoln County, also of State Democratic Executive Committee. K. of P. Baptist. Member executive committee National and Southern Associations of Commissioners of Agriculture.

FRANKLIN DAVIS GRIST

COMMISSIONER OF LABOR AND PRINTING

Frank D. Grist, Democrat, was born at Lenoir, Caldwell County, July 23, 1891. Son of John Taylor and Mary Nancy (Davis) Grist. Elected Commissioner of Labor and Printing, 1924. Served in World War with First Regular Army division in France. Member House of Representatives, session 1923. Married in 1919 to Miss Jessie Deal. Two children. Address: Raleigh, N. C.

STACEY W. WADE

INSURANCE COMMISSIONER

Stacey W. Wade, Democrat, was born in Morehead City, N. C., August 18, 1875. Son of David B. and Sarah (Royal) Wade. Attended public and private schools of home town. Assistant principal clerk of the State Senate, 1903-05-07-08 and 09; City Clerk, 1906-08; Director of the Bank of Carteret, 1907-09; Auditor and member Finance Committee Atlantic and North Carolina Railroad Company, 1911-21; Chief Deputy Insurance Commissioner, 1909-21. Insurance Commissioner, *ex officio* Fire Marshal, January 1, 1921-25. President Southern Group of Securities Commissioners 1923. President of the Fire Marshals Association of North America, 1924. Vice President National Association of Securities Commissioners, 1923. Member Executive Committee of the National Convention of Insurance Commissioners. Reëlected for second term, 1924-1928. Knights Templar, Scottish Rite, Thirty Second Degree Mason. Methodist. Married Miss Clyde Mann, December, 1905; three children. Address: Raleigh, N. C.

RUFUS A. DOUGHTON

COMMISSIONER OF REVENUE

Rufus A. Doughton was born in Alleghany County, N. C., January 10, 1857. Son of J. Horton and Rebecca (Jones) Doughton. Educated at Independence (Va.) High School, 1876-1877; University of North Carolina. Studied law at University of North Carolina,

1880. Lawyer, farmer, and banker. President of Bank of Sparta. Representative in the General Assembly, 1887, 1889, 1891, 1903, 1907, 1909, 1911, 1913, 1915, 1917, 1919, and 1921. Lieutenant Governor, 1893-1897. Speaker of the House, 1891. Member of the State Highway Commission, but resigned that place upon entering upon his duties as Commissioner of Revenue to which he was appointed in January, 1923, by Governor Morrison. He was elected Commissioner of Revenue, November 4, 1924. Mason. Methodist. Married, January 3, 1883, Miss Sue B. Parks. Address: Raleigh, N. C.

JUSTICES OF THE SUPREME COURT

WALTER PARKER STACY
CHIEF JUSTICE

Walter Parker Stacy was born in Ansonville, N. C., December 26, 1884. Son of Rev. L. E. and Rosa (Johnson) Stacy. Attended Weaverville College (N. C.), 1895-1898; Morven (N. C.) High School, 1899-1902; University of North Carolina, degree of A.B., 1908; University of North Carolina Law School, 1908-1909. Member of North Carolina Bar Association. Represented New Hanover County in North Carolina General Assembly of 1915. Judge Superior Court, Eighth Judicial District, 1916-1920. Elected Associate Justice of the Supreme Court of North Carolina, 1920; appointed Chief Justice by Governor A. W. McLean, March 16, 1925, to succeed Chief Justice Hoke, resigned; nominated without opposition in the primary and elected to the same position for a term of eight years, 1926. President General Alumni Association, University of North Carolina, 1925. Lecturer, University of North Carolina Summer Law School, 1922, 1923, 1924, 1925; tendered deanship of the University of North Carolina Law School, 1923. LL.D. (University of North Carolina, 1923). Lecturer, Northwestern University School of Law, Summer Session, 1926. Democrat. Methodist. Residence: Wilmington, N. C. Office: Raleigh, N. C.

HERIOT CLARKSON
ASSOCIATE JUSTICE

Heriot Clarkson, Democrat, of Charlotte, N. C., was born at Kingville, Richland County, S. C., August 21, 1863. Son of Major William and Margaret S. (Simons) Clarkson. Educated at the Carolina Military Institute of Charlotte, University Law School at Chapel Hill. Licensed by the Supreme Court of North Carolina to practice law, 1884. Immediately thereafter began the practice of law at Charlotte, N. C. Alderman and Vice Mayor of Charlotte, 1887-88, same posts in 1891-92. In 1899 member of House of Representatives, known as "White Supremacy Legislature." City attorney of Charlotte, 1901-04. Twice codified the city ordinances of Charlotte, in 1887 and 1901; legal adviser under administration of Mayor T. L. Kirkpatrick. Solicitor of Twelfth Judicial District, 1904-10. Author of "The Hornet's Nest," appearing in the *North Carolina Booklet* of October, 1901. Delivered address to the Society of the Cincinnati on "The Heroic Incidents of the Life of General Francis Marion." On December 10, 1889, married Miss Mary Lloyd Osborne, of which union were born nine children. Mason; life member Lodge No. 31, A. F. and A. M. at Charlotte; Noble of the Mystic Shrine (Oasis Temple); Knight of Pythias; Jr. O. U. A. M. Member the Society of Sons of the Revolution, Society of the Cincinnati, and the Huguenot Society of South Carolina. At one time was lieutenant of the Hornet's Nest Riflemen of Charlotte. Thirty odd years director in the Charlotte Y. M. C. A. One of the original founders of the Crittendon Home and the Mecklenburg Industrial Home for Women. For many years a director of the Chamber of Commerce and "Made in the Carolinas" Exposition. Chairman Anti-Saloon League when the saloon was voted out of Charlotte, July 5, 1904. Also President Anti-Saloon League when the saloon and distillery were voted out of the State on May 27, 1908. Governor Robt. B. Glenn presented him with the pen with which he signed the Prohibition proclamation. Trustee State Association Y. M. C. A. of North Carolina. Was Chairman of the Good Roads Association Committee that drafted the tentative good roads act passed by the Legislature of 1921 substantially as drawn. He drafted the Mecklenburg Drainage Act and was the leader in establishing the Belmont Vocational School at Charlotte, the first of its kind in the State. Episcopalian; built St. Andrew's Chapel in Charlotte; vestryman and senior warden of St. Peter's Protestant Episcopal Church for many years. Appointed Justice of the Supreme Court of North Carolina by Governor Morrison, May 26, 1923; elected, November 2, 1926. Residence: Charlotte, N. C. Office: Raleigh, N. C.

GEORGE WHITFIELD CONNOR

ASSOCIATE JUSTICE

George W. Connor was born on October 24, 1872, at Wilson, N. C. Son of Henry Groves and Kate Whitfield Connor. Prepared for college by Rev. B. S. Bronson, Wilson, N. C.; University of North Carolina, class 1892, A.B. Member of House of Representatives from Wilson County, 1909, 1911, 1913; Speaker of House of Representatives, 1913. Judge Superior Court, 1913-1924. Appointed by Governor Morrison Associate Justice of the Supreme Court; elected at election of 1924.

WILLIAM JACKSON ADAMS

ASSOCIATE JUSTICE

William Jackson Adams, Democrat, Associate Justice of the Supreme Court, was born at Rockingham, January 27, 1860. Son of Rev. S. D. and Mary (Jackson) Adams. A.B. University of North Carolina, 1881; LL.D., 1924. Two-year law course at the University; admitted to the bar in 1883 and began practicing at Carthage. Member of the North Carolina House of Representatives in 1893; of the State Senate in 1895, and of the Board of Internal Improvements, 1899-1901. Appointed by Governor Glenn as Judge of the Superior Court for the unexpired term of Judge Walter H. Neal in December, 1908; elected to the same office in 1910 and in 1918 for a term each of eight years. Resigned in September, 1921, upon appointment by Governor Morrison as Associate Justice of the Supreme Court to fill the unexpired term of Justice W. R. Allen, deceased; elected to same office in 1922 for the unexpired term, and in 1926 for a full term. Member of the American and State Bar Associations. Married Miss Florence Wall, of Rockingham. Methodist. Home address: Carthage, N. C.; office, Raleigh, N. C.

WILLIS JAMES BROGDEN
ASSOCIATE JUSTICE

Willis James Brogden, Democrat, Associate Justice of the Supreme Court, was born in Goldsboro, October 18, 1877. Son of Willis H. and Virginia (Robinson) Brogden. Attended Goldsboro Graded Schools, 1891-1894; Ph.B., University of North Carolina, 1898; Trinity College and University Law School. Licensed to practice in 1907. Member American and North Carolina Bar Associations. Mayor of Durham, 1911-1915. A. F. & A. M.; Past Master Durham Lodge No. 352; Member Kiwanis Club. Appointed by Governor McLean as Associate Justice of the Supreme Court to fill the unexpired term of Judge Varser; elected to same office for the unexpired term, November 2, 1926. Baptist. Married Miss Lila Markham, January 9, 1917. Address: Durham, N. C.

UNITED STATES SENATORS

FURNIFOLD McLENDEL SIMMONS

F. M. Simmons, Democrat, of New Bern, Craven County, was born January 20, 1854, in the county of Jones. Educated at Wake Forest College and at Trinity College, graduating at Trinity College with the degree of A.B., in June, 1873. Was admitted to the bar in 1875, and practiced the profession of law until his election to the United States Senate in 1901. In 1886 was elected a member of the Fiftieth Congress from the Second Congressional District of North Carolina. In 1893 was appointed Collector of Internal Revenue for the fourth (the eastern) Collection District of North Carolina, and served in that office during the term of Mr. Cleveland. In the campaigns of 1892, 1898, 1900, 1902, 1904 and 1906, was chairman of the Democratic Executive Committee of the State. LL.D. of Trinity College, N. C., 1901; University of N. C., 1915. He was elected to the United States Senate to succeed Marion Butler, Populist, for the term beginning March 4, 1901, and reëlected in 1907, and again in 1913, having been chosen in the Democratic primary, November 5, 1912, over two opponents, Governor W. W. Kitchin and Chief Justice Walter Clark; Chairman of Finance Committee in the Sixty-third, Sixty-fourth and Sixty-fifth Congresses during Democratic control of the United States Senate. One of the authors of the Underwood-Simmons Tariff Act of 1913-1921, and of the revenue measures which provided for the financing of the World War on the part of the United States. In 1918, reëlected to the Senate for term, March 4, 1919 to March 3, 1925. Led the Democrats of the Senate in their great fights against the Republican Revenue Bills and the Fordney-McCumber Tariff Bill in 1921 and 1922. Member of Democratic National Senatorial Committee in campaign of 1922, and was offered its chairmanship but declined it. Author of the Simmons plan (Income Tax Rates now the law) adopted by the Republican Congress of 1924, defeating the Mellon plan proposed by the President and Secretary of the Treasury Mellon. Is now the senior Democratic member of the United States Senate in length of service, and is ranking minority member of the committee on Finance, member of the Steering Committee, the Committee on Commerce, Committee on Irrigation and Reclamation, and of other committees of the Senate. Was honored with the vote of North Carolina for the presidency of the United States in the Democratic National Convention of 1920. Was chosen as North Carolina member of the Democratic National Committee at the Democratic National Convention of 1924. Reëlected to the Senate for his fifth term (1925-1931) without opposition in his party. His majority in the general election, November 7, 1924, over his Republican opponent, was 111,011, the largest ever given in North Carolina to a Senatorial candidate.

LEE SLATER OVERMAN

Lee Slater Overman, Democrat, of Salisbury, was born January 3, 1854, in Salisbury, Rowan County. Graduated at Trinity College, North Carolina, with the degree of A.B., June, 1874; the degree of M.A. was conferred upon him two years later. Since that time the degree of LL.B., also degree of LL.D. conferred by the University of North Carolina in 1917; also LL.D. conferred by Davidson College, North Carolina, in 1922. Taught school two years. Was private secretary to Governor Zebulon B. Vance in 1877-78; private secretary to Governor Thomas J. Jarvis in 1879. Began the practice of law in his native town in 1880; was five times a member of the Legislature, sessions of 1883, 1885, 1887, 1893 and 1899. Was the unanimous choice of his party and elected Speaker of the House of Representatives, session of 1893. Was president of the North Carolina Railroad Company in 1894. Was the choice of the Democratic caucus for United States Senator in 1895, and defeated in open session by Hon. Jeter C. Pritchard, through a combination of Republicans and Populists. Was president of the Democratic State convention in 1900 and 1911. For ten years a member of the Board of Trustees of the State University; is also trustee of Trinity College. Was chosen Presidential Elector for the State-at-large in 1900. Married Miss Mary P. the eldest daughter of United States

Senator (afterwards Chief Justice) A. S. Merrimon, October 31, 1878. Was elected to the United States Senate to succeed Hon. Jeter C. Pritchard, Republican, for the term beginning March 4, 1903, and reëlected in 1909; was elected on November 3, 1914, for a third term, being the first Senator elected to the United States Senate by direct vote of the people of his State. Elected on the 2d day of November, 1920, for a fourth term; reëlected November 2, 1926, for a fifth term.

REPRESENTATIVES IN CONGRESS

LINDSAY CARTER WARREN

(First District—Counties: Beaufort, Camden, Chowan, Currituck, Dare, Gates, Hertford, Hyde, Martin, Pasquotank, Perquimans, Pitt, Tyrrell and Washington. Population (1920) 206,137.)

Lindsay Carter Warren, Democrat, was born at Washington, N. C., December 16, 1889. Son of Charles F. and Elizabeth Mutter (Blount) Warren. Received his preparatory education at Bingham School, Asheville, 1903-1906. Student University of North Carolina, 1906-1908, Law School, U. N. C., 1911-1912. Admitted to the bar, February, 1912. Chairman Democratic Executive Committee of Beaufort County, 1912-1925. County Attorney of Beaufort County, 1912-1925. State Senator, 1917 and 1919. President *pro tempore* State Senate, 1919. Member Code Commission compiling Consolidated Statutes, 1919. Representative from Beaufort County, 1923. Trustee University North Carolina, 1921-1925. Director First National Bank of Washington. Member Alpha Tau Omega (College) fraternity. Elk. Episcopalian. Married Miss Emily D. Harris, February, 1916; three children. Elected to Sixty-Ninth Congress, and reëlected to Seventieth Congress, without Republican opposition.

JOHN HOSEA KERR

(Second District—Counties: Bertie, Edgecombe, Greene, Halifax, Lenoir, Northampton, Warren and Wilson. Population (1920) 233,111.)

John Hosea Kerr, Democrat, of Warrenton, was born at Yanceyville, N. C., December 31, 1873. Son of Capt. John H. Kerr, of the Confederate Army, and Eliza Katherine (Yancey) Kerr. Was a student in Bingham School, and graduated from Wake Forest College, North Carolina, with degree of A.B., in 1895; studied law and was admitted to the bar in 1895, when he moved to Warrenton and entered upon the practice of his profession. Married Miss Ella Foote, of Warrenton, and they have two sons—John Hosea and James Yancey. Elected Solicitor of the Third District and served eleven years; while solicitor, was elected Judge of the Superior Court and served seven years. While serving on the bench, was nominated for Congress to succeed Hon. Claude Kitchin, deceased, and was elected at a special election held November 6, 1923, only one vote being cast against him. Reëlected to the Sixty-ninth Congress, November 4, 1924, and unopposed for election to the Seventieth Congress.

CHARLES LABAN ABERNETHY

(Third District—Counties: Carteret, Craven, Duplin, Jones, Onslow, Pamlico, Pender, Sampson and Wayne. Population, 202,760.)

Charles Laban Abernethy, Democrat, from the Third District, was born at Rutherford College, N. C., March 18, 1872. He is the son of Rev. Turner Abernethy and Martha Ann Scott Abernethy. He was educated at Mount Olive preparatory schools, Rutherford College, and the Law School of the University of North Carolina. Lawyer. Member of the Kiwanis Club of New Bern and New Bern Chamber of Commerce. County Attorney of Carteret County, 1896. Presidential elector, 1900 and 1904. Solicitor Third and Fifth Judicial Districts for about twelve years. Elected to the Sixty-eighth and Sixty-ninth Congresses. Reëlected to Seventieth Congress, November 2, 1926. Odd Fellow, K. of P., B. P. O. E., Red Men, Jr. O. U. A. M., Woodman of the World. Mason. Shriner. Methodist. Married Miss Minnie May, in 1895. Has one son, Charles L. Abernethy, Jr., now practicing law with him.

EDWARD WILLIAM POU

(Fourth District—Counties: Chatham, Franklin, Johnston, Nash, Vance and Wake. Population, 238,594.)

Edward William Pou, Democrat, of Johnston County, was born at Tuskegee, Ala., September 9, 1863. Son of Edward W. and Anna Maria (Smith) Pou. Was married to Carrie Haughton Ihrie in 1887 and has three living children. Presidential Elector in 1888. Elected Solicitor of the Fourth Judicial District of North Carolina in 1890, 1894 and 1898. Elected to the Fifty-seventh, Fifty-eighth, Fifty-ninth, Sixtieth, Sixty-first, Sixty-second, Sixty-third, Sixty-fourth, Sixty-fifth, Sixty-sixth, Sixty-seventh, Sixty-eighth and Sixty-ninth Congresses. Reëlected to Seventieth Congress, November 2, 1926. Address: Smithfield, N. C.

CHARLES MANLY STEDMAN

(Fifth District—Counties: Alamance, Caswell, Durham, Forsyth, Granville, Guilford, Orange, Person, Rockingham, Stokes, Surry. Population, (1920) 408,138.)

Charles Manly Stedman, Democrat, of Greensboro, N. C., was born January 29, 1841, in Pittsboro, N. C. He entered the University of North Carolina at the age of sixteen, and graduated from that institution in 1861. He received his diploma, but before the commencement exercises responded to a call for volunteers and enlisted as a private in the Fayetteville Independent Light Infantry Company, which was in the First North Carolina (or Bethel) Regiment. Upon the disbanding of this regiment, he joined a company from Chatham County; was lieutenant, then captain, and afterwards major. He served with Lee's Army during the entire war, and was wounded three times. Surrendered at Appomattox. Immediately after the war he read law and procured his license to practice. On January 8, 1866, he married Miss Katherine deRossett Wright, daughter of Joshua G. Wright, of Wilmington, N. C. In 1867 he moved to Wilmington and practiced law under the firm name of Wright & Stedman. In 1880, was chosen a delegate to the Democratic National Convention. Was elected Lieutenant-Governor in 1884, holding the position until the expiration of the term. In 1888, after a prolonged contest, he was defeated for Governor by a very small majority. In 1898, moved to Greensboro and practiced law under the firm name of Stedman & Cooke. Served as president of the North Carolina Bar Association. In 1909, was appointed by Governor Kitchin as director of the North Carolina Railroad Company, and afterwards elected its president. Was elected to the Sixty-second Congress, and reëlected to the Sixty-third, Sixty-fourth, Sixty-fifth, Sixty-sixth, Sixty-seventh, Sixty-eighth and Sixty-ninth Congresses. Reëlected to Seventieth Congress, November 2, 1926.

HOMER LeGRAND LYON

(Sixth District— Counties: Bladen, Brunswick, Columbus, Cumberland, Harnett, New Hanover and Robeson. Population 223,434.)

Homer LeGrand Lyon, Democrat, of Whiteville, was born March 1, 1879, in Elizabethtown. Educated at Davis Military School and the University of North Carolina. Licensed to practice law in September, 1900. Had been Solicitor of the Eighth Judicial District for seven years preceding his election to Congress. Elected to the Sixty-seventh, Sixty-eighth, Sixty-ninth Congresses. Reëlected to the Seventieth Congress. Married Miss Kate M. Burkhead in 1904.

WILLIAM C. HAMMER

(Seventh District—Counties: Anson, Davidson, Davie, Hoke, Lee, Montgomery, Moore, Randolph, Richmond, Scotland, Union, Wilkes and Yadkin. Population, 295,917.)

William C. Hammer, Democrat, was born in Randolph County, March 24, 1864. Son of William C. and Hannah Jane (Burrows) Hammer. Educated in the public schools, Yadkin College, Western Maryland College, University of North Carolina Law School. Lawyer. Member American Bar Association; North Carolina Bar Association; National Editorial Association; North Carolina Press Association. Mayor of Asheboro. Town Commissioner. County Superintendent of Schools. Solicitor Tenth, afterwards the Fifteenth Judicial District, of North Carolina. United States Attorney Western

District of North Carolina. Delegate from North Carolina to Democratic National Convention, 1896, at Chicago. Delegate-at-large to Democratic National Convention at Baltimore, 1912. President North Carolina Press Association, 1914-1915. Elected to the 67th, 68th and 69th Congresses. Reëlected to the 70th Congress, November 2, 1926. Mason, Odd Fellow, Jr. O. U. A. M., Woodman of the World. Methodist. Married Miss Minnie Lee Hancock, 1893. Address: Asheboro, N. C.

ROBERT LEE DOUGHTON

(*Eighth District*—Counties: Alexander, Alleghany, Ashe, Cabarrus, Caldwell, Iredell, Rowan, Stanly and Watauga. Population, 217,254.)

Robert L. Doughton, Democrat, Laurel Springs, was born at Laurel Springs, November 7, 1863. Educated in the public schools and at Laurel Springs and Sparta High Schools. Farmer and stock raiser. Appointed a member of the Board of Agriculture in 1903. Elected to the State Senate from the Thirty-fifth District in 1908. Served as a director of the State Prison from 1909 to 1911. Elected to the Sixty-second, Sixty-third, Sixty-fourth, Sixty-fifth, Sixty-sixth, Sixty-seventh, Sixty-eighth and Sixty-ninth Congresses. Reëlected to the Seventieth Congress.

ALBERT LEE BULWINKLE

Ninth District—Counties: Mecklenburg, Gaston, Cleveland, Lincoln, Catawba, Burke, Madison, Mitchell, Yancey and Avery. Population, 297,996.

A. L. Bulwinkle, Democrat, Gastonia, born April 21, 1883. Attended school in Dallas. Studied law at the University of North Carolina. Lawyer. Member of the firm of Bulwinkle & Cherry. Prosecuting Attorney in the Municipal Court of the city of Gastonia, 1913-1916. Nominated for the State Senate, withdrew on account of being in the military service on the Mexican Border. Captain, First Infantry, N. C. N. G., 1909-1917. Major, commanding

Second Battalion, 113th F. A., 55th F. A. Brigade, 30th Division, 1917-1919. Married Miss Bessie Lewis, 1911; two children. Elected to the Sixty-seventh, Sixty-eighth, and Sixty-ninth Congresses. Reëlected to the Seventieth Congress.

ZEBULON WEAVER

(*Tenth District*—Counties: Buncombe, Cherokee, Clay, Graham, Haywood, Henderson, Jackson, McDowell, Macon, Polk, Rutherford, Swain, Transylvania. Population, 231,483.)

Zebulon Weaver, Democrat, of Buncombe County, was born in Weaverville, May 12, 1872. He is the son of W. E. and Hannah E. (Baird) Weaver. A.B. of Weaverville College, 1899. Studied law at the University of North Carolina, 1894. Lawyer. Represented Buncombe County in the General Assembly of North Carolina in 1907 and 1909. State Senator, 1913 and 1915. After a close contest with James J. Britt, Republican, in 1916, was declared elected Representative in the Sixty-fifth Congress. Was elected to the Sixty-sixth, Sixty-seventh, Sixty-eighth, Sixty-ninth and Seventieth Congresses. Methodist. Married Miss Annie Hyman of New Bern. Has five children. Address: Asheville, N. C.

MEMBERS OF THE GENERAL ASSEMBLY

SENATORS

JACOB ELMER LONG

PRESIDENT OF THE SENATE

Jacob Elmer Long, Democrat, Lieutenant Governor, was born in Yanceyville, July 31, 1880. Son of Jacob A. and Esta T. Long. Educated at Graham College, 1888-1890; Elon College, 1891-1895; Horner Military School, 1896-1898; University of North Carolina, 1900-1903. LL.B., University of North Carolina, 1903. Lawyer. Chairman Congressional Executive Committee, Fifth District, 1912-1917. Private Secretary to Charles M. Stedman, Member of Congress from Fifth North Carolina District, 1912-1916. Representative in General Assembly from Alamance County, 1911-1913. Senator Eighteenth District, 1917 and 1921. Elected Lieutenant Governor, November 4, 1924. Fraternal Orders: Sigma Nu Fraternity (college); Omega Tau Legal Fraternity (college); Order of Sphinx (college). Presbyterian. Married, November 10, 1909, Miss Lessie Ermine Peay. Address: Durham, N. C.

EDWARD STEPHENSON ASKEW

(*Third District*—Counties: Bertie and Northampton. One Senator.)

Edward Stephenson Askew, Democrat, Senator from the Third Senatorial District, was born in Windsor, February 17, 1874. Son of Richard Watson and Elizabeth (Webb) Askew. Attended Windsor Academy and Norfolk Academy, Randolph Macon College, and the University of North Carolina, A.B. 1899, *cum laude*. Attended University Law School and was licensed to practice law in 1907. Farmer and Banker. Member Windsor Chamber of Commerce; Secretary Peanut Congress, Jamestown Exposition; President Citizens Bank of Windsor; Manager Roanoke-Chowan Telephone Company; Ex-Mayor of Windsor; Chairman Bertie County Democratic Executive Committee; Member N. C. Fisheries Commission Board.

Odd Fellow; Phi Delta Theta; Gorgon's Head. Episcopalian; vestryman. Married Miss Nellie Ashburn Bond, July 15, 1919. Address: Merry Hill, N. C.

JOHN LEMON BAILEY

(*Sixth District*—Counties: Franklin, Nash and Wilson. Two Senators.)

John L. Bailey, Democrat, Senator from the Sixth Senatorial District, was born in Wilson County, 1850. Son of Birt and Mahala (Braswell) Bailey. Attended public school in Wilson County, 1866. Farmer, banker and merchant. Justice of the Peace, 1871. Member House of Representatives, 1883, 1915, 1917. State Senator, 1925. Mason—Worshipful Master and all the other offices in Masonic Lodge. Presbyterian. Married Miss Emma Braswell, 1881. Address: Elm City, N. C.

MARVIN KEY BLOUNT

(*Fifth District*—County: Pitt. One Senator.)

Marvin K. Blount, Democrat, Senator from the Fifth Senatorial District, was born at Bethel, March 18, 1892. Son of Marion Orlando and Florence Blount. Attended Culver Military Academy, Culver, Indiana. A.B., 1914. University of North Carolina, 1914-1916; LL.B., 1916. Lawyer. Member N. C. Bar Association and Kiwanis Club. Director and attorney for Bank and Building and Loan Association. Chairman Pitt County Democratic Executive Committee, 1924-1926. Special Agent U. S. Department of Justice, 1918. Member Phi Delta Theta Fraternity. Shriner. Methodist, chairman board of stewards, 1926. Married Miss Ruth Elizabeth Baldwin, January 22, 1920. Address Greenville, N. C.

JOSEPH MELVILLE BROUGHTON

(*Thirteenth District*—Counties: Wake, Chatham and Lee. Two Senators.)

Joseph M. Broughton, Democrat, Senator from the Thirteenth Senatorial District, was born in Raleigh, November 17, 1888. Son of Joseph Melville and Sally Elizabeth (Harris) Broughton. Attended Raleigh Public Schools and Hugh Morson Academy; A.B., Wake Forest College, 1910; Harvard Law School, 1912-1913. Lawyer. Member Wake County Bar Association, North Carolina Bar Association and American Bar Association. Chairman Wake County Democratic Executive Committee, 1916-1918; City Attorney, 1921-1923; Member Raleigh Township School Committee, 1925-1926. Mason; member Jr. O. U. A. M. Baptist; Deacon; Superintendent of Sunday School; Married Miss Alice Harper Willson, December 14, 1916. Three children. Address: Raleigh, N. C.

CLARENCE CALL

(*Twenty-fourth District*—Counties: Davie, Wilkes and Yadkin. One Senator.)

Clarence Call, Republican, Senator from the Twenty-fourth Senatorial District, was born in Wilkesboro, April 7, 1869. Son of Isaac Slater and Martha (Masten) Call. Attended Wilkesboro School and Moravian Falls Academy. President and General Manager Oak Furniture Company. Merchant. Farmer. Banker. Sheriff and Treasurer Wilkes County, 1894-1898. Member Board of Elections, twenty-five years. Mason; Knight of Pythias. Episcopalian—Vestryman, church treasurer, Junior and Senior Warden. Married Miss Sallie Green Cook, of Greensboro, December 4, 1901. Delegate Republican National Convention at Cleveland, 1924. Address: Wilkesboro, N. C.

CLAUDE CARL CANADAY

(*Eighth District*—Counties: Johnston and Wayne. Two Senators).

Claude Carl Canaday, Democrat, Senator from the Eighth Senatorial District, was born in Johnston County, January 8, 1890. Son of John Henry and Lucy D. (Williams) Canaday. Attended Benson High School, 1908-1911; University of North Carolina, 1911-1912;

University Law School, 1912-1914. Lawyer and Farmer. Member North Carolina Bar Association. Kiwanis Club. Mayor of Benson, 1918. Married Miss Willie Duncan, September 12, 1915. Address: Benson, N. C.

WADE HAMPTON CHILDS

(*Twenty-fifth District*—Counties: Catawba, Iredell and Lincoln. Two Senators.)

Wade H. Childs, Democrat, Senator from the twenty-fifth Senatorial District, was born in Lincolnton, May 31, 1890. Son of C. E. and Katie (Motz) Childs. Attended Lincolnton Graded Schools. Entered University of North Carolina in 1908. Attended University Law School. Lawyer. City attorney for Lincolnton, 1913-1923; re-elected in September, 1926. Government appeal representative as attorney on the Local Exemption Board during the World War. Sigma Chi, U. N. C., Mason; Shriner. Presbyterian. Married Miss Miriam B. Johnstone, March, 1914. Address: Lincolnton, N. C.

W. G. CLARK

(*Fourth District*—Counties: Edgecombe and Halifax. Two Senators).

W. G. Clark, Democrat, from Edgecombe County, Senator from the Fourth District. Address: Tarboro, N. C.

CLAUDE CURRIE

(*Eighteenth District*—Counties: Davidson, Montgomery, Richmond, and Scotland. Two Senators.)

Claude Currie, Democrat, Senator from the Eighteenth Senatorial District, was born in Candor, December 8, 1890. Son of J. C. and Louise (McKinnon) Currie. Attended Oak Ridge Institute, 1911-1914; University of North Carolina, 1914-1917; 1923-1926; A.B., LL.B., 1926. Lawyer. Sergeant United States Army, 1917-1919. Mason. Phi Delta Phi. Presbyterian. Address: Troy, N. C.

FRANK LEMUEL DUNLAP

(*Nineteenth District*—Counties: Anson, Stanly and Union. Two Senators.)

Frank L. Dunlap, Democrat, Senator from the Nineteenth Senatorial District. Born at Wadesboro, Anson County. Son of Joseph I. and Charlotte B. (Bennett) Dunlap. Educated at Horner's Military School, 1902-1903-1904; University of North Carolina, LL. B., 1908. Lawyer and farmer. Civitan. Clerk of Superior Court, Anson County, 1910. Solicitor Recorder's Court, Anson County, 1911-1914. Senator General Assembly, 1921 and 1925. Served in World War, 1917-19; First Lieutenant Infantry, U. S. A., A. E. F. Episcopalian. Address: Wadesboro, N. C.

PLATO DURHAM EBBS

(*Thirty-first District*—County: Buncombe. One Senator.)

Plato Durham Ebbs, Democrat, Senator from the Thirty-first Senatorial District, was born in Madison County. Son of Jasper and Tolitha (Flemmons) Ebbs. Wholesale grocer. Director Asheville Chamber of Commerce and Merchants Association. Representative from Madison County, 1915-1917; in Senate, 1923-24 and 1925. United Commercial Travelers. B. P. O. E. Married Miss Katie Sprinkle, December, 1903. Address: Asheville, N. C.

HORATIO THOMAS FULTON

(*Twenty-seventh District*—Counties: Cleveland, Henderson, McDowell, Polk and Rutherford. Two Senators.)

Horatio Thomas Fulton, Democrat, Senator from the Twenty-seventh Senatorial District, was born in Kings Mountain, March 4, 1874. Son of Horatio Decalb and Sarah Beattie (Dixon) Fulton. Attended county public schools, 1880-1886; Kings Mountain High School until 1892; Brown School of Embalming in 1921. Funeral director. President North Carolina Funeral Directors' Association. Member Board of Aldermen, Kings Mountain, 1906-1908; member school board, 1908-1910; County Commissioners, 1912-1918, chairman from 1914-1918. Private in Bell's Military School, Kings Mountain. 1887. Knight of Pythias, Mason, Blue Lodge, Royal Arch, Knight Templar; Worshipful Master Masons, 1912-1916; Chancellor Commander Knights of Pythias. Methodist—Steward, 1902-1926; Sunday school Superintendent, 1918-1926. Married Miss Sarah Salina Baker, November 30, 1898. Address: Kings Mountain, N. C.

LEMUEL CLAYTON GRANT

(*Ninth District*—Counties: Duplin, Pender, New Hanover and Sampson. Two Senators.)

Lemuel Clayton Grant, Democrat, Senator from the Ninth Senatorial District, was born in Wilmington, January 17, 1882. Son of Reuben and Elizabeth (McMillan) Grant. Attended Wilmington Public Schools, 1889-1901; University of North Carolina, 1901-1902; University Law School, 1907. Lawyer. Member Wilmington and North Carolina Bar Associations. Chairman Committee Four Minute Men, New Hanover County, 1917-1918; Chairman Committee Public Instruction, 1917-1918. Representative from New Hanover County in the General Assemblies of 1917 and 1919. Mason, Knight of Pythias; Chancellor Commander Stonewall Lodge No. 1, Knights of Pythias, 1910. Baptist. Married Miss Margaret E. Montgomery, November 24, 1908; three children, Margaret, Elizabeth and Eleanor. Address: Wilmington, N. C.

FRANK LUTTRELL GRIER

(*Twenty-fifth District*—Counties: Catawba, Iredell and Lincoln. Two Senators.)

Frank L. Grier, Democrat, Senator from the Twenty-fifth Senatorial District, was born in Statesville, October 24, 1898. Son of H. P. and Marietta (Leinster) Grier. Attended Statesville High School, 1914-1917 and Marion Military Institute, 1917-1918; U. S. Military Academy, West Point, and University of North Carolina. University Law School, 1920-1922. Lawyer. Member Iredell County Bar Association and North Carolina Bar Association. Kiwanian. Attorney for City of Statesville, 1922-1926. Cadet Marion Military Institute; R. O. T. C. and United States Military Academy. Alpha Tau Omega (social) and Phi Delta Phi (legal) fraternities. Associate Reform Presbyterian. Married Miss Juliet Bristol, November 21, 1925. Address: Statesville, N. C.

FRANKLIN WILLS HANCOCK, JR.

(Fifteenth District—Counties: Granville and Person. One Senator.)

Franklin Wills Hancock, Jr., Democrat, Senator from the Fifteenth Senatorial District, was born in Oxford, November 1, 1894. Son of Franklin Wills and Lizzie (Hobgood) Hancock. Attended Horner Military School and Warrenton High School and the University of North Carolina. Lawyer. Member North Carolina Bar Association; Oxford Rotary Club. Mason; Sudan Temple, A. A. O. N. M. S.; Kappa Alpha Fraternity. Baptist. Married Miss Lucy Osborne Landis, May 12, 1917. Address: Oxford, N. C.

J. S. HARGETT

(Seventh District—Counties: Carteret, Craven, Greene, Jones, Lenoir and Onslow. Two Senators.)

J. S. Hargett, Democrat, Senator from the Seventh Senatorial District, was born May 28, 1874. Attended Richland High School and University. Married twice, first wife Olivia Steed, of Richland. Of this union six children, four living. Second wife, Mrs. Susan Koonce Burt. No children by this union. Methodist—Steward and District Lay Leader. Sheriff Jones County, twelve years. Chairman County Democratic Executive Committee since 1916. Member State Executive Committee. Mason—Shriner. State Senator since 1921. Address: Trenton, N. C.

CLYDE PEEBLES HARRIS

(Sixth District—Counties: Franklin, Nash and Wilson. Two Senators.)

Clyde Peebles Harris, Democrat, Senator from the sixth Senatorial District, was born in Franklin County, September 19th, 1864. Son of Col. Harville and Roxanna (Daniel) Harris. Attended Louisburg Academy, 1880-1881, and rural schools. Farmer. Was Director and Vice President of Farmers and Merchants Bank, Louisburg, for many years and in January, 1920, was made President. Baptist. Church treasurer, 1905-1920. Married Miss Annie Fleming in 1891. State Senator in 1923. Address: Mapleville, N. C.

FAB J. HAYWOOD

(*Twentieth District*—Counties: Cabarrus and Mecklenburg. Two Senators).

Fab J. Haywood, Democrat, from Cabarrus County, Senator from the Twentieth District. Address: Concord, N. C.

CHARLES ANDERSON HINES

(*Seventeenth District*—Counties: Guilford and Rockingham. Two Senators.)

Charles A. Hines, Democrat, Senator from the Seventeenth Senatorial District, was born in Guilford County, February 14, 1886. Son of E. D. and Isabel (Wright) Hines. Attended Jefferson Academy, Elon College; University of North Carolina Law School, 1907-1908. Member North Carolina and American Bar associations. Director Greensboro Chamber of Commerce. City Attorney, 1917-1922. Emergency Judge Superior Court, 1925. Chairman Guilford County Democratic Convention, 1908, 1916, 1918. Member State Democratic Executive Committee, 1916-1926. Mason, Junior Order; Woodmen of World; Moose. Delegate to National Convention of Woodman of World, 1917-1927 inclusive. Methodist; Steward; Teacher Bible Class. Author Extension Charter of Greater Greensboro, 1923. Married Miss Ida Winstead, November 12, 1912. Three children. First president Greensboro Civitan Club; leader in 1922-1925, Building and Loan Campaign; director in several business companies. Lawyer; member firm of Hines, Kelly & Boren. Address: Greensboro, N. C.

WILLIAM BANKS HORTON

(*Sixteenth District*—Counties: Alamance, Caswell, Durham and Orange. Two Senators.)

William B. Horton, Democrat, Senator from the Sixteenth Senatorial District, was born at Corning, Kansas, November 20, 1879. Son of Thomas and Mary Ellen (Wilkins) Horton. Attended Chapel Hill High School; University of Chicago Law School, 1915-1916; Wake Forest College Law School, 1922-1923. Lawyer. Twenty years in Navy, resigning with the rank of Lieutenant, July 20, 1921. Veteran of Spanish American and World War. Cited for meritorious service by Federal Government. Mason. Shriner. Methodist. Address: Yanceyville, N. C.

WILKINS PERRYMAN HORTON

(*Thirteenth Senatorial District*—Counties: Chatham, Lee and Wake. Two Senators.)

Wilkins Perryman Horton, Democrat, of Chatham County, Senator from Thirteenth District, was born at Kansas City, Kansas, September 1, 1889. Son of Thomas B. and Mary E. (Wilkins) Horton. Was educated in the public schools of Chatham County; Draughn's Business College, 1910-1911. University of North Carolina, 1912-1914. Lawyer. County Attorney from 1916-1919 and from 1924-1926. Chairman of Democratic Executive Committee of Chatham County. Senator from Chatham, 1919. Mason. Methodist. Married Miss Cassandra C. Mendenhall, June 12, 1918.

JAMES LEE HYATT

(*Thirtieth District*—Counties: Avery, Madison, Mitchell and Yancey. One Senator).

James Lee Hyatt, Republican, of Yancey County, Senator from the Thirtieth District, was born at Burnsville, March 14, 1865. Son of Jason L. and Sarah Eliza (McClelland) Hyatt. Was educated at Burnsville Academy, 1899. Real estate dealer. County Superintendent of Schools. State Senator, 1899, 1911, and 1919. Mason; Odd Fellow; Knight of Pythias. Methodist. Married Miss Margarite C. Griffith, June 12, 1892. Four children. Address: Burnsville, N. C.

RIVERS DUNN JOHNSON

(*Ninth District*—Counties: Duplin, New Hanover, Pender and Sampson. Two Senators).

Rivers Dunn Johnson, Democrat, Senator from the Ninth Senatorial District, was born in Wilson, December 29, 1885. Son of Seymour Anderson and Annie E. (Clark) Johnson. Educated at James Sprunt Institute, Warsaw High School and Wake Forest. Attended Wake Forest Law School, 1908, 1909. Lawyer. Member American Bar Association, North Carolina Bar Association, and Duplin County Bar Association. Mayor Warsaw, 1909-1910. State Senator, 1911, 1915, 1923. Cadet, First Officers Training Camp, Fort Oglethorpe, Ga. Thirty-second Degree Mason—Scottish Rite Bodies; Shriner—Sudan Temple; Jr. O. U. A. M.; Eastern Star. Member Warsaw Rotary Club. Master Masonic Lodge, 1911-1915; Councilor, Jr. O. U. A. M., two years; President Shrine Club, 1919-1926; President Rotary Club, 1926-1927. Episcopalian. Married Miss Olivia R. Best, May 23, 1921. Address: Warsaw, N. C.

LLOYD J. LAWRENCE

(*First District*—Counties: Camden, Chowan, Currituck, Gates, Hertford, Pasquotank and Perquimans. Two Senators.)

Lloyd J. Lawrence, Democrat, Senator from the First Senatorial District, was born at Murfreesboro, in 1871. Son of James N. and Mary Elizabeth (Pruden) Lawrence. Attended Murfreesboro High School, 1883-1888; Murfreesboro Military Academy, 1888-1890; University of North Carolina Law School, 1890-1892. Lawyer. Member State Bar Association, Commercial Law League of America. President of Citizens Bank, 1911-1919; President of the First National Bank of Murfreesboro, 1919-1922; Mayor of Murfreesboro, 1893-1901; Chairman of Board of Education; Chairman Board of

Elections; County Attorney; Town Attorney; Representative in General Assembly of 1901 and 1923. Supervisor first North Carolina District, 1920 Census. Methodist. Married in 1895, to Miss Eva Alberta Eldridge; in 1919 to Miss Olive B. Vinson. Address: Murfreesboro, N. C.

WILLIAM LUNSFORD LONG

(*Fourth District*—Counties: Halifax and Edgecombe. Two Senators.)

William Lunsford Long, Democrat, of Halifax County, Senator from the Fourth District, was born February 5, 1890, at Garysburg. Son of Lemuel McKinney and Bettie Gray (Mason) Long. A.B. of the University of North Carolina, 1909. Lawyer and Manufacturer. Director of First National Bank of Roanoke Rapids, and Rosemary Banking and Trust Company of Rosemary. President of the Rosemary Manufacturing Company, and Vice President and Treasurer of the Roanoke Mills Company, of Roanoke Rapids. Representative in the General Assembly, 1915. State Senator, 1917-1919, 1921, 1923. S. A. E. (College Fraternity), Gimghoul, Phi Beta Kappa of University of North Carolina. Mason; K. of P. Married Miss Rosa Arrington Heath of Petersburg, Va. President *pro tem* of North Carolina Senate, 1921 and 1923. Trustee of the University of North Carolina. Address: Roanoke Rapids, N. C.

DANIEL ALLEN McDONALD

(*Twelfth District*—Counties: Hartnett, Hoke, Moore and Randolph. Two Senators.)

Daniel A. McDonald, Democrat, Senator from the Twelfth Senatorial District, was born at Currieville, Moore County, June 13, 1851. Son of Allan and Mary Ann (McIver) McDonald. Attended old field school at Currieville, and Commercial College, at Lexington, Ky., 1874. Farmer. Mason. Shriner. County Surveyor, 1878-1879. Clerk Superior Court, 1886-1906. Representative in the General Assembly of 1909 and Senator in 1911 and 1923. Director of Insane Asylum, six years. President Bank of Carthage at one time and of the Randolph and Cumberland Railroad. Presbyterian; deacon, 1886-1900; elder since 1900. Married Miss Ida Ann Martin in 1884. Address: Carthage, N. C.

GEORGE B. McLEOD

(*Eleventh District*—County: Robeson. One Senator).

George B. McLeod, Democrat, Senator from the Eleventh District. Senator in 1913. Address: Lumberton, N. C.

PETER THURMAN McNEILL

(*Twenty-ninth District*—Counties: Alleghany, Ashe, Watauga. One Senator.)

Peter Thurman McNeill, Democrat, Senator from Twenty-ninth District, was born in Jefferson, 1896. Son of P. G. and Cynthia Alice (McMillan) McNeill. Attended Jefferson High School, finished in 1916; King College, Bristol, Va.; Berea College, Berea, Kentucky. Farmer and merchant. Member Ashe County Commercial Club. Appointed by Judge Webb of the Federal Court as United States Commissioner, February, 1925, for a period of six years. Primitive Baptist. Married, September 22, 1918, Miss Martha Ellen Fletcher, Somerset, Kentucky. President Jefferson Democratic National Club; Campaign Manager of Governor A. W. McLean for Ashe County. Address: West Jefferson, N. C.

DONALD McRACKAN

(*Tenth District*—Counties: Bladen, Brunswick, Columbus and Cumberland. Two Senators).

Donald McRackan, Democrat, Senator from the Tenth District, was born in Columbus County, in 1866. Educated at Wake Forest College. Studied law at Greensboro under Judge Robert P. Dick and John H. Dillard. Lawyer. Representative in the General Assembly, 1907 and 1917. State Senator, 1915. Married Miss Ada McKeithan. Address: Whiteville, N. C.

SAMUEL OSCAR MAGUIRE

(*Twenty-third District*—Counties: Stokes and Surry. One Senator).

Samuel Oscar Maguire, Republican, Senator from the Twenty-third District, was born in Madison, Dorchester County, Maryland, February 10, 1863. Son of Edwin Oscar and Julia Francis (Williams) Maguire. Attended High School, Dorchester County, Maryland, and Baltimore City College. Traveling salesman. Member of the General Assembly, 1919, 1921. Elkin Lodge, No. 545, A. F. &. A. M.; North Wilkesboro Chapter Royal Arch Masons, No. 78; Piedmont Commandery No. 6, Winston-Salem; Oasis Temple, Charlotte, A. A. O. N. M. S.; Jr. O. U. A. M. Held every office in Masonic Lodge and elected to Master station twice. Methodist. Married, August 20, 1910, Miss Rebecca Emeline Bray. Address: Elkin, N. C.

CLAYTON MOORE

(*Second District*—Counties: Beaufort, Dare, Hyde, Martin, Pamlico, Tyrrell and Washington. Two Senators.)

Clayton Moore, Democrat, Representative from Martin County, was born at Williamston in 1888. Son of James E. and Jane Sykes) Moore. Attended Williamston High School; Oak Ridge Institute; A. and M. College; Virginia Polytechnic Institute, and University of North Carolina Law School. Attorney. Member State Bar Association. Representative from Martin County in General Assembly of 1921, 1923, 1925. Mason. B. P. O. E. Episcopalian—member of vestry. Married Miss Jennie Swanner in 1914. Address: Williamston, N. C.

J. CLYDE RAY

(*Sixteenth District*—Counties: Alamance, Caswell, Durham and Orange. Two Senators.)

J. Clyde Ray, Democrat, Senator from the Sixteenth Senatorial District. Born in Orange County, February, 1890. Son of John W. and Lila (Williams) Ray. Attended Hillsboro High School, 1909-1912; University of North Carolina, graduating in 1916 with A.B.

degree. Attorney. Member North Carolina Bar Association. Private in the Army from September 7, 1918, to January 7, 1919. Methodist Steward, 1916-1922. State Senator from the Sixteenth District in 1923. Married Miss Mamie E. Brown, 1918. Address: **Hillsboro, N. C.**

ROBERT J. ROANE

(*Thirty-third District*—Counties: Cherokee, Clay, Graham, Macon, Swain. One Senator.)

Robert J. Roane, Democrat, Senator from the **Thirty-third District**, was born in Macon County, May 30, 1860. Son of **William and Mary (Munday) Roane**. Attended **Franklin common schools**. Merchant. Sheriff of Swain County, 1910-1914; Member Board of Education of Swain County since 1922. Mason. Methodist. Married Miss Mary Lewellyn Siler, October 1, 1884. Address: **Whittier, N. C.**

KENNETH CLAIBORNE ROYALL

(*Eighth District*—Counties: Johnston and Wayne. Two Senators.)

Kenneth Claiborne Royall, Democrat, Senator from the **Eighth Senatorial District**, was born in Goldsboro, July 24, 1894. Son of **George C. and Clara Howard (Jones) Royall**. Attended Goldsboro City Schools, Episcopal High School, Alexandria, Va., 1909-1911. University of North Carolina, A.B. 1914; Harvard Law School, LL.B., 1917. Lawyer. Member North Carolina Bar Association, American Bar Association, Harvard Law School Association, Harvard Law Review Association and American Law Institute. Associate Editor *Harvard Law Review*, 1915-1917. United States Field Artillery, May, 1917 to February, 1919; A. E. F., August, 1918 to February, 1919, 1st Lieutenant F. A. Mason; J. O. U. A. M.; Rotarian; Delta Kappa Epsilon. Episcopalian; vestryman since 1924. Married Miss Margaret Best, August 18, 1917. Two children, **Kenneth C. Jr., and Margaret**. Address: **Goldsboro, N. C.**

JOSEPH WATERS RUARK

(*Tenth District*—Counties: Bladen, Brunswick, Columbus and Cumberland. Two Senators.)

Joseph Waters Ruark, Democrat, Senator from the Tenth Senatorial District. Born at Southport in 1885. Son of J. B. and Sallie (Longest) Ruark. Attended Southport Academy and Law School of the University of North Carolina. Attorney. Member of Southport Chamber of Commerce. Elected Attorney for Brunswick County, 1922; Mayor of Sanford, 1911-1912; Mayor of Southport, 1915-1921; Recorder for Brunswick County, 1921-1922. State Senator 1923. Jr. O. U. A. M.; Past Master Pythogoras Lodge No. 249, A. F. & A. M. Methodist. Married Miss Bessie Cross in 1911. Address: Southport, N. C.

NEILL McKAY SALMON

(*Twelfth District*—Counties: Harnett, Hoke, Moore and Randolph. Two Senators.)

Neill McK. Salmon, Democrat, Senator from the Twelfth Senatorial District, was born in Lillington, July 20, 1887. Son of Silas A. and Mary Louise (McKay) Salmon. Attended Bingham Military School, Asheville, 1913-1915; University of North Carolina, and graduated from Trinity College Law School, 1920. Lawyer. Member North Carolina and American Bar associations. Solicitor for Harnett County, 1922-1924; Secretary Democratic Executive Committee, Harnett County, 1922-1926. Student officer in United States Naval Aviation Forces during World War. Mason—held all offices; Worshipful Master Lillington Lodge, June, 1926; Jr. O. U. A. M. Presbyterian. Address: Lillington, N. C.

J. CHESLEY SEDBERRY

(*Eighteenth District*—Counties: Davidson, Montgomery. Richmond and Scotland. Two Senators.)

J. Chesley Sedberry, Democrat, Senator from the Eighteenth Senatorial District, was born near Troy, Montgomery County, December 13, 1889. Son of John W. and Ellen (Morris) Sedberry.

Attended country public schools until 1909; Wadesboro High School, 1909-1912. Attended the University of North Carolina, 1914-1916. Lawyer. Member North Carolina and Richmond County Bar Associations. Attorney for town of Rockingham, 1920-1925. Methodist. Married Miss Lottie Brigman, June 1, 1916. Address: Rockingham, N. C.

JAMES MERRITTE SHARP

(*Seventeenth District*—Counties: Guilford and Rockingham. Two Senators.)

James M. Sharp, Democrat, Senator from the Seventeenth Senatorial District, was born in Rockingham County, September 26, 1877. Son of James M. and Eliza (Merritte) Sharp. Educated in public schools of Rockingham County, Whitsett Institute, Wake Forest College Law School. Was a teacher in the public schools of the State for several years. Founder and president for seven years of Sharp Institute, a private school in Rockingham County. Lawyer. Kiwanian, Mason, Deputy National Councillor of Junior Order United American Mechanics for State of Georgia. Second Lieutenant, Home Guards, during World War. County Attorney of Rockingham County. Member State Senate from Seventeenth Senatorial District, 1925. Married Miss Annie Britte Blackwell in 1906. Address: Reidsville, N. C.

DAVID BAIRD SMITH

(*Twentieth District*—Counties: Cabarrus and Mecklenburg. Two Senators.)

David Baird Smith, Democrat, Senator from the Twentieth Senatorial District, was born in Greensboro, March 2, 1876. Son of John Y. and Delphina Elizabeth (Kersey) Smith. Attended Greensboro Public Schools, 1882-1893; Ph.B., University North Carolina, 1897; University Law School, 1901. Lawyer. Member North Carolina Bar Association. Member Charlotte School Board, 1904-1908; Recorder, City of Charlotte, 1909-1913; Assistant U. S. District Attorney, 1919-1920; Democratic County Chairman. Elk; Jr. O. U. A. M. Methodist. Married Miss Esther Lotton, of Springfield, Ohio, July 19, 1919. Address: Charlotte, N. C.

WHITMAN ERSKINE SMITH

(*Nineteenth District*—Counties: Anson, Stanly and Union. Two Senators.)

Whitman Erskine Smith, Democrat, Senator from the Nineteenth Senatorial District, was born in Norwood, February 13, 1896. Son of R. L. and Ora (Burgess) Smith. Attended Webb School, Bell Buckle, Tennessee, 1910-1913; Morgan School, Fayetteville, Tenn., 1914-1915. Entered Trinity College in 1915 and graduated from the Law School in 1921. Lawyer. Member North Carolina Bar Association. Prosecuting attorney for Stanly County Court, 1922-1926. United States Navy, 1918-1919. Methodist. Address: Albemarle, N. C.

J. F. SPAINHOUR

(*Twenty-eighth District*—Counties: Alexander, Burke, and Caldwell. One Senator).

J. F. Spainhour, Democrat, from Burke County, Senator from the Twenty-eighth District. Representative in the General Assembly of 1911. Address: Morganton, N. C.

CARROLL BAXTER SPENCER

(*Second District*—Counties: Beaufort, Dare, Hyde, Martin, Pamlico, Tyrrell and Washington. Two Senators.)

Carroll B. Spencer, Democrat, Senator from the Second Senatorial District, was born at Fairfield, April 23, 1888. Son of F. F. and Alice (Harris) Spencer. Educated at Fairfield Academy until 1905; University of North Carolina, A.B. degree, 1910; U. N. C. Law School, 1909-1910, fall of 1910. Summer Law School, Wake Forest College, 1911. Lawyer. Member North Carolina Bar Association. Chairman Democratic Executive Committee, 1914. State Senator, 1925. Mason—Shriner, Sudan Temple. Odd Fellow. Methodist. Married Miss Lucile Mann, 1912. Address: Swan Quarter, N. C.

THOMAS STRINGFIELD

(*Thirty-Second District*—Counties: Haywood, Jackson and Transylvania. One Senator.)

Thomas Stringfield, Democrat, Senator from the Thirty-second District, was born at Mossy Creek, Tennessee, March 18, 1872. Son of W. W. and Maria (Love) Stringfield. Attended Waynesville schools, Emory and Henry College, Trinity College, and the University of North Carolina; M.D., Vanderbilt University, 1898. Banker; President Citizens Bank and Trust Co., Waynesville. Member Haywood County Medical Society and the North Carolina Medical Society. Mayor of Waynesville, 1899-1905. Member North Carolina National Guard, thirty years; First Lieutenant, N. C. Volunteer Infantry, Spanish American War; Major and Inspector General, World War; Colonel and Inspector General, North Carolina National Guard. Mason; Knight of Pythias; Knight Templar; Odd Fellow; Woodman of the World. Methodist. Married Miss Mary Elizabeth Moore, 1906. Address: Waynesville, N. C.

L. P. TAPP

(*Seventh District*—Counties: Carteret, Craven, Greene, Jones, Lenoir and Onslow. Two Senators.)

L. P. Tapp, Democrat, Senator from the Seventh Senatorial District. Born in Orange County, October, 1869. Son of Ruffin R. and Malissa (Dunnagan) Tapp. Educated in the free schools and Caldwell Institute. Tobacconist. Town Alderman at Kinston for six years. President of the Atlantic and North Carolina Railroad. State Senator, 1923, 1925. Methodist. Married Miss Lillie Laws. Address: Kinston, N. C.

ROBERT LEE WHITMIRE

(*Twenty-seventh District*—Counties: Cleveland, Henderson, McDowell, Polk and Rutherford. Two Senators.)

Robert L. Whitmire, Democrat, Senator from the Twenty-seventh Senatorial District, was born in Brevard, January 21, 1898. Son of W. P. and Annie Colman (Floyd) Whitmire. Attended Brevard and Hendersonville High Schools; University of North Carolina; University Law School, 1919-1921. Member Henderson County Bar Association. Secretary Democratic Executive Committee of Henderson County, 1922. Chairman Henderson County Board of Elections, 1922-1924. Hendersonville City Attorney, 1923-1924. Delegate Democratic National Convention, 1924. Sergeant U. S. A. and A. E. F., April, 1917 to February, 1919. Mason; K. of P. Lodge, Chancellor Commander K. of P. Lodge, 1922-1923. Baptist. Married Miss Irene Louise Jones, July 30, 1925. One child, Robert Lee Jr. Address: Hendersonville, N. C.

BUXTON BARKER WILLIAMS

(*Fourteenth District*—Counties: Vance and Warren. One Senator.)

Buxton B. Williams, Democrat, Senator from the Fourteenth Senatorial District, was born in Ridgeway, April 27, 1881. Son of Dr. Thomas B. and Lucy (Jerman) Williams. Attended Graham's High School, 1889-1898. A.B., University of North Carolina, 1902; Law School, 1904-1905. Lawyer. President Kiwanis Club; Director Bank of Warren and of Federal Land Bank, Columbia, S. C. County and city attorney, 1910 and 1926. Trustee University of North Carolina. Methodist. Married Miss Sue P. Williams, September 4, 1911. Address: Warrenton, N. C.

PATRICK HENRY WILLIAMS

(*First District*—Counties: Camden, Chowan, Currituck, Gates, Hertford, Pasquotank and Perquimans. Two Senators.)

Patrick H. Williams, Democrat, Senator from the First Senatorial District, was born in Camden County, 1869. Son of Robert and Marenda (Torksey) Williams. Attended Elizabeth City Schools till 1886; Davis's Military School at LaGrange, 1886-1888. University of North Carolina, 1888-1889; Smith's Business College, 1899, at Lexington, Ky.; Randolph-Macon College, 1892-1896, A.B. degree. Law School of the University of North Carolina, 1897. Banker. Manager, Secretary-Treasurer Elizabeth City Hosiery Company,

1902-1918. Director First National Bank, Elizabeth City, 1900-1917. President Savings Bank and Trust Company, Elizabeth City, 1916 to the present time. Director Atlantic Joint Stock Land Bank, Raleigh. Alderman, 1921. District Supervisor under Revaluation Act, 1919-1920. Kappa Alpha. Odd Fellow—office holder. Methodist—Superintendent Sunday school, Board of Stewards, Board of Trustees, Lay Leader, and Teacher. Member State Senate, 1923 and 1925. Chairman Senate Finance Committee, 1925. Member Advisory Budget Committee, 1925-1926. Married, 1891, Miss Minnie White; in 1898, Miss Ella Kramer. Address: Elizabeth City, N. C.

ALBERT EDGAR WOLTZ

(*Twenty-sixth District*—County: Gaston. One Senator.)

Albert Edgar Woltz, Democrat, Senator from the Twenty-sixth Senatorial District, was born at Dobson, August, 1877. Son of Dr. John R. and Louisa J. (Kingsbury) Woltz. Received his preparatory education at Dobson High School, 1893-1895, and Siloam Academy, 1895-1897. Attended the University of North Carolina, 1897-1901; Central University, 1905-1907; A.B. and A.M., and the University Law School, 1909-1911. Member Gaston County and American Bar Associations. Mayor Granite Falls, 1902. Member Board of Directors, Chamber Commerce, City of Gastonia, 1919-1920; Board of Trustees University of North Carolina since 1919; City School Board of Gastonia, 1912-1916; Board of Directors Gaston Mutual Building and Loan Association, 1919-1920; Legal Advisory Board for Gaston County, 1917-1919; Board of Directors of Gaston County Fair Association, 1916-1920; Congressional Executive Committee, Ninth District, 1920. Superintendent Granite Falls Graded Schools, 1901-1902; Lenoir Graded Schools, 1903-1907; Goldsboro Graded Schools, 1907-1909. Bursar of University of North Carolina, 1909-1912. Mason. I. O. O. F.; Noble Grand, 1919; Grand Guardian, 1920; Deputy Grand Master, 1922; Red Men; Knights of Pythias; Past Councilor, Jr. O. U. A. M.; Kiwanian. Methodist—Steward, 1914-1926. Vice President Alba Cotton Mill, 1920-1922. Married Miss Daisy C. Mackie, 1903. Represented Gaston County in the General Assembly of 1921; Senator from Twenty-sixth District in 1923. Address: Gastonia, N. C.

BUNYAN S. WOMBLE

*(Twenty-second District—*County: Forsyth. One Senator.)

Bunyan S. Womble, Democrat, Senator from Forsyth County, was born in Chatham County, May 2, 1882. Son of Rev. W. F. and Olivia (Snipes) Womble. Educated at public schools of Lincolnton and Belwood Institute; graduated from Trinity College, A.B. degree, 1904. Trinity College Law School and Columbia University. Lawyer. Member North Carolina and American Bar associations. Solicitor City Court, Winston-Salem, 1908-1910. Representative in the General Assembly of 1925. Member Judicial Conference from Eleventh District. Knight of Pythias. Methodist. Married, 1914, Miss Edith Willingham. Address: Winston-Salem, N. C.

WALTER H. WOODSON

*(Twenty-first District—*County: Rowan. One Senator.)

Walter H. Woodson, Democrat, Senator from the twenty-first Senatorial District, was born in Salisbury, April 20, 1875. Son of Horatio Nelson and Margaret Elizabeth (Bostian) Woodson. Attended Salisbury Graded Schools, 1881-1889; James M. Hill's High School at Salisbury, 1889-1892; B.S., University of North Carolina, 1892-1896. University Law School, 1898-1899. Lawyer. Member of North Carolina Bar Association. City Attorney of Salisbury, 1910-1913. Mayor of City of Salisbury, 1913-1919. Chairman Salisbury City School Board, 1913-1919. Chairman of Democratic Executive Committee Rowan County, 1908-1918, and from 1922 to present time. Knight of Pythias. Jr. O. U. A. M. Methodist—Church Trustee. President Rowan County University Alumni Association. Member Legislature, 1921, 1923, and 1925. Chairman Senate Committee on Education, 1921 and 1923. Chairman Senate Committee on Appropriation, 1925. Married Miss Pauline Bernhardt, December 20, 1900. Four sons—Walter, Jr., Paul, Nelson and James Leak. Address, Salisbury, N. C.

REPRESENTATIVES

RICHARD TILMAN FOUNTAIN
SPEAKER

Richard Tilman Fountain, Democrat, Representative from Edgecombe County, was born in same county, February 15, 1885. Son of Almon L. and Louisa (Eagles) Fountain. Was educated in the public schools of Edgecombe County and the Tarboro Male Academy; University of North Carolina, 1905-1907. Lawyer. Member of the North Carolina Bar Association. Vice-President of said Association, 1922-1923; also member of the American Bar Association. President Rocky Mount Bar Association. Judge of the Municipal Court of Rocky Mount, 1911-1918. Trustee of the Rocky Mount Graded Schools; Secretary to the Board, 1917-1921; Chairman of the Board since July 1, 1924. Chairman of the Board of Trustees of the Eastern Carolina Industrial Training School for Boys. Member of the Legislature, sessions of 1919, 1921, 1923 and 1925. Knight of Pythias. Presbyterian. Married Miss Susan Rankin, October, 1918. Three children: Susan Rankin, Anne Sloan, and Margaret Eagles. Address: Rocky Mount, N. C.

WILLIAM BRYANT AUSTIN

William Bryant Austin, Democrat, Representative from Ashe County, was born in Laurel Springs, May 3, 1891. Son of George Bryant and Alice (Woodie) Austin. Attended public schools of Ashe County; Appalachian Training School, 1910-13. A.B., LL.B. University North Carolina, 1919. Lawyer. Member Ashe County Commercial Club, North Carolina Bar Association, American Bar Association, Commercial Law League. President, Ashe County Commercial Club, 1925-26. Chairman, Democratic Executive Committee of Ashe County, 1920-26; Mayor of Jefferson, 1925-26. Private and Second Lieutenant, Machine Gun Corps, World War, 1917-19. Theta Chi; Mason, member of Jefferson Lodge, 219, and Master, 1925-26. Methodist. Married, November 25, 1925, Miss Nona Neal. Address: Jefferson, N. C.

VESTON COULBOURNE BANKS

Veston C. Banks, Democrat, Representative from Pamlico County, was born March 13, 1899, at Grantsboro. Son of N. H. and Deborah A. (Downs) Banks. Graduated from Alliance High School, 1917. Studied law at Wake Forest College, 1917-1920. Teacher. Member North Carolina Education Association. Justice of the Peace. In U. S. Army, 1918. Mason. Free Will Baptist—Church clerk. Married Miss Daisy Mason, June 25, 1925. Address: Grantsboro, N. C.

DANIEL LONG BELL

Daniel Long Bell, Democrat, Representative from Chatham County, was born in Enfield, April 15, 1894. Son of David and Lila (McLin) Bell. Attended Trinity Park School, Durham, 1910-1911; University of North Carolina. A.B., 1915; LL.B., 1917. Lawyer. Town Commissioner and Secretary-Treasurer, Pittsboro, 1919-1926. Second Lieutenant, 25th Field Artillery, 1918-1919. Mason; Knight of Pythias. Episcopalian. Married Miss Allie Peoples, April 6, 1920. Address: Pittsboro, N. C.

WILLIAM H. BELL

William H. Bell, Democrat, Representative from Carteret County, was born at Newport, September 2, 1888. Son of C. A. and Daisy (Newberry) Bell. Attended public schools of Newport. Real Estate dealer. Mayor of Newport, 1923-1925; member Board of Aldermen, 1925-1926. Mason; member Ocean Lodge A. F. and A. M.; Chapter 46, R. A. M.; St. John Commandery No. 10, K. T.; Sudan Temple, A. A. O. N. M. S.; Elm Camp Woodmen of the World; Tent No. 10 The Maccabees; Lodge No. 19 Charitable Brotherhood of North Carolina. Married Miss Leah A. Garner, June 30, 1915. Address: Newport, N. C.

SAMUEL BLACK

Samuel Black, Democrat, Representative from Cabarrus County, was born in same county, January 24, 1875. Son of John M. and

Sarah (Erwin) Black. Attended Mooresville High School, 1889-92. Farmer and merchant. Justice of the peace for twenty years. Presbyterian—Elder. Address: Harrisburg, N. C., R. F. D. No. 2.

WILLIAM BRYAN BOLICH

William Bryan Bolich, Democrat, Representative from Forsyth County, was born in Salisbury, December 16, 1896. Son of John Alonzo and Sallie B. (McMahon) Bolich. Attended Saluda Seminary, 1903-1913; Trinity College, A.B. degree, 1917; University of Budapest, Hungary, Summer School, 1922; Trinity College Law School, 1919-1921; Oxford University, England, 1921-1924; B.A. in Jurisprudence; M.A.; Bachelor of Civil Law. Lawyer. Member of Winston-Salem Junior Bar Association. Ensign U. S. Navy, June, 1918-March, 1919. Member Winston Masonic Lodge, 167; Carolina Consistory of Scottish Rite Masons; Oasis Temple of the Shrine; Kappa Alpha Fraternity; American Legion. Methodist—Chairman Junior Board of Stewards, 1926. North Carolina Rhodes Scholar to Oxford University, England. Address: Winston-Salem, N. C.

LUTHER HUBBARD BOST

Luther H. Bost, Democrat, Representative from Stanly County, was born at Mt. Pleasant, January 28, 1874. Son of S. D. and Martha (Carter) Bost. Attended Albemarle Academy, 1889-1892; Mount Pleasant Collegiate Institute, 1892-1893. Farmer. President Stanly County Cotton Growers' Association for the past four years. County Commissioner, 1907-1908. Representative from Stanly County in the General Assembly of 1915. Member County Board of Education since 1919, chairman since 1924. Methodist—District Steward. Married Miss Sarka Dry, April 1, 1896. Taught school twenty-nine years in Stanly County. Address: Albemarle, N. C., Route 6.

JAMES R. BOYD

James R. Boyd, Democrat, Representative from Haywood County, was born in same county on September 5, 1868. Son of John H. and Rebecca J. (Brown) Boyd. Attended public schools of Haywood County. Banker. Member County Board of Education, 1893-1904. Register of Deeds, 1904-1908. Mayor of Waynesville, 1909-12. Chairman Board of County Commissioners, 1912-16. Chairman Graded School Board, 1915-24. Chairman Democratic Executive Committee, Haywood County, 1910-1914. Odd Fellow; Jr. O. U. A. M.; Royal Arcanum; Noble Grand two terms in I. O. O. F. and Councilor Junior local lodge. Represented both these orders in grand lodge and council meetings. Secretary Royal Arcanum, eighteen years. Methodist—Trustee and Steward, chairman building committee when new $100,000 church was built. Married Miss Sallie Campbell, March 29, 1891. Ten children, all living. Served in House of Representatives, 1925. Address: Waynesville, N. C.

CALVIN O. BOYLES

Calvin O. Boyles, Republican, Representative from Stokes County, was born in that county, April 24, 1878. Son of R. R. and Mary (Newton) Boyles. Attended Mountain View Academy and Boonville High School, 1900. Farmer and Merchant. State Senator, 1905; Postmaster at King, 1922-1924. J. O. U. A. Baptist. Married: first, Miss Jennie Bennett, 1907; second, Miss Beulah Slate, 1921. Address: King, N. C.

SUMTER COE BRAWLEY

Sumter C. Brawley, Democrat, Representative from Durham County, was born in Mooresville, April, 1878. Son of Hiram A. and Susan A. (Mayhew) Brawley. Educated in Mooresville High School and Business College at Charlotte, 1900. Studied law at University of North Carolina, 1905. Lawyer. Member State Democratic Executive Committee since 1912. Elk. Representative in the General Assembly of 1913. Married Miss Margaret Burkett, October, 1907. Three sons. Address: Durham, N. C.

JOHN M. BREWER

John M. Brewer, Democrat, Representative from Wake County, was born in Wake Forest, March 15, 1879. Son of William C. and Louisa M. (Gooch) Brewer. Attended Wake Forest Public Schools and Littleton Male Academy. Graduated from Wake Forest College in 1899 with M.A. Degree. Attended Eastman Business College in 1900. Merchant, farmer, and banker. Member Board of Aldermen, Wake Forest, 1919-1925; School Board, 1919-1925; State Prison Board, 1925-1926. Mason; Jr. O. U. A. M. Baptist. Married Miss Mary Purefoy, August 17, 1904; Miss Loula H. Briggs, October 25, 1922. Address: Wake Forest, N. C.

STACY BREWER

Stacy Brewer, Democrat, Representative from Moore County, was born March 27, 1884. Publisher. Secretary-Treasurer A. and N. C. R. R. Company, 1925-26. Jr. O. U. A. M. Presbyterian. Married Miss Margaret Frye, April 25, 1912. Address: Vass, N. C.

JAMES ALBERT BRIDGER

James A. Bridger, Democrat, Representative from Bladen County, was born in Bladenboro, July 16, 1900. Son of R. L. and Emma (Stone) Bridger. Attended Bladenboro High School. Graduated from Wake Forest College, 1921, with degree of LL.B.; attended Columbia University and Massey's Business College, Richmond. Cotton Manufacturer. Mayor of Bladenboro. Students Army Training Corps, Wake Forest College. Mason; Shriner. Baptist. Address: Bladenboro, N. C.

PRESLEY ELMER BROWN

Presley E. Brown, Republican, Representative from Wilkes County, was born in Mulberry, Wilkes County, March 2, 1879. Son of Millard F. and Alice (Holbrook) Brown. Attended county free school, 1884-1903; Fair View College, Trap Hill, 1904-05. Manufacturer and wholesale lumber dealer. Member Hardwood Lumber Dealers' Association. Sheriff and Treasurer, Wilkes County, 1906-14. Member General Assembly for Wilkes County, 1925. Mason, Odd Fellow and Knight of Pythias. Methodist—Steward since 1921. Married, December 24, 1910, Miss Rosalie Walding. Republican candidate for Congress in Seventh District in 1916. Address: Wilkesboro, N. C.

VON CLINE BULLARD

Von Cline Bullard, Democrat, Representative from Cumberland County, was born in that county, August 9, 1885. Son of Thomas C. Isham and Nancy Matilda Bullard. Attended Salem High School and Oakhurst Academy, 1892-1897, teaching part of the time and going to school part of the time. Studied law at Wake Forest College and obtained license, February, 1900. Lawyer. Member State Bar Association and Ninth District Bar Association. County Attorney for Cumberland County, 1912-1914, and 1924-1926. Representative in the General Assembly of 1903; Mayor of Fayetteville, 1907-1909. Loyal Order of Moose of the World. Baptist. Married Miss Mary B. Kyle, July 5, 1907. Address: Fayetteville, N. C.

JOHN STEWART BUTLER

John S. Butler, Democrat, Representative from Robeson County, was born in Sampson County, August 23, 1887. Son of Robert N. and Alice (Highsmith) Butler. Attended the public schools of Sampson County and Salem High School from 1904-1907. Attended Wake Forest College for three years. Lawyer. Member North Carolina Bar Association and Robeson County Bar Association. Judge of Recorder's Court, St. Pauls District, Robeson County, 1914-1922. Clerk of Town of St. Pauls, 1921-1923. Mason. Baptist— Member Board of Trustees, St. Pauls Church, teacher Bible Class. Married Miss Annie Rebecca Jones, October 25, 1915. Address: St. Pauls, N. C.

ARNOLD W. BYRD

Arnold W. Byrd, Democrat, Representative from Wayne County, was born in Duplin County. Son of N. B. and Bettie C. Byrd. Attended Mount Olive High School, 1905-1909. A.B. of Trinity College, 1913. Attended Trinity College Law School, 1914-1916. Lawyer. Representative from Wayne County in General Assembly, 1919, 1921, 1923, and 1925, and special sessions. Represented North Carolina Colleges in National Peace Oratorical Contest in 1913. Served as First Lieutenant in World War in France, Germany and Belgium, 1918-1919. Mason. Odd Fellow. Rotarian. Methodist—Steward. Address: Mount Olive, N. C.

WILLIAM BAUGHAM CAMPBELL

William Baugham Campbell, Democrat, Representative from New Hanover County, was born at Yatesville, Beaufort County, November 29, 1888. Son of Charles A. and Martha V. (Wilkinson) Campbell. Attended Rhodes Military Institute, 1903-5; Oak Ridge Institute, 1906-7. Attended University Law School, 1912-1913. Lawyer. Member North Carolina Bar Association; New Hanover County Bar Association; and Lions Club. Member National Guard for two years. Jr. O. U. A. M. Episcopalian—Vestryman; Junior and Senior Warden. Married Miss Jeannette Robbins, July 31, 1917. Address: Wilmington, N. C.

THOMAS H. COFFEY

Thomas H. Coffey, Democrat, Representative from Watauga County. Address: Blowing Rock, N. C.

HENRY GROVES CONNOR

Henry G. Connor, Democrat, Representative from Wilson County, was born at Wilson, July 19, 1876. Son of Henry Groves and Kate (Whitfield) Connor. Was educated at Wilson Graded Schools; private schools in Wilson; B.S. of University of North Carolina, 1897. Law School, University of North Carolina, 1898. Lawyer. Chairman

County Democratic Executive Committee. Delegate National Democratic Convention, 1916 and 1924. Sigma Alpha Epsilon (College fraternity). Member of the State Senate, 1919; House of Representatives, 1921, 1923, and 1925. Married Miss Elizabeth Clark, April 17, 1901. Address: Wilson, N. C.

BERIAH THADDEUS COX

Beriah Thaddeus Cox, Democrat, of Pitt County, was born in Pitt County, July 30, 1863. Son of Josiah and Sarah Ann (Tyson) Cox. Educated at Coxville, and at University of North Carolina, 1884-1886; University of Maryland. M.D., 1888. Physician and farmer. Superintendent of Health for Pitt County, 1890-1893. Member Medical Society of North Carolina; Ex-President Pitt County Medical Society. Representative from Pitt County in General Assembly, 1909, 1913. President and director of Winterville Cotton Oil Mills; president and director of Farmers Bank, Greenville; vice president and director of the Bank of Winterville. Primitive Baptist. Married Mary V. Smith in 1891, four daughters living and one son dead. Address: Winterville, N. C.

ROBERT MARTIN COX

Robert Martin Cox, Democrat, Representative from Forsyth County, was born in that county, July 9, 1876. Son of Romulus L. and Susan E. (Barrow) Cox. Farmer and seed merchant. Representative in the General Assembly, 1907, 1917, 1919, 1921, 1923, and 1925. Methodist Protestant. Married, 1917, Miss Lillian Miller. Two children. Address: Winston-Salem, N. C.

WILEY EVERETTE COX

Wiley E. Cox, Democrat, Representative from Alleghany County, was born in Sparta, January 8, 1853. Son of Cloyd and Cynthia (Reeves) Cox. Attended Brown and Phipps School, Independence, Va., 1868-1869. Farmer. Clerk Superior Court, 1890-1898; County

Commissioner four years, member County Board of Education; County Supervisor under the Revaluation Act, 1919-1920. Methodist Steward. Married Miss Laura E. Maxwell, May 11, 1882. Address: Stratford, N. C.

THOMAS CREEKMORE

Thomas Creekmore, Democrat, Representative from Wake County. Born, June 11, 1888. Son of H. T. and Annie C. (Baker) Creekmore. Attended public schools, William and Mary College, 1908; Law Department, George Washington University, 1914. Lawyer. Member Legislature, 1925. American Bar Association, North Carolina Bar Association, Wake County Bar Association, Kiwanis Club, Sigma Phi Epsilon Fraternity, Mason, Shriner, Presbyterian. Secretary Wake County Democratic Executive Committee, 1924-26. Married Miss Christina Friedlin, 1914. Two children. Address: Raleigh, N. C.

WILLIAM DUNN, Jr.

William Dunn, Jr., Democrat, Representative from Craven County, was born in New Bern, August 31, 1882. Son of John and Lucretia R. (Guion) Dunn. Attended private school, 1889-1896; and New Bern High School, 1896-1899. Graduated from University of North Carolina, 1904, with Ph.B. degree. Attended University Law School. Lawyer. Member North Carolina Bar Association. Mason; B. P. O. E.; D. K. E., College Fraternity. Episcopalian. Married Miss Octavia W. Hughes, December 14, 1907. Address: New Bern, N. C.

HALL MORRISON EDDLEMAN

Hall Morrison Eddleman, Democrat, Representative from Gaston County, was born in Mount Holly, June 13, 1858. Son of D. F. and Louisa F. (Summerrow) Eddleman. Attended Denver Academy, 1876-1879; Louisville (Ky.) Medical College, 1880-1881; College of Physicians and Surgeons, Baltimore, Maryland, 1886. Physician. Member North Carolina Medical Society, Gaston County Medical Society, and Southern Medical Association. Presbyterian. Married Mrs. Jennie Parks Williams, 1893. Address: Gastonia, N. C.

TAZEWELL AUGUSTUS EURE

Tazewell A. Eure, Democrat, Representative from Gates County, was born in Gates County, April 5, 1875. Son of Henry A. and Adminter S. (Johnson) Eure. Attended Gatesville High School, 1887-1893; A. and M. College, Raleigh, 1894-1895. Farmer. Director Bank of Gates, Gatesville, since its organization in 1904. Member Board of Education, Gates County, in 1920. Representative from Gates County in General Assembly, 1925. Member Christian Church—deacon since 1900; Sunday school superintendent since 1918. Married Miss Mecy E. Langstun, who died in 1916. Married second time, Miss Lucy P. Johnson, in 1920. Address: Eure, N. C.

JAMES ALPHONSO EVERETT

James A. Everett, Democrat, Representative from Martin County, was born in Hamilton, August 2, 1886. Son of Justus and Elizabeth (Purvis) Everett. Attended Trinity Park High School and graduated from the University of North Carolina in 1910 with the degree of A.B. Farmer. Methodist—Superintendent of Sunday school. Married Miss Minnie Whichard, December 12, 1917. Address: Palmyra, N. C.

REUBEN OSCAR EVERETT

Reuben Oscar Everett, Democrat, Representative from Durham County, was born in October, 1879. Son of Justus and Elizabeth (Purvis) Everett. Graduate of the University of North Carolina, 1903; post graduate work at Duke, Columbia and Harvard Universities. Lawyer. Member House of Representatives, 1921, 1923, 1925. Chairman North Carolina Cotton Commission, and of the Cotton States Commission. Trustee of the University of North Carolina. Represented North Carolina at the World Cotton Conference at Liverpool and Manchester in 1921. President North Carolina Agricultural Society, 1917. President North Carolina Division Bryan Memorial Association. Married Miss Kathrine McDiarmid Robinson, June, 1926. Episcopalian. Address: Durham, N. C.

BAYARD THURMAN FALLS

Bayard T. Falls, Democrat, Representative from Cleveland County, was born in Cleveland County January 28, 1879. Son of J. Z. and Sarah Catherine (Cline) Falls. Attended Belwood Institute; Piedmont High School; Fallston High School; Wake Forest College, 1899-1903, A.B. and M.A. degrees. Wake Forest College Law School, 1907-1908; Columbia University, summer 1906. Lawyer. Member Kiwanis Club. Superintendent Cleveland County schools, 1905-1911. County Recorder and Auditor, Cleveland County, 1916 to December 1, 1924. Representative in the General Assembly of 1925. Member Jr. O. U. A. M. Odd Fellow. Baptist. Married Miss Selma Eskridge, 1909. Address: Shelby, N. C.

EDWARD GASKILL FLANAGAN

Edward G. Flanagan, Democrat, Representative from Pitt County, was born in Greenville, December 3, 1875. Son of John and Mary W. (Gaskill) Flanagan. Attended Greenville High School. President Greenville Bank and Trust Company. Owner and general manager John Flanagan Buggy Company. Odd Fellow; Knight of Pythias; twice Chancellor Commander Local Lodge Knights of Pythias. Baptist—Trustee. Married, October 18, 1899, Miss Rosa M. Hooker. Address: Greenville, N. C.

JOHN HAMLIN FOLGER

John Hamlin Folger, Democrat, Representative from Surry County, was born at Rockford. Son of Thos. Wilson and Ada Dillard (Robertson) Folger. Educated at Dobson High School, 1895; Yadkinville Normal School, 1896-1898. Attended Guilford College and the University Law School in 1901. Lawyer. Member North Carolina Bar Association and the American Bar Association. Mayor of Mount Airy, 1909-1910. Member Granite Lodge A. F. & A. M. No. 322; Blue Ridge Council No. 72. Jr. O. U. A. M. Methodist—Trustee. Married Miss Maude Douglas, November 4, 1899. Address: Mount Airy, N. C.

CLOSS GIBBS

Closs Gibbs, Democrat, Representative from Hyde County, was born in Engelhard, Hyde County, September 12, 1879. Son of Charles E. P. and Sarah Elizabeth (Swindell) Gibbs. Attended schools of Engelhard and LaGrange. Merchant and farmer. Chairman Lakelanding Credit Association; vice president Engelhard Banking and Trust Company. Chairman County Commissioners, 1920-1922; Mayor of Engelhard. Methodist; trustee; steward; chairman building committee. Married Miss Maude A. Gibbs, August 17, 1910. Address: Engelhard, N. C.

JOHN HAMPTON GILES

John Hampton Giles, Democrat, Representative from Burke County, was born in Glen Alpine, February 22, 1867. Son of John M. and Ruth (Butler) Giles. Attended school in Glen Alpine. Lumber and furniture dealer. Register of Deeds, 1898-1900. Knight of Pythias, Odd Fellow and Jr. O. U. A. M. Methodist—steward and chairman of the board. Married, October 8, 1893, Miss Ida E. Pitts. Address: Glen Alpine, N. C.

THOMAS JACKSON GOLD

Thomas Jackson Gold, Democrat, Representative from Guilford County. Graduate University of North Carolina, 1903; University Law School, 1904. Lawyer. Judge Recorder's Court of High Point, 1911-1912. Representative in the General Assembly, 1913, 1919. Presidential Elector, Fifth Congressional District. Trustee University of North Carolina. Elk; Shriner. Address: High Point, N. C.

ALEXANDER HAWKINS GRAHAM

Alexander Hawkins Graham, Democrat, Representative from Orange County, was born at Hillsboro, August, 1890. Son of John W. and Maggie F. (Bailey) Graham. Received his preparatory education in the Episcopal High School, Alexandria, Va., 1906-1908;

A.B. Degree, University of North Carolina, 1912. Attended Law School, University of North Carolina, 1912-1913; also Summer Law School, 1913; and Harvard Law School, 1913-1914. Lawyer. Member North Carolina Bar Association. During recent World War served from May 13, 1917, to July 15, 1919, being commissioned Second Lieutenant at First Officers Training Camp, Fort Oglethorpe, Ga.; promoted to First Lieutenant and then to Captain, serving overseas with the Eighty-first Division. Member of the Legislature since 1921. Episcopalian. Married Miss Kathleen Long in August, 1917. Address: Hillsboro, N. C.

ARCHIBALD McLEAN GRAHAM

Archibald McLean Graham, Democrat, Representative from Sampson County, was born in Wallace, October 28, 1873. Son of Daniel McLean and Elizabeth Ann (Murphy) Graham. Attended Clement School, Wallace, 1888-1891. B.L., University of Virginia, 1899. Lawyer. Mayor of Clinton, 1909-1913. Second Lieutenant North Carolina National Guard, 1905-1908. Mason; Master of Lodge, 1911-1912. Married Miss Allie Moseley Lee, December 12, 1906. Address: Clinton, N. C.

A. TURNER GRANT, JR.

A. Turner Grant, Jr., Republican, Representative from Davie County, was born in Mocksville, June 2, 1876. Son of A. T. and Rebecca (Parker) Grant. Attended Mocksville Academy, 1890-1897, and the University of North Carolina. Lawyer. Representative in the General Assemblies of 1903, 1905, 1907, 1909 and 1921; State Senator, 1913; 1925. Food Administrator for Davie County, 1917-1918; Chairman Liberty Loan Committee, Davie County, during World War. Married Miss Helen Brewster, March 18, 1908. Address: Mocksville, N. C.

JOHN L. GWALTNEY

John L. Gwaltney, Democrat, Representative from Alexander County, was born in Alexander County. Son of James and Clorinda

Gwaltney. Attended Cedar Run Academy, 1866-68; Rutherford College, 1869-1873; studied law in private school. Lawyer. Local counsel for Southern Railroad for ten years. Register of Deeds for six years. Chairman of the Board of Education, two years. City Alderman, two years. County attorney, six years. Director of the Penitentiary during Aycock's Administration. Mason; Eastern Star; Jr. O. U. A. M.; Master of Lodge; Secretary; District Deputy Grand Master; Worthy Patron in Eastern Star. Baptist—Deacon for 20 years. Moderator of Alexander Association for past ten years. Taught school for 15 years. Married March 12, 1876, to Miss Emma E. Connally. Address: Taylorsville, N. C.

FREDERICK WALTER HARGETT, JR.

Frederick W. Hargett, Jr., Democrat, Representative from Onslow County, was born in that county, May 7, 1889. Son of Frederick Walter and Penie S. (Thompson) Hargett. Attended Warrenton High School, 1904-1906; University of North Carolina, 1907-1908. Farmer and live stock dealer. Alderman town of Jacksonville, four years; and mayor for last seven years. Mason and Shriner. Married Miss Leila May Sabiston, November 2, 1910. Address: Jacksonville, N. C.

REGINALD LEE HARRIS

Reginald Lee Harris, Democrat, Representative from Person County, was born in Roxboro, September 9, 1890. Son of William Henry and Rosa Lee (Jordan) Harris. Attended Virginia Military Institute. Cotton Manufacturer. Secretary and Treasurer Roxboro Cotton Mills; Treasurer Laura Cotton Mills; Secretary Greenville Cotton Mills. Member Rotary Club; Kappa Alpha. Methodist. Married Miss Katherine Jones Long, December 10, 1915. Address: Roxboro, N. C.

JOHN ELLIS HART

John Ellis Hart, Democrat, Representative from Anson County, was born in Mecklenburg County, 1876. Son of James T. and Rebecca (McCall) Hart. Attended Union Institute; Bain Academy, 1890-1894; University of North Carolina, 1894-95; University of Maryland, 1895-1897; graduate of medicine in 1897. Physician. Farmer. Member Anson County and North Carolina Medical societies. Life member Board of Directors Anson Sanatorium; Director State Hospital, Goldsboro; Vice President Wadesboro Chamber of Commerce. Director in Bank of Wadesboro. Chairman Board of Commissioners, 1914-1920. Mason—Shriner. Odd Fellow. Knight of Pythias. Presbyterian. Married Miss Josephine Redfern, 1898. Address: Wadesboro, N. C.

MATTHIAS D. HAYMAN

Mathias D. Hayman, Democrat, Representative from Dare County, was born at Kitty Hawk, August 5, 1868. Son of Daniel and Abby (Tillett) Hayman. Attended public schools of Dare County; Business School in Manteo in 1890. Fisherman. Member Wanchese Lodge No. 521 A. F. & A. M. Representative in the General Assembly of 1925. Methodist. Married Miss Zora W. Daniels, 1894. Address: Wanchese, N. C.

OSCAR HAYWOOD

Oscar Haywood, Democrat, Representative from Montgomery County, was born near Mount Gilead. Son of William and Henrietta (Baldwin) Haywood. Attended county schools; Mount Gilead Academy, 1879-1881; Wake Forest College, 1882-1885; honorary degree of D.D. by Southwestern Baptist University, 1906. Farmer, lecturer, and preacher. Life Member Ministers' Conference of New York; International Chautauqua and Lyceum Association. Baptist. Ordained to ministry, Kendal's Church, Stanly County, 1887. Author of *Practical Christianity*, 1894; *Jean Val Jean*, 1901; Address, "A Hundred Years of Contemporaneous History." Married Miss Marion Pleasants, of Huntsville, Ala., 1896. Widower. Pastor Baptist Church of the Covenant, New York City, for twelve years. Address: Mount Gilead, N. C.

T. L. A. HELMS

T. L. A. Helms, Democrat, Representative from Union County, was born near Monroe, January 25, 1857. Son of Joseph C. and Francis A. (McLarty) Helms. Attended public schools in county and Monroe High School about 1878. Farmer. Mayor of Unionville, 1916-1918. Magistrate, 1919. Mayor of Benton Heights, 1926. Corporal in the State Guard. Methodist—Steward; Sunday school Superintendent, 1896-1919. Married Miss Ellie Caldwell, 1885. Address: Monroe, N. C., Route 6.

JOHN BRIGHT HILL

John Bright Hill, Democrat, Representative from New Hanover County, was born in Warsaw, August 25, 1897. Son of William L. and Mary Lou Hill. Attended Warrenton High School. A.B., University of North Carolina, 1917. Attended University of North Carolina Law School and Harvard Law School and obtained license in 1920. Commander Wilmington Post No. 10, American Legion; Phi Delta Phi, legal fraternity; Exchange Club. Judge Juvenile Court of New Hanover County. Attended United States Military Academy, West Point. B. P. O. E.; 32d Degree Mason; Shriner— Sudan Temple. Presbyterian. Married Katherine Taylor, November 9, 1926. Address: Wilmington, N. C.

THEO M. JENKINS

Theo M. Jenkins, Republican, Representative from Graham County, was born in Fairview, Buncombe County, in 1887. Son of C. L. and Sue L. (Redmond) Jenkins. Attended Fairview Collegiate Institute, 1905; University of North Carolina (Summer School), 1908; Wake Forest Law School, 1917. Lawyer. Member North Carolina Bar Association. Mayor of Robbinsville, 1922; County Attorney for Graham County, 1917-1920, 1922; United States Government Appeal Agent, Attorney to Local Board, Graham County, 1917-1919. Representative in General Assembly of 1923; Member North

Carolina Budget Commission, 1923-1925. Mason. Shriner—Oasis Temple. Baptist. Married Miss Winnie V. Mauney, November 23, 1916. Address: Robbinsville, N. C.

EDWIN R. JOHNSON

Edwin R. Johnson, Democrat, Representative from Currituck County, was born near Currituck Court House, September 10, 1868. Son of Silas P. and Carolina (Coulter) Johnson. Attended the public schools of the county and the Atlantic Collegiate Institute of Elizabeth City. Merchant. Chairman of the County Democratic Executive Committee for thirty years. Member State Senate, 1909 and 1917. Member House of Rpresentatives, 1919, 1921, and 1925. Food Administrator for Currituck County during the World War. Chairman County Highway Commission, 1923-1924; Chairman Game Commission, 1923-24; Chairman of the Board of County Commissioners and of the Board of Education. Married Mrs. Genevieve Holleman, 1910. Address: Currituck, N. C.

CHARLES ANDREW JONAS

Charles Andrew Jonas, Republican, Representative from Lincoln County, was born in Lincoln County, August 14, 1876. Son of Cephas and Martha (Scrouce) Jonas. Attended Ridge Academy and Fallston Institute, 1886-1889; Ph.B., 1902; University Law School, 1905. Lawyer. State Senator, 1915-17. Assistant United States Attorney, Western District, 1921-25. Junior O. U. A. M., Odd Fellow; held all offices in local lodge. Methodist. Married, August 23, 1902, Miss Rosa Petrie. Address: Lincolnton, N. C.

HUBERT RANSOM JONES

Hubert Ransom Jones, Democrat, Representative from Johnston County, was born in Johnston County, March 13, 1884. Son of James A. T. and Sara (Barnes) Jones. Attended Mount Zion Academy. Farmer. Mason. Missionary Baptist. Address: McCullers, N. C., Route 1.

A. YANCEY KERR

A. Yancey Kerr, Democrat, Representative from Caswell County, was born in Yanceyville. Son of John H. Kerr and Eliza Catherine (Yancey) Kerr. Attended school at Yanceyville, and Wake Forest College, 1897-99. Editor and insurance writer. Postmaster, Yanceyville, during Wilson administration. Junior O. U. A. M. Married in 1919 to Miss Mary Johnson Oliver. Address: Yanceyville, N. C.

LOOMIS FRANKLIN KLUTZ

Loomis Franklin Klutz, Republican, Representative from Catawba County, was born at Maiden, N. C., May 27, 1888. Son of Dr. P. J. and Luella (Carpenter) Klutz. Attended South Fork Institute, 1900-1903, and Catawba College, 1903-1907. A.B. of Washington and Lee University, 1910. Bachelor of Oratory Degree, Valparaiso University, 1911. Certificate of Highest Honor in Debating from Valparaiso University, 1911. Trinity College Law School, Wake Forest College Law School. Attorney and Farmer. Member North Carolina Bar Association. Attorney for Alexander County, 1914-18; Attorney for Catawba County, 1918-22; Solicitor for Catawba County, 1918-22; Government Attorney for Alexander and Catawba counties during World War; Attorney for Highway Commission for Catawba County since 1919; Attorney for Maiden since 1922; appointed by Governor McLean, delegate to the Pan American Congress held in New York City, December, 1925. Representative in General Assembly, 1925. Mason—Eastern Star; White Shrine; Royal Arch; Secretary of Taylorsville Chapter O.E.S.; Worthy Patron of Maiden Chapter O.E.S.; Grand Sentinel of the Grand Chapter of North Carolina, O.E.S. Member Grace Reformed Church, Newton; former Superintendent of Sunday school. Author of a Post Card description of North Carolina, also a description of Catawba County. Married, September 28, 1922, Mrs. Maggie Lou Turner, formerly Miss Cline. Have one daughter, Mary Ella. Address: Newton, N. C.

CHARLES G. LEE, Jr.

Charles G. Lee, Jr., Democrat, Representative from Buncombe County, was born in Asheville, February 3, 1900. Son of Charles

G. and Mary Lavinia (Justice) Lee. Attended Asheville High School, 1914-1916; North State Fitting School, 1916; Horner Military School, Charlotte, 1916-1918; graduated from the University of North Carolina, 1922, with A.B. degree; University Law School, 1922-1924. Lawyer. Member North Carolina Bar Association and Buncombe County Bar Association. In the navy during World War. A. T. O. Fraternity and Phi Alpha Delta (Law fraternity). Baptist. Married Miss Marie Matthews, April 18, 1925. Address: Asheville, N. C.

LOVIRA WRIGHT LEGGETT

Lovira W. Leggett, Democrat, Representative from Halifax County, was born at Louisville, Ky., August 26, 1877. Son of Dr. Kenelm and Augusta (Wright) Leggett. Attended school at Buies Creek, 1898; Oak Ridge Institute, 1900-1901; Trinity School (Chocowinity), 1901-1905; Wake Forest College, 1905-1909; Summer Law School, 1910; two years medicine and two years law at Wake Forest College. Lawyer. Member Scotland Neck Lodge No. 470 A. F. & A. M.; and William R. Davie Chapter, Rose Croix, No. 4. Representative in the General Assembly of 1925. Married Miss Sallie Hyman, 1914. Address: Hobgood, N. C.

WILLIAM FRANKLIN LITTLE

William F. Little, Democrat, Representative from Polk County, was born at Carmi, Illinois, June 21, 1876. Son of George Robert and Cynthia Anne (Barton) Little. Attended public schools of Carmi and Carmi High School, 1882-1894. Banker. Chairman Liberty Loan Committee and Polk County Chapter Red Cross. Chairman Board of Education, Tryon Graded Schools. Honorary Commission Lieutenant, Spanish-American War, 1898 (Pillows Provisional Regiment, Carmi, Illinois). Keeper records and seal, Tryon Lodge Knights of Pythias, 1917-1918. Congregationalist. Trustee Erskine Memorial Church. Editor Carmi *Times*, 1910; *Polk County News* and Tryon *Bee*, 1914-1917. Married Miss Dale Pritchett, of Denver, Colorado, in 1907. Address: Tryon, N. C

ED S. LOVEN

Ed S. Loven, Democrat, Representative from Avery County, was born in Burke County, 1872. Son of Anderson and Mary (Webb) Loven. Received education in Public Schools. Merchant. Sheriff of Avery County, 1911-1912. Representative from Avery County in 1923. Mason. Presbyterian. Married Miss Myrtle L. Clay in 1895. Address: Linville, N. C.

MALCOM HUGH McBRYDE

Malcom Hugh McBryde, Democrat, Representative from Rockingham County, was born in Linden, September 12, 1877. Son of Rev. D. D. and F. N. (McKay) McBryde. Attended Little River Academy, 1885-92; Boston Latin School, Boston, Mass., 1893-96. A.B., Davidson College, 1896-98; M.D., University College of Medicine, Va., 1898-1901. Physician. Member N. C. Medical Society, Southern Medical Society, Rockingham County Medical Society. President Caswell County Medical Society, 1907-08. Coroner of Rockingham County. Elected Coroner Caswell County, 1904. Commissioner, town of Milton, 1906-08. Knight of Pythias; Chancellor Commander of K. of P. Presbyterian. Widower. Reidsville, N. C.

N. B. McDEVITT

N. B. McDevitt, Democrat, Representative from Madison County, was born in that county, December 22, 1875. Son of Rev. P. and Sarah E. (Rice) McDevitt. Educated at Mars Hill and Wake Forest College. Wholesale Grocer. County Tax Assessor, Madison County; Member Board of County Commissioners, six years—chairman, four years; Clerk Superior Court, Madison County; Member Board of Education, four years; teacher, three years. Baptist. Married Miss Alice Hurt. Address: Marshall, N. C.

ANGUS D. MacLEAN

Angus D. MacLean, Democrat, Representative from Beaufort County, was born in Maxton, July 12, 1877. Son of John A. and

Mary Virginia (Brown) MacLean. Educated in private school at Maxton and Laurinburg High School; attended University of North Carolina, 1894-1895 and 1896-1897; University Law School, 1898. Member North Carolina Bar Association and American Bar Association; B. P. O. E.; Knight of Pythias. Presbyterian. Married Miss Annetta Everett, October 24, 1900. Member law firm of Small, MacLean & Rodman. Address: Washington, N. C.

CARRIE LEE McLEAN

Carrie L. McLean, Democrat, Representative from Mecklenburg County, was born in Lincolnton, September 25, 1873. Daughter of James Logan and Margaret Ann (Smith) McLean. Attended Lincolnton High School and Chowan College in 1894. Studied law under a private teacher and licensed to practice in 1918. Took special course in American Government and Economics at Columbia University. Lawyer. Member Mecklenburg County, North Carolina, and American Bar associations. President Mecklenburg Bar Association in 1925; Public Administrator for Mecklenburg County. Member Altrusa Club and Woman's Club of Charlotte and League of Woman Voters. First vice president from North Carolina of the National Federation of Business and Professional Women's Clubs, holding this office three years and also vice president of the State Association. Baptist. Address: Charlotte, N. C.

WILLIAM HENRY MACON

William Henry Macon, Democrat, Representative from Franklin County, was born at Ingleside, June 1, 1862. Son of Sabastian and Sallie (Thomas) Macon. Attended private school and Louisburg Academy, 1874-1882. County Tax Assessor. Mayor Louisburg, 1900-1908. Member General Assembly, 1919. Methodist—steward. Married Miss Lizzie L. Jones, October 4, 1887. Address: Louisburg, N. C.

OSCAR PERCY MAKEPEACE

Oscar P. Makepeace, Democrat, Representative from Lee County, was born in Noblesville, Ind., February 18, 1883. Son of George Henry and Nannie (Fisher) Makepeace. Attended local schools and Buie's Creek Academy. President and General Manager Sanford Sash and Blind Company. City Alderman. Mayor. Chairman School Board. Highway Commissioner. Rotarian. Representative in the General Assembly, 1925. Member Lodge No. 120, A.F. and A.M.; Lee Chapter No. 72; Southern Pines Commandery No. 16; Charlotte Consistory No. 1. Methodist—Chairman Board of Stewards, 1924-25. Married twice, first to Miss Zelma Turner Austin, 1904; second to Miss Edelweiss King, 1920. Address: Sanford, N. C.

JAMES A. MARSHALL

James A. Marshall, Democrat, Representative from Forsyth County, was born in same county, March 25, 1866. Son of J. Matt and Sallie P. (Haizlip) Marshall. Educated in private and public schools. Farmer. Justice of the peace, twenty-seven years. Representative in General Assembly of 1925. Jr. O. U. A. M.; Knight of Honor. Councilor Jr. O. U. A. M., Past Councilor at present. Married, 1889, Miss Victoria Allen. Address: Walnut Cove, N. C.

LISTER A. MARTIN

Lister A. Martin, Democrat, Representative from Davidson County, was born in Leaksville, October 29, 1885. Son of A. B. J. and Lula W. (Hubbard) Martin. Attended Leaksville Public School; Oak Ridge Institute, 1904; University North Carolina, 1906-08. Lawyer. Member North Carolina Bar Association, Davidson County Bar. Judge Recorder's Court, Thomasville, 1911-13; Solicitor Recorder's Court, Thomasville, 1913-14; Member Board of Aldermen, city of Lexington, 1920; Member Lexington High School Board, 1925-26. Member Rotary Club. Baptist—formerly Superintendent Sunday school, member Board Deacons, teacher Junior Baraca Class. Married, May 24, 1911, Miss Jessie King. Address: Lexington, N. C.

VAN BUREN MARTIN

Van Buren Martin, Democrat, Representative from Washington County, was born in Northampton County. Son of J. V. and Ida (Stancell) Martin. Received his preparatory education at Conway High School and Whitsett Institute. B.L. of Wake Forest College, 1904. Mayor of Plymouth, 1919-1920. Superintendent of Public Schools, Washington County, 1909-1910. Prosecuting attorney for Washington County, 1910-1919. Member of State Senate from Second Senatorial District, 1909 and 1911. Member State Legislature, 1921 and 1923, from Washington County. A. F. and A. M., Knight of Pythias, Royal Arch Mason. Baptist. Married, in 1907, to Miss Estell Johnston. Address: Plymouth, N. C.

OSCAR FERDINAND MASON, JR.

Oscar F. Mason, Jr., Democrat, Representative from Gaston County, was born in Dallas, December 23, 1901. Son of Oscar F. and Fannie (Durham) Mason. Attended Blue Ridge High School, Hendersonville, 1916-1919; N. C. State College, 1920-1922; University of North Carolina, 1922-1924. Lawyer. Member North Carolina Bar Association; Civitan Club. Chairman Gaston County Board of Elections, 1926. Mason. Prelate Knights of Pythias, Kappa Sigma Fraternity. Baptist. Married Miss Lillian Grace McLean, June 2, 1926. Address: Gastonia, N. C.

WALTER JOHNSON MATTHEWS

Walter Johnson Matthews, Democrat, Representative from Scotland County, was born at Wagram, September 29, 1899. Son of Walter Jesse and Mary (Johnson) Matthews. Attended Spring Hill preparatory school. Graduated from Wake Forest College in 1922. Farmer. Private U. S. Army, 1918. Baptist—Sunday school Superintendent, teacher Barca Class. Address: Wagram, N. C.

WILLIAM FOWLER MORGAN

William F. Morgan, Democrat, Representative from Perquimans County, was born in that county, August 9, 1885. Son of Thomas C. and Addie (Speight) Morgan. Life underwriter. Member Democratic Executive Committee. Member North Carolina National Guards, 1909-1912; enlisted as private; discharged as First Quartermaster. Member Farmers' Educational and Coöperative Union of America; Jr. O. U. A. M., Member State Council held at Durham, 1914. Member General Assembly, 1917 and 1919. Baptist. Married October 22, 1907, Miss Neva Clyde Ausborn. Address: Winfall, N. C.

IRA CLEVELAND MOSER

Ira Cleveland Moser, Democrat, Representative from Randolph County, was born at Rock Creek, February 6, 1886. Son of Thaddeus Lucian and Barbara (Garrett) Moser. Attended Friendship Academy and Oak Ridge Institute. Graduated University of North Carolina, 1911; University Law School, 1915. Lawyer. Member North Carolina Bar Association; Asheboro Chamber of Commerce. Member North Carolina General Assembly, 1923. Lutheran. Married, August 14, 1918, Miss Lou Ola Tuttle. Address: Asheboro, N. C.

OTWAY BINNS MOSS

Otway Binns Moss, Democrat, Representative from Nash County, was born in Wilson, October 20, 1890. Son of Vernon F. and Loula A. (Binns) Moss. Attended Wilson graded schools; LL.B., Wake Forest, 1913. Lawyer. Vice Recorder, Nash County Court, 1916-1922; Supervisor Census Fourth Congressional District, 1919-20; Member school board, 1918-1922; Chairman Democratic Executive Committee, Manning's Township, 1916-1926; Member County Executive Committee, 1916-1926. State Senator, 1923. Mason—Shrine, Sudan Temple. Baptist superintendent of Sunday school, 1920. Married Miss Dolly Edwards, June 2, 1915. Address: Spring Hope, N. C.

THOMAS JULIAN MOSS

Thomas Julian Moss, Democrat, Representative from Rutherford County, was born at Forest City in 1900, September 10. Son of W. S. and Mattie Agnew (Goode) Moss. Educated at Forest City High School; Wake Forest College, B.A. and LL.B. degrees, 1922-23. Lawyer. Kiwanis Club. Member Students Army Training Corps, 1918. Mason. Member Kappa Alpha Fraternity, Knights of Pythias, American Legion. Baptist. Member Wake Forest Football Team, 1919-22; All-State Tackle; Track Team, and Athletic Council, 1921; President Athletic Association and President "W" Club. Representative from Rutherford County in the General Assembly of 1925; reëlected in 1926. Member Rutherford County and State Bar associations. City Attorney for Forest City, Attorney for Farmers Bank and Trust Company, Attorney for Industrial Loan and Investment Bank. Discharged from United States Army, December 12, 1918. Address: Forest City, N. C.

WALTER MURPHY

Walter Murphy, Democrat, Representative from Rowan County, was born in Salisbury, N. C., October, 1872. Son of Andrew and Helen (Long) Murphy. Educated at the University of North Carolina. Attended University Law School, 1892-1894. Lawyer. Trustee of University since 1903, and member of executive committee of the Board of Trustees. General Secretary of the Alumni of the University of North Carolina. Trustee, North Carolina Sanatorium for the Treatment of Tuberculosis, 1907-1914. Member State Democratic Executive Committee, 1898, 1913. City Attorney for Salisbury, 1903-1908. Member General Assembly, 1897, 1901, 1903, 1905, 1907, 1913, 1915, 1917, 1921, 1923, 1925; Speaker of House of Representatives, Extra Session, 1913, and Regular Session, 1917. Reading Clerk of the Senate, 1899. Elector at Large, 1908. B. P. O. E., F. O. E., Red Men, Knights of Pythias, Mason. A. A. O. N. M. S. Oasis Temple, Sigma Nu (College) Fraternity. President of the General Alumni Association of the University. President, Salisbury Kiwanis Club. Member of Advisory Budget Commission. Episcopalian. Married Miss Maud Harvey, 1903. Address: Salisbury, N. C.

MARVIN WESLEY NASH

Marvin W. Nash, Democrat, Representative from Richmond County, was born in Greenville, May 13, 1878. Son of Rev. L. L. and Louise (Taylor) Nash. Attended Raleigh Male Academy, 1888-1891; Cape Fear Academy, Wilmington, 1892-1894; Fayetteville Military Academy, 1896-1898; University of North Carolina Law School, 1899-1900. Lawyer. Member North Carolina Bar Association. City Attorney, Hamlet, 1910-1920; Senator Twenty-first District, 1921; Solicitor Thirteenth Judicial District, September, 1921-December, 1922. Mason; Knight of Pythias; Royal Arch, Knights Templar, Shrine. Methodist. Married Miss Rosa R. Hart, 1905. Address: Hamlet, N. C.

HARRY L. NETTLES

Harry L. Nettles, Democrat, Representative from Buncombe County, was born at Biltmore, in 1885. Son of W. M. and Eliza (Joyner) Nettles. Attended public schools, Christ School, and Asheville Business College, 1906. Farmer. Representative in the General Assembly of 1915, 1923, and 1925. Knight of Pythias. Jr. O. U. A. M. Modern Woodmen of America. D. O. K. K. Married Miss Margaret Gibson in 1908. Address: Biltmore, N. C.

CYRUS HERBERT NICHOLSON

Cyrus Herbert Nicholson, Republican, Representative from Jackson County, was born in Cowarts, August 29, 1898. Son of James Marion and Nancy Ellen (Wood) Nicholson. Attended Cullowhee Normal and Industrial School, 1915-1918, 1921-1922; Wake Forest College Law School, 1923-25. Lawyer. Baptist. Address: Cowarts, N. C.

WALTER JAMES NORWOOD

Walter J. Norwood, Democrat, Representative from Halifax County, was born in Ante, Virginia, July 12, 1895. Son of M.D. and Lucy J. (Taylor) Norwood. Cotton Buyer. First Sergeant World War, 1917-1920. Mason; Odd Fellow; Red Man. Baptist—Deacon, Sunday school teacher. Address: Rosemary, N. C.

WILLIAM P. ODOM

William P. Odom, Republican, Representative from Cherokee County, was born in Graham County, April 16, 1888. Son of W. G. and .... (Phillips) Odom. Attended public schools. Real estate and insurance. Register of Deeds, Cherokee County, 1914-1918; Sheriff, 1920-1924. Private; six months in training camp, 1918. Mason. Methodist. Address: Murphy, N. C.

WILLIAM McDUFFIE OLIVER

William McDuffie Oliver, Democrat, Representative from Robeson County, was born August 29, 1886. Son of James S. and Annie (McDuffie) Oliver. Attended Marietta public schools and Trinity Park School, Durham. Farmer and merchant. Mason. Methodist—Sunday school superintendent for ten years. Married Miss Pansy V. Bowles, October 1, 1914; one child. Address: Marietta, N. C.

CARL PUTNAM PARKER

Carl P. Parker, Democrat, Representative from Northampton County, was born in Northampton County, December 9, 1891. Son of Israel Putnam and Sarah Susan (Gay) Parker. Attended Warrenton High School, 1908-1910; University of North Carolina 1910-11; Medical College of Virginia, 1911-1915; M.D. Degree. Physician. Member Northampton County Medical Society, North Carolina State Medical Society. Fellow American Medical Association. Member Eastern Carolina Chamber of Commerce. Past President of Northampton County Medical Society. Chairman Seaboard Township Road Committee, 1920-1926. Member Third Judicial District Committee. Captain, Medical Reserve Corps U. S. Army, December 13, 1917-April 23, 1919; Field Hospital No. 42. Twelve months overseas service. Mason; Knight Templar—Mystic Shrine; W. O. W.; Past Master Seaboard Lodge. Methodist—Steward, 1923-1926, delegate to Annual Conference, 1925 and 1926. Married Miss Bertha Helen Joyner, September 5, 1913. Address: Seaboard, N. C.

WILLIAM I. PARNELL

William I. Parnell, Republican, Representative from Yancey County, was born in Selma. Son of Clemmons and Melvina (Collier) Parnell. Attended public schools from 1894-1908. Cashier Peoples Bank, Burnsville. President Yancey County Building and Loan Association since 1924; vice president North State Feldspar Corporation; vice president Yancey County Chamber of Commerce. Alderman of Burnsville since 1922. Mason, Worshipful Master since 1922. Baptist. Married Miss Kittie Ramsey, August 6, 1916. Address: Burnsville, N. C.

EVERETT WITT PENLAND

Everett Witt Penland, Republican, Representative from Clay County, was born in that county, April 26, 1880. Son of C. N. and Margaret (Maclure) Penland. Attended public schools of county. Farmer and stock raiser. Mason. Methodist. Married Miss Ollie Lance, September 25, 1902. Address: Hayesville, N. C.

CLARENCE McKINLEY POOL

Clarence McKinley Pool, Republican, Representative from McDowell County, was born in Marion, September 3, 1893. Son of John C. and Mary S. (Stroud) Pool. Attended Marion and Nebo High Schools, 1912-1914. Farmer and Merchant. Manager and Secretary of the Farm Supply Company, Marion, 1920-1926; secretary Farmers' Union, 1917-1920. Methodist—trustee, steward, Sunday school Superintendent. Married Miss Nellie S. Noblitt, March 13, 1917. Address: Marion, N. C.

DAVID SCOTT POOLE

David Scott Poole, Democrat, Representative from Hoke County, was born in Montgomery County, August 3, 1858. Son of William R. and Mary Eliza (Ray) Poole. Attended school at Jackson Springs Academy, 1868-80. Printer and publisher. Kiwanian. Reading Clerk in House of Representatives, 1911. Mayor Racford,

1911-12. Justice of the Peace, 1917-18. Private in Company G, Maxton Guards, 1892-93. Mason. Odd Fellow. Jr. O. U. A. M. Noble Grand in Odd Fellows, 1916-1917. Councilor in Junior Order U. A. M., 1902. Presbyterian—Ruling elder; Sunday school superintendent; Clerk of the Session; Representative in Presbytery twenty times; twice in Synod; temporary clerk of Presbytery once; Commissioner to General Assembly once; Representative in the General Assembly of 1925. Married Miss Margaret Lenora Holliday, 1884. Began publication of a newspaper in 1894, continuing to the present time. Address: Raeford, N. C.

WILLIAM EDGAR PRICE

William E. Price, Democrat, Representative from Mecklenburg County, was born at Harrisonburg, Virginia, April 22, 1877. Son of James R. and Mary (Marshall) Price. Attended the county schools of Rockingham County; county high school, Harrisonburg, Virginia; and Shenandoah Institute, Dayton, Virginia. Insurance and Real Estate. President Charlotte Insurance Exchange, 1925; Superintendent County Board of Education, 1918-1922. I. O. O. F.; Past Grand, filled all the chairs past ten years. Presbyterian—Ruling Elder. President Presbyterian Hospital, Inc., Charlotte. Married Miss Robena Lyne Cootes, 1902. Address: Charlotte, N. C.

HAYWOOD CULLEN PRIVOTT

Haywood C. Privott, Democrat, Representative from Chowan County, was born in Chowan County, August 6, 1862. Son of John M. and Susan C. (Bunch) Privott. Attended community and district schools, 1870-1875; Reynoldson Academy and Edenton Academy, 1875-1882; University of North Carolina, 1883. Banker and Farmer. Clerk Superior Court Chowan County, 1890-1906. Baptist. Married Miss Georgie Byrum in 1891. Teacher in public schools of Chowan County, eight years. Address: Edenton, N. C.

HUGHES JENNINGS RHODES

Hughes Jennings Rhodes, Democrat, Representative from Alamance County, was born in Jones County, September 28, 1896. Son of William H. and Sadie (Riggs) Rhodes. Attended New Bern High School; Buies Creek Academy, 1914-15; L.L.B., Wake Forest College, 1921. Lawyer. Member Alamance County Bar Association, North Carolina Bar Association and American Bar Association. Corporal, H. A., U. S. Army, July, 1918-October, 1919. Member Burlington Kiwanis Club; Mason. Baptist—Sunday school Superintendent; Deacon. Married Miss Ethel Marguerite Hotchkiss, July 28, 1920. Address: Burlington, N. C.

JAMES WILEY RIDEOUTTE

James W. Rideoutte, Democrat, Representative from Rowan County, was born at Raleigh in 1878. Son of James Thomas and Nancy Elizabeth (Johnson) Rideoutte. Attended public schools at New Bern, 1884-1887; Columbia (S. C.) High School, 1887-1893. Machinist with Southern Railway Company. Member International Association of Machinists; foreman Southern Railway, 1910; general foreman, 1911. Member Salisbury Board of Aldermen, 1914-1915, 1916-1917. Representative in the General Assembly in 1923 and 1925. Member of Company D, First South Carolina Volunteers 1895-1897. W. O. W. Moose. Episcopalian. Married Miss Agnes D. Crawford in 1899. Address: Salisbury, N. C.

WILLIAM WENDELL ROGERS

William W. Rogers, Democrat, Representative from Hertford County, was born at Winton, August 11, 1874. Son of George H. and Sallie F. (Martin) Rogers. Educated at Winton High School, Littleton High School, and Wake Forest College. Received LL.B. degree from Wake Forest College, 1903. Lawyer. Mayor of Ahoskie, 4 years. Member County Democratic Executive Committee. Mason. Member North Carolina Bar Association; Kiwanis Club.

Representative in the General Assembly of 1925. Episcopalian. Married Miss Nina Hayes December 6, 1911. Address: Ahoskie, N. C.

ROBERT C. ROUSE

Robert C. Rouse, Democrat, Representative from Greene County, was born in same county. Son of Abner and Penniah (Dixon) Rouse. Attended public schools. Farmer. Member Selective Service Board for Greene County, two years. Representative in the General Assembly of 1925. Mason. Methodist. Married Miss Annie E. Croom in 1889. Address: Snow Hill, N. C., Route 2.

SAMUEL JOSEPH SATTERWHITE

Samuel Joseph Satterwhite, Democrat, Representative from Warren County, was born in Vance County, August 3, 1886. Son of James P. and Roberta (Rogers) Satterwhite. Attended public and private schools, 1892-1897; Gilmer's Academy, Henderson, 1897; Graham High School, Warrenton, 1898, 1899; Butler-Ball High School, Dabney, 1901; A. & M. College, Raleigh, 1902, 1903; graduate in bookkeeping from Massey's Business College, Richmond, 1903. Farming and real estate. Methodist Protestant—steward and trustee. Married Miss Madeline Rogers Warren, November 10, 1908. Address: Manson, N. C.

JAMES MATHY SHIPMAN

James M. Shipman, Democrat, Representative from Columbus County, was born in Columbus County, October 18, 1850. Son of John D. and Ester Jane (Baldwin) Shipman. Attended county schools, 1856-1865. Civil Engineer and Farmer. Justice of Peace, 1875-1891; chairman Board of County Commissioners, four years. Member House of Representatives, 1903, 1905 and 1911. United States Census enumerator for Welch's Creek township, three times. Baptist. Chairman Finance Committee and Church Trustee. Superintendent Sunday school. Married Miss Katharine Smith, May 13, 1873. Address: Whiteville, N. C.

THOMAS LAWSON SMITH

Thomas Lawson Smith, Democrat, Representative from Rockingham County, was born in Leaksville, August 19, 1868. Son of Nat Scales and Mary Johns (Lawson) Smith. Attended Leaksville Male Academy, 1880-1884. Brick Manufacturer and Proprietor Bettie Field Inn. Representative in the General Assembly of 1925. Mason. J. O. U. A. M. Presbyterian; elder since 1905. Married Miss Mabel Zell Wall, November 25, 1897. Address: Leaksville, N. C.

WILLIS SMITH

Willis Smith, Democrat, Representative from Wake County, was born in Norfolk, Virginia, December 19, 1887. Son of Willis and Mary (Creecy) Smith. Attended Atlantic Collegiate Institute, Elizabeth City. Graduated from Trinity with A.B. Degree in 1910. Studied law at Trinity, 1910-1912. Lawyer. Member Wake County Bar Association, North Carolina Bar Association, American Bar Association and Commercial Law League. Inheritance Tax Attorney for North Carolina, 1916-1919. Private Company 16, C. B., C. A. C. Fortress Monroe, 1918. Methodist. Married Miss Anna Lee, April 30, 1919. Address: Raleigh, N. C.

ALVIN SYLVANUS SOLESBEE

Alvin Sylvanus Solesbee, Republican, Representative from Macon County, was born in Macon County, June 25, 1875. Son of Asbury and Mary Solesbee. Attended Hiwassee High School, 1893-95. Minister of the Gospel. Appointed Storekeeper and Gauger of Internal Revenue Service, 1898. Taught in Public Schools of North Carolina, fourteen years. Surveyor of Towns County, Georgia. Odd Fellows, Star of Bethlehem, and Rebekah. Chaplain of Lodge I. O. O. F. No. 236 in 1905-07. Missionary Baptist. Married, in 1901, Miss Belle Kilpatrick. Address: Franklin, N. C.

MARK SQUIRES

Mark Squires, Democrat, Representative from Caldwell County, was born in Union County in 1878. Son of John D. and Mary A. (Stevens) Squires. Educated in public schools and the North Carolina State College. Lawyer. Chairman County Executive Committee, 1910-1912. Mayor of Lenoir, 1911-1914. Reading Clerk State Senate, 1909-1911. Member State Senate, special sessions, 1921 and 1924, and regular sessions, 1923 and 1925. Wilson and Marshall elector in 1916. Chairman North Carolina Park Commission. Mason. Married Miss Mary E. Dunlap in 1902. Address: Lenoir, N. C.

J. CLYDE STANCILL

J. Clyde Stancill, Democrat, Representative from Mecklenburg, was born in Mecklenburg County, March 23, 1889. Son of H. J. and Mary Rose (Walker) Stancill. Attended city schools of Charlotte; Charlotte University School and Erskine College, Due West, S. C., from 1909-1912. Studied law at the University of North Carolina, 1913. Lawyer. Prosecuting Attorney of the City of Charlotte, 1914-1919. Mason; Shriner. Associate Reformed Presbyterian. Married Miss Lucia Earle McCormick, November 23, 1913. Address: Charlotte, N. C.

FREDERICK ISLER SUTTON

Frederick I. Sutton, Democrat, Representative from Lenoir County, was born at Kinston, September 7, 1886. Son of L. M. and Cora Elizabeth (Grimsley) Sutton. Educated at Miss Dora Miller's School, 1893-96; Dr. Richard H. Lewis's School; Kinston High School; University of North Carolina, A.B. Degree, 1908; Harvard Summer School, 1907. Harvard Law School, 1908-11, LL.B. Degree. Lawyer. Member Kinston Bar Association, North Carolina Bar Association, Harvard Law School Association. Secretary-Treasurer Carolina Municipal Association. Vice President North Carolina Good Roads Association. Attorney City of Kinston. Director and Attorney Caswell Banking and Trust Company. Director and Attorney National Bank of Kinston. Mayor City of Kinston, 1913-19.

Representative in the General Assembly of 1925. Served as Corporal in Home Guard. Member St. John's Lodge, No. 4, A. F. and A. M., Caswell Chapter, No. 38, Royal Arch Masons, St. Paul's Commandery, No. 18, Knights Templar, Sudan Temple, A. A. O. N. M. S. Jr. O. U. A. M. Lenoir Council, Alpha Tau Omega and Pi Sigma Fraternities. Kiwanis Club. President Kinston Shrine Club and Kinston Kiwanis Club. Married Miss Annie Gray Fry, of Greensboro, 1915. Address: Kinston, N. C.

CURTIS L. TARKINGTON

Curtis L. Tarkington, Democrat, Representative from Camden County, was born at Camden, May 1, 1887. Son of Thomas and Pauline (Robertson) Tarkington. Attended public schools. Farmer. Director and Treasurer Camden Gin Company. Deputy Sheriff Camden County, 1923-24. Member General Assembly of 1925. Mason. Married Miss Sallie Overton, August 1, 1913. Address: Camden, N. C.

CHARLES WALLACE TATEM

Charles Wallace Tatem, Democrat, Representative from Tyrrell County, was born in Columbia, September 25, 1876. Son of Cammilas Etheridge and Ellen E. (McClees) Tatem. Attended Columbia Academy, 1885-1891; Trinity School, 1892-93. Civil Engineer. Married Miss Ella Gertrude Wynne, September 24, 1896. Address: Columbia, N. C.

JOHN H. TIPTON

John H. Tipton, Republican, Representative from Mitchell County, was born at Relief, October, 5, 1890. Son of S. D. and ———— (Bradshaw) Tipton. Farmer. Minister. Secretary-Treasurer, N. F. L. A. County commissioner, 1919-1920. Notary Public. Mason. Junior warden, 1921. Methodist; ordained Local Deacon, 1925. Married Miss Masters, July 23, 1922. Address: Relief, N. C.

N. A. TOWNSEND

N. A. Townsend, Democrat, Representative from Harnett County. Son of Jackson and Sarah M. (Oliver) Townsend. Was born in Robeson County, May 1, 1882. A.B., University of North Carolina, 1905. Studied law at University of North Carolina, 1905-1906. Lawyer. Admitted to bar, February, 1906. Married, 1909, Miss Myrtle Agnes Wade. Mayor of Dunn, 1911-1912. Attorney of Dunn, 1917-21. Member of the House of Representatives, 1921, 1923, and 1925. Address: Dunn, N. C.

ZEBULON VANCE TURLINGTON

Zebulon V. Turlington, Democrat, Representative from Iredell County, was born in Johnston County, in 1877. Son of Eli and Sarah (Woodall) Turlington. Attended Turlington Institute, Smithfield, 1893-1896; University of North Carolina Law School, 1898-1899. Lawyer. Member Rotary Club. Member House of Representatives in 1905, 1907, 1909, 1911, 1923, and 1925. President Board of Regents, Barium Springs Orphanage. Presbyterian. Married Miss Mary Howard Rankin in 1902. Address: Mooresville, N. C.

GEORGE ROBERT WARD

George R. Ward, Democrat, Representative from Duplin County, was born in Wallace, November 4, 1877. Son of George W. and Mary P. (Alderman) Ward. Educated at Rockfish Academy, Duplin County, 1895-1897; Johnson and Wyche High School, 1897-1898; Atlantic and Belvoir High School, Clinton, 1898-1899; Ph.B., University of North Carolina, 1903; University Law School, 1903-1904. Lawyer. Member North Carolina Bar Association and the American Bar Association. Representative in the General Assemblies of 1917 and 1925. Member Duplin County Board of Elections. Member Duplin County Advisory Board during World War. Mason—Master of local lodge No. 595. Presbyterian—Elder. Married Miss Bettie Williams, 1908. Address: Wallace, N. C.

JOHN S. WATKINS

John S. Watkins, Democrat, Representative from Granville County, was born in that county in 1879. Son of John A. and Margaret (Reid) Watkins. Attended Scottsburg Normal College, 1898-1899. Farmer. Secretary and Treasurer of Granville County Branch of Farmers Mutual Fire Insurance Company, 1918 to present date. Member Legislature, 1923 and 1925. Mason. W. O. W. Baptist—Chairman Board of Deacons. Married Miss Belle Norwood in 1905. Address: Virgilina, Va., Route No. 2.

MARVIN BROGDON WATKINS

Marvin B. Watkins, Democrat, Representative from Brunswick County, was born in Ellenboro, July 5, 1889. Son of Rev. D. A. and Sallie (Brogdon) Watkins. Attended Salemburg High School, 1907; Fayetteville Graded School, 1900; Mount Pleasant, 1903. Farmer. Secretary Brunswick County Democratic Executive Committee, 1920-1926; represented Brunswick County in General Assembly, 1923, and Special Session, 1924. Seaman in U. S. Navy during World War. Methodist—Charge Lay Leader, District Steward, Recording Steward. Married Miss Mattie J. Thompson, June 6, 1919. Address: Town Creek, N. C.

JOHN THOMAS WELLS

John Thomas Wells, Democrat, Representative from Pender County, was born at Watha, November 2, 1896. Son of Walter Lee and Elizabeth Brock (Moore) Wells. Attended Burgaw High School, 1914-1920; University of North Carolina, 1921-22. Druggist and farmer. Mayor of Atkinson, 1925-1926. Entered service at Camp Glenn, September 25, 1916, and was discharged with rank of Sergeant at Camp Jackson, S. C., April 7, 1919. Awarded American Distinguished Service Cross and French Croix de Guerre for service in France. Thirty-second Degree Mason; member Knights of Ku Klux Klan. Methodist. Address: Atkinson, N. C.

FRANCIS SAMPSON WETMUR

Francis S. Wetmur, Republican, Representative from Henderson County, was born in Watertown, Carver County, Minnesota. Son of David G. and Harriett M. (Sampson) Wetmur. Attended the schools of Watertown and Minneapolis, Minnesota. Ford dealer. Member Chamber Commerce, Kiwanis Club, Merchants Association, North Carolina Automobile Trade Association. President Chamber Commerce, 1923-1924; delegate to Kiwanis International Convention at St. Paul, June, 1925. Mason; Shriner. Methodist—steward, seventeen years; trustee; charge lay leader, six years. Married Miss Mabel Wininger, January 12, 1892. Address: Hendersonville, N. C.

THOMAS CALVIN WHITAKER

Thomas Calvin Whitaker, Democrat, Representative from Jones County, was born at Cypress Creek, Jones County, January 25, 1855. Son of Thomas J. and Sarah Eliza (Koonce) Whitaker. Educated in neighborhood schools, 1863-74; Rutherford College, 1875. Farmer. Private Secretary to Hon. Charles R. Thomas, M. C., for twelve years, 1899-1911. Trustee A. and E. College, 1925-1933. Two years Director Atlantic and North Carolina Railroad, 1899-1901. Four years State proxy A. and N. C. Railroad (Kitchin administration), 1909-13. Member Democratic State Executive Committee, 1906. Eighteen years a member, twelve years Secretary, Democratic Executive Committee, Third Congressional District, 1894-1912. Eighteen years Chairman Democratic County Executive Committee, Jones County, 1892-1910. A member of the General Assembly, 1921-23-25. Methodist—Superintendent Sunday school, Trenton, since 1894. Married, December 23, 1880, to Miss Elizabeth Murray of Wilson. Address: Trenton, N. C.

GEORGE THOMAS WHITE

George Thomas White, Republican, Representative from Yadkin County, was born at McCurdy, Iredell County, in 1865. Son of W. Pinkney and Adeline (Daniel) White. Attended public schools, Moravian Falls High School. Flour milling and farming. County

Commissioner, 1902-04; Sheriff, 1904-08. State Senator, Twenty-fourth District, 1923. Mason, Woodman of the World. Methodist—Steward since 1900. Married 1887, to Miss Mary McCaullis Johnson; in 1917, to Miss Mallie Thomasson. Address: Hamptonville, N. C.

OLIVER PERRY WILLIAMS

Oliver Perry Williams, Republican, Representative from Swain County, was born in Monroe County, Tennessee, April 24, 1859. Son of William and Amanda (Johnson) Williams. Attended Maryville Normal and Preparatory School, Maryville, Tenn, 1881-1883. Cashier bank since 1913. Clerk Superior Court, Graham County, 1890-1892; Representative from Graham County in the General Assembly of 1899 and from Swain County in 1911. Clerk Superior Court, Swain County, 1904-1910; twice Mayor of Bryson City; member of the County Board of Education; Postmaster and Alderman of Bryson City. Knight of Pythias, Chancellor Commander and Prelate. Baptist—Pastor of churches in the Tennessee River Association, Sunday school Superintendent, and Teacher of Men's Bible Class. Married: first, Miss Artie Grant; second, Miss Etta Shope; widower. Address: Bryson City, N. C.

JOHN KENYON WILSON

John Kenyon Wilson, Democrat, Representative from Pasquotank County, was born at Elizabeth City in 1883. Son of Tully B. and Jennie F. (Kenyon) Wilson. Received his preparatory education in Elizabeth City schools. Attended University of North Carolina, taking A.B. Degree in 1905 and B.L. Degree in 1906. Lawyer. Representative in General Assembly of 1925. Served in World War from April, 1917, to November, 1918, as Lieutenant Commander U. S. Naval Reserve. Mason. Methodist. Married Miss Bessie V. Weatherly, September 21, 1918. Address: Elizabeth City, N. C.

THOMAS J. WILSON

Thomas J. Wilson, Democrat, Representative from Transylvania County, was born in that county. Son of George W. and Laura J. (Miller) Wilson. Farmer. Married Miss Nell Johnson, November 28, 1906. Address: Pisgah Forest, N. C.

FRANCIS DONNELL WINSTON

Francis D. Winston, Democrat, Representative from Bertie County, was born in Windsor, October 2, 1857. Son of Patrick Henry and Martha Elizabeth (Byrd) Winston. Attended Henderson Classical School, 1869-1870; Horner and Graves, Oxford, 1871-1873; Cornell University, 1874-1875. Graduated from University of North Carolina with B.A. Degree, 1879. Attended Dick and Dillard Law School, 1880. Lawyer. Member North Carolina Bar Association; Windsor Chamber of Commerce. Clerk Superior Court, 1881-1882; Judge Superior Court, 1901-1903, and 1916. United States District Atttorney, 1913-1916. Emergency Judge, 1925. President North Carolina Bar Association, 1911. Lieutenant Governor, 1905-1908. Trustee University since 1887. Trustee Bryant's Musical School, Durham. Democratic District Elector, 1892; Democratic Elector at Large, 1912; President State Democratic Convention of 1912; President State Democratic Clubs, 1904. Served two enlistments, Windsor Naval Reserves, 1897-1903. Boatswain. Mason; Grand Master Grand Lodge, 1907-1908. Episcopalian; Vestryman, 1885-1920. Married Miss Rosa Mary Kenney, May 30, 1889. President North Carolina Folk Lore Society and Member State Literary and Historical Association. Address: Windsor, N. C.

J. W. WOOD

J. W. Wood, Democrat, Representative from Johnston County. Address: Benson, N. C.

WILLIAM COLEMAN WOODARD

William Coleman Woodard, Democrat, Representative from Nash County, was born at Rocky Mount, June 8, 1889. Son of William C. and Charlotte (Woodard) Woodard. Attended Wilkinson's School, Tarboro, 1900-1904; A.B., University of North Carolina, 1908; Law School, 1911. Insurance business. Member Chamber of Commerce and Kiwanis Club. Secretary and Past President of Kiwanis Club, Director of Chamber of Commerce, Director Beneview Country Club, and Director Citizens' Building and Loan. Member Board of Aldermen, 1925. Order of Gimghouls, Corinthian Lodge, No. 230, Rocky Mount Chapter, St. Bernard Community, Sudan Temple. Episcopalian. Married, February 4, 1915, to Miss Katharine Bunn. Address: Rocky Mount, N. C.

C. G. WRIGHT

C. G. Wright, Democrat, Representative from Guilford County. Capitalist. Educated at the University of North Carolina, class of 1886. Representative in the General Assembly of 1917, 1919, 1921, 1923 and 1925. Trustee of the University of North Carolina since 1917. Address: Greensboro, N. C.

HARRISON YELVERTON

Harrison Yelverton, Democrat, Representative from Wayne County, was born at Goldsboro, July 16, 1890. Son of William Thomas and Sarah Jane (Sauls) Yelverton. Educated Goldsboro High School; University of North Carolina, 1908-12; Harvard University, one year. Merchant. Member Board of Directors American University Union in London. Appointed by Lord Fortesque to membership on committee for celebration of the Sir Walter Raleigh Tercentenary. Appointed American Consular Assistant, April, 1914, detailed to Department of State at Washington; detailed to Consulate General at London, February, 1915. Made Vice Consul in charge of Consulate at Swansea, Wales, November, 1916. Appointed American Vice Consul at London, February, 1917. Detailed to duty in Department of State, July, 1919. Appointed by Secretary of

State and detailed to duty on Conference for Limitation of Armament, November, 1921, acting as private secretary to Senator Underwood. Member Wayne Lodge, No. 112, A. F. and A. M. North Carolina Beta Chapter of Phi Delta Theta—President, 1912. Representative in the General Assembly of 1925. Address: Goldsboro, N. C.

GEORGE ALEXANDER YOUNCE

George A. Younce, Democrat, Representative from Guilford County, was born in Roanoke, Virginia, April 25, 1899. Son of Charles P. and Elizabeth Frances (Kepley) Younce. Graduated from the Spencer (N. C.) High School, 1915, and from the University of North Carolina in 1919 with a B.A. Degree. Also studied law at the University and obtained license to practice in 1920. Lawyer. Apprentice Seaman, S.A.T.C., University of North Carolina, 1918. Mason, member Corinthian Lodge No. 542, Greensboro; Knights of Pythias, member of Greensboro Lodge No. 80, Past Chancellor and District Deputy Grand Chancellor, Seventh District; Loyal Order of Moose; Sigma Alpha Epsilon Fraternity. Baptist. Married Miss Helyn Louise Stone, June 30, 1925. Catcher University Baseball Club, 1917-1920; President Athletic Association and of the Athletic Council of the University, 1919-1920. Address: Greensboro, N. C.

ISAAC JONES YOUNG

Isaac Jones Young, Representative from Vance County. Born in Henderson, April 25, 1872. Son of W. W. and Annie E. Young. Attended a private school in Henderson. Real estate business. City Alderman, 1906-1909. Methodist. Married Miss Celestia Jones Gill. Four children; two boys and two girls. Member House of Representatives, 1913. Member Democratic County Executive Committee, 1918; also a member of the State Executive Committee until 1917. Appointed Postmaster, April 30, 1917; served four years in that capacity under President Wilson's administration, and two years under President Harding's administration, retiring from office, March 1, 1923. Member of National Democratic Committee; appointed by Hon. Cordell Hull, March 17, 1923, as President of the National Democratic Victory Club. Address: Henderson, N. C.

Lightning Source UK Ltd.
Milton Keynes UK
UKHW040929180920
370091UK00001BA/60